T0073113

Lecture Notes in Electrical Engineering

Volume 853

The book series *Lecture Notes in Electrical Engineering* (LNEE) publishes the latest developments in Electrical Engineering - quickly, informally and in high quality. While original research reported in proceedings and monographs has traditionally formed the core of LNEE, we also encourage authors to submit books devoted to supporting student education and professional training in the various fields and applications areas of electrical engineering. The series cover classical and emerging topics concerning:

- Communication Engineering, Information Theory and Networks
- Electronics Engineering and Microelectronics
- Signal, Image and Speech Processing
- Wireless and Mobile Communication
- Circuits and Systems
- Energy Systems, Power Electronics and Electrical Machines
- Electro-optical Engineering
- Instrumentation Engineering
- Avionics Engineering
- Control Systems
- Internet-of-Things and Cybersecurity
- Biomedical Devices, MEMS and NEMS

For general information about this book series, comments or suggestions, please contact leontina.dicecco@springer.com.

To submit a proposal or request further information, please contact the Publishing Editor in your country:

China

Jasmine Dou, Editor (jasmine.dou@springer.com)

India, Japan, Rest of Asia

Swati Meherishi, Editorial Director (Swati.Meherishi@springer.com)

Southeast Asia, Australia, New Zealand

Ramesh Nath Premnath, Editor (ramesh.premnath@springernature.com)

USA, Canada:

Michael Luby, Senior Editor (michael.luby@springer.com)

All other Countries:

Leontina Di Cecco, Senior Editor (leontina.dicecco@springer.com)

** This series is indexed by EI Compendex and Scopus databases. **

More information about this series at https://link.springer.com/bookseries/7818

Ch. Satyanarayana · Debasis Samanta ·
Xiao-Zhi Gao · Rajiv Kumar Kapoor
Editors

High Performance Computing and Networking

Select Proceedings of CHSN 2021

 Springer

Editors
Ch. Satyanarayana
Jawaharlal Nehru Technological University
Kakinanda, Andhra Pradesh, India

Xiao-Zhi Gao
School of Computing
University of Eastern Finland
Kuopio, Finland

Debasis Samanta
Department of Computer Science
and Engineering
Indian Institute of Technology Kharagpur
Kharagpur, West Bengal, India

Rajiv Kumar Kapoor
Department of Electronics
and Communication Engineering
Delhi Technological University
New Delhi, Delhi, India

Prof. Ch. Satyanarayana is Deceased.

ISSN 1876-1100   ISSN 1876-1119 (electronic)
Lecture Notes in Electrical Engineering
ISBN 978-981-16-9884-2   ISBN 978-981-16-9885-9 (eBook)
https://doi.org/10.1007/978-981-16-9885-9

This Springer imprint is published by the registered company Springer Nature Singapore Pte Ltd.
The registered company address is: 152 Beach Road, #21-01/04 Gateway East, Singapore 189721,
Singapore

Dedicated to

Late Prof. Ch. Satyanarayana
Professor and Registrar
JNTU Kakinada

Program Committee

Dr. Akula Chandrasekhar, Avanthi Institute of Engineering & Technology
Dr. Anish Kumar Saha, National Institute of Technology Silchar
Dr. Anupam Biswas, National Institute of Technology Silchar
Dr. Ayyagari Srinagesh, R. V. R. & J. C. College of Engineering
Dr. B. N. Jagadesh, Srinivasa Institute of Engineering and Technology
Dr. B. Sateesh Kumar, JNTU Hyderabad
Dr. Badal Soni, National Institute of Technology Silchar
Dr. Bhagavan Konduri, KL University
Dr. Bhramaramba Ravi, GITAM University
Dr. Chamundeswari Ganta, Sir C. R. Reddy College of Engineering
Dr. Chandra Sekhar Potala, GITAM University
Dr. Chapram Sudhakar, National Institute of Technology Warangal
Dr. Dalton Meitei, National Institute of Technology Silchar
Dr. Devendra Singh Gurjar, National Institute of Technology Silchar
Dr. E. Suresh Babu, National Institute of Technology Warangal
Dr. Eugénia Bernardino, Instituto Politécnico de Leiria, Portugal
Dr. Firoz Ahmed, University of Rajshahi, Bangladesh
Dr. Gondi Lakshmeeswari, GITAM University
Dr. Gopa Bhaumik, National Institute of Technology Sikkim
Dr. G. V. S. Rajkumar, GITAM University
Dr. J. Harikiran, VIT University, Andhra Pradesh
Dr. J. Avanija, Sree Vidyanikethan Engineering College (Autonomous)
Dr. N. Jayapandian, CHRIST University
Dr. Kabir G. Kharade, Shivaji University
Dr. Kaushal Bhardwaj, Indian Institute of Information Technology Senapati
Dr. Kok-Why Ng, Multimedia University, Malaysia
Dr. D. R. Kumar Raja, REVA University
Dr. L. Dolendro Singh, National Institute of Technology Silchar
Dr. L. Venkateswara Reddy, K. G. Reddy College of Engineering (Autonomous)
Dr. M. Brindha, National Institute of Technology Trichy
Dr. M. Radhika Mani, Pragati Engineering College (Autonomous)

Dr. Malaya Dutta Borah, National Institute of Technology Silchar
Dr. Mohammad Pasha, Muffakham Jah College of Engineering and Technology
Dr. Nagaraju Baydeti, National Institute of Technology Nagaland
Dr. Narendra Kohli, Harcourt Butler Technical University
Dr. Naresh Babu Muppalaneni, National Institute of Technology Silchar
Dr. Naveen Palanichamy, Multimedia University, Malaysia
Dr. P. Satheesh, MVGR College of Engineering (Autonomous)
Dr. P. C. Srinivasa Rao, KL University
Dr. Pao-Ann Hsiung, National Chung Cheng University, Taiwan
Dr. Partha Pakray, National Institute of Technology Silchar
Dr. Prabina Pattanayak, National Institute of Technology Silchar
Dr. R. Kanesaraj Ramasamy, Multimedia University, Malaysia
Dr. R. Murugan, National Institute of Technology Silchar
Dr. Rama Narasingarao Manda, KL University
Dr. Rashmi Saini, G. B. Pant Institute of Engineering and Technology
Dr. Reddymadhavi Konduru, Sree Vidyanikethan Engineering College
(Autonomous)
Dr. Ripon Patgiri, National Institute of Technology Silchar
Dr. S. Srinivas Kumar, Jawaharlal Nehru Technological University Kakinada
Dr. Sanjaya Kumar Panda, National Institute of Technology Warangal
Dr. Sasikumar Gurumoorthy, Vel Tech University
Dr. Shyamapada Mukherjee, National Institute of Technology Silchar
Dr. Sivasutha Thanjappan, Multimedia University, Malaysia
Dr. Srinivas Chakravarthy Lade, GITAM University
Dr. Sunitha Gurram, Sree Vidyanikethan Engineering College (Autonomous)
Dr. T. Jyothrmayi, GITAM University
Dr. Tomasz Rak, Rzeszow University of Technology, Poland
Dr. Tripti Goel, National Institute of Technology Silchar
Dr. Uma N. Dulhare, Muffakham Jah College of Engineering and Technology
Dr. Veenu Mangat, Panjab University
Dr. Venkata Lakshmi Sanapala, GITAM University
Dr. Venushini Rajendran, Multimedia University, Malaysia
Dr. Vishal Saraswat, Bosch Engineering and Business Solutions
Dr. Wei-Chiang Hong, Asia Eastern University of Science and Technology, Taiwan
Dr. Yuen Peng Loh, Multimedia University, Malaysia
Dr. Zhao Yang, American University, Washington
Mr. Satish Kumar Satti, National Institute of Technology Silchar
Mr. Yonten Jamtsho, Royal University Bhutan
Ms. Anchana P. Belmon, Maria College of Engineering and Technology
Ms. Lilapati Waikhom, National Institute of Technology Silchar
Ms. Sabuzima Nayak, National Institute of Technology Silchar
Ms. Sonam Wangmo, Royal University Bhutan

Keynote Speakers

Dr. Pascal Lorenz

University of Haute Alsace, France

Dr. Pao-Ann Hsiung

National Chung Cheng University, Chiayi, Taiwan

Prof. Kurt Tutschku

Blekinge Institute of Technology (BTH), Sweden

Dr. Warusia Yassin

Universiti Teknikal Malaysia Melaka, Malaysia

Kamiya Khatter

Editor, Applied Science and Engineering

Springer Nature

Foreword

The 2nd International Conference on Computer Vision, High Performance Computing, Smart Devices and Networks (CHSN-2021) is aimed to bring researchers together working in this area to share their knowledge and experience. In this conference, topics of contemporary interested would be discussed to provide a holistic vision on latest technologies for computer science and engineering. The scope includes data science, machine learning, computer vision, deep learning, artificial intelligence, artificial neural networks, mobile applications development and Internet of Things, etc. Conference participants are expected to gain relevant knowledge and better understanding of the applications of computer science in various fields.

CHSN-2021 would be both stimulating and informative with the active participation of galaxy of keynote speakers. We would like to thank all the authors who submitted the papers, because of which the conference became a story of success. We also would like to express our gratitude to the reviewers, for their contributions to enhance the quality of the papers. We are very grateful to the keynote speakers, reviewers, session chairs and committee members who selflessly contributed to the success of CHSN-2021. We are very thankful to Jawaharlal Nehru Technological University Kakinada, Kakinada, for providing the basic requirements to host the CHSN-2021.

Last but not least, we are thankful for the enormous support of publishing partner, i.e. Springer, for supporting us in every step of our journey towards success.

Dr. D. Haritha
Convener, CHSN-2021
JNTU
Kakinada, India

Contents

About the Editors

Ch. Satyanarayana is a Professor in the Department of Computer Science and Engineering, Jawaharlal Nehru Technological University, Andhra Pradesh, India. He obtained his Ph.D. degree in 2007 from Jawaharlal Nehru Technological University, Hyderabad. Dr. Satyanarayana has over 20 years of teaching and research experience. He has published over 130 research papers in journals of international and national repute. Few of his research innovations are at different stages of patenting as intellectual reserves. His research interests span image processing, speech recognition, pattern recognition, network security, big data analytics, and computational intelligence.

Debasis Samanta is an Associate Professor in the Department of Computer Science and Engineering, Indian Institute of Technology Kharagpur. Professor Samanta is actively working in the field of human-computer interaction. He aims to develop efficient interaction mechanisms for people with special needs such as motor-impaired people and people with other disabilities, illiterate people, etc. He has developed a multi-modal interaction technique, text entry mechanisms in Indian languages, which are new of their kind to bridge the digital divide. Currently, he is working toward the development of next-generation hands-free and touch-free interaction mechanisms using brain-computer interfaces. He and his research team are developing a BCI-HCI lab in IIT Kharagpur, a unique lab facility in India. He is an author of three books and over 60 journals, and 110 conference papers of international repute.

Xiao-Zhi Gao received his B.Sc. and M.Sc. degrees from the Harbin Institute of Technology, China, in 1993 and 1996, respectively. He obtained his D.Sc. (Tech.) degree from the Helsinki University of Technology (now known as Aalto University), Finland in 1999. He is presently working as a professor of data science at the University of Eastern Finland, Finland. Professor Gao has published over 400 technical papers in refereed journals and international conferences. His research interests are nature-inspired computing methods (e.g., neural networks, fuzzy logic, evolutionary computing, swarm intelligence, and artificial immune systems), optimization, data mining, machine learning, networking, control, signal processing, and industrial electronics.

Rajiv Kumar Kapoor is a professor in Electronics and Communication Engineering at Delhi Technological University, Delhi. His research interests span vision/speech-based tracking, machine learning, activity recognition vision, speech-based signal processing, pattern recognition, and cognitive radio. He published around 70 research papers in reputed International and National Journals and published over 100 articles in various International and National conferences. Nine of his research innovations are at different stages of patenting as intellectual reserves, and four patents have already been awarded. He authored seven books and completed three research projects. He has undertaken Industrial Research work worth 1.8 crores and other Research Consultancy worth 3 crores for various Research Organizations.

An Effective DNLP Optimization Method for Economic Load Dispatch Problem

P. Dinakara Prasad Reddy, K. Ram Prasad, M. Vijayakumar Naik, and Ch. Devisree

Abstract For power system engineers, meeting the rapidly increasing demand for loads with existing generating capacities is the major challenge. The creation of new capacity entails tremendously large capital expenditures, and hence, it is very important to operate with optimum utilization of existing power system. This paper therefore presents a novel DNLP approach using GAMS for generators scheduled to increase economic power generation. Economic load dispatch (ELD) problem is considered as a highly nonlinear constrained optimization problem. It is crucial for the power system operation and planning. The suggested approach is tested on seven different well-known test systems to demonstrate its applicability in the ELD problem. The results are compared to other methods in terms of solution quality, resilience, and computation time, implying that the presented method outperforms the other methods. In this paper, different test systems with 38, 13, 40, 20, 10, and 15 generators are evaluated to address valve point impact, transmission loss, prohibited zone, and ramp rate limits. The results are quite promising, and they outperform various existing optimization techniques.

Keywords Economic load dispatch · Valve point effects · Prohibited operating zones · Ramp rate limits · Transmission line loss

1 Introduction

The economic load dispatch (ELD) problem is used to determine the best allocation of generation across all generating units in order to reduce overall fuel costs while meeting both equality and inequality constraints [1–3]. However, since the 1980s, when many pollution control acts were enacted, determining the minimum generation cost has been a key problem for power generation companies [4, 5]. The valve

P. Dinakara Prasad Reddy (✉) · K. Ram Prasad · M. Vijayakumar Naik · Ch. Devisree
Department of EEE, S V University, Tirupati, Andhra Pradesh, India

© The Author(s), under exclusive license to Springer Nature Singapore Pte Ltd. 2022
C. Satyanarayana et al. (eds.), *High Performance Computing and Networking*,
Lecture Notes in Electrical Engineering 853,
https://doi.org/10.1007/978-981-16-9885-9_1

point effects (VPE) [6–8], prohibited operating zones (POZ) [7, 9], ramp rate limitations [10, 11], and various fuel functions [12] make the ELD problem a nonlinear optimization problem.

Many researchers have introduced numerous heuristic optimization approaches to address the drawbacks of conventional methods in recent years, as evidenced by the literature. Some of these techniques are quasi-oppositional teaching learning-based optimization [13], hybrid differential evolution algorithm [14], hybrid shuffled differential evolution (SDE) algorithm [15], differential harmony search algorithm [16], biogeography-based optimization [17], real coded chemical reaction algorithm [18], modified harmony search algorithm [19], modified artificial bee colony algorithm [20], artificial bee colony [21], krill herd algorithm [22], backtracking search algorithm [23], immune algorithm [24], teaching-learning-based optimization [25], gray wolf optimization algorithm [26, 27], flower pollination algorithm [28], natural updated harmony search [29], colonial competitive differential evolution [30], exchange market algorithm [31], chaotic teaching-learning-based optimization with Levy flight [32], ant lion optimizer [33], opposition-based greedy heuristic search [34], social spider algorithm [35], improved differential evolution algorithm [36], chaotic bat algorithm [37], quasi-oppositional self-learning teacher-learner-based-optimization (QOSLTLBO) [38], semi-definite programming [39], opposition-based krill herd algorithm [40], hybrid artificial algae algorithm [41], modified crow search algorithm [42], parallel hurricane optimization algorithm [43], orthogonal learning competitive swarm optimizer [44], chaotic Jaya algorithm [45], adaptive charged system search algorithm [46], dragonfly algorithm [47], multi-objective spotted hyena optimizer [48], phasor particle swarm optimization [49], artificial cooperative search algorithm [50], ameliorated gray wolf optimization [51], Jaya algorithm with self-adaptive multi-population and Levy flights [52], adaptive differential evolutionary algorithm [53], PSO [54], and firefly algorithm [55].

2 Mathematical Model of Economic Load Dispatch

The classic ELD problem is formulated as minimizing generator fuel costs while maintaining real power balanced with total load demand as well as limiting generator outputs without taking into account any practical constraints.

$$\min \sum_{i=1}^{N} \text{FC}_i(P_{pi}) = \sum_{i=1}^{N} \left(\alpha_i P_{pi}^2 + \beta_i P_{pi} + \gamma_i \right) \tag{1}$$

The generating unit in the ELD model has a quadratic cost function. Thermal units in practical power systems, on the other hand, typically include boilers with valve points for regulating their power outputs. Due to the wire drawing effect, this imposes a significant range in the input–output characteristics. The valve point effect

(VPE) is usually modeled by adding a sinusoidal component to the quadratic cost function.

$$\min \sum_{i=1}^{N} FC_i(P_{pi}) = \sum_{i=1}^{N} \left(\alpha_i P_{pi}^2 + \beta_i P_{pi} + \gamma_i + \left| e_i \left(\sin(f_i(P_{pi}^{\min} - P_{pi})) \right) \right| \right) \quad (2)$$

where FC_i is the fuel cost function of generator i ($/h); P_{pi} is the electrical output power of generator i (in MW); α_i, β_i, γ_i are, respectively, the fuel cost coefficients of generator i; N is the generators number; valve point loading coefficients are μ_i and f_i; minimum power generation limit of generator i (in MW) is $P_{pi}^{\min}$.

2.1 Constraints

A. **Equality Constraints**
The equality constraint is given by

$$\sum_{i=1}^{N} P_{pi} = P_L + P_D \quad (3)$$

where P_D denotes the total demand of system (in MW); P_L represents total transmission line losses (in MW), which are typically approximated using Kron's loss formula, which is shown below.

$$P_L = \sum_{i=1}^{N} \sum_{j=1}^{N} P_{pi} B_{ij} P_{pj} + \sum_{i=1}^{N} B_{0i} P_{pi} + B_{00} \quad (4)$$

where B_{ij} denote the transmission loss coefficient. The sum of total demand for load and total losses of transmission line results the generated power as stated by the criterion of power balance (Eq. 5). Furthermore, the research community has chosen a curtailment version that excludes transmission lines real power losses. It is given by

$$\sum_{i=1}^{N} P_{pi} = P_D \quad (5)$$

The real power balance constraints are most commonly expressed using Eqs. (4) and (5).

B. **Inequality Constraints**

The inequality constraint is given as:

$$P_{pi}^{\min} \leq P_{pi} \leq P_{pi}^{\max} \tag{6}$$

where $P_{pi}^{\min}$ and $P_{pi}^{\max}$ represent the min and max output power (in MW), respectively. The output power P_{pi} ranges in between $P_{pi}^{\min}$ and $P_{pi}^{\max}$.

2.2 *Prohibited Operating Zones (POZ)*

The entire operating range of generator is not always available because of physical operation limitations in practice. As shown in Fig. 1, POZ tend to discontinuous regions for the objective function. The POZ constraints are given as:

$$P_{pi} = \begin{cases} P_{pi}^{\min} \leq P_{pi} \leq P_{pi,1}^{L} \\ P_{pi,z-1}^{U} \leq P_{pi} \leq P_{pi,z}^{L} \\ P_{pi,pzi} \leq P_{pi} \leq P_{pi}^{\max} \end{cases} \tag{7}$$

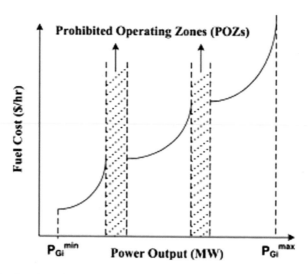

Fig. 1 Objective function with prohibited operating zone

where $P_{pi,z}^{L}$ and $P_{pi,z-1}^{U}$ represents the zth prohibited operating zone lower and upper limits for the ith generation unit, respectively, p_{pzi} denotes the POZ number for the ith unit.

2.3 Ramp Rate Limits

In practice, each generating unit range of operation is constrained by its ramp rate limit, and therefore, the power output P_{pi} cannot be changed instantly. The up-ramp and down-ramp constraints are:

$$P_{pi} - Pp_{i}^{o} \leq UR_{i}$$
$$P_{pi}^{o} - P_{pi} \leq DR_{i}. \tag{8}$$

where P_{pi} is the present power output, P_{pi}^{0} is the previous power output, UR_{i} and DR_{i} is the up-ramp and down-ramp limit of generator i, respectively. Considering together with the generating capacity limit, ramp rate limit can be modified as:

$$\max\left(P_{pi}^{\min}, P_{pi}^{0} - DR_{i} \leq P_{pi}\right) \leq \min\left(P_{pi}^{\max}, P_{pi}^{0} + UR_{i}\right) \tag{9}$$

3 Results

To confirm the efficacy of the proposed method, it is applied to six ELD problems. Its finest outcomes are compared to those that have been reported in the literature. All cases are modeled in GAMS environment and solved using lindo solver (Table 1).

Table 1 Test cases

Characteristics	Case 1	Case 2	Case 3	Case 4	Case 5	Case 6
Unit number	38	13	40	20	10	15
PD (WM)	6000	2530	10,500	2500	2000	2630
Valve point effect		✓	✓		✓	
Transmission loss				✓	✓	✓
Prohibited zone						✓
Ramp rate limits						✓

Considering Case 1, Table 2 represents that the lowest value of cost function is achieved by proposed method, and it is 9418736.1091 ($/h), and also third lowest cost value, which is slightly larger than MHS and ADE-MMS is obtained. In comparison with the proposed method, the costs obtained by other methods like SPSO, PSO_Crazy, New_PSO, and PSO_TVAC are all larger than proposed method.

Considering Case 2, Table 3 represents that by using the TLBO, GA-DE-PS, and ADE-MMS, feasible solution can be obtained. Further, lowest cost value can be obtained by the proposed method, and it is equal to 24,043.8371 ($/h). When compared with other algorithms, MABC is the worst, and its cost value is equal to 24,208.833 ($/h). In the Case 3, when compared to other algorithms in Table 4, the cost value of proposed method is the lowest one, which is equal to 118,651.2350 ($/h). The remaining algorithms CSA, MsEBBO, CCDE, SDP, EMA, GA-DE-PS, DEPSO, and ADE-MMS give the results similar to each other.

In the Case 4, in Table 5, when compared to other algorithms, i.e., CBA, PSO_GSA and ADE-MMS, the proposed method gives slightly more cost value 62,464.8036 ($/h). However, the losses are less when compared to other algorithms. When compared to IA-EDP, the proposed method gives better values in terms of both cost and loss. In the Case 5, from Table 6, among all the methods, the proposed method gives the best cost value as 111,259.6877 ($/h). The cost value with decreasing order is given as TLBO, QOTLBO, RCCRO, ADE-MMS, BSA, and OGHS. In case 6, from Table 7, when compared to IA_EDP, IA_EDP, ACSS, RTO, and PSO-SIF, the proposed method gives the best cost value 32,697.2682 ($/h).

4 Conclusions

This paper proposes DNLP, which is formulated in GAMS for ELD problems. Six test cases related to the ELD problem have been evaluated using the proposed method, including POZ, VPE, ramp rate constraints, and transmission line losses. Furthermore, the results of several ELD problems reported in recent literature are compared with the results of DNLP. The results indicate that in all cases, the cost values of the proposed method, with the exception of case 6, exhibit balanced exploration and exploitation capabilities. In all six cases where the equality constraints are fully fulfilled, the optimal solutions of the proposed method are the smallest.

Table 2 Case 1 results comparison (38-unit PD = 6000 MW)

Unit i	SPSO [2]	PSO_crazy [2]	New PSO [2]	PSO_TVAC [2]	GWO [26]	MHS [19]	EPSO [7]	ADE-MMS [53]	Proposed method
1	519.097	366.631	550	443.659	429.7056	426.6055452	388.2933	426.607294	426.9239
2	437.92	550	512.263	342.956	416.2439	426.604709	388.2933	426.604775	427.0135
3	374.789	467.129	485.733	433.117	408.4052	429.6635302	500	429.667976	429.3957
4	394.877	370.471	391.083	500	412.4527	429.6647862	500	429.658589	429.4222
5	356.603	425.712	443.846	410.539	433.6422	429.6667821	500	429.66264	429.3489
6	380.358	415.226	358.398	482.864	425.6522	429.6628268	500	429.66229	429.3504
7	300.234	339.872	415.729	409.483	435.6207	429.6609836	391.2769	429.664774	429.3794
8	335.871	289.777	320.816	446.079	437.6536	429.6631084	391.2769	429.652296	429.3089
9	238.171	195.965	115.347	119.566	115.2751	114	114	114.000001	114
10	218.563	170.608	204.422	137.274	116.883	114	114	114	114
11	196.63	138.984	114	138.933	130.7939	119.7673921	114	119.757436	120.0882
12	234.5	262.35	249.197	155.401	153.2393	127.0724321	114	127.070702	127.3444
13	111.529	114.008	118.886	121.719	110	110	110	110	110
14	100.731	92.393	102.802	90.924	90.028	90	90	90	90
15	122.464	89.044	89.039	97.941	82.0111	82	82	82	82
16	125.31	130.555	120	128.106	120	120	120	120	120
17	155.981	167.85	156.562	189.108	157.1682	159.598211	154.9601	159.538618	159.6762
18	65	65.754	84.265	65	65	65	65	65	65
19	70.071	65	65.041	65	65.0326	65	65	65	65
20	263.95	199.594	151.104	267.422	271.9524	272	272	272	272
21	245.065	272	226.344	221.383	271.959	272	272	272	272

(continued)

Table 2 (continued)

Unit i	SPSO [2]	PSO_crazy [2]	New PSO [2]	PSO_TVAC [2]	GWO [26]	MHS [19]	EPSO [7]	ADE-MMS [53]	Proposed method
22	191.702	130.379	209.298	130.804	259.81	260	260	260	260
23	99.123	173.544	85.719	124.269	120.8832	130.6483892	117.8994	130.647753	130.7053
24	15.058	13.263	10	11.535	12.3567	10	10	10	10
25	60.06	112.161	60	77.103	107.634	113.3051025	60	113.30554	113.4754
26	91.14	105.898	90.489	55.018	92.4117	88.06710085	55	88.066386	88.1224
27	41.006	35.995	39.67	75	39.6668	37.5056686	35	37.504753	37.5642
28	20.399	22.335	20	21.682	20.005	20	20	20	20
29	34.65	30.045	20.995	29.829	20.0014	20	20	20	20
30	20.957	24.112	22.81	20.326	20.0302	20	20	20	20
31	20.219	20.494	20	20	20.013	20	20	20	20
32	25.424	20.011	20.416	21.84	20.007	20	20	20	20
33	26.517	27.44	25	25.62	25.0032	25	25	25	25
34	18.822	18	21.319	24.261	18.008	18	18	18	18
35	9.173	8.024	9.122	9.667	8.006	8	8	8	8
36	26.507	25	25.184	25	25.002	25	25	25	25
37	24.344	20	20	31.642	22.4379	21.78173191	20	21.784749	21.8085
38	27.181	24.371	25.104	29.935	20.0048	21.06169922	20	21.063428	21.0725
Cost	9,543,984.777	9,520,024.601	9,516,448.312	9,500,448.31	9,419,270.188	9,417,235.785	9,431,139.15	9,417,235.7865	9,418,736.1091

Table 3 Case 2 results comparison (13-unit with VPE PD = 2520 MW)

Unit i	TLBO [25]	GA-DE-PS [8]	ABC [21]	SDP [39]	MABC [20]	SDE [15]	ADE-MMS [53]	Proposed method
1	623.564100	628.317500	628.31190	628.31853	628.318530	628.32	628.318544	680
2	299.252200	298.915900	298.98250	299.1993	299.199300	299.2	299.198497	360
3	299.201900	299.138000	295.77100	299.1993	299.1993	299.2	294.520969	360
4	159.733000	159.726900	159.73290	159.7331	159.733100	159.73	159.731398	153.9712
5	159.735000	159.719000	159.73180	159.7331	159.733100	159.73	159.732749	153.9712
6	159.724200	159.718500	159.72930	159.7331	159.733100	159.73	159.730864	160.144
7	160.382600	159.702000	159.73240	159.7331	159.733100	159.73	159.731722	153.9712
8	159.409800	159.703100	159.72770	159.7331	159.733100	159.73	159.732314	153.9712
9	159.396200	159.727800	159.73090	159.7331	159.733100	159.73	159.730301	153.9712
10	77.399700	74.361100	77.210800	77.39991	77.3999123	77.4	77.393765	40
11	77.404000	76.480000	77.037200	77.39991	77.3999121	77.4	77.392382	40
12	92.398800	92.320700	92.227500	87.68453	87.6845309	92.4	92.396383	55
13	92.398500	92.169500	92.083300	92.39991	92.3999123	87.68	92.390112	55
Cost	24,197	24,171.3467	24,166.2199	24,169.9177	24,169.9177	24,169.92	24,164.12233	24,043.8371

Table 4 Case 3 results comparison (40-unit with VPE $P_D = 10,500$ MW)

Unit i	EMA [31]	GA-DE-PS [8]	CSA [9]	MsEBBO [17]	IDE [36]	DEPSO [14]	CCDE [30]	OLCSO [44]	SDP [39]	ADE-MMS [53]	Proposed method
1	110.7998	110.7998	112.0518	110.7998	111.0958	110.802	110.7998	111.9087	110.7998	110.800416	114
2	110.7998	110.7998	111.4948	110.7998	110.9387	110.802	110.7998	112.3251	110.7998	110.788262	114
3	97.3999	97.3999	97.5626	97.3999	97.42609	97.4	97.3999	97.3999	97.39991	97.398774	120
4	179.7331	179.733	179.8	179.7331	179.7333	179.733	179.7331	179.7331	179.7331	179.734403	190
5	87.7999	87.8	88.9834	87.7999	87.95703	87.8	87.7999	88.7912	87.7999	87.809034	97
6	140	139.9999	140	140	140	140	140	140	140	139.999823	140
7	259.5996	259.5998	299.9993	259.5997	259.6062	259.6	259.5997	259.5996	259.5997	259.613755	300
8	284.5996	284.5996	284.9506	284.5997	284.6818	284.6	284.5997	284.5997	284.5997	284.580315	300
9	284.5996	284.5996	284.9653	284.5997	284.6214	284.6	284.5997	284.5997	284.5997	284.593811	300
10	130	130	130.0006	130	130	130	130	130	130	130.001022	130
11	94	94.0001	94	94	94	94	94	168.7998	94	94.001173	94
12	94	94	94	94	94.0001	94	94	168.7998	94	94.001598	94
13	214.7598	214.7597	214.7621	214.7598	214.7598	214.76	214.7598	214.7598	214.7598	214.753201	125
14	394.2793	394.2794	304.5194	394.2794	394.2794	394.279	394.2794	394.2794	394.2794	394.276278	271.6727
15	394.2793	394.2792	394.2799	394.2794	394.2791	394.279	394.2794	304.5196	394.2794	394.267545	266.6637
16	394.2793	394.2795	394.2793	394.2794	394.2794	394.279	394.2794	394.2794	394.2794	394.280016	266.6637
17	489.2793	489.2793	489.2802	489.2794	489.2796	489.279	489.2794	489.2794	489.2794	489.282007	500
18	489.2793	489.2793	489.2776	489.2794	489.2794	489.279	489.2794	489.2794	489.2794	489.284944	500
19	511.2793	511.2793	511.2797	511.2794	511.2795	511.279	511.2794	511.2794	511.2794	511.288149	550
20	511.2793	511.2795	511.2799	511.2794	511.2794	511.279	511.2794	511.2794	511.2794	511.281076	550
21	523.2793	523.2797	523.3012	523.2794	523.285	523.279	523.2794	523.2794	523.2794	523.273674	550

(continued)

Table 4 (continued)

Unit i	EMA [31]	GA-DE-PS [8]	CSA [9]	MsEBBO [17]	IDE [36]	DEPSO [14]	CCDE [30]	OLCSO [44]	SDP [39]	ADE-MAS [53]	Proposed method
22	523.2793	523.2797	523.2928	523.2794	523.2795	523.279	523.2794	523.2794	523.2794	523.284691	550
23	523.2793	523.2793	523.2892	523.2794	523.2835	523.279	523.2794	523.2794	523.2794	523.283.26	550
24	523.2793	523.2796	523.434	523.2794	523.2978	523.279	523.2794	523.2794	523.2794	523.273e8	550
25	523.2793	523.2796	523.2839	523.2794	523.2805	523.279	523.2794	523.2794	523.2794	523.290698	550
26	523.2793	523.2796	523.281	523.2794	523.2829	523.279	523.2794	523.2794	523.2794	523.278.49	550
27	10	10.0002	10	10	10	10	10	10	10	10.00026	10
28	10	10.0003	10.0009	10	10	10	10	10	10	10.00048	10
29	10	10	10.0014	10	10	10	10	10	10	10	10
30	87.7999	87.8003	92.0666	87.7999	88.13216	87.8	87.7999	88.6662	87.7999	87.804959	97
31	190	189.9999	190	190	190	190	190	190	190	189.990602	190
32	190	189.9999	190	190	190	190	190	190	190	189.9984	190
33	190	189.9999	190	190	190	190	190	190	190	189.991515	190
34	164.7998	164.8002	199.9998	164.7998	165.1617	164.8	164.7998	164.8003	164.7998	164.799331	200
35	200	194.4059	199.9999	200	200	194.395	194.3969	164.9011	194.3978	194.466807	200
36	194.3977	199.9997	200	194.3977	192.9418	200	200	165.1643	200	199.98457	200
37	110	109.9998	110	110	110	110	110	110	110	109.981676	110
38	110	110	110	110	110	110	110	110	110	109.991255	110
39	110	109.9906	110	110	110	110	110	110	110	109.997131	110
40	511.2793	511.278	511.2824	511.2794	511.2794	511.279	511.2794	511.2794	511.2794	511.272926	550
Cost	121,412.5	121,412.8	121,425.6	121,412.5	121,411.5	121,412.6	121,412.5	121,415.8	121,412.5	121,370.821975	118,651.2350

Table 5 Case 4 results comparison (20-unit with line loss, $P_D = 2500$ MW)

Unit i	IA-EDP [24]	CBA [37]	BSA [23]	CSA [9]	PSO-SIF [11]	PSO_GSA [10]	TL_QCP [12]	ADE-MMS [53]	Proposed method
1	498.3856	512.7176	510.4477	512.8467	512.9098	512.7788	512.782	512.90625007	514.62
2	194.5007	169.0294	168.3973	168.8534	170.0314	169.0469	169.102	168.64982970	156.5512
3	109.7942	126.8788	125.9721	126.8549	127.0971	126.8915	126.891	126.86181966	128.4591
4	100.0175	102.8739	103.5291	102.8784	103.1858	102.8666	102.867	103.07182158	103.893
5	118.2894	113.6932	113.8212	113.6863	113.6241	113.6839	113.683	113.78617963	113.3537
6	73.8652	73.5788	73.7901	73.5482	73.5924	73.5798	73.572	73.55105912	73.2614
7	122.2779	115.3014	115.0664	115.4766	115.3039	115.2981	115.29	115.58255999	121.8543
8	119.3704	116.4061	116.3401	116.4497	116.4027	116.4039	116.4	116.42803568	118.5064
9	99.2393	100.4357	100.7093	100.7505	100.322	100.4041	100.405	100.41258505	98.3958
10	97.9034	106.0647	107.1366	106.1438	105.7159	106.0575	106.027	106.23675914	109.1751
11	146.9011	150.2262	150.706	150.2221	150.123	150.2512	150.239	150.06950158	143.5412
12	298.086	292.7687	291.1304	292.7736	292.8279	292.7548	292.766	292.79241993	302.2164
13	116.1543	119.1206	119.1528	118.9029	119.1141	119.1124	119.114	118.95954697	112.9466
14	35.6257	30.8427	32.4521	30.8736	29.6754	30.835	30.832	30.83111600	30.608
15	112.5822	115.8196	116.1479	115.7864	115.8047	115.8097	115.806	115.70642231	116.334
16	36.3446	36.2513	36.2816	36.2102	36.1852	36.2548	36.254	36.25933353	36.2491
17	67.1374	66.8602	67.7355	66.8828	66.8944	66.8649	66.859	66.89719916	65.8331
18	91.289	87.9713	87.2547	87.8848	88.0711	87.965	87.971	87.92517311	88.7134

(continued)

Table 5 (continued)

Unit i	IA-EDP [24]	CBA [37]	BSA [23]	CSA [9]	PSO-SIF [11]	PSO_GSA [10]	TL_QCP [12]	ADE-MMS [53]	Proposed method
19	95.9706	100.8124	101.5359	100.7805	100.7354	100.7982	100.803	100.5894492*	104.4242
20	59.7995	54.3106	54.2861	54.1771	54.3	54.3083	54.305	54.42643219	52.8152
Cost	62,466.8	62,456.63	62,456.69	62,456.63	62,456.67	62,456.63	62,456.63	62,456.507435	62,464.8036
P_L	93.5348	91.9632	91.893	55.8	91.9275	91.9654	91.967	91.94349367	91.7513

Table 6 Case 5 results comparison (10-unit with VPE and line loss, $P_D = 2000$ MW)

Unit i	QOTLBO [23]	TLBO [23]	OGHS [34]	RCCRO [18]	BSA [23]	ADE-MMS [53]	Proposed method
1	55	55	55	55	55	55.00000000	55
2	79.9991	80	80	79.9999	80	80.00000000	80
3	107.9231	105.9616	106.9916	106.922	106.9295	106.93993334	107.0668
4	98.6479	99.9321	100.5354	100.5426	100.6028	100.57627031	99.9515
5	82.018	80.6424	81.445	81.5216	81.499	81.50173667	82.0117
6	83.4878	85.7878	83.067	83.0528	83.0074	83.02088436	83.0112
7	300	300	299.9998	299.9999	300	300.00000000	300
8	340	340	339.9999	339.9999	340	340.00000000	340
9	469.9706	469.6979	470	469.9999	470	470.00000000	470
10	469.9988	469.9943	469.9999	469.9999	470	470.00000000	470
Cost	111,498	111,500	111,490	111,497.6319	111,497.6276	111,497.630810	111,259.6877
P_L	87.045326	87.016061	87.03890848	87.0387	87.0387	87.03882468	87.0412

Table 7 Case 6 results comparison (15-unit with POZ, ramp rate limits and line loss constraints, P_D = 2630 MW)

Unit i	OLCSO [44]	IA_EDP [24]	TLBO [32]	MsEBBO [17]	CSS [46]	ACSS [46]	RTO [21]	PSO-SIF [11]	ADE-MMS [53]	Proposed method
1	455	455	455	455	454.5672	454.9941	455	455	455	455
2	380	379.9999	455	380	379.901	379.9797	380	380	455	380
3	130	130	130	130	129.9512	129.9845	129.9999	130	130	130
4	130	129.9999	130	130	129.9999	129.9344	129.9999	130	130	130
5	170	169.9999	304.99	170	169.5655	169.9251	170	169.997	234.132442	170
6	460	459.9999	460	460	459.9664	459.8311	460	460	460	460
7	430	429.9999	465	430	429.9179	429.9816	430	430	465	430
8	69.4738	67.9628	60	69.4798	81.1328	68.4119	70.225	74.9813	60	71.4285
9	60.1108	65.7269	25.042	60.1049	94.6923	59.1246	60.1965	55.844	25.00000001	58.5957
10	160	156.3294	25	160	108.6934	159.7769	159.9999	160	30.96514737	160
11	80	80	58.749	80	79.8733	79.6671	80	80	76.68369098	80
12	80	79.9999	54.99	80	79.7393	79.825	80	80	80	80
13	25	25	25	25	25.2144	25.0364	25	25.0001	25	25
14	15	15	15	15	16.3491	16.5617	15	15	15	15
15	15	15	15	15	18.2129	15.0816	15	15.0598	15	15
Cost	32,692.4	32,698.2	32,770.721	32,692.4	32,693.31	32,678.13	32,701.81	32,706.88	32,547.369569	32,697.2682
P_L	29.5846	30.0187	28.791	29.5848	29.1089	29.4543	30.4216	30.8822	26.78128031	30.0243

References

1. Sinha N, Chakrabarti R, Chattopadhyay PK (2003) Evolutionary programming techniques for economic load dispatch. IEEE Trans Evol Comput 7:83–94
2. Chaturvedi KT, Pandit M, Srivastava L (2009) Particle swarm optimization with time varying acceleration coefficients for non-convex economic power dispatch. Int J Electr Power Energy Syst 31:249–257
3. Bhattacharya A, Chattopadhyay PK (2010) Biogeography-based optimization for different economic load dispatch problems. IEEE Trans Power Syst 25:1064–1077
4. Basu M (2011) Economic environmental dispatch using multi-objective differential evolution. Appl Soft Comput 11:2845–2853
5. de Athayde Costa e Silva M, Klein CE, Mariani VC, dos Santos Coelho L (2013) Multi-objective scatter search approach with new combination scheme applied to solve environmental/economic dispatch problem. Energy 53:14–21
6. Niknam T, Mojarrad HD, Meymand HZ (2011) Non-smooth economic dispatch computation by fuzzy and self adaptive particle swarm optimization. Appl Soft Comput 11:2805–2817
7. Abdullah MN, Abu Bakar AH, Abd Rahim N, Moklis H (2013) Economic load dispatch with nonsmooth cost functions using evolutionary particle swarm optimization. IEEJ Trans Electr Electron Eng 8:S30–S37
8. Mahdad B, Srairi K (2013) Solving practical economic dispatch using hybrid GA–DE–PS method. Int J Syst Assurance Eng Manage 5:391–398
9. Basu M, Chowdhury A (2013) Cuckoo search algorithm for economic dispatch. Energy 60:99–108
10. Dubey HM, Pandit M, Panigrahi BK, Udgir M (2013) Economic load dispatch by hybrid swarm intelligence based gravitational search algorithm. Int J Intell Syst Appl 5:21–32
11. Ghorbani N, Vakili S, Babaei E, Sakhavati A (2013) Particle swarm optimization with smart inertia factor for solving non-convex economic load dispatch problems. Int Trans Electr Energy Syst 24:1120–1133
12. Yang L, Fraga ES, Papageorgiou LG (2013) Mathematical programming formulations for non-smooth and non-convex electricity dispatch problems. Electr Power Syst Res 95:302–308
13. Roy PK, Bhui S (2013) Multi-objective quasi-oppositional teaching learning based optimization for economic emission load dispatch problem. Int J Electr Power Energy Syst 53:937–948
14. Sayah S, Hamouda A (2013) A hybrid differential evolution algorithm based on particle swarm optimization for nonconvex economic dispatch problems. Appl Soft Comput 13:1608–1619
15. Srinivasa Reddy A, Vaisakh K (2013) Shuffled differential evolution for large scale economic dispatch. Electr Power Syst Res 96:237–245
16. Wang L, Li L-p (2013) An effective differential harmony search algorithm for the solving non-convex economic load dispatch problems. Int J Electr Power Energy Syst 44:832–843
17. Xiong G, Shi D, Duan X (2013) Multi-strategy ensemble biogeography-based optimization for economic dispatch problems. Appl Energy 111:801–811
18. Bhattacharjee K, Bhattacharya A, nee Dey SH (2014) Solution of economic emission load dispatch problems of power systems by real coded chemical reaction algorithm. Int J Electr Power Energy Syst 59:176–187
19. Secui DC et al (2014) A modified harmony search algorithm for the economic dispatch problem. Technical report
20. Secui DC (2015) A new modified artificial bee colony algorithm for the economic dispatch problem. Energy Convers Manage 89:43–62
21. Labbi Y, Attous DB, Mahdad B (2014) Artificial bee colony optimization for economic dispatch with valve point effect. Front Energy 8:449–458
22. Mandal B, Roy PK, Mandal S (2014) Economic load dispatch using krill herd algorithm. Int J Electr Power Energy Syst 57:1–10
23. Modiri-Delshad M, Abd Rahim N (2014) Solving non-convex economic dispatch problem via backtracking search algorithm. Energy 77:372–381

24. Aragón VS, Esquivel SC, Coello Coello CA (2015) An immune algorithm with power redistribution for solving economic dispatch problems. Inf Sci 295:609–632
25. Banerjee S, Maity D, Chanda CK (2015) Teaching learning based optimization for economic load dispatch problem considering valve point loading effect. Int J Electr Power Energy Syst 73:456–464
26. Kamboj VK, Bath SK, Dhillon JS (2015) Solution of non-convex economic load dispatch problem using grey wolf optimizer. Neural Comput Appl 27:1301–1316
27. Pradhan M, Roy PK, Pal T (2016) Grey wolf optimization applied to economic load dispatch problems. Int J Electr Power Energy Syst 83:325–334
28. Abdelaziz AY, Ali ES, Abd Elazim SM (2016) Implementation of flower pollination algorithm for solving economic load dispatch and combined economic emission dispatch problems in power systems. Energy 101:506–518
29. Al-Betar MA, Awadallah MA, Khader AT, Bolaji AL, Almomani A (2016) Economic load dispatch problems with valve-point loading using natural updated harmony search. Neural Comput Appl 29:767–781
30. Ghasemi M, Taghizadeh M, Ghavidel S, Abbasian A (2016) Colonial competitive differential evolution: an experimental study for optimal economic load dispatch. Appl Soft Comput 40:342–363
31. Ghorbani N, Babaei E (2016) Exchange market algorithm for economic load dispatch. Int J Electr Power Energy Syst 75:19–27
32. He X, Rao Y, Huang J (2016) A novel algorithm for economic load dispatch of power systems. Neurocomputing 171:1454–1461
33. Kamboj VK, Bhadoria A, Bath SK (2016) Solution of non-convex economic load dispatch problem for small-scale power systems using ant lion optimizer. Neural Comput Appl 28:2181–2192
34. Singh M, Dhillon JS (2016) Multiobjective thermal power dispatch using opposition-based greedy heuristic search. Int J Electr Power Energy Syst 82:339–353
35. Yu JJQ, Li VOK (2016) A social spider algorithm for solving the non-convex economic load dispatch problem. Neurocomputing 171:955–965
36. Zou D, Li S, Wang G-G, Li Z, Ouyang H (2016) An improved differential evolution algorithm for the economic load dispatch problems with or without valve-point effects. Appl Energy 181:375–390
37. Adarsh BR, Raghunathan T, Jayabarathi T, Yang X-S (2016) Economic dispatch using chaotic bat algorithm. Energy 96:666–675
38. Prakash T, Singh VP, Singh SP, Mohanty SR (2017) Economic load dispatch problem: quasi-oppositional self-learning TLBO algorithm. Energy Syst 9:415–438
39. Alawode KO, Jubril AM, Kehinde LO, Ogunbona PO (2018) Semidefinite programming solution of economic dispatch problem with non-smooth, non-convex cost functions. Electric Power Syst Res 164:178–187
40. Md Ali Bulbul Sk, Pradhan M, Roy PK, Pal T (2018) Opposition-based krill herd algorithm applied to economic load dispatch problem. Ain Shams Eng J 9:423–440
41. Kumar M, Dhillon JS (2018) Hybrid artificial algae algorithm for economic load dispatch. Appl Soft Comput 71:89–109
42. Mohammadi F, Abdi H (2018) A modified crow search algorithm (MCSA) for solving economic load dispatch problem. Appl Soft Comput 71:51–65
43. Rizk-Allah RM, El-Sehiemy RA, Wang G-G (2018) A novel parallel hurricane optimization algorithm for secure emission/economic load dispatch solution. Appl Soft Comput 63:206–222
44. Xiong G, Shi D (2018) Orthogonal learning competitive swarm optimizer for economic dispatch problems. Appl Soft Comput 66:134–148
45. Yu J, Kim C-H, Wadood A, Khurshiad T, Rhee S-B (2018)A novel multi-population based chaotic JAYA algorithm with application in solving economic load dispatch problems. Energies 11:1946
46. Zakian P, Kaveh A (2018) Economic dispatch of power systems using an adaptive charged system search algorithm. Appl Soft Comput 73:607–622

47. Das D, Bhattacharya A, Ray RN (2019) Dragonfly algorithm for solving probabilistic economic load dispatch problems. Neural Comput Appl 32:3029–3045

48. Dhiman G (2019) MOSHEPO: a hybrid multi-objective approach to solve economic load dispatch and micro grid problems. Appl Intell 50:119–137

49. Gholamghasemi M, Akbari E, Asadpoor MB, Ghasemi M (2019) A new solution to the non-convex economic load dispatch problems using phasor particle swarm optimization. Appl Soft Comput 79:111–124

50. Aghay Kaboli SHr, Alqallaf AK (2019) Solving non-convex economic load dispatch problem via artificial cooperative search algorithm. Expert Syst Appl 128:14–27

51. Singh D, Dhillon JS (2019) Ameliorated grey wolf optimization for economic load dispatch problem. Energy 169:398–419

52. Yu J, Kim C-H, Wadood A, Khurshaid T, Rhee S-B (2019)Jaya algorithm with self-adaptive multi-population and Lévy flights for solving economic load dispatch problems. IEEE Access 7:21372–21384

53. Zhang Q, Zou D, Duan N, Shen X (2019)An adaptive differential evolutionary algorithm incorporating multiple mutation strategies for the economic load dispatch problem. Appl Soft Comput 78:641–669

54. Tiwari S, Pal NS, Ansari MA, Yadav D, Singh N (2020) Economic load dispatch using PSO. In: Micro-electronics and telecommunication engineering. Springer, Singapore, pp 51–64

55. Chandra Sekhar JN (2014) Application of firefly algorithm for combined economic load and emission dispatch. Int J Recent Innov Trends Comput Commun 2:2448–2452

Multi-Perspective Reasoning Using Adaptive Learning

P. Kumar, B. Swaminathan, and U. Karthikeyan

Abstract An evaluation and decision of learning methodology is a huge locale in AI, man-made thinking, data mining, model affirmation, etc. There are a large number of learning calculations which exists, and new calculations are being included the AI writing; in any case, it is hard to choose the most reasonable learning calculation for a given dataset. With the data blast of various learning calculations and regularly changing information situations, there is a need of versatile learning framework. A specific learning strategy which is reasonable in a circumstance may not be fruitful for all the sorts of learning. The learning cycle is firmly identified with the learning issue or information within reach or what we are attempting to learn, and henceforth, while choosing learning techniques, it is important to comprehend the learning issue. There is a need to investigate the learning issue and afterward select the most appropriate methodology by versatile learning. It does not simply mean joining more than one learning calculations and it is not exchanging two unique techniques. It is tied in with discovering information attributes and suggesting the most suitable strategy. It is a test to devise an approach which yields the most exact outcomes and manage the evolving condition. Multi-viewpoint learning is fundamental in multi-viewpoint dynamic. The accentuation of the work is on choosing arrangement calculation (s) for a specific choice situation. As highlight determination strategy influences classifier execution, the mixture choice technique utilizing rotation forest is proposed for clinical conclusion. The goal is to build up a versatile learning philosophy with expanded exactness where the learning strategy can be managed, and it tends to be a solitary classifier or it very well may be an outfit of classifiers.

Keywords Data mining · Machine learning · Adaptive learning · k-NN · SVM

P. Kumar (✉) · B. Swaminathan · U. Karthikeyan
Rajalakshmi Engineering College, Chennai, India
e-mail: kumar@rajalakshmi.edu.in

© The Author(s), under exclusive license to Springer Nature Singapore Pte Ltd. 2022
C. Satyanarayana et al. (eds.), *High Performance Computing and Networking*,
Lecture Notes in Electrical Engineering 853,
https://doi.org/10.1007/978-981-16-9885-9_2

1 Introduction

As cited by Rich and Knight [1], "artificial intelligence is the investigation of how to cause PCs to get things done at which, right now, individuals are better." Machine learning is a subfield of AI which includes frameworks that learn dependent on past experience. AI is characterized as "a logical order that includes the plan and improvement of calculations permitting machines to imitate human insight." Herbert Simon characterizes learning as "learning indicates changes in the framework that is versatile as in the empower the framework to do similar assignment or errands all the more proficiently or all the more viably whenever." As per Mitchell [2], AI is characterized as "s PC program is said to gain for a fact E-concerning some class of errands T and execution measure P, if its presentation at assignments in T, as estimated by P, improves with experience E." Machine learning adjusts to new conditions, identifies and extrapolates designs.

Learning is a ceaseless cycle of retaining contributions from different sources and recalling that it and deduce from it to utilize it for the future circumstances. The manner in which person sees the circumstance and learns for the further activity is an extremely intricate cycle. Learning and derivation are significant parts of insight. Learning helps in dynamic and advancing the cycles. The learning is sorted into the accompanying kinds: supervised learning, unsupervised learning, reinforcement learning, and semi-supervised learning. Regulated learning utilizes a named information and finds a component of a named models. There is a couple of information and a normal yield esteem. The solo learning is utilized to gather unlabeled information according to some comparability measure. Since the models provided to the student are not named, a mistake signal is absent for analyzing a forthcoming arrangement. The support learning [3] is the most broad of the over three learning classes. In support learning, the student demonstrations in a situation and gets a prize or punishment for its activities when it is tackling an issue.

Semi-managed taking in [4] is gaining from of both marked and unlabeled information. Semi-regulated learning is most helpful at whatever point a lot of unlabeled information are accessible contrasted with marked information. This happens if gaining information focuses are modest, yet nearly getting names, costs a great deal of time, cash, and exertion. Versatile learning [3] alludes to realizing where expertise is adjusted, concerning the earth, or a learning task. The learning depends on the data assembled and information gained before and experience. A specific technique which is exceptionally effective in a particular circumstance may not give a proficient answer for the various learning issues. The learning cycle is firmly connected with the learning issue or rather what is to be realized and what are realizing goals. Henceforth, determination of learning strategy requests a comprehension of the issue. There is a need to dissect the learning issue and afterward select the correct methodology which is most reasonable methodology progressively in versatile learning. It is not simply changing various techniques or utilizing a board of specialists. It includes choosing information keenly, and consequently, the most proper technique

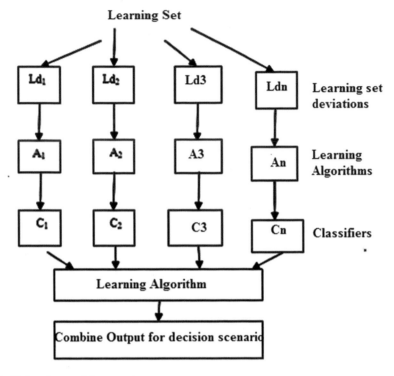

Fig. 1 Various learners' framework

is picked. Versatile learning attempts to improve learning and can have arrangements for changing learning situations.

Versatile learning [3] utilizes numerous students that can choose powerfully. It can have a gathering of calculations and diverse learning sets. This blend and the choice circumstance structure the versatile learning calculation. The troublesome portion of the system is consolidating various students and classifiers. An ordinary structure with a few students and characterization calculations is shown in Fig. 1.

Execution forecast of AI calculations, discovering positions among students, and picking an appropriate classifier for a given information are significant points in AI and information mining [5–7].

2 Literature Review

An assessment and determination of learning strategy is an unmistakable territory in information mining, manmade brainpower, and example acknowledgment [8]. There are a many learning calculations accessible in AI and information mining, and new calculations are included each day. However, it is hard to pick the appropriate student or classifier for a given information. Consequently, there is the data blast of various learning calculations and the changing information situations. A learning technique which is exceptionally effective in a specific circumstance may not be fruitful for all the learning issues. The learning cycle is firmly identified with the learning issue or information within reach or what we are attempting to learn. Consequently, while choosing learning strategies, it is important to comprehend the learning issue. There is a need to examine the learning issue and afterward select the most reasonable calculation which is prescribed to the end client.

The AI field has developed since various years and has given a scope of calculations for performing arrangement, for example, neural organizations [2], choice trees [2], rule inducers, closest neighbor, support vector machine (SVM) [9, 10], and so on. The client needs to pick the appropriate calculation which performs best for his undertaking. This calculation determination issue is a troublesome issue since no calculation can perform superior to all others, independent of explicit issue attributes, as it has been seen in different exact correlations [11]. Later, the experimental outcomes have been affirmed by "sans no lunch hypotheses" [12]. Among others, they express that their presentation found the middle value of overall learning issues characterized over a particular preparing set which will be actually the equivalent. Every calculation has a selective matchless quality [13], for example, it works superior to the rest of the calculations for explicit issues. This is on the grounds that each calculation has "inductive inclination." The calculation makes the presumptions for characterizing concealed models and causes inductive inclination. As indicated by Mitchell [2], "the inductive predisposition of a learning calculation is the arrangement of all suppositions which are required for advocating its inductive surmising as deductive derivations." Subsequently, the client must have a skill in distinguishing the best calculation for the given issue.

Meta-learning [14] implies finding out about learning calculations. Meta-learning is utilized for tackling significant grouping and relapse issues. It helps in the best possible determination of an appropriate classifier or a blend of classifiers. In the event that clients are not given any assistance, they need to confront issues while performing classifier determination and mix. So it is needed to do on an experimentation premise. An answer for this issue can be accomplished by making meta-learning framework. A few meta-learning systems are proposed for calculation choice issue in [5]. Meta-learning chooses a reasonable learning device for a given errand or application. Three choices are given that worry the objective. The best learning calculation is chosen which creates the most ideal decision for the issue in the primary alternative. Second is to pick the quantity of students that incorporate the best one, and different calculations are not extensively less fortunate than the best one. The third gives positioning of the calculations dependent on their exhibition. This positioning enables the client finally to pick the learning calculation. This meta-learning approach dependent on positioning is applied in Esprit Project MetaL [15].

Lemke et al. [16] portray the various settings wherein meta-learning can be applied. Gama and Brazdil [17] use relapse for foreseeing the exhibition of various calculations. They have utilized fifteen meta-highlights for creating direct relapse models. Their outcomes show that it is hard to choose the best student and standardization technique. Lamentably, the investigation utilizes just twenty datasets.

Linder et al. [18] propose meta-getting the hang of utilizing case-based thinking. Here, a case base comprising of known and worked out issue examples is shaped, and the most related issue is utilized for suggesting of algorithm(s). Nonetheless, the suggestion incorporates application limitations that worry sort of the calculation, interpretability of the made model, and the time required for preparing and testing

Positioning is another methodology that is proposed to suggest calculations. Calculations dependent on the positioning score are suggested. The positioning strategy is worthwhile in light of the fact that the client may evaluate the most legitimate calculation for the given information. A k-nearest neighbor approach [19] is utilized by Brazdil et al. [6] to rank the calculations. A score is determined dependent on exactness and absolute running season of the calculation, and the positioning is given.

Choice of highlights relies on the difficult space and chose calculations. There ought to be a legitimate determination of highlights to uncover the shifting complexities of issue occasions. It is not so natural to propose suitable meta-highlights for a given issue.

There are different characterization calculations in information mining. End clients frequently do not have needed involvement with picking a fitting classifier. Additionally, they need to continue with experimentation premise, which is tedious. So an answer is required for this issue. Meta-learning can be utilized to suggest fitting learning calculation which utilizes different kinds of meta-highlights, for example, straightforward, data hypothetical, and factual measures.

3 Proposed Work

Interestingly with the above methodologies, the proposed arrangement calculation suggestion strategy is not quite the same as the above work in the manner to portray a dataset and manage comparative datasets. All the more explicitly, k-closest neighbor (k-NN) [19] technique is recognizing k-closest datasets with the new dataset. At that point, the calculations with the prevalent exhibitions on the nearest datasets are proposed for giving answers for the inconspicuous information. The test results on the 38 UCI datasets [20] and nine distinct classifiers affirm that proposed strategy works viably.

3.1 Multi-perspective Learning

There is a need to catch totally information and framework data that is acquired from alternate points of view. It is essential to utilize more data accessible to adapt ideally. Each snippet of data includes certain point of view. A few viewpoints are imperative while some of them are not really. Dynamic becomes troublesome when information about various potential points of view is not accessible. Henceforth, learning may stay inadequate. Multi-viewpoint learning is vital for multi-point of view dynamic. It signifies "the gaining from the information and data obtained and worked from alternate points of view" [3]. The multi-viewpoint learning requires catching data, framework boundaries, and connections by considering alternate points of view. The multi-viewpoint learning may add to in general learning intricacy; be that as it may, it gives a lot all the more learning possibilities.

According to "No Free Lunch" hypothesis [21], no student is appropriate for the distinctive learning situations. So the work is done to propose a learning strategy which will be appropriate according to the issue or information close by. It applies to the information mining space. Execution of learning strategy or classifier depends not just on the issue or its information qualities, yet additionally the element choice technique utilized.

The work stream as shown in Fig. 2 can be utilized to suggest proper calculation as the information changes. Utilizing information portrayal instrument, measurable, and data hypothetical meta-highlights are determined. This progression is done for both verifiable datasets and new test dataset. Execution of classifiers on the recorded datasets is thought of and put away in knowledgebase.

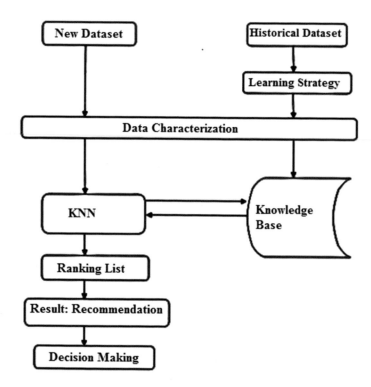

Fig. 2 Work stream of adaptive learning in data mining

The fundamental thought is to propose a calculation (s) for non-master in calculation determination measure. Calculation determination is to discover the most appropriate calculation for a given issue when a few equivalent choices are accessible. The goal is to propose a structure for figuring out how to defeat the disadvantages of existing learning techniques. The proposed learning system will include keen determination of classifiers. As a matter of fact, the recommended technique will focus on flexible taking in based on point of view. The learning philosophy can be past managed or semi-regulated. For example, it very well may be a mix of support vector machine (SVM) like element vector grouping procedure and fake neural organization like managed learning method to bamboozle both the universes. There are different methodologies of calculation choice [22] as given underneath:

(1)   Trial and Error Approach: Existing calculations are tried on each dataset. It gives precise suggestion of calculation, yet it includes more expense.
(2)   Random Selection: Selection of classifier is done arbitrarily. It is savvy, however, less precision is acquired.
(3)   Expert counsel: Every new issue is alluded to a specialist for exhortation. In any case, it is anything but a useful arrangement.
(4)   Case Base Reasoning: Previous case is utilized for proposing characterization, for example, for a dataset, a couple of calculations are tried utilizing the relevance test. A calculation is proposed for each new dataset.

The strategy utilized in the proposed work is as per the following:

1.   Datasets are gathered from UCI AI archive [20].
2.   Meta component extraction is finished utilizing data characteristics tool (DCT) for preparing.
3.   A learning calculation with execution measure is thought of. Characterization precision is utilized as an exhibition basis.
4.   The information base is made by thinking about information qualities or meta-highlights of datasets and execution of learning calculations.
5.   Extraction of meta-highlights is done for new inconspicuous dataset utilizing DCT.
6.   Use k-NN [19] for getting k-comparable datasets from information base.
7.   Obtaining the calculations for the K-comparable datasets.
8.   Ranking of calculation.
9.   Algorithm suggestion which will help in dynamic.

Meta-learning has two stages. The principal stage is called assessment mode. Meta-highlights of authentic or preparing datasets are extricated. Execution of various learning calculations on various datasets and meta-highlights of these datasets are put away in knowledgebase. The subsequent stage is called proposal mode. Here, meta-highlights are separated for another or test dataset. At that point, utilizing k-NN calculation [19] and knowledgebase, initial three best classifiers are suggested. The framework is executed in Java. WEKA [23] is utilized for investigation and approval. MS Access is utilized to store information base.

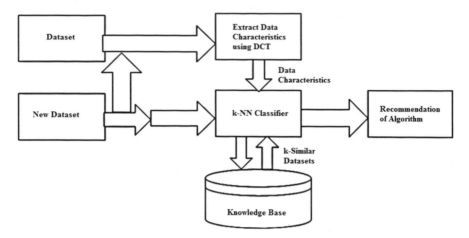

Fig. 3 Engineering of adaptive learning

Engineering of adaptive learning framework is appeared in Fig. 3. Dataset contains both the preparation models and testing models. At first, datasets are given to data characteristics tool (DCT). DCT figures information attributes, for example, number of occasions, skewness, kurtosis, entropy, and so forth, which are alluded as meta-highlights or meta-information. Knowledgebase comprises of the exhibition of classifiers on various datasets. This information can be regarding arrangement exactness, time, and so on. Proposed approach utilizes order exactness. At the point when an obscure tuple is given, a k-NN [19] discovers match of the obscure tuple with the example space for k-nearest preparing tuples.

There are various potential choices for the separation work; however, Euclidean separation is generally utilized in k-NN. Euclidean separation is determined utilizing Eq. (1).

$$d(p, q) = d(q, p) = \sqrt{(q_1 - p_1)^2 + (q_2 - p_2)^2 + \cdots + (q_n - p_n)^2}$$

$$= \sqrt{\sum_{i=1}^{n} (q_i - p_i)^2}. \tag{1}$$

The proposal technique includes two stages. To begin with, the closest neighbor datasets for another dataset are distinguished. Grouping calculations are proposed for the new dataset utilizing the closest neighbors. The accompanying calculation is utilized for recognizing the k-closest neighbors of a case among occasions. The technique is received to choose k most comparable datasets for a given dataset.

3.2 Neighbor Recognition Algorithm

1. $i = 1$;
2. For every $D \in DC$ do
3. DistanceTable [i] = the separation among d and D, for example, |d-D|
4. $i = i + 1$;
5. Sort DistanceTable in rising request
6. Neighbors = top K datasets of separation table
7. $j = 0$;
8. For each $j < K$ do
9. Alg[j] = Dj's Best Algorithm

The dataset change [24] changes a non-parallel dataset into a comparing double dataset. The consideration ought to be taken that semantic data is not lost. The ostensible to twofold change of the characteristic is widely utilized if learning calculations cannot manage multi-esteemed ostensible credits legitimately. So for this situation, the entire dataset is thought of, and all the characteristics are changed into double configuration. The change cycle is a two stages measure. The means are as per the following.

Stage 1: Distinct credits esteem distinguishing proof: In request to help the change cycle, it requires knowing the quantity of unmistakable qualities for each trait. Each characteristic has an alternate number of particular qualities. Accept trait A1 has a1, a2, a3 as unmistakable qualities. A property is then supplanted by that number of particular components. All out number of unmistakable components is meant by m.

Stage 2: Attribute and its worth substitution [24]: In this cycle, each quality is supplanted by its property estimation set CAi, for example, all unmistakable components of a property supplant its characteristic.

First dataset qualities or meta-highlights are determined for a given dataset. An information portrayal apparatus is utilized to separate dataset attributes, for example, meta-information about a given dataset is gathered. New dataset qualities are given to k-NN, and afterward results are given to the knowledgebase. Knowledgebase decides learning calculation execution dependent on dataset qualities. Comparability between predefined datasets and another dataset is utilized to propose a reasonable calculation. Results from knowledgebase structure a premise to suggest a fitting calculation's amplifying execution. Results are utilized further dynamic. This adaptive learning approach contains the aftereffect of nine order calculations and 38 datasets. Directly, the proposed framework is utilized for characterization task. Assume when there are n datasets and m classifiers, at that point to know which classifier is the best for a given dataset, the dataset is prepared over all classifiers. In the versatile learning approach, likeness check is expected to perform for each verifiable dataset.

Verifiable datasets: For each chronicled dataset, correctnesses are determined utilizing Waikato environment for knowledge analysis (WEKA) [23]. In this proposed framework, nine classifiers and 38 authentic datasets are utilized. So in execution assessment stage, 38×9 mixes are inspected for precision and as well as can be expected be resolved.

New dataset: For another dataset, precision is not accessible at preparing time. So information attributes of another dataset are contrasted and authentic datasets, and afterward, classifiers are suggested dependent on k-NN utilizing Euclidean separation.

The boundaries for each classifier are not changed, however, set as default in WEKA. All 43 datasets utilized are in attribute relation file format (ARFF). The endeavor is made to consider classifiers from various classifications of classifiers, for example, likelihood based, sluggish students, tree, meta, rules, and capacities. It is notable from gathering writing that outfits perform better contrasted with single classifier. The trials are led on ten benchmark datasets utilizing gathering classifiers, for example, Adaboost [25], Bagging [26], Logitboost [27], and Stacking. It is discovered that stacking gives 60% or less characterization precision for these datasets and performs ineffectively contrasted with other three outfit classifiers. Thus, stacking is discarded, and Random Forest [28] and J48 [29] work better as they are tree-based classifiers. SMO gives better execution. Thus, every one of these classifiers are chosen for proposed work.

4 Results and Discussions

It is important to assess how the proposed order calculation choice methodology performs and how it is compelling. The exact examination is set up as follows:

1. 38 arrangement datasets from the UCI AI vault [20] are utilized in the experimentation. Table 1 presents the quantity of examples, the quantity of traits, and the quantity of classes for each dataset. Data hypothetical meta-highlights are separated for datasets with nonstop qualities. As depicted in Table 1, the quantity of examples, the quantity of traits, the quantity of classes, the quantity of numeric ascribes, the quantity of representative credits, missing qualities, and the quantity of unmistakable qualities and entropy are essential highlights of dataset utilized for assessment. Additionally, the best classifier for each of the dataset is appeared.

2. Eight various classifiers are picked to characterize datasets. The consideration is taken to choose classifiers from the vast majority of the classes of classifiers. Gullible Bayes (NB) depends on likelihood. J48 [29] and Random Forest [28] are tree-based classifiers. Projective adaptive resonance theory (PART) [20] is a standard-based classifier, IBK [11] is lethargic learning calculation, and sequential minimal optimization (SMO) classifier [23] is a capacity-based classifier. Other than these learning calculations, the outfits, for example, Random Forest, Bagging [26], and Adaboost [25], are likewise utilized. The three classifiers J48, PART, and NB are utilized as the base classifier in Bagging and Adaboost.

3. The cross-approval strategy [30] ascertains order exactness. A 10-overlap cross-approval is utilized in experimental examination. Information is broken into ten sets, each with a size of information n/10. Nine of these datasets are utilized for

Table 1 Synopsis of knowledge base

S. No	Name	Classifier	Attributes	Occurrences	Session	Figurative	Values	Lost significance	Distinct	Entropy
1	Anneal	RF	39	805	4	29	5	0	72	1.09
2	Audiology	LO	58	231	20	70	0	295	201	2.99
3	Balance-scale	NB	5	599	2	0	5	0	2	0.99
4	Beast-cancer	NB	8	301	3	8	0	8	39	0.79
5	Breast-w	SM	8	700	3	1	8	15	3	0.93
6	Bridges1	NB	9	99	5	9	3	69	129	2.28
7	Bridges2	LO	9	110	5	9	0	69	138	2.27
8	Cars	PA	7	109	3	4	2	0	11	0.18
9	Colic	BA	19	359	2	17	5	1896	49	0.96
10	Credit-a	J4	20	702	2	8	7	71	39	0.98
11	Credit-g	NB	19	999	2	11	8	0	49	0.77
12	Cylinder-bands	SM	40	528	3	19	21	1000	541	0.97
13	Diabetes	SM	9	757	2	0	7	1	3	0.94
14	E. coli	LO	8	325	7	0	6	0	7	2.22
15	Flags	LO	30	202	7	4	18	0	221	2.29
16	Glass	RF	8	223	5	0	8	0	5	2.20
17	Heart-c	LO	9	298	2	7	4	6	19	0.98
18	Heart-h	NB	10	302	3	9	6	811	18	0.95
19	Heart-s	SM	9	285	2	0	11	0	3	0.98
20	Hepatitis	SM	20	163	2	15	7	174	31	0.76
21	Hypothyroid	LO	30	4189	3	18	5	6247	48	0.39

(continued)

Table 1 (continued)

S. No	Name	Classifier	Attributes	Occurrences	Session	Figurative	Values	Lost significance	Distinct	Entropy
22	Ionosphere	PA	33	348	2	0	37	0	1	0.95
23	Eyes	SM	5	147	2	0	5	0	4	1.62
24	Labor	SM	18	64	2	11	9	335	31	0.94
25	Lymph	BA	20	153	3	12	3	0	52	1.31
26	Segments	RF	21	2405	6	0	21	0	6	2.78
27	Sick	J4	30	3881	3	25	5	6103	51	0.35
28	Sonar	IB	59	211	2	0	57	0	3	0.98
29	Soybean	SM	33	692	21	41	0	1	147	3.79
30	Sponge	SM	44	81	4	39	2	28	241	0.49
31	tic-tac-toe	IB	8	987	2	7	0	0	35	0.95
32	Play or Not Play	LO	5	18	2	5	0	0	9	0.98
33	Trains	J4	29	9	2	18	18	49	38	1.00
34	Vehicles	RF	20	856	3	0	21	0	3	1.98
35	Votes	RF	17	501	2	21	0	415	41	0.99
36	Vowels	RF	15	1001	13	3	9	0	29	3.52
37	Weather	IB	5	17	2	2	3	0	9	0.99
38	Zoo	SM	20	99	5	21	1	0	147	2.51

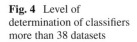

Fig. 4 Level of determination of classifiers more than 38 datasets

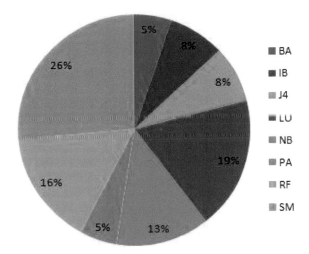

preparing, and testing is completed on one. A mean precision is determined after this cycle is run multiple times. Cross-approval is utilized to analyze the exhibitions of the diverse prescient displaying exhibitions. Utilizing cross-approval, the two unique students or classifiers are analyzed impartially. The presentation measure utilized in the experimental work for the correlation is the arrangement exactness. Best_Classifier is acquired with tests utilizing WEKA, which gives the precision of the classifier and dependent on that the Best_Classifier is distinguished physically.

Figure 4 shows the level of choice of eight classifiers more than 38 datasets. SMO is the most broadly utilized classifier among eight arrangement calculations as it is chosen 26% of the time. Logitboost and Random Forest are the following best classifiers for the majority of the datasets.

The pie diagram in Fig. 4 shows that datasets that are chosen are most appropriate in eight classifiers and not a solitary classifier outweighs everything else (not over 26%), for example, every classifier that is chosen is similarly significant. There is no single classifier which is not suggested in any way.

Figure 5 speaks to the best classifier for 38 datasets among these eight classifiers. For instance, for the first dataset, Random Forest gives the best exactness, though SMO is the best classifier for the last dataset. Figure 5 shows the general image of classifier suggestion, where the exactness suggested is not under 60% of all. So it demonstrates the calculations picked are over normal. Trials are performed on different benchmark datasets (38 datasets) from all spaces, with best classifiers from different classes (nine classifiers). Very nearly fifteen information qualities are utilized. Among these fifteen attributes, numerous blends are shaped, and from that, the best mix is found for the proposal of the classifier. Meta-learning is utilized in proposed adaptive learning. The proposed technique is one endeavor to tackle grouping calculation determination issue in information mining. The trial work shows

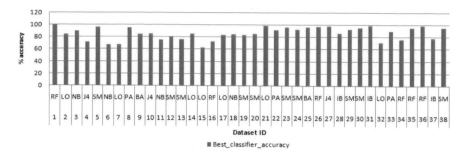

Fig. 5 Chart of level of genuine best exactness more than 38 datasets

that for 76% datasets, for example, 29 out of 38 benchmark datasets, the anticipated precision coordinates intimately with the genuine exactness.

5 Conclusion

From the experimentation and the outcomes, the significance of highlight determination is featured which lessens the time, yet in addition is useful in expanding the precision. Subsequently, one needs to make an appropriate determination of the base classifier just as the component choice so as to accomplish the ideal grouping exactness with respect to the clinical datasets. Three unique kinds of meta-highlights, for example, basic, measurable, and data hypothetical, are misused and analyzed in the current work. Other meta-highlights ought to be thought of and meta-highlights determination ought to be upgraded. Unpleasant sets can help for decreasing and choosing ideally meta-highlights. A ton of time is needed to ascertain all the distinctive meta-highlights, so harsh sets can spare the time needed to choose the calculation and intellectual weight will be diminished for non-specialists.

References

1. Rich E, Knight K, Nair B (1997) Artificial intelligence. Tata McGraw-Hill Publishing Company Ltd.
2. Mitchell T (1997) Machine learning. McGraw Hill
3. Kulkarni P (2012) Reinforcement and systemic machine learning for decision making. IEEE Press
4. Basu S (2005) Semi-supervised clustering: probabilistic models, algorithms and experiments. PhD Thesis, The University of Texas at Austin, USA
5. Soares C, Brazdil P (2000) Zoomed ranking: selection of classification algorithms based on relevant performance information. In: Proceedings of the 4th European conference on principles of data mining and knowledge discovery, pp 126–135
6. Brazdil P, Soares C, Da Costa J (2003) Ranking learning algorithms: using IBL and meta-learning on accuracy and time results. Mach Learn 50:251–277

7. Giraud-Carrier C (2008) Meta-learning tutorial. Technical report, Brigham Young University
8. Kou G, Wu W (2014) An analytic hierarchy model for classification algorithms selection in credit risk analysis, mathematical problems in engineering, vol 2014
9. Joachims T (1997) Text categorization with support vector machines: learning with many relevant features. Technical Report 23, University at Dortmund, LS VIII
10. Joachims T (1999) Making large-scale SVM learning practical. In: Schölkopf B, Burges C, Smola A (eds) Advances in Kernel methods—support vector learning. MIT Press, pp 41–56
11. Aha D (1992) Generalizing from case studies: a case study. In: Proceedings of the 9th international machine learning conference, pp 1–10
12. Wolpert D (1996) The lack of a priori distinctions between learning algorithms. Neural Comput 8:1341–1390
13. Brodley C (1995) Recursive automatic bias selection for classifier construction. Mach Learn 20:63–94
14. Kalousis A, Hilario M (2000) Model selection via meta-learning: a comparative study. In: Proceedings of the 12th International IEEE conference on tools with AI, Canada, pp 214–220
15. MetaL Project. http://www.metal-kdd.org
16. Lemke C, Budka M, Gabrys B (2015) Metalearning: a survey of trends and technologies. Artif Intell Rev 44:117–130
17. Gama J, Brazdil P (1995) Characterization of classification algorithms. In: Springer progress in artificial intelligence, lecture notes in computer science, vol 990, pp 189–200
18. Lindner G, Studer R (1999) AST: support for algorithm selection with a CBR approach. In: Recent advances in meta-learning and future work, pp 418–423
19. Cover T, Hart P (1967) Nearest neighbor pattern classification. IEEE Trans Inf Theory 13(1):21–27
20. Bache K, Lichman M (2013) UCI machine learning repository. School of Information and Computer Science, University of California, Irvine, CA
21. Frank E, Witten I (1998) Generating accurate rule sets without global optimization. In: Proceedings of the fifteenth international conference on machine learning. Morgan Kaufmann Publishers Inc., pp 144–151
22. Smith-Miles K (2009) Cross-disciplinary perspectives on meta-learning or algorithm selection. ACM Comput Surv 41(1):1–25
23. Hall M, Frank E, Holmes G, Pfahringer B, Reutemann P, Witten I (2009) The WEKA data mining software: an update. SIGKDD Explorat 11(1)
24. Song Q, Wang G, Wang C (2012) Automatic recommendation of classification algorithms based on data set characteristics. Pattern Recogn 45:2672–2689
25. Kumar P, Swaminathan B, Karthikeyan U (2021) A novel deep learning model based on Yolo-V2 and Resnet for pedestrian detection. Ann R.S.C.B. 25(4):2258–2268 ISSN: 1583-6258
26. Breiman L (1996) Bagging predictors. Mach Learn 24(2):123–140
27. Friedman J, Hastie T, Tibshirani R (1998) Additive logistic regression: a statistical view of boosting. Ann Stat 28(2):337–407
28. Leo B (2001) Random forests. Mach Learn 45(1):5–32
29. Quinlan J (1993) C4.5: programs for machine learning. Morgan Kaufmann Publishers
30. Kohavi R (1995) A study of cross validation and bootstrap for accuracy estimation and model selection. In: Proceedings of the 14th IJCAI. Morgan Kaufmann, San Francisco, CA, pp 338–345

Ink Recognition Using TDNN and Bi-LSTM

R. Sai Kesav, H. B. Barathi Ganesh, B. Premjith, and K. P. Soman

Abstract The proposed work utilises a combined architecture of time delay neural networks (TDNN) and multi-layered bidirectional long short-term memory (Bi-LSTM) network for the ink recognition from the handwritten text. We added a Trie beam search decoder with three smoothing algorithms such as Kneser–Ney Back off, Kneser–Ney Interpolated, and Stupid Back off to improve the performance of the model. This paper discusses the performance of the combined TDNN and Bi-LSTM network with the above-stated decoder for the ink recognition task. This paper also reports a comparison with the existing models that were implemented for this task. The analysis showed that the model with TDNN and Bi-LSTM architecture with an additional Trie beam search decoder with Kneser–Ney Interpolated smoothing algorithm using 10,000-word lexicon performed better than the model without a decoder.

Keywords Online handwriting recognition · Sequence-sequence learning · Time delay neural network

1 Introduction

Advancements in the present technological era have brought the necessity of human and computer interaction. Since its emergence in the 1900s, optical character recognition (OCR) introduced an alternative method for identifying printed alphabets and

R. Sai Kesav (✉) · B. Premjith · K. P. Soman
Center for Computational Engineering and Networking (CEN), Amrita School of Engineering, Amrita Vishwa Vidyapeetham, Coimbatore, India
e-mail: b_premjith@cb.amrita.edu

K. P. Soman
e-mail: kp_soman@amrita.edu

H. B. Barathi Ganesh
Federated AI Services, Coimbatore, India
e-mail: hb.bg@fai.services

© The Author(s), under exclusive license to Springer Nature Singapore Pte Ltd. 2022   35
C. Satyanarayana et al. (eds.), *High Performance Computing and Networking*,
Lecture Notes in Electrical Engineering 853,
https://doi.org/10.1007/978-981-16-9885-9_3

characters. First-generation OCR emerged between 1960 and 1965; it was developed to read constrained letters and symbols for specific purposes. As time preceded, additional features in fonts and writing patterns featured the need for a new pattern recognition system that matches templates and compares them to recognise characters from a library of words and prototype images for each character given for recognition. A surge of development is followed in OCR, leading to its official release to people in 1986 [1]. Advancements in technology led to the evolution and generation of two separate recognition for handwritten characters offline and online, which was initially proposed for the third-generation OCR. Offline handwriting recognition is a computer vision-based recognition, where pre-written characters are recognised. Online handwriting recognition is a sequence–sequence-based task [2], where each character is recognised [3, 4]. Both recognition systems follow a systematic procedure of optical scanning, location, segmentation, pre-processing, post-processing, extracting the features, with better algorithms for a more significant recognition rate [2].

The introduction of an online handwriting recognition system has improved the accessibility and straightforward input of text into a digital interface to convert handwritten characters into computer-recognised text. Online handwriting recognition system recognises handwritten texts in real time through a digitiser where written words noted with coordinates and specific time frames for characters and words [5]. In online handwriting recognition, written characters are captured and made as input. These inputs differ from offline handwriting recognition as these are real-time inputs. In real-time data, information is captured in sequence–sequence format [2]. There are multiple factors through which the written characters are diversified, based on the temporal style, handwriting patterns, stroke lengths. In comparison with an offline character recogniser, an online character recogniser compares and recognises scanned characters based on the additional input corpus.

Hidden Markov model (HMM)-based recogniser was first implemented [6] for recognition of characters. Multiple methods recognising characters were implemented ranging from convolutional neural networks (CNNs) [7], LSTM cells [8], and independent LSTM cells (Indy LSTM) [9]. These methods were used to build a better recogniser model showing variation in the input and pre-processing and post-processing procedures, using Bezier curves[9], lattice indices, and lattice segmentation [10].

Siyuan et al. [11] introduced time delay neural network (TDNN) in speech processing for spotting individual words. A unique, multi-layered feed-forward neural network used for recognising characters from generated features with over two neurons in successive layers, enabling each layer to propagate with its propagation values and weights. In this work, a combination of TDNN architecture with multi-layered bi-LSTM's [12, 13] was used for recognising the characters using the IAMonDB dataset (IAM Online Database) [6].

In the proposed model, minimum character and word error rate results were achieved by implementing two decoders—Trie beam search decoder and Best path decoder with a 7-gram language model using a 10,000-word lexicon. Three smoothing algorithms: Kneser–Ney Back off [14], Kneser–Ney Interpolated [15], and Stupid Back off [16] were implemented in the Trie beam search decoder resulted in minimum character and word error rates.

2 Related Work

Diversified techniques had been used for better recognition of real-time characters. The HMM-based recogniser is an online character recognition model using the IAM online database (IAMonDB) dataset [6]. IAMonDB dataset consists of words and sentences collected from the Lancaster-Oslo-Berger corpus (LOB corpus) [17] written on a whiteboard.

Due to ambiguity in different writing patterns and styles, online handwriting recognition becomes computationally expensive than offline handwriting recognition [2]. Multiple recognisers were made for online handwriting recognition using different datasets. An HMM-based recogniser was first introduced to recognise characters from the IAMonDB dataset [6]. Since then, numerous advancements were made to develop recogniser models using various deep learning algorithms, LSTM, and Indy LSTMs [8, 9].

Pedro Gonnet et al. [9] introduced Indy LSTM, which differed from normal LSTM cells as Indy LSTM recurrent weights were modelled as a diagonal matrix and smaller when compared with normal LSTM. Victor Carbune et al. [8] introduced a recogniser model using LSTM for multiple languages by combining the methods of sequence recognition using Beizer curves as an input. The sequence–sequence manner had been trained and used as architecture from bidirectional LSTMs and fully connected layers with a CTC loss (Connectionist temporal classification) [18]. The observed results were 8.8% and 29.7% of character and word error rates, respectively.

Zhang et al. [7] used convolutional neural networks (CNN) and bidirectional gated recurrent units (Bi-GRU)-based recogniser model as an alternative to the recurrent neural networks (RNN) architectures and LSTM cells. Features were extracted using the attention mechanism. Bi-GRU was used to decode the characters for recognition. The result of architecture by Zhang et al. [7] had a character and a word error rate of 6.88% and 17.45%, respectively, tested on a 2.4 million word vocabulary.

The initial implementation of the time delay neural network (TDNN) [11] was used for individual word recognition from speech signals isolated in the form of spectrograms, which was a replacement of a state-of-the-art HMM-based recogniser to recognise speech. Later, the same TDNN architecture was implemented for character recognition in Indian languages [10]. It is a multiple layered feed-forward neural network with various connections between any two neurons in successive layers. Each link delays the values and has its weight. The inputs to each neuron comprise outputs of its last neuron in its connection in previous and current time steps [19]. TDNN has unique characteristics of shift invariance similar to convolutional neural networks and increased sub-sampling training speed than LSTMs [19].

3   Dataset Description

In this work, standard IAMonDB dataset (IAM online Database) was used. The data under consideration was acquired via the e-Beam square [6] interface recording users handwriting, resulting in over 1700 handwritten forms by 221 writers with 272 individual word instances from an 11,059-word dictionary written in a complete 12,159 text lines. All the written characters and words were recorded with their x and y coordinates. A total of 83 unique characters had been used to represent the words and sentences [6]. A text sentence (sample) from the IAMonDB dataset is shown in Fig. 1.

4   Methodology

In the proposed methodology, after pre-processing of all the text sentences, features were generated from the IAMonDB dataset comprised of words and characters to be recognised and fed into 1-dimensional (1D) convoluted TDNN and multi-layered Bi-LSTM architecture ending with a dense softmax layer and decoded using two decoders, Trie beam search decoder and Best path decoder beside a 7-gram pruned language model and a 10,000-word corpus to recognise the written characters or words. The proposed methodology is shown in Fig. 2.

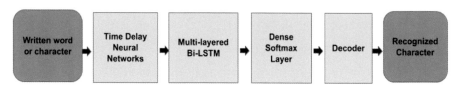

Fig. 1   Image of a text sentence (sample) from IAMonDB dataset

Written word or character → Time Delay Neural Networks → Multi-layered Bi-LSTM → Dense Softmax Layer → Decoder → Recognized Character

Fig. 2   The proposed method TDNN and Bi-LSTM recogniser model

4.1 Pre-processing

In any recognition task, pre-processing of data plays a vital role. The total texts were made homogeneous and in measurable condition for extracting the features. Pre-processing involves the following steps:

- Normalisation: All coordinates of the characters were re-scaled based on their average range between 0 and 1.
- Slope correction: Involved modifying excessive slopes for each character by comparing them with the original samples.
- Sampling distance: Sampled the distance of each stroke after removal of additional strokes.
- Re-sampling distance: Strokes were re-sampled based on the sampling distance and length of strokes in each character.

4.2 Features Generation

Features were extracted by parsing the coordinate data, time frame for each character from each file of the IAMonDB dataset. This dataset consists of coordinate details and time frame of each point, forming all characters and words for a text sentence. The features generated for each stroke were based on stroke beginning and ending point, x and y coordinate directions, and the pen up–down movements while writing all the characters and words in a text sentence.

4.3 Architecture

Time Delay Neural Networks: A multi-layered neural network that classifies patterns with shift-invariance where the classifier takes temporal information by varying it in each hidden layer. It is a 1D CNN without any pooling layers and dilations. Each layer receives inputs from the previous connections in the neural network with certain time delays, avoiding prior segmentation [19]. Time delay neural networks were used effectively in compact and high-performance handwriting recognition systems. The architecture used in this work comprised of six 1D convolutional layers and batch normalisation layers to stabilise the learning process and reduce the training epochs to train the model.

Multi-Layered Bi-LSTMs: Multi-layered Bi-LSTM [20] was used to train the model based on the past and future stroke points with its specific time frame for better recognition of characters. The features generated for word and characters from the IAMonDB dataset were fed into the model comprised of eight LSTM cells with an ending normalisation layer and an additional fully connected softmax layer for assigning probabilities to the 83 individual characters.

Decoder: To attain better results from the proposed network comprised of TDNN and multi-layered bi-LSTM, a connectionist temporal classification decoder (ctc-decoder) [18] and a language model with a 10,000-word lexicon extracted from Google 1 billion word corpus [21] was used. In this work, two decoders—Trie beam search decoder and Best path decoder—were used.

- Trie Beam search decoder: A simple decoder with a Trie switcher for efficient information extraction using the principle concept of maximising the conditional probability for the model, building left-to-right translation and keeping a fixed number of beams (beam width) based on total characters recognised through the decoder. The highest score is achieved by reducing their previous state based on the time frame until zero is attained by normalising the total targeted words for decoding. This results in a highest logarithmic probability of a beam representing the words to be decoded [14]. In the Trie beam search decoder, a 7-gram language model with three smoothing algorithms were implemented Kneser–Ney Back off, Stupid Back off, Kneser–Ney Interpolated. Smoothing algorithms prevent the language model from assigning zero probabilities to the words resulting in a false and higher error rate.

  Kneser–Ney Back off smoothing algorithm [14] focuses on absolute discounting. It uses three different discounts based on the chosen n-gram counts. The absolute-discount smoothing formula is shown below:

$$P_{abs}(w_i \mid w_{i-1}) = \frac{\max(c(w_{i-1}w_i) - d, 0)}{\sum_{w'} c(w_{i-1}w')} + \beta p_{abs}(w_i) \tag{1}$$

  In Kneser–Ney smoothing algorithm, the second word in the lower-order model carries more weight than the first word, whose probability is zero and vice versa. It depends on the continuation probability associated with each unigram in a language model. The count of histories $:|\{w_i : c(w_i, w) > 0\}|$ is replaced by the raw word count and is based on the maximum likelihood estimation of the language model. The Kneser–Ney smoothing equation is:

$$p_{KN}(w) = \frac{d}{\sum_{w_i} c_{1+}(w_i w)} \mid \{w : c(w_i w) > 0\} \mid \tag{2}$$

P_{abs} refers to the Absolute-discount probability, p_{abs} refers to the absolute probability, d refers to the fixed discount value, which is 0.1, and the back off factor is 0. β refers to the normalising constant. w represents the chosen words in the algorithm. p_{KN} represents the probability of the Kneser–Ney algorithm. c_{1+} represents the updated count of word histories.

  Stupid Back off smoothing algorithm [16] uses the differences between dependent contexts and pre-computed probabilities in a word, making it less time-consuming for a distributed environment with a large dataset. In this work, the normalised word probabilities were neglected using a relative score with a back off factor of 0.4.

Kneser–Ney Interpolated is defined as a modified Kneser–Ney smoothing algorithm [15]. Higher-order n-gram language models have sparse counts, making them sensitive to the context. Similarly, lower-order n-grams have robust counts but only limited context; combining them, modified Kneser–Ney smoothing algorithm adjusted the prediction model based on fixed discounts matching the 7-gram model.

- Best path decoder: A simple decoder that generated a word path for its prediction by concatenating the probable characters per each time frame and decoding the blank paths by removing the repeated characters for recognising a given character or word [18].

5   Results and Discussion

The character and word error rates achieved were 6.9% and 23.5% using TDNN and Bi-LSTM architecture without decoder using the IAMonDB dataset. The original and predicted outputs of a text sample from the IAMonDB dataset trained on TDNN and Bi-LSTM layers is shown in Fig. 3.

In this work, three different smoothing algorithms were used in the Trie beam search decoder and achieved less character and word error rate compared to the pre-decoded results of TDNN and Bi-LSTM architecture. Character and word error rate of 6.4% and 22.4% were achieved by Kneser–Ney Interpolated smoothing algorithm pruned on a 7-gram language model using a 10,000-word corpus extracted from billion-word Google corpus [21]. The results were tabulated in Tables 1 and 2 when compared with original samples from both decoders. Predictions from Best path decoder and Trie beam search decoder are shown in Fig. 4. The smoothing algorithm analysed the original sample values, matched and predicted the nearest sample (text sentence), generating the same value as the original sample's value. It gave us the most closely predicted texts as an output. Here, the text sample is shown in Fig. 4, "revision was clearly expressed by nine" took five predictions for being correctly predicted as the original sample.

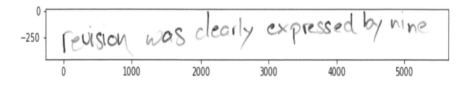

'revision was clearly expressed by nine '

Fig. 3 Original and Predicted sample of a text sentence from IAMonDB dataset using TDNN and Bi-LSTM architecture

Table 1 Character and word error rate achieved using Trie beam search decoder

Smoothing algorithm	Character error rate (%)	Word error rate (%)
Kneser–Ney back off	6.6	23.4
Stupid back off	6.48	22.9
Kneser–Ney Interpolated	6.4	22.4

Table 2 Character and word error rate achieved using best path decoder

Character error rate	Word error rate
7.91%	30.5%

```
Best path:
revision was clearly expressed by nine


Trie beam search:
revision was clearly expressed by nine
revision was clearly expressed by hine
revision was clearly ex pressed by nine
revision was clearly expressed by mine
revision was clearly expressed by nine .
```

Fig. 4 Comparative results of predicted texts from Best path decoder and Trie beam search decoder, respectively

Better word and character error rates were achieved using a 10,000-word lexicon and decoder and three smoothing algorithms, which enabled word recognition through the developed model. Table 3 explained the comparison of character and word error rates achieved in this work with a few state-of-the-art methods using the same IAMonDB dataset. In Table 3, the variables a, b, c represents three smoothing algorithms Kneser–Ney Back off, Kneser–Ney Interpolated, and Stupid Back off smoothing algorithms, respectively. CER and WER represent character error rate and word error rate, respectively.

Compared with other state-of-the-art methodologies implemented using the IAMonDB dataset, a better character error rate was achieved using the Kneser–Ney Interpolated smoothing algorithm compared to LSTM sequence–sequence-based attention mechanism architectures. Less word error rate was achieved using TDNN and Bi-LSTM architecture compared to LSTM and Indy LSTMs. The mentioned state-of-the-art methodologies using the IAMonDB dataset had used more than a million-word lexicon for making the recogniser model.

In this work, five methods were experimented for improving the results of character and word error rates. Referring to the proposed methodology shown in Table 3, minimum character and word error rates of 6.4% and 22.4% were achieved using Kneser–Ney Interpolated smoothing algorithm in Trie beam search decoder with

Table 3 Comparison of character error rate (CER) and Word error rate (WER) with the state-of-the-art methods using IAMonDB dataset

Previous Methodologies	CER (%)	WER (%)
LSTM [8]	8.8	29.7
Indy LSTM [9]	6.25	30
Sequence-sequence based attention mechanism [7]	6.88	17.45
Proposed methodology	CER	WER
TDNN + Bi-LSTM	6.9	23.5
TDNN + Bi-LSTM +Trie Beam search Decoder (a)	6.6	23.4
TDNN + Bi-LSTM +Trie Beam search Decoder (b)	6.4	22.4
TDNN + Bi-LSTM +Trie Beam search Decoder (c)	6.48	22.9
TDNN + Bi-LSTM + Best Path Decoder	7.91	30.5

TDNN and Bi-LSTM architecture. The maximum character and word error rates of 7.91% and 30.5% were achieved using the Best path decoder with TDNN and Bi-LSTM architecture.

6 Conclusion and Future Work

The proposed work mainly focussed on developing an ink recognition model using TDNN and Bi-LSTM architecture based on the IAMonDB dataset, written in 15 broad categories covering significant words from its 11,059-word dictionary ranging in broad categories written by 221 vivid writers in different handwriting styles. The least character and word error rates were accomplished using Kneser–Ney Interpolated smoothing algorithm in the Trie beam search decoder with TDNN and Bi-LSTM architecture. Further, advancements can be made by adding additional layers of 1D convoluted TDNN or a million-word corpus to identify characters. Mobile applications can be made by using a small word corpus for simple processing and recognition of characters.

References

1. Srihari SN, Shekhawat A, Lam SW (2003) Optical character recognition (OCR). Encyclopedia of computer science. Wiley, pp 1326–1333
2. Dharmapala KAKND (2016) Online handwriting recognition systems. Int J Sci Eng Res 7(4):475–481
3. Manjusha K, Kumar M, Soman KP (2018) Integrating scattering feature maps with convolutional neural networks for Malayalam handwritten character recognition. Int J Document Anal Recogn (IJDAR). 21. https://doi.org/10.1007/s10032-018-0308-z
4. Manjusha K, Kumar M, Soman KP (2015) Experimental analysis on character recognition using singular value decomposition and random projection. Int J Eng Technol 7:1246–1255
5. Graves A, Liwicki M, Fernández S, Bertolami R, Bunke H, Schmidhuber J (2009) A novel connectionist system for unconstrained handwriting recognition. IEEE Trans Pattern Anal Mach Intell 31(5):855–868. https://doi.org/10.1109/TPAMI.2008.137
6. Liwicki M, Bunke H (2005) IAM-OnDB—an on-line English sentence database acquired from the handwritten text on a whiteboard. In: Eighth international conference on document analysis and recognition (ICDAR'05), Seoul, South Korea, 2005, Vol 2, pp 956–961. https://doi.org/10.1109/ICDAR.2005.132
7. Zhang J, Du J, Dai L (2017) A GRU-based encoder-decoder approach with attention for online handwritten mathematical expression recognition. In: 2017 14th IAPR International conference on document analysis and recognition (ICDAR), 2017, pp 902–907. https://doi.org/10.1109/ICDAR.2017.152
8. Victor C, Pedro G, Thomas D, Henry R, Alexander D, Marcos C, Li-Lun W, Daniel K, Sandro F, Philippe G (2020) Fast multi-language LSTM-based online handwriting recognition. Int J Document Anal Recogn (IJDAR). 23. https://doi.org/10.1007/s10032-020-00350-4
9. Gonnet P, Deselaers T (2020) Indylstms: independently Recurrent LSTMS. In: ICASSP 2020— 2020 IEEE International conference on acoustics, speech and signal processing (ICASSP), 2020, pp 3352–3356. https://doi.org/10.1109/ICASSP40776.2020.9053498
10. Keysers D, Deselaers T, Rowley HA, Wang L, Carbune V (2017) Multi-language online handwriting recognition. IEEE Trans Pattern Anal Mach Intell 39(6):1180–1194. https://doi.org/10.1109/TPAMI.2016.2572693
11. Myer S, Tomar V (2018) Efficient keyword spotting using time delay neural networks, pp 1264–1268. https://doi.org/10.21437/Interspeech.2018-1979
12. Sreelakhsmi K, Premjith B, Soman KP (2021) Deep learning-based offensive language identification in Malayalam, Tamil and Kannada. In: (EACL2021), pp 249–254
13. Premjith B, Soman KP, Poornachandran P (2018) A deep learning based Part-of-Speech (POS) tagger for Sanskrit language by embedding character level features, pp 56–60. https://doi.org/10.1145/3293339.3293352
14. Chen SF, Goodman J (1999) An empirical study of smoothing techniques for language modeling. Comput Speech Language 13(4):359–394. ISSN 0885-2308
15. Frankie J (2000) Modified Kneser-Ney smoothing of n-gram models
16. Brants T, Popat A, Xu P, Och F, Dean J (2007) Large language models in machine translation.. pp 858–867
17. de Marcken CG (1990) Parsing the LOB corpus. In: Proceedings of the 28th annual meeting on association for computational linguistics (ACL'90) USA, pp 243–251
18. Lu S, Lu J, Lin J, Wang Z, A hardware-oriented and memory-efficient method for CTC decoding. IEEE Access 7:120681–120694. arXiv:1905.03175v1
19. Lang KJ, Waibel AH, Hinton GE (1990) A time-delay neural network architecture for isolated word recognition. Neural Networks 3(1):23–43. ISSN 0893-6080
20. Liu R, Wei W, Mao W, Chikina M (2017) Phase conductor on multi-layered attentions for machine comprehension
21. Chelba C, Mikolov T, Schuster M, Ge Q, Brants T, Koehn P (2013) One billion word benchmark for measuring progress in statistical language modeling. In: Proceedings of the annual conference of the international speech communication association, INTERSPEECH

22. Bluche T, Louradour J, Messina R (2017) Scan, attend and read: end-to-end handwritten paragraph recognition with MDLSTM attention. In: 2017 14th IAPR International conference on document analysis and recognition (ICDAR), 2017, pp 1050–1055. https://doi.org/10.1109/ICDAR.2017.174

23. Graves A, Jaitly N (2014) Towards end-to-end speech recognition with recurrent neural networks. In: Proceedings of the 31st international conference on machine learning, in PMLR, vol 32(2), pp 1764–1772

Sarcasm Detection for Sentiment Analysis: A RNN-Based Approach Using Machine Learning

Rachana P. Rao, Swathi Dayanand, K. R. Varshitha, and Keerti Kulkarni

Abstract With the advent of social media, publicly expressing opinions about businesses are hassle-free. Terms like 'opinion mining' and 'microblogging' have carved a niche. Organizations' concern for brand reputation has accentuated the need for understanding customer's choices and interests. Sentiment analysis scrutinizes users' opinions through machine learning (ML) and natural language processing (NLP), a subset of which is sarcasm detection. The sarcasm detection database was fetched from Kaggle, containing nearly 30,000 tweet headlines curated for sarcasm detection, having high-quality labels with less noise. On implementing four ML algorithms, it is observed that training and testing data accuracies of random forest are 98.83% and 77.22%, linear support vector is 90.69% and 83.23%, logistic regression is 87.78% and 82.52%, Naive Bayes is 79.77% and 71.69%. This paper aims to build an RNN model based on LSTM architecture to accurately classify any given input as sarcastic or not.

Keywords Sarcasm detection · ML · NLP · Sentiment analysis · RNN · LSTM · Random forest · Logistic regression · Linear support vector · Gaussian Naive Bayes

1 Introduction

Sarcasm can be defined in colloquial terms as a sharp, iconic statement that intends to express something ridiculous or humorous. The task of sarcasm detection, simply put, is a method of identifying a text or a sentence as 'sarcastic' or 'non-sarcastic'. It is challenging owing to the multiple complexities involved whilst classifying textual data. Recognition of sarcasm has a very crucial role to play in the case of natural language processing (NLP), when it comes to market research, brand reputation management or even opinion mining [1]. Some of the noted practical uses of sarcasm detection include customer support improvisation, employee/customer feedback tracking, enhanced product analysis and social media monitoring amongst

R. P. Rao · S. Dayanand (✉) · K. R. Varshitha · K. Kulkarni
BNM Institute of Technology, Bengaluru, India

© The Author(s), under exclusive license to Springer Nature Singapore Pte Ltd. 2022   47
C. Satyanarayana et al. (eds.), *High Performance Computing and Networking*,
Lecture Notes in Electrical Engineering 853,
https://doi.org/10.1007/978-981-16-9885-9_4

others. Since, the use of sarcasm is prevalent almost everywhere, a system/method capable of recognizing sarcasm is of grave importance. One of the most common drawbacks of sentiment analysis which is a precursor to sarcasm detection method-ology is that it lacks the ability to properly categorize input data into appropriate polarity as in, positive or negative polarity. There is abundant data available on the Web that could be exploited by organizations aiming to mine or analyze public opinion. Comprehension of vast data is easier said than done because it is not manually feasible to extract features about textual data by mere sentiment analysis [2].

Some of the other issues that need attention include:

- Sentiment detection at different levels of granularities in the text.
- Detection of reader sentiment or those entities mentioned in the text.
- Detection of semantic roles conveyed by the text.

The key factors highlighting the need for sarcasm detection are also the presence of irony, negations, multipolarity in a text.

2 Related Work

It is seen that a sarcasm classifier used in place of a sentiment classifier shows better performance citing that the efficacy of sarcasm detection can boost the overall perfor-mance of sentiment analysis [3]. The paper [4] examines two algorithms, namely adapted machine learning algorithm (AMLA) and customized machine learning algo-rithms (CMLA). The results of the paper have shown that the best results are procured by support vector machine (SVM) along with AMLA that is most widely used for Twitter sarcasm detection. It was found that the combination of convolutional neural network (CNN) and SVM can predict sarcasm with high accuracy. Its applications include microblogging.

In the domain of social media dominated by Twitter, Facebook, Reddit and so on, the detection of sarcasm has become a necessary task in order to realize its influence on business organizations [5]. In [6], there is a mention of a hyperbolic feature-based technique for sarcasm detection in which intensifiers and interjections of the text are present. In [7], the experiments performed have confirmed that correctly detecting sarcasm can lead to improvement of sentiment analysis and sarcasm detec-tion by nearly 50%, nevertheless, though a tweet can be distinguished to be sarcastic, the corresponding sentiment analysis does not yield satisfactorily accurate results. Opinion mining from text and particularly from social media which is difficult to analyze is still not advanced in terms of research which indicates that existing tools are not very useful, despite exhibiting advancement over the ordinary in certain aspects, and hence, there are many issues that remain unresolved [8]. In the study carried out in [9], sarcasm detection has been found to help in the enhancement of efficacy of after-sales services or consumer assistance through analyzing the opinions and real-time reviews of customers. The proposed approach is based on the usage of part of speech tags to extract any kind of patterns in order to characterize the chances of presence of sarcasm in Twitter data. In [10], it has been reviewed that in most research, Twitter dataset is employed because of its distinguishable properties compared to other kinds of datasets. Researchers have an interest in hashtags which can be considered as topical markers, serving as an indicator of the tweet's context and conveying the ideology of the tweet. Two approaches have been employed, out of which the most notable one is based on the approach of machine learning and another approach is rule-based [11]. In general, it opines that the task of detecting and analyzing sarcasm is cumbersome and subjective.

3 Methodology

The proposed methodology (as in Fig. 1) is explained in the following sections:

1. **Data Collection**—Twitter is one of the most preferred social platforms, where consumers and brands have an even playing with concise communication. Thus, many companies have a keen eye on Twitter data to conduct product analysis [12]. The chosen dataset for our experiment is the 'Twitter headlines dataset' having a vast collection of nearly 30 k tweets, sourced from Kaggle [13]. Each record consists of two main attributes which are

   - *headline*: Conveys the heading of the Twitter article.
   - *article_link*: Contains link of the Twitter article.

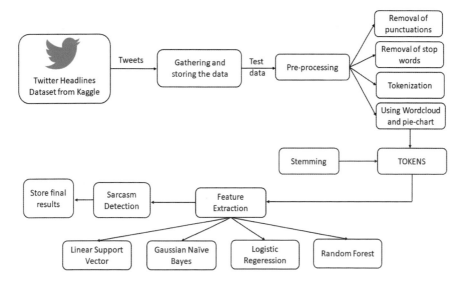

Fig. 1 The flowchart describing the methodology for sarcasm detection

Sarcastic vs Not Sarcastic

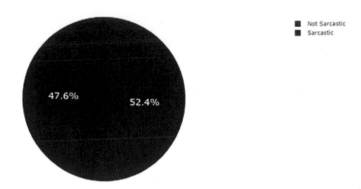

Fig. 2 Using pie chart to represent proportion of sarcastic and non-sarcastic data present in chosen dataset

An added advantage of choosing this dataset is that the news headlines are self-contained. Also, they are written professionally and are less noisy when compared to datasets that have 'hashtags' [14].

2. **Data Pre-Processing in Jupyter Notebook**—Data pre-processing and representation are carried out by utilizing a set of useful Python libraries such as Porter Stemmer, NLTK, TextBlob, SciPy, NumPy, Plotly, Word2Vec and matplotlib [15]. The steps involved in pre-processing are

- *Pictorial representation of data*: The data can be understood using a pie chart as shown in Fig. 2, obtained using 'Plotly' library for effective visualization.
- *Data Cleansing*: The dataset chosen is altered such that it is error-free and does not contain any punctuations, new lines, tabs and/or spaces and is done using pandas and 'NumPy' library.
- *Tokenization*: This process involves breaking down a long paragraph to sentences or a complete sentence into its constituent words. This is achieved using inbuilt libraries of the NLTK module.
- *Word Cloud*: These works in a simple way: The more is the frequency of recurrence of a word appears in the dataset, the bigger it looks in the word cloud [14]. This is depicted in Fig. 3. This is done by using 'matplotlib' library.
- *Stemming*: In NLP, stemming is a step where a word is reduced to its root word ignoring its prefix and suffix. This step is fulfilled with the aid of 'Porter Stemmer' module.
- *Lemmatization*: This process is similar to stemming but it is slower as it cuts the words depending on the context of the sentence before processing. This is realized using 'TextBlob' library from NLTK module.

3. **Feature extraction using word embeddings**—The concept of embedding is used to turn the sentiment of a word to number. The embedding is a vector that

Fig. 3 Using word cloud to represent chosen dataset contents

points at a particular direction to establish meanings in words. The embeddings can be seen as a sentiment for that word. This is accomplished using 'Word2Vec' library of the 'gensim' module.

4. **Building a RNN to train the sarcasm detector**—A class of recurrent neural network (RNN) is a long short-term memory (LSTM) network that can monitor as well as keep a check on dependencies of the input data [16]. A view of this is given in Table 1. LSTM overcomes the vanishing gradient problem encountered by vanilla RNNs.

5. **Training the RNN model**—The model is trained using epochs. Epochs are usually the number of iterations that the entire dataset passes through. As the epochs increase, accuracy also increases (Fig. 4; Table 2).

6. **Confusion matrix and accuracies**—Once a model is developed, its performance can be learnt using confusion matrix [17]. The model's accuracies and losses can also be analyzed as in Fig. 5. A matrix of confusion (Fig. 6) is created for the dataset. This matrix is not sufficient, and thus, $F1$-score is used and its values are as reported in Table 3.

7. **Testing RNN model with user inputs**—Researchers are eager to explore the offerings of sarcasm such as its semantic properties and features like lexical icons. In this context, a RNN model becomes very handy owing to its ability to extract features automatically from the dataset [18]. Moreover, the usage of

Table 1 Description of the LSTM layer type of layer

Type of layer	Output shape	Number of parameters
Embedding	(None, 14, 64)	128,000
LSTM	(None, 96)	61,824
Dense	(None, 1)	97
Activation	(None, 1)	0

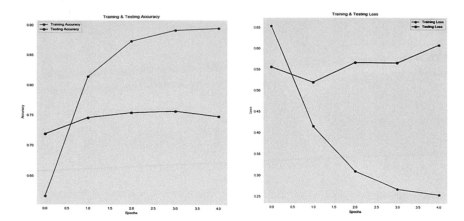

Fig. 4 Graphical representation of training and test accuracy and loss

Table 2 Comparison of various algorithm accuracies for the training and test data	Name of classifier	Accuracy of training data (%)	Accuracy of test data (%)
	Linear support vector	90.69	83.23
	Gaussian Naive Bayes	79.77	71.69
	Logistic regression	87.78	82.52
	Random forest	98.83	77.22

Out[45]: <matplotlib.axes._subplots.AxesSubplot at 0x138aad8f588>

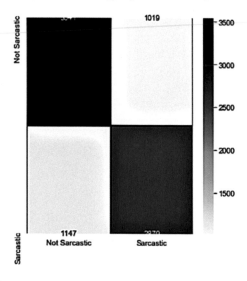

Fig. 5 Output of confusion matrix to check prediction accuracy

```
In [16]:    1  predict_sarcasm("You just broke my car window. Great job.")
Out[16]:  "It's sarcastic!"

In [17]:    1  predict_sarcasm("You just saved my dog's life. Thanks a million.")
Out[17]:  "It's not sarcastic."

In [18]:    1  predict_sarcasm("I want a million dollars!")
Out[18]:  "It's not sarcastic."

In [19]:    1  predict_sarcasm("I just won a million dollars!")
Out[19]:  "It's sarcastic!"
```

Fig. 6 Glimpse of the results of sarcasm detection based on anonymous user inputs

Table 3 A glimpse of classification report showing $F1$-scores and precision

Parameter	Precision	Recall	$F1$-score	Support
Not sarcastic	0.76	0.78	0.77	4560
Sarcastic	0.74	0.72	0.73	4026
Accuracy			0.75	8586
Macro average	0.75	0.75	0.75	8586
Weighted average	0.75	0.75	0.75	8586

RNN can not only make sarcasm detection more efficient but also help in the easy classification of Twitter statements [19].

8. **Comparative Analysis**—Apart from the RNN model, various classifiers are used to draw the important characteristics from the dataset. Table 2 demonstrates the various classifiers, their testing and training accuracies.

In the proposed methodology, testing the model using RNN is the final stage that marks as an interactive measure with the outside world. The model is designed such that it can predict any given user input as sarcastic or non-sarcastic.

4 Results

The ultimate goal of developing a sarcasm detection model using Twitter data was to obtain real-time predictions based on user inputs. The RNN so trained and tested is capable of distinguishing any user input as 'sarcastic' or 'non-sarcastic' quite appropriately. The accuracy of LSTM can reach as high as 92% based on the dataset and number of epochs used.

The model will classify the input based on a prediction variable which is a two-dimensional array. Each time the function 'predict_sarcasm' is called (as shown in Fig. 6), the model refers to the prediction variable to classify the sentence. Based on the value taken by the prediction variable array, the tweet will be classified as sarcastic else it is non-sarcastic.

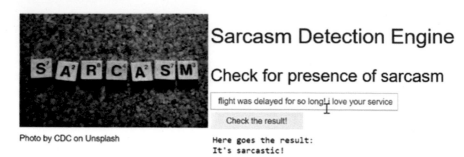

S A R C A S M
Photo by CDC on Unsplash
Sarcasm Detection Engine
Check for presence of sarcasm
flight was delayed for so long! i love your service
Check the result!
Here goes the result:
It's sarcastic!

Fig. 7 Sarcasm detection engine predicting nature of a user input

Furthermore, a front-end engine was developed for the RNN model. The engine can check for sarcasm in a grammatically correct input as seen in Fig. 7 and also alert the user about incorrect input and any spelling mistakes as shown in Figs. 8 and 9, respectively.

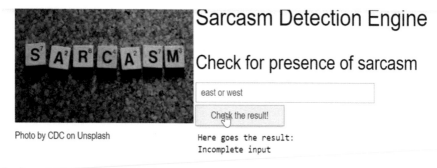

S A R C A S M
Photo by CDC on Unsplash
Sarcasm Detection Engine
Check for presence of sarcasm
east or west
Check the result!
Here goes the result:
Incomplete input

Fig. 8 Sarcasm detection engine detecting incomplete user input

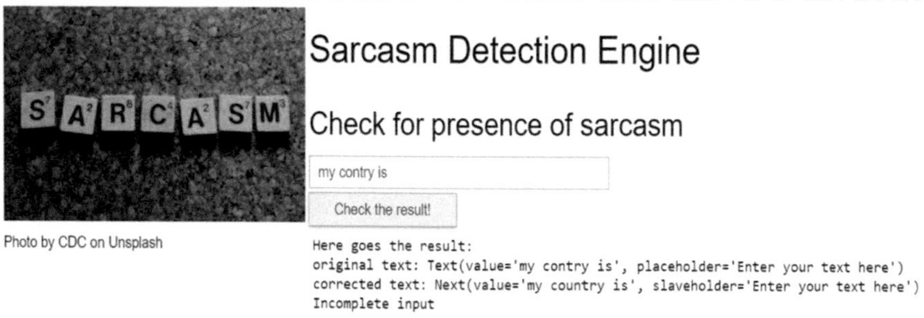

S A R C A S M
Photo by CDC on Unsplash
Sarcasm Detection Engine
Check for presence of sarcasm
my contry is
Check the result!
Here goes the result:
original text: Text(value='my contry is', placeholder='Enter your text here')
corrected text: Next(value='my country is', slaveholder='Enter your text here')
Incomplete input

Fig. 9 Sarcasm detection engine detecting spelling errors in a user input

5 Conclusion and Future Scope

The idea of sarcasm detection and analysis on social media data provides a plethora of real-time insights into the public view about emerging trends. The obstacles of earlier sentiment analysis methods have been addressed by sarcasm detection but further interest lies in discovering the prospect of automatic sarcasm detection as a mainstream problem statement y[20]. Beginning with the first known ideals of sarcasm detection in speech to now, there has been a lot of change with respect to growing interest towards extension of sarcasm detection to various data forms. The research in this field has seen significant growth, reinstating the prominence of the very idea of sarcasm detection. The current trend points to discovering new pragmatic features and lexical symbols in a given text whilst analyzing it for presence of sarcasm. Whilst there is no dearth for datasets today, there is a need for resorting to distant or remote supervising techniques to acquire features of data. There is also scope for the incorporation of versatile context forms whilst employing sarcasm detection.

References

1. Rendalkar S, Chandankhede C (2018) Sarcasm detection of online comments using emotion detection. In: 2018 International conference on inventive research in computing applications (ICIRCA), 2018, pp 1244–1249.https://doi.org/10.1109/ICIRCA.2018.8597368
2. Adarsh MJ, Ravikumar P (2019) Sarcasm detection in text data to bring out genuine sentiments for sentimental analysis. In: 2019 1st international conference on advances in information technology (ICAIT), 2019, pp 94–98. https://doi.org/10.1109/ICAIT47043.2019.8987393
3. Majumder N, Poria S, Peng H, Chhaya N, Cambria E, Gelbukh A (2019) Sentiment and Sarcasm classification with multitask learning. IEEE Intell. Syst. 34(3):38–43. https://doi.org/10.1109/MIS.2019.2904691
4. Sarsam SM, Al-Samarraie H, Alzahrani AI, Wright B (2020) Sarcasm detection using machine learning algorithms in Twitter: a systematic review. Int J Market Res 62(5):578–598
5. Pawar N, Bhingarkar S (2020) Machine learning based sarcasm detection on twitter data. In: 2020 5th international conference on communication and electronics systems (ICCES), 2020, pp 957–961. https://doi.org/10.1109/ICCES48766.2020.9137924
6. Bharti SK, Naidu R, Babu KS (2017) Hyperbolic feature-based Sarcasm detection in tweets: a machine learning approach. In: 2017 14th IEEE India council international conference (INDICON), 2017, pp 1–6. https://doi.org/10.1109/INDICON.2017.8487712
7. Maynard D, Greenwood MA (2014) Who cares about sarcastic tweets? Investigating the impact of sarcasm on sentiment analysis
8. Aboobaker J, Ilavarasan E (2020) A Survey on Sarcasm detection and challenges. In: 2020 6th international conference on advanced computing and communication systems (ICACCS), 2020, pp 1234–1240. https://doi.org/10.1109/ICACCS48705.2020.9074163
9. Bouazizi M, Ohtsuki T (2015) Sarcasm detection in twitter: "all your products are incredibly amazing!!!" - are they really? In: 2015 IEEE global communications conference (GLOBECOM), San Diego, CA, 2015, pp 1–6.https://doi.org/10.1109/GLOCOM.2015.7417640
10. Wicana SG, İbisoglu TY, Yavanoglu U (2017) A review on Sarcasm detection from machine-learning perspective. In: 2017 IEEE 11th international conference on semantic computing (ICSC), San Diego, CA, 2017, pp 469–476. https://doi.org/10.1109/ICSC.2017.74

11. Bouazizi M, Otsuki Ohtsuki T (2016) A pattern-based approach for sarcasm detection on twitter. IEEE Access 4:5477–5488. https://doi.org/10.1109/ACCESS.2016.2594194

12. Das D, Clark AJ (2019) Construct of Sarcasm on social media platform. In: 2019 IEEE international conference on humanized computing and communication (HCC), 2019, pp 106–113. https://doi.org/10.1109/HCC46620.2019.00023

13. News headlines dataset for sarcasm detection. https://www.kaggle.com/rmisra/news-headlines-dataset-for-sarcasm-detection

14. Bindra KK, Gupta A (2016) Tweet Sarcasm : mechanism of sarcasm detection in twitter. ISSN: 0975-9646

15. Shrikhande P, Setty V, Sahani DA (2020) Sarcasm detection in newspaper headlines. In: 2020 IEEE 15th international conference on industrial and information systems (ICIIS), 2020, pp 483–487. https://doi.org/10.1109/ICIIS51140.2020.9342742

16. Misra R, Arora P (2018) Sarcasm detection using hybrid neural network. https://doi.org/10.13140/RG.2.2.32427.39204

17. Raeder J, Gambäck B (2018) Sarcasm annotation and detection in tweets. In: 18th international conference, CICLing 2017, Budapest, Hungary, April 17–23, 2017, Revised Selected Papers, Part II.https://doi.org/10.1007/978-3-319-77116-8_5

18. Porwal S, Ostwal G, Phadtare A, Pandey M, Marathe MV (2018) Sarcasm detection using recurrent neural network. In: 2018 second international conference on intelligent computing and control systems (ICICCS), 2018, pp 746–748. https://doi.org/10.1109/ICCONS.2018.8663147

19. Salim SS, Nidhi Ghanshyam A, Ashok DM, Burhanuddin Mazahir D, Thakare BS (2020) Deep LSTM-RNN with word embedding for sarcasm detection on twitter. In: 2020 international conference for emerging technology (INCET), 2020, pp. 1–4. https://doi.org/10.1109/INCET49848.2020.9154162

20. Gupta R, Kumar J, Agrawal H (2020) A statistical approach for sarcasm detection using twitter data. In: 2020 4th international conference on intelligent computing and control systems (ICICCS), 2020, pp. 633–638. https://doi.org/10.1109/ICICCS48265.2020.9120917

Statistical Analysis of Soil Properties Using Non-imaging Spectral Data for Quantitative Analysis of Raver Tehsil

Vipin Y. Borole and Sonali B. Kulkarni

Abstract The soil properties assessment is very important for identifying the soil content for requirement of fertilizers as well as discovery of fertilizers. In the traditional, soil properties analysis has been obtained through routine soil physicochemical laboratory analysis. However, these laboratory methods do not fulfill the rapid requirements. Accordingly, spectroscopic remote sensing methods can be used to nondestructively detect and characterize soil content without chemical analysis. In the present research, we use spectroscopy techniques for soil properties analysis. The non-imaging spectral data of agglomerated farming soils were acquired by the ASD Field spec 4 spectroradiometer. It provides the large range of data in Visible (350–700 nm) and Near-Infrared (700–2500 nm) region. Total 110 soil specimens were collected in pre-monsoon and post-monsoon, respectively, with mixed, organic, chemical fertilizers treatment applied for banana and cotton crops in the context of surface and subsurface for finding the influence of fertilizers. The soil sample was collected from Raver Tehsil of Jalgaon District of Maharashtra, India. The soil spectra of VNIR region were preprocessed to get pure spectra. Then process the acquired spectral data by statistical methods for quantitative analysis of soil properties. The detected soil properties were carbon, Nitrogen, soil organic matter, pH, phosphorus, potassium, moisture sand, silt, and clay. In this paper, required statistical methods are used for quantitative analysis of soil properties. The quantitative analysis represents the availability of soil properties.

Keywords Soil · Fertilizers · Season · Remote sensing · Spectroradiometer · Statistical methods

V. Y. Borole (✉) · S. B. Kulkarni
Department of Computer Science & Information Technology, Dr. Babasaheb Ambedkar Marathwada University, Aurangabad, India

© The Author(s), under exclusive license to Springer Nature Singapore Pte Ltd. 2022
C. Satyanarayana et al. (eds.), *High Performance Computing and Networking*,
Lecture Notes in Electrical Engineering 853,
https://doi.org/10.1007/978-981-16-9885-9_5

1 Introduction

In the agriculture field, the soil properties are dynamic due to human activities, different agricultural practices, and global climatic change it may change [1]. The soil properties may be varied by spatially and temporally with different agricultural practices. An accurate and reliable soil properties assessment is challenging issue in soil analysis. Due to the lack of knowledge, poor agricultural practices and misuse of fertilizers soil properties were varied in agricultural land. Soil nutrients are the major source of soil fertility that helps for plant growth as well as yield production. In the agriculture field, farmers used the organic, chemical, or mixed fertilizers for fulfillment of nutrients. But accurately use of fertilizers based on the required amount for a certain site or type of crop and soil has always remained a challenge [2]. In the previous research, number of techniques and methods are used for hyper spectral imaging and non-imaging data processing. The ASD Field Spec4 Spectroradiometer also used in agriculture field for soil assessment, crop disease detection, and crop condition monitor but the very less work carried out on soil properties assessment for influence of different types of fertilizers on soil using remote sensing is very less. This study is very important to farmers for knowing the soil or field site for fertilizers management, and it will helpful for reducing the fertilizers cost and increasing the crop yield. Traditional soil assessment procedure is time consuming, costly, labor intensive as well as hazardous chemical are required in this soil testing process. Accordingly, spectroscopic remote sensing methods can be used to nondestructively detect and characterize soil content without chemical analysis. In the present research, we use remote sensing ground based spectroscopy techniques for soil properties analysis. In this domain, spectroscopy technique is one of most important technique is used for soil properties assessment, and it gives most accurate and fast results. ASD Field Spec4 Spectroradiometer device were used for spectral data acquisition in the range of 350–2500 nm. This high range device is capable to detect the various soil properties. The acquired high rage spectral data need to process by applying statistical methods which are required to quantitative analysis.

2 Study Area

The study is carried out in Raver Tahsil of Jalgaon District in Maharashtra, which is located between Lat: 21° 12′ 30″ N, Lon: 75° 56′ 36″ E and Lat: 21° 11′ 42″ N, Lon: 75° 58′ 08″ E in, India with GPS information. Mostly, banana is the main cash crop in the study area. Banana from this area is very famous in the national and international market. Banana and cotton crops are associated with the formation of soils, nature of surface, and availability of groundwater [3–5].

3 Material and Methods

The total 110 soil samples are collected from organic, chemical, and mixed fertilizers treatments used for banana and cotton crops sites in two different season. In pre-monsoon (First week of June) season, 50 soil samples were collected from 25 different locations. Each location containing 2 soil sample one from surface (5–20 cm) and other from subsurface (30 cm). As well as, in post-monsoon (First week of November) season 60 soil samples were collected from 30 different locations where different fertilizers treatment used for different crops. Collected soil samples are classified according to season, fertilizers treatment and cropwise like Premonsoon Organic Cotton (PROC), Postmonsoon Organic Cotton (POOC), Premonsoon Mixed Cotton (PRMC), Postmonsoon Mixed Cotton (POMC), Premonsoon Organic Banana (PROB), Premonsoon Mixed banana (PRMB), Premonsoon Chemical Banana (PRCB), Postmonsoon Organic Banana (POOB), Postmonsoon Mixed Banana (POMB), and Postmonsoon Chemical Banana (POCB) [3, 4, 6, 7].

3.1 Spectral Data Acquisition

ASD Field Spec4 non-imaging spectroradiometer having spectral range (350–2500 nm) is used for data acquisition. As it acquires data in many narrow wavelength bands, it allows the use of almost continuous data in studying the Earth's surface [8–10]. These spectral signatures are acquired using ASD FieldSpec4 Spectroradiometer (Analytical Spectral Devices Inc., USA). Spectroradiometer gives the output in the form of continuous spectral response curve is referred to as the spectral signature of collected soil samples [5–7, 11]. Reflectance spectroscopy provides an alternate method to classical physical and chemical laboratory soil analysis for the estimation of a large range of soil properties. Spectroradiometer giving minimal sample preparation, fast analysis, cost-effective to analyze a single or batch of samples, several constituents can be determined simultaneously, no destruction of samples, no hazardous chemical used, and results can be accurate and fast [12–15]. Data collection and processing of acquired data processing is explain and follow in [3–7, 12–14].

4 Results

The spectroscopic techniques using remote sensing provides acquired data in the form of spectral signature. For knowing the value of available soil properties or quantitative analysis, the spectral data need to convert in numeric values. Therefore, some statistical analysis are required to process the spectral to numeric data. There are calculate the Min, Max, Median, Mean, and S.D. (standard deviation) statistical methods for quantitative analysis. The statistical analysis perform in Table 1. Where

Table 1 Statistical analysis of post-monsoon organic cotton soil samples

POOC

Soil properties	Surface					Subsurface				
	Min	Max	Median	Mean	Std. Dev.	Min	Max	Median	Mean	Std. Dev.
Sand	0.050	0.109	0.107	0.089	0.042	0.095	0.104	0.103	0.101	0.005
Silt	0.048	0.102	0.101	0.083	0.038	0.092	0.100	0.097	0.096	0.004
Clay	0.049	0.108	0.107	0.088	0.042	0.094	0.105	0.104	0.101	0.006
SOM	0.048	0.104	0.101	0.084	0.040	0.090	0.099	0.099	0.096	0.005
Moisture	0.067	0.101	0.081	0.083	0.024	0.095	0.109	0.103	0.102	0.007
pH	0.031	0.097	0.087	0.072	0.031	0.083	0.089	0.084	0.085	0.003
Carbon	0.043	0.111	0.109	0.090	0.043	0.096	0.106	0.106	0.103	0.006
Nitrogen	0.037	0.101	0.100	0.083	0.037	0.093	0.100	0.095	0.096	0.004
Phosphorous	0.041	0.106	0.105	0.087	0.041	0.092	0.103	0.102	0.099	0.006
Potash	0.035	0.094	0.093	0.077	0.035	0.085	0.092	0.089	0.089	0.004

the soil samples are collected in post-monsoon season from surface and subsurface where organic fertilizers are used for cotton crops.

In Table 1, different soil properties are analyzed on the basis of statistical methods (Min, Max, Median, Mean, and Standard Deviation) for surface and subsurface soil samples. On the basis of statistical analysis in Table 1, minimum value for pH are found Min = 0.031, Max = 0.097, Median = 0.087, Mean = 0.072, and minimum value of standard deviation is found for Moisture properties in surface soil samples. In subsurface soil sample also minimum values are found for pH soil properties and maximum values of standard deviation is found for moisture content. On the basis of statistical analysis of mean methods for surface and subsurface, higher content are available in subsurface soil sample as compare to surface soil samples in post-monsoon season for cotton crop.

The statistical analysis performs in Table 2. Where the soil samples are collected in pre-monsoon season from surface and subsurface where organic fertilizers are used for cotton crops.

In Table 2, different soil properties are analyzed on the basis of statistical methods (Min, Max, Median, Mean, and Standard Deviation) for surface and subsurface soil samples. On the basis of statistical analysis in Table 2, minimum value for pH are found in surface and subsurface soil samples also. And minimum value of standard deviation is found for sand and potash properties in surface soil samples. The maximum values of mean are found for carbon soil properties in surface and subsurface soil samples. Maximum values of standard deviation are found for sand content. On the basis of statistical analysis of mean methods for surface and subsurface, higher content is available in surface soil sample as compare to subsurface soil samples in pre-monsoon season cotton crop.

Table 2 Statistical analysis of pre-monsoon organic cotton soil samples

PROC

Soil properties	Surface					Subsurface				
	Min	Max	Median	Mean	Std. Dev.	Min	Max	Median	Mean	Std. Dev.
Sand	0.103	0.139	0.136	0.126	0.025	0.074	0.152	0.086	0.104	0.042
Silt	0.097	0.135	0.131	0.121	0.026	0.072	0.144	0.083	0.100	0.039
Clay	0.102	0.140	0.136	0.126	0.027	0.073	0.152	0.086	0.104	0.042
SOM	0.098	0.135	0.132	0.122	0.026	0.070	0.146	0.082	0.099	0.041
Moisture	0.097	0.155	0.129	0.127	0.041	0.075	0.140	0.094	0.103	0.034
pH	0.084	0.122	0.116	0.107	0.027	0.065	0.124	0.077	0.089	0.031
Carbon	0.105	0.142	0.138	0.128	0.026	0.075	0.154	0.087	0.106	0.042
Nitrogen	0.098	0.134	0.129	0.120	0.026	0.074	0.142	0.084	0.100	0.037
Phosphorous	0.100	0.138	0.135	0.124	0.027	0.072	0.149	0.085	0.102	0.042
Potash	0.090	0.125	0.121	0.112	0.025	0.067	0.132	0.077	0.092	0.035

Table 3 represents the statistical analysis of post-monsoon organic banana soil samples. Where the soil samples are collected in post-monsoon season from surface and subsurface where organic fertilizers are used for banana crops.

In Table 3, soil properties are analyzed on the basis of statistical methods (Min, Max, Median, Mean, and Standard Deviation) for surface and subsurface soil samples. On the basis of statistical analysis in Table 3, minimum value for pH are found in surface and subsurface soil samples also. And minimum value of standard deviation is found for SOM properties in subsurface soil samples. The maximum

Table 3 Statistical analysis of post-monsoon organic banana soil samples

POOB

Soil properties	Surface					Subsurface				
	Min	Max	Median	Mean	Std. Dev.	Min	Max	Median	Mean	Std. Dev.
Sand	0.074	0.107	0.103	0.095	0.018	0.091	0.095	0.095	0.094	0.002
Silt	0.070	0.101	0.097	0.089	0.017	0.086	0.092	0.092	0.090	0.003
Clay	0.073	0.107	0.102	0.094	0.018	0.091	0.094	0.094	0.093	0.002
SOM	0.070	0.101	0.098	0.090	0.017	0.087	0.090	0.090	0.089	0.001
Moisture	0.072	0.097	0.081	0.083	0.013	0.085	0.095	0.095	0.092	0.006
pH	0.062	0.087	0.084	0.078	0.014	0.075	0.083	0.083	0.080	0.005
Carbon	0.075	0.109	0.105	0.096	0.018	0.093	0.096	0.096	0.095	0.002
Nitrogen	0.070	0.100	0.098	0.089	0.017	0.086	0.093	0.093	0.091	0.004
Phosphorous	0.072	0.105	0.100	0.092	0.018	0.090	0.092	0.092	0.092	0.002
Potash	0.065	0.093	0.090	0.083	0.015	0.080	0.085	0.085	0.083	0.003

Table 4 Statistical analysis of pre-monsoon organic banana soil samples

PROB

Soil properties	Surface					Subsurface				
	Min	Max	Median	Mean	Std. Dev.	Min	Max	Median	Mean	Std. Dev.
Sand	0.165	0.181	0.174	0.174	0.008	0.104	0.111	0.110	0.109	0.004
Silt	0.158	0.176	0.169	0.167	0.009	0.100	0.106	0.104	0.103	0.003
Clay	0.166	0.181	0.174	0.173	0.008	0.104	0.110	0.108	0.107	0.003
SOM	0.160	0.176	0.169	0.168	0.008	0.099	0.106	0.105	0.103	0.004
Moisture	0.108	0.173	0.133	0.138	0.033	0.103	0.106	0.104	0.105	0.002
pH	0.139	0.159	0.149	0.149	0.010	0.088	0.094	0.089	0.090	0.003
Carbon	0.169	0.184	0.178	0.177	0.008	0.106	0.113	0.111	0.110	0.004
Nitrogen	0.156	0.174	0.169	0.166	0.010	0.100	0.109	0.103	0.104	0.004
Phosphorous	0.164	0.180	0.172	0.172	0.008	0.102	0.109	0.106	0.106	0.003
Potash	0.145	0.163	0.156	0.155	0.009	0.092	0.098	0.096	0.095	0.003

values of mean are found for carbon soil properties in surface soil samples. Maximum and equal values of standard deviation are found for sand, clay, carbon, and phosphorous content in surface soil samples. On the basis of statistical analysis of mean methods for surface and subsurface soil samples, no more difference is found in post-monsoon season for banana crop.

Table 4 represents the statistical analysis of pre-monsoon organic banana soil samples. Where the soil samples are collected in pre-monsoon season from surface and subsurface where organic fertilizers are used for banana crops.

On the basis of statistical analysis in Table 4, minimum value is found for potash in subsurface. The maximum values of mean are found for carbon soil properties in surface soil samples. On the basis of mean methods, higher contents are available in surface as compare to subsurface soil samples are found in post-monsoon season for banana crop.

The statistical analysis of post-monsoon mixed cotton soil samples shown in Table 5. Where the soil samples are collected in post-monsoon season from surface and subsurface where mixed fertilizers are used for cotton crops.

On the basis of statistical analysis in Table 5, minimum value is found for potash in surface and subsurface as compare other properties in respective layer. The maximum values of mean are found for moisture soil properties in surface soil samples. On the basis of mean methods, higher contents are available in surface as compare to subsurface soil samples are found in post-monsoon season for cotton crop where mixed fertilizers are applied.

The statistical analysis of pre-monsoon organic banana soil samples shown in Table 6. Where the soil samples are collected in pre-monsoon season from surface and subsurface where mixed fertilizers are used for cotton crops.

Table 5 Statistical analysis of post-monsoon mixed cotton soil samples

POMC

Soil properties	Surface					Subsurface				
	Min	Max	Median	Mean	Std. Dev.	Min	Max	Median	Mean	Std. Dev.
Sand	0.074	0.114	0.103	0.097	0.021	0.059	0.069	0.065	0.064	0.005
Silt	0.070	0.110	0.097	0.092	0.020	0.056	0.066	0.062	0.061	0.005
Clay	0.073	0.114	0.102	0.096	0.021	0.059	0.068	0.064	0.064	0.005
SOM	0.070	0.110	0.098	0.093	0.020	0.056	0.065	0.062	0.061	0.005
Moisture	0.069	0.167	0.097	0.111	0.050	0.055	0.065	0.061	0.061	0.005
pH	0.062	0.099	0.084	0.081	0.019	0.049	0.058	0.055	0.054	0.005
Carbon	0.075	0.116	0.105	0.099	0.021	0.060	0.070	0.066	0.065	0.005
Nitrogen	0.070	0.108	0.098	0.092	0.020	0.056	0.066	0.062	0.062	0.005
Phosphorous	0.072	0.113	0.100	0.095	0.021	0.058	0.067	0.063	0.063	0.004
Potash	0.065	0.102	0.090	0.086	0.019	0.052	0.061	0.057	0.057	0.005

Table 6 Statistical analysis of pre-monsoon mixed cotton soil samples

PRMC

Soil properties	Surface					Subsurface				
	Min	Max	Median	Mean	Std. Dev.	Min	Max	Median	Mean	Std. Dev.
Sand	0.112	0.118	0.116	0.115	0.003	0.074	0.098	0.095	0.089	0.013
Silt	0.105	0.116	0.113	0.111	0.006	0.072	0.093	0.092	0.085	0.012
Clay	0.114	0.118	0.116	0.116	0.002	0.073	0.099	0.094	0.089	0.014
SOM	0.106	0.114	0.111	0.110	0.004	0.070	0.093	0.090	0.084	0.013
Moisture	0.104	0.114	0.111	0.110	0.005	0.075	0.096	0.095	0.089	0.012
pH	0.092	0.106	0.103	0.100	0.008	0.065	0.083	0.082	0.077	0.010
Carbon	0.114	0.121	0.118	0.118	0.003	0.075	0.100	0.096	0.091	0.013
Nitrogen	0.105	0.115	0.113	0.111	0.005	0.074	0.093	0.093	0.087	0.011
Phosphorous	0.111	0.117	0.114	0.114	0.003	0.072	0.097	0.092	0.087	0.014
Potash	0.097	0.108	0.104	0.103	0.005	0.067	0.086	0.085	0.079	0.011

On the basis of statistical analysis represented in Table 6, minimum pH value is found in surface and subsurface layer as compare to other properties. The maximum values of mean are found for carbon soil properties in surface soil samples. On the basis of mean methods higher contents are available in surface as compare to subsurface soil samples are found in pre-monsoon season for cotton crop where mixed fertilizers are applied.

Table 7 Statistical analysis of post-monsoon mixed banana soil samples

POMB

Soil properties	Surface					Subsurface				
	Min	Max	Median	Mean	Std. Dev.	Min	Max	Median	Mean	Std. Dev.
Sand	0.063	0.074	0.066	0.068	0.006	0.069	0.087	0.074	0.077	0.009
Silt	0.059	0.070	0.063	0.064	0.005	0.066	0.082	0.071	0.073	0.009
Clay	0.062	0.073	0.065	0.067	0.006	0.068	0.087	0.074	0.076	0.009
SOM	0.060	0.070	0.063	0.064	0.006	0.065	0.083	0.071	0.073	0.009
Moisture	0.059	0.072	0.063	0.065	0.007	0.065	0.082	0.078	0.075	0.009
pH	0.052	0.062	0.056	0.057	0.005	0.058	0.072	0.063	0.064	0.007
Carbon	0.064	0.075	0.067	0.069	0.006	0.070	0.088	0.076	0.078	0.009
Nitrogen	0.060	0.070	0.064	0.064	0.005	0.066	0.083	0.072	0.074	0.009
Phosphorous	0.061	0.072	0.064	0.066	0.006	0.067	0.085	0.072	0.075	0.009
Potash	0.055	0.065	0.058	0.059	0.005	0.061	0.077	0.066	0.068	0.008

The statistical analysis of post-monsoon mixed banana soil samples shown in Table 7, where the soil samples are collected in post-monsoon season from surface and subsurface where mixed fertilizers are used for banana crops.

The statistical analysis represent in Table 7, minimum value is found for pH in surface and subsurface as compare other properties in respective layer. The maximum values of mean are found for sand soil properties in surface and subsurface soil samples. On the basis of mean methods, higher contents are available in subsurface as compare to surface soil samples are found in post-monsoon season for banana crop where mixed fertilizers are applied.

The statistical analysis of pre-monsoon mixed banana soil samples is shown in Table 8, where the soil samples are collected in pre-monsoon season from surface and subsurface where mixed fertilizers are used for banana crops.

Table 8 shows the minimum value is found for moisture in surface and pH in subsurface as compare other properties in respective layer. The maximum values of mean are found for carbon soil properties in surface and subsurface soil samples. On the basis of mean methods, higher contents are available in surface as compare to subsurface soil samples are found in pre-monsoon season for banana crop where mixed fertilizers are applied.

The statistical analysis of post-monsoon chemical banana soil samples is shown in Table 9, where the soil samples are collected in post-monsoon season from surface and subsurface where chemical fertilizers are used for banana crops.

Table 9 shows the minimum value is found for pH in surface and subsurface as compare other properties in respective layer. The maximum values of mean are found for carbon soil properties in surface and subsurface soil samples. On the basis of mean methods, higher contents are available in subsurface as compare to surface

Table 8 Statistical analysis of pre-monsoon mixed banana soil samples

PRMB

Soil properties	Surface					Subsurface				
	Min	Max	Median	Mean	Std. Dev.	Min	Max	Median	Mean	Std. Dev.
Sand	0.147	0.181	0.174	0.167	0.004	0.115	0.158	0.130	0.134	0.022
Silt	0.142	0.174	0.169	0.161	0.004	0.107	0.147	0.122	0.125	0.020
Clay	0.148	0.181	0.174	0.167	0.005	0.116	0.159	0.130	0.135	0.022
SOM	0.143	0.175	0.169	0.162	0.004	0.110	0.150	0.123	0.128	0.020
Moisture	0.101	0.171	0.133	0.135	0.027	0.099	0.164	0.128	0.130	0.033
pH	0.125	0.153	0.149	0.142	0.003	0.091	0.124	0.105	0.107	0.017
Carbon	0.151	0.184	0.178	0.171	0.005	0.117	0.161	0.132	0.137	0.022
Nitrogen	0.140	0.173	0.169	0.161	0.003	0.105	0.147	0.123	0.125	0.021
Phosphorous	0.146	0.178	0.172	0.165	0.005	0.114	0.155	0.128	0.132	0.021
Potash	0.131	0.161	0.156	0.149	0.003	0.099	0.135	0.113	0.116	0.019

Table 9 Statistical analysis of post-monsoon chemical banana soil samples

POCB

Soil properties	Surface					Subsurface				
	Min	Max	Median	Mean	Std. Dev.	Min	Max	Median	Mean	Std. Dev.
Sand	0.057	0.074	0.063	0.064	0.009	0.059	0.074	0.069	0.067	0.008
Silt	0.054	0.070	0.059	0.061	0.008	0.056	0.071	0.066	0.064	0.008
Clay	0.056	0.073	0.062	0.064	0.009	0.059	0.074	0.068	0.067	0.007
SOM	0.054	0.070	0.060	0.061	0.008	0.056	0.071	0.065	0.064	0.007
Moisture	0.054	0.072	0.059	0.062	0.010	0.055	0.078	0.065	0.066	0.011
pH	0.048	0.062	0.052	0.054	0.007	0.049	0.063	0.058	0.057	0.007
Carbon	0.058	0.075	0.064	0.066	0.009	0.060	0.076	0.070	0.069	0.008
Nitrogen	0.055	0.070	0.060	0.061	0.008	0.056	0.072	0.066	0.065	0.008
Phosphorous	0.055	0.072	0.061	0.063	0.008	0.058	0.072	0.067	0.066	0.007
Potash	0.050	0.065	0.055	0.057	0.007	0.052	0.066	0.061	0.059	0.007

soil samples are found in post-monsoon season for banana crop where chemical fertilizers are applied.

The statistical analysis of pre-monsoon chemical banana soil samples is shown in Table 10, where the soil samples are collected in pre-monsoon season from surface and subsurface where chemical fertilizers are used for banana crops.

Table 10 shows the minimum value is found for pH in surface and subsurface as compare other properties in respective layer. The maximum values of mean are found for moisture soil properties in surface and carbon in subsurface soil samples.

Table 10 Statistical analysis of pre-monsoon chemical banana soil samples

PRCB

Soil properties	Surface					Subsurface				
	Min	Max	Median	Mean	Std. Dev.	Min	Max	Median	Mean	Std. Dev.
Sand	0.106	0.140	0.113	0.118	0.015	0.088	0.107	0.103	0.102	0.011
Silt	0.102	0.131	0.110	0.113	0.013	0.083	0.101	0.098	0.096	0.010
Clay	0.105	0.141	0.113	0.118	0.016	0.090	0.107	0.104	0.103	0.011
SOM	0.102	0.135	0.109	0.114	0.015	0.084	0.101	0.098	0.098	0.011
Moisture	0.102	0.139	0.121	0.121	0.016	0.081	0.100	0.096	0.093	0.009
pH	0.090	0.109	0.099	0.099	0.010	0.072	0.087	0.086	0.084	0.008
Carbon	0.108	0.143	0.116	0.120	0.016	0.091	0.109	0.106	0.105	0.011
Nitrogen	0.102	0.126	0.109	0.111	0.011	0.082	0.100	0.097	0.095	0.010
Phosphorous	0.104	0.139	0.112	0.117	0.016	0.088	0.105	0.102	0.101	0.011
Potash	0.095	0.120	0.102	0.105	0.012	0.077	0.093	0.090	0.089	0.009

On the basis of mean methods, higher contents are available in surface as compare to subsurface soil samples are found in pre-monsoon season for banana crop where chemical fertilizers are applied.

In the existing system, number of researchers carried out the work for soil properties assessment, but very less work was found on soil properties assessment for influence of fertilizers in different season, different depth of soil samples, and different crops. On the basis of quantitative results, the soil properties are altered in different season.

5 Conclusion

The remote sensing domain using spectroscopy techniques gives the better results for soil assessment. But it requires appropriate methods and process for analysis of data. This study assessed the efficiency of spectroscopy and its techniques for rapid and inexpensive determination of soil properties parameters. This study covered the required statistical methods that are applied for quantitative analysis of the soil properties. In this analysis, the spectral data converted in numeric format and find out the various soil properties by applying statistical methods and calculate the Min, Max, Median, Mean, and Standard Deviation for quantitative soil properties analysis. On the basis of quantitative analysis, availability of soil properties is higher in pre-monsoon season maximum in surface soil samples category, and in post-monsoon season higher soil properties are available in maximum subsurface soil samples. Overall, the more content availability in organic fertilizers applied soil samples as compare to mixed and chemical fertilizers. On the basis of quantitative analysis, the organic fertilizers can be recommended for maintaining the soil quality. This study is helpful to researcher for analysis of soil parameter using spectral data and process the data as well as to farmers for fertilizers management, and it will help for reducing the fertilizers cost.

References

1. Şeker C, Qzaytekin HH, Negiş H, Gumuş I, Dedeoglu M, Atmaca E, Karaca U (2017) Assessment of soil quality index for wheat and sugar beet cropping systems on an entisol in Central Anatolia. Environ Monit Assess 135:1–11
2. Moore F, Sheykhi V, Salari M, Bagheri A (2016) Soil quality assessment using GIS-based chemometric approach and pollution indices: Nakhlak mining district, Central Iran. Environ Monit Assess 214:1–16
3. Feyziyev F, Babayev M, Priori S, L'Abate G (2016) Using visible-near infrared spectroscopy to predict soil properties of Mugan Plain, Azerbaijan. Open J Soil Sci 6:52–58
4. Feng Y, Astin I (2015) Remote sensing of soil moisture using the propagation of Loran-C navigation signals. IEEE Geosci Remote Sens Lett 12:195–198
5. Liu Y, Pan X-Z, Shi R-J, Li Y-L, Wang C-K, Li Z-T (2015) Predicting soil salt content over partially vegetated surfaces using non-negative matrix factorization. IEEE J Sel Topics Appl Earth Observ Remote Sens 8(11):5305–5317
6. Bhise PR, Kulkarni SB, Borole VY (2019) Preprocessing and statistical analysis of soil parameters using conventional laboratory techniques and non-imaging spectral techniques for Vaijapur Taluka. Int J Recent Technol Eng 8(2):3092–3096
7. Borole VY, Kulkarni SB, Bhise PR (2019) Soil spectral signature analysis for influence of fertilizers on two differen crops in raver Tahshil. Int J Recent Technol Eng 8(3):659–663
8. Sahoo RN, Bhavanarayana M, Panda BC, CArika N, Kaur R (2005) Total information content as an index of soil moisture. J Ind Soc Rem Sens 33(1)
9. Kai T, Mukai M, Araki KS, Adhikari D, Kubo M (2015) Physical and biochemical properties of apple orchard soils of different productivities. Open J Soil Sci 5:149–156
10. Borole VY, Kulkarni SB, Bhise PR (2020) Effect of fertilizers on soil properties for different crops in pre-monsoon season using spectroradiometer for raver tehsil of Jalgaon district. Int J Sci Technol Res 9(2):844–849
11. Chandrasekaran A, Rajalakshmi A, Ravisankar R, Vijayagopal P, Venkatraman B (2015) Measurements of natural gamma radiations and effects of physico-chemical properties in soils of Yelagiri Hills, Tamilnadu India with statistical approach, global challenges, policy framework & sustainable development for mining of mineral and fossil energy resources (GCPF2015). Proc Earth Planetary Sci 11:531–538
12. Borole VY, Kulkarni SB (2019) Soil quality assessment for analyzing the effect of chemical fertilizers on agriculture field using spectroradiometer: a review. In: International conference on electrical, communication, electronics, instrumentation and computing (ICECEIC). IEEE, New York (2019)
13. Bhise PR, Kulkarni SB (2019) Estimation of soil macronutrients from spectral signatures using hyperspectral non-imaging data. In: International conference on electrical, communication, electronics, instrumentation and computing (ICECEIC). IEEE, New York (2019)
14. Bhise PR, Kulkarni SB, Review on analysis and classification techniques of soil study in remote sensing and geographic information system. Int J Emerg Trends Technol Comput Sci (IJETTCS) 6(1):124–138
15. Vibhute AD, Dhumal R, Nagne A, Gaikwad S, Kale KV, Mehrotra SC (2018) Multi-sensor, multi-resolution and multi-temporal satellite data fusion for soil type classification. In: IJCA proceedings on international conference on cognitive knowledge engineering, by IJCA Journal, ICKE 2016—Number 2, 2018

16. Todorova M, Mouazen AM, Lange H, Astanassova S (2014) Potential of near-infrared spectroscopy for measurement of heavy metals in soil as affected by calibration set size. Water Air Soil Pollut 225(8):1–19
17. Khadse K (2011) Spectral reflectance characteristics for the soils on Basaltic terrain of central Indian plateau. J Indian Soc Reomte Sens 40(4):717–724
18. Mahanty T, Bhattacharjee S, Goswami M, Bhattacharyya P, Das B, Ghosh A, Tribedi P (2016) Biofertilizers: a potential approach for sustainable agriculture development. Springer, Berlin, pp 3315–3335
19. Bhise Pratibha R, Kulkarni Sonali B, Remote sensing and data mining techniques applied on soil characteristics data classification. IOSR J Comput Eng (IOSR-JCE), pp 83–91
20. Bhise PR, Kulkarni SB (2018) Evaluation of soil physical/chemical parameters for agriculture production in Vaijapur Taluka using VNIR-SWIR reflectance spectroscopy. Int J Comput Sci Eng 6(12):43–48

Building an Efficient Heart Disease Prediction System by using Clustering Techniques

Kamepalli S L Prasanna and J. Vijaya

Abstract The healthcare management system (HMS) is a key to successful management of healthcare facilities such as clinics or hospitals. In today's world, heart disease is one of the most common causes of illness and death. Heart disease proves to be the leading reason for the death of a person. Heart disease affects human life very badly and its prediction is a complex task. Heart disease predicts a system which can assist medical professionals in predicting the status of a patient's heart condition based on their clinical data or records. We choose 14 attributes such as age, gender, cholesterol, type of chest pain, fasting blood sugar, resting blood pressure (restbps), resting electro cardio graph (ECG (for heart monitoring)), exercise-induced angina, maximum heart rate, slope, old peak and number of vessels coloured. In this paper, we proposed a work to predict the likelihood of heart disease and classify patient risk level using various hybrid techniques. We combined unsupervised and supervised approaches to achieve a higher-level accuracy of classification. The unsupervised approach is very important in the hybrid learning methods. Hence, K-means clustering used for patient segmentation is helpful for grouping of similar types of patients within a cluster. The holdout approach is used to form the training and testing data from each cluster. Then, the model is generated by various classification algorithms such as DT, NB, SVM and KNN. The heart disease predicts at early stage based on risk factors, and this experiment demonstrated that combining the K-means algorithm along with a decision tree improves accuracy.

Keywords HMS · Heart disease · Supervised algorithms · Unsupervised algorithms · Machine learning

Kamepalli. S. L. Prasanna (✉) · J. Vijaya
VIT-AP University, Vijayawada 522237, India
e-mail: prasanna.20phd7157@vitap.ac.in

J. Vijaya
e-mail: vijaya.stephen@vitap.ac.in

1 Introduction

Nowadays, one of the most common illness is heart disease, it is decreasing lifespan of a human because of heart disease every year 17.5 million people are dying [1]. Predicting of heart disease is the most difficult problem in the medical industry and diagnosed based on symptoms, medical assessment and signs of the patient [2]. Factors that effect of heart diseases include body level of cholesterol, smoking habits and obesity, hereditary (due to genetic disorder), blood pressure and working environment [3]. Congestive heart failure, angina pectoris, coronary heart disease, myocarditis, congenital heart disease, arrhythmias and cardiomyopathy are several types of heart illnesses [4]. When coronary arteries become blocked, blood flow to the heart muscles is reduced. The ECG records were examined to see whether there were any irregular heartbeat issues caused by cardiovascular illnesses. When a blood vessel supplying the brain becomes blocked, a stroke occurs. The cause of heart stroke is high cholesterol, high blood pressure, smoking and diabetes. Heart arrhythmias are irregular heartbeats that occur when the heart beats too fast or too slowly. Arrhythmias are significant because they can result in sudden strokes, cardiac death. Because the nature of cardiac disease is complicated, it must be treated seriously. Tumours of the heart, vascular tumours of the brain; disorders of heart muscle that is cardiomyopathy; heart valve diseases; disorders of the lining of the heart. In medical research and machine learning are being utilized to identify different types of metabolic disorder increasing risk of heart disease, stroke, and diabetes. In the prediction of cardiac disease and data research, machine learning techniques with classification play a significant part. Heart disease was predicted using various methods, such as logistic regression (LR), Naive Bayes (NB), support vector machine (SVM), K-nearest neighbour (KNN), artificial neural networks (ANNs) and decision tree (DT), were used to predicting heart disease [5–8]. Especially, given the fact that single-classifier classification is an effective model, their prognosticate accuracy is not considerable. In this paper, we consider dataset from UCI machine learning repository where it consists of 75 attributes amongst them, we are using 14 set of attributes such as cholesterol, age, sex, max heart rate, chest pain type, resting blood pressure (restbps), fasting blood sugar, slope, resting electro cardio graph (ECG (for heart monitoring)), exercise-induced angina, old peak, number of vessels coloured. Hence, currently used hybrid approaches involving combines supervised and unsupervised approaches. However, there are just a few contributions to unsupervised approaches. In hybrid models, unsupervised approaches provide an important role for predicting risk of heart disease based on the risk factors. It focuses on improving the accuracy of risk prediction for heart disease by using a similarity between the patients. Hence, we focus on K-means traditional unsupervised learning approaches which are useful to group the similar symptoms-oriented patients. The holdout approach is used to form the training and testing data from each cluster. Then, the model is generated by various classification algorithms such as DT, NB, SVM and KNN. The heart disease prediction experiment demonstrated that combining the K-means algorithm along with a decision tree improves accuracy.

2 Literature Survey

Anna Karen Garate-Escamila et al. (2020) mainly focus on prediction of heart disease using feature selection technique and different classification they are DT, GBT, NB, RF and MLP but more accuracy is given the combination of principal component analysis (PCA) and chi-square (CHI) with random forest (RF). They considered the three different datasets such as Cleveland, Hungarian and Cleveland-Hungarian [4]. The model achieved accuracy 99.0% for Hungarian, 98.7% for Cleveland and 99.4% for CH. Elham Nikookar et al. (2018) use a hybrid ensemble model based on that predicted heart disease, the dataset consists of 278 samples from single proton emission computed tomography (SPECT) images of patients, we achieved 80% of sensitivity, 96% of classification accuracy and 93% of specificity performance are obtained it not provided feature selection techniques [9]. Beulah et al. (2019) predicting heart disease and improving the accuracy by using ensemble algorithms such as boosting, bagging algorithms and bagging algorithm gives the 6.92% more of the accuracy and boosting algorithm gives 5.94%. So that increases the maximum accuracy 7% for weak classifier with the help of ensemble algorithms using feature selection to improve accuracy of the prediction of disease [2]. Robinson et al. (2020) proposed classification and filter methods for enhanced heart disease prediction. They use different feature extraction and filter methods (symmetrical uncertainty (SU), chi-squared, PCA, Relief F) for UCI dataset, different data mining techniques used such as KNN, Bayes net, logistic, SGD and AdaBoost, they concluded Bayes net classifier and chi-squared feature selection achieved precision of 84.73%, an accuracy of 85.0% and recall of 85.56%. And also, they build another model using the SGD algorithm along with Relief F feature selection had a comparable precision and accuracy is 84.57% and 84.86%, respectively, with an improved recall of 85.83%. The next model is IBK with PCA feature extraction, which had precision of 81.91% and the highest accuracy of 83.89% and recall of any model at 87.22% [6]. Senthil Kumar Mohan et al. (2019) suggested a hybrid approach (HRLFM) collaborate the linear method (LM) and random forest (RF). Using this model provided an accuracy of 88:7% for prediction of heart disease, for better accuracy to apply feature selection method [10]. Indra Kumar et al. (2020) proposed the prediction of heart disease by using K-means algorithm with visualization tool and data analytics, they considering dataset 209 records, using the visualization tool get the accuracy, hybrid model with feature selection combination get more accuracy prediction of disease [3]. Amita Malav et al. (2018) using a hybrid approach combination of K-means and ANN gives the accuracy of 93.52% prediction of disease only concentrated on adults and for better accuracy, use fuzzy logic and crisp set [11]. Youness Khourdifi1 et al. (2018) using different classification algorithms, KNN, RF, SVM, NB, along with feature selection and optimization techniques used fast correlation-based feature selection (FCBF) with two different optimizations. Those are ant colony optimization (ACO) with particle swarm optimization (PSO) approaches. FCBF, ACO and PSO achieve an accuracy of 99.65% with KNN and 99.6% RF [12]. Thippa Reddy et al. (2017)

prediction of heart disease using a novel approach that is a combination of rule-based fuzzy logic (RBFL) and oppositional firefly with BAT (OFBAT). First, select relevant features using the locality preserving projection (LPP) algorithm, dataset considered from the UCI machine learning repository. It provides 78% of accuracy [13]. Padmavathi Kora et al. (2019) coronary heart disease detection is based on fuzzy rules clinical system detection of disease using traditional classifications KNN and SVM. Fuzzy classification gives 99.3% accuracy [8]. Ashir Javeed et al. (2020) based on feature selection to detect heart risk failures using NN classification get the more accuracy used floating window with adaptive size for feature elimination (FWAFE), consider two different approaches, such as ANN and DNN. The combination of FWAFE + ANN achieved an accuracy of 91.11% and FWAFE + DNN achieved an accuracy of 93.33% [5]. Indu Yekkala et al. (2018) heart disease prediction by using three different classifications: KNN, RF, NB and one common feature selection technique, rough set (RS) The best result is given by RF + RS whether the patient was suffering from heart disease or not [14]. Ahmed et al. (2019) using rough set give more accuracy to prediction of heart disease provided by the hybrid model. This model combination of cuckoo search with rough set (CSRS) and accuracy is 93.7%. It compared cuckoo search and decision tree predictive learner (CSDTPL), the CSRS provided more 3.7% of accuracy' [7]. Farman Ali et al. (2020) using ensemble deep learning and feature fusion approaches to provide smart healthcare system using feature selection, feature fusions based on traditional classification and weighting techniques. This model achieved an accuracy 98.5% [1].

3 Parameters and Techniques for Predicting Heart Disease

The proposed work is depicted in Fig. 1 as a block diagram with several phases. The first step reflects pre-processed the data and removing the missing values based on the attributes. Only numerical values are accepted by the clustering algorithm, so string values are converted into numerical format. Patients were divided into groups in order to assess their efficacy. During the holdout process, the clusters are divided into training and testing, with DT, SVM, KNN, and NB used for training and models developed for testing (Fig. 2).

3.1 Dataset Description and Pre-processing

Experiments are carried on a heart disease dataset includes 74 independent features of the UCI machine learning repository. NUM specified whether a patient has been affected by heart disease or not. Every single patient was described by 14 attributes and predicted disease. The attributes included primary age, sex, chol, fbs, restecg, cp, restbp and whether the patient has heart disease or not based on complete information. During the pre-processing stage, non-essentials features, such as (family history of

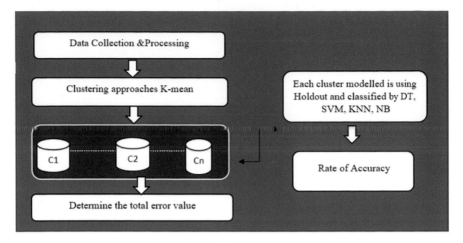

Fig. 1 Hybrid heart disease prediction block diagram

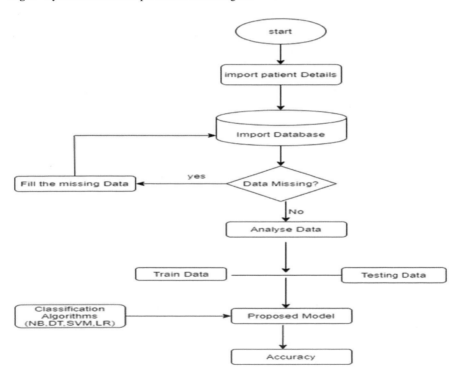

Fig. 2 Flowchart for the early risk reduction of heart disease

coronary heart disease, social security number (CGF), ID and day of exercise ECG reading), are remove from the data collection. Since the clustering algorithms only accept the numerical features, the string values are converted into numerical format, pre-processing which removes noise from data and makes it more reliable, it is one of the most important steps.

3.2   The Algorithm for Clustering

In machine learning, clustering method has broad-spectrum of implementation, including business forecasting, image segmentation and so on. Based on their similarities, the methods classified data objects into classes. The data points with the shortest distance are found in cluster. The distance between two data points is measured using different formulas such as the Euclidean distance, Minkowski distance and Manhattan distance. Clustering is divided into many categories: grid-based clustering, fuzzy clustering, hierarchical clustering, partition clustering, model-based clustering and density-based clustering. We use partitional clustering techniques in this paper.

3.2.1   K-Means

Stuart Lloyd suggested the K-means algorithm based on the partitional clustering method in 1957. It partitioned N input tuples into K partitional, where K was equal or less than N. The following condition for partitional-based clustering (i) each cluster has at least one sample, (ii) each sample must be included in exactly one cluster. The algorithm represents a key stage in K-means clustering.

Algorithm of K-mean

Input: D is whole dataset which contains of N samples.
Output: Total number of clusters K groups.
Level 1: Set K value to be equal or less than N
Level 2: Select K as the initial cluster centre, random.
Level 3: Calculate the variation between an object and the middle of the selected K cluster
Level 4: Objects which have the same minimum distance S are grouped to gathered
Level 5: Replace the cluster means with new cluster centres (Ci) where i = {1 ....
K}
Level 6: If the cluster centre does not change, the algorithm will terminate or return to the step3.

3.3   The Algorithm for Classification

An algorithm defines a collection of data into groups is known as classification. It can be done in both training and testing. The process starts with predicting the class of given data points. It is used to identify the category of new observations based on training data as well as testing data.

3.3.1   Decision Tree

1. Classification of decision tree algorithm to develop the process of learning.
2. The attribute's measure value is used to construct a binary tree.
3. Decision rules are established by following multiple routes from parent node to child node.
4. Identify whether patient suffering with a disease or not using decision rules.

Decision tree rules based on that divided the attributes. The tests consider in three ways they are used commonly: entropy, Gini Index, and gain ratio.

Entropy: The entropy approach selects the splitting attribute that minimizes the value of entropy, thus maximizing the entropy. For each attribute, calculate the entropy and choose the highest entropy. Calculating the entropy for each attribute is given below formula is

$$\text{Entropy} = \sum_{i=1}^{c} -p_i * \log_2(p_i)$$

where c is the number of classes of the target attribute, P_i is the number of occurrences of class i divided by the total number of instances, i.e. the probability of i occurring.

Gini Index: The Gini Index analyzes the data's impurity, it calculates for each attribute in dataset, where C is target attribute the probability of ith class

$$\text{Gini} = 1 - \sum_{i=1}^{c} (p_i)^2$$

Gain Ratio: The entropy measure is biased towards tests with large number of outcomes.

$$\text{Gain Ratio} = \text{Entropy}/\text{Split Information}$$

3.3.2   K-Nearest Neighbours (KNNs) Algorithm

Level 1: Choose number of the Kth neighbour
Level 2: To determine the Euclidean distance between K neighbours

$$d(x_i, x_j) = \sqrt{(x_i, 1 - x_j, 1)^2 + \cdots + (x_i, m - x_j, m)^2}$$

Level 3: By using Euclidean distance value, to find the k closet neighbours.
Level 4: The data points are counted in each group between these k neighbours
Level 5: Apply current data points to group with the maximum number of neighbours.
Level 6: complete calculation.

3.3.3   Naive Bayes Algorithm

Level 1: To calculate the given labels for each class of prior probability.
Level 2: Find likelihood probability with each attribute for each class.
Level 3: Using **Bayes** formula and calculate posterior probability.

$$P(h|D) = \frac{P(D|h)P(h)}{P(D)}$$

3.3.4   Support Vector Machine (SVM) Algorithm

The hyperplane that better divides the tags is generated by SVM, which produces hyperplane from data points. This line serves as a decision boundary for determining the intersection of the lines from both classes. Support vectors are given to these points. A margin is the space between vectors and the hyperplane. The aim of SVM is to increase the greatest margins.

4   Experiment Setup

This experiment consists of three levels. The recognition rate is mainly controlled by the clustering performance based on hybrid techniques.

The first level makes use of the efficiency of the K-means clustering algorithm. The second level measures the performance of hybrid methods, and the third level is compared to the existing method by the following evaluation methods. SSE is the sum of the squared distances between the cluster's centroid and each member. It measures of the variability observations within each cluster. It is mainly used for improving the quality of clustering techniques. If the error level is low, then the objects are clustered. Equation 1 is used to determine the SSE ratio (Figs. 3 and 4; Table 1).

$$SSE = \sum_{i=1}^{k} \sum_{j=1}^{n_i} \|c_i - 0_i\|^2 \tag{1}$$

$$Accuracy = \frac{TP + TN}{TP + TN + FP + FN} \tag{?}$$

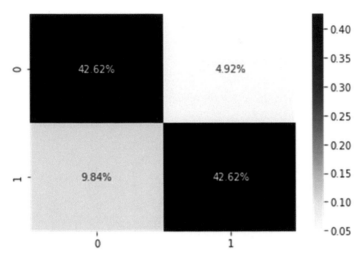

Fig. 3 Confusion matrix

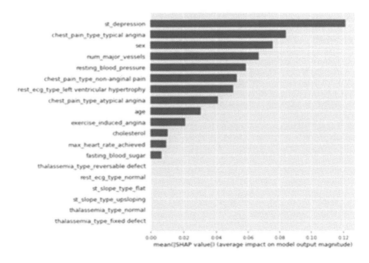

Fig. 4 Average impact on model output

Table 1 Represented mean and averages value based on risk factors

	Count	Mean	Std	Min	25%	50%	75%	Max
age	303.0	54.366337	9.082101	29.0	47.5	55.0	61.0	77.0
sex	303.0	0.683168	0.466011	0.0	0.0	1.0	1.0	1.0
cp	303.0	0.966997	1.032052	0.0	0.0	1.0	2.0	3.0
trtbps	303.0	131.623762	17.538143	94.0	120.0	130.0	140.0	200.0
chol	303.0	246.264.26	51.830751	126.0	211.0	240.0	274.5	564.0
fbs	303.0	0.148515	0.356198	0.0	0.0	0.0	0.0	1.0
restecg	303.0	0.528053	0.525860	0.0	0.0	1.0	1.0	2.0
thalachh	303.0	149.646865	22.905161	71.0	133.5	153.0	166.0	202.0
exng	303.0	0.326733	0.469794	0.0	0.0	0.0	1.0	1.0
oldpeak	303.0	1.039604	1.161075	0.0	0.0	0.8	1.6	6.2
slp	303.0	1.399340	0.616226	0.0	1.0	1.0	2.0	2.0
caa	303.0	0.729373	1.022606	0.0	0.0	0.0	1.0	4.0
thall	303.0	2.313531	0.612277	0.0	2.0	2.0	3.0	3.0
output	303.0	0.544554	0.498835	0.0	0.0	1.0	1.0	1.0

$$\text{Recall} = TP/(TP + FN) \tag{3}$$

$$\text{Precision} = TP/(TP + FP) \tag{4}$$

$$\text{Mis classification} = 1 - \text{Accuracy} \tag{5}$$

4.1 Testing Level I

In the first level testing, concentrated on the K-means algorithm; it comes under an unsupervised approach. Figure 5 represents that k-means produces a sum of squared error result by varying cluster size from 1 to 7. The horizontal line in this graph represents the number of clusters, whilst the vertical line represents the sum of squared errors. Table 2 illustrates a sample result from k-means clustering approaches with a number of clusters equal to 5 and a total of 303 patients.

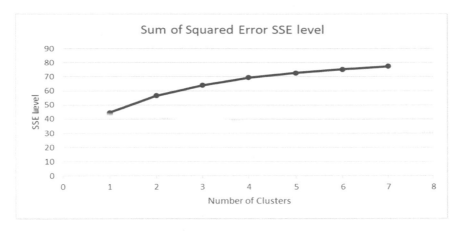

Fig. 5 K-means clustering approaches in SSE

Table 2 Patients in each of the five groups

Name of algorithm	Group1	Group2	Group3	Group4	Group5
K-mean	90	50	81	0	82

4.2 Testing Level II

The second level of testing performance of hybrid models such as K-means clustering with DT, KNN, NB and SVM. Figure 6 shows the results of each model. The percentage clusters and accurate ratio defined by every method are shown by the horizontal and vertical axes, respectively. We have seen in this graph that K-means

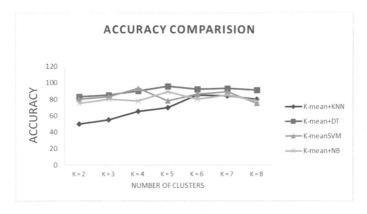

Fig. 6 Various hybrid models of accuracy

Table 3 Accuracy represented to base on K values

No. of clusters	K-means + KNN	K-means + DT	K-means + SVM	K-means + NB
K = 2	50	83	80	75
K = 3	55	85	83	80
K = 4	65	90	93	78
K = 5	70	96	78	89
K = 6	85	92	86	80
K = 7	84	93	89	85
K = 8	80	91	75	78

combined with a decision tree has a higher accurate rate than remaining models. Because K-means clustering has the least SSE value, it may effectively split patients and hence achieve higher classification results. We got an accuracy 96% (Table 3).

4.3   Testing Level III

The final set of tests is analyzed as a result to evaluate various hybrid models. The suggested hybrid model's result is compared to those of other existing models. Robinson et al. (2020) proposed classification and filter methods for enhanced heart disease prediction. For feature selection, they used the chi-squared method with a combination of Bayes net algorithm. They got an accuracy of 85% (Fig. 7).

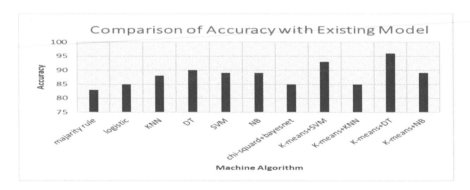

Fig. 7 Comparison of accuracy with existing model and hybrid model

5   Conclusion and Future Work

To improve classification accuracy, both supervised and unsupervised are now merged and unsupervised classification plays a significant role in novel models. This study focuses on unsupervised approaches, specifically k-means clustering with various classification algorithms such as DT, NB, SVM and KNN. As a result, the DT classification algorithm produces better accuracy compared to remaining algorithms. Our model can be used to examine large amounts of data to classify the risk factors associated with various diseases in real-world application.

References

1. Ali F et al (2020) A smart healthcare monitoring system for heart disease prediction based on ensemble deep learning and feature fusion. Inf Fus 63:208–222
2. Latha CBC, Jeeva SC (2019) Improving the accuracy of prediction of heart disease risk based on ensemble classification techniques. Inf Med Unlocked 16:100203
3. Indra Kumari R, Poongodi T, Jena SR (2020) Heart disease prediction using exploratory data analysis. Proc Comput Sci 173:130–139
4. Gárate-Escamila AK, El Hassani AH, Andrès E (2020) Classification models for heart disease prediction using feature selection and PCA. Inf Med Unlocked 19:100330
5. Javeed A et al (2020) Heart risk failure prediction using a novel feature selection method for feature refinement and neural network for classification. Mob Inf Syst 2020
6. Spencer R et al (2020) Exploring feature selection and classification methods for predicting heart disease. Digital Health 6: 2055207620914777
7. Acharjya DP (2020) A hybrid scheme for heart disease diagnosis using rough set and cuckoo search technique. J Med Syst 44(1):1–16
8. Kora P et al (2019) Detection of cardiac arrhythmia using fuzzy logic. Inf Med Unlocked 17:100257
9. Nikookar E, Naderi E (2018) Hybrid ensemble framework for heart disease detection and prediction. Int J Adv Comput Sci Appl 9(5):243–248
10. Mohan SK, Thirumalai C, Srivastava G (2019) Effective heart disease prediction using hybrid machine learning techniques. IEEE Access 7:81542–81554
11. Malav A, Kadam K (2018) A hybrid approach for heart disease prediction using artificial neural network and K-means. Int J Pure Appl Math 118(8):103–110
12. Khourdifi Y, Bahaj M (2019) Heart disease prediction and classification using machine learning algorithms optimized by particle swarm optimization and ant colony optimization. Int J Intell Eng Syst 12(1):242–252
13. Reddy GT, Khare N (2017) An efficient system for heart disease prediction using hybrid OFBAT with rule-based fuzzy logic model. J Circuits Syst Comput 26(04):1750061
14. Yekkala I, Dixit S (2018) Prediction of heart disease using random forest and rough set-based feature selection. Int J Big Data Anal Healthcare (IJBDAH) 3(1):1–12

The GR1 Algorithm for Subgraph Isomorphism. A Study from Parallelism to Quantum Computing

Gheorghica Radu-Iulian ⓘ

Abstract In this paper was described the GR1 algorithm that provides feasible execution times for the subgraph isomorphism problem. It is a parallel algorithm that uses a variant of the producer–consumer pattern. It was designed to easily accept and interchange different pruning techniques. The results obtained are occurrences of different query graphs in a RI human protein-to-protein interaction data graph (Ferro et al., [18], Szklarczyk et al., Nucleic Acids Res 39, 2011 [20]). This is the graph in which the algorithm will execute the search. The execution times are feasible for increasingly larger query graphs (from three up to twenty nodes) and with the included quantum computing approach were obtained superior results. The work consists of implementing and testing the algorithm in an original way starting from a simple multiprocessing example (Python multiprocessing producer consumer pattern, [28]) and then writing and adapting it for use with multiple consumer processes, undirected graphs and motif finding. There are also two tables containing the average execution times. The two tables represent two series of test cases.

Keywords Network Motif · Subgraph isomorphism · Producer-consumer · Parallel programming · Quantum computing

1 Introduction

The subject studied is the subgraph isomorphism problem and obtaining feasible execution times when using large graphs from the perspective of parallel programming and then quantum computing. According to [17] it has applicability in the following domains:

Supervisor Dr. Pârv Bazil, Professor Emeritus.

G. Radu-Iulian (✉)
Faculty of Mathematics and Computer Science, Babeș-Bolyai University, Mihail Kogălniceanu Street, nr. 1, 400084 Cluj County, Cluj-Napoca City, Romania
e-mail: radugheorghica@protonmail.com

© The Author(s), under exclusive license to Springer Nature Singapore Pte Ltd. 2022   83
C. Satyanarayana et al. (eds.), *High Performance Computing and Networking*,
Lecture Notes in Electrical Engineering 853,
https://doi.org/10.1007/978-981-16-9885-9_7

1. World Wide Web.
2. Biochemistry, neurobiology, ecology and engineering.
3. Biomolecules within a cell and synaptic connections between neurons, for example in *Caenorhabditis elegans*.
4. Ecological food webs, genetic networks, for example, *Escherichia coli* and *Saccharomyces cerevisiae*.

The authors of [17] specify that motifs could define universal classes of networks. As stated in [21, 22], if the problems belonging to any domain can be expressed with graphs, then they can benefit from finding motif graphs. The study in the current paper advances the knowledge existent about the subgraph isomorphism problem by presenting a parallel algorithm that can accept any pruning techniques. There is also a quantum computing approach presented. This study was made in the context of parallel programming and quantum computing. The investigated hypothesis is that creating a frame which can combine different pruning techniques, either those existing or with new ones, can yield feasible execution times for increasingly larger graphs, especially when using quantum computing circuits [4]. The parallel programming approach is the following: multiple processes running in parallel, one is a producer and the others are consumers. Each consumer process becomes a producer process for one of the other consumer processes, constructing in a cascading manner the solutions. These are the occurrences of query graphs in a data graph. The following sections present the applicability of the algorithm, terminology used throughout the explanations, details about the input data, preconditions and graph definitions, data storage and access, implementation details about the GR1 Algorithm, test cases and average execution times for the GR1 algorithm and the quantum computing approach. Afterward, there are conclusions, acknowledgment and references.

2 Terminology

1. The words "node" and "vertex" will be used interchangeably in the explanations.
2. Node label—There was used a graph representing human protein-to-protein interactions (PPI) [18, 20]. The same label can be assigned to multiple nodes, or for the example in real life, a multitude of proteins can be associated with the same protein type.
3. Solution—A list which contains nodes. For each node of the query graph, the label is copied. For each position in the solution, there is a corresponding position in the query graph. A solution becomes complete when the following conditions are satisfied:

   (a) Every node has its label equal to the one of the node on the same position in the query graph.
   (b) The number of nodes is equal to the one from the query graph.
   (c) The solution has the same adjacency as the query graph, which is a root vertex and multiple leaf nodes.

4. Motif/Motif finding—Network motifs are patterns that recur much more frequently in the real network than in an ensemble of randomized networks [17].
5. Query graph— The search in the data graph makes use of the label from each of
   the query nodes and the adjacency of the query vertices.
6. Data graph—In this graph, the algorithm executes the search. It represents in this
   case a set of interactions between human proteins [18, 20].

3 Input Data

For testing was used the RI human protein-to-protein interaction graph [18, 20] that
has 12,575 nodes and 86,890 edges as the data graph. For the first series of tests
were used query graphs with the number of nodes ranging from three to six nodes.
For the second series of tests, the query graphs follow this procedure: two of them
have seven nodes and have been split in two parts each. The same is for the next two
graphs that have eight nodes. For the ones that have nine and ten nodes, they were
split into three parts each. For those with twenty nodes, they were split into five parts
each. Let us consider Query Graph 21 with seven vertices from Table 1: ["10", "19",
"16", "27", "26", "30", "12"]. The first node, "10", is the root node, and all the others
are the leaf nodes. It can be split in two parts like this: ["10", "19", "16", "27"] and
["26", "30", "12"]. The first part can be used just like the other query graphs that
were not split. But for the second part, the node on the first position, the position
which is reserved for the root node, is "26" and not "10". The search in the data graph
can still take place, but the output from it will have nothing to do with the results
from the first part. Thus, they will be inserted on the first position of the second part,
the root node of the first part. Then, they will be the following: ["10", "19", "16",
"27"] and ["10", "26", "30", "12"]. For graphs such as these that have more vertices,
they can be split into more parts, and for each part from the second one onward, this
procedure applies. Now, there will be text files containing the output for each part.
Through cartesian product, they can be reconstructed and thus obtain the output data
in a single text file.

4 GR1 Algorithm

Using Dask.distributed [29], a producer process was created for the position of the
root nodes and a consumer process for each subsequent node positions. Afterward,
they will be running in parallel to build solutions. The input data for the algorithm
consists of query graphs having the adjacency of a root and multiple leaf nodes.
They also used a data graph representing RI human protein-to-protein interactions
[18, 20]. The algorithm detects and creates automatically the number of processes
necessary, up to a maximum of six per query graph part. The producer takes the label
of the query graph root node and searches in the part of the data graph assigned by

Dask to it for all the nodes having that label. It can also search, if needed, into the data graph parts of the other processes as well. The first consumer takes root nodes from the producer output queue as soon as it starts being populated. The first consumer then uses the label of the second node (which is the first leaf vertex) from the query graph, and for each root node from the producer, it searches for data graph nodes that have that leaf vertex label. Those nodes must also be adjacent to the selected root vertex. As soon as it finds such nodes, it will store them in its own output queue which will serve as the input queue for the next consumer. This continues for each position corresponding to the query graph nodes. If any queue stops receiving products from the previous process, they will wait until more will be available. When the first producer does not have any more root nodes to transmit, a flag is used to trigger the end of the production across all the processes. This procedure is similar to a real-life factory where a product has to be taken through different machines in order to be complete. A second machine will not wait for the first one to complete its intermediary products before passing them along, but instead, as soon as it completes, one of them it sends it to the next machine which does the same and so on. The GR1 algorithm can work with query graphs that have up to twenty vertices and more if needed. The GR1 algorithm can also serve as a frame on which different pruning techniques can be attached for reducing the search space in the data graph and the execution times.

5   Tests

For GR1 algorithm, the execution times include the starting of the producer and consumer processes in Dask.distributed [29]. They do not include the stopping of the processes after the operations of the algorithm are finished. For tests, there was used the RI human protein-to-protein interaction graph [18, 20]. By using the function "scatter" with the keyword "broadcast" having the value "False" [29, 30], the data graph will not be copied in its entirety on every process, but separated into multiple parts, and then, each part will be assigned to a process. Table 1 contains the comparison of average execution times measured in seconds. Here, the query graphs have been split into multiple parts. Three executions for each part of the query graph.

For future development, another approach will be the parallelization of the MultiRI [19] algorithm. A few details are given in Figs. 1, 2 and 3. Also, quantum computing will be used for that implementation and new algorithms.

6   Quantum Computing Approach

According to [10], an oracle is a way to provide the list items to the quantum computer, a common way to encode such a list is by means of a function f that returns $f(x) = 0$ for the items x that are not marked and $f(w) = 1$ for the element that is the winner. As

Table 1 Execution times for ten query graphs that were split into multiple parts

Query graphs	GR1 (seconds)
Query graph 21, two parts, seven nodes	388.70
Query graph 22, two parts, seven nodes	163.64
Query graph 23, two parts, eight nodes	172.20
Query graph 24, two parts, eight nodes	154.76
Query graph 25, three parts, nine nodes	225.41
Query graph 26, three parts, nine nodes	230.74
Query graph 27, three parts, ten nodes	246.12
Query graph 28, three parts, ten nodes	232.87
Query graph 29, five parts, twenty nodes	501.08
Query graph 30, five parts, twenty nodes	522.66

Fig. 1 Example of SMM with a query Q and a target T. Node ids are drawn outside the circles [19]

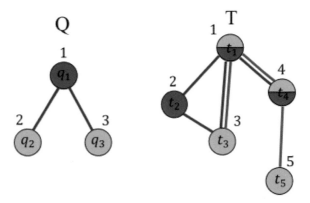

Fig. 2 The application of the automorphisms in Fig. 1 result graphs Q′ and Q″ [19]

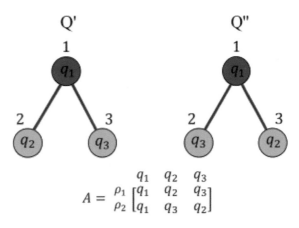

$$A = \begin{array}{c} \\ \rho_1 \\ \rho_2 \end{array} \begin{array}{ccc} q_1 & q_2 & q_3 \\ \left[\begin{array}{ccc} q_1 & q_2 & q_3 \\ q_1 & q_3 & q_2 \end{array} \right] \end{array}$$

Fig. 3 Example of usage of breaking conditions for the query Q and target T of Fig. 1. Matched query and target nodes are linked by dashed edges [19]

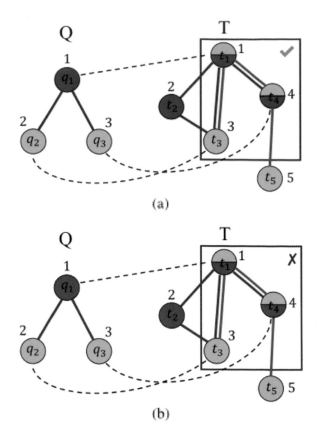

explained in [10], amplitude amplification is the means by which the data sought after is indicated to the user. Gates, both quantum and classical, can be used as operations for the qubits [4, 8]. By using the the details at [15], putting it in practice for query graphs means they will have an index or an identity that will be passed to the quantum computers. As described in the examples of [15, 16], it can be considered a case of an index "011" (for three qubits—other states can also be selected: $|000\rangle$, $|001\rangle$, $|010\rangle$, $|011\rangle$, $|100\rangle$, $|101\rangle$, $|110\rangle$ and $|111\rangle$. For two qubits, the states are $|00\rangle$, $|01\rangle$, $|10\rangle$, $|11\rangle$, as stated by [1]) which will be assigned to a query graph. By activating gates on the quantum circuits and using Grover's Algorithm [10], the amplitude for the "011" outcome will be amplified and represented through a histogram. As specified by user vy32 in their example [15], "abcdefgh" is formed from four elements having two bits each and is checked if ab = 11, cd = 11, ef = 11, gh = 11 for the case when the value "Dio" is the one being searched for, after associating the index 11 with it. Figures 4, 5, 6, 7, 8 and 9 were created by the author using IBM quantum experience [1], with the exception of Figs. 1, 2 and 3 [19]. In the tests with the quantum computing circuits, the execution times are significantly better than the standard parallel approach, as seen in Tables 1 and 2. A quantum circuit with 15 qubits is executed 8192 times in

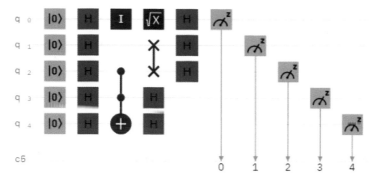

Fig. 4 Quantum circuit 1 [4, 10]

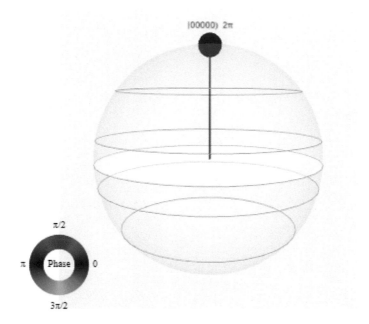

Fig. 5 Quantum circuit 1 Q-sphere [4, 10]

less than a minute, while the largest query graph from Table 1 is executed with the non-quantum parallel approach and has three executions with an average run time of over 500 s.

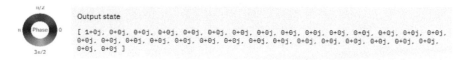

Fig. 6 Quantum circuit 1 statevector [4, 10]

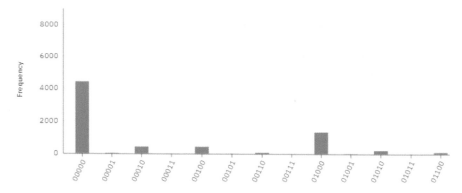

Fig. 7 Quantum circuit 1 measurement outcome histogram [4][10]

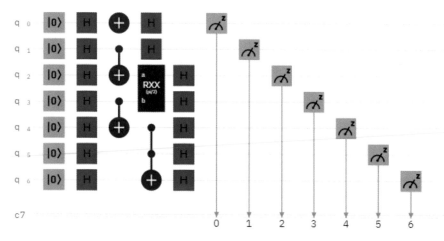

Fig. 8 Quantum circuit 2 [4, 10]

Table 2 Tests with quantum circuits

Quantum circuits	Average execution times (s)
5 qubits, ibmq_lima[13]	9.7
7 qubits, ibmq_16_melbourne[13]	49.9
15 qubits, ibmq_16_melbourne	50.6

The execution times are measured in seconds. There are 8192 shots (executions) for each quantum circuit

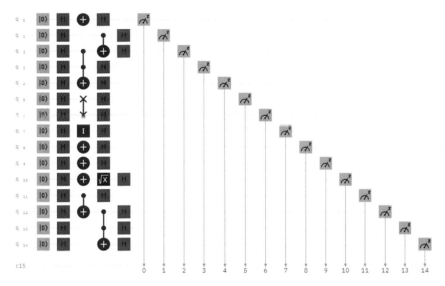

Fig. 9 Quantum circuit 4 [4, 10]

7 Conclusions

In this paper, the GR1 algorithm for parallel searching of motif graphs and then a quantum computing approach were presented. The practical applications, data used, implementation details and test cases were described. The algorithm can be used as a frame on which multiple different pruning techniques can be attached. References [1–16] discuss quantum computing, [17–23] are about motif graphs and references [24–30], detail the tools used by the author for implementing the GR1 algorithm.

Acknowledgements I acknowledge the use of IBM Quantum services for this work. The views expressed are mine, and do not reflect the official policy or position of IBM or the IBM Quantum team.

References

1. IBM quantum experience. https://quantum-computing.ibm.com. Last accessed 21 July 2021
2. The qubit. https://quantum-computing.ibm.com/composer/docs/iqx/guide/the-qubit. Last accessed 21 July 2021
3. How does a quantum bit store exponentially more data? Vinay Phadnis. https://www.youtube.com/watch?v=PDDPXjHdLtg. Last accessed 21 July 2021
4. IBM quantum experience circuit composer. https://quantum-computing.ibm.com/composer/files/new. Last accessed 21 July 2021
5. Creating superpositions and quantum interference. https://quantum-computing.ibm.com/composer/docs/iqx/guide/creating-superpositions. Last accessed 21 July 2021

6. IBM quantum experience visualizations. https://quantum-computing.ibm.com/docs/iqx/visualizations. Last accessed: 15 Feb 2021
7. Quantum phase. https://quantum-computing.ibm.com/composer/docs/iqx/guide/introducing-qubit-phase. Last accessed 21 July 2021
8. IBM quantum experience operations glossary. https://quantum-computing.ibm.com/composer/docs/iqx/operations_glossary. Last accessed 21 July 2021
9. Glossary of terms used within the IBM Quantum site. https://quantum-computing.ibm.com/composer/docs/iqx/terms-glossary. Last accessed 21 July 2021
10. Grover's algorithm. https://quantum-computing.ibm.com/composer/docs/iqx/guide/grovers-algorithm. Last accessed 21 July 2021
11. Qiskit Aqua on GitHub. https://github.com/Qiskit/qiskit-aqua. Last accessed 21 July 2021
12. Qiskit Aqua (Algorithms for QUantum Applications). https://qiskit.org/documentation/apidoc/qiskit_aqua.html. Last accessed on 21 July 2021
13. ibmq_16_melbourne v2.3.22, Processor type: Canary r1.1. ibmq_lima 1.0.11, Processor type: Falcon r4. IBM Quantum. https://quantum-computing.ibm.com, 2021. Last accessed 26 May 2021
14. IBM research blog. https://ibm.com/blogs/research/2019/11/qiskit-for-multiple-architectures/. Last accessed 21 July 2021
15. Grover's algorithm: what to input to Oracle? https://quantumcomputing.stackexchange.com/questions/2149/grovers-algorithm-what-to-input-to-oracle. Last accessed 21 July 2021
16. How can Grover's algorithm be implemented when having a string or other data type as input? https://quantumcomputing.stackexchange.com/questions/16350/how-can-grovers-algorithm-be-implemented-when-having-a-string-or-other-data-typ. Last accessed 21 July 2021
17. Milo R, Shen-Orr S, Itzkovitz S, Kashtan N, Chklovskii D, Alon U (2002) Network motifs: simple building blocks of complex networks. Science 298(5594):824–827
18. Ferro A, Pulvirenti A, Alaimo S, Micale G, Marceca GP, Sciacca E, Maria AD, Sciacca E, Ferlita AL, Martorana E, Giugno R, University of Catania, Department of Clinical and Molecular Biomedicine (MEDBIO). https://www.researchgate.net/profile/Alfredo_Ferro. Last accessed 22 July 2021
19. Micale G, Bonnici V, Ferro A, Shasha D, Giugno R, Pulvirenti A (2020) MultiRI: fast subgraph matching in labeled multigraphs. arXiv:2003.11546v1 [cs.DB] 25 Mar 2020
20. Szklarczyk D, Franceschini A, Kuhn M, Simonovic M, Roth A, Minguez P, Doerks T, Stark M, Muller J, Bork P, Jensen L, von Mering C (2011) The STRING database in 2011 functional interaction networks of proteins, globally integrated and scored. Nucleic Acids Res 2011:39
21. Gheorghica R-I (2020) The GNS1 algorithm for graph isomorphism. In: 26th (Virtual) annual international conference on advanced computing and communications (ADCOM 2020), National Institute of Technology Silchar, Silchar, Assam, India, 16–18 December 2020
22. Gheorghica R-I (2020) Algorithms for graph isomorphism. A Comparative Study on STwig and VF2. In: Proceedings of the 26th workshop on information and communication technologies, 28th international conference on software, telecommunications and computer networks (SOFTCOM 2020), Hvar, Croatia, 17–19 September 2020. ISSN 2623-7350
23. Gheorghica R-I (2018) Algorithms for graph isomorphism. A comparative study. In: 8th international multidisciplinary scientific symposium "challenges and opportunities for sustainable development through quality and innovation in engineering and research management", Universitaria SIMPRO 2018, Petroşani (11–13 October 2018). ISSN–L 1842-4449, ISSN 2344-4754
24. JetBrains s.r.o., PyCharm Professional Edition. https://www.jetbrains.com/pycharm/. Last accessed 22 July 2021
25. van Rossum G, Python Software Foundation. https://www.python.org/. Last accessed 22 July 2021
26. Hagberg A, Shult D, Swart P, Network analysis in python. Available: https://networkx.org/. Last accessed 22 July 2021
27. Oliphant T et al, The fundamental package for scientific computing with Python. https://numpy.org. Last accessed 22 July 2021

28. Python multiprocessing producer consumer pattern. https://stonesoupprogramming.com/2017/09/11/python-multiprocessing-producer-consumer-pattern/. Last accessed 29 July 2021
29. Dask.distributed. https://distributed.dask.org/en/latest/. Last accessed 29 July 2021
30. Dask.distributed Data Locality, User Control, "broadcast" keyword. https://distributed.dask.org/en/latest/locality.html?highlight=broadcast#user-control. Last accessed 29 July 2021

Sliding Windowed Fuzzy Correlation Analysis-Based Marine Motion Detection

M. L. J. Shruthi, B. K. Harsha, and G. Indumathi

Abstract Background subtraction is a widely used technique in motion detection. There are many challenges for motion detection in oceanic video like camera jitter, dynamic background and low visibility. If the background is dynamic or if the background changes overtime, a background update should be done in real time to precisely detect any kind of moving objects. In order to achieve an accurate underwater detection of motion in case of static camera with dynamic background in marine video, a novel detection scheme called sliding windowed fuzzy correlation analysis is proposed. The background modelling is based on sliding window technique, and the detection scheme is based on fuzzy correlation analysis. The window size is fixed to 12 in the algorithm to obtain better results and to reduce the latency in execution. The dataset considered here is 'dataset on underwater change detection' (Kaghyan and Sarukhanyan, Int J Inf Model Anal 1:146–156, 2012) that consists of five marine videos along with its ground truth. We qualitatively and quantitatively prove that the proposed method attains better motion detection as compared to other existing methods. The computational complexity involved is Intel Core i5 processor with MATLAB® software for simulation.

Keywords Background subtraction · Camera jitter · Dynamic background · Sliding window · Underwater motion detection

M. L. J. Shruthi (✉)
Department of ECE, PES University, RR Campus, Bengaluru, Karnataka, India

M. L. J. Shruthi · G. Indumathi
Department of ECE (VTU RC), Cambridge Institute of Technology, Bengaluru, Karnataka, India

B. K. Harsha
Department of ECE, CMR Institute of Technology, Bengaluru, Karnataka, India

C. Satyanarayana et al. (eds.), *High Performance Computing and Networking*, Lecture Notes in Electrical Engineering 853, https://doi.org/10.1007/978-981-16-9885-9_8

1 Introduction

Motion detection is the process of recording the movement of objects. It has many applications which include military, entertainment, sports, robotics, etc. Motion capture is also called motion tracking. The primary task of motion detection in oceanic video is to identify the movement of marine animals. In aquatic videos, wave motion and static movement of aquatic plants form false positives. These are considered to be removed in applications involving movement of aquatic animals. Wave motion forms the most important factor in cyclone prediction, therefore depending upon the requirement, redundancy is exploited.

To avoid time-intensive manual procedures of processing underwater videos, automated process is an attractive alternative. Thus far, a lot of work has been carried out on terrestrial surveillance video based on background subtraction, fuzzy logic, threshold methods, deep-learning based and non-supervised methods [1–21]. Motion detection based on half quadratic minimization procedure is introduced in [22]. In this algorithm, first stage involves initial background estimate and the second stage involves sequential processing using half—quadratic minimization procedures. But this method provides only the soft decision.

Another algorithm based on random forest and SVMs is proposed in [23]. This work is based on building a dataset for human motion (different activities). In [4], a GRAMD method is used to detect motion detection for real-world surveillance. This work concentrates on jitter of camera. Duffner and Garcia [6] use generative and discriminative models using online learning classifier. This algorithm is based on Bayesian probabilistic method to dynamically update the foreground and background model.

In this work, we have used sliding windowed fuzzy correlation analysis to detect moving objects in underwater scenarios. Fuzzy correlation analysis uses the concept of fuzzy theory. Any system which does not have information is represented as black whereas one with full information is represented as white. We use 2 stages for motion detection.

First stage is background generation using sliding window technique, and second stage is motion detection itself. Background generation is used to remove dynamicity in the background and jitter in the camera. Motion detection is employed in 2 stages. First is fuzzy correlation-based motion detection, and second is to remove any kind of false ones and false zeros.

2 Proposed Methodology

Fuzzy correlational analysis is one of the many models that are proposed in fuzzy theory where it uses fuzzy information. System which lacks in any kind of information is represented as no information and system which has all information and complete information has stronger correlation. But in real-world scenarios, ideal situations do

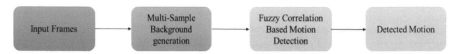

Fig. 1 Proposed fuzzy correlation analysis-based motion detection

not occur. In real-world scenarios, the information is partially known to us and thus becomes haze or fuzzy.

It calculates the fuzzy correlation degree. It is defined as how good 2 systems are correlated. When the changes in two system are very close to each other (or might be same in some cases), then we can say that these two systems will have a very high degree of correlation and when the changes in both the systems are very large, then we can assume the correlation to take a very small value. In this work, we come up with a method for underwater motion detection using fuzzy correlational analysis. There are two stages involved in our work: fuzzy correlation-based background generation model and fuzzy-based motion detection as shown in Fig. 1. First, we created a background generation model which uses sliding window technique with window size as 12. Any change in the considered frame is updated as a background frame. By trial-and-error method, window size is fixed to 12 so as to reduce the processing time with better performance statistics. After this, we use fuzzy correlation analysis to detect the underwater moving object in both static camera where jitter in camera and background changing dynamically might be present. There are two stages in the proposed motion detection algorithm where in the first stage is fuzzy correlation analysis to detect underwater moving object and then we use morphological operations to remove any false positives and false negatives.

2.1 Background Model Generation

We consider luminance component of each pixel in this approach. Each pixel position for every consecutive tth frame is represented by (x, y). We find the correlation between each consecutive background with a reference background which is usually the first frame and create a space of background model. This background model that we generated here using the fuzzy correlation analysis can account for jitter problem by finding the maximum similarity of every incoming frame where we have the impetus for the motion to be detected with respect to the background model space. We check the similarity in the background where similar background will have high positive correlation and dissimilar background will have low positive correlation. Using this, we construct a background model and remove dynamicity from the frames which are being processed. Incoming pixel is given by $p_t(x, y)$, and corresponding candidates are given by $B(x, y)_L$. The Euclidean distance ΔI for each incoming pixel is given by (1):

$$\Delta(i) = \left| p_t(x, y) - B(x, y)_L \right| \tag{1}$$

where $i = 1$ to L and L represents the number of candidates in background model space that we want. Based on the Euclidean distance, the value of fuzzy correlation coefficient Υ is calculated as shown in (2):

$$\Upsilon(p_t(x, y), B(x, y)_L) = \frac{\Delta_{min} + \xi\Delta_{max}}{\Delta(k) + \xi\Delta_{max}} \tag{2}$$

Here, Δ_{min} is the minimum value of the Euclidean distance calculated between the pixels of the present frame and the candidate and Δ_{max} represents maximum distance. These values for our work were set to 0 and 255, respectively. ξ value ranges between 0 and 1. It determines how correlated the pixel values of the present frame p_t is with respect to the reference background. Values of Υ that are close to this ξ value will be said to have very low correlation and hence show changes in the background. For this reason, we keep the value low so as to detect only those objects which show significant motion and motion due to any noise in the background is eliminated. After the calculation of fuzzy correlation coefficient, we find the background variation vector V_k as shown in (3):

$$V_l = \begin{cases} 1 \; for \; \Upsilon(p_t(x, y), B(x, y)_L) \leq \varepsilon \\ 0 \; otherwise \end{cases} \tag{3}$$

ε' value represents empirical tolerance. The variation in background vector is set to 1 if fuzzy correlation coefficient value is less than it else the variation will be 0. The incoming pixel $p_t(x, y)$ is part of background candidates only if the variation in background variation vector is 1. So, the background variation vector will determine whether there is change is pixel values with respect to the background. If so, that pixel value will be the part of background candidates' vector, i.e. when V_k is equal to '1'. Using this, we create the background for the video as in Fig. 2.

2.2   FCA-based Motion Detection

After the background model is created, we use fuzzy correlation analysis scheme to detect motion in objects for underwater scenarios as in Fig. 3.

This approach follows implementation in two stages. The first stage uses pixel wise detection to detect those pixels which show motion. Jitter in the background and dynamic objects moving in background is accounted for by using the concept of fuzzy correlation analysis. The concept is explained as under.

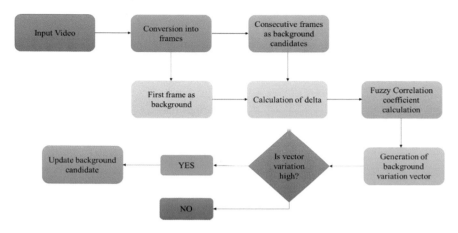

Fig. 2 Flow chart of multi-sample background generation

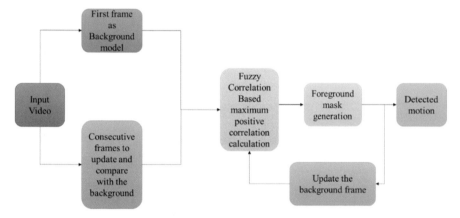

Fig. 3 Flow chart of fuzzy correlation analysis-based motion detection

2.2.1 1st Stage in Underwater Motion Detection

We calculate the maximum positive similarity in the background of each incoming pixel with respect to the background model as in (4):

$$\delta 1 = \max\left(\frac{\Delta_{\min} + \xi\,\Delta_{\max}}{\left(\left\|p_t(x,\,y) - B(x,\,y)_k\right\|\right) + \xi\,\Delta_{\max}}\right) \tag{4}$$

Here, max is used to find the maximum positive similarity of the incoming pixel corresponding to the candidates. In the next step, we have a reference background which is the previous frame for the corresponding video data which is given by $B(x, y)$. We find the correlation of each pixel value with respect to the background frame B as in (5).

$$\delta 2 = \frac{\Delta_{min} + \xi \Delta_{max}}{(\|p_t(x, y) - B(x, y)\|) + \xi \Delta_{max}} \tag{5}$$

Next, we find the maximum positive correlation δ which is $\max(\delta 1, \delta 2)$. By doing this, we are eliminating any kind of changes in the background which is counted as noise. Motion is detected by setting the foreground mask P by setting the β value as in (6):

$$P = \begin{cases} 1, & \text{for } \delta \le \beta \\ 0 & \text{otherwise} \end{cases} \tag{6}$$

When the maximum positive similarity δ (which is max of both the similarities with respect to background model and previous background) exceeds the threshold value, the incoming pixel value is set to '0', i.e., underwater motion is not detected in this case, else the foreground mask P is set to 1, i.e. underwater motion is being detected.

2.2.2 2nd Stage in Underwater Motion Detection

After the potential mask is determined by 1st detection procedure, we apply median filters and morphological erosion and dilation as in (7)

$$D(x, y) = (P(x, y) \odot S) \oplus S \tag{7}$$

$\odot$ means morphological erosion and $\oplus$ means morphological dilation. Morphological filling operation is implemented to reduce false positives. After the motion is detected, the background B is updated for all those pixel values where motion was seen, i.e. P is '1'. This updated background B is made the part of multi-sample background model in order for the algorithm to account for unexpected jitter in the camera and thus reducing false positives.

3 Dataset

Dataset considered is the 'dataset on underwater change detection' [24]. The dataset consists of 5 videos which have 100 hand segmented ground truth frames. All of the videos in the dataset have the challenges like blurry background, haze, low visibility, reflection of light caused by the ripples on the water surface, marine snow or small floating particles. Moreover, the fish often has a colour such that it tends to blend in the background. The resolution of the video captured is 1920 × 1080. The overview of the different videos in the dataset is given below featuring their challenges:

1. Caustics: Complex and dynamic background due to shadows and ripples. The fish blends with the background and hard to detect.
2. Fish Swarm: Haze greenish environment with fish constantly swarming in the scene.
3. Two Fishes: 2 fishes moving very slowly.
4. Marine Snow: Presence of marine snow with good visuals.
5. Small Aquaculture: swarm of fish with clean water.

4 Experimental Results

In this section, the performance analysis for the underwater motion detection using sliding windowed fuzzy correlation analysis with the current methods, namely MOG [25], MOG2 [26], KNN [27] is presented. Figures 4 and 5 reveal the motion detection results and confusion matrix for the 'caustics' video, respectively. Table 1 shows the performance parameters for the 'caustics' video. All the scenes were captured with a static camera. Parameters measured here are accuracy, precision and recall which is given by (8) and (9), respectively:

$$\text{recall} = \frac{\text{tp}}{\text{tp} + \text{fn}} \tag{8}$$

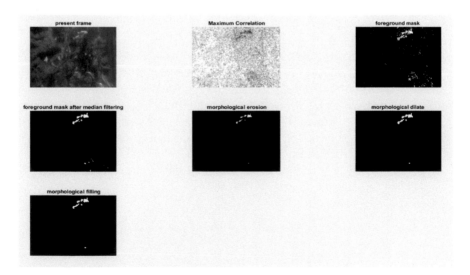

Fig. 4 Motion detection in the 'caustics' video

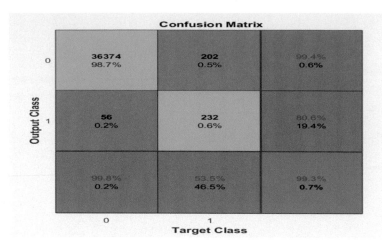

Fig. 5 Confusion matrix for the 'caustics' video

Table 1 Performance evaluation for 'caustics' video

Algorithm	Accuracy	Precision	Recall
MOG1	99	63.58	**88.03**
MOG2	99.39	**91.64**	53.34
KNN	89.9	65.7	11.80
Proposed	**99.42**	89.47	67.54

$$\text{precision} = \frac{tp}{tp + fp} \tag{9}$$

where tp, fp, tn and fn are 'true motion', 'false motion', 'true background' and 'false background', respectively. All the scores here are ranked in terms of percentages where higher the value means better the results.

Similarly, we measure the precision, recall and accuracy for all the videos, namely marine snow, fish swarm, two fishes and small aquaculture, and the same are presented in Tables 2, 3, 4, and 5, respectively. Motion detection results and the confusion matrix for the 'marine snow' video are presented in Figs. 6 and 7, respectively. Figures 8 and 9 show the confusion matrix for the 'small aquaculture' and 'two fishes' videos. Figures 10 and 11 show the motion detection results and confusion matrix for the 'fish

Table 2 Performance evaluation for 'marine snow' video

Algorithm	Accuracy	Precision	Recall
MOG1	97.22	84.1	**82.54**
MOG2	96.3	84.4	49.38
KNN	**97.42**	82.14	75.77
Proposed	96.44	**89.47**	54.10

Table 3 Performance evaluation for 'small aquaculture' video

Algorithm	Accuracy	Precision	Recall
MOG1	91.14	96.86	66.93
MOG2	82.24	98.84	27.52
KNN	94.43	95.18	82.31
Proposed	**94.55**	**99.58**	**83.40**

Table 4 Performance evaluation for 'two fishes' video

Algorithm	Accuracy	Precision	Recall
MOG1	95.52	73.87	84.80
MOG2	**96.09**	**94.67**	63.19
KNN	92.05	56.58	**94.15**
Proposed	94.86	82.69	86.39

Table 5 Performance evaluation for 'fish swarm' video

Algorithm	Accuracy	Precision	Recall
MOG1	85.95	**98.4**	17.92
MOG2	83.6	98.2	2.92
KNN	89.5	98.15	40.21
Proposed	**89.54**	77.86	**72.88**

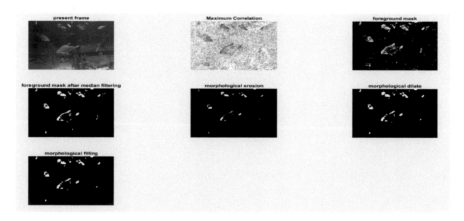

Fig. 6 Motion detection in the 'marine snow' video

swarm' video. The value of eta chosen was 0.1. For 'two fishes' video, for optimum result, this value was updated to 0.06. Number of background candidates chosen was 12. Empirical tolerance value ε chosen was 0.54 for 'caustics' and 'marine snow' videos, 0.53 for 'small aquaculture' and 'two fishes' videos, respectively, and 0.64 for 'fish swarm' video.

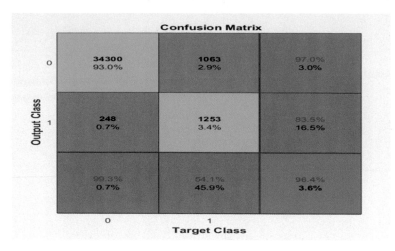

Fig. 7 Confusion matrix for the 'marine snow' video

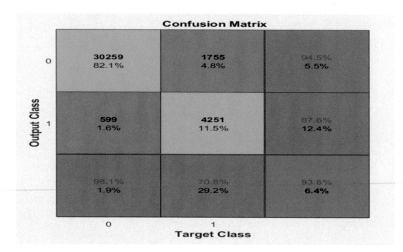

Fig. 8 Confusion matrix for the 'small aquaculture' video

The performance analysis of the results obtained shows that on an average, accuracy is high with 99.42% for the 'caustics' video, average precision is high with 89.47% for the 'marine snow' video and average recall is high with 72.88% for the 'fish swarm' video. Average recall shows 32.67% increase when compared to current methods that is remarkable.

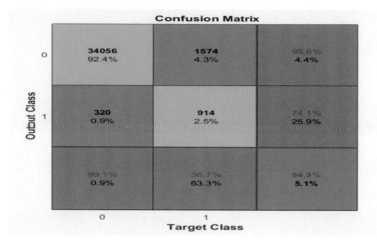

Fig. 9 Confusion matrix for 'two fishes' video

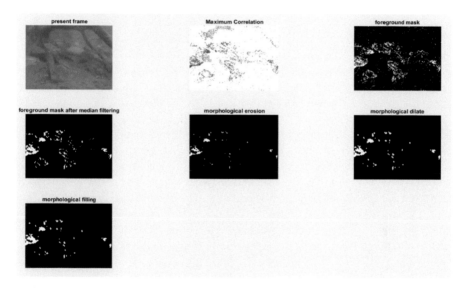

Fig. 10 Motion detection in the 'fish swarm' video

5 Conclusion

In this paper, we proposed an underwater motion detection algorithm which uses sliding windowed fuzzy correlation analysis to accurately and precisely detect moving objects in oceanic video with static camera. The approach uses background model generation that removes any kind of dynamic background and updating of background candidates accurately solves any kind of noise that can be generated by

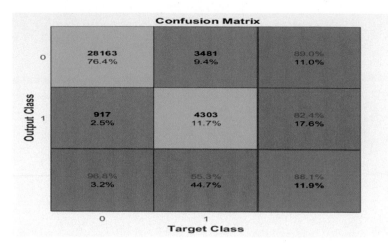

Fig. 11 Confusion matrix for the 'fish swarm' video

jitter in the background. For actual motion detection, fuzzy correlation analysis is used to find the maximum correlation with the background candidates as well as with the previous background so that similar background though in motion can be accounted for. To improve detection and remove any kind of noise that may still be present, morphological erosion followed by morphological dilation and morphological filling was used in addition with median filter. So underwater motion detection using sliding windowed fuzzy correlation analysis can satisfy the pre-processing requirement for video processing applications. The performance of our algorithm is high in terms of average recall with a remarkable increase of 32.67% compared to current methods in case of 'fish swarm' video, 5.07% increased precision in case of 'marine snow' video, 1.09% increased recall, 0.74% increased precision and 0.12% increased accuracy in case of 'small aquaculture' video. The performance is low in cases of very low visibility where the fish tends to blend in with the background and cases where in the fish movement was very slow. So future work may include improving the performance of the algorithm in those areas.

References

1. Mandal M , Vipparthi SK, An empirical review of deep learning frameworks for change detection: model design, experimental frameworks, challenges and research needs. IEEE Trans Intell Transp Syst. https://doi.org/10.1109/TITS.2021.3077883
2. Giraldo JH, Javed S , Bouwmans T, Graph moving object segmentation. IEEE Trans Pattern Anal Mach Intell. https://doi.org/10.1109/TPAMI.2020.3042093
3. Garcia-Garcia B, Bouwmans T, Silva AJR (2020) Background subtraction in real applications: challenges, current models and future directions. Comput Sci Rev 35:100204. ISSN 1574-0137. https://doi.org/10.1016/j.cosrev.2019.100204

4. Huang S, Liu H, Chen B, Fang Z, Tan T , Kuo S (2019) A gray relational analysis-based motion detection algorithm for real-world surveillance sensor deployment. IEEE Sens J 19(3):1019–1027. https://doi.org/10.1109/JSEN.2018.2879187
5. Romero JD, Lado MJ, Méndez AJ (2018) A Background modeling and foreground detection algorithm using scaling coefficients defined with a color model called lightness-red-green-blue. IEEE Trans Image Process 27(3):1243–1258. https://doi.org/10.1109/TIP.2017.2776742
6. Duffner S, Garcia C (2016) Using discriminative motion context for online visual object tracking. IEEE Trans Circuits Syst Video Technol 26(12):2215–2225. https://doi.org/10.1109/TCSVT.2015.2504739
7. Jain R, Nagel H-H (1979) On the analysis of accumulative difference pictures from image sequences of real world scenes. IEEE Trans Pattern Anal Mach Intell PAMI-1(2):206–214. https://doi.org/10.1109/TPAMI.1979.4766907
8. Gustin V, Cufer M (1995) Motion detection using fuzzy logic comparator. IEEE Trans Consum Electron 41(2):360–366. https://doi.org/10.1109/30.391366
9. Miller MI, Grenander U, OSullivan JA , Snyder DL (1997) Automatic target recognition organized via jump-diffusion algorithms. IEEE Trans Image Process 6(1):157–174. https://doi.org/10.1109/83.552104
10. Nguyen HT, Worring M, Dev A (2000) Detection of moving objects in video using a robust motion similarity measure. IEEE Trans Image Process 9(1):137–141. https://doi.org/10.1109/83.817605
11. Paragios N, Deriche R (2000) Geodesic active contours and level sets for the detection and tracking of moving objects. IEEE Trans Pattern Anal Mach Intell 22(3):266–280. https://doi.org/10.1109/34.841758
12. Sheikh Y, Shah M (2005) Bayesian object detection in dynamic scenes. In: 2005 IEEE computer society conference on computer vision and pattern recognition (CVPR'05), San Diego, CA, USA, 2005, vol 1, pp 74–79. https://doi.org/10.1109/CVPR.2005.86
13. Gustafson SC, Costello CS, Like EC, Pierce SJ, Shenoy KN (2009) Bayesian threshold estimation. IEEE Trans Educ 52(3):400–403. https://doi.org/10.1109/TE.2008.930092
14. Benedek C, Sziranyi T, Kato Z, Zerubia J (2009) Detection of object motion regions in aerial image pairs with a multilayer Markovian model. IEEE Trans Image Process 18(10):2303–2315. https://doi.org/10.1109/TIP.2009.2025808
15. Woo H, Jung YM, Kim J, Seo JK (2010) Environmentally robust motion detection for video surveillance. IEEE Trans Image Process 19(11):2838–2848. https://doi.org/10.1109/TIP.2010.2050644
16. Haines TSF, Xiang T (2014) Background subtraction with Dirichlet process mixture models. IEEE Trans Pattern Anal Mach Intell 36(4):670–683. https://doi.org/10.1109/TPAMI.2013.239
17. Han B, Davis LS (2012) Density-based multifeature background subtraction with support vector machine. IEEE Trans Pattern Anal Mach Intell 34(5):1017–1023. https://doi.org/10.1109/TPAMI.2011.243
18. Kim W, Kim C (2012) Background subtraction for dynamic texture scenes using fuzzy color histograms. IEEE Signal Process Lett 19(3):127–130. https://doi.org/10.1109/LSP.2011.2182648
19. Barnich O, Van Droogenbroeck M (2011) ViBe: a universal background subtraction algorithm for video sequences. IEEE Trans Image Process 20(6):1709–1724. https://doi.org/10.1109/TIP.2010.2101613
20. Liu X, Zhao G, Yao J, Qi C (2015) Background subtraction based on low-rank and structured sparse decomposition. IEEE Trans Image Process 24(8):2502–2514. https://doi.org/10.1109/TIP.2015.2419084
21. Chiranjeevi P, Sengupta S (2014) Detection of moving objects using multi-channel kernel fuzzy correlogram based background subtraction. IEEE Trans Cybern 44(6):870–881. https://doi.org/10.1109/TCYB.2013.2274330
22. Zhu R, Long Y, An W (2018) Visual image sequential motion detection via half quadratic minimization method. Progress Electromagnet Res 65:101–109

23. Taylor W. Shah SA, Dashtipour K, Zahid A, Abbasi QH, Imran MA (2020) An intelligent non-invasive real-time human activity recognition system for next-generation healthcare. Sensors 20(9):2653. https://doi.org/10.3390/s20092653
24. Radolko M, Farhadifard F, Von Lukas UF (2016) Dataset on underwater change detection, Ocean. In: 2016 MTS/IEEE Monterey, OCE 2016, 2016. https://doi.org/10.1109/OCEANS.2016.7761129
25. . KaewTraKulPong P, Bowden R (2002) An improved adaptive background mixture model for real-time tracking with shadow detection. Video-Based Surveill Syst pp 135–144. https://doi.org/10.1007/978-1-4615-0913-4_11
26. Kaghyan S, Sarukhanyan H (2012) Activity recognition using K-nearest neighbor algorithm on smartphone with Tri-axial accelerometer. Int J Inf Model Anal 1:146–156. Available: http://www.foibg.com/ijima/vol01/ijima01-2-p06.pdf
27. Zivkovic Z, Van Der Heijden F (2006) Efficient adaptive density estimation per image pixel for the task of background subtraction. Pattern Recognit Lett 27(7):773–780. https://doi.org/10.1016/j.patrec.2005.11.005

Generative Adversarial Network for Music Generation

Suman Maria Tony⊙ and S. Sasikumar

Abstract Generating music artificially using pre-trained Generative Adversarial Networks (GANs) is challenging task as the training involves temporal variations. Unlike training a GAN for synthesizing videos or images, generating music tracks using GAN involves additional inputs. In this paper, we propose a few methods for generating musing using GAN and its variants. The GAN and other variants are trained using a set of midi file accumulated from the piano dataset. The pre-trained model is then used to generate music similar to piano roll. As GAN has both generator and discriminator, the generated music file is similar to the datasets used while training. The accuracy of the network or the quality the music file generated depends both on the generator and on the discriminator. The same pre-trained model is used for several other music tracks like drums, flute, etc., provided the model is trained with appropriate libraries. The outcome of this experiment is evaluated using conventional evaluators and also the esthetics by human observer.

Keywords Music generation · Generative adversarial networks · MIDI · Music synthesis

1 Introduction

Automatic music generation is an interesting and challenging problem as the corresponding algorithm involves both temporal and local parameters to be considered. The challenges are attributed to the following:

- Temporal dependency as time increments
- Multiple tracks and the complex interaction between such tracks or instruments

S. M. Tony (✉)
Department of Electronics and Communication Engineering, Hindustan Institute of Technology and Science, Chennai, India
e-mail: sumanmariatony@licet.ac.in

S. M. Tony · S. Sasikumar
Loyola-ICAM College of Engineering and Technology (LICET), Chennai, India

© The Author(s), under exclusive license to Springer Nature Singapore Pte Ltd. 2022   109
C. Satyanarayana et al. (eds.), *High Performance Computing and Networking*,
Lecture Notes in Electrical Engineering 853,
https://doi.org/10.1007/978-981-16-9885-9_9

DL and ML have found several applications in variety of fields including music generation and medical imaging [1, 2]. The inter-relationship between various tracks (Fig. 1) sometimes and independent tracks at times poses a challenge in generating music.

Melody comprises musical notes in a temporal sequence which can be defined using pitch and duration (Fig. 2). Pitch is explained as a variation of frequencies, and it is played in various patterns which create melodies [3]. Piano keys are numbered in MIDI representation from 21 to 108 denoting the pitch which can be played for a definite time representing the length and there are intervals in between [4, 5].

Section 1 introduces the challenges and temporal dependency in music synthesis and how AI has contributed significantly toward this. Section 2 highlights the related

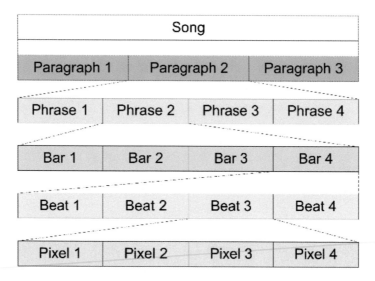

Fig. 1 Relationship between tracks

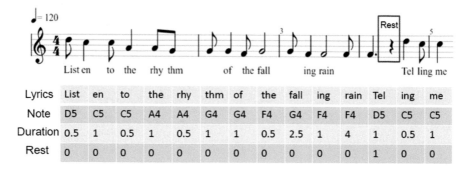

Fig. 2 Example of lyrics and melody alignment

work in music synthesis particularly based on RNN and GAN and explores several proven GAN architectures and its variants which successfully generated music files.

Section 3 explains the proposed model and materials and methods used to conduct the experiment. The simulation results and experiment outcomes are discussed in Sect. 4. Section 5 explains the evaluation methods used to evaluate the outcome which is the synthesized music file. The concluding remarks are given in Sect. 5.

2 Background

2.1 Related Work in Music Generation

A few networks with proven outcome are available for automatic generation of music and music accompaniment [6]. Synthesizing music tracks from each instrument has its own challenges based on the notes involved. Generating piano roll includes more active notes and a few authors have used RNN to generate piano rolls as RNN has significant learning capability [7, 8]. Apart from the temporal learning which RNN possess, local learning is also essential and primary for the problem we have taken, and hence GAN is suitable in this work on music synthesis [9, 10].

The temporal aspects of music generation is addressed by a few researchers by implementing both RNN and GAN together [11, 12], whereas reinforcement learning along with GAN also fixes this problem [12, 13]. Since the feature extraction uses convolutional network, including the temporal features would be challenging [14, 15] and needs additional inputs for the music synthesizer to generate music with harmony.

2.2 Generative Adversarial Networks

2.2.1 Overview of GAN

The discriminator differentiates the real and the randomly synthesized signal by the generator (Fig. 3). The generator synthesizes signal close to the original music track which tries to dupe the discriminator [16].

2.2.2 Existing GAN Architectures

The three models GAN based architecture for synthesizing piano roll was proposed by Dong et al. [17], and it is shown in Fig. 4. The jamming model as in Fig. 4a has N generators and discriminators for generating N tracks. Learning is facilitated by the individual discriminators which back propagate its output. In the composer model,

Fig. 3 General generative
adversarial networks

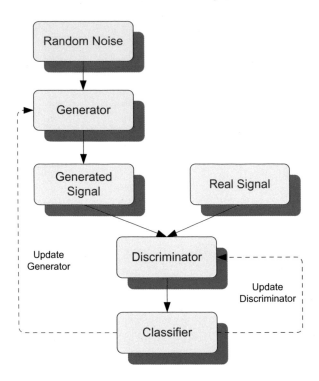

there in a single generator and also one discriminator to mimic a single composer
creating several piano rolls. The random vector Z is shared by all the models as
shown in Fig. 4b. The hybrid model uses M generator and N discriminator, and the
generator takes both intra-random and inter-random vectors (Fig. 4c).

3   Proposed Model

3.1   *Conditional GAN Model*

LSTM has been used to synthesize music and for works related to natural language
processing (NLP). LSTM is a recurrent neural network that can process and
remember time series data and can be used to predict the chain for a defined period.
The generator has as many LSTM cells depending on the number of notes needed.
The first layer of the generator as shown in the Fig. 5a is a rectified linear unit, ReLU.
For example, if the sequence has 10 notes, the generator requires 10 LSTM cells for
learning. The discriminator in Fig. 5b also has LSTM cells, and it helps to differentiate the generated music sequence from the real one. The degree of closeness from
the real music sequence is an important one in the learning process for which the

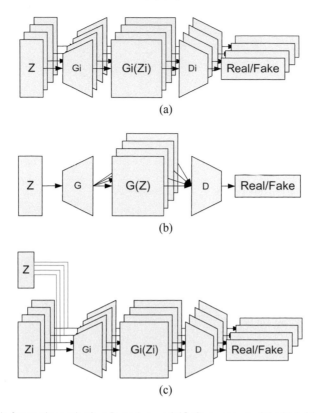

Fig. 4 Models for music synthesis **a** Jamming model **b** Composer model **c** Hybrid model

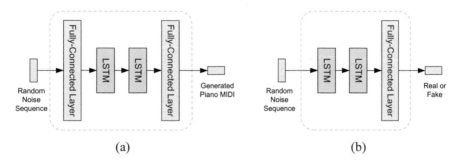

Fig. 5 GAN network with LSTM for music synthesis **a** Generator Network with LSTM **b** Discriminator Network with LSTM

discriminator plays a major role. The output of the hidden layers of the discriminator is given to a sigmoid function for estimating the degree of closeness to the real sequence. Thus the training happens in both the generator and the discriminator and the learning converges.

4 Materials and Methods

4.1 *Music Synthesizer Using Conditional GAN Models*

Incorporating the conditional GAN network in the existing music synthesizer is a good solution to preserve the temporal dependency. Figure 6 shows all the three models originally discussed in Sect. 2.2.2, and it is being modified by adding the conditional GAN architecture shown in Fig. 5.

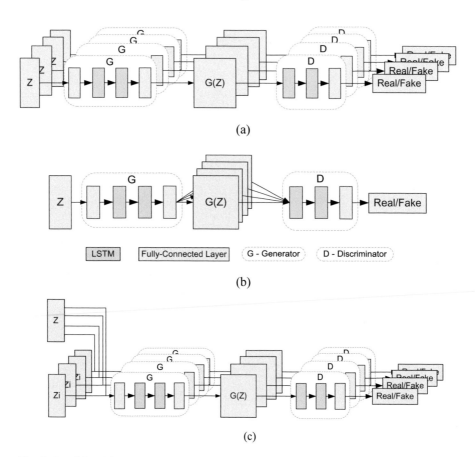

Fig. 6 Conditional GAN models for music synthesis **a** Jamming model **b** Composer model **c** Hybrid model

4.2   Workflow

The MIDI file is encoded to the proper format, and the conditional GAN-LSTM network is trained with that. The model created is used to synthesize piano roll particularly. The midi file from the dataset is converted into song format for a more natural way of learning and synthesizing music based on the learned model. The music file is then encoded into a format suitable for the conditional GAN-LSTM network to recognize the sequence. Here, the music file is converted into a 2 dimensional matrix of samples generated by the music data.

The output of music synthesizer after few epochs of training represents the synthesized music which is converted to a "wav" or encoded to "mp3" format to make the output compatible with a conventional audio player.

5   Results and Discussion

5.1   Generated Piano Rolls

Figure 7 shows the generated piano composition automatically by the proposed algorithm using conditional GAN.

5.2   Evaluation of Models

Music generation models can be evaluated both subjectively and objectively (Fig. 8). The subjective evaluation methods needs the expertise of humans to assess the musical outcome of the models. In this case, the musical Turing test [18] is commonly used to compare the music composed my human and music synthesized by GAN. Whereas the objective evaluation methods use probabilistic methods, parameter metrics both for models and for music generation [19, 20]. The metrics used for music generation includes the analysis of pitch, tone, and rhythm. The evaluation method proposed by Yang et al. [21] is robust as it involves statistical parameters extracted.

5.2.1   Subjective Evaluation Results

The subjective evaluation which is used evaluate most of the automatic music synthesizer [22–25] involves the scoring of music file generated with the help of evaluators. In this experiment, 5 male and 5 female evaluators are chosen, and they scored the music files randomly chosen from the synthesized dataset. The subjects are asked to score on a 5 point scale considering the harmony of the music file. Figures 9 and 10

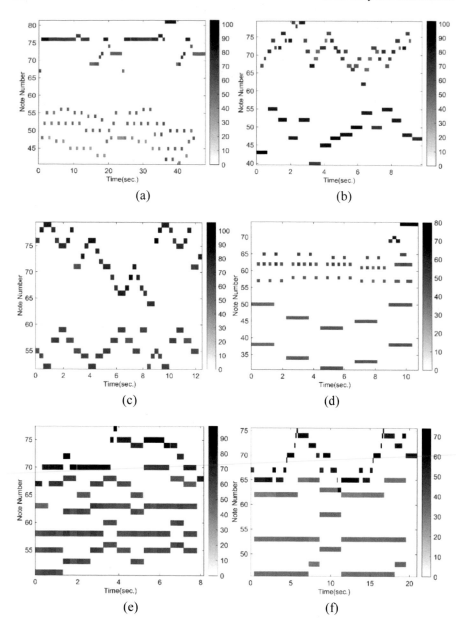

Fig. 7 Generated piano sequences

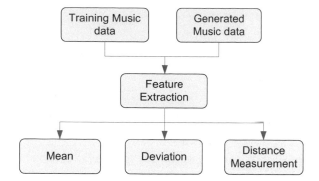

Fig. 8 Features for evaluation of music output

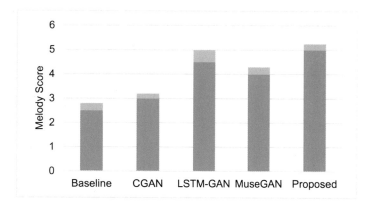

Fig. 9 Subjective evaluation: melody score

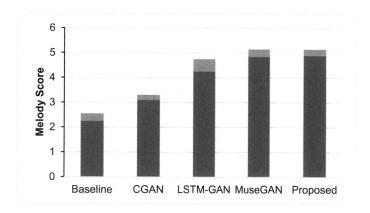

Fig. 10 Subjective evaluation: rhythm score

plot the average subjective evaluation of melody score and rhythm score evaluated by various users.

6   Conclusion

Music synthesis using AI and associated algorithms are in exploration and with the advent of GPUs high computational complexity can he easily handled. To validate the proposed method, we have tested the algorithm with multiple tracks piano roll datasets. After ample training, the trained network synthesized piano roll that is continuous most of the times, and it should be noted that the generated sequence has fragmented notes very occasionally. The evaluation of the generated music sequence shows good result which proves the effectiveness of the proposed method. The loss in temporal dependency happens in a few generated tracks and it needs to be fixed by improving the training accuracy and with a large dataset.

References

1. Kunaraj K, Maria Wenisch S, Balaji S, Mahimai Don Bosco FP (2019) Impulse noise classification using machine learning classifier and robust statistical features. In: Smys S, Tavares J, Balas V, Iliyasu A (eds) Computational vision and bio-inspired computing. ICCVBIC 2019. Advances in intelligent systems and computing, vol 1108. Springer, Cham
2. Bae Y, Kumarasamy K, Ali IM et al, Differences between schizophrenic and normal subjects using network properties from fMRI. J Digit Imaging 31:252–261
3. http://www.musiccrashcourses.com/lessons/pitch.html/
4. https://en.wikipedia.org/wiki/Duration (music)/
5. https://en.wikipedia.org/wiki/Rest (music)/
6. Briot J-P, Hadjeres G, Pachet F (2017) Deep learning techniques for music generation: a survey. arXiv:1709.01620
7. Lim H, Rhyu S, Lee K (2017) Chord generation from symbolic melody using BLSTM networks, arXiv e-prints
8. Hawthorne C, Eck D (2018) A hierarchical latent vector model for learning long-term structure in music. In: Proceedings of ICML
9. Anna Huang C-Z, Cooijmans T, Roberts A, Courville A, Eck D (2017) Counterpoint by convolution. In: Proceedings of the 18th international society for music information retrieval conference, ISMIR
10. Goodfellow IJ et al (2014) Generative adversarial nets. In: Proceedings NIPS
11. Mogren O (2016) C-RNN-GAN: continuous recurrent neural networks with adversarial training. Adv Neural Inf Process Syst
12. Yu L, Zhang W, Wang J, Yu Y (2017) SeqGAN: sequence generative adversarial nets with policy gradient. In: The association for the advance of artificial intelligence, pp 2852–2858
13. Guimaraes GL, Sanchez-Lengeling B, Outeiral C, Farias PLC, Aspuru-Guzik A (2017) Objective-reinforced generative adversarial networks (ORGAN) for sequence generation models. arXiv preprint arXiv:1705.10843
14. Dong HW, Hsiao WY, Yang LC, Yang YH (2018) MuseGAN: multi-track sequential generative adversarial networks for symbolic music generation and accompaniment. In: The association for the advance of artificial intelligence

15. Dong H-W, Yang Y-H (2018) Convolutional generative adversarial networks with binary neurons for polyphonic music generation. In: International society for music information retrieval conference, pp 190–196
16. Goodfellow IJ, Pouget-Abadie J, Mirza M, Xu B, Warde-Farley D, Ozair S, Courville A, Bengio Y (2014) Generative adversarial nets. In: Advances in neural information processing systems, vol 27 (NIPS 2014)
17. Dong H, Hsiao W, Yang L, Yang Y (2018) MuseGAN: multi-track sequential generative adversarial networks for symbolic music generation and accompaniment, AAAI
18. Turing AM (1950) Computing machinery and intelligence. Mind 59(236):433–460
19. Sturm BL, Ben-Tal O (2017) Taking the models back to music practice: evaluating generative transcription models built using deep learning. J Creat Music Syst
20. Huang CZA, Cooijmans T, Roberts A, Courville A, Eck D (2017) Counterpoint by convolution. In: International society of music information retrieval (ISMIR), Suzhou, China
21. Yang L-C, Lerch A (2018) On the evaluation of generative models in music. Neural Comput Appl. https://doi.org/10.1007/s00521-018-3849
22. Agarwala N, Inoue Y, Sly A (2017) Music composition using recurrent neural networks. Stanford University, Technical Report in CS224
23. Hadjeres G, Pachet F (2016) Deepbach: a steerable model for bach chorales generation. In: International conference on machine learning (ICML), New York City, NY, USA
24. Huang KC, Jung Q, Lu J (2017) Algorithmic music composition using recurrent neural networking. Stanford University, Technical Report in CS22
25. Shin A, Crestel L, Kato H, Saito K, Ohnishi K, Yamaguchi M, Nakawaki M, Ushiku Y, Harada T (2017) Melody generation for pop music via word representation of musical properties. arXiv preprint arXiv:1710.11549

Automatic License Plate Recognition for Distorted Images Using SRGAN

Anita Baral, Anupama Koirala, Sanjay Pantha, Rewant Pokhrel, and Bishnu Hari Paudel

Abstract The quality of an image is always a limitation for automatic license plate recognition (ALPR) for its practical and accurate functioning. Distorted low-resolution (LR) images are one of the common issues encountered in ALPR systems. Most of the available algorithms in ALPR systems are effective under controlled circumstances or with intricate image capture systems. Authorities are looking for an improved ALPR system that is primarily concerned with dealing with distorted LR images. In this research, an improved ALPR system is proposed to generate high-resolution (HR) images from LR images using the super-resolution generative adversarial network (SRGAN). On a self-created Nepali dataset, both the networks (ALPR and SRGAN) are trained and assessed. Traditionally, for the identification of vehicles, images of license plates are localized, characters are segmented, and recognized. The accuracy of license plate recognition is heavily reliant on segmentation and recognition accuracy. ALPR with SRGAN comprises a super-resolution process in between. Super-resolution aids to improve the performance of the system by recreating detailed variation of the localized image, thus providing better end-to-end recognition.

Keywords Detection · Localization · Segmentation · Super-resolution · Generative adversarial network · Automatic license plate recognition

A. Baral (✉) · A. Koirala · S. Pantha · R. Pokhrel · B. H. Paudel
Institute of Engineering, Tribhuvan University, Pashchimanchal Campus, Pokhara, Nepal
e-mail: baralanita2@gmail.com

A. Koirala
e-mail: anukoirala55@gmail.com

S. Pantha
e-mail: sanjaypantha.np@gmail.com

R. Pokhrel
e-mail: pokhrelrewant@gmail.com

B. H. Paudel
e-mail: bishnuhari@wrc.edu.n

C. Satyanarayana et al. (eds.), *High Performance Computing and Networking*,
Lecture Notes in Electrical Engineering 853,
https://doi.org/10.1007/978-981-16-9885-9_10

121

1   Introduction

Automatic license plate recognition (ALPR) is an image processing technology that distinguishes vehicles by analyzing the images of their license plates. License plates are rectangular objects attached to a vehicle that display an official set of characters that identify the vehicle. Government organizations implement ALPR technologies for systematic law enforcement and easier investigations when required. ALPR technology allows the creation of a database of relevant data which speeds up time-consuming and labor-intensive manual differentiation of vehicle license plates against records of wanted, stolen, and other vehicles of interest.

ALPR algorithms work best in controlled environments or with complex image capture devices. In an uncontrolled environment, reading license plates accurately remains a significant challenge [1]. It is because a properly detailed image is required to provide enough information during segmentation and recognition to yield accurate results, which is not available in low-resolution (LR) images. In this research, a model is proposed which combines the ALPR system and super-resolution (SR) technique for LR distorted license plates to improve the license plate identification. SR is the task of estimating a high-resolution (HR) image from its LR counterpart [2]. SR can be achieved in many ways and algorithms, including the usage of deep convolutional neural networks and generative adversarial networks [3]. Super-resolution generative adversarial network (SRGAN) is used for super-resolution in this research. It provides a high-frequency detailed and perceptually satisfying counterpart to low-resolution license plates [2].

2   Related Work

Various research has been conducted in the automatic license plate recognition field and ways to improve its accuracy and effectiveness. Li et al. [1] proposed an automatic license plate (LP) detection and recognition system in natural background images using deep neural networks. The network can detect and recognize the plates in a single forward pass which avoids an error during transition and quicken plate processing. Pant et al. [4] proposed an ALPR for Nepali number plates with the use of support vector machines. Silva et al. [5] introduced automatic LP detection and recognition in unregulated conditions for multiple oblique and distorted LPs in a single image. The authors have also presented the solution of detecting LPs from different regions through the employment of manual annotations. In Balamurugan et al. [6], the authors exploit spline interpolation as a super-resolution technique in automatic number plate recognition system that detects plates from surveillance feed and up-scales the image using the SR method then implements OCR for recognition. Various techniques are being designed for the super-resolution of images. Ledig et al. [2] formulated photo-realistic single image super-resolution using generative adversarial network. A perceptual loss function consisting of content and adversarial loss was proposed by the research to obtain photo-realistic images for the $4\times$ up-scaling factor. It has been seen that the implementation of SR techniques has been able to increase the performance of digital image processing techniques [7].

The substantial contribution of this work is a localized national ALPR system. We approach this problem through SRGAN-based techniques for LP detection and some optical character recognition (OCR)-based methods that can handle LP recognition.

3 System Architecture

3.1 Traditional ALPR System

Traditional automatic license plate recognition enacts three major steps: license plate detection and localization, character segmentation, and character recognition [8, 9]. Plate detection entails detecting the plate within the input image frame. Localization extracts the image of the detected plate from the input image and passes it through character segmentation, which further isolates each character. The isolated characters are now sent to OCR, which recognizes them (Fig. 1).

3.2 ALPR System for Distorted Images

The automatic license plate recognition system for distorted LR images enhances the efficiency and accuracy of the traditional ALPR system by refining the quality and resolution of the localized images, unlike the traditional system where the localized plate was directly fed to OCR after segmentation (Fig. 2).

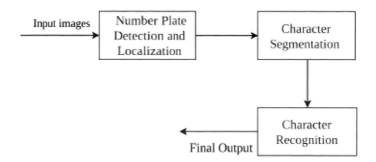

Fig. 1 Architecture of traditional ALPR system

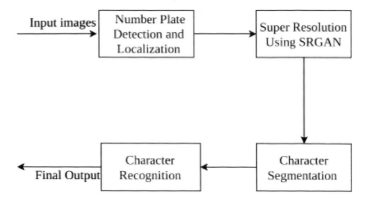

Fig. 2 Architecture of ALPR System for Distorted Images

4 Methodology

The raw input image is fed to the system and goes through various steps of preprocessing and processes to finally extract the characters. Starting from normalization
and plate detection via Warped Planar Object Detection Network (WPOD-NET), a
localized license plate image is obtained and fed to the SRGAN model. After some
extra steps of grayscale and binary conversion, character segmentation is performed.
Finally, segmented characters are fed to OCR model to obtain the result.

4.1 License Plate Detection

To detect license plates, a novel convolutional neural network (CNN) known as the
Warped Planar Object Detection Network (WPOD-NET) [5] has been implemented.
The WPOD-NET was obtained by incorporating ideas from You Only Look Once
(YOLO), Single Shot MultiBox Detector (SSD), and Spatial Transformer Networks
(STN) [5]. This network pursues to detect license plates in various distortions [5].
The following steps are involved for detecting and localizing the license plate:
Normalization In this step, we change the range of pixel intensity for the input image.
The input image is converted in a range of pixel values between 0 and 1.
Plate Detection WPOD-NET is used to obtain coordinates of plate boundaries on
the normalized image. The bounding box is drawn around the license plate with the
help of the acquired coordinates. The coordinates are then used to extract the license
plates from the images.

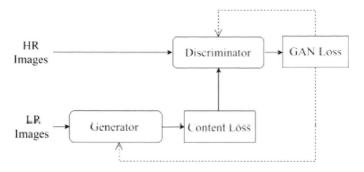

Fig. 3 Block diagram of SRGAN [10]

4.2 Super Resolution

SRGAN consists of two competing models, generator and discriminator [10], which can capture, copy and recreate detail variation within a dataset. The generator portion of SRGAN learns to create HR images by upscaling LR images through the incorporation of feedback from the discriminator output. The discriminator in an SRGAN is simply a classifier. It tries to distinguish real HR images from the HR images created by the generator. The discriminator comes across two types of HR images, real and fake. The real ones are the original HR images, whereas the fake ones are the upscaled HR images by the generator. SRGAN uses perceptual loss that consists of an adversarial and content loss. Perceptual loss function helps to obtain photo-realistic natural images. SRGAN relinquishes the use of pixel-wise mean square error (MSE) loss as content loss which is used by many other state-of-the-art systems because it cannot recover high-frequency contents from LR images which results in over smooth images for obtaining a high peak signal noise ratio (PSNR) (Fig. 3).

Perceptual Loss The overall loss in the generator network of SRGAN is based on perceptual loss l^{SR}, which is the weighted sum of the content loss l_x^{SR} and adversarial loss l_{Gen}^{SR} [2].

$$l^{SR} = l_x^{SR} + 10^{-3} l_{Gen}^{SR} \tag{1}$$

Content Loss The content loss function for this SRGAN is defined as a VGG loss function $l_{VGG/i,j}^{SR}$ that is obtained from the pre-trained VGG network as depicted in Simonyan and Zisserman [11]. VGG loss is calculated as the Euclidean distance between feature map of an SR image $G_{\theta_G}(I^{LR})$ and the HR image I^{HR} [11].

$$l_{VGG/i,j}^{SR} = \frac{1}{W_{ij}H_{ij}} \sum_{x=1}^{W_{ij}} \sum_{y=1}^{H_{ij}} (\phi_{ij}(I^{HR})_{x,y} - \phi_{ij}(G_{\theta_G}(I^{LR}))_{x,y})^2 \tag{2}$$

Adversarial Loss Along with content loss, we add the generative component l_{Gen}^{SR} of the GAN to the perceptual loss. By attempting to deceive the discriminator network, the system is encouraged to prefer alternatives that reside on the manifold of natural images [2].

$$l_{\text{Gen}}^{\text{SR}} = \sum_{n=1}^{N} - \log D_{\theta_D}(G_{\theta_G}(I^{\text{LR}})) \tag{3}$$

4.3 Character Segmentation

Character segmentation segregates an image into constituted parts, each of which contains a character and can be excerpted for further processing. In this system, a contour-based approach has been implemented. This method is a gradient-based segmentation method that finds the boundaries based on the high gradient magnitudes. Before applying character segmentation, we have applied the following processing techniques to reduce noise and emphasize the key features of license characters.

Conversion to grayscale images To reduce the code complexity, for faster processing, and to ease the analysis of localized super-resolved license plates without keeping into consideration the color contrast, the images are primarily converted into grayscale.

Conversion to binary images The grayscale super-resolved license plate is then converted into an image with only black and white pixels. As a fundamental decree, this can be accomplished by establishing a threshold. If the pixel value exceeds the threshold, it is converted into a white pixel; otherwise, it is altered into a black pixel. Since the lighting condition is not uniform in the image, determining the threshold value becomes a crucial task.

4.4 Character Recognition

Individual characters from the localized plate are fed into the OCR system for prediction after being segmented. The OCR system employs learning and prediction algorithms based on support vector machines (SVM) to classify the segmented characters [12]. SVM is a versatile supervised machine learning algorithm that can perform linear or nonlinear classification, regression, and even outlier detection. The SVM algorithm's target is to determine a hyper-plane in an N-dimensional space that classifies the data points. The coordinates of each observation are used to calculate the support vectors. SVMs can yield precise and reliable classification results [12]. In this research, SVM is utilized to classify segmented characters among the twelve trained classes (०-९, ञ and प).

5 Training Details

Datasets

- License Plate Dataset: There are approximately 1400 license plate images captured from various vehicles at different orientations and lighting conditions. The license plates are captured in the Gandaki zone, some in the underground parking while others in the outdoor parking.
- Character Dataset: There are a total of 6481 samples in the character dataset for twelve classes. The dataset is created by segmenting the characters using the contour-based approach in the localized license plate dataset and then manually categorizing them into twelve different classes.

Table 1 shows the number of representatives collected for each class.

SRGAN Training SRGAN model is trained approximately on 1100 localized number plates. The plates were all resized to a size of 200 * 280 for uniformity among the dataset. Two models were developed, one has an up-sampling factor of four while another has an up-scaling factor of eight. In SRGAN, perceptual quality is considered as a metric. The model has been trained for 1000 epochs since it generated a convincing result. Figure 4 illustrates the output of the SRGAN model for up-sampling factor four and eight.

OCR Training To train 4860 (75% of the total data-set) characters from twelve different classes, the Support Vector Classifier with polynomial kernel is used.

Table 1 Character dataset

Character	Sample
०	322
१	866
२	431
३	396
४	446
५	412
६	425
७	498
८	439
९	450
ग	873
प	923
Total	6481

6   Experiments and Results

The purpose of this study is to assess the use of SRGAN to enhance the performance of the ALPR system. Figure 5 illustrates the overall working of the system. Our research is based on Nepali number plates of the Gandaki zone. Our system initially trains all the localized number plates in SRGAN, and then, the trained SRGAN model is used in conjunction with the traditional ALPR system (Fig. 5).

Segmentation Results The proposed system was evaluated on forty arbitrarily selected samples for license plate segmentation where the plates of the vehicles were not clear. Among the samples, twenty were highly pixelated and were up-scaled by factor eight in SRGAN, while the other twenty were up-scaled by factor four in SRGAN. Among the twenty images up-scaled by factor eight, seventeen samples were correctly segmented by the system, and among the images up-scaled by factor four, nineteen samples were correctly segmented.

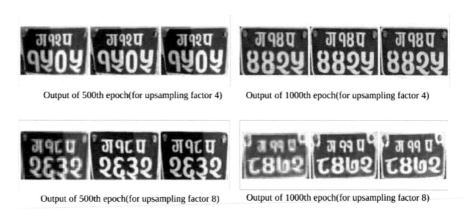

Output of 500th epoch(for upsampling factor 4)   Output of 1000th epoch(for upsampling factor 4)

Output of 500th epoch(for upsampling factor 8)   Output of 1000th epoch(for upsampling factor 8)

Fig. 4   Output of SRGAN model for up-sampling factor four and eight

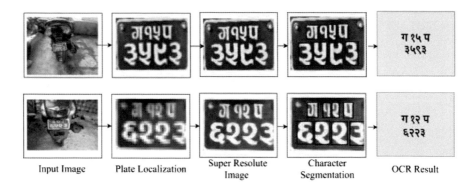

Input Image   Plate Localization   Super Resolute Image   Character Segmentation   OCR Result

Fig. 5   Overall working of the system

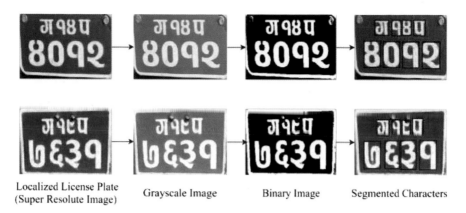

Localized License Plate
(Super Resolute Image)   Grayscale Image   Binary Image   Segmented Characters

Fig. 6 Character segmentation

Table 2 Character recognition results

Metrics	Score
Accuracy	0.9858
Precision	0.9854
Recall	0.9842
$F1$-score	0.9847

Figure 6 illustrates the character segmentation for Super Resolute license plates.
OCR Result Seventy-five percent of the data was used for training, while the remaining twenty-five percent was used for testing. Data samples were chosen at random and exclusively for training and testing in each experiment.

Table 2 shows the accuracy, precision, recall, and F-score of the OCR system. Table 3 displays the experiment's confusion matrix (CM).

Number Plate Recognition Results In total, forty images are tested. Twenty of the images were slightly distorted, while the other 20 were severely distorted. An experiment was conducted first on distorted images and then on up-scaled images. Former experiment shows an accuracy of 50% in slightly distorted images while in the case of heavily distorted images, the segmentation algorithm is not being able to detect the contours. On the later experiment that uses SRGAN with traditional ALPR, the evaluation result shows an accuracy of 90% in slightly distorted images that are up-scaled by factor four in SRGAN, and accuracy of 75% in heavily distorted images that are up-scaled by factor eight in SRGAN.

Table 3 Confusion matrix

Class	०	१	२	३	४	५	६	७	8	९	ग	प	Total
०	81	0	0	1	2	0	0	0	0	0	0	1	85
१	0	209	0	0	0	0	0	0	0	0	0	0	209
२	0	0	101	0	0	0	0	0	0	0	0	0	101
३	1	1	0	96	0	0	0	0	0	0	0	0	98
४	0	0	0	0	108	0	0	0	1	0	1	0	110
५	0	2	0	0	0	101	0	0	0	0	0	0	103
६	0	0	0	0	0	0	114	0	0	0	0	0	114
७	1	1	0	0	0	0	0	138	0	0	0	0	140
८	0	1	0	0	0	0	0	0	90	0	0	0	91
९	1	1	1	0	0	1	0	0	0	120	0	0	124
ग	1	1	0	1	0	0	0	0	0	0	216	2	221
प	0	0	0	0	0	0	1	0	0	0	0	223	224
Total	85	216	102	98	110	102	115	138	91	120	217	226	1620

7 Conclusion

In the real-world scenario, it is not always possible to get a visually understandable license plate taken by the commodity cameras which results in lower accuracy of the traditional ALPR models. ALPR models when combined with super-resolution techniques, SRGAN being one of them, can deliver better results. The research is carried out in the sector where traditional ALPR is failing to perform as expected. In severely and slightly distorted images, the ALPR system for distorted images achieved accuracy rates of 75% and 90%, respectively. In the event of slightly distorted images, the model improves accuracy by 40% when compared to traditional ALPR system, whereas in the case of heavily distorted images where the traditional system is failing, the proposed model shows an accuracy of 75%. The accuracy of model particularly in the case of heavily distorted images can be enhanced with further research in near future. Although the model's accuracy is a significant improvement over traditional ALPR, it can still perform better with better segmentation tools and an SRGAN model trained on a larger dataset and more number of epochs. SRGAN, along with ALPR, is a complex image processing model. This model becomes more viable when there is a larger number of dataset, i.e., ten times more than what has been used in this study. Although the model is complex, it has a great economic advantage in long term over high-end hardware components.

In Nepal, license plates are inconsistent, discolored, and mud-splattered. The above-mentioned factors affect segmentation, recognition accuracy, and, ultimately, the overall accuracy of the system. This study is being conducted for the number plates of Nepal's Gandaki zone, the research can be expanded across the country. Along with this, the dataset consists of only bike and scooter license plates; other automobiles should be included for the system to be realistic. Improving the aforementioned issues can result in a system with cutting-edge performance. Automatic license plate recognition for distorted images thus combines the components of traditional ALPR systems with SRGAN to achieve better results in real-world scenarios.

References

1. Li H, Wang P, Shen C (2017) Towards end-to-end car license plates detection and recognition with deep neural networks. arXiv:1709.08828 [cs], Sep. 2017
2. Ledig C et al (2017) Photo-realistic single image super-resolution using a generative adversarial network. arXiv:1609.04802 [cs, stat], May 2017
3. Dong C, Loy CC, He K, Tang X (2015) Image super-resolution using deep convolutional networks. arXiv:1501.00092 [cs], Jul. 2015
4. Pant AK, Gyawali PK, Acharya S (2015) Automatic Nepali number plate recognition with support vector machines. In: Presented at the international conference on software, knowledge, information management and applications (SKIMA), Dec. 2015
5. Silva SM, Jung CR (2018) License plate detection and recognition in unconstrained scenarios. In: Ferrari V, Hebert M, Sminchisescu C, Weiss Y (eds) Computer Vision ECCV 2018, vol 11216. Springer International Publishing, Cham, pp 593–609
6. Balamurugan G, Punniakodi S, Rajeswari K, Arulalan V (2015) Automatic number plate recognition system using super-resolution technique. In: 2015 International conference on computing and communications technologies (ICCCT), Chennai, India, Feb. 2015, pp. 273–277. https://doi.org/10.1109/ICCCT2.2015.7292759
7. Singh A, Singh J (2016) Super resolution applications in modern digital image processing. IJCA 150(2):6–8. https://doi.org/10.5120/ijca2016911458
8. Indira K, Mohan KV, Nikhilashwary T (2019) Automatic license plate recognition. In: Bhattacharyya S, Mukherjee A, Bhaumik H, Das S, Yoshida K (eds) Recent trends in signal and image processing, vol 727. Springer Singapore, Singapore, pp 67–77
9. Renuka devi D, Kanagapushpavalli D (2011) Automatic license plate recognition. In: 3rd International conference on trendz in information sciences computing (TISC2011), Dec. 2011, pp. 75–78. https://doi.org/10.1109/TISC.2011.6169088
10. Goodfellow IJ et al (2014) Generative adversarial networks. arXiv:1406.2661 [cs, stat], Jun. 2014
11. Simonyan K, Zisserman A (2015) Very deep convolutional networks for large-scale image recognition. arXiv:1409.1556 [cs], Apr. 2015
12. Auria L, Moro RA (2008) Support vector machines (SVM) as a technique for solvency analysis. SSRN J. https://doi.org/10.2139/ssrn.1424949

EEG Signals Classification for Right- and Left-Hand Movement Discrimination Using SVM and LDA Classifiers

Yogendra Narayan and Rajeev Ranjan

Abstract Motor imagery (MI)-based electroencephalogram (EEG) signals classification has been utilized for developing assistive human–robotic interaction in the past few decades. EEG signals have excessive importance in the field of brain–computer interface (BCI) which has different applications in the field of bio-medical. BCI acquires brain signals, extracts features, reduced noise and produces control signal. The objective of this research work is compared to the effectiveness of time-domain (TD) features using two different classifiers, namely linear discriminant analysis (LDA) and support vector machine (SVM), to discriminate between right- and left-hand movements of EEG signals. In this context, the ocular artifact, i.e., electrooculogram (EOG) signal, was rejected by using the independent component analysis (ICA) approach, whereas dimension reduction was done by principal component analysis (PCA). The EEG dataset was acquired from ten healthy human subjects in two sessions followed by band-pass Butterworth filtering for de-noising. In this work, the 12-TD features were compared to each other in terms of classification accuracy with SVM and LDA classifiers. Finally, the top ten features were utilized to make the final feature vector which exhibited the best performance with an SVM classifier with an accuracy of 98.75% as compared to LDA (95.2%). The finding of this study would be utilized for designing the EEG-based wheelchair as well as a prosthetic limb.

Keywords Motor imagery · EEG signal · SVM · LDA · ICA · PCA

1 Introduction

The human head is made up of various layers including the brain, skull, scalp, and other layers. The signal gets attenuated by the skull almost hundred times that of the soft tissues. Noise is produced either by the external part of the scalp which is known as external noise or system noise and by the internal part of the brain which

Y. Narayan (✉) · R. Ranjan
Department of Electronics and Communication Engineering, Chandigarh University, Ajitgarh, India

© The Author(s), under exclusive license to Springer Nature Singapore Pte Ltd. 2022
C. Satyanarayana et al. (eds.), *High Performance Computing and Networking*,
Lecture Notes in Electrical Engineering 853,
https://doi.org/10.1007/978-981-16-9885-9_11

is known as internal noise [1]. So, a large number of active neurons are required to generate the potential that can be recorded by the electrodes [2]. These signals are then amplified and displayed. The central nervous system (CNS) gets fully developed and operational with the development of approximately 10^{11} neurons, i.e., 10^4 neurons per cubic mm. The synapses interconnect the neurons to form a neural net. In the case of an adult, there are approximately 5×10^{14} synapses [3]. The number of neurons starts decreasing with age while the number of synapses increases. Based on its anatomy, the brain is divided into three parts: (i) brain stem, (ii) cerebellum, and (iii) cerebrum [4]. The cerebrum is made up of the right and left lobes of the brain with a surface layer termed the cerebral cortex. The cerebrum consists of the regions for the expression of emotions, behavior, movement initiation, complex analysis, and conscious awareness of sensation [5, 6]. The cerebellum systematizes the voluntary action of the muscles. The brain stem systematizes involuntary actions like biorhythms, neuro-hormone, respiration, and heart regulation [7]. Yang et al. utilized wavelet packet-based features with common spatial pattern method and achieved 95.5% classification accuracy [8].

The study of EEG is thus used to diagnose neurological disorders and other disorders of the body. The EEG signals acquired from the human body can be used to diagnose and treat the following clinical disorders: (i) Epilepsy investigation and finding the seizure origin, (ii) Monitoring coma, alertness, and brain death; (iii) Controlling the depth of anesthesia; (iv) Discovering the areas of damage in the case of stroke, head injury, and tumor; (v) Invigilating the cognitive engagement, (vi) Verifying the afferent pathways, (vii) Providing a hybrid of the recording system with imaging modalities, (viii) Testing the effects of drugs on epilepsy; (ix) Investigating disorders of the brain; (x) Helping in cortical excision of epileptic focus; (xi) Investigating physiology and sleep disorders; (xii) Testing the convulsive effects drugs, (xii) Monitoring the development of the brain, etc. [9]. The above discussions indicate the importance, relevance, and potential of the EEG technique which encourages further research scope for assisting the clinicians as well as the engineers [10].

The research work in this paper is divided into four different portions, the introduction of different EEG signal classification techniques and related work is the first part, materials and method related to current research work is the second part in which EEG acquisition, classification including feature extraction is given. The results obtained from MATLAB© 2020 are given in the third part, whereas the fourth and last part of the work discusses the conclusion including the possible future directions.

2 Materials and Methods

This section describes the EEG data recording steps, feature extraction, and classification process of right- and left-hand movement discrimination. Figure 1 demonstrates the different accessories utilized during the experimental work which includes

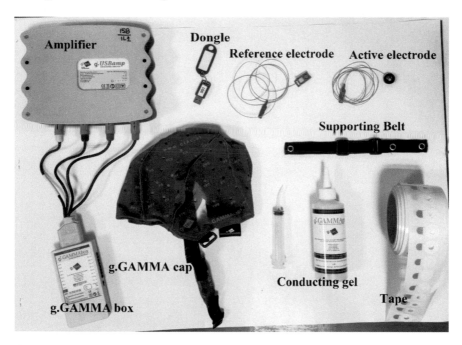

Fig. 1 Different accessories employed for EEG dataset acquisition

g.GAMMAcap, g.LADYbird active electrodes, dongle, and amplifier to acquire the EEG dataset from humans.

2.1 EEG Data Acquisition and Preprocessing

EEG dataset acquisition was done with twenty physically and mentally fit human subjects in two different data recording sessions. A training session was conducted for subjects who participated in data recording. The subjects were instructed to imagine both hand movements, i.e., right and left twenty-time per session. The distance between the subject and the computer monitor was 150 cm, and subjects were sitting on a comfortable armchair with a fully relaxed state. They were instructed to keep the body relaxed and forbidden any arm or foot movement [3]. Before the data acquisition, instructions are provided for learning the correct movements, the concept of MI and BCI setup [11]. Figure 2 shows the block diagram representation of the complete workflow used in the study. Electrodes were placed according to 10–20 international systems nearer to C3 and C4 positions over the motor cortex with a sampling rate of 256 Hz. A total of 16 active electrodes was utilized for EEG acquisition.

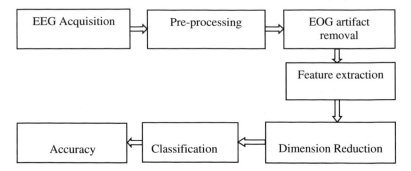

Fig. 2 Complete workflow of EEG signals classification scheme

The EEG signals are converted from analog-to-digital form by using analog-to-digital converters (ADC). EEG signal has a bandwidth of approximately 100 Hz. Hence, the minimum sampling frequency of 200 samples/sec is required for sampling the EEG signals. EEG signals undergo the process of quantization to preserve the diagnostic information. Each signal sample is represented by up to 16 bits for accurate recording [12]. This provides the required memory volume for epileptic seizure monitoring records and storing the signals massively. Generally, the memory size for storing the EEG signal is much smaller than that used for storing the radiological images.

After the preprocessing, the well-known feature extraction method CSP was utilized to extract the features. Different types of bio-medical artifacts like EOG and ECG were rejected by using the ICA technique. The large dimension of the feature vector was reduced by employing the PCA method [13]. The critical step of brain–computer communication is measuring the activities of the brain correctly and effectively. But BCI cannot read the mind or decode the thoughts. It can only identify and recognize the particular patterns of activity of brain signals related to particular events or tasks [14]. So a BCI has the requirement of producing these patterns by mental strategy. The foundation of any brain–computer communication is the mental strategy [15]. The BCI can recognize the mental strategy to decide what the user has to do for generating the brain patterns [16]. The mental strategy decides some constraints on the software as well as on hardware of BCI and also some techniques of signal processing to be applied later [17]. The common mental strategies are motor imagery and selective attention [18].

2.2 EEG Feature Extraction

BCI depends on the electrical measures of the activities of the brain. It also depends on the location of the sensor on the head to measure the activities of the brain [19]. Electrical activities of the brain are recorded from the scalp with electrodes by using

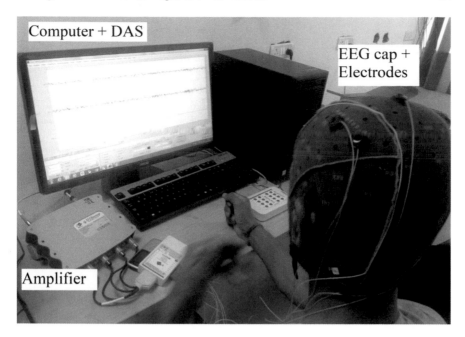

Fig. 3 EEG-based BCI comprising electrode with electrode cap

the technique of EEG. This technique is generally utilized for decades, in various research and clinical activities [20, 21]. Figure 3 represents an EEG-based BCI that has cables that transfer signals to the bio-signal amplifier from electrodes. The whole system consists of a personal computer for processing the EEG dataset and interfacing with the BCI application. EEG signals were converted from analog-to-digital form by exploiting the bio-signal amplifier and required software toolbox.

TD features are the well-known features among the FD and TFD features because ease of extraction approach as well as no transformation is required for their computation. Preprocessed EEG signals time series are exploited to extract meaningful TD features. There are a wide range of application of advance and novel feature extraction technique irrespective of their domain if they have sufficient robustness. Few existing TD features are listed in Table 1.

2.3 Classifiers

Classification is the process in which objects and notions are recognized based upon some identity and then comprehended [22]. In another way, it is an evolution or categorization of objects or people into a faction based on a few qualities or characteristics. For example, classifying galaxies based on the shapes, classifying the emails into spam based on its content, classifying the students of the class based on

Table 1 TD features use in the present work

S. No.	Name of the feature	Equation
1	Integrated absolute value (IAV)	$\text{IAV} = \sum_{i=1}^{N} |X_i|$
2	Mean absolute value (MAV)	$\text{MAV} = \frac{1}{N} \sum_{i=1}^{N} |X_i|$
3	Simple square integral (SSI)	$\text{SSI} = \sum_{i=1}^{N} (X_i)^2$
4	Variance (VAR)	$\text{VAR} = \frac{1}{N-1} \sum_{i=1}^{N} (X_i)^2$
5	Root mean square (RMS)	$\text{RMS} = \sqrt{\frac{1}{N} \sum_{i=1}^{N} X_i^2}$
6	LOG detector (LD)	$\text{LOG} = e^{\sqrt{\frac{1}{N} \sum_{i=1}^{N} X_i^2}}$
7	Waveform length (WL)	$\text{WL} = \sum_{i=1}^{N-1} |X_{i+1} - X_i|$
8	Average amplitude change (AAC)	$\text{AAC} = \frac{1}{N} \sum_{i=1}^{N-1} |X_{i+1} - X_i|$
9	Zero-crossing (ZC)	$\text{ZC} = \sum_{i=1}^{N-1} \left[\text{sgn}(X_i * X_{i+1}) \cap |X_i - X_{i+1}| \geq \text{Threshold} \right]$ $\text{sgn}(X) = \begin{cases} 1 & \text{if } X \geq \text{threshold} \\ 0 & \text{otherwise} \end{cases}$
10	Standard deviation (SD)	$\text{SD} = \sqrt{\frac{1}{N-1} \sum_{n=1}^{N} x_n}$
11	Kurtosis (KUT)	$\sum_{n=1}^{N} \frac{E(x_0 - \mu)^4}{\sigma^4}$
12	Slope sign change (SSC)	$\text{SSC} = \sum_{i=2}^{N-1} \left[f\left[(X_i - X_{i-1}) * (X_i - X_{i-1}) \right] \right]$ $f(X) = \begin{cases} 1 & \text{if } X \geq \text{threshold} \\ 0 & \text{otherwise} \end{cases}$

their grades, etc., and the master who performs this task is known as a classifier. In this study, SVM and LDA classifiers were compared to each other.

3 Results and Discussion

In this study, the critical performance of 12-TD features was carried out in terms of accuracy by employing the LDA as well as SVM classifiers. The computation of accuracy was based on the ratio of true samples to a total number of samples. The acquisition of the EEG dataset was done in two sessions with 20-heathy subjects at NITTTR Chandigarh, India. Results compared individual features performance of both sessions of EEG recording. Standard deviation was calculated for each feature across all subjects using the classification techniques. Results were obtained from MATLAB© 2020 simulation and reposted in Tables 2 and 3. The threefold cross-validation (FCV) approach was implemented to divide the whole dataset into testing and training purposes. In the 3-FCV technique, the whole dataset was segregated into three equal parts so that two-part of the EEG dataset could be employed to train the classification algorithm, whereas the last part of the dataset could be appointed to test the classifier, whereas no dataset was used for validation of classifier.

Table 2 shows the performance as the accuracy (ACC) of EEG data recorded in the first session for 12-TD features by using the SVM and LDA technique. Classification accuracy was reported in percentage (%) for each feature with the corresponding standard deviation during the classification. The results demonstrated that the best five features were VAR, SSI, LD, MAV, and RMS with the accuracy of 59.1 ± 4.7%, 60.9 ± 4.6%, 66.2 ± 4.9%, 67.8 ± 5.2%, and 68.7 ± 5.6%, respectively. Results obtained in Tables 2 and 3 showed that SVM performed better than the LDA classifier for MI-based EEG signal classification to discriminate between right- and left-hand movements. The least performing feature was AAC, IAV, SSC, KUT, and SD. Least performing features can be rejected to form the final feature vector as they can degrade the performance of the classifier.

Table 3 shows the performance of 12-time-domain features during the second session of EEG recording by employing the SVM and LDA classifier. The best feature was founded as RMS, the second was MAV, the third was LD, the fourth was SSI, and the fifth was VAR. Similarly, the worst-performing features were SD, KUT, SSC, IAV, and AAC. Based upon the finding of this work, top features can be utilized for forming the features vector while ignoring the least performing features. Results indicated that the SVM classifier is the best in comparison with the LDA approach.

Table 2 Classification accuracy of time-domain features for left- and right-hand movements classification for session 1

Feature rank	Features	LDA (% ACC + SD)	SVM (% ACC + SD)
1	RMS	68.7 ± 5.6	71.6 ± 5.2
2	MAV	67.8 ± 5.2	69.5 ± 5.9
3	LD	66.2 ± 4.9	68.5 ± 5.4
4	SSI	60.9 ± 4.6	64.3 ± 4.1
5	VAR	59.1 ± 4.7	62.4 ± 4.0
6	WL	56.2 ± 7.7	59.6 ± 7.1
7	ZC	53.5 ± 3.1	56.7 ± 3.5
8	SD	44.7 ± 6.2	47.3 ± 6.8
9	KUT	42.3 ± 12.9	44.9 ± 12.2
10	SSC	41.8 ± 3.2	43.4 ± 3.6
11	IAV	36.4 ± 4.6	40.1 ± 4.9
12	AAC	28.3 ± 2.8	32.7 ± 2.2

Table 3 Classification accuracy of time-domain features for left- and right-hand movements classification for session 2

Feature rank	Features	LDA (% ACC + SD)	SVM (% ACC + SD)
1	RMS	69.4 ± 5.2	72.3 ± 6.8
2	MAV	68.4 ± 5.9	70.1 ± 6.4
3	LD	66.9 ± 5.1	69.2 ± 5.1
4	SSI	61.2 ± 4.9	65.4 ± 4.9
5	VAR	60.5 ± 4.2	63.0 ± 4.7
6	WL	57.3 ± 7.0	60.5 ± 6.8
7	ZC	54.9 ± 3.8	56.7 ± 3.5
8	SD	44.7 ± 5.9	49.2 ± 6.5
9	KUT	43.6 ± 11.2	46.1 ± 11.8
10	SSC	43.0 ± 4.6	44.9 ± 3.8
11	IAV	37.7 ± 5.8	42.1 ± 5.5
12	AAC	30.7 ± 3.1	33.4 ± 3.6

The table showed the rank obtained during the classification of EEG data of right- and left-hand movement discrimination.

Finally, the top ten features were selected to form the feature vector, when the top ten features in the form of feature vector were applied as input to the classifier. Again the SVM classifier was found the best with an accuracy of 98.75%, whereas the LDA with the 95.2% accuracy. So, the SVM method with ICA and PCA can be employed for further improving the performance. Figure 4 shows the scatter plot of SVM classifier during the classification process; initially, the error was 50% but as soon as the time increases the error reduces which indicate that classification accuracy increase. The cross sign shows the wrongly classified sample, whereas the

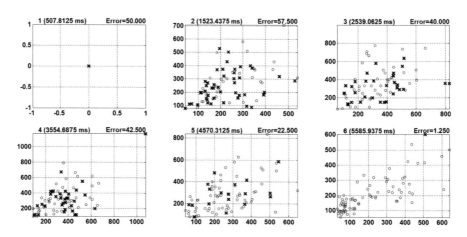

Fig. 4 Scatter plot of SVM classifier with 98.75% accuracy

circle shows the correctly classified. Finally, the SVM classifier achieved the 1.25% error rate at 5.58 s which indicates the 98.75% classification accuracy. As the SVM method was found best; therefore, the scatter plot for SVM was shown only not for the LDA approach.

4 Conclusion

This study compared two classifiers, namely SVM and LDA, for evaluating the performance of 12-time-domain features to discriminate between right- and left-hand movements EEG signals. EEG data recording was done in two sessions, results showed that the SVM method with top ten features in the form of feature vector performed better than the LDA approach. ICA technique was a prominent approach for EOG artifact rejection where PCA was best for dimension reduction with the SVM method. The best five features were VAR, SSI, LD, MAV, and RMS in ascending order which could be utilized for enhancing the performance of the system. The SVM classifier achieved 98.75% accuracy within the 5.58 s. The finding of this study can be applied for designing the online classification-based robotic assistive device for helping disabled persons. Further, the performance of all three domain features could be compared to find more robust feature set combinations.

References

1. Wang M, Hu J, Abbass HA (2020) BrainPrint: EEG biometric identification based on analyzing brain connectivity graphs. Pattern Recognit 300(5):107381. https://doi.org/10.1016/j.patcog. 2020.107381
2. Narayan Y (2021) Motor-imagery EEG signals classification using SVM, MLP and LDA classifiers. Turkish J Comput Math Educ 12(2):3339–3344. https://doi.org/10.17762/turcomat. v12i2.2393
3. Narayan Y, Mathew L, Chatterji S (2018) SEMG signal classification with novel feature extraction using different machine learning approaches. J Intell Fuzzy Syst 35(5):5099–5109. https:// doi.org/10.3233/JIFS-169794
4. Yuan Q et al (2017) Epileptic seizure detection based on imbalanced classification and wavelet packet transform. Seizure 50:99–108. https://doi.org/10.1016/j.seizure.2017.05.018
5. Minguillon J, Lopez-Gordo MA, Pelayo F (2017) Trends in EEG-BCI for daily-life: requirements for artifact removal. Biomed Signal Process Control 31:407–418. https://doi.org/10. 1016/j.bspc.2016.09.005
6. Narayan Y (2021) Mi based brain signals identification using KNN and MLP classifiers. Ann Rom Soc Cell Biol 25(1):3795–3803
7. Li Y, Wei Q, Chen Y, Zhou X (2021) Transfer learning based on hybrid Riemannian and Euclidean space data alignment and subject selection in brain-computer interfaces. IEEE Access 9:6201–6212. https://doi.org/10.1109/ACCESS.2020.3048683
8. Yang B, Li H, Wang Q, Zhang Y (2016) Subject-based feature extraction by using fisher WPD-CSP in brain-computer interfaces. Comput Methods Programs Biomed 129:21–28. https://doi. org/10.1016/j.cmpb.2016.02.020

9. Ko LW, Ranga SSK, Komarov O, Chen CC (2017) Development of single-channel hybrid BCI system using motor imagery and SSVEP. J Healthc Eng 2017. https://doi.org/10.1155/2017/3789386
10. Narayan Y (2020) EEG signals classification using SVM and RF classifier for left and right-hand movement. J Green Eng 10(11):10691–10701
11. Narayan Y, Singh RM, Mathew L, Chatterji S (2019) Surface EMG signal classification using ensemble algorithm, PCA and DWT for robot control. In: International conference on advanced informatics for computing research, vol 10. Springer, Singapore, pp 424–434. https://doi.org/10.1007/978-981-13-3140-4
12. Kim B, Kim L, Kim YH, Yoo SK (2017) Cross-association analysis of EEG and EMG signals according to movement intention state. Cogn Syst Res 44:1–9. https://doi.org/10.1016/j.cogsys.2017.02.001
13. Çınar S, Acır N (2017) A novel system for automatic removal of ocular artefacts in EEG by using outlier detection methods and independent component analysis. Expert Syst Appl 68:36–44. https://doi.org/10.1016/j.eswa.2016.10.009
14. Aranyi G, Pecune F, Charles F, Pelachaud C, Cavazza M (2016) Affective interaction with a virtual character through an fNIRS brain-computer interface. Front Comput Neurosci 10:1–14. https://doi.org/10.3389/fncom.2016.00070
15. Tang Z, Li C, Sun S (2017) Single-trial EEG classification of motor imagery using deep convolutional neural networks. Optik (Stuttg) 130:11–18. https://doi.org/10.1016/j.ijleo.2016.10.117
16. Li M, Chen W, Zhang T (2017) Classification of epilepsy EEG signals using DWT-based envelope analysis and neural network ensemble. Biomed Signal Process Control 31:357–365. https://doi.org/10.1016/j.bspc.2016.09.008
17. Aliakbaryhosseinabadi S, Kamavuako EN, Jiang N, Farina D, Mrachacz-Kersting N (2017) Classification of EEG signals to identify variations in attention during motor task execution. J Neurosci Methods 284:27–34. https://doi.org/10.1016/j.jneumeth.2017.04.008
18. Hamzah N, Zaini N, Sani M, Ismail N (2017) EEG analysis on actual and imaginary left and right hand lifting using support vector machine (SVM). Int J Electr Electron Syst Res EEG 10(6):10–17
19. Vasilyev A, Liburkina S, Yakovlev L, Perepelkina O, Kaplan A (2017) Assessing motor imagery in brain-computer interface training: psychological and neurophysiological correlates. Neuropsychologia 97:56–65. https://doi.org/10.1016/j.neuropsychologia.2017.02.005
20. Virdi P, Narayan Y, Kumari P, Mathew L (2017) Discrete wavelet packet based elbow movement classification using fine Gaussian SVM. In: 1st IEEE international conference on power electronics, intelligent control and energy systems, ICPEICES 2016, 2017, pp 1–5. https://doi.org/10.1109/ICPEICES.2016.7853657
21. Narayan Y, Ahlawat V, Kumar S (2020) Pattern recognition of sEMG signals using DWT based feature and SVM classifier. Int J Adv Sci Technol 29(10):2243–2256
22. Zhang Y, Xie SQ, Wang H, Zhang Z (2021) Data analytics in steady-state visual evoked potential-based brain-computer interface: a review. IEEE Sens J 21(2):1124–1138. https://doi.org/10.1109/JSEN.2020.3017491

A Comparative Study on Network Intrusion Detection System Using Deep Learning Algorithms and Enhancement of Deep Learning Models Using Generative Adversarial Network (GAN)

Ch. Sekhar⬛, Panja Hemanth Kumar⬛, K. Venkata Rao⬛, and M. H. M. Krishna Prasad⬛

Abstract A network intrusion detection system (NIDS) is an approach to continuously monitoring the traffic associated with the network for suspicious activities and raising alarms. The network intrusion detection system is the critical component to detect various attacks from internal and external sources. It is one of the implemented solutions against harmful attacks. Different machine learning techniques are implemented on NIDS, which lack in some aspects. Migrating to deep learning algorithms fulfils the lack obtained in machine learning algorithms. In this research, some deep learning algorithms are executed and evaluated for NIDS. Also, these deep learning algorithms are enhanced using generative adversarial network (GAN) architectural design. In this paper, we have calculated evaluation metrics for every algorithm using various data set NSL-KDD to select the best algorithm to fit for the network intrusion detection system (NIDS) and enhanced its accuracy by generating synthetic data using GAN.

Keywords Network intrusion detection system · NSL-KDD · Deep learning · Generative adversarial network

1 Introduction

Advancements in the Internet over the past few decades are remarkable, and experts believe that more than 49 billion electronic devices are connected over the Internet.

Present Address:
M. H. M. Krishna Prasad
JNTU, Kakinada, India

Ch. Sekhar · P. H. Kumar
Vignan's Institute of Information Technology, Visakhapatnam, India

K. Venkata Rao
Professor in CSE, Guru Nanak Institutions Technical Campus, Manchal, Ibrahimpatnam, Telangana, India

© The Author(s), under exclusive license to Springer Nature Singapore Pte Ltd. 2022
C. Satyanarayana et al. (eds.), *High Performance Computing and Networking*,
Lecture Notes in Electrical Engineering 853,
https://doi.org/10.1007/978-981-16-9885-9_12

143

Since the technology behind the Internet and communications is much integrated and complex, there are vulnerabilities and loopholes which are a threat to safety and security. The security aspects of the technology are pretty significant and need to be advanced with ongoing improvements in the technology of the Internet. Cyberattacks on technologies involving data and networks are becoming quite common these days. Health care, Internet of Things, banking systems and financial systems are some of the technology places where data are generated hugely, and sophisticated network system is present where we are observing hacks. A firewall system to the network can defence up to a specific limit and cannot detect and alarm suspicious activity, which is designed to bypass the firewall and attack the system. This can be achieved with the help of intrusion detection system (IDS) which detects and alarm about the intrusion taken place which can even classify attack into a certain category which can be taken care of with certain countermeasures. An intrusion detection system is a virtual device or application used to monitor hostile attacks in the traffic over the network. Based on the network type, the IDS is classified into two: 1) network-based intrusion detection system (NIDS) 2) host-based intrusion detection system (HIDS). Network-based IDS is used to monitor the hostile activity in traffic over the network. Host-based IDS works on the host system and focuses on the packets coming in and out of the system, and based on that suspicious activity is detected. There are different methods to detect suspicious activities, which are based on signature and anomaly. Signature-based IDS works on the predefined patterns that include the rate of flow of the bytes in the network; the limitation with signature-based IDS is it can only detect the existing patterns and fails to detect when new patterns are encountered. Therefore, signature-based IDS is preferred less in real time. Anomaly-based IDS is used to detect unknown patterns. This IDS includes less-effective performance because of which we go for a combination of both signature and anomaly-based IDS, which is known as full state analysis. This IDS overcomes all the limitations in the signature and anomaly based. This works on the network layer, application layer and transport layer because of the low false-positive rate. State full analysis has predefined protocols with the anomaly-based approach. Most of the organisations use this full state analysis. But nowadays, with the increase of the complex attacks, these methods have also faded down because they depend mostly on parameters related to the traffic of the network, which consists of packet length, inter-arrival time, flows size and so on. In order to overcome this, the intrusion system is made self-learning. The self-learning system is considered to be more powerful as it uses machine learning subject and differentiates the security intrusions by surprised and unsupervised algorithms. Machine learning is related to the self-learning mechanism in which the features and patterns are learned from training data and are successfully identified by the test data. Many solutions were given, but they were found ineffective when imposed in a real-time environment. The output of these solutions had a high false-positive rate with high computational cost. Advancements in machine learning introduced a new subject in it known as deep learning which can be defined as a complex model of machine learning algorithms. They are found to be more effective as they can learn the abstract representation of complex hierarchical features. Recently, we have witnessed deep learning algorithms as more powerful due to their accurate results in various domains like speech processing and language processing. The reason why we are associated with deep learning is because of its two important characteristics: hierarchical feature representation, learning long-term dependencies of temporal patterns in large-scale sequence-related data. Machine learning and deep learning models are classified into supervised and unsupervised learning techniques. Various models are developed to deal with the type of data available for training. Deep learning models have the prime advantage over machine learning models is hierarchical feature representation of data. Feature learning in deep learning is the combination of both local feature learning and inter-relationships with the previously learned features. The shallow architectures are shaped in flat topologies, whereas deep learning architectures are hierarchical in shape. The organisation of the research paper as is as follows: Section 2 discusses about the data set and its problems; Section 3 is all about the literature review made by us during our research; Section 4 and its sub-parts discuss about proposed architectures and enhancements using GAN; Section 6 emphasises on results and analysis of the proposed architectures, and Section 7 discusses about the conclusion and future work of the research work.

2 Data set

The data set used for experiments and analysis is NSL-KDD data set. NSL-KDD data set is proposed to eliminate the limitations of the KDD data set which contains redundant data in both training and testing data sets. This problem with KDD data set leading to poor classification. NSL-KDD has improved from KDD data set in some ways, and those are firstly, all the redundant information from both training and testing data set are removed, and secondly, each record is given particularly difficult in classification based on some learning algorithms. At last, random sampling is used on the records to create distinct records. Even after improvement from KDD data set, the NSL-KDD data set is lacking in some aspects. We can observe in NSL-KDD data set; the normal data are so much large when compared to attack data which are creating imbalance in training phase. To deal with this problem, we implemented GAN on NSL-KDD data set to generate fake data which can be utilised to train the deep learning model which in turn increases the accuracy. Figure 1 shows that bias present in the both KDD and NSL-KDD data sets.

3 Literature Review

The intrusion detection system (IDS) was first developed by Anderson et al. in 1980 and has done significant work [1]. With the development of various types of network intrusion detection system such as signature-based detection, anomaly-based detection, and state full protocol analysis, some of the attacks can be analysed and classified within the turn, helps in the detection of an attack. The above-mentioned

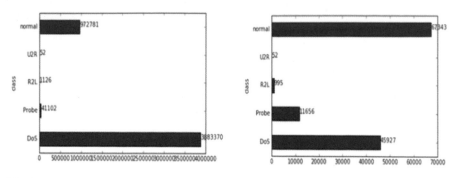

Fig. 1 Number of rows in KDD and NSL-KDD data sets

detection systems absolutely depend on network traffic parameters such as the size of the packet, inter-arrival time and flow. But, some of the complex attacks cannot be detected using these simple techniques. Machine learning techniques are self-learning techniques that learn from data available and detect the attack by analysis and classification of the data [2]. The less time constraint can be dealt with efficiently by machine learning algorithms which have the capability of automation of processes such as identification and classification. The detailed description of comparison of various machine learning algorithms with various data sets and various scenarios such as in IoT devices, smart city, big data environment and mobile networks in the study done by Saranya et al. in their research paper [3], and Figure 2 shows the accuracy performance of the ML algorithms study done by Sekhar et al. [2, 4].

Since the intrusion detection system is a sensitive paradigm, false-positive results may compromise the whole network by the attacker. The usage of deep learning for network intrusion detection system is mainly for the reasons of hierarchical

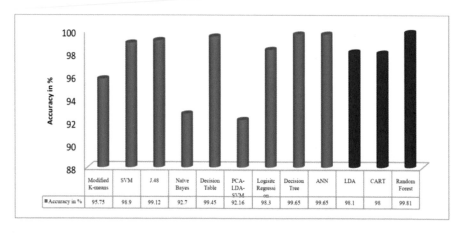

Fig. 2 Performance analysis of machine learning algorithms

representations and learning long-term dependencies of temporal patterns in large-scale sequence data [5]. Vinayakumar et al., in their research paper [6], proposed a convolutional neural network for intrusion detection system and produced results. Vinayakumar et al. also proposed other models of deep learning, which include recurrent neural network, a recurrent neural network with LSTM and other variants of recurrent neural network in a research paper [7]. Vinayakumar et al. also proposed a deep neural network for IDS in a research paper [8]. In real-time, as explained by Liu et al. [9], the network-based intrusion detection system is independent of the operating system and mainly implemented on switches or hosts and can detect the intrusion only on a particular network where it has implemented, whereas host-based intrusion detection system can detect precisely about intrusion components in the network. The host-based intrusion detection system has a major disadvantage in that it is totally dependent on reliability and cannot detect network intrusions. In real-time, the data sources are quite essential, and the time taken to see the intrusion is significant. Before some intrusion has taken place, respective actions are needed. Advancements in deep learning models are pretty complex, which consume computation and time to increase accuracy. Instead of designing deep learning more complexly, we use a generative adversarial network (GAN) [10] to recreate fake data from existing data which is proposed by Shahriar et al. in their research paper [11]. Shahriar et al. also claimed that the data sets available with us now are less and are needed to improve in terms of a size where we use generative adversarial networks (GAN).

4 Proposed Deep Learning Architectures

4.1 Convolutional Neural Network

Convolutional neural networks can extract hierarchical representation from the data fed in and can achieve good performance when compared to previous machine learning models [4]. CNN is simply an extension concept to the basic feed-forward neural networks, which are inspired by biological neurons. Dealing with the time series data, the CNN takes the input in the form of a 1D mesh, in which data are arranged in systematic order with the time interval. Hence, we organised the traffic events of the NSL-KDD data set as time series and fed them into the CNN. In convolutional neural networks, the basic functionality revolves around the convolution operation. Figure 3 shown regular structure of CNN.

The given time series input operated over convolution to generate a feature map with a corresponding filter. The feature map from the set of features is obtained as

$$hl_i^{fm} = \tanh\left(\omega^{fm} x_{i:i+f-1} b\right) \tag{1}$$

where b denotes the bias term, and the filter hl is used on the set of feature to generate the final feature map as

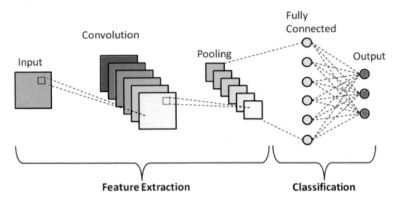

Fig. 3 Basic structure of CNN

$$hl = \left[hl_1, hl_2, hl_3, \ldots, hl_{n-f+1} \right] \tag{2}$$

and then, we apply max-pooling on each feature map obtained as

$$\vec{hl} = \max\{hl\} \tag{3}$$

Max-pooling selects the most significant and essential features and is fed into the fully connected layer, a softmax function. The softmax function can classify by producing probability distribution over each class.

$$o_t = \mathrm{softmax}(\omega_{ho} hl + b_0) \tag{4}$$

4.2 Deep Neural Network

The deep neural network is a multi-layer perceptron network which is basically a feed-forward neural network that is inspired by the biological neuron. DNN is usually made with one input layer, one or more hidden layers and one output layer in its architecture. The information from the input layer is passed onto the corresponding next layers as they are fully connected dense layers. The learning is made through this process in between various connected layers. The mathematical operation in the hidden layer is shown below

$$h_i(x) = f\left(\omega_i^T x + b\right) \tag{5}$$

The function f is the non-linear activation function. Various non-linear activation functions are the sigmoid function, hyperbolic tangent function, softmax function, etc. The softmax activation function is extensively used for multi-label classification purpose. Softmax can even be defined to be multi-class logistic regression architecture. We use the softmax activation function in the output layer in our research as we need to classify multi-label attacks and normal conditions of the network.

$$\mathrm{softmax}(x) = \frac{e^{xi}}{\sum_{j=1}^{n} e^{xj}} \tag{6}$$

In general, the l-layered multi-layer perceptron can be mathematically shown as

$$H_l(H_{l-1}(H_{l-2} \ldots (H_1()))) \tag{7}$$

The stacking of hidden layer functions in this manner is called a deep neural network. The deep neural networks are very dense in nature. The parameters associated with the deep neural network are very high in number. Usually, the parameters are allocated to the network using hyper-parameter estimation techniques. For every hidden layer, we use a special activation function called rectified linear unit (ReLU). ReLU is faster and efficient in terms of computational complexity and time-consuming. ReLU can even eliminate problems such as gradient vanishing and production of error in gradient descent procedure. The network is associated with a loss function to calculate the amount of deviation produced in predicted values from the original values. We employed a multi-class classification model; hence, we used a negative logarithmic of the probability distribution of the predicted values with the original values.

$$d(\mathrm{orig}, p(\mathrm{pred})) = -\log p(\mathrm{pred})_{\mathrm{orig}} \tag{8}$$

And the backpropagation strategy used in the model is stochastic gradient descent.

4.3 Recurrent Neural Network

The recurrent neural network is modelled from a time series analysis model dated back to 1990. RNN is a feed-forward neural network with an additional feedback loop placed internally. This arrangement results in a cyclic graph, and loops are defined in the network, which acts as simple memory elements which have the capability to store and retrieve past information in the data over time. RNN is quite good at dealing with long short-term temporal data. Temporal data can be detailed in CNN up to some extent. RNN can be used to deal with temporal data effectively. RNN shares parameters throughout the network and are avoided from being generalised. Mathematically, the flow of data in RNN can be depicted as

$$H(x, h) = f(\omega_{xh}x + \omega_{hh}h + b) \tag{9}$$

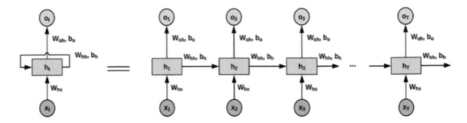

Fig. 4 Recurrent neural network

ω_{xh} and ω_{hh} are weights of the model; x is the input to the model; h is considered as the timestamps of the model. The RNN can be as simple as a feed-forward neural network and can be understood well if it is unrolled, which is shown in Figure 4.

where O_t is output state, h_t is the current timestamp; h_{t-1} is the previous timestamp, and x_t is passed as the input state. A clear understanding of the dynamics of RNN is challenging to understand and manipulate. However, the functionality can be better understood and used to deduce feature maps of the data in the view of temporal data and time-varying data. Even though the backpropagation through time is operated in RNN, it is not advisable because it introduces problems like gradient vanishing and exploding gradient problems.

4.4 RNN-LSTM

The major drawback of RNN is backpropagation through time (BPTT) is not efficient. Modelling sequence data at a large scale is a drawback factor for RNN. Vanishing gradient and exploding gradient problems affect the model severely in terms of accuracy, and results get scattered. This problem can be solved using LSTM. Long short-term memory handles the problems of vanishing gradient and exploding gradient by generating constant error flow. LSTM introduces a memory block instead of a simple RNN unit. Each memory block consists of memory cells, and each memory cell has an inbuilt constant value called constant error carousel (CEC). The value will be active when the model passes through the time-dependent steps, and inactive the memory block is not triggered. Figure 5 shown regular structure of RNN—LSTM.

The mathematics involved behind the recurrent hidden layer function at time step T can be depicted as

$$x_t, h_{t-1}, cl_{t-1} \rightarrow h_t, cl_t \tag{10}$$

$$in_t = \sigma(\omega_{xin}x_t + \omega_{hin}h_{t-1} + \omega_{clin}cl_{t-1} + b_{in}) \tag{11}$$

$$fr_t = \sigma(\omega_{xfr}x_t + \omega_{hfr}h_{t-1} + \omega_{clfr}cl_{t-1} + b_{fr}) \tag{12}$$

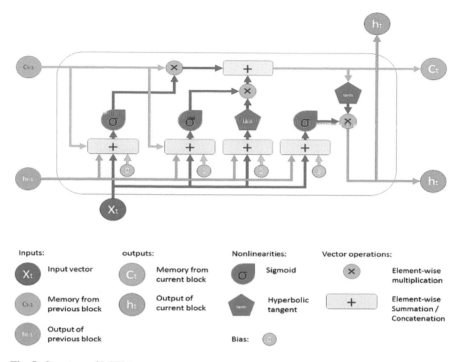

Fig. 5 Structure of LSTM

$$cl_t = fr_t \odot cl_{t-1} + in_t \odot \tanh(\omega_{xcl}x_t + \omega_{hcl}h_{t-1} + b_{cl}) \qquad (13)$$

$$ot_t = \sigma(\omega_{xot}x_t + \omega_{hot}h_{t-1} + \omega_{clot}cl_t + b_{ot}) \qquad (14)$$

$$h_t = ot_t \odot \tanh(cl_t) \qquad (15)$$

LSTM is considered complex, and its enhancement is made to GRU, which we are planning to work on in future work.

4.5 Enhancement Using GAN

The advancements in intrusion detection system using deep learning are suffering from insufficient data. Imbalanced data and missing sample data do not allow the models to train sufficiently to work and give robust results. GAN has the capabilities of generating fake data. Using GAN, we generate synthetic data to fulfil the lack of imbalanced data and missing samples in turn results in an increase in the accuracy of the model. GAN was first proposed by Goodfellow et al. [10], which estimates through adversarial technique.

$$\min_{G} \max_{G} V(D, G) = E_{x\ p_{\text{data}}(x)}\Big[\log D(x)\Big]$$
$$+ E_{z\ p_z(z)}\Big[\log(1 - D(G(z)))\Big]$$

The GAN-assisted intrusion detection system mainly focuses on the data set. The NSL-KDD data set contains 41 features, and each feature has data in terms of nominal, binary and numeric datatypes. Even after thorough enhancement from the KDD data set, some of the problems like imbalanced data and sparsity are known. Hence, we use GAN to create some fake data on which the IDS is trained to increase the accuracy of the prediction. In our proposed model, we have four modules as follows: (1) database module, (2) intrusion detection system module, (3) decision-making module, (4) data collection and data synthesis module. The overall system can be explained using the below figure. The data collection module collects data from the network using various analysers and techniques, which constitutes different features. In our system, we use the NSL-KDD data set, which is collected from the real-time scenario. The data synthesis module contains GAN, which continuously generates data that are similar to the data collected from the real-time scenario. A special field is attached to the data to distinguish the source of the data. The field contains two types of classes: pending and synthetic. The pending states that the data are not tested on the IDS system to result in better accuracy, which is dependent on the decision-making module. The IDS is trained with the data, which contains real data and synthetic data and the results of accuracy on test with some test data. Again, the IDS is trained containing pending data, and accuracy is calculated with some test data. If accuracy with pending data results to be more than real and synthetic data, the pending data are made to synthetic data and stored into the database. Otherwise, pending data are rejected and removed. Figure 6 shows about the enhancement architecture to detect the intrusion in the network.

5   Evaluation Metrics

We consider the following metrics to evaluate the models. The comparison is made before and after enhancement using GAN also. We generate a confusion matrix that consists of the below information. To perform the evolution process, measures are shown in Tables 1 and 2.

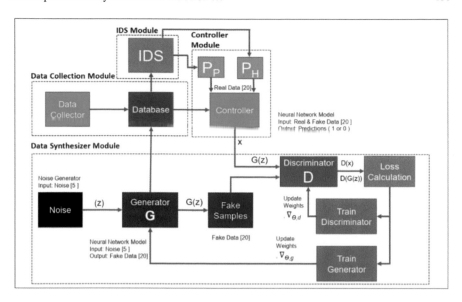

Fig. 6 Architecture of GAN-assisted intrusion detection system

Table 1 Indicators of evaluation

Indicator	Actual label	Prediction
True positive, TP	Attack	Attack
False positive, FP	Normal	Attack
True negative, TN	Normal	Normal
False negative, FN	Attack	Normal

Table 2 Evaluation metrics

Attack type	Description
Accuracy	Defined as the percentage of correctly classified records over the total number of records
Precision (P)	Defined as the % ratio of the number of true positives (TP) records divided by the number of true positives (TP) and false positives (FP) classified records. $P = \text{TP}/(\text{TP} + \text{FP}) \times 100\%$
Recall (R)	Defined as the % ratio of number of true positives records divided by the number of true positives and false negatives (FN) classified records. $R = \text{TP}/(\text{TP} + \text{FN}) \times 100\%$
F-measure (F)	Defined as the harmonic mean of precision and recall and represents a balance between them. $F = 3.P.R/(P + R)$

Table 3 Comparison table of algorithms

Architecture	NSL-KDD data set				Synthetic data set			
	ACC	PRE	REC	$F1$	ACC	PRE	REC	$F1$
CNN	0.76	0.63	0.56	0.59	0.78	0.69	0.64	0.85
DNN	0.79	0.62	0.61	**0.63**	0.8	0.68	0.69	0.67
Simple RNN	0.77	**0.64**	0.56	0.58	0.77	**0.71**	0.68	0.64
LSTM	**0.81**	0.63	**0.61**	0.61	**0.84**	0.7	**0.72**	**0.87**

Bold values shows that improved the performace comparatively to other models

6 Results and Analysis

We made overall evaluation of the deep learning algorithms on the data set NSL-KDD. Trails are executed twice on the NSL-KDD data set and synthetic NSL-KDD data set. The results are tabulated using the evaluation metrics listed. All the experiments are made to run for 100 epochs.

Table 3 shown is comparative analysis of both data sets with deep learning models. We showed results of 100 epochs which are more than enough to show the contrast of variations in the results. Generated data set of NSL-KDD has shown a significant difference in the results in increasing accuracy, recall and f1-score of the classification done. The synthetic data set can eliminate problems faced by the NSL-KDD data set beforehand, which in turn shows less accurate classification.

Deep learning architectures are more robust in the sense of representing data in hierarchical form, and temporal data can be more robustly analysed by deep learning architectures than machine learning architectures.

7 Conclusion and Future Work

The conclusion that can be made clear from the above analysis is that generating fake data using generative adversarial networks can boost up the accuracy of the classification of the deep learning model. The long short-term memory-based deep learning algorithm is producing better accurate results using the synthetic NSL-KDD data set. We are discovering more data sets and mechanisms to work and develop robust intrusion detection system in our future research work.

References

1. Anderson JP et al (1980) Computer security threat monitoring and surveillance. Technical report, James P. Anderson Co., Fort Washington, PA

2. Sekhar CH, Rao KV (2020) A study: machine learning and deep learning approaches for intrusion detection system. In: Smys S, Senjyu T, Lafata P (eds) Second international conference on computer networks and communication technologies. ICCNCT 2019. Lecture notes on data engineering and communications technologies, vol 44. Springer, Cham

3. Saranya T, Sridevi S, Deisy C, DucChung T, AhamedKhan MKA (2020) Performance analysis of machine learning algorithms in intrusion detection system: a review. Proc Comput Sci 171. https;//doi.org/10.1016/j.procs.2020.04.133

4. Sekhar C, Rao KV, Prasad MIIMK (2020) comparison performance of machine learning techniques for intrusion detection system; a review. i-manager's J Comput Sci 7(4).55 61. https://doi.org/10.26634/jcom.7.4.17108

5. Sekhar C, Venkata Rao K, Krishna Prasad MHM (2021) Deep learning algorithms for intrusion detection systems: extensive comparison analysis. Turkish J Comput Math Educ 12(11)

6. Vinayakumar R, Soman KP, Poornachandran P (2017) Applying convolutional neural network for network intrusion detection. ICACCI 2017, pp 1222–1228. https://ieeexplore.ieee.org/abstract/document/8126009

7. Vinayakumar R, Soman KP, Poornachandran P (2017) Evaluation of recurrent neural network and its variants for intrusion detection system (IDS) has accepted in special issue on big data searching, mining, optimization & securing (BSMOS) peer to peer cloud-based networks in IJISMD, 2017. https://www.igi-global.com/article/evaluation-of-recurrent-neural-network-and-its-variants-for-intrusion-detection-system-ids/204371

8. Vinayakumar R, Soman KP, Poornachandran P (2017) Evaluating effectiveness of shallow and deep networks to intrusion detection system. ICACCI 2017, pp 1282–1289. https://ieeexplore.ieee.org/document/8126018

9. Liu H, Lang B (2019) Machine learning and deep learning methods for intrusion detection systems: a survey. Appl Sci MDPI.https://doi.org/10.3390/app9204396

10. Goodfellow I, Pouget J, Mirza M, Xu B, Warde D, Ozair S, Courville AC, Bengio Y (2020) Generative adversarial networks. Commun ACM.https://doi.org/10.1145/3422622

11. Shahriar MH, Haque NI, Rahman MA, Alonso M (2020) G-IDS: generative adversarial networks assisted intrusion detection system. In: 2020 IEEE 44th annual computers, software, and applications conference (COMPSAC), 2020. https://doi.org/10.1109/COMPSAC48688.2020.0-218

Indian Sign Language Detection Using YOLOv3

N. Mallikarjuna Swamy, H. S. Sumanth, Keerthi, C. Manjunatha, and R. Sumathi

Abstract Communication is one of the greatest gifts mankind has ever got. People with communication disabilities find it hard to communicate in a way most people do. Deaf people can communicate or express their thoughts through sign language. In this paper, an attempt has been made to enable deaf people to input the message in sign language that the person is trying to convey. The experimental setup consists of two stages, namely dataset creation and object detection. In the dataset creation phase, the image dataset is created for each Indian sign language (ISL) alphabet. In the object detection phase, the model is trained on the dataset created using the You Only Look Once version-3 (YOLOv3) algorithm, and recognition of ISL alphabets is performed using the trained model. YOLOv3 convolutional neural Network (CNN) uses darknet-53 as a backbone network. CNN is responsible for feature extraction. The effectiveness of the proposed method is validated on a test dataset containing 50 images. The proposed system achieves an average accuracy of 82%.

Keywords Convolutional neural network · You Only Look Once version-3 · Object detection · Darknet-53 · Google Colab · Indian sign language

1 Introduction

The ability to communicate is a special gift to mankind. One cannot deny the fact that communication has shaped human evolution and helped us to share knowledge and express our thoughts. There are people with communication disabilities who find it difficult to communicate in a way most people do. The deaf community forms a major section of this population with communication disabilities. According to World Health Organization (WHO), nearly, 466 million people were identified to have hearing disabilities till 2018. Around 7 million people were found to have

N. Mallikarjuna Swamy (✉) · H. S. Sumanth · Keerthi · C. Manjunatha · R. Sumathi
Siddaganga Institute of Technology, Tumakuru, Karnataka, India

R. Sumathi
e-mail: rsumathi@sit.ac.in

© The Author(s), under exclusive license to Springer Nature Singapore Pte Ltd. 2022   157
C. Satyanarayana et al. (eds.), *High Performance Computing and Networking*,
Lecture Notes in Electrical Engineering 853,
https://doi.org/10.1007/978-981-16-9885-9_13

similar disabilities reported as per the 2011 census of India. Several attempts have been made to overcome the problems faced by people with hearing disabilities like the use of sign languages. Conversing using sign language has proven to be very effective for people with hearing disabilities. The sign languages have their grammar which makes use of hand gestures, facial expressions, etc. Though deaf people can converse effectively using sign language, communication becomes challenging when a deaf person needs to communicate with a person who doesn't know sign language. To overcome this challenge, there is a need for a system that can effectively recognize the sign language in real time.

Today's advanced technology has enabled us to solve a variety of complex problems in our society. In the area of sign language recognition, there are two ways to recognize signs: glove-based and vision-based recognition [1]. Several sensors are used in glove-based recognition in which movements of fingers are captured. Glove-based recognition systems are not feasible in real time because gloves with sensors are not accessible to everyone. The vision-based recognition takes images or video as input and recognizes the sign language.

In this paper, vision-based system is proposed to recognize the ISL alphabets. At first, an image dataset for ISL alphabets is created. Then, the model was trained on the dataset using the YOLOv3 algorithm. The trained model is used to detect the alphabets of ISL. YOLOv3 is an object detection algorithm. The entire image is processed only once with a single CNN; due to which, YOLOv3 is faster in object detection. Further, the algorithm maintains a high range of accuracy. Speed and accuracy make YOLOv3 a better choice for real-time sign language recognition.

Upcoming sections of the paper are organized as follows: Section 2 gives an abstract view of the related works. Section 3 explains YOLOv3, darknet-53 architecture, and the working of YOLOv3. In Sect. 4, we discuss Indian sign language. Section 5 deals with sign language detection using the YOLOv3 algorithm. The experimental setup and results are summarized in Sect. 6. Section 7 concludes the research paper.

2 Related Works

Karishma et al. [2] proposed a system that automatically recognizes ISL and translates it into a textual form, based on features combination of Hu invariant moment and shape descriptors. The system is capable of providing a 96% recognition rate.

A vision-based approach for automatic recognition of hand gestures in ISL is proposed in [3]. Artificial neural networks and digital image processing techniques are used for sign recognition. The trained model achieves an accuracy of 90.11%.

Muneer et al. [4] describe extracting features from the input video using 3DCNN approach. The extracted features are fed to the softmax layer which uses a softmax function that gives the probability for each class. The authors have considered three types of datasets. The system achieved accuracy rates of 100, 98.12, and 76.7% in signer-dependent mode and 34.9, 84.33, and 70% in signer-independent mode on same dataset.

Sun [1] also published a paper on hand gestures recognition using the Gaussian mixture model. The hand gesture (area) is extracted from the input image using AdaBoost, which is based on Haar features. After extraction of the area of the hand, gesture tracking is achieved using the CamShift algorithm. Then, the classification of the gesture is achieved using a CNN.

Trupti et al. [5] developed a portable-assistive text reader using Raspberry Pi. Text detection is achieved by the optical character recognition method, but it fails to recognize the text in Italic format. To overcome this drawback, convolutional recurrent neural network (CRNN) method is used. The recurrent layers predict a label distribution for each sequence, and the transcription layer finds the label sequence with the highest probability for frame prediction.

The paper by Muthu et al. [6] uses dynamic gesture recognition to recognize Indian sign language gestures. A machine learning algorithm called fuzzy c-means (FCM) clustering is to train the model and to predict the hand gestures. They classify the video and extract features using OpenCV. The proposed model had an accuracy of 75% while detecting gestures in ISL.

In a similar work by Bhumika et al. [7] to detect the gestures in ISL, the system uses k-nearest correlated neighbor (K-NCN) algorithm. Histograms of oriented gradients (HOG) and scale invariant feature transform (SIFT) are used for feature extraction, and the features are fused using the K-NCN algorithm. Classification when performed on the complete set of 26 gestures yielded an accuracy of 78.84% using HOG features, 80% using SIFT features, and 90% using the fusion of both.

Suharjito [8] developed a real-time hand gesture recognition system by implementing the i3d inception model. When the model was trained for the first time, it achieved accuracy around 0–20%; then, the model was trained with a unique signer which resulted in 100% accuracy. The authors concluded that this model is too overfit because of very-low validation accuracy.

3 YOLOv3 Algorithm

YOLOv3 algorithm, darknet-53 architecture, and working of YOLOv3 are discussed in the subsequent sub-sections.

3.1 Introduction to YOLOv3

YOLOv3 is a neural network-based real-time object detection algorithm. YOLO is an acronym for "You Only Look Once" because it requires only one forward pass through the network to detect objects [13]. YOLOv3 is an improvement over the previous version of YOLO [14] with a 28.2 mean average precision (mAP) and detection speed of 22 ms for a 320 × 320 image. YOLOv3 CNN makes use of darknet-53 as a backbone network for feature extraction [9] which is explained in the next sub-section. It not only predicts classes but also identifies the location of the object in the image in the form of a bounding box. Here, class refers to the label of the object in the output, for example, an object identified might have the label as a car in the output. The bounding box is a rectangular box enclosing the object in the image. Since it uses a single deep CNN, it is fast and accurate, making it a better option for real-time object detection. YOLOv3 is also generalizable, meaning that the model performs well on new kinds of images in a class.

3.2 Darknet-53 and YOLOv3 CNN

Darknet-53 is a convolutional neural network and is composed of 53 convolutional layers. A CNN is a kind of deep neural network which is mainly used in object detection, image classification, and other tasks. CNN is specialized for detecting the patterns in data.

Darknet-53 is particularly useful for analyzing image data. CNN has convolutional layers. Each convolutional layer applies various filters to the image. These filters extract features from the image. The filters in the initial layers detect geometric features in the image such as edges, shapes, and curves. The convolutional layers and the deeper layers detect features particular to an object like face, hands and a complete object like a person, respectively.

Darknet-53 is a hybrid of 19 layers deep darknet-19 and residual network (ResNet) [9]. Improvement in darknet-53 is achieved by the introduction of skip connections and the addition of more convolutional layers to darknet-19 CNN. Skip connections are introduced by ResNet to improve the training of a deeper neural network, in which the output of one layer is fed as an input to the next layers by skipping some layers. Figure 1 shows the architecture of darknet-53 [9].

YOLOv3 CNN uses darknet-53 as a backbone network. In YOLOv3 CNN, there are 106 fully convolutional layers, in which 53 additional layers are stacked over 53 layers of darknet-53.

3.3 YOLOv3 Algorithm

Definitions of the terms used in YOLOv3 algorithm are listed below:

- Class probability—class probability is a measure of the probability of the presence of an object in the grid cell.
- Ground truth box—the ground truth box is the actual bounding box of the object in the test image.

Type	Filters	Size	Output
Convolutional	32	3 × 3	256 × 256
Convolutional	64	3 × 3 / 2	128 × 128
Convolutional	32	1 × 1	
1× Convolutional	64	3 × 3	
Residual			128 × 128
Convolutional	128	3 × 3 / 2	64 × 64
Convolutional	64	1 × 1	
2× Convolutional	128	3 × 3	
Residual			64 × 64
Convolutional	256	3 × 3 / 2	32 × 32
Convolutional	128	1 × 1	
8× Convolutional	256	3 × 3	
Residual			32 × 32
Convolutional	512	3 × 3 / 2	16 × 16
Convolutional	256	1 × 1	
8× Convolutional	512	3 × 3	
Residual			16 × 16
Convolutional	1024	3 × 3 / 2	8 × 8
Convolutional	512	1 × 1	
4× Convolutional	1024	3 × 3	
Residual			8 × 8
Avgpool		Global	
Connected		1000	
Softmax			

Fig. 1 Darknet-53 architecture [9]

- Intersection over Union (IoU)—IoU gives a measure of how accurate is the predicted bounding box. Figure 2 illustrates the area of intersection and area of union between the predicted bounding box and the ground truth box. IoU is calculated using the formula given below:

$$IoU = \frac{\text{Area of intersection}}{\text{Area of union}} \qquad (1)$$

- *Confidence score*—confidence score for a bounding box reflects:

  - how sure the model is that the box contains an object.
  - how accurate the predicted bounding box is.

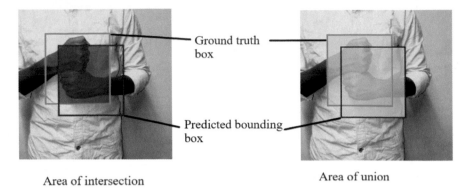

Area of intersection   Area of union

Fig. 2 Intersection and union of area between predicted bounding box and ground truth box

The value for the confidence score ranges from 0—indicating the absence of an object, to 1—indicating the presence of an object with full confidence. It is the product of class probability and IoU.

For object detection, YOLOv3 divides the input image into $S \times S$ grid cells as shown in Fig. 3. For every grid cell, it works by predicting the class and a bounding box for objects present in that grid cell. The algorithm calculates class probability, bounding box coordinates in each cell. Then, it calculates the confidence score for each predicted bounding box. After calculating the confidence score, two-stage filtering is applied. In two-stage filtering, first, it filters out bounding-boxes

Fig. 3 Division of image into $S \times S$ grid (e.g., $S = 10$)

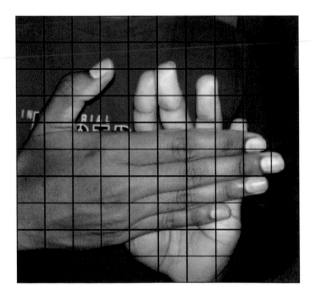

whose confidence score is lesser than the threshold value. Then, it applies non-max-suppression (NMS) to eliminate predictions with lower-class probability. Finally, it outputs the object detected along with the accuracy and bounding box.

In brief, the pseudocode for YOLOv3 object detection is as follows.

Input: *an image of size PxP pixels.*
Output: *object detected, bounding box, and accuracy*
begin
Divide input image into SxS grid
for each cell in grid-cells do:
  Predict the objects present in the cell
  Calculate the class probabilities and bounding box coordinates for each object predicted

  for each bounding-box in bounding-boxes do:
    Calculate IoU
    Calculate confidence score
    Append confidence score attribute to the bounding-box
  end for
end for
Apply two-stage filtering on bounding-boxes
Output object detected along with accuracy and bounding box
end

4 Indian Sign Language

A set of languages that use predefined gestures and expressions to communicate a message are known as sign languages. Fingerspelling, word-level sign vocabulary, and non-manual features are the three main parts of sign language. To pronounce words letter by letter, a fingerspelling is used. Sign language incorporates a variety of expressions like hand signals, body movements, and facial expressions to communicate. Deaf and other verbally impaired people use these expressions to convey their messages. Many countries have their own sign language, which vary greatly in terms of grammatical structure. Some of examples are American sign language (ASL), British sign language (BSL), Korean sign language (KSL), and Indian sign language. Couple of countries use sign language in accordance with their culture, such as India, which uses ISL [15].

ISL is a sign language that has its own syntax and semantics that originated in India. Both isolated and continuous signs are generated by ISL. An isolated sign is a precise hand arrangement and position depicted by a single image that relies on a specific hand gesture. A continuous sign is a sequence of images that depicts a moving gesture. ISL differs from other sign languages in a number of ways, for example, two

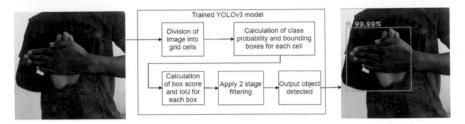

Fig. 4 Proposed system architecture

hands are used to frame various characters. The ISL gestures comprise of alphabets, numbers, animals, colors, days, family, and relations, food, fruits, games, months, places, travel, etc. ISL is used as a standard reference to capture sign language gestures for the image dataset.

5   Sign Language Detection Using YOLOv3 Algorithm

The architecture of the proposed system is depicted in Fig. 4. The proposed system recognizes Indian Sign Language alphabets. To achieve this, the system makes use of an object detection model trained on a custom ISL dataset using YOLOv3.

The system takes a test image or a video containing an ISL gesture as input. Before processing, the image is resized to 320×320 pixels as per the model configuration. Then, the image is processed in a single forward pass. After processing, the model outputs recognized ISL alphabet. The output consists of detected ISL alphabet, bounding box enclosing the gesture, and prediction accuracy. Similarly, detection can also be performed on frames from the camera feed.

6   Experiments and Results

6.1   Experimental Setup

The experimental setup consists of two stages, namely dataset creation and object detection.

Dataset Creation. The dataset is created for each alphabet. The dataset comprises 1000 images for each alphabet. Then, labeling is carried out using Make-sense [10] online tool. Figure 5 depicts the labeling of the images using the Make-sense tool. It is free to use online tool which offers labeling in various formats such as CSV, YOLO, and COCO-JSON. The captured images are loaded into the tool. Then, labeling is done for each image by locating the object with a bounding box. Once the labeling is completed, annotations are exported in YOLO format.

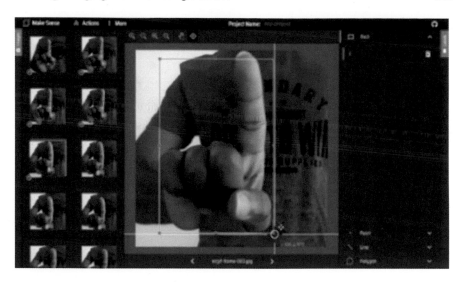

Fig. 5 Labeling images using Make-sense tool [10]

Figure 6 depicts sample ISL alphabet images used to create the dataset.

Object Detection. Object detection comprises of training and detection/inference phase. Phases are as follows:

Training Phase. The model has been trained on the Google-colab [11] cloud platform which offers 12.72 GB of GPU for free. The darknet-53 framework is built after cloning darknet from the GitHub repository [12]. The training dataset is loaded from Google drive to the data directory in darknet. The YOLOv3 configuration file is customized for training based on our dataset and model requirements. Then, the pre-trained weights for convolutional layers are downloaded. The model is trained on the custom dataset using pre-trained weights.

During training, the image dataset is divided into batches which are further divided into sub-batches according to the specifications in the configuration file. YOLOv3 performs 2000 iterations for each alphabet (i.e., per class). YOLOv3 saves the weights as a backup for every 1000 iterations. In each iteration, a batch of images is processed to adjust the weights of the neural network accordingly. This weights file is a binary file that stores the weights of the neural network model efficiently. Once the training is completed, the final weights of the custom object detector are saved.

Detection or Inference Phase. The detection process is done on the Google Colab cloud platform using the trained model. Before testing, the configuration file is customized for the testing process. Then, testing of the custom object detector is performed over a set of 50 images of size 320 × 320. For each test image, the model returns the ISL alphabet identified, the accuracy of detection, and a bounding box enclosing the gesture in the image.

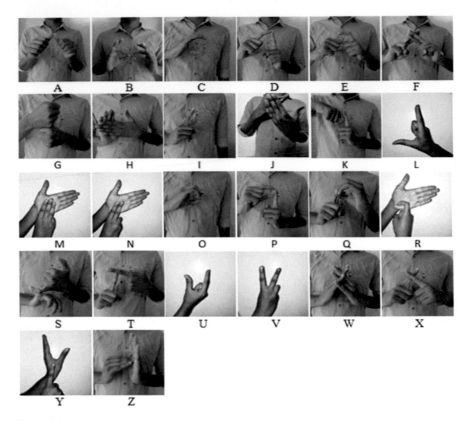

Fig. 6 ISL image dataset

6.2 Results

When the person with a hearing disability inputs an ISL alphabet as a gesture, the model detects the intended alphabet the person wants to input. The detection process recognizes the ISL alphabets in the image along with accuracy and bounding box. Some of the letters were detected with slightly less accuracy. For a test dataset of 50 images containing different ISL alphabet gestures, an average accuracy of 82% is achieved at a threshold of 0.3.

The proposed system gives better results in comparison to the models trained using FCM which has an accuracy of 75% [7]. Figure 7 shows accuracy of detected ISL alphabet gestures.

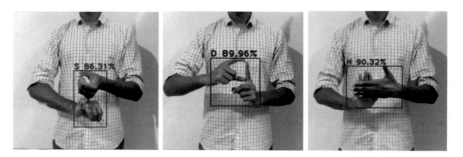

Fig. 7 Recognition of ISL alphabets *S*, *D,* and *H* along with accuracy

7 Conclusion

Communication is an important aspect of life. People with hearing disabilities converse using sign languages more conveniently than any other method. This method is difficult to follow for normal people and a computer system. By recognition of ISL alphabets, the proposed system aims to ease the communication between the deaf and people who don't know ISL. Sign language gesture detection in real time is done using a neural network model trained using YOLOv3. The model recognizes the ISL alphabet from the given input which can be an image or a video. Using the model, an average accuracy of 82% was achieved in the detection process. Unlike RCNN and faster RCNN, the detection is performed in a single forward pass which makes the proposed technique very fast, accurate, and suitable for real-time object detection. In future work, the model can be improved by training the model to detect more sign language gestures like numbers, colors, family, relations, and emotions.

References

1. Sun J-H, Zhang S-B, Yang J-K, Ji G-R (2018) Research on the hand gesture recognition based on deep learning. In: 12th international symposium on antennas, propagation and EM theory (ISAPE), Hangzhou, China
2. Dixit K, Jalal AS (2016) Automatic Indian sign language recognition system. Journal 2(5):99–110
3. Adithya V, Vinod PR, Gopalakrishnan U (2013) Artificial neural network based method for Indian sign language recognition. In: IEEE conference on information and communication technologies
4. Al-Hammadi M, Muhammad G, Abdul W, Alsulaiman M, Bencherif MA, Mekhtiche MA (2020) Hand gesture recognition for sign language using 3DCNN. IEEE
5. Shah T, Parshionikar S (2019) Efficient portable camera based text to speech converter for blind person. In: International conference on intelligent sustainable systems (ICISS), Palladam, India
6. Muthu Mariappan H, Gomathi V (2019) Real-time recognition of Indian sign language. In: Second international conference on computational intelligence in data science (ICCIDS-2019). Chennai, India

7. Gupta B, Shukla P, Mittal A (2016) K-nearest correlated neighbor classification for indian sign language gesture recognition using feature fusion. In: International conference on computer communication and informatics (ICCCI-2016), 2016/01/08, Coimbatore, India
8. Suharjito HG, Thiractta N, Nugroho A (2018) Sign language recognition using modified convolutional neural network model. In: The first 2018 INAPR international conference, 7 Sept 2018, Jakarta, Indonesia
9. Redmon J, Farhadi A (2018) YOLOv3: an incremental improvement. arXiv
10. Make-sense. https://www.makesense.ai/. Last accessed 2021/07/30
11. Google Colab. https://colab.research.google.com. Last accessed 2021/07/30
12. Redmon J. Darknet: open source neural networks in C. https://pjreddie.com/darknet, 2013–2016
13. Redmon J, Divvala S, Girshick R, Farhadi A (2016) You only look once: unified, real-time object detection. In: IEEE conference on computer vision and pattern recognition. Honolulu, HI, USA
14. Redmon J, Farhadi A (2017) Yolo9000: better, faster, stronger. In: IEEE conference on computer vision and pattern recognition (CVPR). IEEE
15. Talking hands. https://www.talkinghands.co.in. Last accessed 2021/07/30

Feature Extraction-Based Phishing URL Detection Using Machine Learning Techniques

Kolati Sri Rama Chandra Murthy, Tanay Bhattacharya, and Narendran Rajagopalan

Abstract Phishing URLs are one of the major contributors in cybercrimes. Internet users are trapped by phishing URLs that are difficult to distinguish from legitimate URLs. The purpose of this research is to identify phishing URLs based on address bar features along with behavioral features. We have considered and performed cross-validation technique on multiple machine learning algorithms and derived that decision tree algorithm works effectively in classifying phishing URLs based on the certain identified features. The dataset used in this research has 9581 data points and 41 features. Finally, we are able to achieve 97% accuracy in finding phishing URLs which is relatively better accuracy than other existing detection models.

Keywords Phishing URLs · Machine learning algorithms · Support vector machine · Decision tree · Naïve Bayes

1 Introduction

Phishing is the most popular and easiest way to steal user's sensitive information in a fraudulent manner. Millions of new domain names are getting registered every day worldwide and finding out phishing domain/URL among them is a challenging task.

As per Anti-Phishing Working Group (APWG), phishing is a crime employing both social engineering and technical subterfuge to steal consumer's personal identity/sensitive data [1]. As per recent statistics from APWG, phishing that target webmail and software as a service (SaaS) users continued to be the biggest category

K. S. R. C. Murthy (✉) · T. Bhattacharya
NCIIPC, New Delhi, India
e-mail: sreeram.kolati@nciipc.gov.in

T. Bhattacharya
e-mail: tanay.b@nic.in

N. Rajagopalan
NIT, Puducherry, India
e-mail: narendran@nitpy.ac.in

© The Author(s), under exclusive license to Springer Nature Singapore Pte Ltd. 2022   169
C. Satyanarayana et al. (eds.), *High Performance Computing and Networking*,
Lecture Notes in Electrical Engineering 853,
https://doi.org/10.1007/978-981-16-9885-9_14

with 34.7% of total identified phishing domains followed by financial institutions with 18% phishing domains [2]. By looking at the large amount of domain registration on daily basis, our research focus should be to adopt automated technique to effectively detect phishing URLs.

There are numerous approaches that have been proposed by various researchers to detect phishing URL. The very first mechanism works on blacklist method. Here, a list of blacklisted domains/URLs is maintained and any input URL can easily check against existing blacklisted domains/URLs to confirm whether it is phishing URL or not. But blacklist mechanism cannot hold all the phishing URLs at all times, and most of the cases, the list is not up to date. The second mechanism depends on finding out the crucial domain features to help to decide any given URL is phishing URL or not. In our research, we have identified vulnerable features of a domain name/URL and applied machine learning techniques to design detection model to classify phishing URLs.

Section 2 describes literature survey done to find out phishing URLs, Sect. 3 describes existing methodologies used for the detection of phishing URLs and our proposed solution. Section 4 describes implementation details. Section 5 describes results and discussions. Section 6 describes conclusion and future scope.

2 Literature Survey

Identifying phishing domains is challenging because of enhancements in technology and lack of proper cyber security awareness among Internet users. As per APWG report, 78% of all phishing domains use SSL protection [2] so identifying phishing URLs is not that much easy for normal Internet user.

Phishing Web sites features classification based on *extreme learning machine model* proposed by Yasin Sonmez and team have designed a model to find out phishing URLs using machine learning algorithms [3]. This research considered phishing Web site features such as address bar-based features, abnormal-based features, HTML, and Java script-based features and domain-based features. Considering these features to determine the URL legitimacy works well but most of the times user's sensitive information has been stolen by using forms or input dialog boxes as and when Web site is loaded, this research did not consider those dynamic-natured features in the process of evolution. Yasin Sonmez and team achieved 95.3% of accuracy in classifying the phishing domains by using extreme learning machine model.

Extreme learning machine model formula:

$$y(p) = \sum_{j=1}^{m} \beta j.g \left(\sum_{j=1}^{n} Wi, j.Xi + bj \right) \tag{1}$$

- *Xi* indicates input vector
- *y(p)* indicates output vector
- *m* and *n* are neuron count
- *Wi, j* indicates input layer to hidden layer weights
- *βj* indicates output layer to hidden layer weights
- *bj* represents the threshold value of neurons in the hidden layer
- *g()* is an activation function.

Nuttapong Sanglerdsinlapachai and ArnonRungsawang proposed a model named Carnegie Mellon Anti-Phishing and Network Analysis Tool (CANTINA) to find out phishing URLs using top page similarity feature [4]. This research proposed address bar features and domain top page similarity as input to machine learning models to train the model. Cosine similarity is used to calculate domain top page similarity. The evaluation result in terms of F-measure was up to 0.9250 with 7.50% of error rate. Phishing Web sites use *typo squatting* on URL as well as on webpage. This will change the similarity score based on common words as the same is computed using TF-IDF algorithm.

$$\text{Cosine Similarity}(A, B) = \frac{A.B}{|A| * |B|} \tag{2}$$

Detecting phishing Web site using machine learning has been proposed by Alkawaz and Steven [5] focused on blacklist URLs and effectiveness of their work relies only if input URL is in blacklist database, and hence, detection engine may miss out phishing URLs that are newly created. Therefore, considering only blacklist database or address bar feature may not give accurate results.

3 Methodology

3.1 Existing Methodology

Phishing Web site features classification based on extreme learning machine model proposed by Yasin Sonmez and team mentioned address bar-based features, abnormal-based features, HTML, and Java script-based features, and domain-based features that are useful in the process of identifying phishing URLs. Table 1 shows the list of features considered in their research.

Classification section in Yasin Sonmez's research was built on extreme learning machine (ELM) algorithm and achieved 95.3% accuracy. However, their dataset was tested on various other machine learning algorithms such as Naïve Bayes and support vector machine and produced similar results. During our research, we observed that 78% of all phishing sites are using SSL protection so considering SSL protection (HTTPS) as a feature to train model may not generate accurate results. Our research aimed at finding out phishing domain as and when it is registered so we removed age

Table 1 Features considered in existing methodology

S. No.	Input feature	S. No.	Input feature
1	Using IP address	16	SFH
2	Long URL to hide suspicious part	17	Submitting info to E-Mail
3	Using URL shortening service	18	Abnormal URL
4	URL having '@' symbol	19	Web site forwarding
5	Redirecting using '//'	20	Status bar customization
6	Adding prefix or suffix separated by '-'	21	Disabling right click
7	Sub-domain and multi-sub-domain	22	Using pop-up window
8	HTTPS	23	Iframe redirection
9	Domain registration length	24	Age of domain
10	Favicon	25	DNS record
11	Using non-standard port	26	Web site traffic
12	Existence of HTTPS in the domain part of the URL	27	Page rank
13	Request URL	28	Google Index
14	URL of anchor	29	No. of links pointing to page
15	Links in <Meta>, <Script> and <link> tags	30	Statistical reports-based feature

of the domain feature from model evolution since all the input domains/URLs are just born there is no difference in the age of the domain and we also do not consider page rank and Google page index features because those newly registered URLs may not get the top score in the indexing algorithms by the Google. In this process, we observed URL shortening service feature is the most commonly used feature by the banking and financial institutions for their regular use such as premium payment and all, so we discarded URL shortening service from the evolution.

3.2 Proposed Methodology

The objective of the proposed model is to achieve high phishing Web site detection accuracy as and when new phishing domain/URL is registered. Usually, all the newly registered domain are available in the Internet with one day delay so we are trying to find phishing domains as early as possible using our proposed methodology. In our proposed model, we have incorporated 41 features to classify phishing Web sites. These features are listed in Table 2. We did not consider few features which were considered in the existing research such as URL shortening service, Google Index,

Table 2 Proposed features

S. No.	Input feature	S. No.	Input feature
1	Using IP address	22	Favicon
2	Number of sub-domains	23	Host name length
3	Number of sensitive words	24	Insecure forms
4	Length of the URL	25	Relative form action
5	No. of Hyphen (-)	26	External form action
6	Path level	27	Abnormal form action
7	Number of Hyphen (-) in host name	28	Null self-redirected hyperlinks
8	Presence of '@' symbol	29	Domain name mismatch
9	Presence of '~' symbol	30	Fake link in status bar
10	Presence of '_' symbol	31	Submit information to E-Mail
11	Number of query components in URL	32	Iframe redirection
12	Number of '#' symbols in URL	33	Missing title in webpage
13	Number of '&' symbols in URL	34	Pop-up window
14	Number of numeric characters in URL	35	Images only in forms
15	Random string	36	External meta script links
16	Number of '.' In URL	37	Query length
17	Domain Name in sub domain	38	Double slash in path
18	Domain name in path	39	Number of '%' symbols
19	HTTPS in host name	40	Path length
20	External resource URLs	41	External hyper links
21	Embedded brand name		

HTTPS, and Page rank since these features won't contribute much in the process of identifying phishing URLs.

In our proposed model, we have considered 41 features and 9581 data points and trained the model using machine learning algorithm to identify phishing Web site. Figure 1 describes the block diagram for the proposed model. Since user data can be theft using *form actions* in a Web site, we proposed a model that considered on form actions as well. Table 3 shows additional features considered in our proposed model. Table 4 shows the excluded features in proposed model.

Ranganayakulu and Chellappan [6] have introduced a unique feature named sensitive words in phishing content, and we have considered number of such sensitive words that are used in the detection model. Table 5 shows those eight sensitive words.

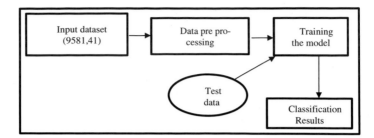

Fig. 1 Block diagram

Table 3 Additional features

S. No.	Input feature	S. No.	Input feature
1	Number of sensitive words	15	Hostname length
2	Number of '-'	16	Embedded brand name
3	Path level	17	External resource URLs
4	Number of '-' in host name	18	Insecure forms
5	Presence of '~'	19	Relative form action
6	Presence of '_'	20	External form action
7	Number of query components	21	Abnormal form action
8	Number of '#'	22	Null self-redirected links
9	Number of '&'	23	Domain name mismatch
10	Number of numerical characters	24	Missing title in page
11	Random string	25	Images on in forms
12	Number of '.'	26	Query length
13	Domain name in sub domain	27	Number of '%'
14	Domain name in path	28	Path length

Table 4 Excluded features

S. No.	Excluded feature	S. No.	Excluded feature
1	Google index	9	URL of anchor
2	Page rank	10	Request URL
3	Statistical report-based feature	11	Number of links pointing to page
4	Web site traffic	12	Using non-standard ports
5	DNS record	13	Domain registration length
6	Age of a domain	14	HTTPS
7	Disabling right click	15	Using URL shortening service
8	SFH	16	Abnormal URL

Table 5 Sensitive words

S. No.	Sensitive word	S. No.	Sensitive word
1	Account	5	Confirm
2	Login	6	Verify
3	Sign-in	7	Secure
4	Banking	8	Update

Based on the outcome of results generated post-cross-validation, we found decision tree algorithm that shows efficient results in classifying phishing Web sites than other machine learning algorithms such as SVM-Linear, SVM-RBF, and Naïve Bayes.

3.2.1 Support Vector Machine (SVM)

Data classification is the most common task in machine learning problems. The goal of classification algorithm is to keep the new data point in appropriate class. In case of support vector machine [7], a data point is viewed as a n-dimensional vector (Here $n = 41$) and we want to know whether we can separate such data points with $n - 1$ dimensional hyperplane. This is called linear classification model. We may use hyperplane to classify data instead of simple plane to classify data instead of simple line then the distance from hyperplane to the nearest data point on each side is maximized.

3.2.2 Naïve Bayes

Naïve Bayes [8] is an easiest model for constructing classification models. This model assumes that the value of a particular feature is independent of the value of any other feature given that class variable. In this model, each feature is going to contribute its decision probability independently to classify the data points.

$$P(A|B) = \frac{P(B|A).P(A)}{P(B)} \tag{3}$$

3.2.3 Decision Tree

Decision tree [9] is widely used predictive model in machine learning, statistics, and data mining. It is a tree-structured model constructed by inferring rules from the training data points. Internal nodes always represent decisions, and leaf nodes represent predictive classes. There are many implementations of decision trees available such as ID3 and more. In our model, we use Gini impurity to measure the quality of splits at each level.

$$\text{Gini Coefficient} = 1 - \sum_{k=1}^{n} (Pi, k) * (Pi, k) \tag{4}$$

$K = 1$ to n represents number of classes
Pi, k represents the fraction of nodes labeled with class 'k' in the ith node.

4 Implementation

Feature extraction-based phishing URL detection model has been implemented using decision tree machine learning algorithm. This model implementation follows the below steps:

1. Feature Extraction module: This module extracts 41 features from input URLs which are required for model building.
2. Data preprocessing module: This module eliminates duplicate data points and null values in the data points.
3. Cross-validation: K-fold cross-validation algorithm to find the best suitable machine learning model. We considered K as 10.
4. Model Training: Train the model using best suitable machine learning algorithm determined by K-fold cross-validation.
5. Model Testing: Test the model accuracy using test data.

Initially, we have collected 10000 data points and 48 features [10] and data preprocessing stage eliminated duplicate data points and less/no contribution features to make dataset more effective. Finally, input dataset is having 9581 data points and 41 features to train the model. Our dataset contains 4585 phishing domains and 4996 legitimate domains.

We performed tenfold cross-validation using input dataset on SVM, decision tree, and Naïve Bayes algorithms to test the mean accuracy of the models and found decision tree is giving efficient accuracy when compared with other machine learning algorithms. Finally, we implemented a model using decision tree algorithm with depth as '6' to classify phishing Web sites and achieved 97% accuracy which is higher than the existing models. We have taken depth as '6' because to make tree balanced and height of tree should not cross ($\log 2n$) where $n = $ number of features. Our model takes 41 features as input so max depth of the tree equals to 6.

4.1   Pseudocode

Algorithm 1: Feature extraction based phishing URL detection using Machine Learning Techniques

---

1. Import all required modules to perform data reading, cross validation and training the model.

2. load data.

3. Remove duplicate data points and low variance attributes.

4. use max_depth = 6 for decision tree.

5. Compute cross validation score, decision_tree_CV = cross_val_score(decision_tree_object,X,Y).

6. Train the model using decision tree classifier.

7. Test the model using test data.

---

5   Results and Discussions

The proposed model using 41 features of URL exhibits 97% of accuracy, whereas existing ELM model exhibited only 95.34% of accuracy. Table 6 describes the results when applied on different models. Table 7 describes the confusion matrix for decision tree model. Figure 2 shows how accuracy varies for all four-machine learning algorithm.

Table 6   Results on different ML models

Algorithm	Accuracy %	Precision %	Recall %	F1-Score %
SVM-Linear	94.5	95	95	95
SVM-RBF	90	91	91	91
Decision tree with max depth as '6'	97	97	97	97
Naïve Bayes	85	85	85	85

Table 7   Confusion matrix for decision tree

Confusion matrix	Predicted NO	Predicted YES
Actual NO	981	32
Actual YES	25	879

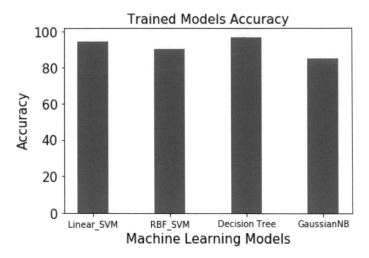

Fig. 2 Accuracy graph

6 Conclusion and Future Scope

Phishing attacks are accounted for more than 80% of all reported security incidents [11]. It is quite essential to prevent phishing attacks to control cybercrimes. Our proposed model takes 41 features of URL as input and shows 97% accuracy in finding out phishing Web sites. We recommend machine learning techniques to find out phishing Web sites as it proves to be an effective tool in finding out patterns in the Web site URLs. This research main was to identify phishing domains accurately for some specific organizations.

This research work can be proceeded further to enhance the accuracy of the model by using artificial neural networks (ANN) which can identify hidden patterns in Web site URLs more effectively.

References

1. Anti-Phishing Working Group Home page. https://apwg.org
2. Anti-Phishing Working Group's Phishing activity trends report 2nd quarter 2020. https://docs. apwg.org/reports/apwg_trends_report_q2_2020.pdf
3. Sonmez Y, Tuncer T. Phishing web sites features classification based on extreme learning machine. https://ieeexplore.ieee.org/document/8355342
4. Sanglerdsinlapachai N, Rungsawang A. Using domain top-page similarity feature in machine learning-based web phishing detection. https://ieeexplore.ieee.org/document/5432672
5. Alkawaz MH, Steven S. Detecting phishing website using machine learning. https://ieeexplore. ieee.org/document/9068728
6. Ranganayakulu D, Chellappan C. Detecting malicious URLs in E-Mail. https://www.sciencedi rect.com/science/article/pii/S2212671613000218

7. Detailed explanation on Support Vector Machine (SVM) by Wiki. https://en.wikipedia.org/wiki/Support_vector_machine
8. Detailed explanation on Naïve Bayes classifier (NB) by Wikipedia. https://en.wikipedia.org/wiki/Naive_Bayes_classifier
9. Detailed explanation on decision tree Classification by Wikipedia. https://en.wikipedia.org/wiki/Decision_tree_learning
10. Phishing dataset for machine learning. https://data.mendeley.com/datasets/h3cgnj8hft/1
11. Top cyber security facts, figures and statistics. https://www.csoonline.com/article/3153707/top-cybersecurity-facts-figures-and-statistics.html

A Slant Transform and Diagonal Laplacian Based Fusion Algorithm for Visual Sensor Network Applications

Radha Nainvarapu, Ranga Babu Tummala, and Mahesh Kumar Singh

Abstract Multi-focus image fusion has developed as a promising research area in the field of visual sensor networks, and its objective is to combine multiple images of the same scene into a single image with enhanced reliability and interpretation. But, the current fusion methods based on focus measures are not able to get the entire focused fused image as they neglect the diagonal neighbor pixels during the selection of the focused objects. In this paper, slant transform and diagonal Laplacian-based fusion algorithm is proposed. The slant transform with its less computational complexity, good energy compaction, and orthogonal properties make the fusion process simple and fast. And the diagonal Laplacian focus measure supports developing a focused image considering the diagonal pixels during the selection of focused objects. So the benefits of slant transform and diagonal Laplacian are utilized in our fusion algorithm for better fusion results. The performance of the proposed method is tested on artificial, natural, and mis-registered multi-focus images. The simulation outcomes specify that our fusion scheme show improved fusion results than other methods in terms of performance measures.

Keywords Diagonal Laplacian · Image fusion · Performance measures · Slant transform · Visual sensor networks

Supported by Aditya Engineering College.

R. Nainvarapu (✉)
Department of ECE, Aditya Engineering College, Surampalem, India
e-mail: radha.nainavarapu@aec.edu.in

R. B. Tummala
Department of ECE, RVR & JC College of Engineering, Chowdavaram, India

M. K. Singh
Accendere Knowledge Management Services, New Delhi, India
e-mail: mahesh.singh@accendere.co.in

1   Introduction

Due to the narrow depth of focus of sensors in visual sensor networks (VSN), it is not possible to get an image with all areas in focus. This makes it tough for VSN to analyze the images in surveillance, traffic, and industrial applications. The multi-focus image fusion overcomes this problem by combining images captured by cameras into a single fused image for better visualization and detection. The spatial and transform-based fusion methods are available in the literature. But, the spatial domain methods-[1–15] suffer from blurring and contrast reduction. Several multi-scale transform domain methods were developed in the literature like pyramid-based methods, multi-resolution singular value decomposition [7], wavelet-based methods, shearlet transform, and DCT-wavelet method [15]. But, kernels calculation is complex in [3–15] fusion methods. The problem of complexity in kernel calculation is reduced by using a fast and simple slant transform. Focus measures are also important for identifying the focused coefficients in the transform domain for effective image fusion. Diagonal Laplacian (DL) has recognized to be an effective focus measure in [4]. Thus, the advantages of slant transform (ST) and Diagonal Laplacian are deliberated for fusion in this paper.

2   Slant Transform

The 2-D Slant Transform (ST) of an image A is represented using Eq. (1)

$$[ST] = [S_N][A][S_N]^T \tag{1}$$

where $[S_N]$ is an $N \times N$ slant matrix. The inverse slant transform is given by Eq. (2)

$$[A] = [S_N]^T [ST][S_N] \tag{2}$$

The ST, recursive matrix of order $N \times N$ is given by Eq. (3)

$$S_N = \frac{1}{\sqrt{2}} \begin{bmatrix} 1 & 0 & & 1 & 0 & \\ a_N & b_N & 0 & -a_N & b_N & 0 \\ 0 & I(N/2)-2 & 0 & 0 & I(N/2)-2 \\ 1 & 0 & & 1 & 0 & \\ -b_N & a_N & 0 & b_N & a_N & 0 \\ 0 & I(N/2)-2 & 0 & 0 & I(N/2)-2 \end{bmatrix} \begin{bmatrix} S_{N/2} & 0 \\ 0 & S_{N/2} \end{bmatrix} \tag{3}$$

where I_N is the identity matrix of order $N \times N$, for $N = 2$, ST is defined as in Eq. (4)

$$S_2 = \frac{1}{\sqrt{2}} \begin{bmatrix} 1 & 1 \\ 1 & -1 \end{bmatrix} \tag{4}$$

The coefficients are calculated as in Eqs. (5) and (6)

$$a_N = \left[\frac{3N}{4(N^2 - 1)}\right]^{\frac{1}{2}} \tag{5}$$

$$b_N = \left[\frac{(N^2 - 4)}{4(N^2 - 1)}\right]^{\frac{1}{2}} \tag{6}$$

ST Properties:

i. It is real and orthogonal and is represented using Eq. (7)

$$[ST] = [ST]^T \tag{7}$$

ii. The ST is a non-sinusoidal fast transform, realized in $(N \log_2 N)$ operations on an $N \times 1$ vector.
iii. It has very good to excellent energy compaction for images.

3 Diagonal Laplacian (DL) Focus Measure

Diagonal Laplacian is used for the extraction of focused blocks of source images. Thelen et al. [4] proposed a DL for a pixel at (x, y) within its neighborhood $\Omega(x, y)$ and is calculated as in Eq. (8)

$$\phi(x, y) = \sum_{(i,j) \in \Omega(x,y)} \Delta_m I(i, j) \tag{8}$$

And the $\Delta_m I$ is calculated as in Eqs. (9–11) (considering neighbors in the x, y-directions and the diagonal neighbors):

$$\Delta_m I(i, j) = |I * L_X| + |I * L_Y| + |I * L_{X1}| + |I * L_{X2}| \tag{9}$$

$$L_X = [-1\ 2\ 1]; L_Y = L_X^T \tag{10}$$

$$L_{X1} = \frac{1}{\sqrt{2}} \begin{bmatrix} 0 & 0 & 1 \\ 0 & -2 & 0 \\ 1 & 0 & 0 \end{bmatrix}; L_{X2} = \frac{1}{\sqrt{2}} \begin{bmatrix} 1 & 0 & 0 \\ 0 & -2 & 0 \\ 0 & 0 & 1 \end{bmatrix} \tag{11}$$

where L_X and L_Y are convolution masks in x, y-directions and L_{X1} and L_{X2} are convolution masks in diagonal-directions.

4 Proposed Algorithm

The following steps are employed in the proposed algorithm:

1. Read A and B source images.
2. Transform RGB images in step1 to YCbCr images.
3. Divide the transformed images in step2 into blocks of size 16×16.
4. Apply 1-level Slant Transform for each block using (1). Denote the ith coefficients of blocks of transformed image A and B by TA_i and TB_i.
5. Compute the Diagonal Laplacian of each block TA_i and TB_i using (8–11).
6. Compare the Diagonal Laplacian focus measures of two corresponding blocks TA_i and TB_i, using the fusion rule in Eq.(12), to construct the ith focused fused block TF_i.

$$TF_i = \begin{cases} TF_i, & \text{if } \phi_i^A \geq \phi_i^B \\ TF_i, & \text{otherwise} \end{cases} \tag{12}$$

where TF_i are the focused blocks of fused image and ϕ_i^A, ϕ_i^B are the diagonal Laplacian focus measures of TA_i and TB_i block.

7. Apply Inverse Slant Transform on TF_i using Eq. (2) on selected focused blocks.
8. Convert fused image (F) in YCbCr to RGB.
9. Calculate PSNR, SSIM and FSIM of fused images using Eqs. (13–15).
10. Calculate SD, SF and MI of fused images using Eqs. (16–22).

5 Performance Measures

The performance measures for evaluating the performance of proposed method are.

5.1 Reference Measures

These measures are used to compare the fused image quality with a reference image.

i. Peak Signal to Noise Ratio (PSNR): It assesses the quality of fused image and is calculated using Eq. (13): where R is reference image, F is fused image, and RMSE is root mean square error.

$$PSNR = 10 \log_{10} \left(\frac{P_{max}^2}{\frac{1}{N \times N} \sum_{x=1}^{M} \sum_{y=1}^{N} [R(x, y) - F(x, y)]^2} \right) \tag{13}$$

ii. Structural Similarity Index Measure (SSIM): Similarity between R and F is calculated using SSIM as in Eq. (14):

$$\text{SSIM} = \frac{(2\mu_R\mu_F + C_1)(2\sigma_{\text{RF}} + C_2)}{(\mu_R^2 + \mu_F^2 + C_1)(\sigma_R^2 + \sigma_F^2 + C_2)} \tag{14}$$

iii. Feature Similarity Index Measure (FSIM): It measures the fused image quality using phase congruency (PC_m) and gradient (S_L) features as in Eq. (15).

$$\text{FSIM} = \frac{\sum_{x,y\in\Omega} S_L(x,y)PC_m(x,y)}{\sum_{x,y\in\Omega} PC_m(x,y)} \tag{15}$$

5.2 Non-reference Measures

These measures are used to compare the fused image quality without a reference image.

i. Standard Deviation (SD): It calculates the fused image contrast, using Eq. (16):

$$\sigma = \sqrt{\sum_{x=1}^{M}\sum_{y=1}^{N}[F(x,y) - \overline{F}]^2}, \overline{F} = \frac{1}{N \times N}\sum_{x=1}^{N}\sum_{y=1}^{N}F(x,y) \tag{16}$$

ii. Spatial Frequency (SF): It measures the fused image clarity level using Eqs. (17–19):

$$\text{RF} = \sqrt{\frac{1}{N \times N}\sum_{x=1}^{N}\sum_{y=2}^{N}[F(x,y) - F(x,y-1)]^2} \tag{17}$$

$$\text{CF} = \sqrt{\frac{1}{N \times N}\sum_{x=1}^{N}\sum_{y=2}^{N}[F(x,y) - F(x-1,y)]^2} \tag{18}$$

$$\text{SF} = \sqrt{\text{RF}^2 + \text{CF}^2} \tag{19}$$

iii. Mutual Information (MI): The information transferred from A, B to F is calculated using Eqs. (20–22):

$$I_{\text{AF}}(F, A) = \sum p(F, A)\log_2\left(\frac{p(F, A)}{p(F)p(A)}\right) \tag{20}$$

$$I_{\text{BF}}(F, B) = \sum p(F, B)\log_2\left(\frac{p(F, B)}{p(F)p(B)}\right) \tag{21}$$

$$\text{MI} = I_{\text{AF}} + I_{\text{BF}} \tag{22}$$

6 Simulation Results and Analysis

The proposed method is experimented on different multi-focus images. The first experiment is executed on artificial images produced by the convolution of the reference image with a 5×5 Gaussian filter. Lena and Airplane standard reference images of the USC-SIPI database are considered for fusion. Both the reference and artificial source images of Lena are presented in Fig. 1.

The fusion results of Lena and Airplane are analyzed by applying the slant transform-based proposed fusion method and the existing transform-based fusion methods [2, 7, 8, 10, 14, 15]. Fused images of Lena from different fusion methods are compared in Figs. 2a –2g. One can observe from Fig. 2a that the shift-variance property of the method [8] produces ringing artifacts in a fused image. The fused image of method [7] in Fig. 2b displays edge breaks. The fused image of method [10] in Fig. 2c shows a contrast reduction. The fused image of method [14] in Fig. 2d also shows edge discontinuities at the border of blurred and distinct regions. The fused image of method [2], in Fig. 2e presents the blurring of edges and decreases in contrast. In Fig. 2f, the fused image of method [15] shows blocking artifacts. It can be perceived from Fig. 2g that the fused image of the proposed method is free from artifacts and have good contrast. Similar annotations are found in experiment with Airplane.

The performance measures of different fusion methods are defined in Table 1. The high values of PSNR, SSIM, FSIM as well as MI, SD, and SF of the proposed method in Table 1, specify that diagonal Laplacian can well extract the focused coefficients in slant transform domain compared to the methods in [2, 7, 8, 10, 14, 15].

Natural multi-focus Lytro database standard images, Man and map with foreground and background focus areas are considered for fusion in the second experiment. The man source images are shown in Fig. 3a, b. The man fused images in Fig. 3c–i demonstrates that both foreground and background areas are focused in the fused image of proposed method compared to other methods. Similar annotations are established in an experiment with map images.

(a)   (b)   (c)

Fig. 1 **a** Reference image, **b**, **c** artificial images

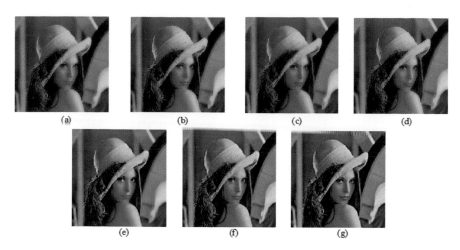

Fig. 2 Fused images of Lena **a** Wang et al. [8], **b** Naidu [7], **c** Li et al. [10], **d** Pujar [14], **e** Li et al. [2], **f** Kumar [15] and **g** proposed method

Table 1 Performance measures comparison

Images	Fusion method	Reference measures			Non-reference measures		
		PSNR	SSIM	FSIM	MI	SD	SF
Lena	Wang et al. [8]	29.9914	0.9811	0.9387	6.2473	56.3316	14.8567
	Naidu [7]	31.1280	0.9863	0.9584	6.2639	56.6330	16.7739
	Li et al. [10]	31.9994	0.9893	0.9636	6.4135	56.5674	15.8821
	Pujar [14]	32.3161	0.9903	0.9675	6.3738	56.6504	17.0004
	Li et al. [2]	32.6201	0.9904	0.9631	6.5828	57.2927	17.2714
	Kumar [15]	35.8492	0.9948	0.9915	6.4995	57.9588	18.7344
	Proposed method	36.8034	0.9956	0.9989	7.0062	58.6740	19.6177
Airplane	Wang et al. [8]	27.5595	0.8718	0.9100	4.6188	39.0008	15.6667
	Naidu [7]	29.0045	0.9090	0.9403	4.5308	39.7408	19.6532
	Li et al. [10]	30.3525	0.9296	0.9509	4.6955	39.6483	18.0650
	Pujar [14]	30.7365	0.9324	0.9547	4.6182	39.8764	19.5565
	S. Li et al. [2]	33.0941	0.9680	0.9697	5.2074	42.4839	21.6502
	Kumar [15]	35.1145	0.9798	0.9874	4.7392	42.2842	22.0153
	Proposed method	36.1687	0.9862	0.9976	5.5167	43.3580	23.0050

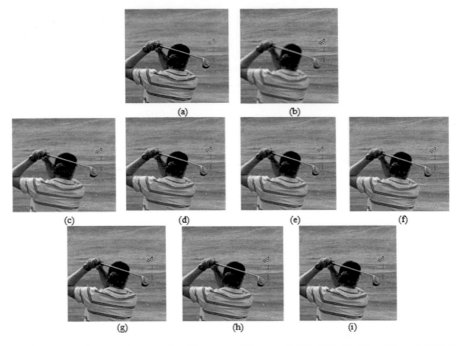

Fig. 3 Man: **a**, **b** source images; fused images, **c** Wang et al. [8], **d** Naidu [7], **e** Li et al. [10], **f** Pujar [14], **g** Li et al. [2], **h** Kumar [15] and **i** proposed method

The proposed method attains the highest values of non-reference measures in Table 2, which indicates that our method works well on natural images to get a fused image with a focused foreground and background regions. To evaluate the strength of the proposed method, the next experiment is done on misregistered multi-focus images. The misregistered source and fused images are shown in Fig. 4. Although the temple images in Fig. 4a, b are extremely misregistered due to the change of viewpoint, it can notice from Fig. 4i that the boundaries and edges of the fused image are clear in the proposed method compared to other fusion methods in Fig. 4c–h. The performance measures MI, SD, and SF are given in Fig. 5–7. The high MI in Fig. 5 shows that the proposed method can combine the focused information of the source images into the fused image. The high SD in Fig. 6 indicates that the proposed method creates a good contrast fused image, and the high SF in Fig. 7 describes that the proposed method preserves detail information in fused image.

Table 2 Performance measures comparison

Fusion method	Man image			Map image		
	MI	SD	SF	MI	SD	SF
Wang et al. [8]	2.1128	44.4744	20.2360	2.5392	70.0910	20.3644
Naidu [7]	6.2384	44.8545	21.4021	6.6877	71.7271	32.6054
Li et al. [10]	6.5242	44.7263	20.5984	6.9301	71.3852	31.3513
Pujar [14]	6.5699	45.0619	22.4433	6.9519	71.9554	34.0584
Li et al. [2]	6.5768	45.5081	22.4940	7.9401	73.1470	35.1219
Kumar [15]	6.4994	45.3556	22.7262	7.1596	72.6975	35.2238
Proposed method	7.0343	46.1979	24.3165	8.4175	73.7496	36.8239

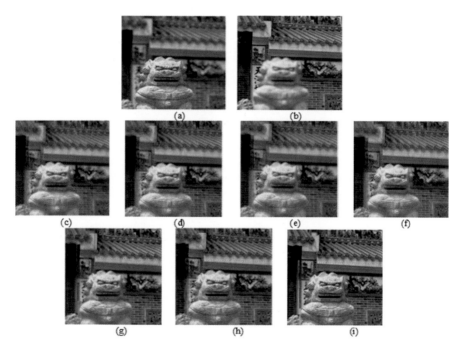

Fig. 4 Temple: **a**, **b** source images; fused images, **c** Wang et al. [8], **d** Naidu [7], **e** Li et al. [10], **f** Pujar [14], **g** Li et al. [2], **h** Kumar [15] and **i** proposed method

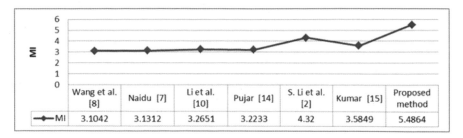

Fig. 5 MI

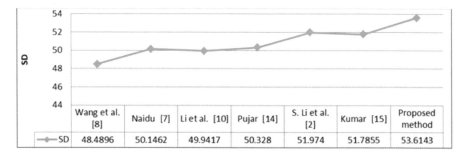

Fig. 6 SD

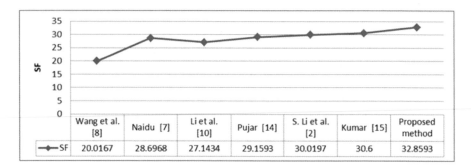

Fig. 7 SF

7   Conclusions

A fast, efficient, image fusion method using slant transform and diagonal Laplacian focus measure is proposed. The properties of slant transform make the fusion process fast, and diagonal Laplacian effectively extracted the focused blocks from source images. The fusion results show that the proposed method can extract visual saliency of the whole scene from the individual source images.

References

1. Pu T, Ni G (2000) Contrast-based image fusion using the discrete wavelet transform. Opt Eng 39(8):2075–2083
2. Li S, James T, Kwok WY (2001) Combination of images with diverse focuses using the spatial frequency. Inf Fus 2(3):169–176
3. Sabre R, Wahyuni IS (2016) Wavelet decomposition in Laplacian pyramid for image fusion. Int J Signal Process Syst 4(1):37–44
4. Thelen A, Frey S, Hirsch S, Hering P (2009) Improvements in shape-from-focus for holographic reconstructions with regard to focus operators, neighborhood-size, and height value interpolation. IEEE Trans Image process 18(1):151–157
5. Pertuz S, Puig D, Garcia MA (2013) Analysis of focus measure operators for shape-from-focus. Pattern Recogn 46(5):1415–1432
6. Jing H, Vladimirova T (2014) Novel PCA based pixel-level multi-focus image fusion algorithm. In: 2014 NASA/ESA conference on adaptive hardware and systems (AHS), pp 135–142. https://doi.org/10.1109/AHS.2014.6880169
7. Naidu VPS (2011) Image fusion technique using multi-resolution singular value decomposition. Defence Sci J 61(5):479–484
8. Wang WW, Shui PL, Song GX (2003) Multifocus image fusion in wavelet domain. In: International conference on machine learning and cybernetics. IEEE, pp 2887–2890. https://doi.org/10.1109/ICMLC.2003.1260054
9. Abhishek S, Tarun G (2017) Change detection from remotely sensed images based on stationary wavelet transform. Int J Electr Comput Eng 7(6):3395–3401
10. Li S, Yang B, Hu J (2011) Performance comparison of different multi-resolution transforms for image fusion. Inf Fus 12(2):74–84
11. Huang W, Jing Z (2007) Evaluation of focus measures in multi-focus image fusion. Pattern Recogn lett 28(4):493–500
12. Hu Z, Liang W, Ding D (2021) An improved multi-focus image fusion algorithm based on multi-scale weighted focus measure. Appl Intell 51(7):4453–4469
13. Li C, Yang X (2021) Multifocus image fusion method using discrete fractional wavelet transform and improved fusion rules. J Mod Opt 68(5):246–258
14. Pujar J, Itkarkar RR (2016) Image fusion using double density discrete wavelet transform. Int J Comput Sci Netw 5(1):6–10
15. Shreyamsha Kumar BK (2013) Multifocus and multispectral image fusion based on pixel significance using discrete cosine harmonic wavelet transform. SIViP 7:1125–1143

Tracking Industrial Assets Using Blockchain Technology

**N. B. L. V. Prasad, M. N. A. Pramodh, R. V. S. Lalitha⃝,
Kayiram Kavitha⃝, and K. Saritha**

Abstract There are several methods to track the movement of goods using different custom developed software applications. This paper presents the implementation of blockchain technology for tracking the movement of assets/equipment within the organization effectively and to share the asset/equipment without any formal authorizations. In this paper, software application is developed to implement transactions. Usage of blockchain technology for this application makes it superior than the other applications in terms of data security and immutability of data. Asset transfer can be made transparent or private to all the users in the chain subject to the application. Once after the submission of the data, it can never be overridden or countermanded. This application allows us to work with improved accuracy and without involvement of human verification.

Keywords Blockchain · Docker · Ec2 · Equip-chain · MultiChain · MQTT

1 Introduction

Tracking the assets is to know the whereabouts of the assets or tools being used in the industry, and traditionally, this was done by maintaining a paper ledger which includes the details like name of the tool, issuer, and receiver names. The asset sharing process between the organization and the employee involves a hectic process of employee requesting for permissions to access that asset, and usually it takes time

N. B. L. V. Prasad (✉)
Technical Hub Pvt Ltd., Rajahmundry, A.P., India
e-mail: techprasad@technicalhub.io

M. N. A. Pramodh · R. V. S. Lalitha
Aditya College of Engineering and Technology, Surampalem, India

K. Kavitha
Gokaraju Rangaraju Institute of Engineering and Technology, Hyderabad, India

K. Saritha
Aditya Engineering College, Surampalem, India

© The Author(s), under exclusive license to Springer Nature Singapore Pte Ltd. 2022   193
C. Satyanarayana et al. (eds.), *High Performance Computing and Networking*,
Lecture Notes in Electrical Engineering 853,
https://doi.org/10.1007/978-981-16-9885-9_16

as the one who authorizes it might not be available all the time. Later, the technology advancement replaced the paper ledger process with a digital ledger. Programming languages and concepts were used to develop these digital ledgers. Even these digital solutions come with the problem where people who are responsible to monitor and update the assets/tools movement in the databases can overwrite the details of the goods at any point of time, which means they can manipulate a particular transaction detail. This is where blockchain can play a crucial role, as by design it is well known for its immutability of data which enables people in the chain to have their own copy of data. Blockchain does not have the concept of having central authority to approve the transactions but enables us to avoid the request permission process to access the asset. Blockchain is a decentralized ledger, distributed across the nodes to store the sequence of the transactions between the parties in the chain. A transaction can be sending money to person/company from one another or exchange process of goods in return for either currency or other goods. A computer that runs the software related to blockchain is often called as a node in this process. Every individual willing to participate in the chain to do some transactions with other participants within the chain should have a computer that runs the blockchain software.

2   Related Work

Bons, R. W. illustrated potential limits of blockchain process [1–3]. Sun applied blockchain process for online language processing [4]. All these transactions are cryptographically approved by the parties involved in the chain. No one in the chain can modify these transactions once after they were committed. Because present transaction is linked to its previous transaction and that will be linked to its predecessor, and that is how they form chain of blocks where each block holds the transaction-related data, the digital fingerprint of the node who approved that transaction, and the previous transaction's hash value as suggested by Sathoshi [5]. A trading company/person from Japan called *Satoshi Nakamot* implemented and started using blockchain technology to implement the first crypto-currency called Bitcoin [6–9]. There are two types of blockchains. First one is called public chain, where anyone in the chain can approve your transaction and we will not have any control over the people in the chain. Bitcoin and Ethereu are the examples for public blockchains. Second one is called private chain, where a limited number of people in the chain will have control over the network, and those can decide who can participate in the chain and who can send and receive a transaction. We can also decide who can be our transaction approvers called miners. If we try to modify one block, we must start modifying all the blocks from then in the sequence. Even if we dare to do that, we need a lot of super computer power. Aida discussed about MultiChain blockchain platform as it is a private and permitted blockchain. We can start running our own blockchain network in our environment with minimal effort, barely just two simple steps to create a new blockchain, and three to connect to an existing one. We can have control (optional) over the participants in the chain who can connect, send, and receive transactions, who can create assets (any tangible and intangible things) [10]. We can issue millions of assets, and we can perform multi-asset and multi-party atomic exchange transactions. MultiChain uses Round Robin Scheduling Algorithm to do the mining process. Blockchain is one of the most happening things in the present fast-growing world, even though it became popular with the Bitcoin, eventually people started realizing the potential of the blockchain in the other industries like health care, food supply chains, Internet of things, financial sector, etc. We needed blockchain to bring trust between the untrusted entities. Namasudra [11, 12] gave the overview and future trends of the blockchain. Konstantinos Demestichas [13] published on how blockchain can be used to revolutionize the agri-food supply chain traceability, and this method uses RFID technology and blockchain together where they connect farmers, warehouse people, and the retailer to the same chain to keep the details of these entities transparent to one another. This can bring the change in tracking the quality and safety of the agri-food by Fang [14] which emphasizes the possibilities of using blockchain in the supply chain industry. Let the supply can be related to agri-food or tracking a goods shipment or tracking the journey of a diamond from the rocks to the diamond store considering post COVID-19 as case study. Sodhro, A. H. discussed IoT-based blockchain technology application using master key generation for encryption process [15]. Dinesh Kumar K. explored the concept of blockchain technology using RFID tags [16] for virtual identity. Pankaja Alappanavar discussed supply chain management using QR code for quick response [7, 17, 18]. Table 1 gives what has been considered as the organization, sample assets, and people involved in the blockchain of this application.

The primary objective of this paper is to show the implementation of blockchain-based solution to track the industrial assets, and to prove how can a blokchain brings trust in the asset exchange process in an organization. The paper is well ordered as follows. Section 2 discusses the overview of the application. Section 3 gives application architecture. Section 4 explains the working of this application. In Sect. 5, we discuss the example scenario of this application. Finally, this paper concludes with a summary described in Sect. 5.

Table 1 Application-specific details

S. no.	Role	Example
1	Blockchain platform	MultiChain
2	Organization	Technical department (Engineering College)
3	Assets	Arduino, Raspberry pi, sensors
4	Admin (participants)	Technical department
5	User (participants)	Employees, and students

3 Overview

This application is named as the equip-chain. The idea of this equip-chain is to trace the movement of the assets that are being used in the organization without any authorization process request permissions to access the asset. Equip-chain installed organization allows the employees to join in the chain. After the registration, the employee will be given access to the Web application where he can check the assets that are available in the organization and the assets that are with him, and to perform send and receive asset operations. The organization itself and each employee will act as a node in the chain usually called as admin and user nodes, respectively. The admin node will create the assets that are available in the organization. Employee requests the admin for an asset of his choice when he is in need. From then, the asset journey in the chain will start, the user can give back the asset to the admin or he can pass the asset to another employee who is in the equip-chain using the Web application. Admin can track the asset at any given time and he can know the journey of an asset from the time it was created in the chain to till date within the company.

Figure 1 illustrates the equip-chain application concept, as we can see the employees and the company are connected. I have taken Raspberry pi and Arduino as the sample assets that were created by the organization as sample assets. We can see at this point of time that the admin wallet has the details of assets that are with

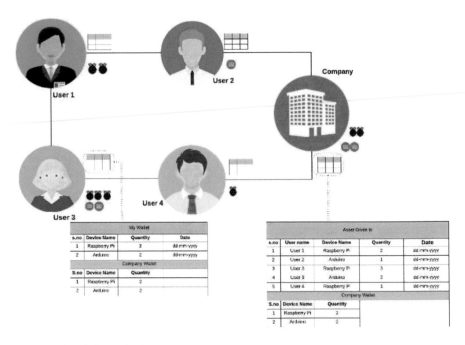

Fig. 1 Equip-chain application

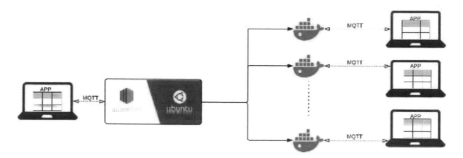

Fig. 2 Architecture overview

others and assets that are with itself. And the employee (user 3) wallet has the details of assets with him/her and assets with the company.

3.1 Equip-Chain Architecture

To run this application, first we must have the nodes those have blockchain setup installed and running. The application used the Docker containers to act as a node. These Docker containers are running in Amazon EC2. The EC2 instance will act as the admin node, and the individual Docker containers in the EC2 instance act as the nodes for the employees and students. By doing this, we can make sure each employee will have a node to participate in the chain, and we can avoid having practical problems like having a computer dedicated to run this application, and even maintenance of the node will become easy. The equip-chain mentioned in this paper contains two software programs, those are user interface and application server, and the overview of the architecture is shown in Fig. 2.

3.2 Tracking of Industrial Assets Using Blockchain

The software application developed using HTML, CSS, and JavaScript enables the user to interact with the equip-chain application server program. This is just to make the application user friendly for operational purpose.

3.3 Blockchain Implementation Through Application Server

This application server is developed using Python, where we have functions defined to interact with the MultiChain using Python SDK to connect/send/receive/check asset

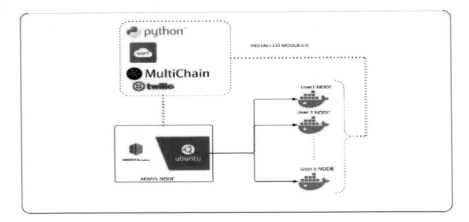

Fig. 3 Modules installed in EC2 and container

balances. Figure 3 shows the modules that were installed in each node. Blockchain implementation is done through MultiChain concept in Python.

Twilio api is used to send/receive OTP whenever a transaction is performed. In this, virtual machine (VM) instances are created using Docker to access EC2 resources. Whenever user creates profile to access blockchain application, automatically nodes will be created in the EC2 server for allowing access to blockchain-related transactions. For test run, two or three nodes are created on payment basis. Let us go through the details of the technologies that have been used in this application.

Amazon Web Services (AWS) is a secure cloud services platform, offering computer power, database storage, serverless computing, mobility, and other functionalities those can help you to build your own business requirements at one place. Amazon Elastic Compute Cloud (EC2) is computing service in AWS. Instead of having in-house hardware setup for servers to host your applications of your business requirements, we can depend on AWS EC2 which is readily available and easy to develop and deploy. The maintenance of your application will be taken care by AWS. Depending on the traffic to our application, we can scale up or down when we want to do so. Docker is used to run software packages called "containers." Containers are isolated from each other and bundle their own tools and libraries. These containers run by a single operating system kernel. Containers are created by source called images. Images can be created from an operating system (Linux/windows) with some other libraries or tools of our choice. Message Queuing Telemetry Transport has been used in the application as communication medium between the user interface and the server application in real time. Twilio is a cloud platform for SMS, voice, and messaging application using the API's PHP,.NET, Java, Node.js, Ruby, and Python.

4   Working Methodology

Once after the installations and registrations have been done, we are ready to start using this application. Admin node will start creating the assets like Arduino and RPI that are available in the organization. Any employee/student who wants one of these assets will have to approach the person who holds that asset currently, and initially it will be the admin. The issuer will log into the Web application and will start the asset sending process. As part of the transaction, the employee will receive an one time password) to his mobile phone, only if the receiver shares the OTP to the sender, then only the asset transfer will be successful. By doing this, we can assure the confirmation from the receiver. Now both the issuer and the receiver (employee) can check their asset balances by just checking their respective Web application's *Dashboard* tab. Like this, people in an organization can send and receive the assets securely without any authorization involved. Blockchain's decentralization and immutability of data assure the security of this application.

Example Scenario

These are the images that show the example asset sending process scenario. The user interface that we can open in the Web browsers and the application server programs is being run in the Ec2 instance and the Docker container.

Step 1   Figs. 4 and 5 show the login process for both admin and the user of this application.

Step 2   Figure 6 shows the assets that are with the organization. We can see the asset details under the Dashboard tab of this application. We can see the organization have assets RPI- 01, RPI-02, RPI-03, ARD-01, ARD-02, and ARD-03 each quantity as one.

Step 3   Figure 7 shows the asset transfer procedure, and we can select one of these assets that are available in the organization and names of the sender and receiver in the respective fields. Then, we can start initiating the transfer

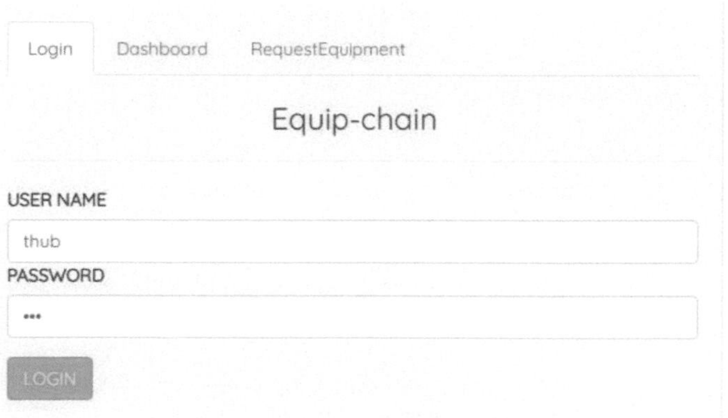

Fig. 4 Admin login

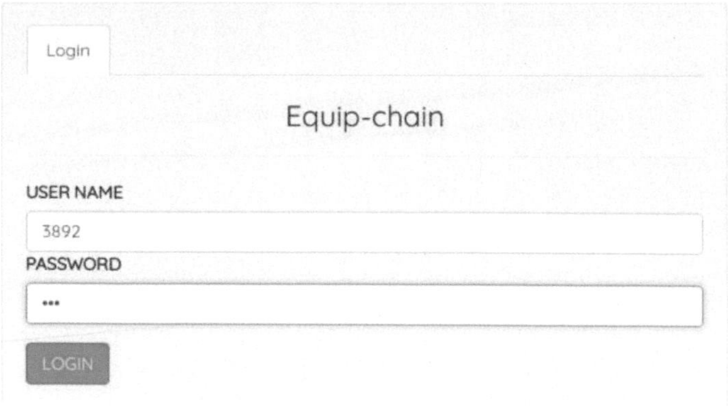

Fig. 5 User login

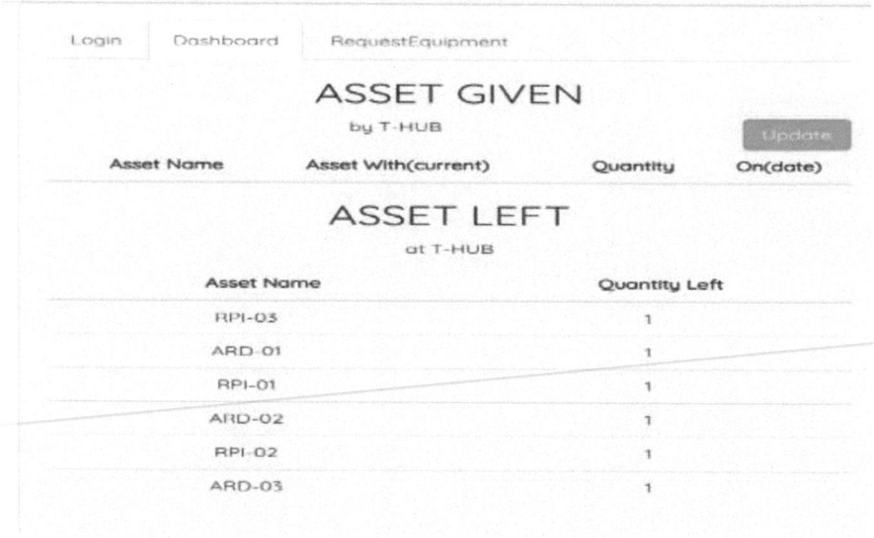

Fig. 6 Asset updated balances

process by clicking on the "**send OTP**" button. The OTP will be sent to the user from the application server program.

Step 4   Figure 8 shows the completing of the transaction by entering the OTP that received by the user. Once after the OTP verification process, that transaction will be completed.

Figures 9 and 10 show the updated asset balances in both admin and the user applications. In the above example scenario, I have sent two assets, namely *RPI-03* and *ARD-01* to user *3892*.

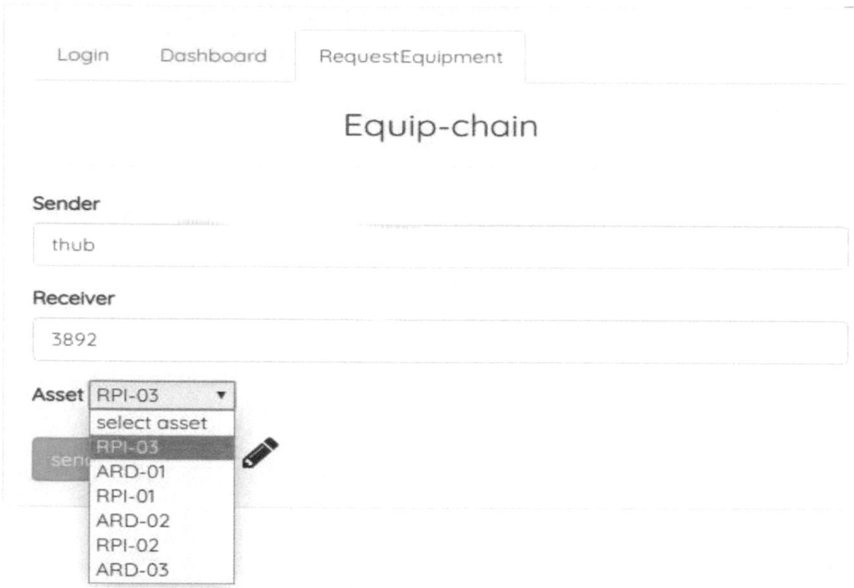

Fig. 7 Asset transfer process

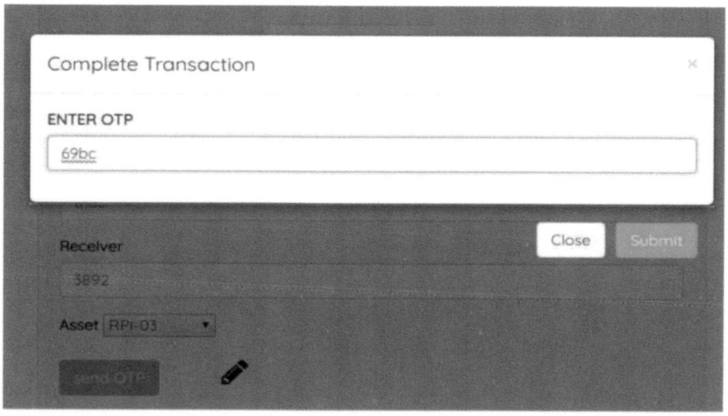

Fig. 8 Completing OTP

5 Conclusion

This paper presented the possibilities of using blockchain to track the movement of the assets being used in the organizations. This paper showed the feasibility of the multi-chain based blockchain solution with the minimal effort and the minimal cost and maintenance using Amazon Ec2 and Docker containers effectively to act as nodes. Equip-chain's ease of access made it very simple to use, even a person

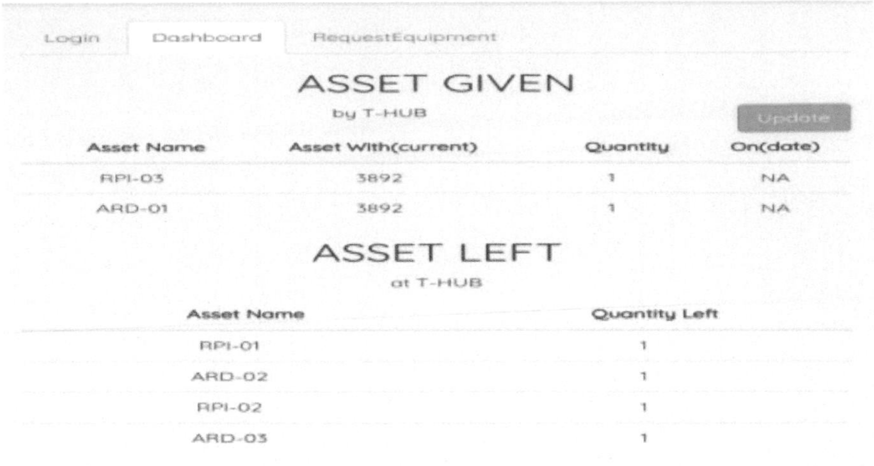

Fig. 9 Updated asset balances in admin application

Fig. 10 Updated asset balances in user application

who is not a technical buff can use it. The application mentioned in this paper being implemented and tested in Aditya College of Engineering and Technology and can be used in a place where the tracking of the assets from time to time is very crucial. In this system, user as well as transaction authentication is included for making transactions more secure. This application is made as private and can be useful for specific organizations or for set of people. Decentralization principle is achieved by implementing this blockchain technology.

References

1. Bons RW, Versendaal J, Zavolokina L et al (2020) Potential and limits of blockchain technology for networked businesses. Electron Markets 30:189–194. https://doi.org/10.1007/s12525-020-00421-8
2. Xu M, Chen X, Kou G (2019) A systematic review of blockchain. Financ Innov 5:27. https://doi.org/10.1186/s40854-019-0147-z
3. Casino F, Dasaklis TK, Patsakis C (2019) A systematic literature review of blockchain-based applications: current status, classification and open issues. Telematics Inform 36:55–81. ISSN 0736-5853. https://doi.org/10.1016/j.tele.2018.11.006
4. Sun X, Zou J, Li L et al (2020) A blockchain-based online language learning system. Telecommun Syst.https://doi.org/10.1007/s11235-020-00699-1
5. Nakamoto S (2009) Bitcoin: a peer-to-peer electronic cash system
6. Luo X, Wang Z, Cai W, Li X, Leung VCM (2020) Application and evaluation of payment channel in hybrid decentralized ethereum token exchange. Blockchain Res Appl 1(1–2):100001. ISSN 2096-7209. https://doi.org/10.1016/j.bcra.2020.100001
7. Douglas A, Holloway R, Lohr J, Morgan E, Harfoush K (2020) Blockchains for constrained edge devices. Blockchain Res Appl 1(1–2):100004. ISSN 2096-7209.https://doi.org/10.1016/j.bcra.2020.100004
8. Peng C, Wu C, Gao L, Zhang J, Alvin Yau KL, Ji Y (2020) Blockchain for vehicular internet of things: recent advances and open issues. Sensors (Basel) 20(18):5079. https://doi.org/10.3390/s20185079
9. Dubovitskaya A, Novotny P, Xu Z, Wang F (2020) Applications of blockchain technology for data-sharing in oncology: results from a systematic literature review. Oncology 98:403–411. https://doi.org/10.1159/000504325
10. Ismailisufi A, Popovic T, Gligoric N, Šandi S, Radonjić S (2020) A private blockchain implementation using multichain open source platform, conference: 2020 24th international conference on information technology (IT) Feb 2020. https://doi.org/10.1109/IT48810.2020.9070689
11. Namasudra S, Deka GC, Johri P et al (2020) The revolution of blockchain: state-of-the-art and research challenges. Arch Computat Methods Eng.https://doi.org/10.1007/s11831-020-09426-0
12. Sujana C, Lalitha RVS, Ram MK, Kumar Pullela SVVSR. Disabled chronicle management using Blockchain technology. Int J Adv Sci Technol (IJAST). ISSN: 2005-4238 (print), ISSN: 2207-6360 (online) IF0.43. http://sersc.org/journals/index.php/IJAST/article/view/27158/14871
13. Demestichas K, Peppes N, Alexakis T, Adamopoulou E (2020) Blockchain in agriculture traceability systems: a review. Appl Sci 10:4113. https://doi.org/10.3390/app10124113
14. Fang H, Wang V (2020) Blockchain technology in current agricultural systems: from techniques to applications. IEEE Access 8(143920):143937
15. Sodhro AH, Pirbhulal S, Muzammal M et al (2020) Towards blockchain-enabled security technique for industrial internet of things based decentralized applications. J Grid Computing.https://doi.org/10.1007/s10723-020-09527-x
16. Dinesh Kumar K, Manoj Kumar DS, Anandh R (2020) Blockchain technology in food supply chain security. Int J Sci Technol Res 9(01). ISSN 2277-8616
17. Alappanavar P, Jyoti VK, Kulkarni I, Varade A (2019) Blockchain based product ownership management for the supply chain using QR code: a survey. J Emerg Technol Innov Res (JETIR) 6(4). ISSN-2349-5162
18. Cheng S, Zeng B, Huang YZ (2017) Research on application model of blockchain technology in distributed electricity market. IOP Conf Ser Earth Environ Sci 93:012065. https://doi.org/10.1088/1755-1315/
19. Weking J, Mandalenakis M, Hein A et al (2020) The impact of blockchain technology on business models—a taxonomy and archetypal patterns. Electron Markets 30:285–305. https://doi.org/10.1007/s12525-019-00386-3

20. Salah D, Ahmed MH, ElDahshan K (2020) Blockchain applications in human resources management: opportunities and challenges. In: EASE'20: proceedings of the evaluation and assessment in software engineering, Apr 2020, pp 383–389. https://doi.org/10.1145/3383219.3383274

Prototype for Recognition and Classification of Textile Weaves Using Machine Learning

Rafael Padilha and Raimundo Cláudio da Silva Vasconcelos

Abstract Textile weave of a fabric gives a garment unique characteristics. It is very difficult to manually classify textile patterns because threads are very small and the classes are very similar. The goal for this project was to create a prototype using machine learning and deep learning techniques to classify textile fabrics from their images. Using the bilinear convolutional neural network, 97.91% accuracy was achieved.

Keywords Textile weave · Machine learning · Convolutional neural networks

1 Introduction

Fabric is the material made of natural, artificial or synthetic yarns, manufactured by methods such as weaving, knitting, flocking, crochet, felting, among others [1]. Weaving is the process of manufacturing flat fabrics through the intertwining of warp yarns and weft yarns at right angles. The way these sets of threads are interwoven forms a pattern that gives the fabric a unique characteristic. The study of these patterns is called patterning. The main types of patterning are canvas (or taffeta), satin and twill. Each pattern has its own characteristics, such as brightness, resistance, flexibility, among others, which can be used differently in a garment [1]. If the fabric is not pre-classified, discovering its pattern manually can be a challenge for those with little experience and/or visual impairments.

In this project, a prototype was developed to classify the pattern of the fabric from a digital image. The proposal was to use machine learning techniques that use previous experiences (data) to find correlations between inputs and classes. As a fabric dataset with the pre-classified pattern was not found, it was necessary to create

R. Padilha (✉) · R. C. da Silva Vasconcelos
Instituto Federal de Brasília (IFB), Brasília, DF, Brazil
e-mail: rafael.padilha@estudante.ifb.edu.br

R. C. da Silva Vasconcelos
e-mail: raimundo.vasconcelos@ifb.edu.br

one from the collected samples. Some architectures with good performances in the literature were tested, such as Alexnet, DenseNet, Inception and even an advanced bilinear convolutional neural network technique, where it reached 97.91% accuracy.

2 Background

2.1 Fabrics

Is the product resulting from the crossing of two sets of threads perpendicularly. Generally, these sets of threads can be separated into warp (threads in the longitudinal direction) and weft (threads in the transverse direction). Weaving field is responsible for studying and understanding the formation of tissue structure [2].The way in which interlacing is done during the weaving process can give different characteristics to the fabric. The variety of interlacing that exists is enormous; however, most of it came from three basic types as we can see in Fig. 1:

(A) Taffeta is the simplest, most versatile and common of the three. It is found in fabrics such as tarpaulins, tricolines and poplins. [2]. In this pattern, the weft yarns pass alternately one by one through the warp yarns [3].

(B) Twill is produced with the warp thread passing over a series of weft threads before passing under one or more weft threads. This pattern makes a diagonal appearance more evident on one side, in addition to making the fabric more resistant [3].

(C) Satin is produced by passing the warp thread over the largest possible number of weft threads, or vice versa, which creates gaps between the interlacing giving shine and softness to this fabric, in spite of decreasing its resistance [1].

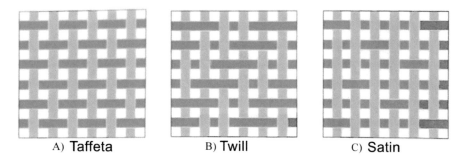

A) Taffeta   B) Twill   C) Satin

Fig. 1 Taffeta, twill and satin fabrics [3]

2.2 Artificial Neural Networks

These are computational models composed of a set of artificial neurons inspired in the biological neurons structure [4]. The training process consists of feeding the Artificial neural network with the training data so that the weights of each neuron adjust in an iterative way, providing the learning of the problem by the artificial neural network. Supervised learning is a training method where the input is previously classified with the expected output. The error can be considered the difference between the obtained and desired output, being used afterward to recalculate the weights of the neurons seeking to increase the accuracy rate [5].

The convolutional neural network architecture can be defined by the repetition and combination of the convolution and pooling layers, among with other transformation functions. Those layers can be mainly defined as:

- **Convolutional layer**
  It is responsible for applying several filters to a set of pixels from the previous layer with predefined weights, which adjust as the convolutional neural network learns to identify the most significant regions. The number of filters is directly related to the depth of the output. Deeper layers tend to identify more details in the identified features [6].

- **Pooling Layer**
  So that the computational cost does not increase significantly at each layer, pooling is useful to reduce the spatial size of the input, and the fact that it reduces the parameters to be learned contributes to controlling overfitting. One of the methods used is max pooling, which selects only the highest value of an area from the input [5].

After the convolution layer, the feature vectors generated by the pooling layer are converted into a column vector (flattening process). This vector is then passed as input to a fully connected artificial neural network, producing the output that will classify the image [7].

Looking at Fig. 2, VGG16 and VGG19 are two architectures of convolutional neural networks proposed by Simonyan and Zisserman that managed to achieve about 90% top-5 accuracy in ImageNet. The structure of the two models is very similar, changing only the number of convolutional layers, while VGG16 has 13 layers of convolution and 3 layers fully connected, while VGG19 has 16 layers of convolution and 3 layers fully connected. Finally, the main structure between the two remain the same; the kernel size in the convolution layers is 3×3, and the max pooling size is 2×2.

2.3 Bilinear Convolutional Neural Networks

It consists of two layers of characteristics extraction based on convolutional neural networks where the two architectures need to be similar, with the same dimensions.

Fig. 2 VGG16 and VGG19 architecture

An image passes through the two layers of feature extraction where the output is multiplied by the external product in each area of the image and then goes through a pooling layer in which a bilinear vector of characteristics is obtained. This vector is finally passed as input to the classification layers [8].

2.4 Related Works

The paper [9] proposes the creation of a system for recognizing patterns of fabric textures. To do this, it extracts the vector of characteristics from the image, which is composed of energy, contrast, homogeneity and correlation. After extraction, this vector is compared with the vector of images already classified. Calculates the distance between the two vectors using the Euclidean distance algorithms, dLog and Pearson, and those with the shortest distance have a tendency to belong to the same pattern.

In [7], the author to assist in the work of biologists in the task of classifying leaves, as it is a long and manual process that depends on the knowledge of the professional. To develop a method of classifying images, its initial objective was to build a convolutional neural network with a structure similar to a VGG16 architecture. Starting with simple binary classification implementations until reaching your final goal.

Still in the biology field, [10] built a solution to classify two genetic types of guaranazeiro cultivars through digital images of their leaves, using the convolutional neural network *LeNet* and *AlexNet* architectures. Sousa et al. [10] propose a methodology where the user takes a picture of a cell phone and sends it to an API using RESTFul technology, thus centralizing all image processing and classification on a machine with sufficient computational power for these tasks.

Currently, some problems studied in the convolutional neural networks field are: classification of images where there is a lot of similarity between classes, images where their characteristics are refined and training with little data. Lin et al. [8] proposes a solution for these problems using the bilinear convolutional neural network architecture, which is composed of two convolution layers of existing architectures, pre-trained in the dataset *ImageNet* [11]. The author tested its implementation on some fine-grained datasets which share the problem of similarity between classes, and they yielded very interesting results.

3 Development

The main characteristic used to define the technologies involved in the project was the use of open-source technologies: Python, OpenCV, TensorFlow, Keras, Pickle.

As we can see in Fig. 3, the development of the project was separated into the following steps.

3.1 Sampling

With the support of a professor from the technical fashion course, a total of 93 samples of various fabrics pre-classified in their respective patterns were loaned for the execution of this project. Of these samples, 40 are of taffeta, 31 of twill and 22 of satin fabrics.

3.2 Dataset Creation

Initially, the goal of the project was to create the dataset from images taken from a smartphone. However, during the development of the project, it was observed that the images recorded by the smartphone did not capture enough details to identify its class. To get around the reported problem, a test was performed using a digital microscope, and it was observed that the result was significantly better than the previous images as it captured more details of the tissue structure. With that, the entire dataset was recreated using the images captured by the digital microscope. The images were saved in JPEG format with the size of 1600 px wide and 1200 px wide.

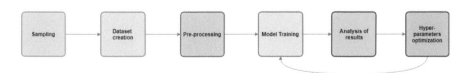

Fig. 3 Flow of project development stages

3.3 Pre-processing

This step was focused on taking the raw data generated by the previous step and preparing it to serve as input to the models to be trained. One of the tasks was to cut the images to fit the defined input sizes for each convolutional neural network architecture, after which the images were separated by 20% for validation and 80% for training.

Next step was the application of data augmentation, set to $2x$ doing only the 90° rotation. Finally, each image was joined with an integer corresponding to its classification in a tuple, saving the data in two binary files of pickle format, separating the training and validation data.

3.4 Model Training

The first step of this step was the creation of a Python algorithm capable of:

- Receive different architectures of Convolutional Neural Networks;
- Load preprocessed data;
- Define the training parameters;
- Perform model training;
- Save the trained model;
- Generate metrics reports;

With this, it was possible to perform several experiments training models using convolutional neural network architectures known in the literature such as: *Alexnet, VGG19, VGG16, DenseNet, ResNet* e *Inception*. An implementation was created in *Keras* for each architecture, where the model was saved in JSON format so that it could be loaded again during training.

Model training was performed on a machine with an Intel Core i5-8400 processor, 8GB of DDR4 2600MHz RAM, and using parallel processing on an NVIDIA GTX 1060 graphics card with 6GB of VRAM and 1280 CUDA Cores.

3.5 Analysis of Results

There are several metrics in the literature to measure the performance of a machine learning model, and in this project, accuracy was used as a metric. At the end of all training, a graph was generated showing the progress of accuracy over the epochs. Comparing the results obtained with the training and validation data, it was possible to estimate the efficiency of the model, if it was not learning, or even to identify signs of overfitting or underfitting.

Based on the results obtained after training the bilinear convolutional neural network, among the architectures tested, the one that had the best result, considering

Table 1 Results of architectural combinations in the bilinear model

	VGG16	VGG19
VGG16	0.9783	0.9791
VGG19	0.9565	0.9513

the metrics defined, were the architecture *VGG19* and *VGG16*, which were tested together, given the nature of the architecture allowing only similar architectures to train together. Next in Table 1, we can see the accuracy values achieved in the validation data after 100 training epochs.

When observing very high values of accuracy, it was estimated that the model could be suffering from overfitting. One way to analyze this is by comparing the accuracy of the training dataset with that of validation and observing if both are not distancing during the seasons and, as we can see in Fig. 4 for each combination of architectures in the bilinear model, where the items refer to the following configurations: (a) vgg16 with vgg16, (b) vgg16 with vgg19, (c) vgg19 with vgg16 and (d) vgg19 with vgg19, this did not happen. Therefore, either the model was learning correctly, or the dataset was not enough to train and validate the model, given that with little data it becomes more difficult for the model to generalize and obtain more accurate results.

Another metric used to check the model performance was the confusion matrix, that is a table which show us the frequency of prediction for each class. As we can see in Fig. 5, the results are quite good for most classes; only the twill class have some wrong guesses.

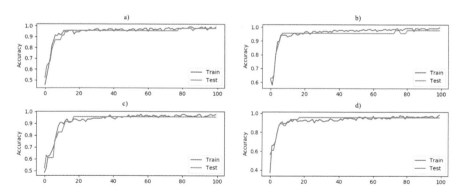

Fig. 4 Graph showing the accuracy progress during the epochs **a** vgg16-vgg16, **b** vgg16-vgg19, **c** vgg19-vgg16, **d** vgg19-vgg19

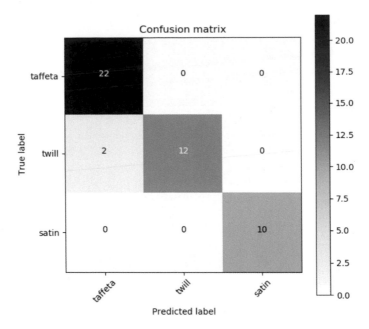

Fig. 5 Confusion matrix for model VGG19-VGG16

3.6 Hyperparameters Optimization

After analyzing the generated graphics, some models needed some adjustments. For example, if the model was overfitting, or it was achieving high hit rates but the error did not decrease, one of the hyperparameters to be adjusted was the model's learning rate; decreasing this value results in a more time-consuming convergence of values. In addition to the learning rate, other parameters adjusted in this step are: batch size due to the computational capacity of the machine available and epochs. The final values can be seen in Table 2.

Table 2 Parameters table

Parameter	Value
Train size	80%
Validation size	20%
Epochs	100
Learning rate	10^{-4}
Batch size	64

4 Conclusion and Recommendations

The initial proposal of this work was to develop a prototype that would classify the pattern of a fabric from a smartphone photograph. During the tests, several difficulties were identified in the attempt to achieve the proposal. One of them was that there is a lot of similarity of data between classes; what differentiates one class from another in the image are very small details.

Another difficulty was the quality of the data. The first version of the dataset created, from the smartphone, had some images that did not allow observing the pattern or even the threads of the fabric, depending on the thickness of the threads or the material. Finally, the number of samples collected was not sufficient to validate the model's accuracy.

With the obtained results reaching 97.91%, it is believed that the tested architecture has the potential to learn this problem but needs a good quality, balanced and high volume dataset to obtain more accurate values.

It can be considered to continue this work and focus on solving the problems detected, such as:

- Build a larger, balanced and good quality dataset with more classes of patterns;
- Find a way to adapt different architectures to the bilinear model or test new methodologies;
- Highlight some features to assist the neural network, such as the Fourier descriptor;

References

1. Frings G (2012) MODA - DO CONCEITO AO CONSUMIDOR. BOOKMAN, Porto Alegre
2. Cuccato F (2015) Manual Técnico Têxtil e Vestuário - Tecelagem
3. Pimentel J, Vasconcelos R (2018) Identificação das estruturas de tecidos planos através da câmera de smartphone
4. Haykin S (2009) Neural networks and learning machines. Pearson, Upper Saddle River
5. Chaves E (2019)Detecção de câncer de mama por meio de imagens infravermelhas utilizando Redes Neurais Convolucionais
6. Vargas A, Paes A, Vasconcelos C (2016) Um estudo sobre redes neurais convolucionais e sua aplicação em detecção de pedestres. In: Proceedings of the xxix conference on graphics, patterns and images, pp 1–4
7. Massucatto J (2018) Aplicação de conceitos de redes neurais convolucionais na classificação de imagens de folhas
8. Lin T, RoyChowdhury A, Maji S (2018) Bilinear convolutional neural networks for fine-grained visual recognition. IEEE Trans Pattern Anal Mach Intell 40:1309–1322
9. Silva L (2017) Desenvolvimento de um sistema para reconhecimento de padrões de texturas de tecidos
10. Sousa A, Salame M, Filho F, Atroch A (2017) Redes neurais convolucionais aplicadas ao processo de classificação de cultivares de guaranazeiros. XIV Encontro Nacional de Inteligência Artificial e Computacional, Uberlândia, MG, Brasil
11. Fei-Fei L, Deng J, Li K (2010) ImageNet: constructing a large-scale image database. J Vis 9:1037

Development of Deep Neural Network Algorithm for Identification of Cerebral Microstructural Changes in Brain Tumor for Post-COVID-19 Patients

Kunal Khadke

Abstract The year 2019 brought the once in hundred years' experience for the whole world. COVID-19 pandemic shaken almost all segments of everyone's life and scientists all over the world are engaged in saving our existence. As there is a need of capturing microstructural changes like tumor boundary pixel level shifts and/or growth, deep learning can be a very promising to identify the pixel level changes occurred in brain MR images. The multi-layer execution using CNN architecture is possible, but there is a need for fast convolution and de-convolution with lowered strides. Conventional methods can provide acceptable results, but to identify the microstructural changes in (COVID-19 patient) MR image, accuracy and visibility at pixel level need to be very precise. Hence, this paper presents the methodology for analysis of pre- and post-COVID-19 brain tumor microstructures by means of development of novel CNNPostCoV deep learning algorithm. Proposed research uses IIARD-19 and IIARD-20 dataset of COVID-19 patient. Algorithm framed with convolution neural network architecture which provides better performance of dice score, sensitivity, and PPV parameters. Paper also presents the training and validation analysis for HGG, LGG, and combined dataset of multi-modal brain tumors.

Keywords COVID-19 pandemic · Brain tumor · Convolution neural network · Deep learning · Dataset · Segmentations · Tumor classification

1 Introduction

COVID-19 [1, 2] is a new type concerning a huge group of viruses known as corona viruses. The disease triggers flu-like signs of illness, by way of the significant consequence coming up with effects to the respiratory system. The disease can easily propagate via individual to individual, because of tiny droplets via the nasal way and mouth which usually can propagate in the event that a person coughs or else sneezes. Some other person may capture COVID-19 by means of inhaling in this kind of tiny

K. Khadke (✉)
Sri SatyaSai University of Technology & Medical Sciences, Sehore, India

© The Author(s), under exclusive license to Springer Nature Singapore Pte Ltd. 2022
C. Satyanarayana et al. (eds.), *High Performance Computing and Networking*,
Lecture Notes in Electrical Engineering 853,
https://doi.org/10.1007/978-981-16-9885-9_18

droplets and by reaching an area that the tiny droplets have ended up with one and so after that reaching most of the eyelids, nostril, or mouth area [3]. People above the age group of 60 as well as all those that have severe complaints and/or weakened resistant power are most likely at major-risk for contracting the virus and also suffering from an even more critical condition after predicament. Various brain tumor sufferers, specifically cancerous brain tumor individuals, are deemed significant concerns, as radiation treatment can endanger a patient's resistant power, carrying out all of them considerably more vulnerable to COVID-19 [4].

As researchers using the globe are positioning plenty of initiatives for detection of genome sequences of corona virus [5], likely effects on individuals that have different comorbidities and so investigating impact of several medications, the computational approaches are turning out to be even more distinguished for immediate analysis.

Through a latest methodical analysis, 6 analyzes [6, 7] are covered that stated on the occurrence of neurological symptoms in individuals with COVID-19. All of these features fatigue, reduced awareness, distress, headaches, seizures, ischemic stroke as well as hemorrhage [8, 9]. Most recent research explained 3 brain patterns and post research enlightened hypotheses on just how every brain layout could communicate with cutbacks in human association to underlie cerebral wellness difficulties in the circumstance of COVID-19 [10].

1.1   Background

As COVID-19 pandemic impacted whole world, the data management becomes very difficult. The parameters for evaluation fall under patient treatment management, bed availability, and various patients with different comorbid conditions, impact of medicines and their impact of various comorbid conditions are different. Further, task force segregated high-level parameters as diabetic patients, cancer patients, kidney diseases patients, etc. But, it becomes difficult for data scientists to collect information for every parametric condition as a workload on health professionals is tremendous.

In year 2019–2020, the whole world was waiting for vaccine for COVID-19. During the initial pandemic wave, the rate of mortality was higher than various medicines were under trial. Now, second wave of pandemic is rendering in many parts of countries facing higher mortality rate as vaccination is in progress but not done fully. Most trials were conducted with parametric samples of population. But as of year 2021, many vaccines drives are in progress throughout world. Now, the post-COVID-19 complications are raising head and yet fewer data are available. However, numerous researches have been done to prove that COVID-19 virus is impacting brain functions and this can be a very serious long-term phase for patient.

1.2 Advantages of CNN for Post-COVID-19 Analysis

The proposed research is focusing on identification of microstructural changes in brain of patients with brain tumor using convolution neural network (CNN) framework. This can also be useful for non-tumor patients but comparative analysis needs normal brain MRI which is not possible for every COVID-19 patients. But, in case of patients with pre-existing brain tumor, conditions can produce their historical MRI data. Hence, this approach can assist scientists to know the precise influence of post-COVID-19 conditions and relation with brain traumatic impact.

Advantages of CNN for post-COVID-19 are as follows:

1. Fast processing of brain MR images is possible and can assist to decide the line of action of treatment of patient.
2. Accurate analysis of brain MR images.
3. Data analysis can be done with comparison of pre- and post-COVID-19 brain microstructure.
4. Segmentation of brain can provide the changes in overall brain structure and tumor structure.
5. Classification can be done to identify the changes in brain due to COVID-19 and due to existing tumor.
6. Due to the max-pooling layers, more accuracy can be achieved.

As per recent literatures, it is confirmed that there is an impact on brain because of COVID-19 virus. Hence, it is necessary to develop such a system which can assist medical professionals in analysis of impact of virus on microstructure of brain. As manual MR image of CT scan report may prone to errors, it is beneficial to develop an algorithm for automated analysis of brain structure and/or tumor. The data published recently are not very huge as the patient MRI registrations under the domain of post-COVID-19 are not done in huge amount hence for COVID-19 patients, proposed research uses IIARD dataset.

Brain MR image is predominantly employed to identify the tumor advances modeling procedure. This data are primarily applied for growth diagnosis as well as medication procedures. MR image provides much more details regarding offered therapeutic image when compared to the CT. MR image presents complete details relating to brain pattern as well as abnormality prognosis in brain cells.

The brain tumor segmentation and classification are necessary for survival prediction and CNN can play an important role in the development of prediction analysis too. Analysis of hyperparameters as dice scores (DSC), sensitivity, and positive prediction values (PPV) can prove the feasibility of proposed method. Previously, there was the classification of brain tumor in two ways as cancerous and non-cancerous but now there is need of the classification of tumor based on the changes in the microstructure of tumor. Hence, feature extraction can be done with focus of pre- and post-COVID-19 brain tumor structure.

The brain is patterned by means of applying execution of neural network (NN). The NN is predominantly utilized for data clustering, structure matching, improvement characteristics as well as classification approaches. In the single layer, the hidden layer is not proclaimed. However, it consists of merely input and output layer. On the other hand, the multi-layer consists of input layer, hidden layer, and output layer. The closed-loop structured responses network is referred to as a recurrent network. The convolution neural network (CNN) is composed of input layer, convolution layer, rectified linear unit (ReLU) layer, pooling layer, and fully connected layer. In the convolution layer, the provided input is segregated right into different modest parts. Component-wise initialization function is executed in ReLU layer. Pooling layer is elective. Even so, the pooling layer is primarily employed to find the down-sampling. Fully connected layer is applied to deliver the score value depending on the likelihood among 0–1 [11].

This paper is organized as Sect. 2 presents the review of related literature focusing on COVID-19 neurological research and the methods proposed for segmentation and classification of brain tumor using deep learning CNN architectures, Sect. 3 discusses the proposed algorithm "CNNPostCoV" along with the flow of execution, in Sect. 4, results and discussion presented for proposed algorithm training and validation, and lastly Sect. 5 concludes the paper.

2   Related Work

In this section, we focused on the latest studies in the domain of impact of COVID-19 on brain health. As pandemic spreading at a very higher rate, researchers throughout the world are working on uncountable parameters. As pharmaceutical scientists are working on medicines, the similar responsibility has been over the data scientists to gather, analyze, and predict the decisions, models of virus like genome sequencing, maintaining the huge data and provide genuine models for scientists. Data science became a sharp weapon in this pandemic which can provide the quick results and decision-making became fast.

As per [12], coronaviruses (CoV) indicate neuro-tropic characteristics and may equally induce nerve system ailments. It is testified the fact that CoV is often discovered through the brain. The pathobiology of such neuro-invasive infections is, however, insufficiently seen, and so it is subsequently essential to research the influence of CoV issues relating to the nervous-system. Author analyzed the exploration straight to neurological problems in CoV issues and so the conceivable processes of injury to the nervous-system. Author in [13] mentioned that a damaged breathing core in the brainstem may be responsible for breathing dysfunction in COVID-19 sufferers. Subsequently, breathing inability pertaining to loss of life may be resulting from the failure of the respiratory core in the brainstem, which is often not too noticeable at the time of medical diagnosis. Research in [14] disclosed that CoV can attain the cerebral vasculature because of the overall circulation, breaking the blood–brain obstacle and so entering as well as wounding the brain parenchyma. CoV may hole to its receptor enzyme indicated in endothelial panels of cerebral capillary vessels as well as through the brain parenchyma in each of those neurons as well as microglia. Artificial intelligence (AI) is additionally important through this discipline and so to develop alternatives to assist medical diagnosis. AI strategies are generally employed to generate computerized programs for COVID-19 examination. In [15], author suggested CNN model applying EfficientNet in which he discovered the binary distinction benefits by employing images from COVID-19 individuals as well as normal individuals. Additionally, the multi-class outcomes implementing images from COVID-19, pneumonia as well as normal patients are mentioned. Author in [16] applied CNN to sort out the COVID-19-infected indi viduals as well as non-infected. Besides that, the preliminary variables of CNN are configured by using multi-objective differential evolution (MODE). Considerable trials are conducted with consideration of the developed approaches. As per research in [17–19], all researchers are searching for powerful alternatives as well as efficient solution strategies intended for this pandemic. To decrease the requirement for medical professionals, quick and reliable automatic recognition methods are presented. Deep learning CNN solutions are featuring exceptional effects for discovering occurrences of COVID-19. In [20], author mentioned that appropriate segmentation is an important stage during the scientific administration of brain tumors. Nevertheless, the process remains to be complicated because of not merely significant modifications in the weights as well as patterns of brain tumors, however, even huge modifications between sufferers.

3 Proposed Method

This section discusses the proposed algorithm. The BRATS-2020 dataset is obtained from Kaggle, which is pre-operative MRI dataset, and IIARD datasets are obtained from IIARD repository. This method classifies brain tumor as pre- and post-COVID-19 microstructures. The newly developed algorithm is given subsequently:

Algorithm 1: CNNPostCoV.

Input: X – BRATS 2020 image dataset, IIARD19/20 dataset.

Output: Y - Segmented brain tumor image set and classification of T1, T2, T1ge images.

1. Register the MRI/CT images for patients for pre-and post-COVID-19 phases
2. Input the BRATS 2020 dataset as [HGG], [LGG], [Combined] (IIARD datasets used for comparative analysis)
3. Apply convolution layers with constant stride 2 for HGG, LGG, and combined dataset
4. Set max pooling layers to tenfold
5. Apply ReLU layer filter for extraction of tumor boundary
6. Add check points to initiate de-convolution phase
7. Store the segmentation and classified T1, T2, T1ge images for further augmentation

8.   Set epoch size to 50
9.   Conduct training and validation with epoch 50 on GPU.
10.   Compute the performance of hyperparameters - DSC, sensitivity, and PPV
11.   Compare the performance for complete, core, and enhanced brain tumor for
      HGG, LGG, and combined dataset

For development and execution of proposed system, hardware used as Windows 10, GPU machine with 12 GB memory size. Algorithmic coding was done by using Python 3.6 version. The dataset used is BRATS-2020. The dataset contains 369 samples, 4 slices for pre-operative conditions.

Figure 1 shows the flowchart for proposed research execution using the novel "CNNPostCoV" algorithm. As CO ID-19 patient's brain MRI dataset is globally under development, the image registration is the key step. Further, BRATS 2020 dataset is used as an input for CNN processing similarly the algorithm also tested for IIARD19/20 datasets. The proposed algorithm can identify the gray pixels boundary which further can be compared with MRI and/or CT images of brain tumor. The training and validation for MR image segmentation and classification are conducted for HGG and LGG. Here, brain images of single patient can be compared to understand the microstructural changes in brain tumor in pre- and post-COVID-19 subject studies. This is the first study in the field of CNN which analyzing the difference between pre- and post-COVID-19 brain tumor structure.

In subsequent Sect. 4, detailed results are provided.

4   Results and Discussion

As discussed in the previous section of this paper, we conducted training and validation for proposed algorithm using CNN framework. We also modified convolution and de-convolution strides and max pooling layers and recorded hyperparameter. Initially, we achieved training for HGG dataset, further we trained LGG dataset, and lastly, combined dataset was trained. Similar sequence is executed for validation of training results.

The segmented images for microstructural changes are shown in following Fig. 2. Result shows that microstructural extraction clearly. As such microstructural surgical events can be erroneous; hence, proposed algorithm can be used as a plug-in for robotic surgery too by human-machine-interfacing (HMI).

Further, the following Table 1 depicts the training and validation setup details.

Further, training of datasets provided hyperparameter results as shown in Table 2. It shows that proposed system performance is better than the existing system as DSC and sensitivity give better results.

Thus, the overall flow of proposed work is to train BRATS dataset images using the proposed algorithm, followed by validation and comparison of proposed and existing parameters as dice similarity coefficient (DSC), sensitivity, and positive predictive

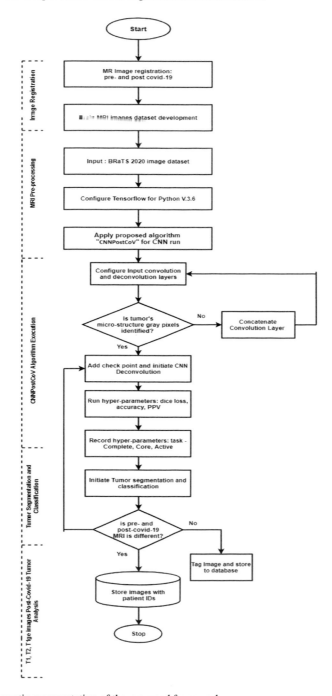

Fig. 1 Schematic representation of the proposed framework

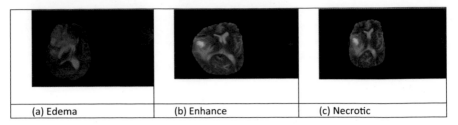

| (a) Edema | (b) Enhance | (c) Necrotic |

Fig. 2 Input and output MR image segmentation

Table 1 Training and validation setup

Targeted data	Training set	Validation set
HGG	259	30
LGG	110	20
HGG + LGG	259 + 110 = 369	30 + 20 = 50

Table 2 Dataset run performance comparison

Method	Dataset	DSC			Sensitivity		
		Complete	Core	Enhanced	Complete	Core	Active
Proposed System	HGG	**0.91**	0.96	0.14	**0.90**	0.91	0.17
	LGG	1.82	3.66	1.56	1.52	3.60	1.74
	Combined	0.93	2.78	2.09	0.91	2.76	2.17
Xue et al. [20]	HGG	0.89	0.95	0.15	0.87	0.90	0.21
	LGG	1.78	3.54	1.69	1.45	3.58	1.86
	Combined	0.97	2.38	2.35	0.94	2.78	2.23

value (PPV). The proposed system performance is compared with the existing system in [20] and depicted in following Table 3.

As per the hyperparameter comparison, it is proven that the proposed system can perform better and classification of T1, T2, and T1ge is efficient with epoch size 50.

Figure 3 shows the percentage of segmentation done for BRATS 2020 dataset with novel CNNPostCoV algorithm. The training epochs are 50 for both training and validation of brain tumor images. The pre- and post-COVID-19 brain tumor

Table 3 CNNPostCoV comparison analysis

Hyperparameters	Proposed system	Existing system [20]
DSC	0.91	0.83
Sensitivity	0.90	0.86
PPV	0.92	0.84

Fig. 3 Performance
comparison between
proposed system and
existing system

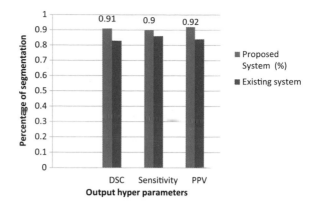

Fig. 4 Dataset comparison

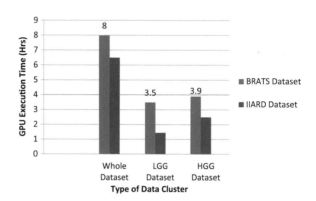

microstructure analysis predicts the survival based on classification of HGG as well as LGG tumors.

Figure 4 depicts the execution time comparison while using GPU for whole dataset, LGG data cluster and HGG data cluster. The comparison is accomplished for BRATS and IIARD-19/20 datasets. As BRATS uses compressible file format ".nii," it takes time for data conversion whereas IIARD-19/20 dataset is precisely considers the formatted images. Hence, BRATS dataset takes more time for execution of data clusters.

5 Conclusion

As the COVID-19 pandemic raised the need of fast and accurate computations, we demonstrated new the efficient solution using deep learning for accurate image processing in identification of microstructure changes in brain tumor for pre-and post-COVID-19 patients. Also, proposed CNNPostCoV deep learning algorithm implemented for training and validation using BRATS 2020 dataset. A result depicts that

HGG, LGG, and combined dataset validation are better for the proposed system. The GPU processing is fast for the training and validation of a dataset with the tenfold convolution and de-convolution layers. The strides are constant for both HGG and LGG and give more promising results. The analysis is conducted for pre-COVID-19 and post-COVID-19 brain images too and proven positive performance in the evaluation of medical conditions of patient, i.e., impact of COVID-19 on brain tumor patients. Furthermore, the classification is done for T1, T2, and T1ge, which are pathologically important for health professionals. The microstructure analysis is important for COVID-19 patients with brain tumor and proposed algorithm can be very useful for increasing survival rate of COVID-19 patient or to control psychological effect if any.

References

1. Filetti S (2020) The COVID-19 pandemic requires a unified global response, p 1–1
2. Sanyaolu A et al (2020) Comorbidity and its impact on patients with COVID-19. SN Compr Clin Med 1–8
3. Singh DR et al (2020) Knowledge and perception towards universal safety precautions during early phase of the COVID-19 outbreak in Nepal. J Commun Health 45:1116–1122
4. Bougakov D, Podell K, Goldberg E (2021) Multiple neuroinvasive pathways in COVID-19. Mol Neurobiol 58(2):564–575
5. Vaid S, Kalantar R, Bhandari M (2020) Deep learning COVID-19 detection bias: accuracy through artificial intelligence. Int Orthopaedics 44:1539–1542
6. Bhattacharya S et al (2021) Deep learning and medical image processing for coronavirus (COVID-19) pandemic: a survey. Sustain Cities Soc 65:102589
7. Vieira S, Pinaya WHL, Mechelli A (2017) Using deep learning to investigate the neuroimaging correlates of psychiatric and neurological disorders: methods and applications. Neurosci Biobehav Rev 74 (2017):58–75
8. Finsterer J, Stollberger C (2020) Update on the neurology of COVID-19. J Med Virol 92(11):2316–2318
9. Asadi-Pooya AA, Simani L (2020) Central nervous system manifestations of COVID-19: a systematic review. J Neurol Sci 116832
10. Hagerty SL, Williams LM (2020) The impact of COVID-19 on mental health: The interactive roles of brain biotypes and human connection. Brain Behav Immunity-Health 100078
11. Seetha J, Raja SS (2018) Brain tumor classification using convolutional neural networks. Biomed Pharmacol J 11(3):1457
12. Wu Y et al (2020) Nervous system involvement after infection with COVID-19 and other coronaviruses. Brain Behav Immun 87:18–22
13. Gandhi S et al (2020) Is the collapse of the respiratory center in the brain responsible for respiratory breakdown in COVID-19 patients? ACS Chem Neurosci 11(10):1379–1381
14. Saavedra JM (2020) COVID-19, angiotensin receptor blockers, and the brain 667–674
15. Marques G, Agarwal D, de la Torre Díez I (2020) Automated medical diagnosis of COVID-19 through EfficientNet convolutional neural network. Appl Soft Comput 96:106691
16. Singh D, Kumar V, Kaur M (2020) Classification of COVID-19 patients from chest CT images using multi-objective differential evolution–based convolutional neural networks. Euro J Clin Microbiol Infect Dis 39(7):1379–1389
17. Saad W et al (2021) COVID-19 classification using deep feature concatenation technique. J Ambient Intell Humanized Comput 1–19

18. Sadoon TM (2021) Classification of medical images based on deep learning network (CNN) for both brain tumors and covid-19. Diss. Ministry of Higher Education, 2021
19. Sharif MI et al (2021) An improved framework for brain tumor analysis using MRI based on YOLOv2 and convolutional neural network. Complex Intell Syst 1–14
20. Xue et al (2020) Hypergraph membrane system based F2 fully convolutional neural network for brain tumor segmentation. Appl Soft Comput 94:106454

A Codebook Modification Method of Vector Quantization to Enhance Compression Ratio

Dibyendu Barman, Abul Hasnat, and Bandana Barman

Abstract The performance of an image compression algorithm is based on the amount of compression ratio achieved keeping the visual quality of the decompress image up to the mark. In an image compression algorithm, two performance measurement parameters, compression ratio, and visual quality of the decompress image are inversely proportional. So, improving the compression ratio of the compression algorithm, keeping visual quality of the decompress image as close to the original is a major challenging task. Vector quantization is one of the widely used lossy image compression techniques found in literature. The compression ratio of this algorithm basically depends on the size of the index matrix and codebook generated during the process. In this present work, a new technique is proposed which represents each and every value of the codebook by 5 bits instead of 8 bits that means it reduces the amount of memory required to store the codebook by 37.50% and which increases the compression ratio of the algorithm significantly. The proposed method is applied on many standard color images found in literature and images from UCIDv.2 database. Experimental results show that the proposed method increases the compression ratio significantly, keeping the visual quality of the decompressed image almost same or slightly lower.

Keywords Codebook · Codevector · Compression ratio · Image compression · PSNR · SSIM · Vector quantization

1 Introduction

Image compression is a technique that removes the redundancy present in the image that reduces the amount of memory required to store it in a storage medium and also reduces the required bandwidth to transfer the image through a communication

D. Barman (✉) · A. Hasnat
Government College of Engineering and Textile Technology Berhampore WB, Berhampore, India

B. Barman
Kalyani Government Engineering College, Nadia, West Bengal, India

© The Author(s), under exclusive license to Springer Nature Singapore Pte Ltd. 2022   227
C. Satyanarayana et al. (eds.), *High Performance Computing and Networking*,
Lecture Notes in Electrical Engineering 853,
https://doi.org/10.1007/978-981-16-9885-9_19

medium [1–4, 7–9]. The image is basically compressed by taking advantage of three types of redundancies [7, 8]. (i) Coding redundancy: Present in the image when less optimal codeword is used. (ii) Inter-pixel redundancy: Causes due to correlation of the neighboring pixels, (iii) Psychxo-visual redundancy-causes due to data ignored by human visual system [8]. Image compression technique broadly classifies into two categories, i. Lossless image compression [8] technique: Visual quality of the decompressed image is the same as original, but the compression ratio achieved is not up to the mark. Normally, this type of compression technique is used where the visual quality of the decompressed image is a major issue rather than compression ratio. Run length encoding (RLE) [7, 8], arithmetic encoding (AE), [7, 8] and Lempel–Ziv–Welch (LZW) [7, 8] are some well-known lossless image compression techniques. ii. Lossy image compression [8]: In the case of lossy image compression, the amount of compression ratio achieved is very high, but at the same time, a huge amount of data is lost due to which the visual quality of the image is degraded. Vector quantization (VQ) [7, 8], color image quantization (CIQ) [7, 8], JPEG [4], and JPEG2000 [4] are some well-known lossy image compression techniques.

The article is organized as follows: Section 2 discusses the literature review. A brief explanation of the proposed method is discussed in Sect. 3. Experimental results are shown in Sects. 4, and 5 concludes the article.

2 Literature Review

In literature study, a sufficient amount of code vector matrix or codebook modification process are found. A few of them are discussed below.

In 2019, Abul Hasnat et al. [4] proposed a method where multiple images of same size can be compressed together by combining code vector matrices or codebook of the chrominance channels of all the images in a three-dimensional matrix. This method improves the compression ratio of the algorithm but at the same time degrade the visual quality of the image. In 2018, Rui Li et al. [5] proposed a new general codebook (GCB) design method based on bit rate and distortion which improves the performance of VQ significantly. Pradeep Kumar Shah et al. [6] in 2016 generate codebook by two steps i. The training set is sorted based on the magnitudes of the training vectors. ii. From the sorted list, training vector from every nth position is selected to form the codevectors. The method reduces the amount of memory required to store the codebook, but at the same time, it degrades the visual quality of the decompressed image.

3 Proposed Method

The size of the codebook of vector quantization plays a vital role for measuring the amount of space required to store the compressed image. The aim of this work is to reduce the number of bits required to store the codebook. The proposed method works in two steps (i) Compression: Reduce the size of each value of the codebook to 5 bits from 8 bits (ii) Decompression: Just reverse process of compression.

3.1 Compression

Input: Codebook of vector quantization **Output**: Compressed codebook.

Step 1: Let CB be a codebook of size $p*q$, generated by a normal vector quantization algorithm. The number of elements in the codebook is $n = p*q$.

Step 2: Divide each value of CB by 64, the one fourth value of the maximum value that can be represented by 8 bits, i.e., $255/4 = 64$, and generate the first quotient matrix Q which contains 0,1, 2, and 3 which can be represented by 2 bits and a remainder matrix R which contains values between 0 to 63 (Fig. 1).

$$Q_{i,j} = CB_{i,j}/64 \quad R_{i,j} = \text{MOD}(CB_{i,j}, 64) \tag{1}$$

Step 3: Divide each value of remainder matrix R by second threshold value 8 and store the nearest integer value in Q' (Fig. 2).

$$Q'_{i,j} \cong R_{i,j}/8 \tag{2}$$

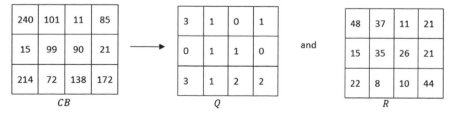

Fig. 1 Quotient matrix Q and remainder matrix R formation

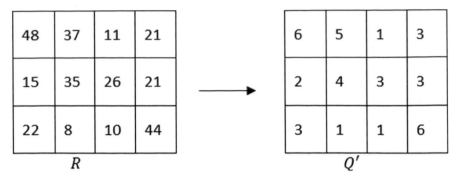

Fig. 2 Second quotient matrix Q' formation

3.2 Decompression

Input: Compressed codebook **Output**: Decompressed codebook.

Step 1: Multiply each value of Q' by second threshold value 8 and generate Q'' (Fig. 3).

$$Q''_{i,j} = Q'_{i,j} * 8 \tag{3}$$

Step 2: Multiply each value of Quotient matrix Q of equation no 1 by first threshold value 64 and then add matrix Q'' to generate decompressed codebook CB' (Fig. 4).

$$CB'_{i,j} = Q_{i,j} * 64 + Q''_{i,j} \tag{4}$$

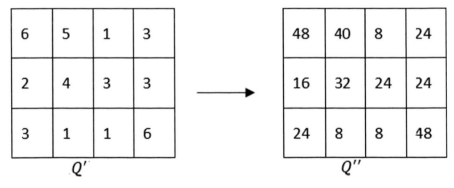

Fig. 3 Creation of Q'' by multiplying Q' by threshold value 8

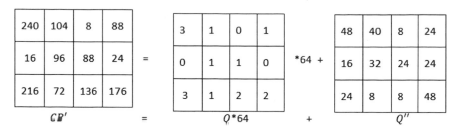

Fig. 4 Decompressed codebook CB' formation from Q and Q''

3.3 Memory Requirements for Proposed Method

Decompressed codebook CB' can be recovered by quotient matrices Q and Q'. The number of bits required to store the uncompressed codebook CB is $12 * 8 = 96$ bits. The maximum value of Q is 3 and requires 2 bits to represent it, whereas the maximum value of Q' is 6, i.e., maximum 3 bits are required to store it. So, memory required for $Q = n*$ no of bits require to represent MAX element, i.e. $= 12 * 2 = 24$ bits. Similarly, the number of bits required to store Q' is $12*3 = 36$ bits. Total number of bits require to recover decompressed codebook $CB' = 24 + 36 = 60$ bits. So, it saves $(96–60)/96\% = 37.50\%$ memory.

4 Experimental Results

The proposed method is implemented using MATLAB2018 and tested on standard color images found in literature and images from UCIDv.2 [4, 7–9] database. The performance of the proposed method is measured by three metrics, compression ratio (CR) [10], peak signal-to-noise ratio (PSNR) [10] and structural similarity index measure (SSIM) [10, 11].

Figure 5a–c shows the original pepper image, decompressed pepper images using vector quantization algorithm and the proposed method, respectively.

From Fig. 5, it can be easily observed that the visual quality of decompressed image using vector quantization and proposed method are almost same. Comparative result of space reduction between vector quantization and proposed method is given in Table 1.

From Table 1, it is observed that space reduction using proposed method lies between 90.81 and 93.81% which is much higher than 88.47–93.23% of VQ.

Table 2 shows computed PSNR [10] between original image and decompressed image using vector quantization and proposed method.

From Table 2, it is observed that visual quality of decompressed image using the proposed method is almost same or slightly lower than VQ in terms of PSNR [10].

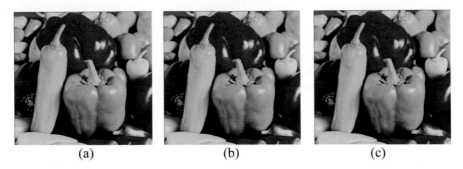

(a)   (b)   (c)

Fig. 5 **a** Original image, **b** decompressed image using vector quantization, **c** decompressed image using proposed method

Table 1 Space reduction using vector quantization and proposed method

Image name	Space for original image	Vector quantization		Proposed method	
		Total	% Reduction	Total	% Reduction
Girl	196,608	22,659	88.47	18,051	90.81
Jelly beans	196,608	20,767	89.43	16,159	91.78
House	196,608	21,335	89.14	16,727	91.49
Tiffany	786,432	54,097	93.12	49,489	93.70
Baboon	786,432	58,172	92.60	53,564	93.18
Pepper	786,432	53,232	93.23	48,624	93.81
ucid00006	589,824	42,174	92.84	37,566	93.63
ucid00007	589,824	47,456	91.95	42,848	92.73
ucid00008	589,824	41,521	92.96	36,913	93.74

Table 2 PSNR between original image and decompressed image using vector quantization and proposed method

Image name	Vector quantization			Proposed method		
	Y	Cb	Cr	Y	Cb	Cr
Girl	34.66	38.39	36.87	32.97	37.45	36.57
Jelly beans	37.06	37.98	37.14	34.49	36.72	36.52
House	35.52	37.10	35.48	33.86	36.87	34.53
Tiffany	34.62	34.91	36.80	33.66	34.36	36.45
Baboon	26.04	30.65	31.54	25.16	30.79	31.70
Peppers	33.51	35.17	34.73	32.22	34.95	34.45
ucid00006	25.82	36.11	35.53	24.95	36.49	35.92
ucid00007	25.06	33.76	34.37	23.91	34.52	35.40
ucid00008	28.34	37.65	37.39	27.29	37.45	37.40

Table 3 SSIM between original image and decompressed image using vector quantization and proposed method

Image name	Vector quantization	Proposed method
Girl	0.8936	0.8569
Jelly beans	0.9793	0.9662
House	0.9553	0.9482
Tiffany	0.9660	0.9591
Baboon	0.8067	0.8020
Peppers	0.9689	0.9637
ucid00006	0.7725	0.7588
ucid00007	0.8374	0.8294
ucid00008	0.8624	0.8381

From Table 3, it can be seen that the quality of the decompressed image using the proposed method slightly lower than vector quantization algorithm in terms of structural similarity index measure (SSIM) [10, 11].

5 Conclusion

This study proposes a method which is used to reduce the number of bits require to store the codebook of a vector quantization algorithm. The proposed method represents each value of the codebook by 5 bits instead of 8 bits that mean it reduces the memory required to store the codebook by 37.50% which increases the compression ratio (CR) of the overall algorithm significantly keeping the visual quality of the decompressed image almost same or slightly lower. Future work may be focused on improving the compression ratio more, keeping the visual quality of the image exactly the same as the original.

References

1. Gonzalez RC, Woods RE, Eddins SL (2011) Digital image processing using MATLB, Mc-Graw Hill
2. Gan G, Ma C, Wu J (2007) Data clustering theory, algorithms and applications. SIAM (2007)
3. Leitao HAS, Lopes WTA, Madeiro F (2015) PSO algorithm applied to codebook design for channel-optimized vector quantization. IEEE Lat Am Trans 13(4):961–967. https://doi.org/10.1109/TLA.2015.7106343
4. Hasnat A, Barman D (2019) A proposed multi-image compression technique. J Intell Fuzzy Syst IOS Press 36(4):3177–3193. https://doi.org/10.3233/JIFS-18360
5. Li R, Pan Z, Wang Y (2018) A general codebook design method for vector quantization. Multi Tolls Appl Springer 77(18):23803–23823. https://doi.org/10.1007/s11042-018-5700-7
6. Shah PK, Pandey RP, Kumar R (2016) Vector quantization with codebook and index compression In: IEEE International conference system modeling and advancement in research trends, India. https://doi.org/10.1109/SYSMART.2016.7894488

7. Hasnat A, Barman D, Halder S, Bhattacharjee D (2017) Modified vector quantization algorithm to overcome the blocking artefact problem of vector quantization algorithm. J Intell Fuzzy Syst IOS Press 32(5):3711–3727. https://doi.org/10.3233/JIFS-169304

8. Hasnat A, Barman D, Barman B (2021) Luminance approximated vector quantization algorithm to retain better image quality of the decompressed image. Springer 80:11985, 12007. https://doi.org/10.1007/s11042-020-10403-9

9. Barman D, Hasnat A, Sarkar S, Rahaman MA (2016) Color image quantization using gaussian particle swarm optimization (CIQ-GPSO). In: IEEE International conference on inventive computation technologies, India. https://doi.org/10.1109/INVENTIVE.2016.7823295

10. Sara U, Akter M, Uddin MS (2019) Image quality assessment through FSIM, SSIM, MSE and PSNR—a comparative study. J Comput Commun 7(3):8–18. https://doi.org/10.4236/jcc.2019.73002

11. Mandal JK (2020) Reversible steganography and authentication via transform encoding. Springer. ISBN: 9789811543975

Intra Change Detection in Shelf Images Using Fast Discrete Curvelet Transform and Features from Accelerated Segment Test

T. Bagyammal, Parameswaran Latha, and Vaiapury Karthikeyan

Abstract Detecting the changes within a single image is significant for applications like planogram compliance where objects of same type are arranged in a sequence. This article discusses on detection of such objects which differ in color, texture and shape from other objects in the given image. In this proposed algorithm, the given image is converted to HSV color space and it is partitioned into regions; Fast Discrete Curvelet Transform (FDCT) coefficients are extracted. In order to identify changed regions in the given image, salient points are detected using the Features from Accelerated Segment Test (FAST) corner detection algorithm. It has been observed that the value channel content of the HSV image is much significant in extracting useful features for change detection. Experimental results show an efficacy of 87% in detecting changes in a single row of a shelf image having same items arranged in a linear fashion.

Keywords (FAST) corner detection · HSV color space · Change detection · FDCT · Image processing

1 Introduction

Change detection is the process of recognizing the differences in the state of the object by monitoring it over a period of time [1]. Change Detection (CD) is useful in remote sensing applications for detecting changes in land-use or land-cover [1, 2]. In

T. Bagyammal (✉) · P. Latha
Department of Computer Science and Engineering, Amrita School of Engineering, Amrita
Vishwa Vidyapeetham, Coimbatore, India
e-mail: t_bagyammal@cb.amrita.edu

P. Latha
e-mail: p_latha@cb.amrita.edu

V. Karthikeyan
TCS Research and Innovation, IIT Madras Research Park, Tata Consultancy Services Limited,
Chennai, India
e-mail: karthikeyan.vaiapury@tcs.com

235
C. Satyanarayana et al. (eds.), *High Performance Computing and Networking*,
Lecture Notes in Electrical Engineering 853,
https://doi.org/10.1007/978-981-16-9885-9_20

computer vision, change detection algorithms are widely used for quality inspection, background detection, image or video compression [4]. Change detection can be done by using pre-classification and post classification techniques. Output of the change detection algorithms is binary pixel map indicating the not changed pixels by using the binary value "0" and changed pixels using the value "1" [1].

Pre-classification techniques exploit the characteristic of a pixel to determine the change without considering the spatial context. One common approach for the decision function element to identify change and no change in CD algorithms is the threshold value. Selecting an optimal threshold is a challenging task. A variety of algorithms have been proposed to learn the threshold automatically and the performance of these algorithms often depends on the scene-content [1, 4]. Post classification techniques use various image features to determine the change. Supervised and unsupervised techniques are used for CD. Accuracy of the classification of individual image is influenced by the accuracy of post classification techniques [1, 5]. Gunes ali et al. [6] have discussed that color-to-grayscale conversion algorithm followed by the National Television Standards Committee (NTSC) loses important details and optimization of this is required to extract more discriminative features. HSV color space features have been proven to give more accurate result for classification task [7].

The goal of this study is to identify and localize changes within the given image. To find changed regions within the same image, transform domain features and interest points are analyzed in grayscale image and Value channel from HSV color space.

2 Background Study on Change Detection

Many researchers have developed algorithms for change detection in images and videos, some of such prominent work relevant to the proposed work is discussed here:

Zhang et al. [1] discussed object based change detection algorithm by combining the change map obtained from coarse to fine scale based on image fusion concept. Liu et al. [2] discussed an image processing algorithm to perform change detection (CD) in heterogeneous remote sensing images. Image transformation technique has been used to obtain the change map and it has been further analyzed using Fuzzy c-means clustering algorithm. Bagyammal et al. [4] have proposed statistical based approach for scene change detection using the saliency feature. Segmentation algorithm using convolutional neural network (CNN) features [4, 5] is useful for scene CD at the object level.

Wu et al. [8] proposed an unsupervised change detection algorithm for remote sensing images using SURF and SVM. SVM classifier has been trained so that the difference image will be segmented into changed and unchanged region. From the given pair of images, SURF keypoints had been extracted and matched using RANdom Sample Consensus (RANSAC) algorithm. Matched keypoints were selected as the samples for unchanged class and rest of the keypoints were for the changed class. SURF feature was found to be effective to locate the matched regions between the pair of images.

Lin et al. [9] proposed an unsupervised change detection algorithm using SURF and Gabor wavelet features for remote sensing images. Initial difference image from the two given images was obtained by comparing Gabor wavelet feature which also takes care of incorporating pixels contextual information. SVM classifier was used to segment the difference image into changed and unchanged regions. SURF keypoints were matched between the two given images using RANSAC algorithm. Matched keypoints were the samples for the unchanged class and samples from remaining keypoints which were selected using Gaussian mixture Model (GMM) were used for changed class. Multispectral image processing algorithms and pattern recognition have gained attention amidst deep learning era. For example, Zhaozhen et al. [10] proposed a change detection algorithm for which image registration has been done using the combination of wavelet transform and SURF algorithm. Moorthy et al. [11] discussed an image processing algorithm, to detect items out-of-stock, misplaced products, count the number of products under each category and void space detection in a shelf. Muthugnanambika et al. [12] have proposed an image processing algorithm for planogram compliance application including void space detection, counting the products in the shelf. Product recognition was done using multiclass discriminative classifier using the statistical features of the segmented products from the input images.

Intra change detection analyzes the content of the image to find the changed region. Cohen Niv et al. [13] proposed a sub-image anomaly detection algorithm for an image containing single object as an image alignment algorithm. Wei et al. [14] proposed anomaly detection based on a deep neural network trained using the negative samples for medical images. Our proposed work on intra change detection algorithm works for images containing multiple images and doesn't require training algorithm.

From the literature survey, it is understood that change detection within an image is an area of research to be explored and image processing features can be used for this study. In this work, we have proposed a novel algorithm to detect changes within the given image without any references or user intervention.

3 Concepts Used

3.1 Wavelets

Wavelet transform based methods are a well-known tool for multi-resolution analysis which is useful to extract fine details as well as coarse details in the image and also for extracting frequency space information from given images [15]. The Curvelet transform is a higher dimensional generalization of the Wavelet transform designed to represent images at different scales and different angles [16].

3.1.1 Fast Discrete Curvelet Transform (FDCT)

Curvelets enjoy two unique mathematical properties, namely: (i) Curved singular-ities can be well approximated with very few coefficients and in a non-adaptive manner—hence the name "curvelets". (ii) Curvelets remain coherent waveforms under the action of the wave equation in a smooth medium. Objects in the image with curved shape can be better represented using FDCT; it represents curves using few coefficients and handles curve discontinuities well [16]. Noise in an image can be reduced effectively using Curvelet transform [17]. FDCT is done using the following steps:

i.   Sub-band decomposition
ii. Smooth partitioning
iii. Renormalization and Ridgelet analysis

i. **Sub-band decomposition**

Image f is filtered into sub-bands of different frequencies containing low and high frequency bands giving resolution layers obtained by performing convolution operation using the corresponding filters. Image f is filtered into sub-band:

$$f \rightarrow (P_o f, \Delta_1 f, \Delta_2 f, \ldots) \tag{1}$$

where, filter P_o contains with frequencies $|\xi| \leq 1$. Band-pass filter Δ_s contains frequencies $|\xi| \in [2^{2s}, s^{2s+2}]$, where s corresponds to the sth sub-band.

ii. **Smooth partitioning**

Sub-band content can be represented using the wavelet transform. Low pass filtered output can be represented using wavelet base. High frequency content can be repre-sented efficiently by dissecting the layer into small partitions called as grid of dyadic squares. This is obtained by multiplying sub-band content with non-negative smooth window function which produces the smooth dissection of the function f into squares. Sub-band decomposition imposes the parabolic scaling law, where width is proportional to square of the length so that the frame elements are anisotropic.

$$h_{Q} = w_Q . \Delta_s f \tag{2}$$

where w_Q corresponds to the window function and $\Delta_s f$ represents the sth sub-band.

iii. **Renormalization and Ridgelet analysis**

Renormalization is centering each dyadic square to the unit square $[0,1] \times [0,1]$ and the renormalized ridges are encoded efficiently using the Ridgelet transform.

Ridgelet are an orthonormal set $\{\rho_\lambda\}$ in domain $L^2(R^2)$ given by,

$$\widehat{\rho_\lambda}(\xi) = \frac{1}{2} |\xi|^{\frac{-1}{2}} \left(\hat{\psi}_{j,k}(|\xi|) . \omega_{i,l}(\theta) + \hat{\psi}_{j,k}(-|\xi|) . \omega_{i,l}(\theta + \pi) \right) \tag{3}$$

where, $\omega_{i,k}$ are periodic wavelets for $[-\pi, \pi)$. i is the angular scale and $l \in [0, 2i - 1 - 1]$ is the angular location. $\omega_{i,l}$ are Meyer wavelets for $\mathfrak{R}$. j is the Ridgelet scale and k is the Ridgelet location. Ridgelet transform divides the frequency domain to dyadic coronae in the frequency $|\xi| \in [2^s, 2^{s+1}]$ in the angular direction, samples the sth corona at least 2^s times using local wavelets. The ridge fragment has an aspect ratio of $2^{-2s} \times 2^{-s}$, ridge fragment needs very few Ridgelet coefficients to represent it. Two scales have been used in the proposed algorithm.

3.2 FAST Algorithm

FAST algorithm has been proposed by Drummond et al. [18] for recognizing interest points in an image for real time applications. "An interest point is a pixel in an image which has a precise position and can be robustly detected. Interest points have high local information content and they should be ideally repeatable between different images. Interest point detection has applications in image matching, object recognition, tracking etc".

The idea is to do the segment test criterion to choose the corners promptly by reducing the number of calculations using machine learning approach which involves two stages. In stage 1, a candidate pixel is compared with its neighboring pixels in Bresenham circle of radius 3 as shown in Fig. 1, and corners are detected using the segment test condition for m and a threshold t. Each pixel (say x) in these 16 pixels can have one of the following three states:

$$S_{p \to x} = \begin{cases} d, & I_{p \to x} \leq I_p - t \,(\text{darker}) \\ s, & I_p - t < I_{p \to x} < I_p + t \,(\text{similar}) \\ b, & I_p + t \leq I_{p \to x} \,(\text{brighter}) \end{cases} \qquad (4)$$

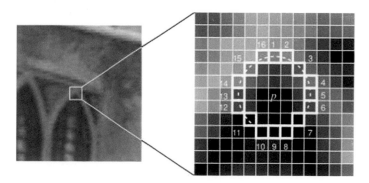

Fig. 1 Image showing the interest point under test and the 16 pixels on the circle [18]

where $S_{p \to x}$ is the state, $I_{p \to x}$ is the intensity of the pixel x and t is a threshold. It classifies p as a corner if there exists a set of m neighboring pixels in the circle which are all brighter than the intensity of the candidate pixel I_p plus a threshold t, or all darker than $I_p - t$. Define a variable K_p which is true if p is an interest point and false if p is not an interest point. In stage 2, decision tree is learned using Iterative Dichotomiser3 (ID3) algorithm for the training set which uses entropy of the pixel to select the x value in order to achieve maximum information gain about whether the candidate pixel is a corner using the entropy measure. The entropy for K for the set P is:

$$H(P) = (c + \hat{c}) \log_2 (c + \hat{c}) - c \log_2 c - \hat{c} \log_2 \hat{c} \qquad (5)$$

where $c = \left| \{ p | k_p \text{ is true} \} \right|$ (number of corners) and $\hat{c} = \left| \{ p | k_p \text{is false} \} \right|$ (number of non-corners). The choice of x then yields the information gain:

$$H(P) - H(P_d) - H(P_s) - H(P_b) \qquad (6)$$

After selecting x the same process is applied to the three subsets i.e., x_b is selected to divide P_b into $P_{b,d}, P_{b,s} P_{b,b}$, x_s is selected to divide P_s into $P_{s,d}$, $P_{s,s}$, $P_{s,b}$ and so on. The process ends when the entropy of a subset is zero.

4 Proposed Change Detection Algorithm

4.1 Misplaced Object Detection and Localization

Detection of misplaced object, that is identifying the region containing a different object with respect to its shape, size, texture and color when compared to its adjacent objects in the given image is done by two steps: (a) Image partitioning and feature extraction (b) Feature matching and misplaced item detection. It has been done using the following algorithm.

Proposed Algorithm: Detecting misplaced object in the shelf (Input: Image I from the dataset).

(1) Read image I.
(2) Repeat step 3 through step 8 for the number_of_ partitions in the image from M to 2.
(3) Partition the image vertically into number_of_partitions. Initialize the 1D array A of size equal to the number of partitions. Extract curvelet features from each partition and then find salient points of curvelet coefficients using FAST corner detection algorithm and represent using SURF feature descriptor.
(4) Salient points are matched between the partition and to all of its adjacent partitions.

(5)   Array elements (A) are incremented when the number of matching salient points between the partitions is greater than α1 and decremented when there are no matching salient points in the corresponding position.

(6)   If all the elements of the array A are non-zero and positive then display "All the objects in the image are same" and goto step 9.

(7)   If the elements of the array A have a negative value less than α2 then misplaced object is in the position corresponding to the minimum negative value, display the image and highlight the partition having the misplaced object and goto step 9.

(8)   If the array A has a negative value greater than α2 then decrement M by 1 and goto step 2.

(9)   Stop.

Parameters used after feature matching are α1 and α2; α1 corresponds to the minimum number of salient point matches for incrementing the element in the array A. Accuracy in the detection of a misplaced object is good when α1 is set as 10. Parameter α2 indicates the minimum number of non-matches between the partitions, to find the partition containing the misplaced object. Value for α2 has been empirically found to be equal to the number of partitions or one less than the number of partitions. The proposed algorithm has been experimented with the maximum of 10 and a minimum of 2 partitions, for detection of the misplaced object. Novelty in this proposed algorithm is summarized below:

i   .In this algorithm, change detection is successful even if the images vary in color, shape and texture

ii   .Change detection has been done without using machine learning approach which requires large amount of time and data for training.

5   Experimental Results and Discussion

Up to our knowledge, we use FDCT based salient points for change detection for the first time. However there exist works for object matching between multi cameras [19] and video [20] using wavelet salient features.

5.1   Dataset

Dataset to evaluate the performance of the proposed algorithm has been obtained by combining the images available in COIL 100 [20] dataset. The object images from COIL 100 are combined to simulate the shelf image in the retail store. It comprises of 647 images, of which 320 images contain the same product and 327 images have a misplaced object among them.

5.2 Results and Discussion

Performance of the proposed algorithm has been measured using accuracy [4] as given in Eq. (6) using the confusion matrix.

$$\text{Accuracy} = \frac{\text{TP} + \text{TN}}{\text{N}} \tag{6}$$

where, N denotes the total number of images. TP denotes the number of images containing an object having different features when compared to its adjacent objects being detected correctly using the proposed algorithm. TN denotes the number of images containing similar objects being detected correctly using the proposed algorithm. The result pertaining to this experimentation is shown in Tables 1 and 2. The following are the observations made on quantitative analysis:

- From Table 1, it may be observed that change detection gives higher accuracy of 84.69% when SURF features are extracted from V channel.
- From Table 2, it may be observed that change detection gives higher accuracy of 87.32% when FAST features are extracted from V channel.
- It is inferred from Tables 1 and 2 that FAST features extracted from V channel are best suitable for intra change detection.

Table 1 Confusion matrix for CD using FDCT, SURF in H and V channel

Predicted	Actual			
	Image has change content (P)		Image does not have changed content (N)	
	V channel	H channel	V channel	H channel
Image has changed content (P)	264 (TP)	259 (TP)	36 (FP)	40 (FP)
Image does not have changed content (N)	63 (FN)	58 (FN)	284 (TN)	280 (TN)
Accuracy H channel	83.30%			
Accuracy V channel	84.69%			

Table 2 Confusion matrix for CD using FDCT, FAST in H and V channel

Predicted	Actual			
	Image has change content (P)		Image does not have changed content (N)	
	V channel	H channel	V channel	H channel
Image has changed content (P)	253 (TP)	253 (TP)	8 (FP)	38 (FP)
Image does not have changed content (N)	74 (FN)	74 (FN)	312 (TN)	282 (TN)
Accuracy H channel	82.69%			
Accuracy V channel	87.32%			

The following are the observations made on qualitative analysis:

• Fig. 2a–d shows the localization, the position of the misplaced object, detected correctly by the proposed algorithm.
• Fig. 3a–d does not have any changes, which is correctly recognized by the proposed algorithm.
• Fig. 4 contains a void space which has been correctly detected by the proposed algorithm when using SURF.
• Fig. 5a, b shows correct detection of misplaced objects of smaller size, by using the proposed algorithm when using FAST.

In the literature, the authors in [13] have reported an average Area Under Curve of Receiver operating Characteristic (ROCAUC) of 85.5% for image level anomaly detection on a few datasets. In [14] the authors have reported an ROCAUC as 84% on a medical image dataset. In this work, the dataset is a collection of shelf images from a retail store where intra change detection is important for computer vision based automated inspection in order to improve the quality of service to the consumers. Thus the proposed algorithm shows higher efficacy in intra change detection scenarios.

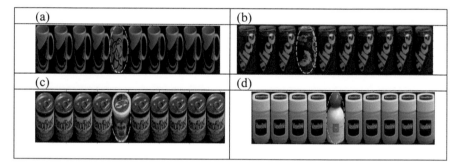

Fig. 2 **a–d** contains image with misplaced object, detected using the proposed algorithm and highlighted the region containing the misplaced object

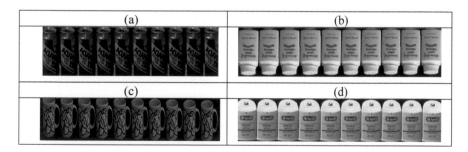

Fig. 3 **a–d** contains images of the same object, which has been recognized correctly using the proposed algorithm

Fig. 4 Image containing void space detected using SURF interest points

| (a) | (b) |

Fig. 5 a, b Image containing small changed object and detected using the proposed algorithm

Fig. 5a, b Image containing small changed object and detected using the proposed algorithm.

6 Conclusion

We have proposed a computer vision based intra change detection algorithm using salient points of the Fast Discrete Curvelet Transform (FDCT) wavelet coefficients from HSV image. Proposed algorithm has been tested with a large number of images and it is found to return satisfactory results. FAST salient points of curvelets have better accuracy in Value channel content when compared to SURF feature and hue channel content. This algorithm can be extended to detect changes in multiple positions. Further extensions are possible by applying deep learning models.

References

1. Zhang Y, Peng D, Huang X (2018) Object-based change detection for VHR images based on multiscale uncertainty analysis. IEEE Geosci Remote Sens Lett 15(1):1–5. https://doi.org/10.1109/LGRS.2017.2763182
2. Liu Z-g, Li G, Mercier G, He Y, Pan Q (2017) Change detection in heterogenous remote sensing images via homogeneous pixel transformation. IEEE Trans Image Process 27(4):1822–1834. https://doi.org/10.1109/TIP.2017.2784560
3. Bagyammal T, Latha P, Karthikeyan V (2018) Visual based change detection in scene regions using statistical based approaches. J Electron Imaging 27(5):051217. doi:https://doi.org/10.1117/1.JEI.27.5.051217
4. Sakurada K, Okatani T (2015) Change detection from a street image pair using CNN features and superpixel segmentation. BMVC 61–1. doi:https://doi.org/10.5244/C.29.61
5. Jong D, Louis K, Bosman AS (2019) Unsupervised change detection in satellite images using convolutional neural networks. In: 2019 International joint conference on neural networks (IJCNN), pp 1–8. IEEE
6. Güneş A, Kalkan H, Durmuş E (2016) Optimizing the color-to-grayscale conversion for image classification. SIViP 10(5):853–860

7. Sachin R, Sowmya V, Govind D, Soman KP (2017) Dependency of various color and intensity planes on CNN based image classification. In: International symposium on signal processing and intelligent recognition systems, pp 167–177. Springer, Cham
8. Wu L, Liu B, Zhao B (2017) Unsupervised change detection of remote sensing images based on SURF and SVM. In: 2017 International conference on computing intelligence and information system (CIIS), Nanjing, pp 214–218
9. Wu L, Feng G, Tu K (2019) An unsupervised change detection approach for remote sensing image using SURF and gabor wavelet features. In: Proceedings of the 2019 international conference on artificial intelligence and computer science, pp 282–287
10. Jiang Z, Zhang Y, Zhai H (2019) Image registration and change detection method based on wavelet transform and SURF algorithm. In: MIPPR 2019: automatic target recognition and navigation. International society for optics and photonics, Vol 11429, p 114291B. doi: https://doi.org/10.1117/12.2542897
11. Moorthy R et al (2015) Applying image processing for detecting on-shelf availability and product positioning in retail stores. In: Proceedings of the third international symposium on women in computing and informatics. ACM. doi: https://doi.org/10.1145/2791405.2791533
12. Muthugnanambika M, Bagyammal T, Latha P, Karthikeyan V (2018) An automated vision based change detection method for planogram compliance in retail stores. In: Computational vision and bio inspired computing, pp 399–411. Springer
13. Cohen N, Hoshen Y (2020) Sub-image anomaly detection with deep pyramid correspondences. arXiv preprint arXiv:2005.02357
14. Wei Q, Ren Y, Hou R, Shi B, Lo JY, Lawrence C (2018) Anomaly detection for medical images based on a one-class classification. In: Medical imaging 2018: computer-aided diagnosis. International society for optics and photonics, Vol 10575, p 105751M
15. Gonzales RC, Wood RE (2002) Digital image processing
16. Candes E, Demanet L, Donoho D, Ying L (2006) Fast discrete curvelet transforms. Multiscale Model Simul 5(3):861–899
17. Zhang Z-y, Zhang X-D, Hai-yan Y, Pan X-H (2010) Noise suppression based on a fast discrete curvelet transform. J Geophys Eng 7(1):105–112
18. Do MN, Vetterli M (2005) The contourlet transform: an efficient directional multiresolution image representation. IEEE Trans Image Process 14(12):2091–2106
19. Cai X, Zheng H, Zhang B (2009) Matching objects between multiple cameras based on wavelet salient features. In: 2009 International conference on information engineering and computer science, pp 1–4. IEEE
20. Zhang F, Wu T-Y, Zheng G (2019) Video salient region detection model based on wavelet transform and feature comparison. EURASIP J Image Video Process 1:58
21. Nene SA, Nayar SK, sMurase H (1996) Columbia object image library (COIL-100). Technical Report CUCS-006–96, Feb 1996

Mucormycosis Vaccine Design using Bioinformatic Tools

Saurabh Biswas and Yasha Hasija

Abstract Mucormycosis is an infection that occurs due to the presence of filamentous molds. Rhizopus delemar is a major cause of mucormycosis. The infection may be due to the inoculation of spores into wounds, inhalation of the spores, or the consumption of contaminated food. Mucormycosis cases have risen during the second wave of COVID-19 infections in India. Therefore, there is an urgent requirement for a vaccine against mucormycosis. The development of these vaccines is costly and time-consuming. Different methods have been used to decrease the expense and duration of time required for the development of a vaccine. One such method is the use of bioinformatics techniques for the development of vaccines. In this paper, the screening of epitopes through the bioinformatic tools predicts that the RO3G_11882 protein of Rhizopus delemar can be used for preparing immunological constructs. Binding and molecular simulation tests predict that the nanomeric epitope VLAL-HNFLL has low energy minimization values which provide stability to the peptide-MHC complex and sufficient binding with MHC class II molecules. This peptide sequence needs to further go through wet lab tests, for developing a vaccine against Mucormycosis.

Keywords Mucormycosis · Bioinformatics · Vaccine design

1 Introduction

Mucormycosis is an infection that occurs due to the presence of filamentous molds. Rhizopus delemar is a major cause of mucormycosis. The infection may be due to the inoculation of spores into wounds, inhalation of the spores, or the consumption of contaminated food. The infection tends to spread to blood vessels, causing infarction, necrosis, and thrombosis. Mortality due to mucormycosis is more than 30%, while it is 90% for the circulated disease [1].

S. Biswas · Y. Hasija (✉)
Department of Biotechnology, Delhi Technological University, Delhi 110042, India
e-mail: yashahasija@dtu.ac.in

© The Author(s), under exclusive license to Springer Nature Singapore Pte Ltd. 2022
C. Satyanarayana et al. (eds.), *High Performance Computing and Networking*,
Lecture Notes in Electrical Engineering 853,
https://doi.org/10.1007/978-981-16-9885-9_21

247

Mucormycosis cases have risen during the second wave of COVID-19 infections in India. Steroids for COVID-19 can reduce the inflammation in the lungs. However, steroids also increase blood sugar levels and decrease immunity in COVID-19 patients. It is believed that this decrease in immunity leads to mucormycosis infections. Therefore, there is an essential requirement for a vaccine against mucormycosis.

Vaccines are pharmaceutical products utilized in the treatment or prevention of diseases. The development of these vaccines is costly and time-consuming. Different methods have been used to decrease the expense and duration of time required for the development of a vaccine. One such method is the use of bioinformatics techniques for the development of vaccines. Vaccines are developed against viruses, bacteria, or parasites through the use of immunoinformatics, reverse vaccinology, and structural vaccinology methods [2]. This paper will use bioinformatic methods for the design and development of a vaccine for mucormycosis.

Reverse vaccinology, immunoinformatics, and structural vaccinology methods for vaccine design are described below:

1.1 Reverse Vaccinology

Reverse vaccinology (RV) is a technique used to discover antigens by searching the complete collection of antigens in an organism encoded as genomic data. The reverse vaccinology method does not need the culturing of pathogens in a lab, making it more easily usable in the case of pathogens that cannot be easily grown but have an obtainable genome sequence.

Reverse vaccinology has transformed vaccine development through the in-silico screening of polypeptide sequences from pathogens for selecting a subset of the novel vaccine candidates. The reverse vaccinology process has been effectively used to produce vaccines against other pathogens like C.pneumoniae [3], where open reading frames code for the surface proteins having homology to the virulence factors of other selected bacteria.

1.1.1 Types

Reverse vaccinology packages are classified according to their algorithmic procedures into filtering and classifying RV tools. Table 1 summarizes some of these RV tools.

Filtering Reverse Vaccinology Tools

These tools are designed like flowcharts. The vaccine candidates are selected by passing polypeptide sequences through a collection of filters till a subset of vaccine

Table 1 Comparison of the reverse vaccinology tools

Tool	Category	Description	Recall (%)
NERVE	Filtering RV tool	Imports polypeptide sequences of the pathogens and 5 different features are predicted	64
Vaxign	Filtering RV tool	Works through a Web interface. Similar to NERVE regarding the predicted protein features	58
VaxiJen	Classifying RV tool	Tool based on the ACC (autocross) conversion of polypeptide sequences into vectors of the same length	76
Heinson-Bowman	Classifying RV tool	Combines the features of Vaxijen and NERVE tools	75

The performance of reverse vaccinology tools was compared by Dalsass et al. [4]

candidates are selected. These filters can be the probability of being an adhesion protein, or in-silico predictions like subcellular localization, or directly quantification like the molecular weight. An a-priori cut-off is utilized when a numerical feature is passed through the filter. These tools differ from each other by the quantity of filters utilized. Some examples of these tools are NERVE and Vaxign.

Classifying Reverse Vaccinology Tools

These tools are a collection of features quantified or predicted on the microorganism's polypeptide sequence in a matrix. An input of a known set of vaccine candidates and non-vaccine candidates is used as the training set. A model is then built by an algorithm that classifies the input polypeptides into one of the two classes. Classifying reverse vaccinology place the complete set of input polypeptides according to their probability of being a vaccine candidate. Some examples of these tools are VaxiJen and Heinson-Bowman.

1.2 Immunoinformatics

The major goal of immunoinformatics is to use different factors like genetic variations in humans, variations in antigens, and the occurrence of infectious diseases are used to develop vaccines. Immune system activation utilizes immune memory induction and the efficacy of vaccines is determined by the strength of this induction. The immunological factors mediated by the vaccine are the T-cells and antibodies. Vaccines mediating T and B-cell responses show better efficacy. Even though B-cells

Table 2 Comparison of the B-cell prediction tools

Tool	Category	Description	Recall (%)
BCPred	Linear B-cell epitope prediction	Uses a kernel-based SVM classifier for prediction	99
ABCPRED	Linear B-cell epitope prediction	Uses networks for predicting linear B-cell epitopes	50.7
DISCOTOPE	Conformational B-cell epitope prediction	Uses surface exposure, spatial knowledge, and amino acid statistics for the predictions	93
SEPPA	Conformational B-cell epitope prediction	Based on continual segment clustering and single residue propensity scales	28.9

The performance of B-cell prediction tools was compared by Hu et al. [6]

are known as the major immune effectors, T-cells can induce antibodies with high-affinity and memory cells. This discovery has led to advancements in the design of vaccines.

1.2.1 Immunoinformatic Tools

Epitopes are structures that can induce an immune response after they are identified by the immune system. Determination of epitopes through experiments is time-consuming and difficult. Therefore, computational methods are being produced for the identification of epitopes. Different methods for the prediction of B and T-cells are described below:

B-cell Epitope Prediction

B-cells generate proteins known as antibodies. On the surface of microorganisms, the B-cell epitopes are present, which interact with the receptors of B-cells. These epitopes can be classified as conformational/discontinuous or linear/continuous epitopes [5]. Discontinuous epitopes make up most of these B-cell epitopes. Linear epitopes are mostly based on experiments. A few B-cell epitope prediction tools have been described in Table 2.

T-cell Epitope Prediction

For T-cells to identify antigenic peptides, the antigens must bind with MHC. There-fore, for predicting T-cell epitopes, detection of MHC binding peptides plays a crucial role. Different techniques for predicting the MHC binding peptides are described in Table 3.

Table 3 Comparison of the B-cell prediction tools

Tool	Category	Description	Recall (%0
NetMHC4	MHC class I antigen prediction	Predictions can be made for MHC class I alleles of humans, mice, pigs, cattle, and monkeys	83.6
NetMHCpan4	MHC class I antigen prediction	Useful in the identification of epitopes, cancer neoantigens, and naturally processed ligands	83.6
NetMHCII2	MHC class II antigen prediction	Predictions for HLA-DP, HLA-DQ, HLA-DR, and H2 class II alleles can be obtained using this tool	57.7
NetMHCIIpan	MHC class II antigen prediction	Predicts the binding of MHCII molecules with peptides of different lengths using ANN	32.6

The performance of T-cell prediction tools was compared by Zhao et al. [7]

1.3 Structural Vaccinology

Structural vaccinology is based on the structural properties of molecules, including polypeptides that are good vaccine candidates. This method for designing vaccines is mainly utilized for designing and the selection of polypeptide vaccines or antigens with the ability to produce immunity against a variety of pathogens. Structural information is useful in the selection of the surface epitopes near the functional site of the polypeptides like binding sites or catalytic sites, or conformational epitopes located on the surface. The structural knowledge is used for mapping antigenic epitopes used for identifying conformational properties like the selection of antigenic regions present in different microorganisms, exposure of the peptides to the solvent, and factors affecting the immunogenicity. For example, using structural modeling and epitope prediction, vaccine candidates were identified against Streptococcus pneumoniae [8].

Molecular docking tools can be used for designing and selecting the desired antigens. This approach generates a complex of two molecules (either protein–ligand or protein–protein) with the structure having the least binding energy. Molecular docking is used for predicting the binding of epitopes with MHC receptors or antibodies.

AutoDock Vina is a program for virtual screening and molecular docking [9]. This program is faster and more accurate for binding predictions as compared to the AutoDock 4.

2 Materials and Method

2.1 Sequence Retrieval and Analysis

CotH3 (RO3G_11882), CotH2 (RO3G_08029), and CotH1 (RO3G_05018) were predicted to be cell surface proteins on Rhizopus oryzae (also known as Rhizopus delemar). The fungal ligands belonging to the CotH family bind to the GRP78 during the endothelial invasion. It has been discovered that blocking the function of CotH proteins reduces the ability of the fungus to enter and damage the cells and reducing the severity of the disease in mice [10].

The protein sequences were analyzed using bioinformatics tools. ExPaSy server's ProtParam tool was utilized for calculating the length, isoelectric point, molecular weight of the proteins. VaxiJen server was utilized to analyze the antigenicity of the three sequences. Allergenicity was computed using Allertop. Allertop is a server for the in-silico prediction of allergens [11]. For analyzing the properties of the sequences, both the VaxiJen and the Allertop techniques utilize z descriptors and auto cross-covariance (ACC) preprocessing to convert the sequences into vectors of equal lengths for making the predictions. The formula for autocovariance A_{jj}(lag) is given below:

$$A_{jj}(l) = \sum_{i}^{n-l} \frac{z_{j,i} \times z_{j,i+1}}{n-l} \tag{1}$$

where index i is the location of the amino acids, j represents the Z scales and l is the lag(1, 2…L). The equation for cross-covariance C_{jk}(lag) between the j and k scales is given below:

$$C_{jk}(l) = \sum_{i}^{n-l} \frac{z_{j,i} \times z_{k,i+1}}{n-l} \tag{2}$$

2.2 Prediction of B-cell and T-cell Epitopes

The CotH proteins sequences of Rhizopus delemar were analyzed for B-cell epitopes using ABCPred and BCPred tools. B-cell epitopes were chosen for the three CotH proteins using ABCPred and BCPred. HLA DRB1-matched-Rhizopus specific T-cells are known to mediate antifungal activity [12]. HLA-DRB1 is an MHC class II cell surface receptor. Therefore, the selected epitopes were further subjected to analysis using NetMHCII2 and NetMHCIIpan. The DRB1 alleles occurring in Indians with the highest frequency are DRB*I 5/16 and DRBI*07 [13]. Epitope sequences

Fig. 1 Methodology for epitope prediction

for these alleles were selected. VaxiJen server was utilized to analyze the antigenicity of the epitopes. Allergenicity was computed using Allertop. The antigenic and non-allergenic sequences are selected.

2.3 Retrieval of the Protein and Epitope Structures

The 3D structure of DRB1*15:01 (54VM) was obtained from PDB. The epitope (VLALHNFLL) was designed using the DISTILL tool. This tool designed the 3D structures of the epitope on the basis of similarity with PDB structures [14].

2.4 Molecular Docking Studies

Molecular docking of the protein (DRB1*15:01) and epitope (VLALHNFLL) was performed using AutoDock Vina. AutoDock Vina can automatically generate the grid maps and collect the results that are present to the users in a transparent way. Negative Gibbs free energy (ΔG) scores were used for predicting the epitope-binding affinities. The best binding pose of the epitope was selected. After the completion of docking, Discovery Studio Biovia was used to visualize the interactions of the epitope with the protein.

Figure 1 represents the methodology used in this paper.

3 Results

3.1 Prediction of Antigenicity and Physicochemical Analysis

The physicochemical features of the proteins obtained from the ProtParam tool are displayed in Table 4. The pH at which the protein has no net charge is the pI value or the isoelectric point of a protein. The pI values for the proteins range between 4.94 and 5.29. The length, molecular weights, and accession number to identify the sequences are also given in Table 4. All the proteins were determined to be antigens

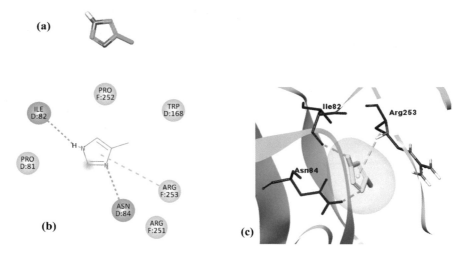

Fig. 2 **a** Structure of VLALHNFLL, **b** interactions between VLALHNFLL and DRB1*15:01 as a 2D diagram, **c** interactions between VLALHNFLL and DRB1*15:01 as a 3D diagram

Table 4 The physicochemical properties of the proteins

Protein name	Accession	Length	M.W.	pI value
RO3G_05018	EIE80313	609	68,759.40	5.29
RO3G_08029	EIE83324	594	65,254.26	4.94
RO3G_11882	EIE87171	601	65,759.18	5.07

Table 5 The antigenicity and allergenicity of the proteins

Protein name	Antigenicity	Allergenicity
RO3G_05018	Antigen	Non-allergen
RO3G_08029	Antigen	Non-allergen
RO3G_11882	Antigen	Non-allergen

and non-allergens using the VaxiJen and Allertop tools, respectively, as shown in Table 5.

3.2 B- and T-cell Epitope Prediction

The epitopes that can induce both T-cell and B-cell immunity are recognized as good vaccine candidates. For identifying the B-cell epitopes from the three proteins, BCPred and ABCPred tools were used, as depicted in Table 6. The protein sequences were given as inputs, and the epitopes were selected using both the tools. These epitopes were further used for identifying the T-cell epitopes. The T-cell epitopes

Table 6 Epitopes predicted using the BCPred and ABCPred servers

Protein	Position	Sequence	Antigenicity	Allergenicity
RO3G_05018	224	ILRKMGTYANEANMVRFFIN	Antigen	Allergen
RO3G_05018	153	KTKITFIGPETINTFEGCTL	Non-antigen	Non-allergen
RO3G_05018	568	SSPSNFIVKIKQGTVSSSSS	Antigen	Allergen
RO3G_08029	446	NRVLAIHNFLSPDLEWDRSI	Antigen	Non-allergen
RO3G_11882	456	VLALHNFLLPDLEWDRSIVQ	Antigen	Allergen
RO3G_11882	437	KYLTETVRVLFNNVTLTNRV	Non-antigen	Non-allergen
RO3G_11882	204	FFKLRHMEEDPTQIRERLYS	Antigen	Allergen

Table 7 T-cell epitopes were predicted by using the B-cell epitopes

Protein	Sequence	Allele	Antigenicity	Allergenicity
RO3G_05018	FIVKIKQGT	DRB1_1602	Non-Antigen	Non-Allergen
RO3G_08029	VLAIHNFLS	DRB1_1501	Antigen	Allergen
RO3G_08029	IHNFLSPDL	DRB1_1501	Antigen	Allergen
RO3G_11882	VLALHNFLL	DRB1_1501	Antigen	Non-Allergen
RO3G_11882	FFKLRHMEE	DRB1_1602	Antigen	Allergen

were detected using the NetMHCII2 and NetMHCIIpan tools, as shown in Table 7. The T-cell epitope predicted as an antigen and non-allergen was selected. Among the T-cell epitopes, VLALHNFLL (highlighted in yellow) peptide was selected as it was predicted as an antigen and a non-allergen.

3.3 Retrieval of the Protein and Epitope Structures

The structure of the DRB1*15:01 was retrieved from the PDB database. The structure of VLALHNFLL was constructed using the DISTILL tool.

3.4 Molecular Docking Analysis

Docking simulations of VLALHNFLL with DRB1*15:01 had the best score of − 3.4 kcal/mol. The two molecules and their interactions are represented in Fig. 2.

4 Discussion

In this study, three CotH proteins of Rhizopus delemar were utilized to predict antigenic sequences. ProtParam tool was utilized to compute the physicochemical properties of the sequences. VaxiJen tool was utilized to analyze the antigenicity of the four sequences. Allergenicity was computed using Allertop.

Epitopes having the ability to induce the immunity of both B- and T-cells are recognized as good vaccine candidates. The CotH proteins sequences of Rhizopus delemar were analyzed, and the B-cell epitopes were selected using ABCPred and BCPred tools. The selected epitopes were used for identifying the T-cell epitopes. The T-cell epitopes were detected using the NetMHCII2 and NetMHCIIpan tools. The DISTILL tool was utilized for designing the 3D structure of the selected epitope. The analysis revealed that a suitable epitope sequence from the protein sequences may be used to construct a vaccine.

5 Conclusion

The screening of epitopes through the bioinformatics tools predicts that the RO3G_11882 protein of Rhizopus delemar can be used for preparing immunological constructs. Binding and molecular simulation tests predict that the nanomeric epitope VLALHNFLL has low energy minimization values which provide stability to the peptide-MHC complex and sufficient binding with MHC class II molecules. This peptide sequence needs to further go through wet lab tests, for developing a vaccine against Mucormycosis. A similar method can be used for selecting vaccine candidates for other diseases, which can reduce the expense and time taken by the experiment.

References

1. Lee JH, Hyun JS, Kang DY, Lee HJ, Park SG (2016) Rare complication of bronchoesophageal fistula due to pulmonary mucormycosis after induction chemotherapy for acute myeloid leukemia: a case report. J Med Case Reports 10:195
2. Seib KL, Zhao X, Rappuoli R (2012) Developing vaccines in the era of genomics: a decade of reverse vaccinology. Clin Microbiol Infect 18:109–116
3. Capo S, Nuti S, Scarselli M, Tavarini S, Montigiani S, Mori E, Finco O, Abrignani S, Grandi G, Bensi G (2005) Chlamydia pneumoniae genome sequence analysis and identification of HLA-A2-restricted CD8+ T cell epitopes recognized by infection-primed T cells. Vaccine 23(42):5028–5037
4. Dalsass M, Brozzi A, Medini D, Rappuoli R (2019) Comparison of open-source reverse vaccinology programs for bacterial vaccine antigen discovery. Front Immunol 10:113
5. Greenbaum JA, Andersen PH, Blythe M, Bui HH, Cachau RE, Crowe J, Davies M, Kolaskar AS, Lund O, Morrison S, Mumey B, Ofran Y, Pellequer JL, Pinilla C, Ponomarenko JV, Raghava GP, van Regenmortel MH, Roggen EL, Sette A, Schlessinger A, Peters B (2007) Towards a

consensus on datasets and evaluation metrics for developing B-cell epitope prediction tools. J Mol Recogn JMR 20(2):75–82

6. Hu YJ, Lin SC, Lin YL, Lin KH, You SN (2014) A meta-learning approach for B-cell conformational epitope prediction. BMC Bioinformatics 15(1):378

7. Zhao W, Sher X (2018) Systematically benchmarking peptide-MHC binding predictors: from synthetic to naturally processed epitopes. PLoS Comput Biol 14(11):e1006457

8. Cornick JE, Tastan Bishop Ö, Yalcin F, Kiran AM, Kumwenda B, Chaguza C, Govindpershad S, Ousmane S, Senghore M, du Plessis M, Pluschke G, Ebruke C, McGee L, Sigaùque B, Collard JM, Bentley SD, Kadioglu A, Antonio M, von Gottberg A, French N, PAGe consortium (2017) The global distribution and diversity of protein vaccine candidate antigens in the highly virulent Streptococcus pneumoniae serotype 1. Vaccine 35(6):972–980

9. Trott O, Olson AJ (2010) AutoDock Vina: improving the speed and accuracy of docking with a new scoring function, efficient optimization, and multithreading. J Comput Chem 31(2):455–461

10. Gebremariam T, Liu M, Luo G, Bruno V, Phan QT, Waring AJ, Edwards JE Jr, Filler SG, Yeaman MR, Ibrahim AS (2014) CotH3 mediates fungal invasion of host cells during mucormycosis. J Clin Investig 124(1):237–250

11. Dimitrov I, Flower DR, Doytchinova I (2013) AllerTOP--a server for in silico prediction of allergens. BMC Bioinform 14(6):S4

12. Castellano-González G, McGuire HM, Luciani F, Clancy LE, Li Z, Avdic S, Hughes B, Singh M, Fazekas de St Groth B, Renga G, Pariano M, Bellet MM, Romani L, Gottlieb DJ (2020) Rapidly expanded partially HLA DRB1-matched fungus-specific T cells mediate in vitro and in vivo antifungal activity. Blood Adv 4(14):3443–3456

13. Mehra NK, Rajalingam R, Kanga U, McEnemy L, Cullen C, Agarwal S, Middleton D, Pollack MS (1997) Genetic diversity of HLA in the populations of India, Sri Lanka and Iran. In: Charron D (eds) Genetic diversity of HLA: functional and medical implications, pp 314–320. EDK Publishers, Paris

14. Baú D, Martin AJ, Mooney C et al (2006) Distill: a suite of web servers for the prediction of one-, two- and three-dimensional structural features of proteins. BMC Bioinformatics 7:402

Blockchain Implementation in IoT Privacy and Cyber Security Feasibility Study and Analysis

Yodida V R S Viswanadham and Kayalvizhi Jayavel

Abstract The Internet of Things (IoT) has a significant role in next-generation information technology, and its value and importance are broadly recognized. Internet of Things is rising at a huge level; hence there is an extensive scope to explore and improve the data privacy and security in IoT. Evolving research in IoT applications exploits blockchain technology to record transactions, optimize performance, provide additional security, and decentralized platforms. Blockchain has gained a lot of acceptance and started implementing in various arenas such as security of Internet of Things, Banking and Finance, Automobile, Manufacturing, Healthcare, and Supply Chain. We believe that this survey will assist readers in gaining a thorough understanding of blockchain security and privacy features and possible options to implement in various domains which are integrated with IoT.

Keywords Blockchain · IoT · Cyber security · Ethereum · IOTA

1 Introduction

Technological revolutions take a significant change periodically, which creates a new prospect of innovation, ideas, and products. Integration of Blockchain technology and Internet of Things (IoT) is one such example, which is implemented and proved its importance in the industry and business domains. The combination of these two emerging technologies is certainly an important step which will impact the daily human activities in the coming years [1]. IoT applications are facing multiple challenges due to integration of a massive number of devices like data integrity, security,

Y. V. R. S. Viswanadham (✉) · K. Jayavel
Department of Networking and Communications, School of Computing, SRM Institute of Science and Technology, Chennai, Tamilnadu, India
e-mail: yv8261@srmist.edu.in

K. Jayavel
e-mail: kayalvij@srmist.edu.in

© The Author(s), under exclusive license to Springer Nature Singapore Pte Ltd. 2022   259
C. Satyanarayana et al. (eds.), *High Performance Computing and Networking*,
Lecture Notes in Electrical Engineering 853,
https://doi.org/10.1007/978-981-16-9885-9_22

and performance. Blockchain offers a reasonable solution to address these limitations of existing IoT applications to ensure data integrity and security by removing third-party involvement.

Additionally, blockchain provides a secure and scalable solutions for an IoT network to transfer a sensitive information having right identification and authentication keys without any central server. Blockchains have newly attracted the attention across the various industries and sectors. The reason for this increase of interest is, by implementation of blockchain, components that could run before on a trusted net, can execute in a decentralized approach, without any need of any central repository and authority [2]. Blockchain is a Distributed Ledger Technology (DLT) which captures and store all the transactions between different entities. The data stores into the form of blocks and newly data appends at the end of the ledger.

The relational database design is primarily focus on a centralized storage, data stores in a central repository. Blockchain is specifically designed for a decentralized storage where the replica of the data stores in all the nodes of the blockchain [3]. Unlike relational database systems, there is no need of admin permissions within a blockchain to modify the data [3]. This paper conducts a methodical review of implementing IoT Security by using blockchain technology along with the areas of application.

2 Security Challenges and Role of Blockchain in IoT

IoT is a growing segment with a lot of potential to change and has quickly become a part of industries, people life, communications, and business sectors. IoT had resolved many issues in different sectors and fetched huge benefits to the business and industries across the globe.

There are many challenges to expand the IoT implementation through providing a secure functioning device at global network. In addition, some further challenges are lack of standards, interoperability, legal challenges, regulatory issues, rights issues, evolving IoT economy issues, and other developmental issues [4].

2.1 Challenges

The major concerns for many business and public organizations are cybersecurity and privacy threats. Most of these concerns are mentioned by the scholars and security experts. Most of the prominent cybersecurity related attacks have proved the vulnerabilities of IoT technologies. All these vulnerabilities exist due to the network connectivity in the Internet of Things that allows access between anonymous and untrusted devices. New security solutions require to safeguard the Internet of Things devices and environment [6]. Out of all the challenges that are aware, more important elements to adopt IoT are security and privacy. It is unfortunate, that there is no mechanism in place to acknowledge the users in case of any security treats till the time a breach occurs, causing major damages like critical data loss and confidential information [6]. Configuring the operational efficiency to populate alerts and notifications is also a challenge in IoT devices [6].

Existence and presence of IoT will increase in future and have opened new several possibilities for industries and exchanging information among several distributed units to improve the productivity, reduce the effort and cost. Data privacy and security are one major focus area and concerned while configuring IoT network. Better results can be provided by resolving IoT security and risks. The loss will be huge if the vulnerabilities in IoT environment are exploited. The privacy and security of the data are the major concern while implementing IoT environment [6].

2.2   IoT Categories

There are 3 IoT categories, based on client's base and usage of devices [5]:

- **Consumer—IoT**: Users buy goods and services for their personal use. Devices like smart mobile phones, smart home appliances, smart cycles, health care sensors, smart security and fire alarms, smart thermostats [5].
- **Commercial—IoT**: Denotes the daily atmosphere outside of the house. Things like inventory controls, device trackers, connected health care devices, vending machines, smart ordering, and payment [5].
- **Industrial—IoT**: Industrial IoT denotes mechanized systems looks for improvement in productivity. Things like connected electric meters, water quality systems, monitoring systems, robots in production units, and other types of associated industrial sensors and systems [5].

2.3   Role of Blockchain and Integration with IoT

Several IoT devices and things communicates with multiple devices and sensors in IoT environment to perform different tasks. There are chances of occurring offensive actions in the network during this course. Blockchain technology has been generally used for encryption and confidentiality to share the information between IoT devices. Blockchain integration with IoT will improve the control of the present system [12].

Lot of data is capturing from IoT sensors on day-day basis which needs to be stored in a secured manner. Blockchain is a distributed ledger and some of the features are security transparency, privacy, and no downtime. There is a great potential for IoT systems in blockchain that rely on device identities and reputation systems [10].

Some of the applications that are developed to address the challenges based on the smart contract-based blockchain and IoT are listed in Table 1, data sourced from Internet.

Table 1 Challenges
Addressed

Platform	Category	Challenges addresses
Multiplatform	Industrial IoT	Privacy, security
	Electric vehicle charging	Access control
	Asset management	Access control
	Blockchain based IoT	Identity, security
Ethereum	Smart transportation	Authentication, privacy
	Wireless IoT systems	Security, authentication
	Internet of things	Access control
	Smart meters	Access control

Integration of Blockchain and IoT opens more opportunities in the industry. Some of these opportunities are defined here:

- Building Trust between objects: The integration of blockchain and IoT model builds a trust among the devices and helps in increasing the levels of security. All the transactions of the devices will be verified by miners of blockchain before storing it into the blocks [11].
- Cost reduction devices can communicate directly without any middleman in between the sender and the receiver. There is a cost saving due to elimination of third party [11, 11].
- Reduction in Transaction Time: Blockchain and IoT integration model will help in reduction of transaction time from days to seconds [11].
- Privacy and Security: The integration model will help in communicating and transforming information between devices in secured environment and ensures the privacy as well [11, 11].

2.4   Blockchain IoT Market Growth Rate

Blockchain IoT market has huge prospects to grow up to 13.2 $ Billion by 2024 as shown in Fig. 1. The major growth factors are operational efficiency, IoT security needs and requirements, decentralized architecture and cryptography, and smart contract-based solutions for IoT.

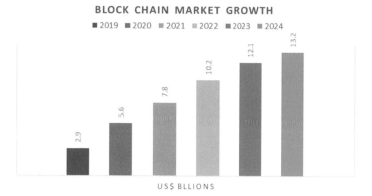

Fig. 1 Blockchain market growth

3 Overview of Blockchain Technology

An individual named Satoshi Nakamoto innovated the idea of blockchain in 2008, to manage the public transaction ledger of the crypto currency Bitcoin [10].

Blockchain is defined as a set of linked transactional data generates in a network by several users like consumers, suppliers, service provider, etc. The data stores in the form of a public ledger format permanently in a decentralized environment. Blockchain doesn't requires any central authority to approve or monitor all the transactions as it works in a peer-t-peer network. Blockchain is a constantly growing ledger that keeps a permanent record of all transactions in a secure, chronological, and unchallengeable manner. Blockchain data is stored in uniformly sized blocks.

3.1 Properties of Blockchain

- Anonymity: Refers to the capability to exchange information between parties without revealing any off-chain identity information or other transactions they have done.
- Availability: Distributed nodes within the blockchain network maintain a replica of the whole record as a public ledger which helps in safeguard from failures and attacks [7].
- Consistency: Distributed consensus and immutability ensure that all committed information is visible to all future data modifications by creating a single truth.
- Decentralization: Decentralization refers to the handover of control and decision-making from a centralized entity to a distributed network [7].
- Persistency: The miner validates transaction record and stores a copy in network. Once the record stores, it cannot be deleted or rollback from the blockchain network [7].

- Security: Information is secured using cryptography on a blockchain. Blockchain uses the asymmetric cryptographic technique to secure and protect the entire blockchain network.
- Transparency: Records stored on a blockchain are available to all members in network. Any changes in the blockchain network are accessible to all members in the public network.

All the transactions in the blockchain network are stored as immutable records, meaning they cannot be modified or deleted [2].

3.2   Types of Blockchain

Briefly, there are 4 types of blockchain technologies as show in Fig. 2.

- Public: A public blockchain is a non-restrictive and permission less distributed ledger technology where everyone in the blockchain network can access and perform transactions. Ex: Bitcoin and Ethereum
- Private: A private blockchain works in a restricted environment under the governance of an organization where only selected members can join the blockchain network. Ex: Hyperledger and R3 Corda
- Hybrid: A hybrid blockchain contains the features of both public and private blockchain. Some of the nodes are formed as public and other nodes as private. Ex: Dragon chain
- Federated or Consortium: A consortium blockchain is another type where more organizations are managing the blockchain network.

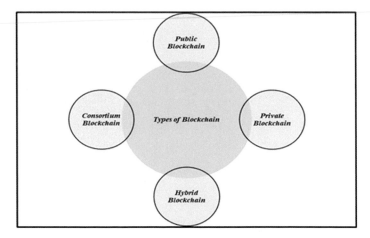

Fig. 2 Types of blockchain

3.3 Categories of Blockchains

- Permissioned
- Permission less.

A permissioned blockchain is a private blockchain which can be accessed by assigned users and requires pre-verification process, where as a permission less blockchain is a public blockchain which is accessible by everyone in the network [3].

3.4 Benefits of Blockchain

Blockchain technology has the following advantages for large scale IoT systems, as follows [8]:

- Building trust between devices
- Reduction of collusion risks
- Cost reduction
- Accelerate transactions
- Authentication of devices
- Removal of single point for failure
- Elimination of intermediaries
- Tamper proof data.

3.5 Blockchain Platforms for IoT

There are a few platforms that are explicitly designed for IoT systems based on features and characteristics:

- IoT chain is a blockchain platform for IoT which provides Industrial IoT infrastructure support and Middleware. IoT chain is using distributed ledger technology to solve the present IoT security and privacy issues [17].
- IOTA is another open-source distributed ledger technology designed for the Internet of Things. IOTA uses a DAG (Directed Acyclic Graph) structure to save the transactions on its ledger. Tangle is IOTA's system which records unaltered transactions of data. It confirms that the data is trustworthy and cannot be altered nor delete [17, 18].
- Walton chain [19] is another platform that is specifically designed for IoT to work as decentralized network. It uses RFID to communicate between various IoT devices. With the self-developed reader and tag chips, data movement is automatically storing into blockchain [17, 17].

3.6   Blockchain Implementation in Different Domains

Blockchain offers a decentralized environment to IoT devices, platforms, and products. The Internet of Things (IoT) opens multiple opportunities for businesses to execute smart processes. Every device around us is now armed with sensors, comminating and sending data to the storage.

Therefore, combining blockchain and IoT technologies can make the systems effective as Blockchain of Things (BCoT) as mentioned below [9]

- Agriculture
- Automotive Industry
- Business
- Distribution
- Energy
- Food
- Finance
- Healthcare
- Manufacturing
- Smart city.

Figure 3 shows the of adoption percentage and implementation of blockchain in different industries [13–15, 20].

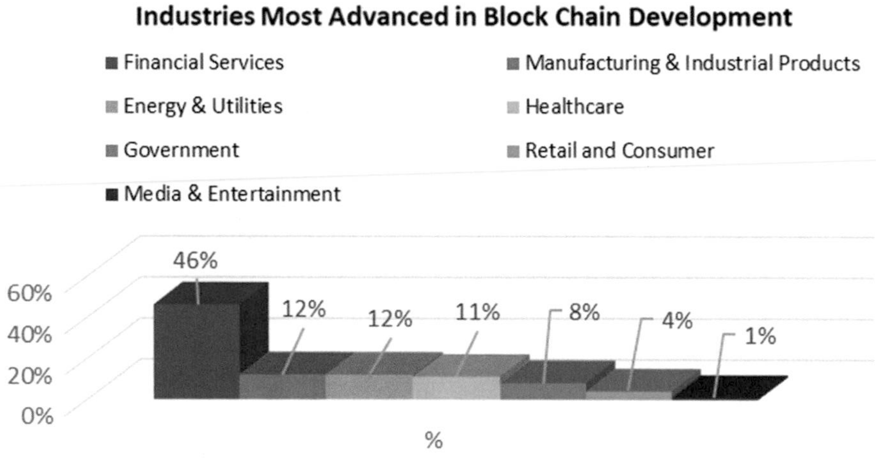

Industries Most Advanced in Block Chain Development

- Financial Services
- Manufacturing & Industrial Products
- Energy & Utilities
- Healthcare
- Government
- Retail and Consumer
- Media & Entertainment

Fig. 3 Most advanced industries in blockchain development

4   SWOT Analysis of Blockchain

SWOT analysis provides the summary of all the key issues to be taken into consideration while implementing blockchain technology [8], illustrated in Fig. 4.

- Strengths: Operational efficiency and resiliency are the major strengths; transactional costs can be lowered, and data can be shared directly between parties without any third-party intervention by removing middlemen [8]
- Weakness: Major weaknesses are immature status of the technology, high implementation costs, high energy consumption, low performance, slow process [8]

Strengths:	*Weakness*:
• *Integrity & Tamper Proof*	• *Low performance*
• *Privacy Protection*	• *Scalability*
• *Elimination of Intermediaries*	• *Energy Consumption*
• *Fast & low-cost money transfers*	• *Early stage of development & Immature*
• *No Data Loss \ Modifications*	• *Lack of High Skilled Human Resources*
Opportunities:	*Treats*:
• *New Business Model Enabler*	• *Lack of Awareness*
• *Data Security Improvement*	• *Low Adoption from external actors*
• *High Data Availability for Analytics*	• *Medium or long-term investment*
• *Fraud Detection*	• *Unfavorable government policies*
• *Reduction of Verification procedures*	• *Perception in insecurity*

Fig. 4   SWOT analysis

Fig. 5   Elliptic curve

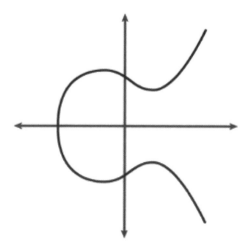

- Opportunities: Secure IoT, Cybersecurity, data integration of supply chain management [8]
- Treats: Scalability, legal regulations, and government policies to implement the technology [8].

5 Ethereum Blockchain

Ethereum is a decentralized, open source, and distributed computing platform. It also provides a platform to develop decentralized applications, also known as DApps also to create and run the smart contracts [21].

5.1 Smart Contract

Smart contract is a conditional agreement among peers used to enable monetary dealings and to store important data in a distributed ledger. The contract permits the exchange of money, property, data, or any asset. Gas and Ether are the types of currencies in Ethereum. Ether is the crypto currency which used to transfer money. Gas is the ether to pay to run smart contracts.

- **Gas limit**: Maximum amount of gas to spend on a transaction.
- **Gas used**: Actual amount of gas used to finalize the transaction.
- **Gas price**: Amount to pay for every unit of gas, denominated in Gwei.
- **Transaction fee**: Actual fee associated with a finalized transaction, equal to gas used * gas price.

Transaction costs is calculated in following manner [22]: **TxCost** = gasLimit * gasPrice.

5.2 Cryptography in Ethereum

ECC (Elliptic Curve Cryptography) is the cryptography use in Ethereum to generate a public key and a private key. The private key is always maintaining as secure, and the public key is used to create the Ethereum address. Elliptic Curve Cryptography (ECC) is a specific flavor of asymmetric cryptography which is using in blockchain technology.

The equation of elliptic curve is $y^3 = x^3 + ax + b$ where a and b are constants like real numbers, rational numbers. Figure 5 shows the elliptic curve defined by a cubic equation.

Key generation is the primary process in ECC to generate both public and private keys. The equation to generate the public key Pk = dn * pc, dn = Random number

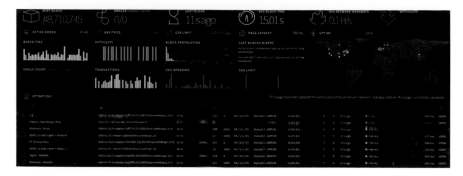

Fig. 6 Rinkeby real time dashboard

within the range (1 to n − 1). pc is the point on the curve. "Pk" is the public key and "dn" is private key.

5.3 *Implementation and Testing*

Remix IDE is a web based Integrated Development Environment that can be used to create, debug, deploy, and test Ethereum Smart Contracts. Remix IDE is a beginning point to trial the smart contract [23]. There are different public primary and test nets available to read and create the transactions to anyone.

Some of the test nets are:

- **Gorli**: Proof of authority (PoA) testnet that works across clients
- **Kovan**: Proof of authority (PoA) testnet for OpenEthereum clients
- **Rinkeby**: Proof of authority (PoA) testnet for Geth client. The Rinkeby testnet real time dashboard shows in Fig. 6
- **Ropsten**: Proof of work (PoW) testnet.

6 Discussion and Analysis

Blockchain is one of the advancements where focus is increasing to implement and use in recent period and has shown extraordinary guarantee to provide data privacy and security in different applications. Numerous investigations are being directed to completely understand blockchain's capacities. We are especially intense on blockchain as a security conspire for ensuring the protection of data and assets to be expanded in IoT projects. The proposed paper depicts the different potentials, structures, and noticeable uses of blockchain and its applications. Keeping that in mind, we have given an overview of how a blockchain can be used in IoT to implement security and privacy and verified the secured data flow using Ethereum IDE and testnet. We used Remix IDE to perform sample validations to check data security features of the Blockchain. Tests yet to conduct using Hyperledger Fabric.

7 Conclusion

IoT security and privacy are key elements to implement and develop the smart systems which further helps in generating new opportunities and brings a change in the environment, economic requirements, and fulfill industrial needs. IoT devices are communicating around the environment and a lot of data is generating from these IoT sensors on day to day. The current IoT Architecture is configured based client server model which may not be sufficient to accomplish the IoT privacy and security future requirements. Blockchain provides a feasible solution to address the IoT issues in current environment. Integration of blockchain in based IoT architecture handles most of the security and privacy treats. In this paper, we provided a basic level overview about blockchain integration with IoT by highlighting its advantages, benefits, and challenges. The conclusion at the end is that integrating blockchain with IoT can improves IoT environment and brings many advantages to secure the IoT data in multiple sectors. There is a scope and still requires additional research to examine blockchain implementation with IoT.

References

1. Choo KKR, Yan Z, Meng W (2020) Editorial: blockchain in industrial IoT applications: security and privacy advances, challenges, and opportunities. IEEE Trans Indus Inform 16(6):4119–4121. [8957273]. https://doi.org/10.1109/TII.2020.2966068
2. Christidis K, Devetsikiotis M (2016) Blockchains and smart contracts for the internet of things. IEEE Access 4:2292–2303. https://doi.org/10.1109/ACCESS.2016.2566339
3. Koshy P, Babu S, Manoj BS (2020) Sliding window blockchain architecture for internet of things. IEEE Internet Things J 7(4):3338–3348. https://doi.org/10.1109/JIOT.2020.2967119
4. Manoj Kumar N, Pradeep Kumar M (2018) Blockchain technology for security issues and challenges in IoT. Procedia Comput Sci 132:1815–1823. ISSN 1877–0509, https://doi.org/10.1016/j.procs.2018.05.140
5. Ahmed B (2018) 6 Three major challenges facing IoT. In Secure and smart internet of things (IoT): using blockchain and AI, River Publishers, pp 33–44
6. van Oorschot IPC, Smith SW (2019) The internet of things: security challenges. In: IEEE Secur Priv 17(5), pp 7–9, Sept–Oct 2019. doi: https://doi.org/10.1109/MSEC.2019.2925918
7. Yanglu, Yadav A (2019) Internet of things based wireless garbage monitoring system, pp 103–107. https://doi.org/10.1109/I-SMAC47947.2019.9032540
8. Fraga-Lamas P, Fernández-Caramés TM (2019) A review on blockchain technologies for an advanced and cyber-resilient automotive industry. IEEE Access 7:17578–17598. https://doi.org/10.1109/ACCESS.2019.2895302
9. Xu M, Chen X, Kou G (2019) A systematic review of blockchain. Financ Innov 5:27. https://doi.org/10.1186/s40854-019-0147-z

10. Hassija V, Chamola V, Saxena V, Jain D, Goyal P, Sikdar B (2019) A survey on IoT security: application areas, security threats, and solution architectures. IEEE Access 7:82721–82743. https://doi.org/10.1109/ACCESS.2019.2924045

11. Al Sadawi A, Hassan MS, Ndiaye M (2020) A review on the integration of blockchain and IoT. In: 2020 International conference on communications, signal processing, and their applications (ICCSPA), pp 1–6. doi:https://doi.org/10.1109/ICCSPA49915.2021.9385757

12. Sisodiya VS, Garg H (2020) A comprehensive study of blockchain and its various applications. In: 2020 International conference on power electronics and IoT applications in renewable energy and its control (PARC), Mathura, India, pp 175–180. doi: https://doi.org/10.1109/PARC49193.2020.236659

13. Wazid M, Das AK, Shetty S, Jo M (2020) A tutorial and future research for building a blockchain-based secure communication scheme for internet of intelligent things. IEEE Access 8:88700–88716. https://doi.org/10.1109/ACCESS.2020.2992467

14. Shahnaz A, Qamar U, Khalid A (2019) Using blockchain for electronic health records. IEEE Access 7:147782–147795. https://doi.org/10.1109/ACCESS.2019.2946373

15. Fernández-Caramés TM, Fraga-Lamas P (2019) A review on the application of blockchain to the next generation of cybersecure industry 4.0 smart factories. IEEE Access 7:45201–45218. https://doi.org/10.1109/ACCESS.2019.2908780

16. Fan C, Ghaemi S, Khazaei H, Musilek P (2020) Performance evaluation of blockchain systems: a systematic survey. IEEE Access 8:126927–126950. https://doi.org/10.1109/ACCESS.2020.3006078

17. Ali Syed T, Alzahrani A, Jan S, Siddiqui MS, Nadeem A, Alghamdi T (2019) A comparative analysis of blockchain architecture and its applications: problems and recommendations. IEEE Access 7:176838–176869. doi: https://doi.org/10.1109/ACCESS.2019.2957660.

18. Shafeeq S, Zeadally S, Alam M, Khan A (2020) Curbing address reuse in the IOTA distributed ledger: a cuckoo-filter-based approach. IEEE Trans Eng Manage 67(4):1244–1255. https://doi.org/10.1109/TEM.2019.2922710

19. Mo B, Su K, Wei S, Liu C, Guo J (2018) A solution for internet of things based on blockchain technology. In: 2018 IEEE international conference on service operations and logistics, and informatics (SOLI), pp 112–117. doi: https://doi.org/10.1109/SOLI.2018.8476777

20. Gonczol P, Katsikouli P, Herskind L, Dragoni N (2020) Blockchain implementations and use cases for supply chains-a survey. IEEE Access 8:11856–11871. https://doi.org/10.1109/ACCESS.2020.2964880

21. Ramesh VKC, Kim Y, Jo JY (2020) Secure IoT data management in a private ethereum blockchain. In: 2020 IEEE 44th annual computers, software, and applications conference (COMPSAC), pp 369–375. doi: https://doi.org/10.1109/COMPSAC48688.2020.0-219

22. Calastry R, Vinay Kumar (2019) Storing IOT data securely in a private ethereum blockchain. UNLV Theses, Dissertations, Professional Papers, and Capstones. 3582. http://dx.doi.org/ https://doi.org/10.34917/15778410

23. Mtetwa N, Tarwireyi P, Adigun M (2019) Secure the internet of things software updates with ethereum blockchain. Int Multi Inform Technol Eng Conf (IMITEC) 2019:1–6. https://doi.org/10.1109/IMITEC45504.2019.9015865

24. Aich S, Chakraborty S, Sain M, Lee H, Kim H (2019) A review on benefits of IoT integrated blockchain based supply chain management implementations across different sectors with case study. In: 2019 21st International conference on advanced communication technology (ICACT), pp 138–141. doi: https://doi.org/10.23919/ICACT.2019.8701910

Modified ResNetModel for MSI and MSS Classification of Gastrointestinal Cancer

C. H. Sai Venkatesh, Caleb Meriga, M. G. V. L. Geethika, T. Lakshmi Gayatri, and V. B. K. L. Aruna

Abstract In this work, a modified ResNet model is proposed for the classification of Microsatellite Instability (MSI) and Microsatellite Stability (MSS) of gastrointestinal cancer. A 41 layer modified ResNet model is proposed. The performance of this model is analyzed and compared with existing models such as Logistic regression, CNN, VGG-16, ResNet: 18, 34, 50, 101, 152. The proposed model surpassed the existing models with an accuracy, F1 score, True positive and True Negative of 89.81%, 0.9178, 6338, and 10,936. The training loss and validation loss are 0.2149 and 0.2488.

Keywords CNN · VGG 16 · ResNet · MSI · MSS · Gastrointestinal cancer

1 Introduction

During the "Genesis of Cancer," the word "Cancer" was rarely heard, and we never thought that we would be hearing it so often. As per IARC (International Agency for Research on Cancer), 1 in 5 people develop cancer [1]. Among all cancer related deaths, gastrointestinal cancer constitutes to 35% of global cancer related deaths. Computer vision was used to detect cancer tumors through histological images which drastically cut down both the time and money to carry out conventional testing methods [2–6].

Microsatellite is defined as the rudimentary repetitive sequence of the Deoxyribonucleic Acid (DNA). DNA comprises of many microsatellites. DNA Mismatch Repair (MMR) is a system which monitors the replication process of microsatellites and DNA, if it finds any error in the DNA recombination and replication it performs

C. H. Sai Venkatesh (✉) · C. Meriga · M. G. V. L. Geethika · T. Lakshmi Gayatri ·
V. B. K. L. Aruna
Department of Electronics and Communication Engineering, VR Siddhartha Engineering College
(Autonomous), JNTU, Kakinada, India
e-mail: 178w1a0411@vrsec.ac.in

V. B. K. L. Aruna
e-mail: aruna@vrsiddhartha.ac.in

© The Author(s), under exclusive license to Springer Nature Singapore Pte Ltd. 2022   273
C. Satyanarayana et al. (eds.), *High Performance Computing and Networking*,
Lecture Notes in Electrical Engineering 853,
https://doi.org/10.1007/978-981-16-9885-9_23

repair with the help of MMR proteins. Failure of MMR leads to unstable microsatellites/DNA which is the genesis of cancer. Based on global genomic status, cancer tumor is classified into "Microsatellite instable" (MSI) and "Microsatellite Stable" (MSS) tumor. High amount of instability in tumor classifies it as MSI-H, and it can be inherited, in which the immune cells are shut off from fully doing their job. By using "Immunotherapy," MSI-H can be cured. In MSS, the DNA in tumor cell has the same number of microsatellites that of a healthy cell, and this can be cured by "radiation" and "chemotherapy"-treatments which are opposite to immunotherapy. 26.4% of gastrointestinal cancer patients are classified as MSI-H and the rest, i.e., 73.6% as MSS. Therefore, detection of MSI or MSS of cancer has the same significance as detection of cancer to give appropriate treatment.

In this paper, we trained different pre-trained models and proposed a "Modified ResNet" model to classify MSI or MSS. 192,000 histological images have been sorted into 10% for test, 80% for training, and 10% for validation by "Justin lin" [7]. The original data set is provided by "Kather, Jakob Nikolas" [8]. This model can be further improved by using full pre-activation ResNet blocks and data augmentation techniques. But this model cannot be used for dynamic inputs such as "ECG." The modified ResNet model architecture and the results obtained are explained below (Fig. 1).

Fig. 1 Sample images of MSI and MSS

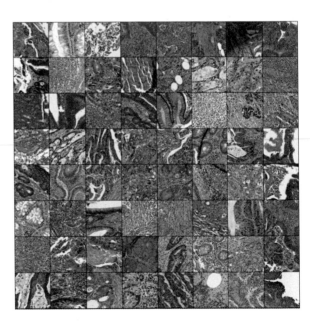

2 Model Description

To build a custom model, the performances of existing architectures on this data set have to be analyzed. It has been proven in many recent publications that "ResNet" architecture is the cream of image classification [9]. In this paper two approaches are used, each containing a group of architectures to determine their performance on the current data set.

2.1 Baseline Approach

In this approach, three baseline architectures were simulated they are "Logistic Regression," "4-Layer Feed Forward Neural Network," and "Convolution Neural Network" (CNN). CNN architecture consists of five convolution layers, two linear layers with dropout rate of 0.5. Each convolution layer is followed by batch normalization. Since "RELU" is computationally efficient, it is used as the activation function except for the output layer. "Max pool 2D" with stride two is used to reduce the image size by half.

2.2 Transfer Learning Approach

VGG16 and various versions of ResNet pre-trained models are simulated in this approach. VGG16 architecture is simple and efficient which performed well in many computer vision Tasks [10]. ResNet and its various versions such as ResNet-18, 34, 50, 101, 152 are tested to find the sweet spot for this dataset. ResNet due to identity mapping function there is no loss of the input image unlike VGG architecture the information is lost as it propagates deeper. "RELU" activation and "MaxPool 2D" with stride two is used in every model.

2.3 Modified ResNet Model

In this modified ResNet architecture, a 2D convolution layer, maxpool 2D layer are followed by four residual blocks which are sequentially connected. An adaptive average pool 2D is used to convert into single dimension; a sigmoid function is used for binary classification. To ramp up the training, after every convolution layer batch normalization is used. For the first residual block stride is one and for the remaining residual blocks stride two is taken. A convolution layer of 1 * 1 is employed to match input and output, when the sizes of input and output blocks are unequal. In fully connected network dropout with different dropout rates have been incorporated to

Table 1 Modified ResNet architecture

Layer name	Specific's	Output size	
Convolution	2D, (3 * 3, 64, stride 2)	112 * 112 * 64	
Maxpool	2 * 2, Stride-2	56 * 56 * 64	
ResNet block 1	$\begin{bmatrix} 1*1 & 64 \\ 3*3 & 64 \\ 1*1 & 256 \end{bmatrix} * 2$	56 * 56 * 256	
ResNet block 2	$\begin{bmatrix} 1*1 & 128 \\ 3*3 & 128 \\ 1*1 & 512 \end{bmatrix} * 3$	28 * 28 * 512	
ResNet block 3	$\begin{bmatrix} 1*1 & 256 \\ 3*3 & 256 \\ 1*1 & 1024 \end{bmatrix} * 5$	14 * 14 * 1024	
ResNet block 4	$\begin{bmatrix} 1*1 & 512 \\ 3*3 & 512 \\ 1*1 & 2048 \end{bmatrix} * 2$	7 * 7 * 2048	
Average pool	Adaptive 2D (output size = (1, 1))	1 * 1 * 2048	
FC1	2048		
FC2	512		
FC3	128		
FC4	1, Sigmoid		

reduce overfitting. The total architecture consists of 41 layers. Table 1 provides the parameters of the architecture.

3   Results and Discussion

The provided dataset images are preprocessed and are available in standard image size of 224 * 224 * 3. The data set is imported into "Google Colaboratory" from "Kaggle." Code is written for every model using "PyTorch" framework to obtain accuracy, F1 score, and confusion matrix.

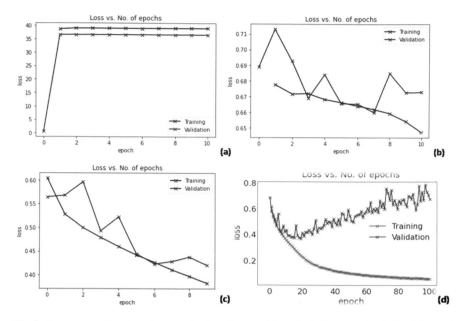

Fig. 2 Loss versus Number of epochs for baseline models: **a** logistic regression. **b** Feed forward neural network. **c** Convolutional neural network upto 10 epochs. **d** Convolution neural network upto 100 epochs

3.1 Baseline Models

Figure 2a shows the loss Vs number of epochs for logistic regression model; the training loss and validation loss remain constant at 39.0352 and 36.6357 (at 10th epoch). Figure 2b illustrates the loss Vs number of epochs for feed forward neural network model; we can observe that the number of epochs increase the training loss decreases but whereas the validation loss is fluctuating. The training loss and validation loss are 0.6473 and 0.6728 (at 10th epoch). The loss Vs number of epochs graph for CNN is shown in Fig. 2c in this graph as we can see the at 10th epoch both losses seem to be declining but when we increase the epochs, and it can be seen that they diverge which indicates over fitting shown in Fig. 2d. The training loss and validation loss are 0.0613 and 0.6774 (at 100th epoch).

3.2 Transfer learning Models

VGG 16's loss versus number of epochs graph is shown in Fig. 3; it can be observed that there is a spike at 16th epoch after that, the training loss and validation loss remain at 0.2829 and 0.2989(at 30th epoch) (Fig. 3).

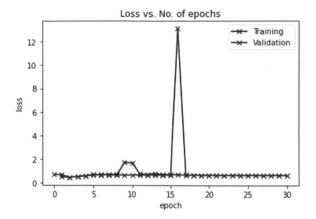

Fig. 3 Loss versus Number of epochs for VGG 16

Figure 4 contains the loss versus number of epochs graphs of ResNet-18, 34, 50, 101, 152. The training loss and validation loss of ResNet18 are 0.2651 and 0.3111 (at 40th epoch) shown in Fig. 4a. The training loss and validation loss of ResNet-34 are 0.3092 and 0.3203 (at20th epoch) shown in Fig. 4b. Similarly, forResNet50-0.2829 and 0.2989 (at 25th epoch) Fig. 4c, ResNet101-0.3102 and 0.3161 (at 15th epoch) Fig. 4e, ResNet152-0.3173 and 0.3307 (at 15th epoch) Fig. 4d. From the graphs of the ResNet family, it can be observed that as the order of the layers increase (such as 18, 34, 50 ... etc.) the sooner the training and validation losses converge and be in proximity. In ResNet-18, 34 base block is used and for the rest, i.e., ResNet-50, 101, 152 bottle neck block is incorporated.

3.3 Modified ResNet Model

From the results of the ResNet family, it is observed that the models having minimum number of layers have better performance even though they take more number of epochs to train. So, with this in mind "Modified ResNet Model" was built; initially base block was used but it didn't show any promise but when replaced by bottle neck block it surpassed the existing models. Here are a few parameters that were considered in this paper learning rate is 0.001, grad-clip = 0.1, weight decay = 1E-4, loss function = binary cross entropy and Adam optimizer. Figure 5 shows the loss versus number of epochs for modified ResNet model; it can be seen that the training loss and validation loss are less than other models 0.2149 and 0.2488 (at 25th epoch).

The confusion matrix is shown in Fig. 6. Class-0 represents MSI, and class-1 represents MSS. True Positive (TP) is defined as when MSI is predicted, and the actual output is MSI. True Negative (TN) is defined as when MSS is predicted, and the actual output is MSS. Similarly, when MSI is predicted but the actual output is

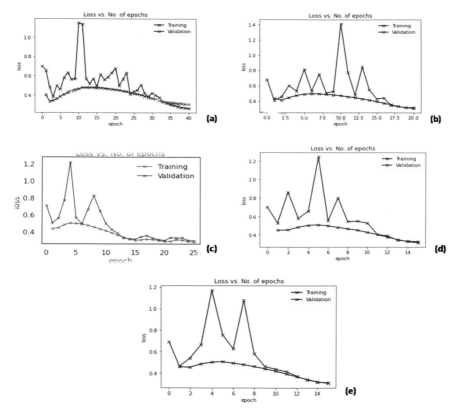

Fig. 4 Loss versus number of epochs of ResNet: **a** ResNet18, **b** ResNet34, **c** ResNet50, **d** ResNet152, **e** ResNet101

Fig. 5 Loss versus number of epochs of modified ResNet model

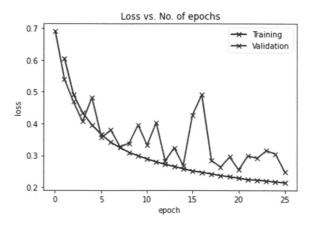

Fig. 6 Confusion matrix

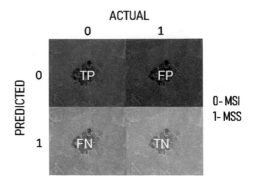

MSS then it is False Positive (FP), when MSS is predicted but the actual output is MSI its False Negative (FN).

From Table 2, it can be observed that the TP and TN values of the modified ResNet surpass other models which are desirable.

Figure 7 shows the comparison of accuracy and F1-score with different baseline, transfer learning models, and existing literature. Basha et al. proposed an efficient CNN based architecture for classification of histological routine colon cancer nuclei named as RCCNet. The main objective of this is to keep the CNN model as simple as possible, and it has achieved a classification accuracy of 80.61% and 0.7887 weighted average F1-score [11]. Lu et al. proposed a new method for training a deep neural network that distills particularly representative training examples and augments the training data by mixing these samples from one class with those from the same and other classes to create additional training samples the accuracy obtained

Table 2 Confusion matrix values of simulated models

Model	True positive (TP)	False positive (FP)	False negative (FN)	True negative (TN)
Logistic regression	0	7505	0	11,728
Feed forward neural network	523	6982	833	10,895
Convolution neural network	5880	1625	1855	9873
VGG16	0	7505	0	11,728
ResNet 18	6182	1323	1072	10,656
ResNet 34	6015	1490	1218	10,510
ResNet 50	6164	1341	972	10,756
ResNet 101	5940	1565	950	10,778
ResNet 152	5828	1677	943	10,785
Modified ResNet (proposed model)	6338	1167	792	10,936

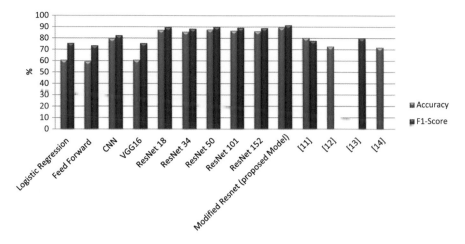

Fig. 7 Comparison of accuracy and F1score with various simulated models and existing literature

by this model is 73% [12]. Khairnar et al. proposed a modified Bayesian CNN for Breast Histopathology Image Classification and Uncertainty Quantification, and the obtained F1-score is 0.8031[13]. Hasan and Kabir developed a new algorithm for lung cancer This method has been tested on 198 slices of CT images of various stages of cancer, and the accuracy of the proposed method in this dataset is 72.2% [14] It is noted that the accuracy and F1-score of proposed modified ResNet model are 89.81%, and 0.9178 are better than remaining models.

4   Conclusion

A "Modified ResNet" model is proposed to classify MSI and MSS of gastrointestinal cancer. The results were compared with baseline, transfer learning models, and with existing literature. From the observations the proposed model exceeded other models with accuracy, F1-score, TP and TN of 89.81, 91.78%, 6338, and 10,936.This model can be further improved by using full pre-activation ResNet blocks and data augmentation techniques. But this model cannot be used for dynamic inputs such as "ECG." This network can be implemented to classify MSI and MSS of other cancers.

References

1. GLOBOCAN 2020: New Global Cancer Data|UICC
2. He K, Zhang X, Ren S, Sun J (2016) Deep residual learning for image recognition. In: Proceedings of the IEEE conference on computer vision and pattern recognition, pp 770–778

3. Dhanasekaran SM, Barrette TR, Ghosh D, Shah R, Varambally S, Kurachi K, Pienta KJ, Rubin MA, Chinnaiyan AM (2001) Delineation of prognostic biomarkers in prostate cancer. Nature 412(6849):822–826

4. Brinker TJ, Hekler A, Utikal JS, Grabe N, Schadendorf D, Klode J, Berking C, Steeb T, Enk AH, Von Kalle C (2018) Skin cancer classification using convolutional neural networks: systematic review. J Med Internet Res 20(10):e11936

5. Iizuka O, Kanavati F, Kato K, Rambeau M, Arihiro K, Tsuneki M (2020) Deep learning models for histopathological classification of gastric and colonic epithelial tumours. Sci Rep 10(1):1–11

6. https://www.kaggle.com/linjustin/train-val-test-tcga-coad-msi-mss

7. Kather JN, Pearson AT, Halama N, Jäger D, Krause J, Loosen SH, Marx A, Boor P, Tacke F, Neumann UP, Grabsch HI (2019) Deep learning can predict microsatellite instability directly from histology in gastrointestinal cancer. Nat Med 25(7):1054–1056

8. Ilhan U, Uyar K, Iseri EI (2020) Breast cancer classification using deep learning. In: International conference on theory and applications of fuzzy systems and soft computing. Springer, Cham, pp 709–714

9. Yamada M, Saito Y, Imaoka H, Saiko M, Yamada S, Kondo H, Takamaru H, Sakamoto T, Sese J, Kuchiba A, Shibata T (2019) Development of a real-time endoscopic image diagnosis support system using deep learning technology in colonoscopy. Sci Rep 9(1):1–9

10. Basha SS, Ghosh S, Babu KK, Dubey SR, Pulabaigari V, Mukherjee S (2018) Rccnet: an efficient convolutional neural network for histological routine colon cancer nuclei classification. In: 2018 15th international conference on control, automation, robotics and vision (ICARCV). IEEE, pp 1222–1227

11. Lu D, Polomac N, Gacheva I, Hattingen E, Triesch J (2021) Human-expert-level brain tumor detection using deep learning with data distillation and augmentation. In: ICASSP 2021–2021 IEEE international conference on acoustics, speech and signal processing (ICASSP). IEEE, pp 3975–3979

12. Khairnar P, Thiagarajan P, Ghosh S (2020) A modified Bayesian convolutional neural network for breast histopathology image classification and uncertainty quantification. arXiv:2010.12575

13. Hasan MR, Kabir MA (2019) Lung cancer detection and classification based on image processing and statistical learning. arXiv:1911.10654ss

An IoT-Enabled Healthcare System: Auto-predictive Colorectal Cancer with Colonoscopy Images Combined with the Convolutional Neural Network

Akella S. Narasimha Raju, Kayalvizhi Jayavel, and T. Rajalakshmi

Abstract Colonoscopy images play a vibrant role in predicting the intensity of the patient's colorectal cancer and there are many techniques for diagnosis and investigation. Colonoscopy image datasets and colorectal cancer analysis were used because of their generalized use. With the evolution of deep learning technologies, input datasets are automatically classified. Deep learning is the largest machine learning procedure widely utilized in a wide variety of applications, including image classification, image analysis, clinical records and object recognition. The classification and segmentation of diseases in intelligent systems is a significant challenge for these image analysis and computer vision systems. Convolutional Neural Network (CNN) is a class of deep neural networks that have spread in computer-assisted diagnosis systems. CNN is designed to learn unavoidably and flexibly the spatial classification of features by back propagation using several building blocks such as convolution layer(s), pooling layer(s) and fully connected layer(s). A method based on deep learning is proposed to automatically measure and predict cancer intensity accurately.

Keywords Colorectal cancer · Convolutional neural network · Deep learning · Colonoscopy · Prediction · Computer-assisted diagnosis

A. S. N. Raju (✉)
Department of Computer Science and Engineering, SRM Institute of Science and Technology, Kattankulathur, Chennai, India
e-mail: akellan@srmist.edu.in

K. Jayavel
Department of Information Technology, SRM Institute of Science and Technology, Kattankulathur, Chennai, India
e-mail: kayalvij@srmist.edu.in

T. Rajalakshmi
Department of Biomedical Engineering, SRM Institute of Science and Technology, Kattankulathur, Chennai, India
e-mail: rajalakt@srmist.edu.in

1   Introduction

Today, around the world, most people who suffer from cancer have the highest mortality rate as a result of the disease. In this cancer, there are numerous types and it affects the various organs of the body. With this dangerous disease most people suffer across the globe. Colorectal cancer (CRC) is the most widespread malignancy and is the second most common type of cancer affecting people. Today 2020–21 across the globe, 12% of people suffer from this colorectal cancer [1]. In this CRC, Non-polyps are not cancers and polyps are possibly depicted as and conversion in cancer. The diagnosis of colorectal cancer may prolong human life and be vital to combat this disease. Therefore, early cancer detection is being vigorously tested by a variety of biological scientists.

The field of AI plays a crucial role in the search for the best results for cancer detection with Machine Learning (ML), and Deep Learning (DL) is the sub-sectors of artificial intelligence.

With these advanced technologies on a daily basis, the new technologies involved in artificial intelligence technologies, computer-assisted detection (CAD) and computer vision concepts. In this CAD system, feature extraction presents certain weaknesses which will occur if the results are less accurate [2].

Computed tomography (CT) and magnetic resonance imaging (MRI) are new colon imaging techniques that are comparable to conventional colonoscopy. Most patients agreed with conventional colonoscopy [3, 4]. All of these studies offer 100% accuracy with respect to conventional colonoscopy. This colonoscopy gives you plenty of high-quality pictures of the discovery of the disease.

2   Proposed Computer-Assisted Detection (CAD) System

Before post-processing, the input images must be evaluated for image quality and abnormalities using Computer Aided Detection (CAD) [5, 6] used to identify colorectal cancer. The intelligent computer-assisted detection (CAD) block diagram for colorectal detection is illustrated in Fig. 1.

The colonoscopy technique provides several image numbers as image datasets. Keep in mind that these source image data sets must be of the highest possible quality. The larger the input images, the easier it becomes to detect the difference in the qualities of the pre-processing images [6, 7]. The intelligent CAD system concept is described in the following steps.

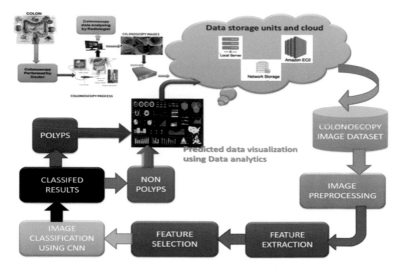

Fig. 1 Functional diagram for the computed detection of colorectal cancer

2.1 Large Intestine

The large intestine measures approximately 1.5 m in length, its primary purpose is to absorb salts and water from the food consumed. It can be divided into four sections: ascending, descending, sigmoid and rectal.

2.2 Colonoscopy

Colonoscopy is the screening method used to detect and identify tumors in the colon as a whole [8, 9, 10]. During this colonoscopy procedure, the physician checks the abnormality of the tumors. The doctor checks the entire colon with the camera fixed thin, light tube that is inserted in the starting point of the colon which is rectum. The camera generates the images which are monitored on the computer display. These images can be looked at in detail by the radiologist. Subsequent images are then stored on the local server for future references.

2.3 Data Storage and Cloud Storage

Cloud storage [11, 12] is an essential part of this computer-assisted diagnosis (CAD). This enables you to analyze large data obtained from the date the image is stored from the local servers. High-speed access to image data represents data stored in the cloud. It is a highly valuable and vital concept for cloud computing. Through a read–write operation, respectively, the Amazon Cloud system is the best choice for storage in the cloud.

The computing platform is essential to the analysis of big data. Thus, the execution of computational tasks at the same time is a reduction of time with high performance calculations. Additional GPU and CPU are introduced for parallel processing. Whereas Map reduce is primarily used by programmers for various calculation tasks for deep learning and machine learning techniques.

2.4 Colonoscopy Image Datasets

The first step in the implementation of the Deep Learning Architecture is to properly identify the issue. Next, enough input data set for deep learning architectures.

2.5 Image Pre-processing

Image pre-processing improves image prominence [13]. To do so, the grayscale of the image pixels is upgraded. In this image augmentation is done like flipping, rotation, Zooming, clipping.

2.6 Feature Extraction

Feature extraction is a dimensional reduction method used in colonoscopy data sets [13]. It eliminates unnecessary and duplicate images from pre-processed images.

2.7 Feature Selection

From the feature extraction, the best subset of features was taken from the pre-processed medical image [13]. The best choice of characteristics has therefore been chosen where the most significant characteristics are selected.

2.8 Convolutional Neural Networks (CNN)

The best model of deep learning prevails and is effective for colorectal cancer (CRC) is the Convolutional Neural Networks (CNN) [14], illustrated in Fig. 2. This class of

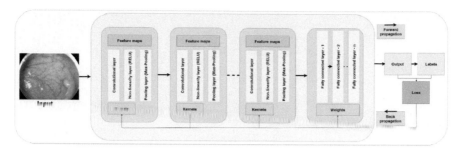

Fig. 2 Development of a convolutional neural network

deep learning algorithms uses high dimensional and hard-to-interpret data to obtain classification results. CNN has a tendency to recognize visuals directly from raw pixels. CNN architecture is usually made up of convolution layers, nonlinear, pooling, dropout and fully connected [15, 16].

2.9 Convolutional Layer

There is a Convolutional layer that is the primary layer that creates the source for Convolutional neural networks [17]. This is dependent upon the stream of a specific filter through the image. Indeed, this is a fact; an image of the kernel is multiplied by the pixel values of the image by stirring left or right on the input image or the image of the prior layer. Formerly its sum is engaged and input into the equivalent pixel area of the output data. The filter which reaches the edge of the matrix is moved down to the anticipated unit and the same procedures are repeated. Following the distribution of the whole image, a feature matrix or feature map is created. The Features Map comprises data on the specific features of a piece filter.

2.9.1 Nonlinearity Layer

One method that has a significant influence on CNN performance is the adoption of nonlinear activation features. Nonlinear activation function is a task, which enhances the nonlinearity of the network which becomes linear by following the preceding layers. Furthermore, it generates a function map by accumulating the non-conventionality of neurons in the next layer deprived of superfluous data values, thus growing the permanence of the whole network. Figures 3 and 4 illustrate some common types of nonlinear activation functions known as ReLU, Sigmoid and Tanh.

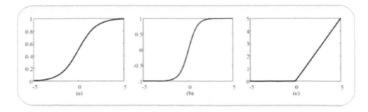

Fig. 3 Activation functions. **a** sigmoid; **b, c** ReLU

$$f_{RELU}(x) = \max(0, x) = \begin{pmatrix} 0 \ if \ x < 0 \\ x \ if \ x \geq 0 \end{pmatrix}$$

$$f_{sigmoid}(x) = \frac{1}{1 + e^{-x}}$$

$$f_{tanh}(x) = \frac{2}{1 + e^{-2x}} - 1$$

Fig. 4 Equation of the ReLU, sigmoid and Tanh

2.9.2 Pooling Layer

The pooling layer reduces the magnitude of the acquired characteristics of the previous layer and makes the similar characteristics more predominant. This is done with ephemeral filters around the image. This means that it is subsample. Consequently, the magnitude of the data for the next layer will be reduced and the model cannot be over fitted. But we must not forget that this reduction translates into the loss of some imperative evidence. The greatest advantage of this layer is the reduction of the numerous factors to be computed on the network. This leads to a reduction in network computing effort and rapid training. There are three options for pooling: maximum pooling, average pooling and minimum pooling. Maximum pooling, this is the fortitude of the highest value among the pixel values in the filter size area. Minimal pooling is the assortment of the lowest value. Average pooling is based on the standard of dividing the sum of the pixel values that enter the filter size area by the size of the filter window.

2.9.3 Dropout Layer

The Dropout layer is the symmetrical layer that disconnects certain nodes to keep the network from storing too much data from the drive. In that manner, further effective learning may happen because certain network parameters are erratically ruined. It may be operational for any network layer and the network recital may be increased accordingly.

2.9.4 Fully Connected Layer

The fully connected layer is in the vicinity of the convolution. Nonlinear and pooling of layers within CNN. The entity matrices affected by the outputs of these layers are deformed into entity vectors by placing them together. That is to say, flatness is attained. The number of that layer can be greater than one, according to its architecture. This featured vector is then tagged which is classified as a traditional neural network. Softmax grew up in one of the most popular options for classifying task. The result is generated within the range of [0, 1] for each object class. The object categorization is included in a class and then mapped to the output neuron that has the highest value.

2.9.5 Image Classification

After the Convolutional neural network classification stage, colonoscopy images can be segmented into two classifications of colonoscopy image data sets. These images are presented in the form of Polyps and Non-polyps images. Polyps that are discovered from CNN could be danger of Cancer. In this way, self-identification of polyps can identify colorectal cancer.

2.9.6 Visualization

Segmented [18] results are polyps and non-polyps from the colonoscopy image will be analyzed to identify colorectal cancer. With the help of various visualization techniques, the information is then stored in a public or private cloud storage. Various users, such as patients and healthcare professionals, could have access to it.

3 Results

Cloud storage is an essential aspect of CAD. This allows you to analyze the resulting big data from the date the picture is stored from the local servers. Fast access to image data represents the data stored within the cloud. That's a very important and critical concept of cloud computing. Through a read and write operation, respectively, our Google Drive Personal Cloud system is the best choice for cloud storage for a single set of data access. The computing platform is key to big data analysis. So, performing computational work in parallel is to decrease the time with high performance calculations. Additional GPU and CPU are introduced for parallel processing.

3.1 Datasets

In this experiment, the CVC-clinicDB dataset was utilized, this dataset includes 606 endoscopic gastrointestinal diseases and includes 2 different classes with original and Ground truth. Datasets used for training and testing 563 and 259 each classification. Images have a resolution of 384 × 288 pixels.

3.2 Split Polyps and Non-polyps

Use polyps and non-polyps from cropped copy files into the train and validation from data polyp. We may use the data set divided into 75 and 25% presented in Fig. 5.

3.3 Convolutional Neural Networks

After extracting polyps and non-polyps images to create a data set, divide the data set in train and validation subfolders. In what we show is that it is possible to get small CNN classifier with CPU i3, 4 GB of RAM and GPU NVIDIA Xp.

We begin our calculations using a CNN with fully connected convolution and layers. The following section is a function of this type of CNN with 5 parameters: the number of filters, the size of the convolution, the epochs, the size of the batch

```
[ ]    sourceFiles1 = os.listdir(sourceFolderClass1)
       sourceFiles2 = os.listdir(sourceFolderClass2)
       print("Class 1 - polyps:", len(sourceFiles1))
       print("Class 2 - non-polyps:", len(sourceFiles2))

       Class 1 - polyps: 606
       Class 2 - non-polyps: 606

        --> Dataset: data_polyps
       > Train - polyps: 563
       > Train - non-polyps: 561
       > Validation - polyps: 259
       > Validation - non-polyps: 257
```

Fig. 5 Splitting of polyps and non-polyps

Table 1 CNN parameters

Model	Topology	Filters	Dimension	Accuracy
Model1_1	1CONV-FC	32	3 × 3	0.84375
Model1_2	1CONV-FC	32	5 × 5	0.66015625
Model1_3	1CONV-FC	64	3 × 3	0.859375
Model1_4	1CONV-FC	128	3 × 3	0.70703125
Model2_1	2CONV-FC	32, 64	3 × 3	0.91015625
Model2_2	2CONV-FC	64, 128	3 × 3	0.88671875
Model3_1	3CONV-FC	32, 32, 64	3 × 3	0.8515625
Model3_2	3CONV-FC	64, 64, 128	3 × 3	0.94921875

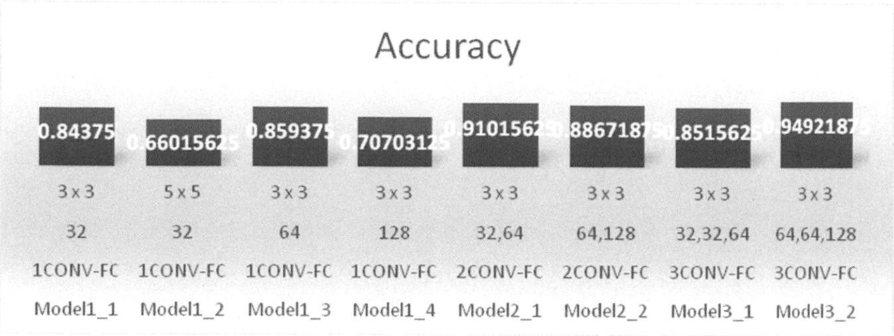

Fig. 6 Comparing CNN parameters

and the size of the entries. You could personalize this function with other parameters such as the dropout rate, activation function, etc. CNN_1Conv_1FC, 2CONV-FC, 3CONV-FC will have the following characteristics shown in table and best accuracy shown from this model are 91% shown in Table 1 and shown in Fig. 6

3.4 Optimized Hyperparameters for 3 Conv—FC

I shall use the topology Conv-Conv-Conv-FC (64, 64, 128 filters) and try to find the best hyperparameters. These results are shown in Table 2 and a comparison of parameters is shown in Fig. 7.

The best colonoscopy model using a small CNN could have a test accuracy of 93.35% using a limited amount of images but using an increase in keras data.

Table 2 Hyperparameters

Batch_size	Drop_rate	Active function	Optimizer	Loss	Accuracy
8	0.1	relu	Adam	0.312158	0.861486
8	0.5	relu	Adam	0.393979	0.837838
8	0.9	relu	Adam	0.693124	0.506757
16	0.1	relu	Adam	0.233646	0.927083
16	0.5	relu	Adam	0.388975	0.871528
16	0.9	relu	Adam	0.398614	0.847222
32	0.1	relu	Adam	0.219862	0.920139
32	0.5	relu	Adam	0.356632	0.878472
32	0.9	relu	Adam	0.493361	0.75
64	0.1	relu	Adam	0.18095	0.933594
64	0.5	relu	Adam	0.225566	0.933594
64	0.9	relu	Adam	0.322688	0.890625
128	0.1	relu	Adam	0.259164	0.90625
128	0.5	relu	Adam	0.272556	0.886719
128	0.9	relu	Adam	0.253681	0.914063

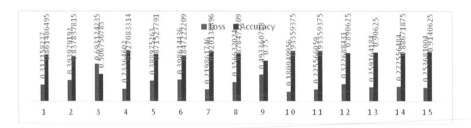

Fig. 7 Comparing hyperparameters

4 Conclusion

For classification purposes, a frame based on deep learning for the classification of colorectal images of the training is proposed. In this regard, diagnostic self-prediction is one of the significant demands of the dominant period and has studied or examined specific polyps. Using computer-assisted tools and analyzing trusted images are key areas that can enhance the effectiveness of health experts. This is a prerequisite of today's times to advance such methods of image processing which can help medical professionals in Gastroenterological surgery of medical science. These approaches are valuable for saving human lives and it is clear that colorectal cancer (CRC) can be anticipated before affecting the colon. For many decades, computer vision specialists have tried to bridge this gap with emerging automated systems that can develop colonoscopy images using machines to make decisions. We were looking at a new IOT-based healthcare system with a deep convolutional network approach that is supported by physicians and physicians in making sensible decisions. The outcomes of the suggested scheme in the dataset are 93.35%.

References

1. https://gco.iarc.fr/, GLOBOCAN [Online]
2. Ponzio F, Macii E, Ficarra E, Di Cataldo S (2018) Colorectal cancer classification using deep convolutional networks an experimental study. In: 5th international conference on bioimaging
3. Fenlon HM, Nunes DP, Schroy PC III et al (1999) A comparison of virtual and conventional colonoscopy for the detection of colorectal polyps. N Engl J Med 341(20):1496–503
4. Taha B, Werghi N, Dias J (2017) Automatic polyp detection in endoscopy videos: a survey. In: Proceedings of the IASTED international conference biomedical engineering (BioMed 2017), Innsbruck, Austria, February 20, 21
5. Sareena AM, Kaur M (2016) Computer-aided-diagnosis in colorectal cancer: a survey of state of the art techniques. In: International conference on inventive computation technologies (ICICT)
6. Patel K, Li K, Tao K, Wang Q, Bansal A, Rastogi A, Wang G (2020) A comparative study on polyp classification using convolutional neural networks. PLoS ONE 15(7): e0236452
7. Li Q, Yang G, Chen Z, Huang B, Chen L, Xu D, Zhou X, Zhong S, Zhang H, Wang T (2017) Colorectal polyp segmentation using a fully convolutional neural network. In: 10th international congress on image and signal processing, biomedical engineering and infromatics (CISP-BMWI2017)
8. Pittma (2019) Colorectal carcinoma screening: established method. In: Hissong E, Meredith E (eds) Colorectal carcinoma screening: established methods and emerging technology. ISSN: 1040-8363 (Print) 1549-781X
9. Wu W, Li D, Du J, Gao X, Gu W, Zhao F, Feng X, Yan H (2020) An intelligent diagnosis method of brain MRI tumor segmentation using deep convolutional neural network and SVM algorithm. Comput Math Methods Med 10
10. Yu L, Chen H, Dou Q, Qin J, Heng PA (2017) Integrating online and offline three-dimensional deep learning for automated polyp detection in colonoscopy videos, vol 21, no 1
11. Cao R, Tang Z, Liu C, Veeravalli B (2020) A scalable multicloud storage architecture for cloud-supported medical internet of things. IEE IoT J 7(3)
12. Dhayne H, Haque R, Kilany R, Taher E (2019) In search of big medical data integration solutions—a comprehensive survey. IEEE Access 7:91265–91290
13. Joshua Samuel Raj R, Jeya Shobana S, Pustokhina IV (2020) Optimal feature selection-based medical image classification using dee learning model in internet of medical things. IEEE ACCESS
14. Deep convolution neural network for big data medical image classification. IEEE ACCESS (2020)
15. Ribeiro E, Uhl A, Wimmer G, Häfner G Exploring deep learning and transfer learning for colonic polyp classification. Comput Math Methods Med
16. Tang H, Hu Z Research on medical image classification based on machine learning. In: IEEE access, pp 93145–93154, 11 May 2020
17. Pacal I, Karaboga D, Basturk A, Akay B, Nalbantoglu U (2020) A comprehensive review of deep learning in colon cancer. Comput Biol Med
18. Makkie M, Li X, Quinn S, Lin B, Ye J, Mon G, Liu T (2019) A distributed computing platform for fMRI big data analytics. IEEE Trans Big Data 5(2)

Akella S. Narasimha Raju is a present pursuing Ph.D. from SRM Institute of Science and Technology. He is presently doing research on the various applications of the Machine learning and Deep learning on Health Internet of Things concept. He was 17 years of teaching experience in various organizations.

Dr. Kayalvizhi Jayavel is a founder IoT Alliance club, a not to profit unit to train students in the field of IoT, www.iotalliance.in. IT Coordinator for National Family Health Survey (NFHS5) for Tamilnadu-South under Ministry of Health and Family Welfare, Government of India. Published papers in reputed journals with international collaborations with countries including Japan, Oman, Rwanda etc., Invited Professor, and research supervisor at the African Centre of Excellence of Internet of Things (ACEIoT), University of Rwanda (2019 to 2020). Visiting researcher to NEC (Japan) for a collaborative research project in the domain of WSN (2011). Recipient of SRM's best teaching performance award (2007).

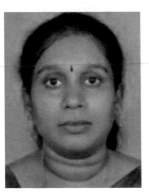

Dr. T. Rajalakshmi is working as an Assistant professor in SRM Institute of Science and Technology. She has 19 years' experience in teaching. She is a life member of ISTE, ISCA and Biomedical Engineering society. She published a number of papers in various journals.

Unfair Review Detection on Amazon Reviews Using Sentiment Analysis

M. Dolly Nithisha, B. Divya Sri, P. Lekhya Sahithi, and M. Suneetha

Abstract Reviews provided by the user have significant value of product within the world of e-market. Individuals and organizations depend heavily on social media now a days for customer reviews in their decision-making on purchases. However, for private gains like profit or fame, people post fake reviews to market or demote certain target products also in order to deceive the reader. To get genuine user experiences and opinions, there's a requirement to detect such spam or fake reviews. Sentiment Analysis (SA) has been used which is now the topic generating the major attentiveness in the text analysis field. Sentiment classification methods are used on a dataset of user reviews for unfair reviews detection and trend patterns. Various supervised and deep learning approaches like Logistic Regression, Support Vector Machine (SVM), and Long Short-Term Memory (LSTM) are used to determine the overall semantic of customer reviews by classifying them into positive and negative sentiment. The performance of sentiment classification is also evaluated by using accuracy, precision, and recall as performance measures and select the best approach for classification.

Keywords Fake review · Supervised learning · Sentimental analysis · LSTM · SVM · Logistic regression

1 Introduction

Nowadays, a large number of user reviews are performed on almost all content on websites in the e-commerce environment (such as Amazon, eBay). Reviews can include user-generated product reviews to help other users make purchasing decisions. Their existence prevents consumers from reading all content and making choices. In addition, when customers read multiple product reviews, it is difficult for

M. Dolly Nithisha · B. Divya Sri · P. Lekhya Sahithi (✉) · M. Suneetha
Department of IT, V.R. Siddhartha Engineering College, Vijayawada, India

M. Suneetha
e-mail: hodit@vrsiddhartha.ac.in

C. Satyanarayana et al. (eds.), *High Performance Computing and Networking*,
Lecture Notes in Electrical Engineering 853,
https://doi.org/10.1007/978-981-16-9885-9_25

them to distinguish between honest and unfair comments [1]. However, depending on the level of trust, they can increase or decrease the value of the product or website.

Our research focuses on the literature level of sentiment analysis, that is, on Amazon review records. Sentiment analysis technology will have a positive impact on the organization, especially when identifying bad reviews in e-commerce and other areas. They are an important source of information for customers to reduce product uncertainty when making purchasing decisions [2].

This study presents two supervised machine learning and deep learning techniques including Logistic Regression (LR), Support Vector Machine (SVM), and Long-Term Short Memory (LSTM) to classify and identify unfair positive reviews, unfair neutral reviews, and unfair negative reviews using this method. The main objective of our study is to classify the polarity of documents in the Amazon review datasets as fair or unfair reviews using sentiment analysis algorithms and supervised learning techniques. The practices performed by sentiment classification algorithms have demonstrated the performance measures of precision, recall, and accuracy. In the electronic Realme Buds case, we have applied LSTM, LR, and SVM classifiers.

2 Literature Review

In some articles, latest Amazon snapshots and various methods of feature selection were not used, and also due to the unbalanced data, the accuracy is not high enough [3]. Hence, more data is added to the actual dataset in order to reduce the imbalance. In some cases, preprocessing of text reviews is not done before it was given as input to the classifier. Only the text of the review is used in some research, which is not an effective way to identify unfair reviews. Many papers don't include collecting live review data from different review websites. A similar process for unsupervised learning for unlabeled data to detect fake reviews is not developed and is not compared with other machine learning algorithms. Our aim is to classify Amazon product reviews into groups of positive, negative, or neutral polarity by using various algorithms.

3 Proposed Work

3.1 Introduction

This project proposes to distinguish all such spammed false reviews by classifying them into fake and genuine in order to solve the major problem faced by online websites due to opinion spamming. The method attempts to classify reviews obtained from live data via website URL and categories such as service-based, product-based, customer feedback, experience-based, and crawled Amazon dataset with a service-based, product-based, customer feedback. We use various algorithms like Logistic

Regression, Support Vector Machine (SVM), and Long Short-Term Memory Model (LSTM).

3.2 System Architecture Diagram

The high-level architecture of the implementation can be seen in the figure (see Fig. 1), and the problem is solved in the following steps:

1. **Amazon Reviews Collection**. The data is collected directly from the Amazon website through the URL of the product. Dataset consists of a list of over 5000 consumer reviews for the Amazon product—Realme Buds (Ear phones). Reviews are collected using the Beautiful soap module and Docker. We use reviews extracted from the unlabeled data in this learning method.
2. **Data Preprocessing**. In preprocessing, only useful information is extracted and also redundant, noisy, and inaccurate information is also identified and analyzed.

    Phase 1: Data Cleaning. Data Cleaning is the phase of data preprocessing in which incomplete, meaningless, and unwanted data is removed. Amazon product dataset needs data cleaning because some fields of rows may have null values. The proposed method cleans the data by filling the null values or removing the rows with many missed values.

    Phase 2: Deletion of Punctuation Marks. The punctuation marks used at the beginning and end of the tests are withdrawn along with the additional spaces.

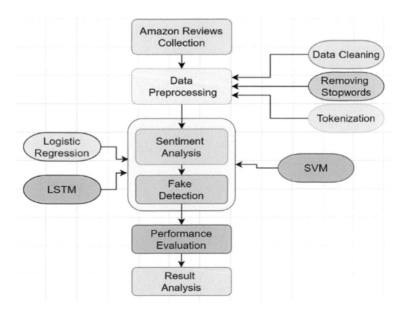

Fig. 1 Architecture diagram

Phase 3: Word Tokenization. In word tokenization, the large text is split into words for simple retrieval, through this process, the document can be converted into classifiable as the text is changed to a set of features.

Phase 4: Removal of Stopwords. Stopwords are removed as they are unwanted and they don't comprise any meaning; hence, those stopwords are eliminated as part of the removal of the stopwords step. Generally "a," "the," "of" "it," "and" etc., are some of the stopwords that do not possess any meaning and they confuse the model instead.

3. **Sentiment Analysis**. Classifying the reviews according to their emotions or feelings as positive, negative, or neutral ones. It includes predicting that the reviews will be positive or negative according to the words used in the text, the emojis used, the ratings given to the review, and so on. Linked studies suggest that fake reviews have stronger positive or negative feelings than actual reviews [4]. The reasons are that false reviews are used to sway people's views, and conveying opinions is more important than describing the facts clearly. Various algorithms such as SVM, LSTM, Logistic Regression were used for performing sentiment analysis.

4. **Fake Detection**. This step involves predicting the performance of the models while testing the datasets and then creating a confusion matrix that classifies the feedback into positive, negative, or neutral ones.

   The confusion matrix is not only used for performance evaluation but also used to obtain fair and unfair percentage reviews. The confusion matrix is a particularly significant part of our research as it allows us to classify Amazon datasets. The below-shown confusion matrix (see Fig. 2.) is the major part that was used in every algorithm.

5. **Performance Evaluation**. We evaluate the performance of the algorithms by calculating the accuracy, precision, recall, and F1_score for each and every algorithm.

		Predicted class A Fair	Predicted class B Unfair	Predicted class C Unfair
Actual class A	Fair	True Negative Reviews (TNR)	False Neutral Reviews (FNeR)	False Positive Reviews (FPR)
Actual class B	Unfair	False Negative Reviews (FNR)	True Neutral Reviews (TNeR)	False Positive Reviews (FPR)
Actual class C	Unfair	False Negative Reviews (FNR)	False Neutral Reviews (FNeR)	True Positive Reviews (TPR)
Unfair Negative Reviews Rate = FNR/TNR + FNeR + FPR				1
Unfair Neutral Reviews Rate = FNeR/FNR + TNeR + FPR				2
Unfair Positive Reviews Rate = FPR/FNR + FNeR + TPR				3
Fair Negative Reviews Rate = TNR/TNR + FNeR + FPR				4
Fair Neutral Reviews Rate = TNeR/TNeR + FPR + FNR				5
Fair Positive Reviews Rate = TPR/TPR + FNeR+FNR				6
Accuracy = TPR + TNR + TNeR/TNR + FNRclassB + FNRclassC + FNeR + TNeR + FNeR + FPRclaasA + FPRclassB + TPR				7
Precision = TNR/TNR + FNR class B + FNRclass C				8
Recall = TNR/TNR + TNeR + FPR				9

Fig. 2 The confusion matrix

6. **Result Analysis**. The most significant classification algorithm to identify the unfair positive, negative, and neutral reviews was identified based on the comparison of accuracy, precision, and F1_score of the different classification.

4 Description of Algorithms

4.1 Logistic Regression

Logistic Regression predicts the value of a particular variable which is dependent on a set of variables and these are independent of each other. This can also be used to predict the value for a categorical variable [5]. The categorical variables can either be Yes or No, 0 or 1, fake or real, etc., so logistic regression outputs a probabilistic value between 0 and 1. Logistic Regression can be said efficient because it works well for both continuous and discrete variables and provides probabilities for those variable and can classify any kind of new data.

Logistic Regression Equation. The Equation of Logistic Regression can be derived from the equation linear regression. The following are the mathematical steps to be followed to derive logistic regression.

Straight line equation can be written as follows:

$$y = b_0 + b_1 x_1 + b_2 x_2 + b_3 x_3 + \cdots + b_n x_n \tag{1}$$

As the required range is $-\infty$ to $+\infty$, to get that let's take logarithm of the equation which gives the following equation:

$$\log\left[\frac{y}{1-y}\right] = b_0 + b_1 x_1 + b_2 x_2 + b_3 x_3 + \cdots + b_n x_n \tag{2}$$

Support Vector Machine. Goal of SVM is to identify the hyperplane that classifies or divides the n-dimensional space into groups or classes. It helps in such a way that if there is any new point, then the model correctly classifies and places it in appropriate class [6]. This hyperplane has its orientation and position through which it is identified. The points which are close to the hyperplane are helpful in constructing the hyperplane. These extreme points are called as support vectors and hence the algorithm is Support Vector Machine.

Long Short-Term Memory (LSTM). LSTM is a kind of RNN that is used in deep learning. LSTM can learn long-term dependencies, and unlike other algorithms it has feedback connections. In general, a LSTM unit has a cell, an input gate, an output gate, and a forget gate. LSTM can remember long sequences of information that is important, leaving the unimportant information behind. For a cell, what to be given as input is decided by input gate, and output is decided by the output gate, and the forget gate is responsible for retaining the important information. These three gates collectively regulate the flow of cell in LSTM. This can be mainly used in speech recognition, text suggestion etc. [7].

As it is known that LSTM is a kind of RNN. It is easy for LSTM to remember previous long sequences of data due to its cell structure. The problem of RNN that is vanishing gradient is sorted out in LSTM.

5 Description of Tools and Dataset

The data is collected directly from Amazon website using the link of the product. The URL of the product used for extracting the data from Amazon website is as follows: https://www.amazon.in/Realme-Buds-Android-Smartphones-Black/pro duct-reviews/B07XMFDHSG/ref=cm_cr_dp_d_show_all_btm?ie=UTF8&review erType=all_reviews.

It consists of a list of more than 5000 customer reviews for the Amazon product Realme Buds. The dataset contains basic product information such as title, review texts, and more for each product (see Fig. 3).

Features and Description in Dataset:

Name—Name of the reviewer

Product—Product's name

Title—Title of the review

Rating—Product's rating out of 5

Review_text—The full text of the review

Review_date—The date on which the review was posted.

Name	Product	Rating	Review_date	Review_text	Title
Aman Singh	Realme Buds 2 with Mic	4.0	Reviewed in India on 9 September 2020	I bought this Earphone as a replacement for my ...	Awesome Overloaded W.R.T Sound Quality
Abdul Karim	Realme Buds 2 with Mic	4.0	Reviewed in India on 14 September 2019	am currently using Sennheixer cx213thats a...	Not Like my Sennheixer cx213
Praveen Kumar	Realme Buds 2 with Mic	5.0	Reviewed in India on 11 September 2019	Built-Boat bassheads build quality is great b...	Boat bassheads 225 vs realme buds 2
Abhishek	Realme Buds 2 with Mic	5.0	Reviewed in India on 25 November 2019	I'm a diehard audiophile and have been using a...	Honest review from a JBL fanboy. Only Rs. 599, seriously??
Pankaz	Realme Buds 2 with Mic	2.0	Reviewed in India on 14 September 2019	Wire Quality is good but most important is sou...	Not so Good

Fig. 3 Dataset

Description of tools. As we cannot directly download the data from the Amazon website, we will be using the tools/libraries such as Requests, Beautiful Soup, and Splash. By using these libraries, the data from any website can be extracted in form of csv file.

Requests. Requests library is one among the integral part of Python for creating HTTP requests to a specified URL.

Beautiful Soup. It is a python library that extracts data from html and xml that makes an easy scraping out information from web pages.

Splash. It is a JavaScript rendering service. It is a light-weight web browser with an HTTP API, implemented in Python 3 with an http API that we can send pages to, it will render it for us and then send us the results back.

6 Results and Observations

6.1 Stepwise Description of Results

1. Loading the Amazon reviews live dataset is created from the URL of the website.
2. Extracting "Rating" and "Review text" from the entire dataset is shown in Table 1.
3. Plotting a bar chart for ratings of the product given by the customers (see Fig. 4). Assign class 0(negative) for ratings 1 and 2, class 1(neutral) for the ratings 3, and class 2(positive) for ratings 4 and 5.
4. Tokenization- Individual analysis is tokenized into words and stored in a list (see Fig. 5). Here we remove numerical data and spaces and extract only words.
5. Stopwords removal- Stopwords like ["a", "is", "the", "on", "an", ...] are removed before training the classifier (see Fig. 6).
6. Converting the textual data into numerical data using the TfidfVectorizer() function of python. It gives a value that tells us how much that a particular word is related to the entire data (see Fig. 7).
7. Divide the entire dataset into test and train datasets.
8. Import Logistic Regression module from sklearn.linear_model and SVC (Support Vector Classifier) from sklearn.svm module in python, fit the models

Table 1 "Rating" and "review text" extraction	Rating	Review_text
	4.0	I bought this Earphone as a replacement for my...
	4.0	am currently using Sennheixer cx213thats a leg...
	5.0	Built-Boat bassheads build quality is great b...
	5.0	I'm a diehard audiophile and have been using a...
	2.0	Wire Quality is good but most important is sou...

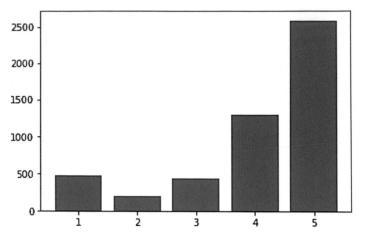

Fig. 4 Ratings-bar chart

```
0       [i, bought, this, earphone, as, a, replacement...
1       [am, currently, using, sennheixer, cx, thats, ...
2       [built, boat, bassheads, build, quality, is, g...
3       [i, m, a, diehard, audiophile, and, have, been...
4       [wire, quality, is, good, but, most, important...
                            ...
1396    [disappointed, they, don, t, support, alexa, i...
1398    [absolute, bag, of, rubbish, wont, connect, to...
1400    [not, as, described, the, sidetone, feature, m...
1401    [sound, is, very, poor, outdoors, pretty, unco...
1410    [use, these, with, an, ipod, touch, th, gen, m...
Name: Review_text, Length: 5267, dtype: object
```

Fig. 5 Tokenization

```
0     bought earphon replac boat earphon mostli use ...
1     current use sennheix cx that legend headphon u...
2     built boat basshead build qualiti great realm ...
3     diehard audiophil use lot headphon dont usual ...
4     wire qualiti good import sound qualiti good ri...
Name: cleaned, dtype: object
```

Fig. 6 Stopwords removal

```
5262    0.0   0.000000    0.0   0.0   0.0   0.0   0.0   0.0   0.0
5263    0.0   0.244872    0.0   0.0   0.0   0.0   0.0   0.0   0.0
5264    0.0   0.000000    0.0   0.0   0.0   0.0   0.0   0.0   0.0
5265    0.0   0.000000    0.0   0.0   0.0   0.0   0.0   0.0   0.0
5266    0.0   0.000000    0.0   0.0   0.0   0.0   0.0   0.0   0.0

[5267 rows x 5655 columns]
```

Fig. 7 Converting textual data to numerical data

Fig. 8 Logistic regression report

```
Train accuracy : 92.57061476382626
Test accuracy : 79.88614800759012


CONFUSION MATRIX
[[ 95  12  60]
 [ 28  12  78]
 [ 22  12 735]]


CLASSIFICATION REPORT
                precision    recall  f1-score   support

           0       0.66      0.57      0.61       167
           1       0.33      0.10      0.16       118
           2       0.84      0.96      0.90       769

    accuracy                           0.80      1054
   macro avg       0.61      0.54      0.55      1054
weighted avg       0.76      0.80      0.77      1054
```

and obtain Confusion matrix and calculate the test and train accuracies. Also generate classification reports (see Figs. 8 and 9).

9. Calculate the Positive, Negative, Neutral reviews percentages for both fair and unfair reviews that the Logistic Regression and SVM Model have predicted.

10. *LSTM*—Import LSTM from keras layers module in python to perform LSTM algorithm, fit the model, and obtain Confusion matrix and calculate the test and train accuracies (see Fig. 10). When the no of epochs increases, the accuracy of the model increases.

6.2 Observations from the Work

The comparison between different algorithms is shown in the table (see Table 2). It is observed that LSTM produced better accuracy when compared to Logistic Regression and SVM.

```
Train accuracy : 90.12580109185853
Test accuracy : 81.02466793168881

 CONFUSION MATRIX
[[105   8  54]
 [ 34  12  72]
 [ 28   4 737]]

CLASSIFICATION REPORT
              precision    recall  f1-score   support

           0       0.63      0.63      0.63       167
           1       0.50      0.10      0.17       118
           2       0.85      0.96      0.90       769

    accuracy                           0.81      1054
   macro avg       0.66      0.56      0.57      1054
weighted avg       0.78      0.81      0.78      1054
```

Fig. 9 SVM report

```
885/885 [==============================] - 30s 33ms/step - loss: 0.0974 - accuracy: 0.9528
Train accuracy : 95.27831673622131
295/295 [==============================] - 10s 35ms/step - loss: 0.1990 - accuracy: 0.9018
Test accuracy : 90.18235802650452

   [[ 425  118  101]
    [ 130  307  304]
    [  49  224 7774]]
   Unfair Negative Reviews Percentage :  10.141657922350472
   Unfair Neutral Reviews Percentage  :  9.939393939393945
   Unfair Positive Reviews Percentage :  7.7778053933142783
   Fair Negative Reviews Percentage   :  48.596012591815324
   Fair Neutral Reviews Percentage    :  13.515151515151516
   Fair Positive Reviews Percentage   :  96.60743134087238
```

Fig. 10 Result analysis for LSTM

Table 2 Accuracy comparisons for the algorithms

Algorithm	Test accuracy (%)	Train accuracy (%)
Logistic regression	79.88	92.57
SVM	81.02	90.12
LSTM	90.18	95.27

Table 3 Evaluation parameters on the dataset

Algorithm	Unfair negative (%)	Unfair neutral (%)	Unfair positive (%)	Fair negative (%)	Fair neutral (%)	Fair positive (%)
Logistic regression	11.89	10.71	10.14	51.35	10.71	95.57
SVM	13.40	3.57	9 36	58.01	10.71	95.83
LSTM	10.14	9.93	7.77	48.59	13.51	96.60

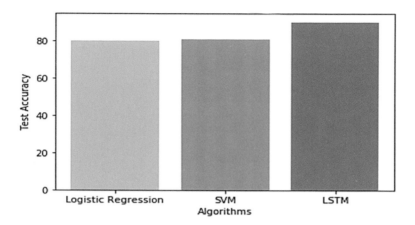

Fig. 11 Test accuracy versus algorithms

Fair and Unfair Reviews percentages of different algorithms are shown in Table 3.

Graph is plotted between algorithms and test accuracy. LSTM produced more test accuracy (see Fig. 11)

7 Conclusion

The unfair review detection technique is designed for filtering the fake reviews. In this research work, LSTM provided a better accuracy of classifying than the Logistic Regression and SVM classifier. Revealing that it predicts the fake reviews efficiently. The data visualization helped in exploring accuracy among different classifiers.

The research to detect unfair reviews brings great value that can ensure the trust of reviews and provide customers with a great shopping experience. Makers can use this unfair review detection methodology to get real data. Business organization can check their product sales and reach by analyzing what the customers are feeling about products. Customers can take decision whether they can purchase or not. Thus, this system makes e-commerce websites trustworthy.

References

1. Ashwini MC, Padma MC (2020) Efficiently analyzing and detecting fake reviews through opinion mining. Int J Comput Sci Mob Comput 9(7)
2. Li L, Qin B, Ren W, Liu T (2017) Document representation and feature combination for deceptive spam review detection. Neurocomputing 254:33–41
3. Reis JCS, Correia A, Murai F, Veloso A, Benevenuto F (2019) Supervised learning for fake news detection. IEEE Intell Syst 34(2):76–81
4. Lakshmi Holla A, Kavitha KS (2018) A comparative study on fake review detection techniques. IJERCSE 5(4):641–645
5. Elmurngi E, Gherbi A (2018) Detecting fake reviews through sentiment analysis using machine learning techniques. Data Anal 11(1, 2)
6. Liu W, He J, Han S, Cai F, Yang Z, Zhu N (2019) A method for the detection of fake reviews based on temporal features of reviews and comments. IEEE Eng Manage Rev 47(4), Fourthquarter
7. Viji D, Asawa N, Burreja T (2020) Fake reviews of customer detection using machine learning models. Int J Adv Sci Technol 29

Decentralized Coded Caching for the Internet of Things (IoT) Using User Cooperation

Tasnimatul Jannah and Asaduzzaman ⓟ

Abstract The Internet of things (IoT) connects embedded devices to the Internet and enables them to collect and share data. It allows devices to communicate and cooperate. These devices include anything from simple household items to sophisticated industrial tools. The collected data in IoT is extremely broad and diverse; however, the majority of data sent over the network are cache able. So caching can play a vital role to improve the performance of the IoT network. In the caching process, copies of files are kept in a temporary storage location to make them available locally. There are some distinct ways of caching. Finding the optimal caching approach for the IoT network is of great importance. The existing approaches may not be suitable for an IoT network. If conventional approaches are applied directly without any modification, the IoT network loses some fundamental properties of its own such as user cooperation, decentralization, and data aggregation. Hence, redesign of existing caching techniques is required to apply them on IoT networks. Our proposed work has replaced the caching approaches with a decentralized caching approach in the IoT network. The existing decentralized caching approach has been modified to accommodate user cooperation. The need for a coordinating central server to exploit coded multicasting opportunities has been eliminated. A generalized equation has been developed to quantify the memory-rate tradeoff of the proposed caching scheme. Results show that the proposed cooperative caching greatly reduces the bottleneck rate of the IoT network.

Keywords User cooperation · Decentralized coded caching · Coded multicasting opportunity

T. Jannah · Asaduzzaman (✉)
Chittagong University of Engineering & Technology, Chattogram 4349, Bangladesh
e-mail: asad@cuet.ac.bd

© The Author(s), under exclusive license to Springer Nature Singapore Pte Ltd. 2022
C. Satyanarayana et al. (eds.), *High Performance Computing and Networking*,
Lecture Notes in Electrical Engineering 853,
https://doi.org/10.1007/978-981-16-9885-9_26

1 Introduction

The Internet of things (IoT) is the latest communication paradigm in which devices that are connected can communicate with each other [1]. The main constraint in designing an IoT network is the size of the devices' memory. For this purpose, caching is an effective technique to mitigate these difficulties. Caching, also known as prefetching, is a network load reduction strategy that involves storing a portion of the content to be transmitted at user nodes cache [2]. Any caching-aided network has two phases in network operation, content placement, and content delivery phase. Caching can be both uncoded and coded. Coded caching is a caching approach where either the placement phase or delivery phase uses coding. The placement and delivery phases of coded caching are designed to allow coded multicasting among users with varying needs [3]. There are distinct approaches used in coded caching. As an IoT network is a network of devices connected, cooperation in caching is highly expected. Cooperative caching can improve caching efficiency of an IoT network. Recently, some caching approaches have been showing remarkable performance. We have to find out a coded caching approach to replace the caching approaches used in the existing IoT network to exploit multicasting opportunities. Our selected caching approach cannot be deployed directly. It has to be modified to be fitted into the requirement of an IoT network. So we can say the main motivation of our work is to deploy our proposed caching scheme in an IoT network where multicasting opportunities have been introduced and user nodes can enjoy each other's cooperation with an improved delivery rate.

2 Related Works

As IoT is growing so fast, designing an efficient IoT network is quite challenging. So many ideas are being proposed. Combining cooperative caching with social networking is suggested in [1]. They have shown a comparative analysis of the performance of both coded and uncoded approaches. Moreover, they used the maximum distance separable (MDS) coded caching scheme [4]. But these approaches of caching cannot exploit multicasting opportunities, and thus,, they cannot enjoy the global caching gain.

A centralized coded caching is described in [5]. In a centralized coded caching scheme, the central server knows the number of users and their identities. As a result, cache contents can be configured jointly in advance to optimize multicasting opportunities [3]. A centralized approach can exploit coded multicasting opportunities but requires a central coordinating server.

In [6], the authors showed that the multicasting gain can still be achieved in a more decentralized setting that gives us more flexibility, and rate is closer to the centralized approach. Decentralized coded caching can handle some issues more effectively than centralized coded caching. It can handle asynchronous demands. The server identifies the collection of active users sharing a bottleneck connection before attempting delivery. It then uses a decentralized coded caching delivery scheme for that group of users. Thus, it can handle dynamic networks also [5]. The popularity of content files often varies by many orders of magnitude. Niesen and Maddah-Ali [7] recommends splitting the collection of files into many groups of similar popularity within each group for such non-uniform distributions. Thus, it can handle non-uniform demands. Pedarsani et al. [8] show how it exploits the property of decentralized coded caching approach in online caching. But decentralized coded caching does not support user cooperation. User cooperation is highly needed in any IoT network. So decentralized coded caching is not directly applicable to any IoT network.

So, we have modified the existing decentralized coded caching algorithm. In the modified algorithm, user cooperation has been introduced to make the caching approach adaptable to an IoT network. It makes the network less dependent on a central coordination system.

3 Overview of Proposed Methodology

3.1 System Setup

Our proposed approach is based on an IoT network which is described with appropriate details and showed in Fig. 1. This network has a base station (BS) that is connected with several user nodes. The base station is connected with the user nodes with a shared bottleneck link. The BS has an access to a database with N files. Each of the K user nodes has independent cache memories of size M that can cache a certain amount of any files. User nodes can communicate and cooperate. The cooperation relies on their social relationship and desire to exchange cache content.

Fig. 1 The IoT network

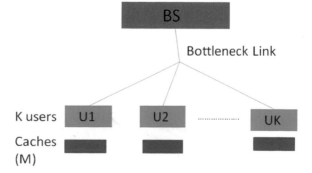

3.2 *Proposed Algorithm*

Content placement: The content placement of our proposed approach is identical to the placement phase of decentralized coded caching described in the paper [6]. It is shown in Fig. 2.

Content delivery: Our initial assumption is that all nodes have a strong social relationship among them and they trust each other. So they can assist each other. Now, the delivery phase starts with $s = K$, the coded transmission satisfies K users at once. Whenever s reaches the value of 2, BS stops sending coded messages. At that iteration, user cooperation will be invoked. Users interchange file fragments to satisfy each other's requirements. When $s = 1$, again the BS sends messages that are useful for only one user at a time. Figure 3 shows us the flowchart of the delivery phase.

Fig. 2 Content placement phase of the proposed algorithm

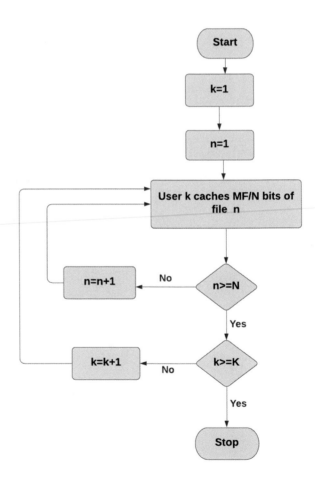

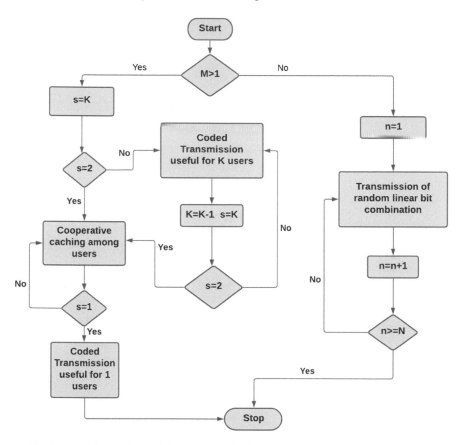

Fig. 3 Content delivery phase of the proposed algorithm

3.3 *Reason Behind Choosing* s = 2 *to Incorporate User Cooperation*

Consider a decentralized coded caching system where $N = K = 3$. Here, N is the number of files in the database and K is the number of user nodes in the network. We have only considered the delivery phase. The delivery phase starts with $s = K$. Here, $K = 3$, and we have considered the worst-case scenario.

1. At the first iteration $s = 3$, the server transmits coded signals which are simultaneously useful for 3 users. Therefore, the server multicasts $A_{23} \oplus B_{13} \oplus C_{12}$.
2. At second iteration $s = 2$, the server transmits coded signals useful simultaneously for 2 users. Therefore, the server multicasts $A_2 \oplus B_1$, $A_3 \oplus C_1$, $B_3 \oplus C_2$.
3. At third iteration $s = 1$, the server transmits coded signals useful only for 1 user. Therefore, the server unicasts A_0, B_0, C_0 to user1, user2, user3, respectively.

We can see that when $s = 3$, if we consider user cooperation, users have to decide from whom they should take the file fragments. Suppose user1 requires A_{23} which is available at both user2 and user3, it is time-consuming and requires additional computation to determine the appropriate sender. When $s = 1$ it is obvious that the server must transmit A_0, B_0, C_0 as these fragments are not present in the cache of the users. When $s = 2$ it is very convenient to consider user cooperation as the user can easily get required fragments. Suppose user2 needs B_3 which is available at user3's cache and user3 needs C_2 which is at user2's cache, so they can easily cooperate to get the desired portion of the file.

3.4 Development of Generalized Equation

We considered a network with $N = K = 3$ [6]. By the law of large numbers, we can write

$$|A_S| \approx (M/3)^{|S|} \times (1 - M/3)^{3-|S|} F$$

The same goes for file B, C. Now, $S \subset \{1, 2, 3\}$ [as we have user1, user2, and user3]. Consequently, the following approximations are considered-

1. When, $|S| = 0$, $|A_0|/F$ can be approximated as $(1 - M/3)^3$. [$s = 1$]
2. When, $|S| = 1$, $|A_1|/F$, $|A_2|/F$, and $|A_3|/F$ are approximated as $(M/3) \times (1 - M/3)^2$. [$s = 2$], and the same approximation goes for B and C.
3. When $|S| = 2$, $|A_{1,2}|/F$, $|A_{1,3}|/F$, $|A_{2,3}|/F$ are approximated as $(M/3)^2 \times (1 - M/3)$. [$s = 3$], and the same approximation goes for B, C.
4. When $|S| = 3$, $|A_{1,2,3}|/F$ is approximated as $(M/3)^3$, and the same goes for B, C. Butas these file fragments are already found in local caches, it won't be considered.

When $s = 3$, the server has to send $A_{23} \oplus B_{13} \oplus C_{12}$. [1 transmission] When $s = 2$, the user cooperation will eliminate the need for transmission from the server. [No transmission] When $s = 1$, the server has to send A_0, B_0, C_0. [3 transmissions] So, we can write the rate as

$$R_{UC}(M) = 3 \times (1 - M/3)^3 + (M/3)^2 \times (1 - M/3) \tag{1}$$

By using similar approximations considered to develop Eq. 1, we can obtain the rate $R_{UC}(M)$ for a decentralized coded caching system where, $N = K = 4$

$$R_{UC}(M) = 4 \times (1 - M/3)^4 + 4 \times [(M/4)^2 \times (1 - M/4)^2] + (M/4)^3 \times (1 - M/4) \tag{2}$$

Now from the above calculation, we can write a generalized equation for our proposed algorithm as

$$R_{UC}(M) = K \times (1 - M/N)^K + \sum_{i=2}^{K-1} \binom{K}{i+1} \times (M/K)^i \times (1 - M/N)^{K-i} \quad (3)$$

where K = No. of users N = No. of files M = Cache memory size $i = |S|$.

3.5 Verification of Generalized Equation

Let consider a network with $N = K = 5$.

Content Placement: In the placement phase, each user will populate their cache with appropriate file fragments. Table 1 shows the cached content of the user1. The other users also fill up their caches accordingly.

Content Delivery: The delivery phase starts with $s = K$. Here, $K = 5$ and we have considered the worst-case scenario.

Now, calculating the rate,

- When $s = 5$, as BS transmits 1 coded message of 5 file fragments which are 1/32th of corresponding files. So the rate is = 1/32. [as 1 coded transmission]
- When $s = 4$, as BS transmits 5 coded messages of 4 file fragments which are 1/32th of corresponding files. So the rate is = 5/32. [as 5 coded transmissions]
- When $s = 3$, as BS transmits 10 coded messages of 3 file fragments which are 1/32th of corresponding files. So the rate is = 10/32. [as 10 coded transmissions]
- When $s = 1$, as BS transmits 5 file fragments which are 1/32th of corresponding files. So the rate is = 5/32. [as 5 coded transmissions]

So, the rate will be
$R_{UC}(M) = 1/32 + 5/32 + 10/32 + 5/32 = 21/32$
Now, calculating rate by using the equation generated for user cooperation

Table 1 Placement phase (cached content of user1)

Fragments of file A	Fragments of file B	Fragments of file C	Fragments of file D	Fragments of file E
A_1	B_1	C_1	D_1	E_1
A_{12}, A_{13}	B_{12}, B_{13}	C_{12}, C_{13}	$D_{12} D_{13}$	E_{12}, E_{13}
A_{14}, A_{15}	$B_{14} B_{15}$	C_{14}, C_{15}	D_{14}, D_{15}	$E_{14} E_{15}$
A_{123}, A_{124}	B_{123}, B_{124}	C_{123}, C_{124}	D_{123}, D_{124}	$E_{123} E_{124}$
A_{125}, A_{134}	B_{125}, B_{134}	C_{125}, C_{134}	D_{125}, D_{134}	$E_{125} E_{134}$
A_{145}, A_{135}	B_{145}, B_{135}	C_{145}, C_{135}	D_{145}, D_{135}	$E_{145} E_{135}$
A_{1234}, A_{1345}	B_{1234}, B_{1345}	C_{1234}, C_{1345}	D_{1234}, D_{1345}	$E_{1234} E_{1345}$
$A_{1245}, A_{1235}, A_{12345}$	$B_{1245}, B_{1235}, B_{12345}$	$C_{1245}, C_{1235}, C_{12345}$	$D_{1245}, D_{1235}, D_{12345}$	$E_{1245}, E_{1235}, E_{12345}$

$$R_{UC}(M) = 5 \times (1 - M/5)^5 + {}^5C_3 \times (M/5)^2 \times (1 - M/5)^3 + {}^5C_4 \times (M/5)^3$$
$$\times (1 - M/5)^2 + {}^5C_5 \times (M/5)^4 \times (1 - M/5)$$
$$= 5 \times (1\text{--}2.5/5)^5 + 10 \times (2.5/5)^2 \times (1\text{--}2.5/5)^3 + 5 \times (2.5/5)^3 \times (1\text{--}2.5/5)^2$$
$$+ 1 \times (2.5/5)^4 \times (1\text{--}2.5/5)$$
$$= 5/32 + 10/32 + 5/32 + 1/32 = 21/32.$$

From the above calculation, we observe that the rate calculated by using the new generalized equation is equal to the rate calculated manually. It provides the proper justification for our equation.

4 Performance Analysis

The proposed algorithm is evaluated by comparing it with other existing algorithms of caching. Firstly, the proposed algorithm is compared with the existing decentralized coding approach as well as with the uncoded caching approach used in the existing IoT network. Finally, the proposed algorithm is compared with some existing caching approaches.

Figure 4 shows that the memory-rate tradeoff for both decentralized coded caching and the proposed caching scheme with $K = 15$ and $K = 30$. The horizontal axis shows the cache memory size, M, and the vertical axis shows the bottleneck link rate, R. The blue and green curves represent the rate achieved by the decentralized coded caching approach. The orange and red curves represent the rate achieved by the proposed coded caching approach. Here, the curves are higher degree polynomial. But they have different slope values. As our proposed caching approach has the smallest slope, that means it has a rate less than the decentralized caching approach.

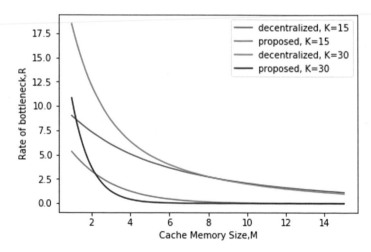

Fig. 4 Bottleneck rate, R versus the cache memory size, M for $K = 15$ and 30 users

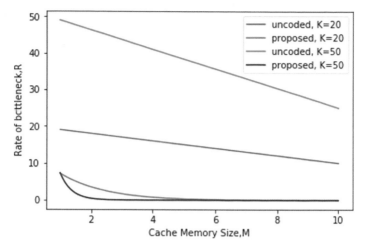

Fig. 5 Bottleneck rate, R versus the cache memory size, M for $K = 15$ and 30 users

So, it provides a better rate. We can see for both the values of K, proposed scheme achieves a better rate.

Figure 5 shows us the memory-rate tradeoff for the uncoded and the proposed caching scheme with $K = 20$ and $K = 50$ to observe the rates of both approaches. For a large number of users in the network, a huge difference between the rates of both approaches is observed. The curves of the uncoded caching are linear. On the other hand, the curves representing the rate of the proposed algorithm are non-linear, but the value of its slope is far less than the uncoded caching approach. The performance of our proposed caching approach is undoubtedly superior.

In Fig. 6, we have compared the performance of proposed caching approach with existing approaches. Our proposed caching scheme should have a better rate than the uncoded and decentralized caching approach. We already know that centralized caching has a better rate but less flexibility. Our target was to make the rate almost the same as centralized caching but to provide better flexibility for decentralized caching. Moreover, the proposed algorithm has accommodated user cooperation to make it suitable for the IoT network. We have observed the rate of the existing approaches including the proposed one for varying cache size, M. Performance of all the approaches are the same for values $M = 1$ and $M = 1.5$. We can see that the proposed approach works better than both decentralized coded caching and the uncoded caching used in the IoT network. When $M = 2$, it even achieves a better rate than centralized coded caching. But when $M = 3$, it shows good performance as it offers a rate almost the same as centralized coded caching. The overall rate of our proposed algorithm is better than the existing caching approaches.

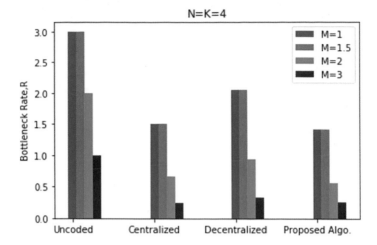

Fig. 6 The comparison between the rate of the existing caching schemes and our proposed caching scheme

5 Conclusion

We presented a decentralized coded caching approach that allows user cooperation for IoT networks. We modified the existing coded caching technique to make it appropriate for an IoT network. The proposed caching scheme created a multicasting opportunity that was not exploited before in IoT networks. By invoking decentralized coded caching in the IoT network, we eliminated the need for any central coordination system to manage the placement phase. Thus a flexible and better caching approach has been introduced for the IoT network. Quantification of user cooperation, identification of complexities due to increase in the number of users, and investigation of adverse effects of user cooperation may consider as future work.

References

1. Ai Y, Wang L, Han Z, Zhang P, Hanzo L (2018) Social networking and caching aided collaborative computing for the internet of things. IEEE Commun Magazine 56(12):149–155
2. Zanella A, Bui N, Castellani A, Vangelista L, Zorzi M (2014) Internet of things for smart cities. IEEE IoT J 1(1):22–32
3. Amiri MM, Yang Q, Gündüz D (2016) Coded caching for a large number of users. In: 2016 IEEE information theory workshop (ITW). IEEE, pp 171–175
4. Wang L, Wu H, Ding Y, Chen W, Poor HV (2016) Hypergraph-based wireless distributed storage optimization for cellular d2d underlays. IEEE J Sel Areas Commun 34(10):2650–2666
5. Maddah-Ali MA, Niesen U (2016) Coding for caching: fundamental limits and practical challenges. IEEE Commun Mag 54(8):23–29
6. Maddah-Ali MA, Niesen U (2014) Decentralized coded caching attains order-optimal memory-rate tradeoff. IEEE/ACM Trans Netw 23(4):1029–1040

7. Niesen U, Maddah-Ali MA (2016) Coded caching with nonuniform demands. IEEE Trans Inf Theory 63(2):1146–1158
8. Pedarsani R, Maddah-Ali MA, Niesen U (2015) Online coded caching. IEEE/ACM Trans Netw 24(2):836–845

Cryptanalysis of SIMON (32/64) Cipher Using Satisfiability Modulo Theories

Praveen Kumar Gundaram, Appala Naidu Tentu, and Naresh Babu Muppalaneni

Abstract SMT stands for Satisfiability Modulo Theories, and it is an efficient framework for solving constraint satisfaction challenges expressed in first-order logic. It uses for software and hardware verification. We show the power of SMT solvers in cryptanalysis specific block ciphers. We represent a block cipher in Boolean equations and translate them into a suitable format that is solved by existing SMT solver and recover the key. The fact that our approach requires a plaintext–ciphertext pair to extract the potential key is a significant feature. We demonstrate the cryptanalysis of the lightweight SIMON block cipher using the proposed procedure. We compare the results of known plaintext attacks on SIMON using the $z3py$ tool up to 8 rounds.

Keywords Block ciphers · ARX ciphers · Cryptanalysis · SMT solvers · Algebraic attacks

1 Introduction

Satisfiability Modulo Theories (SMT) [1, 2] problem is a decision problem for logical formulas involving many background theories like as arithmetic, bit-vectors, arrays, and uninterpreted functions [3]. SMT solver is a tool for determining whether formulas in these theories are satisfiable (or valid). Extended static checking, predicate abstraction, test case generation, and bounded model checking over infinite domains, to state a few, are all possible with SMT solvers.

SMT solver [4] uses three simple steps for cryptanalysis as follows: Firstly, it uses bit-vector theory to convert the cipher structure into equations by taking plaintext, ciphertext, and key as variables. In the second step, plaintext–ciphertext (PT-CT)

P. K. Gundaram (✉)
Department of CSE, Acharya Nagarjuna University, Guntur, Andhra Pradesh, India

P. K. Gundaram · A. N. Tentu
C R Rao AIMSCS, UoH Campus, Gachibowli, Hyderabad, Telangana, India

N. B. Muppalaneni
Department of C.S.E, NIT Silchar, Silchar, Assam, India

© The Author(s), under exclusive license to Springer Nature Singapore Pte Ltd. 2022　　319
C. Satyanarayana et al. (eds.), *High Performance Computing and Networking*,
Lecture Notes in Electrical Engineering 853,
https://doi.org/10.1007/978-981-16-9885-9_27

assigns known values to plaintext and ciphertext variables in the equations defined by bit-vector theory. These we call as constraints to the system [5]. Here, master secret key is unknown and to be recovered. In the third step, solve the system of equations by SMT solvers, the solution satisfies the assigned values for an unknown master key. Then, the solution becomes a possible key. This process directly recovers the secret keys of reduced-round variants of the cipher [5].

List of all SMT Solvers: Currently, the most popular available solvers are Boolector, Z3 [6] CVC4, and STP. Table 1 refers to the status of the solver and the tool usage. All solvers use the SAT solver-based technique inside the SMT solver.

Contribution In this work, we use power of SMT solvers to demonstrate cryptanalysis attack on SIMON lightweight block cipher. The main contribution of this paper is summarized as follows:

a. Develop a framework for transform cipher structure into equations of $z3py$ algebraic formats.
b. Develop an interface for the plaintext–ciphertext pairs as inputs and get the possible keys as output for SIMON ciphers.
c. Generate the equations for fixed plaintext–ciphertext pairs, add each round constraint to the solver.
d. Calculate the possible keys and verifies every key used on the SIMON cipher.

Organization of the paper: In Sect. 2, we describe SMT solver-based cryptanalysis. Section 3, reviews design specifications of the SIMON block cipher with all variants. In Sect. 4, crytanalysis of SIMON (32/64) is discussed using SMT solvers. In Sect. 5 shown the experiment results of SIMON (32/64), and conclusions are in Sect. 6.

Table 1 Comparison between existing SMT-related solvers

SMT tools	Pre-installation theories	Description about the tool
Boolector	Bit vector, arrays	Among the available SMT solvers, this one is the best
Z3 [6]	L-NLA, Bit vector, arrays	After Boolector solver, this is the best
CVC4	int-LA, arrays, BV,	It makes use of a lot of memory and heavyweight computing
STP	BV, arrays	STP is a fast recovery solution in its own theory due to its use of heuristics for preprocessing

2 SMT Solver-Based Cryptanalysis

2.1 Z3 Standard Algorithm

Microsoft Research has released Z3, a new SMT solver [6]. It is designed to address issues that develop during software verification and analysis. As a result, it incorporates support for a wide range of theories. Z3 is a powerful SMT solver with advanced background theory solution techniques [4, 7].

Z3 solver is a computational tool for evaluating a system of equations, which gives an unknown value as result. Suppose individuals in the population(in terms of variables), i.e., Z3 solving techniques, are subjected to the evolution loop. This is a steady-state evolutionary algorithm in which an evolution rule is determined at each iteration. The chosen rule selects and processes the individuals (as many as the rule requires). The individuals so produced are then typically introduced into the population.

The following example demonstrates uses of Z3 solver with better optimization. Initially, create an SMT framework instance o as a $Optimize()$ function. For example, m is variable. $Z3Py$ uses the operators like Python = for assignment. The operators < and > for comparison. The expression $m > 10, m < 15$ are a Z3 constraint. Z3 can solve constraints and assign the maximize value. In this given example, problem has four solutions so that Z3 produced the maximize value 14 as a output.

```
from z3 import *
o = Optimize()
m = Int( 'm' )
o.add(And(m > 10, m < 15))
o.maximize(x)
print(o.check())   # prints sat
print(o.model())   # prints [m = 14]
```

3 SIMON Block Cipher

SIMON cipher is a lightweight block cipher family. It expressed as $2n/mn$ [4, 8] where m is the number of keywords, $2n$ is the block size, and mn represents the key size with $m = 2, 3$ or 4 is the number of keys and $n = 16, 24, 32, 48$ or 64.

3.1 SIMON Design Description

Encryption: For each round, it uses the standard Feistel design on two n-bit parts. Each SIMON round [9] introduces a nonlinear, non-bijective function.

Fig. 1 SIMON round function

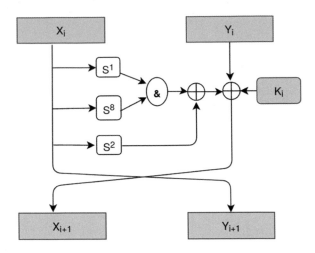

$$\text{Function}(F) : \{0, 1\}^n \times \{0, 1\}^n \rightarrow \{0, 1\}^n \times \{0, 1\}^n \tag{1}$$

The round function uses bitwise circular shift (S^a means a left circular shift and S^{-a} means right circular shift), AND($\&$) and XOR($\oplus$) operators. There are t rounds in SIMON (in SIMON (32/64), $t = 32$). The structure of ith round function is shown in Fig. 1. If x_i and y_i are the left and right parts of the inputs, then round function R_i at round "i" is given by:

$$R_i(x_{i+1}, y_{i+1}) = (f(x_i) \oplus k_i \oplus y_i, x_i) \tag{2}$$

where

$$f(x) = (S^1(x) \& S^8(x)) \oplus S^2(x) \tag{3}$$

Key Scheduling: SIMON key schedule algorithm (KSA) [9] is used to transform master key into a round keys [9]. Let the key variables are $K_0, \ldots, K_{n-1}$ (where $n \in \{2, 3, 4\}$ is the number of keywords), the round keys are $k_0, k_1, k_2, \ldots$, where

$$k_{i+2} = S^{-3}(k_{i+1}) \oplus S^{-1}(S^{-3}(k_{i+1})) \oplus c_i \oplus k_i \tag{4}$$

$$k_{i+3} = S^{-3}(k_{i+2}) \oplus S^{-1}(S^{-3}(k_{i+2})) \oplus c_i \oplus k_i \tag{5}$$

$$k_{i+4} = S^{-3}(k_{i+3}) \oplus S^{-1}(S^{-3}(k_{i+3})) \oplus S^{-1}(k_{i+1}) \oplus c_i \oplus k_i \oplus k_{i+1} \tag{6}$$

c_i represents round constant, with rest of the bits fixed through all rounds. In this research paper, we experiment with SIMON32/64 uses four keywords K_1, K_2, K_3 and K_4.

Decryption: It is the reverse process of encryption. It produces the plaintext by taking ciphertext and round keys as input.

4 SIMON (32/64) Cryptanalysis Using SMT Solvers

Suppose plaintext(P) represents (X_0, Y_0), ciphertext(C) represents (X_n, Y_n) where n is the total number of rounds, and key scheduling represents $K \in \{K_0, K_1, \ldots K_n\}$. The following 16-bit operations are used in SIMON32/64 [10] encryption and decryption. For all P, C, and K words represent in bit variables as shown below.

Key schedule	P-C variables in bit format
$K_0: k_{15} \ldots k_0$	$X_0: x_{15} \ldots x_0$
$K_1: k_{31} \ldots k_{16}$	$Y_0: y_{15} \ldots y_0$
$K_2: k_{47} \ldots k_{32}$	$\ldots$
$K_3: k_{63} \ldots k_{48}$	$\ldots$
$\ldots$	$X_{i+1} := S^1(X_i) \& S^8(X_i) \oplus S^2(X_i) \oplus Y_i \oplus K_i$
$K_{31}: k_{511} \ldots k_{496}$	$Y_{i+1} := X_i$ where i $\in \{1, 2, \ldots 32\}$

The following approach recovers the partial key or possible key. The method for resolving these equations is as follows: initially, place the plaintext and ciphertext pairs and form SIMON equations [11, 12] till up to 8 rounds. Z3 solver interface code examines constructed equations for unknown plaintext and ciphertext pairs to look at if there are any possible key or keys [10].

SIMON equations are generated from plaintext bits to ciphertext are as follows. SIMON structure have Shift($<<$), AND(&), XOR ($\oplus$) operators. SIMON (32/64) encryption function transforms into 16-bits equations. Let us assume X (left side block), Y (right side block) of plaintext.

$X_0 = [x_0, x_1, x_2 \ldots x_{15}]$, $Y_0 = [y_0, y_1, y_2 \ldots y_{15}]$ and $K_0 = [k_0, k_1, \ldots k_{15}]$.

Operation	Function description	Initial variable	Updated variable
S^1	Crcular shift to the left for 1 time	$[x_0, x_1, x_2 \ldots, x_{15}]$	$[x_1, x_2 \ldots x_{15}, x_0]$
S^8	Circular shift to the left for 8 time	$[x_0, x_1, x_2 \ldots, x_{15}]$	$[x_8, x_9, x_{10} \ldots, x_7]$
S^2	Circular shift to the left for 2 time	$[x_0, x_1, x_2 \ldots, x_{15}]$	$[x_2, x_3, x_4 \ldots, x_1]$

- $S^1 \& S^8$—Output $[x_1 \cdot x_8, x_2 \cdot x_9, x_3 \cdot x_{10}, \ldots x_{15} \cdot x_6, x_0 \cdot x_7]$
- Ciphertext $= (S^1 \& S^8) \oplus Y_0 \oplus S^2 \oplus K_0$
- $x_1 \cdot x_8 + y_0 + x_2 + k_0, x_2 \cdot x_9 + y_1 + x_3 + k_1, x_3 \cdot x_{10} + y_3 + x_4 + k_2 \ldots x_0 \cdot x_7$
  $+ y_{15} + x_1 + k_{15}$

  - $C_0 = x_1 \cdot x_8 + y_0 + x_2 + k_0$
  - $C_2 = x_2 \cdot x_9 + y_1 + x_3 + k_1 \ldots$
  - $C_{15} = x_0 \cdot x_7 + y_{15} + x_1 + k_{15}$

Example for one round *SIMON32/64* fixed PT-CT pairs: Initially, declare and assign 16-bit words [7] as given below example and get the model using the Z3 Solver framework. Generate a system of equations for one round where the inputs are plaintext (0x6565, 0x6877) ciphertext(0xbca2, 0x6565) and recover the key $(k_0) =$ 0x0100.

Cipher Model for Solver:

```
from z3 import *
p0,p1,c0,c1=BitVecs('p0 p1 c0 c1',16)
k0=BitVecs('k0',16)
ct0,ct1,ct2=BitVecs('ct0 ct1 ct2',16)
s1 = Solver()
s1.add(p0==0x6565)
s1.add(p1==0x6877)
s1.add(c0==0xbca2)
s1.add(c1==0x6565)
s1.add(c0==simplify(((RotateLeft(p0,2))^p1^k0)^
                    (RotateLeft(p0,1)&RotateLeft(p0,8))))
s1.add(c1==p0)
print s1.check()
print s1.model()
```

The following proposed procedure provides an impression of the algebraic crypt-analysis [13] problem in the SMT framework [1, 2]. The main aim of this procedure is solving boolean equations and recover the related key.

Procedure: Algebraic Cryptanalysis of SIMON (32/64)
SIMON-generated equations are the target to key recovery attack/algebraic cryptanalysis for
r rounds where $r \in \{1, 2, \ldots, 8\}$
PT–CT pairs parse the input and recover the possible key as output
begin
  Declaration: Declare given number of rounds key k_i $(i = \{1, 2, \ldots n\})$ bits
  Initialization: Declare and assign plaintext (P_i) and ciphertext(C_i) bits
  (PT–CT pair information is known)
  Create SMT solver as instance S
  Generate system of equations from encryption algorithm
  Add the each round constraints to the solver
  $R_i(X_{i+1}, Y_{i+1}) = (Y_i \oplus f(X_i) \oplus K_i, X_i)$
    where $f(X) = (S^1 \& S^8) \oplus S^2$ where X is input
  Check satisfiability for given system of equations
  if unsatisfiable
    Invalid equations are supplied. (it gives error as output)
  else
    Continue: Get the model which satisfiability the constraints and add it into solver
  end if
  for all $i \in \{K_1, K_2 \ldots K_n\}$
    Compute $C_i = Enc(PT_i, K_i)$, where (K_i) possible key models
    Verify the C_i is same as original ciphertext
    K_i is a correct key, out of possible keys
  end for
end

5 SIMON (32/64) Experiment Results

SIMON cryptanalytic technique [8, 14] used in SMT framework and execute for known pairs of each round. The following table measures execution duration in terms of seconds possible keys. If suppose plaintext (PL, PR) = (0x6565, 0x6877) and various ciphertext of each round as given in the Table 2, then calculate execution time for 10 or 1024 possible keys as follows. Measure the time for CPU, 12 CPUs. Note: actual master key (k0 = 0x0100, k1 = 0x0908, k2 = 0x1110, k3 = 0x1918).

Z3 solver computational time measured in seconds for reduced round SIMON32/ 64 cryptanalysis is given in the graph, X-axis represents number of rounds, and Y-axis represents execution time in seconds (in terms of logarithmic scale) as shown in the Fig. 2.

5.1 SMT Result Developed for the Following SIMON (32/64)

In this section, we simulate the key recovery algorithm on SIMON (32/64) [4] variant using the Z3py solver [15]. We have shown some of the reduced round (up to 8th round) results when fixing random plaintext and ciphertext pairs and plaintext as zero. Tables 3 and 4 showed the possible key.

Table 2 Execution time to recover possible keys of random (PT-CT) pair

#Rounds	PC pair (PL, PR) = (0x6565, 0x6877)	1 CPU (exe. time) 10 possible keys	12 CPUs (exe. time) 1024 possible keys
1	$(X_1, Y_1) = (0\text{xbca2}, 0\text{x6565})$	0 m 0.133 s	0 m 0.81 s
2	$(X_2, Y_2) = (0\text{xbee3}, 0\text{xbca2})$	0 m 0.136 s	0 m 1.93 s
3	$(X_3, Y_3) = (0\text{x37ba}, 0\text{xbee3})$	0 m 0.138 s	0 m 6.70 s
4	$(X_4, Y_4) = (0\text{x5327}, 0\text{x37ba})$	0 m 0.157 s	0 m 7.141 s
5	$(X_5, Y_5) = (0\text{x2ca6}, 0\text{x5327})$	0 m 0.159 s	0 m 10.58 s
6	$(X_6, Y_6) = (0\text{x57fa}, 0\text{x2ca6})$	0 m 0.461 s	52 m 17.23 s
7	$(X_7, Y_7) = (0\text{x8fcf}, 0\text{x57fa})$	0 m 51.638 s	252 m 1.45 s
8	$(X_8, Y_8) = (0\text{x873b}, 0\text{x8fcf})$	354 m 42.835 s	–

Table 3 Recover the possible keys for SIMON32/64 where plaintext is random

#Rounds	Input PT-CT Pairs	Output: Intermediate Round	Output: Probable Key
2	$(X_0, X_0) = (0x6565, 0x6877)$ $(X_2, Y_2) = (0xbee3, 0xbca2)$	$(X_1, Y_1) = (0xbca2, 0x6565)$	$k_0 = 0x100$ $k_1 = 0x908$
3	$(X_0, X_0) = (0x6565, 0x6877)$ $(X_3, Y_3) = (0x37ba, 0xbee3)$	$(X_1, Y_1) = (0x0, 0x6565)$ $(X_2, Y_2) = (0xbee3, 0x0)$	$k_0 = 0xbda2$ $k_1 = 0xdb86$ $k_2 = 0xadb2$
4	$(X_0, X_0) = (0x6565, 0x6877)$ $(X_4, Y_4) = (0x5327, 0x37ba)$	$(X_1, Y_1) = (0x3458, 0x6565)$ $(X_2, Y_2) = (0xf6b, 0x3458)$ $(X_3, Y_3) = (0x37ba, 0xf6b)$	$k_0 = 0x89fa$ $k_1 = 0xf35e$ $k_2 = 0x3448$ $k_3 = 0xa890$
5	$(X_0, X_0) = (0x6565, 0x6877)$ $(X_5, Y_5) = (0x2ca6, 0x5327)$	$(X_1, Y_1) = (0x7245, 0x6565)$ $(X_2, Y_2) = (0x57bd, 0x7245)$ $(X_3, Y_3) = (0x731d, 0x57bd)$ $(X_4, Y_4) = (0x5327, 0x731d)$	$k_0 = 0xcfe7$ $k_1 = 0xbfcf$ $k_2 = 0xf2ff$ $k_3 = 0xccdd$ $k_4 = 0x3564$
6	$(X_0, X_0) = (0x6565, 0x6877)$ $(X_6, Y_6) = (0x57fa, 0x2ca6)$	$(X_1, Y_1) = (0xfd40, 0x6565)$ $(X_2, Y_2) = (0xc0d5, 0xfd40)$ $(X_3, Y_3) = (0xfa84, 0xc0d5)$ $(X_4, Y_4) = (0x2314, 0xfa84)$ $(X_5, Y_5) = (0x2ca6, 0x2314)$	$k_0 = 0x40e2$ $k_1 = 0x1032$ $k_2 = 0x8513$ $k_3 = 0x8dda$ $k_4 = 0x5e52$ $k_5 = 0xc67a$
7	$(X_0, X_0) = (0x6565, 0x6877)$ $(X_7, Y_7) = (0x8fcf, 0x57fa)$	$(X_1, Y_1) = (0xaef5, 0x6565)$ $(X_2, Y_2) = (0x26ef, 0xaef5)$ $(X_3, Y_3) = (0xff69, 0x26ef)$ $(X_4, Y_4) = (0x2ffd, 0xff69)$ $(X_5, Y_5) = (0xb05a, 0x2ffd)$ $(X_6, Y_6) = (0x57fa, 0xb05a)$	$k_0 = 0x1357$ $k_1 = 0xadf6$ $k_2 = 0x8726$ $k_3 = 0x9c66$ $k_4 = 0xaded$ $k_5 = 0xf9dd$ $k_6 = 0xca28$
8	$(X_0, X_0) = (0x6565, 0x6877)$ $(X_8, Y_8) = (0x873b, 0x8fcf)$	$(X_1, Y_1) = (0x6c28, 0x6565)$ $(X_2, Y_2) = (0xfca5, 0x6c28)$ $(X_3, Y_3) = (0xcc0e, 0xfca5)$ $(X_4, Y_4) = (0xe8ee, 0xcc0e)$ $(X_5, Y_5) = (0x77f3, 0xe8ee)$ $(X_6, Y_6) = (0x3605, 0x77f3)$ $(X_7, Y_7) = (0x8fcf, 0x3605)$	$k_0 = 0xd18a$ $k_1 = 0x2121$ $k_2 = 0xf3f9$ $k_3 = 0x2c7c$ $k_4 = 0xd88e$ $k_5 = 0xe240$ $k_6 = 0x242a$ $k_7 = 0x818f$

Table 4 Recover the possible keys for SIMON32/64 where plaintext is zeros

#Rounds	Input PT-CT Pairs	Output: Intermediate Round	Output: Probable Key
2	$(X_0, X_0) = (0x0000, 0x0000)$ $(X_2, Y_2) = (0xd08, 0x100)$	$(X_1, Y_1) = (0x100, 0x0)$	$k_0 = 0x100$ $k_1 = 0x908$
3	$(X_0, X_0) = (0x0000, 0x0000)$ $(X_3, Y_3) = (0x2c30, 0xd08)$	$(X_1, Y_1) = (0x0, 0x0)$ $(X_2, Y_2) = (0xd08, 0x0)$	$k_0 = 0x0$ $k_1 = 0xd08$ $k_2 = 0x1010$
4	$(X_0, X_0) = (0x0000, 0x0000)$ $(X_4, Y_4) = (0xb4f0, 0x2c30)$	$(X_1, Y_1) = (0xd49a, 0x0)$ $(X_2, Y_2) = (0xaa0d, 0xd49a)$ $(X_3, Y_3) = (0x2c30, 0xaa0d)$	$k_0 = 0xd49a$ $k_1 = 0x7072$ $k_2 = 0x5496$ $k_3 = 0xbe1d$
5	$(X_0, X_0) = (0x0000, 0x0000)$ $(X_5, Y_5) = (0xee91, 0xb4f0)$	$(X_1, Y_1) = (0xdf7a, 0x0)$ $(X_2, Y_2) = (0x6b6c, 0xdf7a)$ $(X_3, Y_3) = (0xac06, 0x6b6c)$ $(X_4, Y_4) = (0xb4f0, 0xac06)$	$k_0 = 0xdf7a$ $k_1 = 0x2c52$ $k_2 = 0x9a85$ $k_3 = 0x6f8a$ $k_4 = 0xf1f5$
6	$(X_0, X_0) = (0x0000, 0x0000)$ $(X_6, Y_6) = (0x29dc, 0xee91)$	$(X_1, Y_1) = (0xefb1, 0x0)$ $(X_2, Y_2) = (0x645d, 0xefb1)$ $(X_3, Y_3) = (0xbf10, 0x645d)$ $(X_4, Y_4) = (0x5f15, 0xbf10)$ $(X_5, Y_5) = (0xee91, 0x5f15)$	$k_0 = 0xefb1$ $k_1 = 0x4bf9$ $k_2 = 0x89f4$ $k_3 = 0xd72b$ $k_4 = 0x39de$ $k_5 = 0x5dac$
7	$(X_0, X_0) = (0x0000, 0x0000)$ $(X_7, Y_7) = (0x4f1d, 0x29dc)$	$(X_1, Y_1) = (0xcf09, 0x0)$ $(X_2, Y_2) = (0xfe4, 0xcf09)$ $(X_3, Y_3) = (0x7a09, 0xfe4)$ $(X_4, Y_4) = (0x202d, 0x7a09)$ $(X_5, Y_5) = (0xd8e9, 0x202d)$ $(X_6, Y_6) = (0x29dc, 0xd8e9)$	$k_0 = 0xcf09$ $k_1 = 0x3bc0$ $k_2 = 0x8e98$ $k_3 = 0xc7fe$ $k_4 = 0x2254$ $k_5 = 0xcb86$ $k_6 = 0x60ac$
8	$(X_0, X_0) = (0x0000, 0x0000)$ $(X_8, Y_8) = (0xe9d3, 0x4f1d)$	$(X_1, Y_1) = (0xc516, 0x0)$ $(X_2, Y_2) = (0x7e13, 0xc516)$ $(X_3, Y_3) = (0xbbe7, 0x7e13)$ $(X_4, Y_4) = (0x6581, 0xbbe7)$ $(X_5, Y_5) = (0xc12a, 0x6581)$ $(X_6, Y_6) = (0xa269, 0xc12a)$ $(X_7, Y_7) = (0x4f1d, 0xa269)$	$k_0 = 0xc516$ $k_1 = 0x684d$ $k_2 = 0x969a$ $k_3 = 0x9387$ $k_4 = 0x6dc8$ $k_5 = 0xc102$ $k_6 = 0x4713$ $k_7 = 0x6bc5$

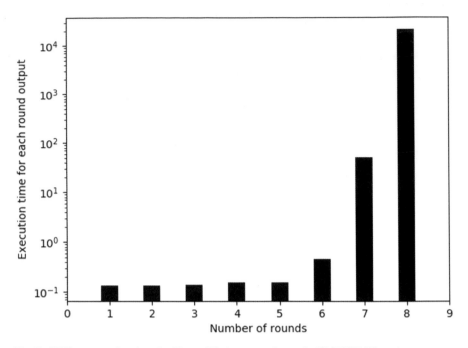

Fig. 2 CPU computation time for 10 possible keys upto 8 rounds SIMON32/64

6 Conclusion

In this paper, we proposed the procedure for cryptanalysis of SIMON block cipher by using Z3 theorem prover (SMT solver). This SMT solver approach is also proved to be an efficient technique to retrive the partial key of block ciphers. We use the SMT solvers to recover the probable sub keys up to 8 rounds of SIMON (32/64) by solving cipher equations, and results are given in Tables 3 and 4. Examine the reduced round SIMON cipher CPU performance by using the Z3 tool. In future work, we apply the attack an complete cipher by the proposed procedure combining with statistical distinguisher.

References

1. De Moura L, Bjorner N (2011) Satisfiability modulo theories: introduction and applications. Commun ACM 54(9):69–77
2. Ranise S, Tinelli C (2006) The satisfiability modulo theories library (smt-lib) Available at http://goedel.cs.uiowa.edu/smtlib
3. Brummayer R (2009) Efficient SMT solving for bit-vectors and the extensional theory of arrays. PhD thesis, Johannes Kepler University Linz, Austria

4. Beaulieu R, Shors D, Smith J, Treatman-Clark S, Weeks B, Wingers L (2015) SIMON and SPECK: block ciphers for the internet of things. IACR Cryptology ePrint Archive 2015/585. http://eprint.iacr.org/2015/585
5. Pascal J, Marco M (2009) Revisiting the idea philosophy. In: Orr D (ed) Fast software encryption. 5665 of lecture notes in computer science. Springer, Berlin Heidelberg, pp 277–295
6. de Moura L, Bjorner NS (2008) Z3: an efficient SMT Solver. In: Ramakrishnan CR, Rehof J (eds) TACAS 2008. LNCS, vol 4963, pp 337–340. Springer, Heidelberg; Lecture Notes in Computer Science, vol 4963
7. Jovanovic P, Neves S, Aumasson JP (2014) Analysis of Analysis of NORX, Cryptology ePrint Archive, Report 2014/317. http://eprint.iacr.org/2014/317
8. AlKhzaimi H, Lauridsen MM (2013) Cryptanalysis of the simon family of block ciphers. IACR Cryptology ePrint Archive 543
9. Beaulieu R, Shors D, Smith J, Treatman-Clark S, Weeks B, Wingers L The Simon and speck families of lightweight block ciphers. http://ia.cr/2013/404
10. Courtois N, Mourouzis T, Song G, Sepehrdad P, Susil P (2014) Combined algebraic and truncated differential cryptanalysis on reduced-round simon. In: 2014 11th international conference on security and cryptography (SECRYPT). IEEE, pp 1–6
11. Bard G, Courtois N, Jefferson C (2006) Efficient methods for conversion and solution of sparse systems of low-degree multivariate polynomials over GF(2) via SAT-Solvers. Cryptology ePrint Archive, Report 2007/024. Available at http://eprint.iacr.org/2007/024.pdf
12. Beaulieu R, Shors D, Smith J, Treatman-Clark S, Weeks B, Wingers L (2013) The Simon and Speck families of lightweight block ciphers. National Security Agency, pp 16-45
13. Gundaram PK, Tentu AN, Muppalaneni NB Performance of various SMT solvers in cryptanalysis, Published in IEEE. In: International conference on computing, communication, and intelligent systems (ICCCIS-2021). https://doi.org/10.1109/ICCCIS51004.2021.9397110
14. Bard GV (2008) Algebraic cryptanalysis. www.springer.com/book/978-0-387-88756-2
15. Sahu HK, Pillai NR, Gupta I et al (2020) SMT solver-based cryptanalysis of block ciphers. SN Comput Sci 1:169. https://doi.org/10.1007/s42979-020-00181-4

Personal Safety Monitoring Devices in Wake of COVID19: Application of IoT and Sensor Technology

Satyabrata Dash ⓘ and Vadhul Suryanarayana ⓘ

Abstract There are constraints to provide the effective treatment for COVID19 patients in hospitals due to infectious nature of the disease. Quality treatment and continuity in the healthcare of patient is difficult in case of patients of diseases of infectious nature. In the process of treatment, many patients are not been properly monitored to their clinical events for better diagnosis. Patients are uncomfortable for the delay in medical attention as cost of such treatments is too high as various devices are to be included in the care. Therefore, it is required to provide the unrestricted medical advice and support to avoid further spread of the disease and better cure of the patient. In this manuscript, we proposed two ICT enabled centralized patient monitoring devices along with usage of other IoT-based systems which are to be used for COVID19 hospitals to help the Paramedic's staff to monitor the body temperature of the COVID19 patients in emergency medical situations for serious patients with the aim of stabilizing them without moving to their place.

Keywords Smart device · COVID19 · ICT enabled centralized patient monitoring

1 Introduction

Pathogens are not certainly responsible for a disease. When bacteria, viruses, or any other microbes enter into the human body and start replicating them then infection occurs. This infection starts damaging body cells, and symptoms of the illness appear in an individual. The intensity of the infection depends on the type and strength of the pathogen, also the degree of immunity of an individual. Once the infectious disease capture a living being, then it make that living being a carrier of that infectious disease [1]. Therefore, identification and cure for the infected living being is compulsory.

S. Dash (✉) · V. Suryanarayana
Department of Computer Science and Engineering, Ramachandra College of Engineering, Eluru, Andhra Pradesh, India

V. Suryanarayana
e-mail: vs@rcee.ac.in

© The Author(s), under exclusive license to Springer Nature Singapore Pte Ltd. 2022
C. Satyanarayana et al. (eds.), *High Performance Computing and Networking*,
Lecture Notes in Electrical Engineering 853,
https://doi.org/10.1007/978-981-16-9885-9_28

331

Medicines play its own roles in the cure but care of the patient is another aspect which is crucial in the care of infectious diseases like COVID19. Therefore, specific devices are to be used for the extensive care of the patients. Present devices for this purpose are either too costly or very inconvenient in use. Hence, we put an effort to provide a low-cost, mass-produced, portable hand-held device having features including an integrated screen, user-friendly controls, and a serial port. Clinicians can take this light, easily usable, and portable instrumentation device to a remote location very easily [1, 2]. It is an ICT enabled centralized patient monitoring device for COVID19 hospitals which helps the Paramedics hospital staff to routine monitor the body temperature of the COVID19 patients with the aim of stabilizing them without moving to their place except for un-avoidable condition. This invention relates to monitoring of person safety requirements during this COVID19 situation. More particularly, the proposed invention is similar to an IoT-based Smart device for monitoring of personal parameters so that to avoid for infection of possibility of COVID19.

2 COVID19: A Case Study

An understanding about the behavior about the diseases has to be identified before proposing a solution; and therefore, we have considered the COVID19. It is a pandemic in today's world and all related research communities are fighting against it. Therefore, let us consider the following different parameters used to understand the behavior of COVID19 to counter it [3, 4].

2.1 Test Cases or Total Number of Sample Tested

It is one of our most important tools/process in the fight with COVID19 to sluggish and diminishes the impact of the virus spread. Different types of cases like Non-vulnerable Cases, Susceptible Cases, Positive Cases, or Vulnerable Cases are identified by the tests after clinical identification [4–6].

2.2 Non-vulnerable Cases

These are the accumulation of the negative test cases and the recovered cases after clinical treatment from the vulnerable category and having no symptom of COVID19 infections.

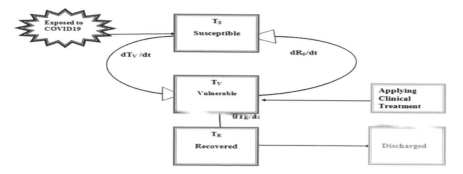

Fig. 1 Susceptible-vulnerable-recovery cases

2.3 Susceptible or Vulnerable Cases

The susceptible cases are the cases that exposed to COVID19 and don't help in transmission of infection after infection. Some susceptible cases which are exposed to infection of COVID19 and affected by the infection and carried out transmission is called vulnerable cases and some are exposed but still they cannot help in transmission of infection are susceptible cases. Some cases are the recovered and discharged after successful clinical treatment as shown in Fig. 1 [4, 7].

2.4 Positive Cases or Active Cases

The positive cases are the infected by virus, and they are identified by the appropriate laboratory testing. They are supposed to be reported by different countries as per their standard protocols. Some of the active cases may be recovered and some may not so; we can calculate total active case as given below:

The total Active Cases = Total cases–Total recovered Cases − Total deaths cases [5].

2.5 Transmission Rate

The *attack rate or transmissibility* tells how rapidly the disease spreads. Reproductive number represented by R_0 provides the information that how many persons are infected by a single person [6].

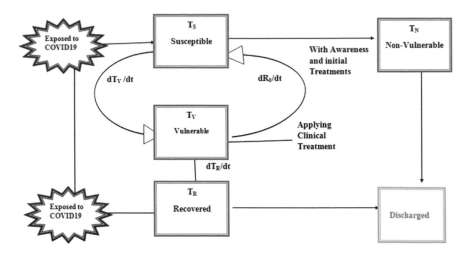

Fig. 2 Susceptible-vulnerable-recovery-susceptible cases

2.6 Recovered Cases

These are the recovered and discharged cases after successful clinical treatment. This statistic is highly important for COVID19 treatment. They are represented by [5, 8] as given below—

The total recovered Cases = Total cases − Active Cases − total deaths.

The recovered cases are the subset of vulnerable cases. After successful recovery from the COVID19 infection, it is recommended to check the symptoms are resolved successfully and two negative tests are there within 24 h and additional 14 days isolations are directed [4, 5]. But after the recovery, if again, the recovered case is exposed to COVID19 then the case can be susceptible case and may help in transmission of infection as shown in Fig. 2.

2.7 Infection Outbreak

If an infection is spreading at an unexpected high rate, then it is known as outbreak of a disease. It is due to the huge size contact with a spreading agent including a person, animal, an environmental factor, or another media. Once it occurs then it will take days or even years to come at an end [5, 9].

2.8 Rate of Positive Cases

Rate of positive cases R_0 is the ratio between the total number of affected positive cases or vulnerable cases to the underlying cases that are susceptible to infection and can be made per cases with transmission rate R_0. This is the rate which gives the number of newly infected people from a single case. The average positive rate is the difference of total susceptible case to total negative cases in a day. A number of groups have estimated the positive rate for COVID19 to be somewhere approximately between 1.5 and 5.5 [4, 6, 10]

2.9 Rate of Negative Cases

Rate of negative cases is the ratio of total negative test cases to total number of test conducted. In the best case, it should be approaching to total number of tests conducted.

2.9.1 Rate of Recover Cases

The rate of recovery is ratio between the total recovery cases in cumulative to total number of affected positive cases [5]. It is represented as below—

The total recovered Cases = Total cases − Active Cases − total deaths.

2.9.2 Rate of Death Cases

Total deaths cases are the cumulative number of deaths among detected positive cases [5].

The values of above discussed parameters present the current intensity of the pandemic. On the basis of the values of these parameters, we conclude that what type of remedy has to be followed to counter the pandemic. To control these parameters defiantly, the medication plays an important role but it is not available then using masks, keep distance, curfews at public places, etc., help to restrict the infection. On the other side of the coin, patients are to be handled in a very conscious manner so that a very limited or no infection spreads. Generally, these patients are to be kept in isolation and hospital staff has to take care of them with a minimal contact. This is only possible by using the technological devices. The availability of such devices at a minimal cost has to be ensured [6, 8]. Therefore, we have made an effort by proposing such devices at minimal cost to provide quality treatment and continuity of patient care particularly for COVID19 hospitals [10, 11].

We proposed two (02) ICT enabled centralized patient monitoring and public safety devices which are to be used for COVID19 hospitals and help to the

Paramedic's hospital staff to monitor the body temperature of the Paramedics patients in emergency medical situations for those who are seriously ill with the aim of stabilizing them without moving to their place.

3   Literature Survey

Detection of more patients in an advanced stage and keeping them for medication is a significant part of the hospital management. It also leads to a financial burden to the healthcare system of that nation as there are different infrastructures which are involved for the patients including "ADML-COVID19 Protected Room," "IFQCK-COVID19 Kit," "CMSP-Suit," and "COVID19 killer." Contamination in a room or surface is disinfected and sterilized by the use of an apparatus like "ADML-COVID19" Protected Room. In case of rough surfaces, "IFQCK-COVID19 Kit" is used to non-destructive advanced testing. "CMSP-Suit" is used as a structural material for protection cloths for COVID19 [6].

On the basis of literature review about COVID19, we infer that none of the work is suggesting or claiming about the "ICT Enabled Centralized Patient Monitoring Device" in the treatment of an infectious disease. Due to this above backdrop, it is desired to have a device which can operate automatically to providing data related to the patient's diagnosis and medical advice in quick, efficient, and accurate way. This proposed system and device will better configure the patient health and provide the data for analysis with elementary medical diagnosis along with different modules including patient's data module, conversion module for generating an output file representing the health of patient, and a display module to display output.

4   IoT for COVID19

IoT plays a significant role during the COVID19 pandemic for healthcare systems to monitor the patients with intertwined devices. IoT industry helps a lot during these days to protect the people from infection and spread of the pandemic. IoT network is a collection of interconnected devices to collect data and communicate it to a device for analysis on wireless network without human intervention. Once the data is gathered at a common platform with a common language, it can be analyzed by a distributed environment [6]. The analysis helps to take the proper countermeasures against the pandemic. IoT devices are integrated in many systems used to sluggish the impact of COVID19 pandemic and contributes to the COVID19 safety norms. The architecture of the IoT varied from solutions to solutions and also depends on the functional area. But the major technology consists of four major components including sensors/ devices, gateways, networks/cloud, and application layers.

There are different layers of IoT which is shown in the Fig. 3. Sensors and actuators are the first stage in the IoT architecture. Sensors are the electronics devices which are

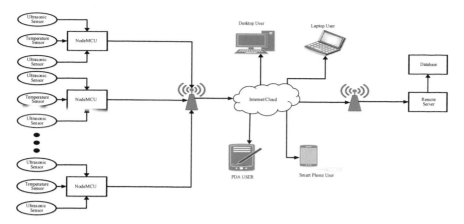

Fig. 3 Block diagram

used to sensors the environmental parameters, and the actuators are the transducers which converts the electrical signals into the motion. They are connected to the node devices through wired or wireless medium and send–receive corresponding data over the network. The second stage is the gateways through which data are transferred in a very high speed. These may be the WiFi, Ethernet, GSM, 5G, etc. After that, the third stage is the cloud where the information through analytics, management of devices, and security controls are done. The last stage is the cloud that transfers the information or data to end users applications. In case of COVID19, healthcare systems devices/sensors including temperature sensor, heartbeat sensor, blood pressure sensor, etc., are responsible to sense the data. Through the gateway, this collected information goes to the cloud where it is analyzed by different required modules, and the resultant has to be provided to the medical attendant using APIs of application layer [12].

5 IOT Enabling Personal Safety Methodology and Equipment

5.1 ICT Enabled Wrist Band

The proposed device is an ICT enabled centralized patient monitoring device which can be used for COVID19 hospitals and will help the hospital staff (Paramedics) to monitor the body temperature of the COVID19 patients in emergency medical situations who are seriously ill with the aim of stabilizing them without moving to their place. It will also monitor the patient's movement activity with respect to other persons and give warning to maintain social distancing.

By using the ICT enabled wrist band, one can do the centralized patient monitoring from a remote distance. It will help the Paramedics hospital staff to monitor the body temperature of the COVID19 patients in emergency medical situations who are seriously ill with the aim of stabilizing them without moving to their place. It can also be used for the hospital staffs to monitor their body temperature in frequent basis and helps in social distance maintaining [6].

It will also monitor the patient's movement activity with respect to other persons and give warning to maintain social distancing. As it is a low-cost wearable device, it can be also used for quarantine peoples or for personal use. As list of wearable devices are connected to a centralized database, it will help the Paramedics to analysis the statistics of temperature monitoring of the total patients so in time and accurate clinical and medical treatments can be provided at the earliest. An initial diagram for ICT enabled wrist band is depicted in Fig. 4.

Figure 5 is representing the possible usage description of ICT enabled wrist band, and Fig. 6 depicts the complete on board design of this device.

The foregoing detailed description of the device implemented is better understood when read in conjunction with the attached drawings. For better understanding, each component is represented by labeled which is further illustrated for the components used with the figure. The simulation is done through a virtual simulator software. The

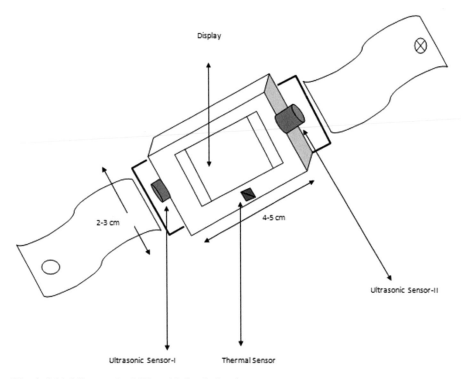

Fig. 4 Initial diagram for ICT enabled wrist band

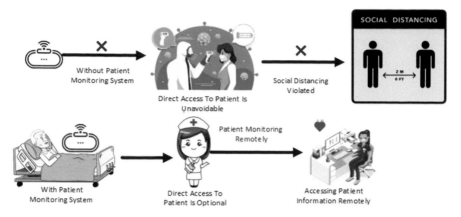

Fig. 5 Description for ICT enabled wrist band

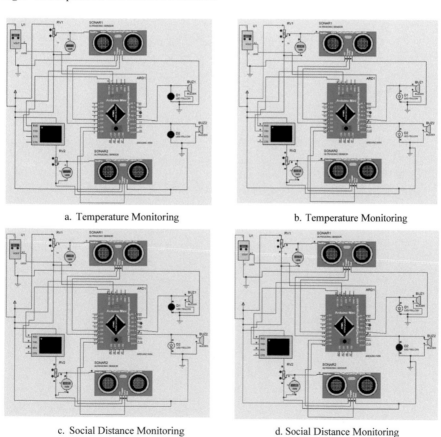

a. Temperature Monitoring

b. Temperature Monitoring

c. Social Distance Monitoring

d. Social Distance Monitoring

Fig. 6 On board diagram for ICT enabled wrist band

software consists of virtual devices in which ultrasonic sensor, MCU unit, Buzzer. The ultrasonic senor is used to sense the distance between the user and the public around. The alert is given up as a glowing led and the corresponding buzzers. When the sensor placed in the top detects a presence in the proximity, it gives up a signal to the left buzzer and the led. The bottom sensor also operates in the same manner. When both the sensor detect proximity together both leds and the buzzers turns on giving alert. When there is no alert, it is cleared that no proximity presence is detected.

5.2 ICT Enabled Face Shield

The proposed research is a battery operated ICT enabled smart face shield structure which can be used as a personal safety monitoring equipment as shown in Fig. 7. It can help to monitor the body temperature of a person and intimate about not maintaining the social distance. This smart face shield is to provide an extra layer of protection and to protect the eyes when in close contact with someone that has or is suspected to have COVID19.

There are many possible utilizations of the ICT enabled Face Shield, some of them are given as below—

- This smart face shield structure can be used as a personal safety monitoring equipment.
- It can help to monitor the body temperature of a person and intimate about not maintaining the social distance.
- It can be also used for the hospital staffs to monitor their body temperature in frequent basis and helps in social distance maintaining.

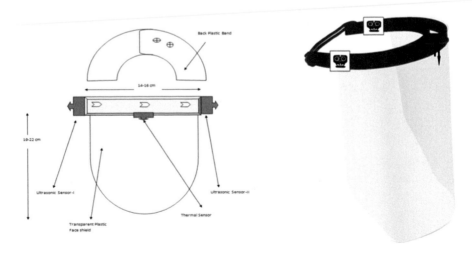

Fig. 7 Initial diagram for ICT enabled face shield and prototype

- As it is a low-cost wearable device, it can be also used for quarantine peoples or for personal use.
- This smart face shield is to provide an extra layer of protection and to protect the eyes when in close contact with someone that has or is suspected to have COVID19.
- It is also a reminder to maintain social distancing, and at the same time it allows visibility of facial expressions and lip movements for speech perception.
- It is also suggested that if wearing face shields in a regular basis, it could also help to reduce the number of COVID19 infections. Figure 8 depicts the complete on board design of this device.

The detailed description of the device is depicted by Fig. 11. The drawings are well-labeled to each component for its better understanding. The simulation is done through simulation software where electronics devices can be automated without the use of the real hardware. This is the software best suited for the PCB design. From

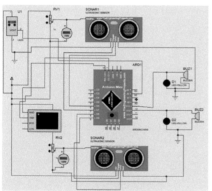

a. Temperature Monitoring

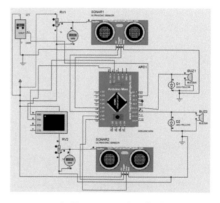

b. Temperature Monitoring

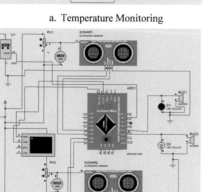

c. Social Distance Monitoring

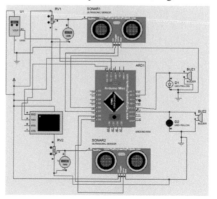

d. Social Distance Monitoring

Fig. 8 On board diagram for ICT enabled face shield

the Fig. 13, it is clear that when the sensor detects any obstacles within the range specified in the program then automatically a signal will go to the microcontroller. Based on the signal received by the MCU, the actuation will be taken place in the form of sound. This in turn notifies the patients who are wearing the device that it's essential to maintain the social distancing.

6 Conclusion

In this manuscript, we have proposed Personal Safety Monitoring Devices in wake of COVID19 by application of IoT and sensor technology. In the process of treatment, many patients are not been properly monitored to their clinical events for better diagnosis. Patients are uncomfortable for the delay in medical attention as cost of such treatments is too high as various devices are to be included in the care. As there are constraints to provide the effective treatment for COVID19 patients in hospitals due to infectious nature of the disease, we proposed the devices to maintain the quality treatment and its continuity in the healthcare. Before proposing our inventions, we studied different parameters helpful to understand the behavior of COVID19. Later, the role of IoT enabling technology is described and how it will be helpful for the purpose. We hope that in this pandemic time these devices will be helpful to sluggish the impact of pandemic.

References

1. WHO (2020) Coronavirus disease 2019 (COVID-19). Situation report 24. February 13, 2020. World Health Organization, Geneva
2. Li Y, Wang B, Peng R, Zhou C, Zhan Y, Liu Z, Jiang X, Zhao B (2020) Mathematical modeling and epidemic prediction of COVID-19 and its significance to epidemic prevention and control measures. annals of infectious disease and epidemiology, 5(1), Article 10521
3. nCoV-2019 Data Working Group (2020) Epidemiological data from the nCoV-2019 outbreak: early descriptions from publicly available data. 2020. Available at: http://virological.org/t/epidemiological-data-from-the-ncov2019-outbreak-early-descriptions-from-publicly-available-data/337. Accessed on 13 Feb 2020
4. Brahma B (2021) Mathematical model for analysis of COVID-19 outbreak using VON Bertalanffy growth function (VBGF). Turkish J Comput Math Educ (TURCOMAT) 12(11):6063–6075
5. Chesbrough H (2020) To recover faster from Covid-19, open up: managerial implications from an open innovation perspective. Ind Market Manage 0–1. https://doi.org/10.1016/j.indmarman.2020.04.010
6. Berglund ME, Duvall J, Dunne LE (2016) A survey of the historical scope and current trends of wearable technology applications. In: Proceedings of the 2016 ACM international symposium on wearable computers, pp 40–43
7. Bai L, Yang D, Wang X, Tong L, Zhu X, Zhong N, Bai C, Powell CA, Chen R, Zhou J, Song Y, Zhou X, Zhu H, Han B, Li Q, Shi G, Li S, Wang C, Qiu Z, Tan F (2020) Chinese experts' consensus on the internet of things-aided diagnosis and treatment of coronavirus disease 2019 (COVID-19). Clin EHealth 3:7–15. https://doi.org/10.1016/j.ceh.2020.03.001

8. Haleem A, Javaid M, Khan IH (2020) Internet of things (IoT) applications in orthopaedics. J Clin Orthop Trauma 11(xxxx):S105–S106. https://doi.org/10.1016/j.jcot.2019.07.003
9. Haleem A, Javaid M, Vaishya R, Deshmukh SG (2020) Areas of academic research with the impact of COVID-19. Am J Emerg Med. https://doi.org/10.1016/j.ajem.2020.04.022
10. Dash S, Chakravarty S, Mohanty SN, Pattanaik CR, Jain S (2021) A deep learning method to forecast COVID-19 outbreak. New Gen Comput 1–25
11. Behera MK, Chakravarty S, Gourav A, Dash S (2020) Detection of nuclear cataract in retinal fundus image using radial basis function based SVM. In: 2020 sixth international conference on parallel, distributed and grid computing (PDGC). IEEE, p 281
12. Javaid M, Haleem A, Vaishya R, Bahl S, Suman R, Vaish A (2020) Industry 4.0 technologies and their applications in fighting COVID-19 pandemic. Diabetes Metabolic Syndrome Clin Res Rev 14(4):419–422. https://doi.org/10.1016/j.dsx.2020.04.032
13. Healthcare spend in wearables to reach $60 billion by 2023, as monitoring devices & hearables become must haves in delivering care. https://www.juniperresearch.com/press/press-releases/healthcare-spend-in-wearables-reach-60-bn-2023. Accessed 04 July 2020

A Systematic Review of Deep Learning Approaches for Computer Network and Information Security

Khushnaseeb Roshan and Aasim Zafar

Abstract The massive use of the Internet, online data, and information transfer has made the computer network vulnerable to cyberattacks. Deep Learning and Machine Learning approaches are providing efficient solutions to these automated attacks and intrusions. Previously known conventional methods are no longer appropriate as intruders are smart enough to avoid these methods easily. Also, the conventional approaches are not capable enough to detect the latest and previously unknown scenarios. In this article, we have studied and analyzed the latest Deep Learning methods. These methods are widely applied in network anomaly detection, intrusion detection, network traffic analysis, and classification. Through the literature review, we have observed that researchers are using the combination of Machine Learning, Deep Learning, and Hybrid Deep Learning methods to achieve a better result in terms of accuracy and real-time detection. Hence, we have included comprehensive Machine Learning and Deep Learning methods, both single and hybrid approaches. Then, we discuss some open issues and future recommendations for further improvement. And finally, we conclude with an overall summary.

Keywords Deep Learning · Intrusion detection system · Network anomaly · Network attack · Network security

1 Introduction

Information and computer network security is increasingly becoming a focus area of many researchers' nowadays. A secure computer network must have data and information security, integrity, confidentiality, and availability. The integrity of the computer network and hosts is compromised when malicious events, unauthorized access, abnormal profiling behavior, and viruses enter the network. They try to harm, disrupt, the normal flow, and even steal private data and information [1, 2]. The internal weakness within the configuration and implementation of the devices

K. Roshan (✉) · A. Zafar
Aligarh Muslim University, Aligarh, Uttar Pradesh 202002, India

© The Author(s), under exclusive license to Springer Nature Singapore Pte Ltd. 2022
C. Satyanarayana et al. (eds.), *High Performance Computing and Networking*,
Lecture Notes in Electrical Engineering 853,
https://doi.org/10.1007/978-981-16-9885-9_29

345

and networks creates vulnerabilities for the intruders. Intrusion detection, Anomaly detection, Network traffic analysis and classification, Antiviruses, and Firewall are the widely known approaches to provide computers and networks security [3, 4].

Deep Learning (DL) methods are playing an important role in network and information security. These methods have been proved to effectively detect zero-day attacks and provide better accuracy, as shown in Table 1. Researchers also used Machine Learning (ML) techniques in this area like intrusion detection [5], fraud detection [6], phishing [7]. However, the purpose of this study is to tell how researchers are combining different Deep Learning approaches like supervised, unsupervised, and hybrid methods to get better performance, as shown in Table 1.

This article comprises widely known ML and DL methods applied in network anomaly, intrusion detection, and computer network traffic analysis. This paper is organized as follows. Section 2 explains the methodology. Section 3 describes motivation. Section 4 discusses the literature review. Section 5 and its subsection present detailed descriptions of each method. Section 6 provides recommendations for open issues, and finally, Sect. 7 concludes this article.

2   Methodology

"Deep Learning," "Intrusion Detection," "Anomaly Detection," "Network Security," and "Network Attack" are the important key phrase (keywords for searching) that we have used for this study. We have considered all areas related to computer network security with DL approaches. We have used mainly IEEE Xplore, Science Direct, Scopus, and Web of Science (WoS) datasets for target research articles. After that, we have skimmed through the abstract and titles of selected resources. Finally, we have selected the most appropriate and latest articles that lie within the scope of this study. We have considered mainly journal and conference articles. We did a comprehensive review, especially on hybrid DL approaches, as they play a vital role in computer network and information security. Section 5 provides a detailed description of each hybrid DL method.

3   Motivation

Deep Learning approaches are very efficient in discovering the hidden patterns and relationships in highly complex data without human intervention. Network traffic is also highly complex data for which Deep Learning methods are an efficient solution for feature selection and data classification. Below, we have discussed some important points that motivate us to apply Deep Learning approaches in computer networks and information security.

Table 1 Hybrid technique

Category	DL Approach	Datasets	Metric	Performance	Year
NTC [19]	GAN + SVM/DT/RF	NIMS dataset	ACC, F, AUC	99.89% ACC	2017
NTC [20]	CNN + RNN	RedIRIS	ACC, P, R, F	99.59% ACC	2017
IDS [21]	CNN + LSTM (HAST-IDS)	DARPA1998,ISCX2012	ACC, DR, FAR	99.89% ACC	2018
NTC (RT) [31]	ImCNN + ImGWO	DARPA1998, KDD-CUP99, Synthetic datasets	ACC, P, R, F, FPR	98.42% ACC	2019
IDS and NTC [24]	LSTM + AE	NSL-KDD, UNSW-NB15,CICIDS2017	ACC, P, R, F	99.6% DR	2019
IDS and NTC [25]	1D-CNN + LSTM + SAE	ISCX 2012 IDS, ISCX VPN-nonVPN	ACC, P, R, F	99.85% ACC	2019
IDS [26]	DNN + IGASAA + SAA	CICIDS2017, NSL-KDD, CIDDS-001 and Simulated Environment	P, FPR, ACC, DR, F, AUC	99.93% ACC	2019
NTC [27]	CNN + SAE	UNB ISCX VPN-nonVPN	P, R, F	0.98 DR	2019
NTC (RT) [28]	DBN + SVM	CICIDS2017 + Simulated Environment	ACC, P, R, F	97.67% DR	2020
IDS (RT) [22]	CNN + LSTM	REAL-TIME HTTP DATASETS (KF-ISAC), CSIC-2010 HTTP, CICIDS2017	ACC, P, R, F, S	98.07% ACC	2020
IDS [29]	AE + LSTM	MAWILab, IDS2017	ACC, P, R, F, FPR, AUC	99.7% DR	2020
IDS [30]	GAN + AE	NSL-KDD, UNSW-NB15	ACC, P, R, F	95.19% ACC	2020

GAN Generative Adversarial Network; *RNN* Recurrent Neural Network; *LSTM* Long Short-Term Memory; *AE* Autoencoder; *SAE* Stacked AE; *SVM* Support Vector Machine; *CNN* Convolutional Neural Network; *SDA* Stacked Denoising Autoencoder; *SA* Sparse AE; *RBM* Restricted Boltzmann Machine; *DBM* Deep Boltzmann Machine; *DBN* Deep Belief Network; *DNN* Deep Neural Network; *DL* Deep Learning; *DT* Decision Tree; *RF* Random Forest; *SAA* Simulated Annealing Algorithm; *GA* Genetic Algorithm; *IGA* Improved Genetic Algorithm; *S* Specificity; *RT* Real-Time; *ACC* Accuracy; *FAR* False alarm rate; *DR* Detection Rate; *R* Recall; *P* Precision, *F* F-measure; *FPR* False positive rate; *TPR* True positive rate; *NTC* Network traffic classification; *ML* Machine Learning

Deep Learning can provide real-time or zero-day attack detection and prevention mechanism with extensive computational support like multi-core CPU and GPU. As a result, it can give a better response to any security threat.

Deep Learning model can work efficiently with high-dimensional and large volume data. Consequently, DL methods can give better detection accuracy once the model is trained on real-time and massive network traffic data.

Attackers are also using more advanced adversarial techniques (GAN DL) for modifying actual data which can lead to disaster. Consequently, a traditional approach like Machine Learning cannot deal with these advanced attack scenarios [8].

Researchers can apply a combination of Machine Learning and Deep Learning approach to provide a better result and real-time detection of network attacks. Also, many research articles have been published where authors used the combination of various Deep Learning and Machine Learning approaches in a hybrid manner, as shown in Table 1.

4   Literature Review

Deep Learning techniques provide defense against computer networks and information security. Intrusion detection, Network traffic analysis and its classification, Anomaly detection, and Network attack detection, all are various aspects related to the scope of this study. This section reviewed the recent research articles published in this area based on Deep Learning approaches.

In [9], the authors proposed anomaly-based IDS to detect abnormal network traffic. Autoencoder is used to learn features and memetic algorithm for final classification. The model has trained on NSL-KDD and KDD-99 datasets and achieved 98.11% detection rate. Another approach based on Autoencoder proposed in [10]. Here, the authors presented a framework for Network Intrusion Detection Systems named SU-IDS. Two datasets NSL-KDD and CICIDS2017 were used for the experiment and showed acceptable detection rate and accuracy.

The authors of [11] proposed the model for IDS based on CNN. The authors used graphical conversion techniques and NSL-KDD dataset for model training and testing.

However, results did not improve the state-of-the-art method, but future work can be done to improve model performance with a better image conversion approach. Another approach in [12] presented for anomaly-based IDS named TR-IDS. This method utilizes both statistical and payload features of traffic data and showed the effective result. The authors used the random forest algorithm as a final classifier and did extensive experiments to show a promising result.

The authors of [13] presented the new model named BAT-MC for network traffic anomaly detection. This model is based on long short-term memory and attention mechanism. The proposed model did not require feature engineering and can learn key features automatically. In [14], another approach based on LSTM is proposed for cyberattack detection. This model showed a better detection rate for different cyber-attacks. NSL-KDD datasets were used and showed improved results as compared to other methods.

In [15], the authors proposed Stacked AE based approach to detect network anomalies. The model can detect new attacks and also able to classify them accurately. The model can classify four types of attacks: legitimate traffic, flooding type attacks, injection type attacks, and impersonation type attacks with an overall accuracy of 98.6688%. The authors of [16] proposed a method to detect application-layer DoS attacks by applying anomaly-based techniques. This approach can analyze encrypted network traffic without its decryption. This method tested on the realistic cyber environment and resulted in a low false alarm rate.

All the proposed DL approaches include mainly single DL techniques like AE, CNN, LSTM, etc. But nowadays, researchers are moving toward more effective solutions, i.e., ensemble and hybrid DL methods. Section 5 discusses DL approaches where researchers used different DL techniques to provide accurate and real-time detection of security threats. The purpose of this paper is to encourage researchers to apply the combination of advanced DL methods (AE, GAN etc.) for an improved result.

5 Deep Learning Approaches

This review analysis included Deep Learning solutions for network and data security from various attacks and intrusion. Below we have discussed recently applied DL methods in this domain.

5.1 AC-GAN and SVM/DT/RF

Generative Adversarial Networks (GAN) are comprised of two competing neural networks, namely the Generator and the Discriminator, and both are trained in opposition manner. Generators generate the sample data, and discriminators try to distinguish between the actual and the generated data. The training process of both networks is done simultaneously, and this race leads to generate samples that are indistinguishable from the real data [17]. The auxiliary classifier GAN (AC-GAN) is a variant of GAN with a difference that input data of auxiliary classifier GAN includes both the noise and class label [18].

The authors of [19] proposed the model based on AC-GAN and addressed the challenging issue of the imbalanced property of network data. The performance of the network classification model can be improved by enriching the dataset and balancing the minor and the major classes. The authors used AC-GAN to generate synthetic network traffic data. They combined it with the original dataset, i.e., NIMS, to train the three supervised learning algorithms, namely Support Vector Machine,

Decision tree, and Random forest. The model achieved impressive results, but future studies can be done to improve the model by using Deep Learning techniques instead of Machine Learning classification algorithms.

5.2   CNN and RNN

A new technique is proposed for network traffic classifier (NTC). The authors combined the CNN and RNN Deep Learning model to detect and classify IoT network traffic [20]. The method demonstrates that CNN can be extended from image-processing to vector time-series data analysis. Furthermore, the model does not require to process a large number of packets to have an excellent result. This model can provide better detection rate by extracting data from the packet header because the payload data might be confidential and encrypted.

5.3   CNN and LSTM

The authors of [21] proposed the IDS model called hierarchical spatial–temporal features-based intrusion detection (HAST-ID) by combining the advantage of both Deep Learning approaches, i.e., CNN and LSTM. The HAST-IDS learns the spatial features of network traffic data using CNN and then learns temporal features using LSTM. A high false alarm rate (FAR) is a challenging issue for any anomaly-based IDS, and this restricts it for real-life implementation. The authors evaluated the model on the two benchmark datasets, DARPA1998 and ISCX2012, and achieved quite impressive results in terms of FAR. However, future studies can be done to improve the performance of the model in the imbalanced nature of network traffic data, as mentioned in the previous approach.

In a recent study [22], the same technique is applied by combining the CNN and LSTM architecture to focus on payload-level learning and a high-performance computing environment. The proposed Artificial Intelligence-based Intrusion Detection System (AI-IDS) model utilized the normalized UTF-8 character encoding for Spatial Feature Learning (SFL) and the effective extraction of real-time HTTP traffic characteristics. The earlier work was mostly based on accuracy and detection rate, but here the authors also mentioned that scalability and precision are also important factors for real-time IDS.

5.4   ImCNN and ImGWO

The authors of [23] proposed a hybrid anomaly-based IDS model for cloud data center, which leverages Grey Wolf Optimization (GWO) and Convolutional Neural

Network (CNN). Both the techniques, GWO and CNN, further improved to detect anomalies in real-time network traffic streaming data. Here, GWO is improvised in terms of initial population, exploration and exploitation capabilities and Convolutional Neural Network are changed with respect to dropout layer functionalities. The extensive evaluation has been done on two well-known datasets, i.e., DARPA1998 and KDD-CUP99, And the resultant model achieved acceptable detection and false alarm rate. However, researchers can extend the same approach to detect malware in cloud environments.

5.5 LSTM and Autoencoder

A novel multimodal-sequential IDS approach is presented in the study of [24]. The authors used the special structure of the hierarchical progressive network. This approach is supported by the multimodal deep autoencoder (MDAE) and LSTM technologies. Here, features extraction is done at a different level from the network traffic, which is different from the long feature vector used in the traditional approaches mentioned earlier. The three different features views presented are quite novel and intelligent approaches to understand the rich nature of the network behavior. This would be a new perspective for the other researcher in the same domain.

The extensive evaluation is performed using three benchmark datasets, NSL-KDD, UNSW-NB15, and CICIDS 2017. The achieved accuracy of the model in both the binary and multi-class classification is 94% and 88%, respectively. However, the proposed approach can be improved further and implemented in real-world data to increase applicability.

5.6 1D-CNN, LSTM, and SAE

The authors of [25] presented a novel lightweight framework capable of classifying encrypted traffic and detecting malware traffic. The proposed model called Deep-full-range (DFR) is based on Convolutional Neural Network (CNN), Long Short-Term Memory (LSTM), and Stacked AutoEncoder (SAE) architecture. It does not require manual feature extraction and human intervention to analyze private details and information. The experimental results on two benchmark datasets (ISCX 2012 IDS, ISCX VPN-nonVPN) show impressive results in terms of improved F1-score.

5.7 DNN, IGASAA, and SAA

The authors of [26] developed an anomaly-based IDS for the detection and prevention of both inside and outside cloud environment attacks. The resulted model is called "MLIDS" (Machine Learning based Intrusion Detection System). This model is comprised of Deep Neural Network (DNN) and a hybrid optimization framework (IGASAA) based on Improved Genetic Algorithm (IGA) and Simulated Annealing Algorithm (SAA). Here, genetic algorithm improved with optimization techniques, namely Parallel Processing and Fitness Value Hashing. Furthermore, SAA also improved to optimize its heuristic search. The simulation of the proposed approach is done on CloudSim 4.0 simulator. The authors used three datasets, i.e., CICIDS2017, NSL-KDD, and CIDDS-001. Moreover, the optimization strategies applied over GA and SAA have significantly reduced execution time and processing power.

5.8 CNN and SAE

The authors of [27] presented Deep Packet, a framework that embedded stacked autoencoder and one-dimensional convolution neural network to classify encrypted network traffic as well as application identification (e.g., BitTorrent, Email, Youtube, Skype, etc.). The approach of automatic features extraction is somewhat similar, as mentioned in previous methods, but the application identification is an additional implementation. The model was tested on UNB ISCX VPN-nonVPN datasets and performed well in terms of detection and classification of the traffic.

5.9 DBN and SVM

The study presented by the authors of [28] is based on real-time IDS; they addressed the issue of slow detection speed and low detection accuracy from nonlinear massive and high-dimensional network traffic. Here, DBN architecture is used to reduce the feature dimensions of original nonlinear data and then, one-to-all classification is done with multiple SVM classifiers. The sliding window concept is used for data streaming corresponds to CICIDS2017 dataset and to enable real-time detection. Although the model proved a feasible and efficient lightweight intrusion detection system, future work can improve performance accuracy by combining it with other hybrid Deep Learning approaches, as shown in Table 1.

6 Autoencoder and LSTM

The authors of [29] combined the idea of ensemble learning in the field of network traffic anomaly detection and developed a model called HELAD (Heterogeneous Ensemble Learning Anomaly Detection). Here, three major issues of the anomaly detection system were introduced, i.e., real-world environments, changes in the attacks (unknown attacks) environment, and multi-dimensionality of network traffic.

Additionally, the features extraction task is done by the Damped Incremental Statistics algorithm from network traffic data. And, the two well-known datasets, MAWILab and IDS2017, were used for extensive experiments and achieved an impressive detection rate of 99.7%.

6.1 GAN and Autoencoder

A novel model named SAVAER-DNN is proposed by the authors of [30]. The model is based on adversarial learning (GAN) and autoencoder DL architecture. The proposed model is better as compared to the previously mentioned approaches because it detects unknown attacks and is efficient to identify low-frequency attacks. And hence increasing its overall detection rate. The issue of the imbalanced nature of network traffic data is also addressed by generating new attack samples, which provide a balance to the training data by increasing the diversity of the samples. The overall accuracy of 93.01% is achieved by the model, and two benchmark datasets NSL-KDD and UNSW-NB15 were used for evaluation. Furthermore, researchers can improve the detection rate as it is the major factor of anomaly-based IDS.

7 Current Issues and Future Directions

In this article, we have studied recent state-of-the-art Machine Learning and Deep Learning methods for intrusion detection, network anomaly detection, computer network traffic analysis, and its classification. Many issues and future research directions are there to explore for researchers. Some of the current open challenges have been discussed below with further suggestions.

Most publically available datasets used by the researchers are outdated and do not represents the real-world environment and latest attacks. Most of the information in datasets are redundant and do not have balanced categories of the attacks. The large volume of data having real-world network traffic and new attacks could be a key solution for it. Also, to get efficient results from Deep Learning model, developing the standard and benchmarks datasets should be another research direction.

There are different evaluation metrics used to measure the performance of Deep Learning model, as shown in Table 1. Many researchers use a few of them as per their problem needs, even on the same datasets. There should be some criteria to make a standard for metric selection for Deep Learning model's evaluation and further enhancement.

Deep Learning model should also be capable enough to detect real-time and zero-day attacks. The time complexity and the detection efficiency of the model should be one of the key solutions for this. Also, new attacks are evolving on a daily basis to know the vulnerabilities of the system. Researchers should try to reduce the false positive scenario of the detection model as it takes lots of investigating time unnecessarily.

Now day's cybercriminals are using adversarial inputs to fool the classification model. As a solution, the model training should be done in adversarial settings. The authors of [32] presented an approach named DeepCloak. DeepCloak increases the robustness of the prediction model by removing unnecessary features which limit the generation of adversarial inputs.

Deep Learning methods are highly computational. It requires a massive amount of data with multi-core CPUs and GPUs to perform in real-time. Hence providing better hardware and software support would be a solution in a critical situation, for example, like credit card fraud detection where one false negative can cause a major loss. The other issue is the opacity of the Deep Learning model. Sometimes, it is like a black box to us where we cannot find the cause of the error.

8   Conclusion

Network and information security are gaining the attention of many researchers day by day due to various attacks and other cyber-criminal activities. ML and DL techniques are playing an important role in detecting and react against these attacks. This short review paper has shown the rapidly growing interest of researchers in this domain in Table 1. Authors are combining different ML and DL methods to get better detection accuracy. Here, we have included mainly intrusion detection, anomaly detection, and network traffic analysis latest articles. From these articles, we have analyzed some open issues that need to be addressed in further research. Section 6 describes open issues, future directions for improvement, and these challenges are worthy enough for further research.

References

1. Ambalavanan V, Shanthi Bala P (2019) Cyber threats detection and mitigation using Machine Learning. In: Handbook of research on machine and deep learning applications for cyber security, pp 132–149
2. Fernandes G, Rodrigues JJPC, Carvalho LF, Al-Muhtadi JF, Proença ML (2019) A comprehensive survey on network anomaly detection. Telecommun Syst 70(3):447–489
3. Choo KKR (2011) The cyber threat landscape: challenges and future research directions. Comput Secur 30(8):719–731
4. Aldweesh AD, Emam AZ (2020) Deep learning approaches for anomaly-based intrusion detection systems: a survey, taxonomy, and open issues. Knowl Syst 189:105124
5. Dey S, Ye Q, Sampalli S (2019) A machine learning based intrusion detection scheme for data fusion in mobile clouds involving heterogeneous client networks. Inf Fusion 49:205–215
6. Gupta BB, Nedjah N, Prusti D, Padmanabhuni SSH, Rath SK (2020) Credit card fraud detection by implementing machine learning techniques. Safety Secur Reliab Robot Syst, pp 205–216
7. Rao RS (2019) Detection of phishing websites using an efficient feature-based machine learning framework. Neural Comput Appl 31(8):3851–3873

8. Gao J, Lanchantin J, Lou Soffa M, Qi Y Black-box generation of adversarial text sequences to evade deep learning classifiers. In: Proceedings—2018 IEEE symposium on security and privacy workshops, SPW, 2018, pp 50–56
9. Mohammadi S, Namadchian A (2017) A new deep learning approach for anomaly base IDS using memetic classifier. Int J Comput Commun Control 12(5):677–688
10. Min E, Long J, Liu Q, Cui J, Cai Z, Ma J (2018) Su-ids: a semi-supervised and unsupervised framework for network intrusion detection. In: International conference on cloud computing and security, pp 322–334
11. Li Z, Qin Z, Huang K, Yang X, Ye S (2017) Intrusion detection using convolutional neural networks for representation learning. In: Lecture notes computer science (including subseries lecture notes artificial intelligence, lecture notes bioinformatics), vol 10638 LNCS, pp 858–866
12. Min E, Long J, Liu Q, Cui J, Chen W (2018) TR-IDS : anomaly-based intrusion detection through text-convolutional neural network and random forest. Secur Commun Netw
13. Su T, Sun H, Zhu J, Wang S, Li Y (2020) BAT: deep learning methods on network intrusion detection using NSL-KDD dataset. IEEE Access 8:29575–29585
14. Hou H et al (2020) Hierarchical long short-term memory network for cyberattack detection. IEEE Access 8:1–1
15. Thing VLL (2017) IEEE 802.11 network anomaly detection and attack classification: a deep learning approach. In: 2017 IEEE wireless communication networks conference, pp 1–6
16. Zolotukhin M, Hamalainen T, Kokkonen T, Siltanen J (2016) Increasing web service availability by detecting application-layer DDoS attacks in encrypted traffic. In: 2016 23rd international conference on telecommunication ICT 2016
17. Goodfellow IJ et al (2014) Generative adversarial nets. Adv Neural Inf Process Syst 3(January):2672–2680
18. Odena A, Olah C, Shlens J (2017) Conditional image synthesis with auxiliary classifier gans. In: 34th international conference on machine learning ICML 2017, vol 6, pp 4043–4055
19. Vu L, Bui CT, Nguyen QU (2017) A deep learning based method for handling imbalanced problem in network traffic classification. In: ACM international conference proceeding series, pp 333–339
20. Lopez-martin M, Member S, Carro B (2017) Network traffic classifier with convolutional and recurrent neural networks for internet of things. IEEE Access 5:18042–18050
21. Wang WEI et al (2018) HAST-IDS: learning hierarchical spatial-temporal features using deep neural networks to improve intrusion detection. IEEE Access 6:1792–1806
22. Kim A, Park M, Lee DH (2020) AI-IDS: application of deep learning to real-time web intrusion detection. IEEE Access 8:70245–70261
23. Garg S, Kaur K, Kumar N, Kaddoum G, Zomaya AY, Ranjan R (2019) A hybrid deep learning based model for anomaly detection in cloud datacentre networks. IEEE Trans Netw Serv Manag 1
24. He H, Sun X, He H, Zhao G, He L, Ren J (2019) A novel multimodal-sequential approach based on multi-view features for network intrusion detection. IEEE Access 7:183207–183221
25. Zeng Y, Gu H, Wei W, Guo Y (2019) Deep-full-range: a deep learning based network encrypted traffic classification and intrusion detection framework. IEEE Access 7:45182–45190
26. Chiba Z, Abghour N, Moussaid K, El omri A, Rida M (2019) Intelligent approach to build a deep neural network based IDS for cloud environment using combination of machine learning algorithms. Comput Secur 86:91–317
27. Lotfollahi M, Zade RSH, Siavoshani MJ, Saberian M (2017) Deep packet: a novel approach for encrypted traffic classification using deep learning. Soft Comput 24(3):1999–2012
28. Zhang H, Li Y, Lv Z, Sangaiah AK, Huang T (2020) A real-time and ubiquitous network attack detection based on deep belief network and support vector machine. IEEE/CAA J Autom Sin 7(3):790–799
29. Zhong Y et al (2020) HELAD: a novel network anomaly detection model based on heterogeneous ensemble learning. Comput Netw 169:107049
30. Yang Y, Zheng K, Wu B, Yang Y, Wang X (2020) Network intrusion detection based on supervised adversarial variational auto-encoder with regularization. IEEE Access 8:42169–42184

31. Garg S, Kaur K, Kumar N, Kaddoum G, Zomaya AY, Ranjan R (2019) A hybrid deep learning based model for anomaly detection in cloud datacentre networks. IEEE Trans Netw Serv Manag 16(3):924–935
32. Gao J, Wang B, Lin Z, Xu W, Qi Y (2017) DeepCloak: masking deep neural network models for robustness against adversarial samples

Online Mail Junk Penetration by Using Genetic Algorithm Probabilistic Weights and Word Compute

S. Pradeep, G. Sreeram, and M. Venkata Krishna Reddy

Abstract Junk email sifting is a high volume space for exploration, and they are developing with time. The vast majority of the spam sends are limited time in nature. Consequently, spam sends are not unsafe for the PCs, but rather these sends are irritating for client. Spam sends can be separated utilizing spam sifting techniques like Bayes and Gullible Bayes arrangements. Arrangement is one based on substance of the by email and based on specifically on names or likelihood can determined of discovering an instruction from junk and non-spam classifier words. As the count is not many names or weight of information which can be found in both junk and non-spam sends, hence limit based component is attractive for right characterization. For right arrangement utilizing Bayes and Innocent Bayes dataset ought to be colossal in a perfect world number of sends ought to be boundless. However, in genuine applications a plan is wanted which is versatile in nature and can furnish great outcomes with a couple of sends. The comparative way, in this paper a hereditary calculation based spam identification strategy is definite which is basic and give great outcomes restricted dataset.

Keywords Genetic algorithm · Spam · Naive Bayes · Bayes · Ham

S. Pradeep (✉)
Department of Computer Science and Engineering, Malla Reddy Engineering College for Women (UGC Autonomous Institution), Hyderabad, Telangana, India

G. Sreeram
Department of Computer Science and Engineering, Vignana Bharathi Institute of Technology, Ghatkesar, Hyderabad, Telangana, India
e-mail: sreeram@vbithyd.ac.in

M. V. K. Reddy
Department of Computer Science and Engineering, Chaitanya Bharathi Institute of Technology (CBIT)(A), Gandipet, Hyderabad, Telangana, India
e-mail: krishnareddy_cse@cbit.ac.in

© The Author(s), under exclusive license to Springer Nature Singapore Pte Ltd. 2022   357
C. Satyanarayana et al. (eds.), *High Performance Computing and Networking*,
Lecture Notes in Electrical Engineering 853,
https://doi.org/10.1007/978-981-16-9885-9_30

1 Introduction

As of now, quite possibly the most essential components of interchanges over Web is email. Not this, couple of moments of our valuable time is gone through consistently in dispose of spam managing items promotion, offering visas, banking sends, and so forth despite the fact that current spam channels dependent on rules are productive to make the recognizable proof of spam sends and impeding them to entomb post box [1]. In any case, spammers are continually delivering progressed strategies/methods to sidestep channels and send spam messages to enormous gathering of individuals. It is presently very simple and modest to impart across the world because of the headway of innovation. Twitter, Facebook, and other informal communities are regular intends to associate with companions across world. However, this has likewise opened a fresher crowd for spammers to abuse. Spam is not simply restricted to email any more, it is on Voice over Web Convention (VoIP) as spontaneous showcasing or promoting calls, or advertising, publicizing, and sexual entertainment joins on informal community. Spam is all over. As spams are not quite the same as infection, accordingly they do not hurt our PC, PC, and so forth. Yet, they are undesirable message which slither into our letter drop. There is no all-inclusive meaning of spam sends, as they rely upon client interest a mail can be delegated spam or ham sends. Notwithstanding the reality, various scientists everywhere on the world are occupied in broad examination with the intend to battle spam [2]; still a powerful arrangement is inaccessible. Because of the way that spam sifting is mind boggling issue, it is beyond the realm of imagination to expect to spam messages with one arrangement. As the spam messages structure is not consistent, henceforth we require an answer which can be adjusted according to junk process. Subsequently, this is important that from characterization, strategy ought to be versatile in nature, and variation ought to be close by of the each mail client.

From this paper, we commence a hereditary calculation-based information mail arrangement strategy for right distinguishing proof of ham and spam sends. This paper is coordinated into six areas. Section 2 of the paper examines the connected work, and Sect. 3 of the paper talks about Bayes and Credulous Bayes classifier. Hereditary calculation is itemized in Sect. 4 of the paper. In Sect. 5, test results are introduced. Significant finishes of the paper are gritty in Sect. 6.

2 Related Work

In the past history of scrutiny conducted on junk email separation, essentially every one of them depends on the substance of the email. In the comparative setting, Bayes and Innocent Bayes strategies in various structures are utilized [3]. Past investigations including man-made consciousness molecule swarm improvement, confided in reports, AI, and hereditary programming. In any case, these papers generally focus on how these techniques can be utilized in spam sifting. The establishment of the work introduced in this paper was set somewhere around Shrivastava et al., in their underlying exploration where creators have depicted spam arrangement utilizing hereditary calculation in detail. Be that as it may, their work just depends on score point, and along these lines, exactness is restricted. As of late, Choudhary et al., expansion tells about efforts and puts forward prospect weight technique in efficiency of characterization. From this work, we move to expound on the hereditary-based junk sifting method utilizing both loads of junk names and count of words in the resultant. The incorporation of word tally expands the exactness of the email order. The information word reference gives corpus consideration in this work; it is the matching those thought by Shrivastava et al. to make correlation more attractive.

3 Bayes and Naive Bayes Classifiers Related Work

At the commenced work, the two things of junk words loads and absolute quantities in information of an email are utilized toward email order. In attempt of understanding, the impact on junk word and complete count of words depend on junk grouping. Innocent Bayes classifiers and Bayes are examined in this segment [1, 2]. Email separating measure is vigorously subject to the substance holding the information, or all the additional explicitly, numeral of words, and their blends utilized. Allow us to mean number of words in a specific process mail (M) as w_1, w_2, …, w_n. At that point, likelihood of getting mail is likeness accepting words.

$$P(M) = P(W_1, W_2, \ldots, W_n) \tag{1}$$

As we process with the theorem Bayes [4], we are looking over the possible words and the mixed data are turned which needs a large scale of training dataset. As for clarification the count of words are been taken self-sufficient to each other, it can be as Wi is the self-sustaining of Wj Naive Bayes.

At this case,

$$P(M) = \prod_{i=1}^{n} P(W_i) \tag{2}$$

As we go with define spam as M_s and ham as M_H, it will calculate

$$P\left(\frac{M_s}{M}\right) = \frac{P\left(\frac{M}{M_s}\right) P(M_s)}{P(M)} = P(M_s) \prod_{i=1}^{n} \frac{P\left(\frac{W_i}{M_s}\right)}{P(M)} \tag{3}$$

This represents probability of an email that given in the spam uniformly prospect of the email ham is

$$P\left(\frac{M_{\mathrm{H}}}{M}\right) = \frac{P\left(\frac{M}{M_{\mathrm{H}}}\right) P(M_{\mathrm{H}})}{P(M)} = P(M_{\mathrm{s}}) \prod_{i=1}^{n} \frac{P\left(\frac{W_i}{M_{\mathrm{H}}}\right)}{P(M)} \tag{4}$$

Bisecting the two equations, we will get

$$\log \frac{P\left(\frac{M_{\mathrm{s}}}{M}\right)}{P\left(\frac{M_{\mathrm{H}}}{M}\right)} = \log \frac{P(M_{\mathrm{s}})}{P(M_{\mathrm{H}})} + \sum_{i=1}^{n} P\left(\frac{W_i}{M_{\mathrm{s}}}\right) / P\left(\frac{W_i}{M_{\mathrm{H}}}\right) \tag{5}$$

$$\text{If } \log \cdot \frac{P\left(\frac{M_{\mathrm{s}}}{M}\right)}{P\left(\frac{M_{\mathrm{H}}}{M}\right)} > 0$$

it can be given as spam. In the extension of Eq. 3

$$P\left(\frac{M_{\mathrm{s}}}{M}\right) = \frac{P\left(\frac{M}{M_{\mathrm{H}}}\right) P(M_{\mathrm{H}})}{P(M)} = \frac{P\left(\frac{M}{M_{\mathrm{s}}}\right) P(M_{\mathrm{s}})}{P(M_{\mathrm{s}}) P\left(\frac{M}{M_{\mathrm{s}}}\right) + P(M_{\mathrm{H}}) P\left(\frac{M}{M_E}\right)} \tag{6}$$

Applying self-dependence, we can

$$P\left(\frac{M_{\mathrm{s}}}{M}\right) = \frac{P\left(\frac{M}{M_{\mathrm{s}}}\right) \prod_{i=1}^{n} P\left(\frac{W_i}{M_{\mathrm{s}}}\right)}{P(M_{\mathrm{s}}) \prod_{i=1}^{n} P\left(\frac{W_i}{M_{\mathrm{s}}}\right) + P(M_{\mathrm{H}}) \prod_{i=1}^{n} P\left(\frac{M}{M_{\mathrm{H}}}\right)} \tag{7}$$

Regardless of the value, $P(M_s/Wi)$ is known as

$$P\left(\frac{W_i}{M_{\mathrm{s}}}\right) = \frac{P\left(\frac{M_{\mathrm{s}}}{W_i}\right) P(W_i)}{P(M_{\mathrm{s}})} \tag{8}$$

Therefore,

$$P\left(\frac{M_{\mathrm{s}}}{M}\right)$$

$$= \frac{P(M_{\mathrm{s}}) \prod_{i=1}^{n} (P(M_{\mathrm{s}}/W_i) P(W_i)/P(M_{\mathrm{s}}))}{P(M_{\mathrm{s}}) \prod_{i=1}^{n} (P(M_{\mathrm{s}}/W_i) P(W_i)/P(M_{\mathrm{s}})) + P(M_{\mathrm{H}}) \prod_{i=1}^{n} (P(M_{\mathrm{H}}/W_i) P(W_i)/P(M_{\mathrm{H}}))} \tag{9}$$

For the given input of liability spam

$$P\left(\frac{M_{\mathrm{s}}}{M}\right) = \frac{P(M_{\mathrm{s}}).^{1-n} \prod_{i=1}^{n} P\left(\frac{M_{\mathrm{s}}}{W_i}\right).}{P(M_{\mathrm{s}}).^{1-n} \prod_{i=1}^{n} P\left(\frac{M_{\mathrm{s}}}{W_i}\right) + P(M_{\mathrm{H}}).^{1-n} \prod_{i=1}^{n} P\left(\frac{M_{\mathrm{H}}}{W_i}\right)} \tag{10}$$

If the liability of the presented information (M) is Junk, (J) is > than procedures brink for the spam mails and the liability is given as.

$$P(M_H/M) = 1 - P(M_J/M) \qquad (11)$$

Nonetheless, the exceeding definition depends on the expectation of discovering different names in various sends, as on the off chance that specific count is misplaced, 1 term will be 0, and ultimately item 0 and technique comes up short. To upgrade technique, likelihood for misplaced information ought to leave.

The mail consists an enormous count of term, all things considered, barely any information are normal in both junk and non-spam sends. Hence, limit position instrument additionally needed for decision for junk and non-spam information. In addition, all things considered, barely any words are bound to be in spam data, so weighted likelihood would give better outcomes [4]. The complete count of weights specifically sends likewise significant, and this can influence prospect in obtaining words specifically considered. For improving precision, common normal words those can probably be available in found both junk and non-spam mails which can be disposed of characterization.

Mostly Bayes strategy intensely depends over word and cannot be their recurrence, it rather discovering a few words does not imply that the information being scrutinized is junk. In consideration of better recognition, it goes with underneath model. As the objective perspective; it can be carried with 2458 non-spam and 765 junk mails [5]. From the data in the tabular 1 information, 'She', 'will', 'Send', 'love', and 'Data' are thought of and their event in spam and ham sends alongside characterized likelihood. To start with, we have thought about just a word 'Free' for assessment. We process likelihood utilizing condition 5, and we get the calculation part of the test mails and values [6] (Table 1).

$$P(M_s) = \frac{510}{510 + 2462} = 0.1716 \text{ and } P(M_H) = \frac{2462}{510 + 2462} = 0.8284$$

$$P(W_i/M_s) = \frac{337}{510} = 0.6608 \text{ and } P(W_i/M_H) = \frac{471}{2462} = 0.1913$$

$$\log\frac{P(M_s/M)}{P(M_H/M)} = \log\frac{0.1716}{0.8284} + \log\frac{0.6608}{0.1913}$$

Table 1 Resultant data and prospective evaluation

Word	Spam	Ham	P(S/Wi)
She	19	411	0.04622
Will	25	1177	0.02124
Send	175	225	0.77777
Love	135	401	0.33665
Data	156	248	0.62903

$$\log \frac{P(M_s/M)}{P(M_H/M)} = \log 0.2071 + \log 3.45 = -0.1454$$

This can be considered as ham mails

$$P(M_s).^{1-2} \prod_{i=1}^{n} P\left(\frac{M_s}{W_i}\right) = 0.5068$$

$$P(M_H).^{1-2} \prod_{i=1}^{n} P\left(\frac{M_H}{W_i}\right) = 0.0309$$

To tackle above issues, followings should be possible

1. starting with of all recognize junk (spam) words and build up junk information word reference.
2. Splitting the weights of information into certain gatherings holding specific sorts of information.
3. Enumerate gathering likelihood rather than singular word likelihood utilizing above philosophy.
4. Use heuristic to rule for ham/spam sends.

4 Proposed Algorithm

Here, we are commencing with algorithm of genetic which tells the count of junk names, and weights recurrence and complete number of words in a mail are utilized as boundaries in order of non-spam and junk information [7]. From the channel of Bayesian toward the vector, trademark contains recurrences small count of words regularly chose by character specialists. In the development process, it is connected in reality to definitive yield channel. At allusion, this technique in assembling consequently a channel proposed as Bayesian. The procedure establishes framework for the hereditary instruction. The comparative way hereditary calculation was commenced. We are doing calculation arrangement in advanced for every individual resulting emphasis. As into this underlying populace was chosen and amusement was behavior and efficiency, the arrangement hybrid and change is complete in producing current posterity exceptional wellness esteem, in interaction is attentively rehashed arrangement in wanted exactness was accomplished.

The genetic algorithm interaction process are appeared in Fig. 1 [8, 9]. Wellness esteems ensure that the posterity's attributes are over some clear limit. Wellness capacity or wellness esteem is issued, ward and edge are likewise chosen, so that we chat to the arrangement of given issue in least number of cycles. In our trial, wellness esteem relies over the couple of account focuses and no. of words in an email.

For the cycle, first absolute weight words in email tallied, from that point catchphrases to remove is finished [10]. Each junk word is assessed based on the resulting

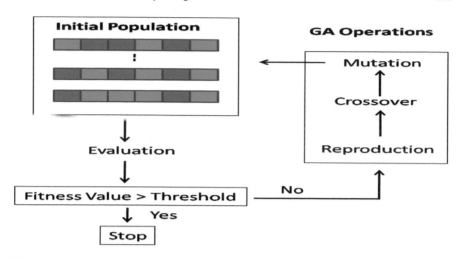

Fig. 1 Genetic algorithm direction steps

process, and from there on, hereditary calculation is requested to acquiring point and on the premise in allowing the acquiring point choice in making with respect to non-spam or junk mail. Its definite methodology is talking about in other segment (FIg. 2).

For the commenced strategy, the most important weights are distinguished and which are chosen weights of words, junk information word reference is outlined. As The weights of the words are considered by taking junk dataset [11]. From the weights, information word reference is isolated into a few gatherings $g_1, g_2, g_3, \ldots, g_n$, individual information dataset with words for every gathering and their recurrence is distinguished, and words gathering is determined. Acquired loads changed onto paired series of zero's and one's. In this way, for a data information to complete quantities of 'zero's' and 'one's' in a string are 10n. We are thinking about some M messages the information base from which m messages are non-spam and the rest M-m are junk information [12]. It is characterization on accessible ahead of time from the downloaded data set.

Hence, we are going with M chromosomes pointing to information M, and we are pointing next which is to plan hereditary calculation to such an extent that it effectively perceives over junk and non-spam data. As the identity of junk and non-spam mail gives idea of the result which is presented toward the depending on strand coordinating with resultant mail with effectively ordered junk and non-spam messages [13]. Solitary quality coordinating with builds score a point by one. Be that as it may, just score point cannot be utilized for non- spam and junk groupings, we are putting a quantity of weight information changes with no. of weighted words in an email and result mail with more number of words is bound to have a bigger score. Thusly, in arrangement, the pair of words in number in an email and score ought to be thought of [14]. The principle process in genetic algorithm depending junk location has appeared in Fig. 2 (Table 2).

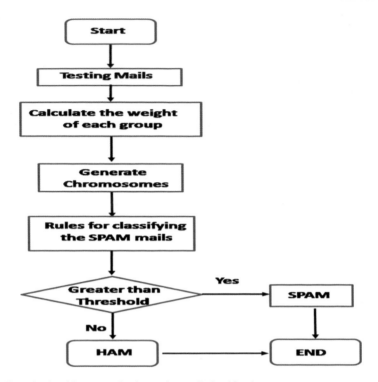

Fig. 2 Genetic algorithm procedural steps in email classification

Table 2 Rules for classification

Acquiring points	No of words (email)
0–5	0–25
6–10	26–50
11–15	51–100
16–20	101–150
21–25	150–200

With reference to count of 353 words taken into consideration and are separated these into seven gatherings 'Grown-up', 'Monetary', 'Business', 'Excellence', 'Voyaging', 'Locally established' and 'Betting'. The quantity of words in each gathering differs and point by point in table for subtleties of words in each gathering peruse can alluded to. Most importantly utilizing these words, chromosome line of 70 pieces is made, and the heaviness of each gathering is addressed by a line of ten pieces [15, 16]. Presently utilizing quality coordinating with score focuses is assessed lastly by taking pair of score focuses and count of words' orders which is functioned. On the off chance, measure data in Table 2 is not fulfilled that picked information is non-spam (Table 3).

Table 3 Data dictionary words classification in each group

Group	No. of words
Group1 (Gambling)	20
Group2 (Home based)	10
Group3 (Travel)	25
Group4 (Beauty)	100
Group5 (Commercial)	86
Group6 (Financial)	68
Group7 (Adults)	44
	353 words

5 Experimental Output

Out-and-out interaction can be clarified utilizing beneath notice email model. As a matter of first importance, all-out names in email are checked, and weights which are regular in information word reference weights to be removed from recurrence were tallied. Based on the weight, W_{wi} is given by name word W_i.

$$W_{Wi} = f/N \tag{12}$$

As the 'f' is recurrence to a specific length of word and absolute no. of words 'N' are specifically informed, this acquired loads are introduced for the length of words via post visible the table data-4. As a matter of first importance, we have included all-out names into the mail. The next count of names that include information of word reference is removed from each word recurrence of data Table 4 loaded (Table 5).

This consolidated load of individual gathering appears for in data Table 5. At this point of view, we cannot find information based no words and subsequently weight for bunch Group 1, Group 3, 4 is zero. This record of heaviness of the gathering is addressed by ten pieces, where the exactness is of the request for 10-3. The genetic code utilizing for the above data table similarity is from the (Fig. 3).

Here, 'X' puts as—'000,000,000'.

Table 4 Weight of considered mail

Group	Word	Frequency	Weight
G1	Single	3	0.00302
G2	Hello	6	0.02125
G3	Maker	1	0.03125
G4	Offline	2	0.03000
G5	Receive	1	0.01212
G6	Current	1	0.02215
G7	Fresh	2	0.02145

Table 5 Group weight of each group

Group	Weight
Group1 (Gambling)	0
Group2 (Home based)	0.00381
Group3 (Travel)	0
Group4 (Beauty)	0
Group5 (Commercial)	0.017010
Group6 (Financial)	0.50211
Group7 (Adults)	0.00389

Group1	Group2	Group3	Group4	Group5	Group6	Group 7
X	0000110010	0000001001	X	X	000000011	0000000011

Fig. 3 Genetic code construction contemplation email

Fig. 4 Uncertainty matrix

	P	N
Y	True Positions	False Positive
N	True Negative	False Negative
	P	N

This resultant things will be grasped through digital simulation. The data of junk and non-spam considerations uncertainty lattice is used Fig. 4 it has four possible methods.

[TP]-True positives—Non-spam emails are truly addressed

[TN]-True negatives—Junk emails are truly addressed

[FP]-False positives—Non-spam emails are not truly addressed

[FP]-False negative—Junk emails are not truly addressed.

$$\text{Precision} = \frac{TP}{TP + FP}, \text{Recall} = \frac{TP}{TP + FN}$$

$$F\text{ - Compute} = \frac{1}{\text{Precision}} + \frac{1}{\text{Recall}}$$

The trial process of F-computer is precision in twofold arrangement. This relies upon over primary review. Supremacy is action that takes place exactness review of a proportion to immenseness of accuracy. As the situation exactness is proportion, precisely junk is distinguished for the review estimates that the number of junk information is accurately recognized. Exactness thinks about just obvious instance

Table 6 Test results

Parameters	Value
True positive	1124
True negative	65
False positive	50
False negative	11
Recall	0.91255
Priority	0.93545
F-score	0.97

in characterization, as F-compute thinks about either valid or bogus qualities order. It is immediate proportion of categorize rightness. F-compute is a more extensive calculation which is consider to variety of information and grouping.

Here the technique is tried on 1250 data information and the outputs are appeared data tabular form 6. Out of 1250, accurately distinguished junk information is 1124, 65 junk data information is recognized as junk mails. 50 junk mails are distinguished as junk. 11 junk mails are recognized as non-spam. Priority is 0.93545 and review is 0.91255 (Table 6).

The efficiency can be given as

$$\text{Accuracy} = \frac{\text{TN} + \text{TP}}{\text{TN} + \text{TP} + \text{FN} + \text{FP}} = 0.971$$

F-Compute = 0.91 (Fig. 5).

From the picture five, the acknowledgment price versus bogus P + ve rate is lay over different strategies. It can be bogus P + ve rate which is expanded than the acknowledgment price that additionally makes. From this picture, it has been contrasted among outcomes and as of late distributed outcomes. In the normal technique commenced by Srivastava et al. [9], the acknowledgment rate is 82%, with probabilistic strategy acknowledgment cost is 86%, a fluffy combination of normal and prospect strategy of acknowledgment rate is 90% with the proposed strategy, the acknowledgment cost that goes with is 95%. As we input that spam word loads the absolute weights include in a mail which is likewise vital other way ruling for junk or non-spam mails.

6 Conclusion

Overall, the paper talks about the hereditary calculation which goals to play in shifting email. This process is going to get the information in separating junk emails to an unlocked issue, and it is difficult to tackle process the issue with 100% fulfillment. It can get a result of 0.97 with genetic algorithm-based technique. As significant discoveries about different process:

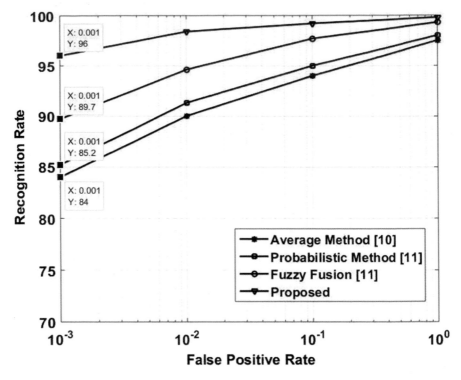

Fig. 5 Identification of recognition rate versus false positive (absolute results)

- Junk email separating wellness work is significant and ought to be chosen cautiously.
- Junk information base is likewise vital in characterizing mail as Junk and non-spam mail.
- Edge estimation is to preface work cannot be set ahead of time, it shifts with information and kind of issue.
- The expression of the information word reference ought to be picked cautiously, as based on these words spam and ham sends will be ordered.

Acknowledgements This research did not receive any specific grant from funding agencies in the public, commercial, or not-for- profit sectors. I would like to thank the editor and anonymous reviewers for their comments that help in improve the quality of this work.

References

1. Schneider KM (2003) A comparison of event models for Naive Bayes anti-spam e-mail filtering. In: Proceedings of the tenth conference on European chapter of the association for computational linguistics, vol 1, pp 307–314
2. Metsis V, Androutsopoulos I, Paliouras G (2006) Spam filtering with naive bayes-which naive bayes. In: CEAS, vol 17, pp 28–69
3. Fdez-Riverola F, Iglesias EL, Díaz F, Méndez JR, Corchado JM (2007) Applying lazy learning algorithms to tackle concept drift in spam filtering. Expert Syst Appl 33:36–48
4. Zhang Y, Wang S, Phillips P, Ji G (2008) Binary PSO with mutation operator for feature selection using decision tree applied to spam detection. Knowl-Based Syst 64:22–31
5. Zheleva E, Kolcz A, Getoor L (2008) Trusting spam reporters: a reporter-based reputation system for email filtering. ACM Trans Inf Syst (TOIS) 27:3
6. Lai CC, Tsai MC (2004) An empirical performance comparison of machine learning methods for spam email categorization. In: 4th International conference on (HIS'04), pp 44–48
7. Ahluwalia M, Bull L, Banzhaf W (1999) A genetic programming-based classifier system. In: GECCO, vol 1, pp1–18
8. Katirai H (1999) Filtering junk e-mail: a performance comparison between genetic programming and naïve bayes. Unpublished manuscript: citeseer.nj.nec.com/katirai99filtering.html, p 10
9. Shrivastava JN, Maringanti HB (2014) E-mail spam filtering using adaptive genetic algorithm. Int J Intell Syst Appl 6:54
10. Shrivastava JN, Bindu MH (2013) E-mail classification using genetic algorithm with heuristic fitness function. Int J Comput Trends Technol (IJCTT) 4(8):2956–2961
11. Singh M, Saxena PS (2017) E-mail classification using fuzzy fusion of average and probabilistic methods. Int J Appl Eng Res 12:7816–7822
12. Chowdhary M, Dhaka VS (2015) E-mail spam filtering using genetic algorithm: a deeper analysis. Int J Comput Sci Inf Technol 6(3):2272–2276
13. Tang KS (1996) Genetic algorithm and their applications. IEEE Signal Process Mag, pp 22–37
14. Koproski GJ, Spam accounts for most e-mail traffic. http://www.technewsworld.com/story/510 55,html
15. Briand L, Labiche Y, Shousha M (2006) Using genetic algorithms for early schedulability analysis and stress testing in real-time systems. Genet Program Evolvable Mach 7(2):145–170. https://doi.org/10.1007/s10710-006-9003-9
16. Salehi S, Selamat A, Bostanian M (2011) Enchanced genetic for spam detection in email. In: IEEE—2nd international conference on software engineering and service science. https://doi.org/10.1109/ICSESS.2011.5982390

A Novel Study and Analysis on Global Navigation Satellite System Threats and Attacks

Krishna Samalla and P. Naveen Kumar

Abstract Due to rapid increase of GNSS functions usage for civilian applications, it is fact that it has some security concern and threatened by variety of attacks, the signals which are given by GNSS are very low power, and hence, the interference may takes place, it will effect on usage, also accuracy will decrease, and the important concern is "spoofing attack" in GNSS, and also it divides GNSS output signals, by the aim of putting receivers control of a receiver also make by calculating its time place and position. The wide usage of GNSS for people's everyday life all aspects of works the integrity and the authenticity is very much concern for satellite navigation signals, the signals are prone to suffer from jamming and spoofing hence it effect on receiver signals and it will impact on cause to position deviation (Humphreys TE, Ledvina BM, Psiaki ML, O'Hanlon BW, Kintner PM (2008) Assessing the spoofing threat: development of a portable GPS civilian spoofer. In: ION GNSS 21st. International technical meeting of the satellite division, pp 2314–2325 [1], Ledvina BM, Bencze WJ, Galusha B, Miller I (2010) An in-line anti-spoofing device for legacy civil GPS receivers. In: Proceedings of the 2010 international technical meeting of the institute of navigation, 25–27 Jan 2010, San Deigo CA, pp 698–712 [2]). Based on the available literature about GNSS spoofing attacks, this article is to analyze various technologies used for anti-spoofing methods and also discuss about strategies which are articulated by various researchers, protection procedures, and implementation schemes of anti-spoofing techniques caused by spoofing attacks which are also analyzed more specifically in different signal level, and therefore, the paper will analyze the performance of various methods for detecting the different types of anti-spoofing techniques.

Keywords GNSS civilian signal · Spoofing · Anti-spoofing · Jamming attack · Signal-level · Data-level · Attacks

K. Samalla (✉)
Sreenidhi Institute of Science and Technology, Hyderabad 501301, India

P. N. Kumar
Osmania University College of Engineering, Hyderabad 500007, India

© The Author(s), under exclusive license to Springer Nature Singapore Pte Ltd. 2022   371
C. Satyanarayana et al. (eds.), *High Performance Computing and Networking*,
Lecture Notes in Electrical Engineering 853,
https://doi.org/10.1007/978-981-16-9885-9_31

1 Introduction

Era evolves in increase of demand and the related for safety in every digital and inter communication enhancement as well. This situation implies to many specific categories of these days' society, in every of GNSS applications, it may be visible, present society completely is based on GNSS, for uninterrupted and stable increase of variety activities and services, but the problem associated with the safety of such kind of structures are from time to time underestimated. At the time of this, a few kinds of applications and services depend on GNSS civilian satellite signals. In fact, the threat of global frequency interface of radio waves is like spoofing or jamming threats and attacks, attempting to detect approaches to guard GNSS users and other civil customers from these spoofing threats [3, 4]. These navigation and informatics centers are used for different sections of society like transportation, business centers, electronic and electric systems, communication centers, and military applications.

The GNSS receiver consists of: to capture and separate the security intelligence service transmitted by the satellites and compute the pseudo range for each satellite by means of a time of arrival measurement.

As depicted in Fig. 1, we can observe that the satellites' trilateration consists of three. If we expect that the clock of receiver is flawlessly adjusted with the time of GPS, the time of arrival computation will become trivial regrettably, and it is not in case of GNSS receivers. Therefore, indicators acquired from the satellite TV for PC will have diverse because of change variation among both the GPS time and the clock time of reverted, and the computation measurements performed with the receiver are referred to as pseudo ranges.

By defining device coordination position, we make outline time reference of device we want to outline the time reference machine. In the GNSS, where the location is acquired via through the measurement of time its miles crucial to have a unique synchronization of the satellite every clock.

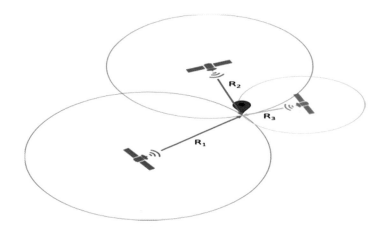

Fig. 1 Example of satellite trilateration

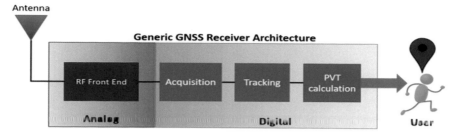

Fig. 2 Receiver architecture of GNSS

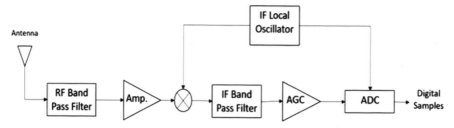

Fig. 3 Generic GNSS front-end receiver

But due to interferences among those signals, the GNSS receiver positioning will deviate. Hence, if the satellite communication system may destroy, and the receiver receives the false information which may lead the user in incorrect positioning (Fig. 2).

The satellite signals are received by GNSS receivers, process it, and calculate through PVT methods. The architecture of a typical GNSS receiver has multiple blocks that work together to obtain the final solution, as shown in Fig. 3. The computational blocks are tracking, acquisition, and the front end of radio frequency (RF) [5]. The ultimate aim of the GNSS navigation system is to find the position, time, and velocity of any user.

In general, the complexity of the front-end presents a trade-off that is proportional to the quality of the signal processing performed. Being the first stage of the process, the quality of the signal delivered by the front-end will improve or degrade all the receiver results. The input of the front-end is the RF analog signal transmitted by the satellite, and the output will be the digitized version of the IF signal. This digitized signal is the input for the acquisition stage.

2 The Spoofing Attack Chronology

Due to advancement in latest technological aspects in real world, the high-speed technologies and innovations are in, hence, the security and threats also increasing accordingly. Therefore, it is fact that these latest advancements are used by GNSS for

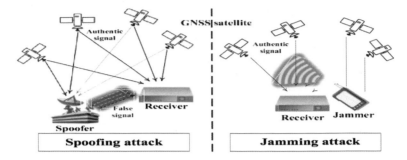

Fig. 4 Source of spoofing and jamming

variety of civilian applications as known that these receivers signals might be effected by different types of attacks and threats, because the receivers signals of GNSS have very poor amplitude once they pass on to the surface of the globe (Fig. 4).

3   The Spoofing Attacks Background Survey

The attacks of spoofing include the various broadcasting navigations of a satellite GNSS-signal to furtively take manage of the end receiver, the signal which is aligned is transmitted and forwarded by the spoofing with the present-day constellation, and the spoofer is capable of taking manage by the end receiver.

It can smoothly alter the place and position solution except the receiver identifying any kind of in consistency within the analysis of solutions [6, 7]. In this work, the assaults of spoofing are the important consciousness of the studies, growing methods, and procedures for detecting spoofing mitigating and other spoofing result.

Many civilian applications of GNSS are proper goals for threats and attacks by spoofing in particular if the target of signal is to detect and carry out unwanted movements in a place as relaxed position or to surreptitiously disrupt accurate operate of the purpose of the receiver [8]. As described in an example, a fisher man he may moreover need to adjust the placement of a vessel, if you want to get entry to misguided waters without elevating the danger indication of the particular geophone. As a substitute, by the way, an attacker or a spooler may need to alter the direction of a drone wings flying close by as a manner to make it crash after which be recovered with the aid of the attacker. However, a massive variety of packages based totally on the important use and applications of GNSS can be identified vital phrases of protection and accountability and liability, and therefore, they have demanding requirements of reliability. In like models, not handiest systems for transportation and swift management depend on the network location that acquire from the satellite navigation signal indicators; however, additionally power generation station, grids intercommunication networks, business activates, and many others may depend on GNSSs for integration purposes [9, 10]. In preferred, in an effort to do manipulate of the Navigation signal, solution of assault of a spoofing will try to change and modify the postpone records of every satellite TV for PC in this manner (Table 1).

Survivalence of civil GNNS: The attacking methods mainly classified in two categories which are spoofing attack and jamming attack; they are mainly caused by satellite navigation signals at the receivers end, and spoofing attack may vary in two versions like spoofing attack in forward direction and source of the spoofing attack by misleading navigation signals, its fact that the spoofer must have an idea about structure of the satellite not only the navigation satellite information, the spoofer independently introduce the generated signal in to the receiver and the jamming attack accurse in transmitters to pass on strong signal' interference and hide the navigation satellite signals therefore the output waveform is suppressed thereby GNNS signals will be deviates, these two threats (Jamming and Spoofing) will show a major impact on the signals of Civil and military applications of GNSS. Attack process (Four ways of attacking) the classifications and characteristics of Spoofing threats and attacks are depicted in Tables 1 and 2.

The above said Classifications are observed by various authors for anti-spoofing methods, and implementation process is described as well; indeed to observe it, the

Table 1 Spoofing attack characteristics

Type of attack	Replay spoofing attack (RSA) [11–14]
Implementation difficulty	Low
Effect of attack	Moderate
Characteristics	Here, the spoofing signal delays by which is transmitted by the
Type of attack	Forgery spoofing attack (FSA) [14–19]
Implementation difficulty	Medium
Effect of attack	Moderate good
Characteristics	In this case, adjust the ant parameters related to the signal by generation a signal which contains spoofing signal
Type of attack	Estimation spoofing attack (ESA) [14, 20, 21]
Implementation difficulty	Medium–High
Effect of attack	Good
Characteristics	This method cannot only affect general signals of civil applications, and also it says that it can misguide the signals of satellite without knowing the security programs. In this method, it can estimate and generate satellite signals
Type of attack	Advanced spoofing attack (ASA) [10, 21]
Implementation difficulty	High
Effect of attack	Good
Characteristics	The receivers are integrated, complex, and methods of anti-spoofing. It can hold multiple strategies of spoofing, and it can include the characteristics of signal not only adopts multiples spoofing strategies for implementation of another strong signal spoofing, hence more effectively and directly the spoofing of the receiver

Table 2 Analysis of various spoofing and anti-spoofing techniques

Methodology	Spoofing detection method based on spoofing attack [22]
Characteristics	In this method, a couple state method of estimation is used to analyze and solve the angle of phase unit measurement problem of optimization while entrancing dynamic estimation and by unknowing estimation of time
Inadequacy/Fault in	In the spoofing detection method, considers less to nonlinear delay the dynamic system of monitoring in the real environment
Configuration required/difficulty in implementation	The receiver depends on combined estimation state capability/less
Implementation phase	Track and compute
Methodology	The methods for sampling suppression [23]
Characteristics	To perform signal estimation in spoofing, it combines to methods (RF and phase) controlling technology in signal processing estimation
Inadequacy/fault in	By applying this method, the receivers' front end for spoofing the suppression needs to improve for better performance reliability
Configuration required/difficulty in implementation	The RF receiver phase control needs capability of analysis/medium
Implementation Phase	Track and capture
Methodology	Time hopping anti-spoofing methods [24]
Characteristics	In this paper, it says that analysis of time hoping by the method of linear regression through the algorithms for signal processing techniques
Inadequacy/Fault in	Optimization techniques are required, and calculation procedure is too large
Configuration required/difficulty in implementation	Receiver needs signal delay decision capability/high
Implementation phase	Trace/track
Methodology	Regenerative spoofing signal detection method [25]
Characteristics	To implement the model for spoofing estimation, this method works on spectral analysis method
Inadequacy/fault in	Interference can increase due to multipath in fake alarm probability; it has drawback of the multipath interface for considering complete plan
Configuration required/difficulty in implementation	The capability of signal output phase detector/medium
Implementation phase	Track and capture
Methodology	Frequency phase two-dimensional search spoofing detection method [26]

(continued)

Table 2 (continued)

Methodology	Spoofing detection method based on spoofing attack [22]
Characteristics	To operate time authenticity for identified networks and desired locations, two methods are combined cross (checking and correlation)
Inadequacy/fault in	During the implementation, it has some problems and have very high complexity in computational process
Configuration required/difficulty in implementation	Capability in cross (correlation and checking)/high
Implementation phase	Capture and track
Methodology	A new method of spoofing detection in the capture phase [27]
Characteristics	In this method, it can monitor peaks of correlation numbers beyond the threshold power which depends on power of signal
Inadequacy/fault in	Due to low sampling rate the performance of spoofing direction is unstable
Configuration required/difficulty in implementation	The satellite clock difference of receiver requires difference and drift monitoring capability/track and capture
Implementation Phase	Track and capture
Methodology	Slope detection method for multi-correlator structure [28]
Characteristics	The method performs spoofing detection based on the difference of correlation vale among the multi path and spoofing signals
Inadequacy/fault in	The method can affect the effective recognition performance of spoofing signals
Configuration required/difficulty in implementation	Receiver needs to configure multi correlator/high
Implementation phase	Track and capture
Methodology	GPS spoofing signal detection method [29]
Characteristics	The detection of spoofing depends on the variation correlation among the two between spoofing signal ratio and original satellite signals
Inadequacy/fault in	To identify the delay spoofing process of detection of ratio gain between more than path, it can take large time and the real-time application is poor
Configuration required/difficulty in implementation	Correlation peak detection capability/high
Implementation phase	Track and capture

(continued)

Table 2 (continued)

Methodology	Spoofing detection method based on spoofing attack [22]
Methodology	Real-time synchronization attack suppression and mitigation techniques [30]
Characteristics	It can observe and monitor satellite drift bias and other models of different attacks of spoofing
Inadequacy/fault in	This operation method is detecting in real time, and it is in less
Configuration required/difficulty in implementation	The satellite clock difference of receiver requires difference and drift monitoring capability/track and capture
Implementation phase	Medium
Methodology	Signal authenticity test using signal quality signal quality monitoring indication [31]
Characteristics	In this method, an effective processing of signal performance
Inadequacy/fault in	The method can affect the effective recognition performance of spoofing signals
Configuration required/difficulty in implementation	The equipment of receiver needs to have a high correlation peak detection correlation property/high
Implementation phase	Track and capture
Methodology	Spoofing detection on Doppler offset and satellite signal amplitude indicator [32]
Characteristics	Multiple satellite signals for different satellite signals will be transmitted by a single spoofing signal
Inadequacy/fault in	This scheme effectively detects the signal which is transmitted by single spoofing interference source
Configuration required/difficulty in implementation	Needs to have un interrupted monitoring of the signal value and amplitude and Doppler shift value/medium
Implementation phase	Track and capture
Methodology	Anti-spoofing method based on Doppler shift [32]
Characteristics	This method enables detection spoofing from influencing factors and considering in all the informative data influencing factors
Inadequacy/fault in	In this case, computational complexity will increase, and for high power mobiles, the reliability of suppressing poor signals is less
Configuration required/difficulty in implementation	The receiver has Doppler shift analysis capability/medium
Implementation phase	Track and capture

suppression methods for spoofing and detection of spoofing, required configuration, characteristics, and methodology is described in detail, the Doppler shift method is employed for the given satellite signal and its parameter due to the elative movement between receiver and the navigation satellite, meanwhile as the detection of spoofing can be operated by the receiver capture or during the tracking. The analysis gives the performance of signal navigation, and some sort of information processed by the signal of satellite, it may consists that within the understandable scene and without any spoofing.

4 Conclusion and Future Scope

The method of anti-spoofing and its attack for a given receiver can be treated separately between the method of signal processing level and also with information processing level. In this paper, we analyzed the various performances of the receiver anti-spoofing methods for navigation satellite and also described the data processing anti-spoofing methods in tables that we summarized the anti-spoofing and other anti-spoofing methods, and the characteristic performance for resistance has been summarized and analyzed in detailed, and also discussed various implementation procedure methods for every anti-spoofing techniques to different spoofing attacks in different domains also highlighted.

The attacks in navigations signal is affecting more on its performance. In Table 1, it is described that four attack effects of spoofing (RSA) (FSA), (ESA), and (ASA) are discussed one by one to lead the research in enhanced manner.

Comparatively speaking, for these sorts of spoofing, the tactic of anti-spoofing is extremely weak. Considering the performance of the spoofing attack comprehensively with that of the combination spoofing strategy, the problem of implementing direct replay spoofing is a smaller amount than that of multi-antenna receiver replay spoofing.

From this survey, it is summarized during this article, it is identified that any of the deception method may do the configured technologies of anti-spoofing ineffective, and any of these anti-methods of anti-spoofing can counter all kind of deception attacks. In view of this, the longer-term directions to review a more complete anti-deception system because the deception model continues to advance. At an equivalent time, we must also specialize in the suppressed signals of spoofing-affected signals in order that the navigation system of satellite can give services in safer and stable position.

Even though technologies, innovative research, and theories belong to GNSS related which have been improved rapidly in the last decade, still there is a huge demand for civilian applications of GNNS, and it is not reaching the required service increases, meanwhile the GNSS encounter the spoofing and anti-spoofing technologies other side, the loopholes of the navigation systems of satellite that it leads a major issues and great challenges to the applicants, the key challenges and regular problems, emerging challenges of the navigation system have today is addressed in this paper and analyzes with summary of further research.

References

1. Humphreys TE, Ledvina BM, Psiaki ML, O'Hanlon BW, Kintner PM (2008) Assessing the spoofing threat: development of a portable GPS civilian spoofer. In: ION GNSS 21st. International technical meeting of the satellite division, Savannah GA, pp 2314–2325, 16–19 Sept 2008
2. Ledvina BM, Bencze WJ, Galusha B, Miller I (2010) An in-line anti-spoofing device for legacy civil GPS receivers. In: Proceedings of the 2010 international technical meeting of the institute of navigation, 25–27 Jan 2010, San Deigo CA, pp 698–712
3. Margaria D, Motella B, Anghileri M, Floch J-J, Fernández-Hernández I, Paonni M (2017) Signal structure-based authentication for civil GNSSs: Recent solutions and perspectives. IEEE Signal Process Mag 34(5):27–37
4. Lo S, Lorenzo DD, Enge P, Akos D, Bradley P (2009) Signal authentication, a secure civil GNSS for today. Inside GNSS 4(5):30–39
5. Akos DM (2012) Who's afraid of the spoofer? GPS/GNSS spoofing detection via automatic gain control (AGC). J Inst Navig 59(4)
6. Jovanovic, Botteron C, Fariné P-A (2014) Multi-test detection and protection algorithm against spoofing attacks on GNSS receivers. In: Proceedings of IEEE/ION position, location navigation symposium (PLANS), Monterey, CA, USA, pp 1258–1271
7. Jiang, Chen S, Chen Y, Bo Y, Xia Q, Zhang B (2018) Analysis of the baseline data based GPS spoofing detection algorithm. In: Proceedings of IEEE/ION position, location navigation symposium (PLANS), Monterey, CA, USA, pp 397–403
8. Caparra G, Ceccato S, Sturaro S, Laurenti N (2017) A key management architecture for GNSS open service navigation message authentication. In: Proceedings of European navigation conference (ENC), Lausanne, Switzerland, pp 287–297
9. Humphreys TE (2013) UT Austin researchers spoof supery-acht at Sea. The University of Texas at Austin. [Online]. Available: http://www.engr.utexas.edu/features/superyacht-gps-spo ofing
10. Shi, Chen S, Liu Z (2017) Analysis and optimizing of time-delay in GPS repeater deception. J Chongqing Univ Posts Telecommun (Natural Sci. Edition) 29(1):56–61
11. Psiaki ML, Humphreys TE (2016) GNSS spoofing and detection. Proc IEEE 104(6):1258–1270
12. Gao Z, Meng F (2011) Principle and simulation research of GPS repeater deception jamming. J Telemetry Tracking Command 32(6):44–47
13. Scott L (2003) Anti-spoofing & authenticated signal architectures for civil navigation systems. In: Proceedings of the 16th international technical meeting of the satellite division of the institute of navigation (ION GPS/GNSS), Portland, OR, USA, pp 1543–1552
14. Humphreys TE (2013) Detection strategy for cryptographic GNSS anti-spoofing. IEEE Trans Aerosp Electron Syst 49(2):1073–1090
15. Humphreys TE, Ledvina BM, Psiaki ML, O'Hanlon BW, Kintner PM (2009) Assessing the spoofing threat. GPS World 20(1):28–39
16. Dai, Xiao M, Huang S (2017) GPS spoofing and inducing model of UAV. Commun Technol 50(3):496–501
17. He L, Li W, Guo C (2016) Study on GPS generated spoofing attacks. Appl Res Comput 33(8):2405–2408
18. Shi M, Chen S, Wu H, Mao H (2015) A GPS spoofing pattern based on denial environment. J Air Force Eng Univ (Natural Sci. Edition) 16(6):27–31
19. Huang S, Chen S, Yang B, Wu H (2017) A power control strategy of multiple GNSS spoofing signals. J Air Force Eng Univ (Natural Sci. Edition) 18(1):76–80

20. Wesson K, Rothlisberger M, Humphreys T (2012) Practical crypto-graphic civil GPS signal authentication. Navigation 59(3):177–193
21. Curran JT, O'Driscoll C (2016) Message authentication, channel coding & anti-spoofing. In: 29th International technical meeting of the satellite division of the institute of navigation (ION GNSS), Portland, OR, pp 2948–2959
22. Risbud P, Gatsis N, Taha A (2019) Vulnerability amnalysis of smart grids to GPS spoofing. IEEE Trans Smart Grid 10(4):3535–3548
23. Kim TH, Sin CS, Lee S, Kim JH (2013) Analysis of effect of anti-spoofing signal for mitigating to spoofing in GPS L1 signal. In: 13th International conference on control automation and systems (ICCAS), Gwangju, South Korea,pp 523–526
24. Berardo M, Manfredini EG, Dovis F, Presti LL (2016) A spoofing mitigation technique for dynamic applications. In Proceedings of 8th ESA workshop satellite navigation technology European workshop GNSS signals signal process. (NAVITEC), Noordwijk, The Netherlands, pp 1–7
25. Zhao L, Miao Z, Zhang B, Liu B, Li G, Zhou X (2015) A novel spoofing attack detection method in satellite navigation tracking phase. J Astronaut 36(10):1172–1177
26. Bhamidipati S, Mina TY, Gao GX (2018) GPS time authentication against spoofing via a network of receivers for power systems. In: Proceedings of IEEE/ION position, location navigation symposium (PLANS), Monterey, CA, USA, pp 1485–1491
27. Wang, Li H, Cui X, Lu, M (2013) A new method in acquisition to detect GNSS spoofing signal. In: Proceedings of international conference on mechatronic sciences, electric engineering and computer (MEC), Shenyang, China, pp 2913–2917
28. Cai, Sun X, Fan G, Wu C (2017) Deception detection method in multipath environment. Mod Defence Technol 45(5):72–77
29. Li H, Wang X (2016) Detection of GPS spoofing through signal multipath signature analysis. In: Proceedings of IEEE Canadian conference on electrical and computer engineering (CCECE), Vancouver, BC, Canada, pp 1–5
30. Khalajmehrabadi, Gatsis N, Akopian D, Taha AF (2018) Real- time rejection and mitigation of time synchronization attacks on the global positioning system. IEEE Trans Ind Electron 65(8):6425–6435
31. Jahromi AJ, Broumandan A, Daneshmand S, Lachapelle G, Ioannides RT (2016) Galileo signal authenticity verification using signal quality monitoring methods. In: Proceedings of international conference on localization GNSS (ICL- GNSS), Barcelona, Spain, pp 1–8
32. Broumandan A, Jafarnia-Jahromi A, Dehghanian V, Nielsen J, Lachapelle G (2012) 'GNSS spoofing detection in handheld receivers based on signal spatial correlation. In: Proceedings of IEEE/ION position, location navigation symposium, Myrtle Beach, SC, USA, pp 479–487

Modified Gaussian Mixture Distribution-Based Deep Learning Technique for Beamspace Channel Estimation in mmWave Massive MIMO Systems

V. Baranidharan, N. Hariprasath, K. Tamilselvi, S. Vignesh, P. Chandru, A. Srinigha, and V. Yashwanthi

Abstract In recent times, the evolution of cellular networks has an exponential growth. Millimeter-wave provides higher spectral efficiency and wider bandwidth; it solves the problem of adopting a greater number of users to the mobile network in the future. The beamforming in the mm-wave system is introduced to narrow down the beam which is highly directional and reduces the path loss in the systems. To deploy the beamforming in the existing systems, it requires more cost and performance also gets affected. To reduce the hardware cost, lens antenna array is used in the existing systems in order to reduce the RF chains and improve the performance. While deploying the large lens antenna with a smaller number of RF chains, channel estimation becomes more difficult and crucial. Recently, several deep learning-based channel estimation schemes for mm-Wave are proposed to improve the efficiency of the system. In order to improve the performance of the channel, sparsity of the beamspace channel is exploded. This results in considering the beamspace channel estimation as the sparse signal recovery problem. The sparse signal recovery problem can be solved by AMP which is the classic iterative-based algorithm. However, these systems do not satisfy the performance and accuracy. The modified GM-based LAMP system uses the prior information for the channel estimation to improve the performance.

Keywords Massive MIMO · Sparse signal · mmWave band · Channel estimation · LAMP network

V. Baranidharan (✉) · N. Hariprasath (✉) · K. Tamilselvi · S. Vignesh · P. Chandru · A. Srinigha · V. Yashwanthi
Department of Electronics and Communication Engineering, Bannari Amman Institue of Technology, Sathyamangalam, India

© The Author(s), under exclusive license to Springer Nature Singapore Pte Ltd. 2022 383
C. Satyanarayana et al. (eds.), *High Performance Computing and Networking*,
Lecture Notes in Electrical Engineering 853,
https://doi.org/10.1007/978-981-16-9885-9_32

1 Introduction

In recent days of the wireless communication, wireless evolution of the generation is more challenging and on among the field which shows exponential growth in the world. In the connected world, the current 4G fails to serve its intentional needs due to rapid increase of connected community and technological development. The increase in the number of users and insufficient bandwidth forced to move to the next generation. 5G has more demands due to its wide bandwidth, latency and its massive MIMO concepts. In fact, advancement of the current digital technology such as IoT and AI is purely depending on the 5G as it has a more throughput. The advantage of having massive MIMO is all about adapting a greater number of users within the same spectrum [1]. The implementation of more antennas either in transmitter or receiver side will provide possible paths as much as possible and high data rate. We receive a higher frequency beam width by reducing its antenna size [2]. The introduction of the lens array helps in reducing the power consumption and hardware cost and supports large number of antennas with energy-efficient hybrid precoding realization [1]. Beamspace channel parameters is derived from the spatial channel by adding the lens array antenna at the base station.

Investigating the different DL algorithms will reduce the high computational problems and it also helps to reduce the complexity for achieving accuracy in systems [3]. There are a few existing algorithms which uses the DL techniques for accuracy improvement such as learned AMP. These algorithms use DL algorithms which gives promising results, but it has some difficulties in solving computational complexities.

.

2 Related Works

Xie Zwang et al. have proposed a new Deep Learning-Based Channel Estimator for Massive MIMO Systems [1]. In this section, the channel estimation has the USP of concentrating only on the pilot symbols which are lesser than the count of the transmitter antenna. The estimation system is divided into two sub stages. In first stage, the channel is estimated based on the pilot and the channel estimator. In the second stage, another DNN is used for improving the accuracy of the channel estimation. Evangelos Vlachos has proposed a new Massive MIMO Channel Estimation for Millimeter Wave System via Matrix Completion [2]. The beamforming in the millimeter-wave technology requires a most efficient method of channel estimation technique in the wireless channel. The channels which use mm waves have a large variability difference in which it severely affects the short training period recovery problem.

R. Dai, Y. Liu have proposed a new Channel Estimation by Reduced Dimension Decomposition for Millimeter Wave massive MIMO Systems [4]. This work aims to provide the channel estimation with by decomposing the channel matrix H into channel gain information and angle information estimation. The decomposition is made to the received signal with respect to the dimensionality so that the transmitting and the receiving end angles are separated. In this proposed system, the initial spare support set is obtained sparse signal recovery algorithm. Chang-Jac Chun have proposed an AMP-Based Network with DEEP Residual Learning for mm Wave Beam space Channel Estimation [5]. In this scheme, the AMP algorithm is used as the iterative channel estimation algorithm. This is mainly divided into two components, the first part is of learned AMP and the second part is of residual learning-based AMP network. The previous works on beamspace channel estimation works exploits the sparsity property of the channel matrix where this explicitly reduces the impact of noise in the channel and improves the performance.

Kiran Venugopal has proposed a Channel Estimation for Hybrid Architecture-Based Wideband Millimeter Wave Systems [6]. In millimeter wave systems, both array gain and multiplexing gain can be achieved by implementing the hybrid analog and digital precoding techniques. The basic channel knowledge helps to design the precoders and the combiners. In previous channel estimation techniques, which use hybrid architectures focus only on the channels with narrowband. Pierluigi V. Amadori, Christos Masouros have proposed a Low RF-Complexity Millimeter-Wave Beam space-MIMO Systems by Beam Selection [7]. The increase in the high-capacity wireless links and short range due to wide bandwidth in the mm Wave communication channels have provided many numbers of use cases. By combining the beam selection and the beamspace multiple input multiple output, the hardware cost is reduced with the performance to the near-optimal state.

In overall, the existing beamspace channel estimation using iterative and deep learning methods fail to achieve the satisfactory performance metrices, low computational complexity. The tradeoff between computational complexity and algorithm performance determines the accuracy of the system and the existing systems fails in providing that accuracy. Hard utilization of channel state information in the existing system also degrades the efficiency of the systems.

3 System Model

In order to improve the efficiency, constructing the beamspace channel model, and then formulating the beamspace channel estimation problem as sparse signal recovery problem.

3.1 Copyright Forms

To formulate the beamspace channel estimation problem, assume conventional mmWave massive MIMO in spatial domain. The Saleh Valenzuela channel model [8] is widely used in all the channel estimation, and its channel vector h_k of size N

$\times$ 1can be represented in (1) where k—number of users, N—number of antennas in base station, L_k–number of resolvable path, $c_{k,li}$—lth path component, $\beta_{k,l}$—complex gain, $\theta_{k,l}^{azi}$—azimuth angle, $\theta_{k,l}^{ele}$- elevation angle.

$$h_k = \sqrt{\frac{N}{L_k}} \sum_{l=1}^{L_k} \beta_{k,l} a(\theta_{k,l}^{azi}, \theta_{k,l}^{ele}) = \sqrt{\frac{N}{L_k}} \sum_{l=1}^{L_k} c_{k,l} \tag{1}$$

Array steering vector [8] for simpler uniform linear arrays (ULAs) is

$$\alpha_{ULA}(\theta) = \frac{1}{\sqrt{N}} [e^{-j2\pi d\sin(\theta)n/\lambda}] \tag{2}$$

where $n = [0, 1, 2, ..., N-1]^T$.

For UPAs with $N_1 \times N_2$ antennas,

$$a_{UPA}(\theta^{azi}, \theta^{ele}) = \frac{1}{\sqrt{N}} \left[e^{-j2\pi d\sin(\theta^{azi})\sin(\theta^{ele})n_1/\lambda} \right] \otimes \left[e^{-j2\pi d\sin(\theta^{azi})\sin(\theta^{ele})n_2/\lambda} \right] \tag{3}$$

where $n_1 = [0, 1, 2, ..., N_1-1]^T$, $n_2 = [0, 1, 2, ..., N_2-1]^T$, λ—wavelength of carrier, d—antenna spacing.

Since lens antenna array plays the role of spatial discrete Fourier transform (DFT), it can easily transform spatial domain channel into beamspace channel by including the DFT matrix U of size $N \times N$ [9]. Therefore, the channel vector equation will be

$$\tilde{h}_k = Uh_k = \sqrt{\frac{N}{L_k}} \sum_{l=1}^{L_k} \tilde{c}_{k,l} \tag{4}$$

where $\tilde{c}_{k,l} = Uc_{k,l}$.

3.2 Problem Formulation

To know the channel state information (CSI), all the users have to transmit their known pilot symbol to base station for a times. Since the TDD channel have reciprocity, considering only the uplink, so that the downlink will be directly obtained for channel estimation problem. So that channel vector can be estimated one by one between K users and base station. Due to pilot orthogonality, channel estimation method is same for all K users hence the overall measurement signal can be expressed as

$$y = A\tilde{h} + n \tag{5}$$

The beamspace channel $\tilde{h}$ is more or less sparse since there is a few propagation path due to limited scattering at mmWave frequencies [10]. Therefore, applying for sparse signal recovery in order to complete the estimation with low pilot overhead.

$$\min \left\| \tilde{h}_0 \right\|, \text{S} \cdot \text{t} \cdot \left\| y - A\tilde{h}_2 \right\| \leq \varepsilon \tag{6}$$

where $\left\| \tilde{h}_0 \right\|$ is number of non-zero element of $\tilde{h}$, and ε is error tolerance parameter.

3.2.1 AMP and LAMP Network

IThe mmWave massive MIMO system is generally large due to the number of antennas; hence, the dimension of sparse signal is high. But the iterative AMP algorithm can overcome the problems by providing low computational complexity with sparse signal recovery also [3].

3.2.2 AMP Algorithm

Input: y - Measurement vector, **A** - sensing matrix, **T** - number of iterations.
Initialization: $v_{-1} = 0$, $b_0 = 0$, $c_0 = 0$, $\hat{\tilde{h}}_0 = 0$
for $t = 0,1,…,T-1$ **do** $v_t = y - A\hat{\tilde{h}}_t + b_t v_{t-1} + c_t v_{t-1}^*$
$\quad \sigma_t^2 = \frac{1}{M} \|v_t\|_2^2$
$\quad r_t = \hat{\tilde{h}}_t + A^T v_t$
$\quad \hat{\tilde{h}}_{t+1} = \eta_{st}\left(r_t : \lambda_t, \sigma_t^2\right)$
$\quad b_{t+1} = \frac{1}{M}\sum_{i=1}^{N} \frac{\partial \eta_{st}(r_{t,i}:\lambda_t,\sigma_t^2)}{\partial r_{t,i}}$
$\quad c_{t+1} = \frac{1}{M}\sum_{i=1}^{N} \frac{\partial \eta_{st}(r_{t,i}:\lambda_t,\sigma_t^2)}{\partial r_{t,i}^*}$
end for
Output: Sparse signal recovery results: $\hat{\tilde{h}} = \hat{\tilde{h}}_T$

Even though the AMP algorithm is fine in dealing the sparse signal recovery problem, there comes the two more problem which arises in the sparse beamspace channel estimation. Firstly, the same empirical value will be followed in all the iteration for the shrinkage parameter [11] λ_t. Secondly, the prior distribution of the beamspace channel cannot be exploited by the general AMP algorithm. To change the value of λ_t for each iteration, the classical AMP algorithm called LAMP network has been proposed. where the inputs of the t th layer are $y \in C^M, \hat{\tilde{h}}_t \in C^N$, and $v_t \in C^M$, y is measurement vector $\hat{\tilde{h}}$, and v_t are outputs of $(t-1)$th layer.

$$\hat{\tilde{h}}_{t+1} = \eta_{st}(r_t : \lambda_t, \sigma_t^2) \tag{7}$$

$$v_{t+1} = y - A\hat{\tilde{h}}_t + b_{t+}v_t + c_{t+1}v_t^* \tag{8}$$

Here, A^T was replaced by B^T which can choose different linear coefficients for each layer t. By giving enough training data, we can find the LAMP network with better shrinkage parameter. Still, the second problem of AMP algorithm has not been solved. The AMP algorithm and LAMP network only considers the sparsity of signals to be recovered, which are general for any sparse signal recovery problem. The shrinkage function of LAMP network is not specifically designed for beamspace channel estimation.

3.3 Modified GM-Based LAMP Network for Beamspace Channel Estimation

Based on the Gaussian mixture distribution of beamspace channel, obtaining a new shrinkage function. Then, the GM-based LAMP beamspace channel estimation scheme is proposed, based on obtained shrinkage function. In order to gain the sparse signal recovery problems, extending our idea of GM-based LAMP network.

3.3.1 Gaussian Mixture Distribution and Its Corresponding Shrinkage Function

Knowing the need of getting the channel estimation with prior information. Then, to refine the LAMP network, using more specific prior distribution [12, 13]. Precisely, the probability density function of element $\tilde{h}$ of the beamspace channel $\tilde{h}$ can be showed as

$$p\left(\tilde{h}, \theta\right) = i \sum_{K=0}^{N_c-1} P_k CN\left(\tilde{h}; \mu_k, \sigma_k^2\right) \tag{9}$$

Considering the ULA, the rationality of the Gaussian mixture distribution can be expressed on the basis of two ways. The n th element $\tilde{h}_n$ of the beamspace channel $\tilde{h}$ can be expressed as

$$\tilde{h}_n = i\sqrt{\frac{N}{L}}i \sum_{l-1}^{L} \beta_l \sin c(\Delta\psi_n) \tag{10}$$

where $\Delta\psi_n = i\overline{\psi}_n - \psi_l$. Hence, the Gaussian mixture distribution is expected to model the distribution of beamspace channel elements.

The new shrinkage function is

$$\eta_{\mathrm{gm}}\left(r; \theta, \sigma^2\right) = i\frac{\sum_{K=0}^{N_c-1} p_k\tilde{\mu}_k(r)CN\left(r; \mu_k, \sigma + \sigma_k^2\right)}{\sum_{K=0}^{N_c-1} p_k CN\left(r; \mu_k, \sigma + \sigma_k^2\right)} \tag{11}$$

compared with η_{st} (soft threshold function) in the existing LAMP network, the η_{gm} (Gaussian shrinkage function) considering the prior distribution of the beamspace channel.

3.3.2   Modified GM-Based LAMP Network

Our proposed GM-based LAMP network is still constructed on the AMP algorithm because replacing the soft threshold shrinkage function in the existing LAMP network by Gaussian mixture shrinkage function. Similar to LAMP network, the GM-based LAMP network also has T homogeneous layers, where the inputs and outputs of each layer are same as those of LAMP network. The only difference is that each layer has the soft threshold shrinkage function η_{gm}. To obtain this, $\widehat{h}_{t+1}$ of the t th layer in GM-based LAMP network can be obtained by,

$$r_t = \widehat{h}_t + B_t v_t \tag{12}$$

$$\widehat{h}_{t+1} = \eta_{\mathrm{gm}}\left(r_t; \theta_t, \sigma^2\right) \tag{13}$$

The linear transform coefficients B_t and non-linear shrinkage parameters θ_t are trainable variables that can be optimized in training phase. This GM-based LAMP network mainly works in two phases: offline training phase and online estimation phase. In offline training mode, the large number of known training data are given; the GM-based LAMP network tries to optimize overall trainable variables $\Omega_{T-1} = \{B_t, \theta_t\}_{t=0}^{T-1}$ by minimizing the loss function. In online estimation phase, by inputting the new measurements y, the trained GM-based LAMP network can output the estimated beamspace channel $\widehat{h}$.

Acquired the supervised learning to train GM-based LAMP network. The training dataset is represented by $\{y^d, h^d\}_{d=1}^{D}$. To avoid overfitting, the layer-by-layer training method [11] is used which helps in training GM-based LAMP network. The layer-by-layer training method can be explained in three steps:

Firstly, the entire training procedure can be divided into T sequential training sub-procedures [11]. And for t th training sub-procedure, we aim to refine the trainable variables $\Omega_t = \{B_i, \theta_i\}_{i=0}^{t}$ where $i = 0, 1,..., t$ th layer. Every layer of GM-based LAMP has its own loss function. Secondly, two types of loss function are as follows which are related to linear transform operation and non-linear shrinkage function:

$$L_t^{\text{linear}}(\Omega_t) = \frac{1}{D} \sum_{d=1}^{D} \left\| r_t^d(y^d, \Omega_t) - \tilde{h}^d \right\|_2^2 \tag{14}$$

$$L_t^{\text{non linear}}(\Omega_t) = \frac{1}{D} \sum_{d=1}^{D} \left\| \hat{\tilde{h}}_{t+1}^d(y^d, \Omega_t) - \tilde{h}^d \right\|_2^2 \tag{15}$$

Thirdly, the hybrid method of "individual" and "joint" optimization is further adopted in linear training and non-linear training sub-procedure[11]; only the linear transform coefficients B_t are first optimized individually, all trainable variables Ω_{T-1} of the previous $i = 0, \ldots, (t-1)$th layer together with B_t are optimized jointly. Similarly in non-linear training of the t th training sub-procedure, the non-linear shrinkage parameters θ_t are first optimized individually, and then, all trainable variables Ω_{T-1i} of the previous $i = 0, \ldots, (t--1)$th layer together with B_t and θ_t are optimized jointly.

3.3.3   Layer-By-Layer Training Method

See Fig. 1.

4   Simulation Results and Discussion

4.1   Simulation Setup

In the simulation, the base station (BS) equipping of 256 (N) lens antenna array with 16 (N_{RF}) RF chains is considered. The measurement (M) and the total number of users of single antenna (K) are set to the values 128 and 16, respectively. For channel estimation in uplink, $1/\sigma_n^2$ is defined as the signal-to-noise ratio (SNR). Then, in accordance to the channel model Saleh-Valenzuela and the dataset DeepMIMO, the samples for spatial channel is generated. For each k user in the channel model Saleh-Valenzuela, the parameters of the channel are set to be same, and it is as follows: (1) $L_k = 3$ (the total number of paths). (2) The path gain is $\beta_{k,l} \sim CN(0, 1)$ for all the paths $l = 1, 2$ and 3. 3). The angle for ULA is $\theta_{k,l} \sim U\left(-\frac{\pi}{2}, \frac{\pi}{2}\right)$, the angle of azimuth in UPA is $\theta_{k,l}^{\text{azi}} \sim U\left(-\frac{\pi}{2}, \frac{\pi}{2}\right)$, and the angle of elevation in UPA is $\theta_{k,l}^{\text{ele}} \sim U\left(-\frac{\pi}{2}, \frac{\pi}{2}\right)$ for all the paths $l = 1, 2$, and 3.

The modified GM-LAMP network is trained and tested with the generated samples as 80,000 samples for the training phase, 2000 samples for the testing phase, and 2000 samples for the validating phase. Further, the process of obtaining the channel samples from the DeepMIMO dataset is introduced. The Ray-tracing method is used to generate the samples for the channel from the dataset DeepMIMO. The

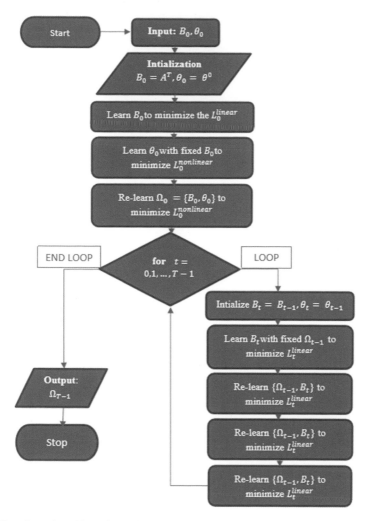

Fig. 1 Flowchart of working of modified LAMP algorithm

raytracing scenario involves the complete definition of the parameter sets needed for the simulation, and this stands as the main prospective of the DeepMIMO dataset. In the simulations carried out, the scenario of ray-tracing 'O1' in the outdoor of the dataset DeepMIMO with the parameters mentioned in Table 1 and working at the mmWave frequency of 28 GHz are considered.

About 54,000 channel samples between the 3 base stations and 16 single-antenna users are generated as per the setup shown in Table 1. Then, the 54,000 samples are split into 50,000, 2000, and 2000 for training, validating, and testing, respectively. The beamspace channel samples and the measurement samples can be generated from the obtained samples of the spatial channel of the channel model Saleh-Valenzuela

Table 1 Parameters adopted for simulation from DeepMIMO dataset

Parameters	Value
Number of base stations	3
Number of users	16
Number of antennas	$(N_x, N_y, N_z) = (1, 256, 1)$—ULA; $(1, 16, 16)$—UPA
Spacing between antennas	0.5
Number of paths	3

and the dataset DeepMIMO. The optimization of the trainable variables are carried out via a layer-by-layer training method which is described in the system model above using the Adam optimizer. The each update uses a batch wise usage of samples in which each batch constitutes of samples of training with the value 128.

4.2 Simulation Results of the Channel Model—Saleh Valenzuela

In this subsection, the beamspace channel estimation performance comparison of the [11] GM-LAMP network and the modified GM-LAMP network based on the channel.

The model Saleh-Valenzuela is provided. The NMSE performance comparison of two algorithmic schemes in the ULA against different SNRs considered is shown in Fig. 2. Table 2 statistically shows the SNR and NMSE of GM-LAMP and modified GM-LAMP.

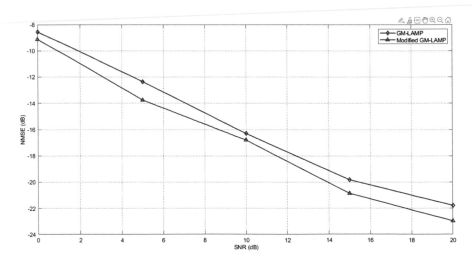

Fig. 2 NMSE performance comparison for ULAs based on the Saleh Valenzuela channel model

Table 2 Comparison of SNR and NMSE for proposed and existing based on the Saleh Valenzuela channel model

Parameters	SNR	NMSE	
		GM-LAMP	Modified GM-LAMP
Minimum	0	−21.87	−22.83
Maximum	20	−8.631	−9.264
Mean	10	−15.82	−16.71
Median	10	−16.39	−16.86
Mode	0	−21.87	−22.83
S.D	7.908	5.414	5.434
Range	20	13.24	13.57

4.3 Simulation Results of the Dataset—DeepMIMO

In this subsection, the NMSE performance of two algorithmic schemes are compared based on the DeepMIMO dataset is provided. Figures 3 and 4 show the NMSE performance comparison of four different schemes against different SNRs for the 256×1 uniform linear array (ULA) and the 16×16 uniform planar array (UPA), respectively. Tables 3 and 4 statistically show the SNR and NMSE of GM-LAMP and modified GM-LAMP for DeepMIMO using ULA and UPA.

The modified GM-LAMP network is found to be having the lowest estimation errors and higher accuracy in the comparison with the various algorithmic schemes in comparison with others schemes under investigation.

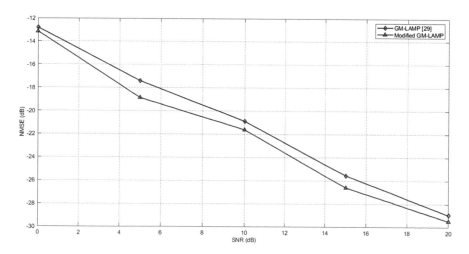

Fig. 3 NMSE performance comparison for ULAs based on the DeepMIMO dataset

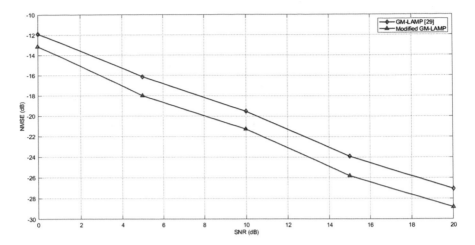

Fig. 4 NMSE performance comparison for UPAs based on the DeepMIMO dataset

Table 3 Comparison of SNR and NMSE for proposed and existing based on the ULA of DeepMIMO

Parameters	SNR	NMSE	
		GM-LAMP	Modified GM-LAMP
Minimum	0	−28.93	−29.93
Maximum	20	−12.9	−13.23
Mean	10	−21.12	−21.94
Median	10	−20.87	−21.58
Mode	0	−28.93	−29.45
S.D	7.908	6.367	6.388
Range	20	16.02	16.22

Table 4 Comparison of SNR and NMSE for proposed and existing based on the UPA of DeepMIMO

Parameters	SNR	NMSE	
		GM-LAMP algorithm	Modified GM-LAMP algorithm
Minimum	0	−27.06	−28.73
Maximum	20	−11.89	−13.17
Mean	10	−19.74	−21.48
Median	10	−19.57	−21.4
Mode	0	−27.06	−28.83
S.D	7.908	6.041	6.194
Range	20	15.18	15.66

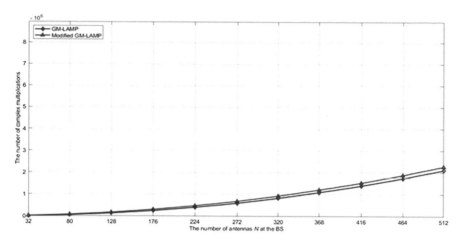

Fig. 5 The number of complex multiplications against the number of antennas

4.4 Simulation Results of the Computational Complexity Analysis

The 5.3×10^5 and 6.1×10^5 complex multiplications are required by the GM-LAMP network and the modified GM-LAMP network, respectively.

It is found from Fig. 5 that more computational complexity is required for GM-LAMP algorithmic scheme when compared to the modified GM-LAMP algorithmic scheme. It is because of the reason that the presence of on-sager functions in the GM-LAMP and modified GM-LAMP networks accelerates the convergence of the algorithm harnessing the powerful learning capacity of DNNs. But achieves better estimation performance compared with the existing GM-LAMP network. Table 4 statistically shows the SNR and NMSE of GM-LAMP and modified GM-LAMP for complexity analysis.

5 Conclusions

In order to solve the millimeter wave massive MIMO system's estimation of the beamspace channel problem, a modified GM-LAMP network with prior channel state information (prior-aided) is proposed in this work. By harnessing the elements of the channel of the beamspace via Gaussian mixture distribution, a new shrinkage function is derived. Therefore, the modified Gaussian mixture learned approximate message parsing network is deployed by integrating the existing learned AMP algorithm network with the derived Gaussian mixture distribution's shrinkage function. The simulation results show that the comparison of the proposed modified GM-LAMP network which has considered the prior distribution of channel state information with the conventional existing schemes in terms of NMSE and SNR. It is evident from the graph and the tabulation statistics that the proposed modified GM-LAMP algorithm gives better performance accuracy with less error and less pilot overhead.

References

1. Wei Y, Zhao MM, Zhao M, Lei M, Yu Q (2019) An AMP-based network with deep residual learning for mmWave beamspace channel estimation. IEEE Wirel Commun Lett 8(4):1289–1292
2. Vlachos E, Alexandropoulos GC, Thompson J (2018) Massive MIMO channel estimation for millimeter wave systems via matrix completion. IEEE Signal Process Lett 25(11):1675–1679
3. Donoho DL, Maleki A, Montanari A (2010) Message passing algorithms for compressed sensing: I. motivation and construction. In Proceedings of information theory workshop, (ITW'10), Cairo, Egypt, pp 1–5
4. Dai R, Liu Y, Wang Q, et al (2021) Channel estimation by reduced dimension decomposition formillimeter wave massive MIMO system. Phys Commun 44
5. Chun C-J, Kang J-M, Kim I-M (2018) Deep learning based channel estimation for massive MIMO systems. IEEE Wireless Commun 6(8):245–267
6. Venugopal K, Alkhateeb A, Prelcic NG, Heath RW (2017) Channel estimation for hybrid architecture-based wideband millimeter wave systems. IEEE J Sel Areas Commun 4(2):112–115
7. Amadori PV, Masouros C (2015) Low RF-complexity millimeter-wave beamspace-MIMO systems by beam selection. IEEE Trans Commun 63(6):1112–1126
8. Alkhateeb A, El Ayach O, Leus G, Heath RW (2014) Channel estimation and hybrid precoding for millimeter wave cellular systems. IEEE J Sel Top Signal Process 8(5):831–846
9. Gao X, Dai, L, Han S, Chih-Lin I, Wang X (2017) Reliable beamspace channel estimation for millimeter-wave massive MIMO systems with lens antenna array. IEEE Trans Wireless Commun 16(9):6010–6021
10. Brady J, Behdad N, Sayeed A (2013) Beamspace MIMO for millimeterwave communications: System architecture, modeling, analysis, and measurements. IEEE Trans Ant Propag 61(7):3814–3827
11. Borgerding M, Schniter P, Rangan S (2017) AMP-inspired deep networks for sparse linear inverse problems. IEEE Trans Signal Process 65(16):4293–4308
12. Huang C, Liu L, Yuen C, Sun S (2019) Iterative channel estimation using LSE and sparse message passing for mmwave MIMO systems. IEEE Trans Signal Process 67(1):245–259
13. Mo J, Schniter P, Heath RW (2018) Channel estimation in broadband millimeter wave MIMO systems with few-bit ADCs. IEEE Trans Signal Process 66(5):1141–1154
14. Mumtaz S, Rodriguez J, Dai L (2017) mmWave massive MIMO, A Paradigm for 5G
15. Amadori P, Masouros C (2015) Low RF-complexity millimeter-wave beamspace-MIMO systems by beam selection. IEEE Trans Commun 63(6):2212–2222
16. Gao X, Dai L, Chen Z, Wang Z, Zhang Z (2016) Near-optimal beam selection for beamspace mmWave massive MIMO systems. IEEE Commun Lett 20(5):1054–1057
17. Yang L, Zeng Y, Zhang R (2018) Channel estimation for millimeterwave MIMO communications with lens antenna arrays. IEEE Trans Veh Technol 67(4):3239–3251
18. Tao J, Qi C, Huang Y (2016) Regularized multipath matching pursuit for sparse channel estimation in millimeter wave massive MIMO system
19. Li X, Fang J, Li H, Wang P (2018) Millimeter wave channel estimation via exploiting joint sparse and low-rank structures. IEEE Trans Wireless Commun 17(2):1123–1133

20. Alkhateeb A (2019) DeepMIMO: a generic deep learning dataset for millimeter wave and massive MIMO applications. In Proceedings of information theory and applications workshop (ITA'19), San Diego, CA, pp 1–8
21. Gao X, Dai L, Han S, Chih-Lin I, Heath RW (2016) Energy-efficient hybrid analog and digital precoding for mmWave MIMO systems with large antenna arrays. IEEE J Sel Areas Commun 34(4):998–1009

Efficient Structural Matching for RNA Secondary Structure Using Bit-Parallelism

Muhammad Yusuf Muhammad, Salu George Thandekkattu⬝,
Sandip Rakshit⬝, and Narasimha Rao Vajjhala⬝

Abstract The idea of matching parameters, complements, and constants symbols is referred to as structural matching or s-matching for short. In this paper, an efficient exact pattern matching bit-parallel algorithm is proposed to address RNA secondary structure queries using the concept of s-matching. This algorithm has good application in finding structural similarity between RNA sequences which could help in infer its biological function. We developed a new bit-parallel algorithm that can be implemented and advance the well-known shift-OR algorithm by adding a transformative approach of working with s-strings through coding techniques that were portable in the area of s-matching. Our algorithm advances for the exact s-matching problem on RNA secondary structure assumed to be optimal on average time. The proposed algorithm could help answer RNA matching queries, such as discovering precisely similar RNA and structurally similar RNA sequences, critical to the characterization of functional annotation of a newly discovered RNA.

Keywords Parallelism · Parameterized matching · Structural matching · Encoding · RNA · Algorithm · Sequences

M. Y. Muhammad · S. G. Thandekkattu · S. Rakshit
American University of Nigeria, Yola, Nigeria
e-mail: muhammad.muhammad@aun.edu.ng

S. G. Thandekkattu
e-mail: george.thandekkattu@aun.edu.ng

S. Rakshit
e-mail: sandip.rakshit@aun.edu.ng

N. R. Vajjhala (✉)
University of New York Tirana, Tirana, Albania
e-mail: narasimharao@unyt.edu.al

© The Author(s), under exclusive license to Springer Nature Singapore Pte Ltd. 2022   399
C. Satyanarayana et al. (eds.), *High Performance Computing and Networking*,
Lecture Notes in Electrical Engineering 853,
https://doi.org/10.1007/978-981-16-9885-9_33

1 Introduction

Ribonucleic acid (RNA) molecule plays a vital role in biological processes like the transfer of genetic code necessary for protein synthesis, priming in DNA replication, inducing gene splicing, and gene activation. RNA can fold into a 3-dimensional structure like protein. However, these functions are critically dependent on their structure [1]. Figure 1 shows the basic secondary structure elements formed in RNA molecules during folding. Four types of a nitrogenous base (nucleotides), namely adenine (denoted as A), cytosine (denoted as C), guanine (denoted as G), and uracil (denoted as U), form a single-strand RNA molecule. Watson–Crick base pairs (A, U) and (C, G) complement one another, which during folding can pair up to form essential elements like stems and stalk. So, productions over the set of alphabet $\sum_{RNA}$ = [A, C, G, U] are RNA string sequences. Therefore, string pattern matching methods can analyze RNA sequences or structures appropriately. For example, approaches that match RNA secondary structure using the edit distance between bases and complementary base pairs [2, 3].

An $O(nm^2)$ algorithm that finds an exact match between an **n**-length text and RNA secondary structure expression of size **m** was introduced by Xu, Wang and Deng [4]. Heyne et al. [5] and Mauri and Pavesi [6] proposed indexing algorithms for finding both exact and approximate matches for RNA structure using bidirectional affix tree with $O(n)$ space and $O(nm)$ worst-case time complexities. Strothmann [7] proposed a method that uses a more efficient data structure for pattern matching problems on RNA structure. Structural matching (S-matching for short) was previously proposed by Beal and Adjeroh [1] and Shibuya [8] to extend the parameterized matching (p-matching for short) to deal with the issues of complementary base pairing that is essential in RNA structure formation [9, 10]. Shibuya [8] introduces the idea of structural string (s-string) for exact pattern matching on RNA structure by constructing a structural suffix tree data structure (s-suffix tree for short) for the s-matching problem. Beal and Adjeroh [1] propose the use of structural suffix array (s-suffix array for

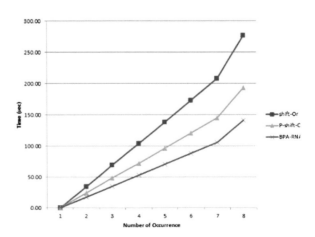

Fig. 1 Running time for 8-bits pattern length

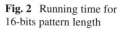

Fig. 2 Running time for 16-bits pattern length

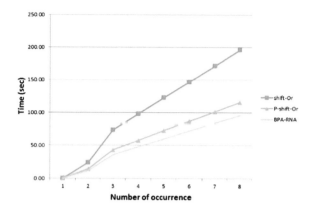

short) as a more efficient alternative and lightweight data structure than s-suffix tree and the structural Longest common prefix (sLCP) to address s-matching problems. However, geometric increase in the number of RNA sequence databases as a result of improved sequencing technology and practical space requirement that are associated with data structures such as affix tree, suffix tree, s-suffix tree, and their lightweight data structures like suffix array, s-suffix array, etc., have remained the significant bottlenecks.

Recently, the bit-parallelism approach was applied to address these problems [11, 12]. This approach efficiently simulates non-deterministic finite automata by allowing bit operations parallel to computer words per clock cycle [13]. This method enhances the searching process by reducing the number of these bit operations to a certain level depending on the ward size, which is either 32 or 64 bits [14, 15]. This has made bit-parallel algorithms to be faster than the benchmark pattern matching algorithms such as the Knuth-Morris-Pratt algorithm (KMP) [16], Boyer-Moore (BM) [17], and BMH [18], BMHS [19, 20]. Figure 2 shows how bit-parallel operations are carried out on a 16 bits computer word.

Since the first introduction of this technique in many researchers has proposed different algorithms for exact and approximate pattern matching using the shift-OR/ AND bit operations or an automaton [21, 22]. An algorithm using bits operations and edit distance on longest common subsequence to address sequence alignment problem on biological sequences was proposed by Benson et al. [23]. Backward non-deterministic matching (BNDM) is a benchmark algorithm using AND or shift operation in parallel to address false matches associated with the shift-or algorithm [24–26]. An improved BNDM named 2-way non-deterministic matching (TNDM) was proposed by Peltola and Tarhio [27] and many other variants like SBNDM, shift-OR with q-gram [28], BNDM [29], etc. Other methods that use the concept of parameterized matching for exact [30], approximate [31, 32], and multi-pattern matching [33, 34] were also proposed. This paper developed an algorithm that advances the standard shift-OR algorithm for exact s-matching on RNA secondary structure.

2 Review of Literature

2.1 Definitions

The following definitions are adopted throughout the paper. Let $T = [t_1, \ldots, t_n]$ be a large string sequence and $P = [p_1, \ldots, p_m]$ be a string pattern where $m \leq n$. Ordinary matching problem is to find all occurrences of a string P such that P matches the text substring $t_j \ldots t_m$ in a given sequence T.

Definition 1 Parameterized string (p-string): A production from finite set of constants (or fixed) symbols $\sum$ and set of parameter symbols $\prod$ such that $(\sum \cap \prod) = \emptyset$. For example: Let $\sum = (G, H)$ be finite sets of fixed symbols and $\prod = [v, w, x, y, z]$ be finite set of parameter symbols then strings S = GxHzzywv, T = GwHyyzxv, and U = GwHyyxzv are said to be p-strings.

Definition 2 Structural string (s-string): A p-string with complementary parameter pairing $\pi(p_i, p_j)$ in $\prod$ such that each p in $\prod$ is used in exactly one pair and the complement(p_i) $=$ p_j, complement $(p_j) = p_i$ when $i \neq j$ or the complement $(p_i) = p_i$ when $i = j$. For example: Let $\sum = [G, H]$ be finite set of fixed alphabets and $\prod = [y, w, z, v, x]$ be finite set of parameter alphabets with complementary parameter mapping $\Gamma = [(y \leftrightarrow y), (z \leftrightarrow w), (v \leftrightarrow x)]$ then the p-strings S = GxHzzywv, T = GwHyyzxv, and U = GwHyyxzv are said to be s-strings.

Definition 3 Prev-encoding: Given an n-length text string T and a nonnegative integer R, a mapping $(\sum \cup \prod)^* \to (\sum \cup R)^*$ encodes a given constant symbol C as same symbol and a given parameter symbol r to the distance of the previous r. For example: Let $\sum = \{G, H\}$, $\prod = \{y, w, z, v, x\}$ be finite sets of fixed alphabets and parameter alphabets with parameter complementary mapping $\Gamma = \{(y \leftrightarrow y), (z \leftrightarrow w), (v \leftrightarrow x)\}$ and let S = GxHzzywv, T = GwHyyzxv, and U = GwHyyxzv be s-strings then the prev (S) = G0H01000, prev (T) = G0H01000, and prev (U) = G0H01000.

Definition 4. Complement encoding: Given an n-length text string and a nonnegative integer R, the function $(\sum \cup \prod)^* \to (\sum \cup Q)^*$ encodes a given constant alphabet $C \in \sum$ as the same alphabet and a given parameter alphabet $r \in \prod$ to the distance of its previous complementary alphabet, as formally defined in [1]. For example 4: Let $\sum = \{G, H\}$, $\prod = \{y, w, z, v, x\}$ be two finite sets of fixed symbols and parameter symbols with complementary parameter mapping $\Gamma = [(y \leftrightarrow y), (z \leftrightarrow w), (v \leftrightarrow x)]$ and let S = GxHzzywv, T = GwHyyzxv, and U = GwHyyxzv be s-strings then the compl(S) = G0H00150, compl(T) = G0H00150, and compl(U) = G0H00420.

Definition 5. Structural encoding (sencode): Given an n-length text T and two nonnegative integers R and Q, the function $(\sum \cup \prod)^* \to (\sum \cup R \cup Q)^*$ encodes constant symbols C as the same symbol and encodes parameter symbol r1 $\in$ R to the distance of its previous r1 or r2 $\in$ Q to the distance of its previous parameter complement as defined in [1]. For example: Let $\sum = \{G, H\}$ be finite set of fixed alphabets and $\prod = \{y, w, z, v, x\}$ and parameter symbols with complementary parameter mapping $\Gamma = [(y \leftrightarrow y), (z \leftrightarrow w), (v \leftrightarrow x)]$ and let S = GxHzzywv, T = GwHyyzxv, and U = GwHyyxzv be s-strings then the sencode(S) = G0H01150, sencode (T) = G0H01150, and sencode (U) = G0H01420.

2.2 Parameterized Matching Problem

Parameterized matching is a variation of string-matching methodologies used to detect duplicate code but is now widely used in many other applications [35]. The p-matching problems support its application on RNA sequence AND/OR structure. Thus, the p-matching problem is to find equality between two p-strings (see Definition 1), say S and T where all the constant symbols in $\sum_c$ of S and T exactly matched and a bijection function can rename one parameter symbols in $\sum_p$ to transform it to another.

Two p-strings, T and P, are said to be p-matched if and only if one p-string can be transformed into the other by a bijection that renamed its parameters. A naive way to parameterized matching is performed by left–right traversal of the two p-strings while constructing a table establishing the mapping allowing the transformation of the p-string. This process continues until a mismatch occurred. A mismatch occurs when:

- One of the alphabets is non-parameter, and the rest are parameters.
- Non-parameter alphabets are all different from one another.
- All the alphabets are parameters such that either of them is assigned to a different parameter alphabet in the mapping table.

This approach was transformed by the introduction of the prev-encoding (Ref. Definition 3) by Baker [10], where p-suffix tree was constructed by pre-encoding each of the suffixes in p-string in $O(n(|\sum_p| + log(|\sum_p| + |\sum_c|)))$ worst-case time. An improvement over this time was presented by several researchers [36, 37]. A more optimal time of $O(n\ log(min[m, |\sum_p|])$ methods was proposed by researchers [38, 39], where m = pattern length. An automata-based multiple p-matching was also proposed by Ben Nsira et al. [40]. Cantone et al. [41] proposed the first more optimal time solution by constructing p-suffix array for binary string with $|\sum_p| = 2$ in $O(n)$.

2.3 S-Matching Problem

Shibuya [8] introduced the s-suffix tree and later used the s-suffix array with structural LCP array by adding the complementary parameter alphabet to p-string to a level of structure p-matching. An s-string comprises two finite sets of constant symbol $\sum_c$

and parameter symbols $\sum_p$ where each symbol in $\sum_p$ may complement one another (Ref. Definition 2). The concept of matching that involves fixed, parameterized, and complementary alphabets are referred to as s-matching. Shibuya proposes using a complement encoding (compl-encode) (Ref. Definition 4) scheme to ensure that all the complementary symbols in the p-strings are consistently structured. This shows that s-matching exist between two s-strings if and only if prev(S) = prev(T) and comp-encode(S) = comp-encode(T) [42]. The structural encoding (sencode) scheme (as in Definition 5) that is composed of the previous encoding (as in Definition 3) and complement encoding (as in Definition 4) was also proposed to simplify s-matching. It easily detects s-matching by comparing the encodings rather than considering the bijective mapping between parameter symbols in the s-strings. Thus, an s-match between two s-strings is detected by matching up the strings under sencode as in Theorem 1.

Theorem 1 s-strings, S and T, are said to be s-match if sencode(S) = sencode(T).

3 Proposed Algorithm

For our proposed algorithm, the following notations for bit-parallel operations were adopted. A computer word w and bitwise AND, | bitwise OR, $\wedge$ XOR, ~ bit negation, left shift with 0 paddings, right shift with 0 paddings and assumed that m £ w. To advance the standard shift-OR algorithm for s-matching, we ensure that in the pre-processing stage, prev-encoding, and compl-encoding for both text T and pattern P are computed in $O(n)$ via Lemma 1. The new algorithm (BPA-RNA) builds tables Bp and Bc for each of the prev- and compl-encodings indexed from [0, ..., $m-1$]. During the computation of the sencode for each c $\hat{I}$ $\prod$, two arrays prev[c] and compl[c] are, respectively, maintained for the prev- and compl-encodings to store the position of its last occurrence. At the searching phase, to detect s-match, an array Bs (called sencode array) is formed to hold sencode of pattern P and text T determined by comparing the character (say c) bits of the two encodings (prev-encoding and compl-encoding) and taking the character with higher value. Initially, all bits in the state vector D are set to all 1's (i.e., $D = 1$ m), then D is updated as

$$D = \begin{cases} (D \ll 1)|B_p[c] \text{ if } c \text{ prev - encoding} \\ (D \ll 1)|B_c[c] \text{ if } c \text{ compl - encoding} \end{cases} \tag{1}$$

After each update, a match is reported when the most significant bit in D is 0, which can be achieved via Theorem 1.

At the searching phase; to detect s-match, an array Bs (called sencode array) is formed to hold sencode of pattern P and text T determined by comparing the character (say c) bits of the two encodings (prev-encoding and compl-encoding) and taking the character with higher value. Initially, all bits in the state vector D are set to all 1's (i.e., $D = 1$ m) then D is updated as

$$D = \begin{cases} (D \ll 1)|B_p[c] \text{ if } c \text{ prev - encoding} \\ (D \ll 1)|B_c[c] \text{ if } c \text{ compl - encoding} \end{cases}$$

After each update, a match is reported when the most significant bit in D is 0 which can be achieved via Theorem 1.

3.1 Bit-Parallelism Example

Consider the sets of fixed alphabets $\sum_{RNA} = [\emptyset]$ (no fixed alphabet in RNA sequence), parameterized alphabets $\sum_p = [A, C, G, U\}]$, and complementary symbols $\Gamma = [(A, U), (C, G)]$. Let text (T) = UCGAGCA, pattern (P) = AGCA be a text and the pattern, respectively. The problem is to locate all the occurrence of P in T.

Pre-processing stage.

Text (T) = AGCAGCAG, prev-encode(T) = 00033333, comp-encode(T) = 00,102,102, sencode (S) = 00133333.

Pattern (P) = UCGUC, prev-encode(P) = 00033, comp-encode(P) = 00132, sencode (P) = 00133.

4 Experimental Results

The new algorithm (BPA-RNA) was implemented in C# on Intel core (™) i7 computer with CPU that runs at 2.10 GHZ, 4 GB Ram with 64-bit processor running on 32bit windows operating system. We extracted an RNA text sequence data input file of size 7.66 mb from NCBI database. The comparison was done between our new algorithm and two other standard bit-parallel algorithms shift-OR and parameterized shift-OR as shown in Figs. 1, 2, 3, and 4.

5 Results

Prior researchers have used the indexing approach to address the s-matching problem for exact string pattern matching problems on RNA secondary structure. Shibuya [8] introduced the notion of s-string and constructed the s-suffix tree data structure to address the exact p-matching problem in $O[n(\log |\Sigma c| + \log |\Sigma p|)]$ time, while Beal and Adjeroh [1] have proposed the use of s-suffix and LCP arrays data structures to address the exact pattern RNA s-matching problem in $O(\log n + m + \eta_{occ})$. Though the use of lightweight data structures proposed in Beal and Adjeroh [1] has made it possible to achieve a reasonable improvement over that of Shibuya [8] and Baker [10], the practical space requirement of these data structures remained their major bottleneck. Our new algorithm proposes using a bit-parallelism approach by advancing

Fig. 3 Running time for
32-bit pattern length

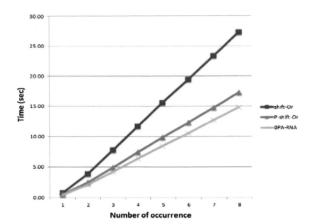

Fig. 4 Running time for
64-bits pattern length

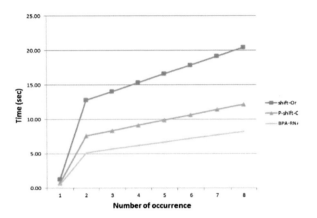

the standard shift-OR algorithm using the encoding scheme instead of data structures to address these bottlenecks. The only time required in our new algorithm is
for the computation of the encodings and that of the matching process, which could,
respectively, be achieved in $O(n)$ via Lemma 1 and $O(n + \eta_{occ})$ time via Theorem 2,
which suggest that our new algorithm is simple and can practically be implemented.

Our asymptotic analysis shows that the new algorithm (BPA-RNA) performs
better than other algorithms discussed in this study. This is because our algorithm
uses the bit-parallelism approach as an efficient alternative to data structures like
the s-suffix tree in [3] and the s-suffix array in [1]. Hence, the new algorithm can
address practical space requirements associated with the previous research that used
data structures. The experimental results show that the comparison between the
standard bit-parallel algorithms, i.e., shift-OR and parameterized shift-OR, and our
new algorithm (BPA-RNA) run for different pattern length (representing 8, 16, 32
and 64 bits computer word length) has better performance (has lower running time
with any pattern length) as shown in Figs. 1, 2, 3, and 4. Therefore, our proposed

algorithm can sufficiently answer the various queries on matching RNA secondary structure, i.e., finding RNA structural similarity, so that newly discovered RNA can be easily annotated to understand its functions better.

6 Conclusion

In summary, we have proposed a bit-parallel algorithm as an efficient alternative to the previous indexed based-algorithms. It can also be practically implemented and be used to address exact RNA pattern matching problems. We have also shown that using the bit-parallelism approach has made our algorithm more space and time efficient than others. Extending the algorithm to handle inexact pattern matching queries on RNA secondary structure could be the task of future research. Our algorithm advances for the exact s-matching problem on RNA secondary structure assumed to be optimal on average time. The proposed algorithm could help answer RNA matching queries, such as discovering precisely similar RNA and structurally similar RNA sequences, critical to the characterization of functional annotation of a newly discovered RNA.

References

1. Beal R, Adjeroh D (2015) Efficient pattern matching for RNA secondary structures. Theoret Comput Sci 592:59–71. https://doi.org/10.1016/j.tcs.2015.05.016
2. Allali J, Sagot M (2005) A new distance for high level RNA secondary structure comparison. IEEE/ACM Trans Comput Biol Bioinf 2(1):3–14. https://doi.org/10.1109/TCBB.2005.2
3. Zhang K et al (1999) Computing similarity between RNA structures. In: Proceedings of combinatorial pattern matching. Springer Berlin Heidelberg, pp 281–293
4. Xu Y et al (2004) Exact pattern matching for RNA secondary structures. In: Book Exact pattern matching for RNA secondary structures, Series Exact pattern matching for RNA secondary structures. Australian Computer Society, Inc., pp 257–263
5. Heyne S et al (2009) Lightweight comparison of RNAs based on exact sequence-structure matches. Bioinformatics 25(16):2095–2102. https://doi.org/10.1093/bioinformatics/btp065
6. Mauri G, Pavesi G (2005) Algorithms for pattern matching and discovery in RNA secondary structure. Theoret Comput Sci 335(1):29–51. https://doi.org/10.1016/j.tcs.2004.12.015
7. Strothmann D (2007) The affix array data structure and its applications to RNA secondary structure analysis. Theoret Comput Sci 389(1):278–294. https://doi.org/10.1016/j.tcs.2007.09.029
8. Shibuya T (2004) Generalization of a suffix tree for RNA structural pattern matching. Algorithmica 39(1):1–19. https://doi.org/10.1007/s00453-003-1067-9
9. Lewenstein M (2016) Parameterized pattern matching. In: M-Y Kao (ed) Encyclopedia of algorithms. Springer New York, pp 1525–1530
10. Baker BS (1993) A theory of parameterized pattern matching: algorithms and applications. In: Book A theory of parameterized pattern matching: algorithms and applications, Series A theory of parameterized pattern matching: algorithms and applications. Association for Computing Machinery, pp 71–80
11. Chhabra T et al (2017) Engineering order-preserving pattern matching with SIMD parallelism. Softw Pract Exp 47(5):731–739. https://doi.org/10.1002/spe.2433

12. Vajjhala NR et al (2021) Novel user preference recommender system based on twitter profile analysis. In: Proceedings of soft computing techniques and applications. Springer Singapore, pp 85–93
13. Hirvola T, Tarhio J (2017) Bit-parallel approximate matching of circular strings with <i>k</i> mismatches. ACM J Exp Algorithmics 22, Article 1.5. https://doi.org/10.1145/3129536
14. Cantone D et al (2010) A compact representation of nondeterministic (suffix) automata for the bit-parallel approach. In: Proceedings of combinatorial pattern matching. Springer Berlin Heidelberg, pp 288–298
15. Petrović S (2018) Approximate search in digital forensics. In: Daimi K (ed) Computer and network security essentials. Springer International Publishing, pp 355–367
16. Wu P, Shen H (2012) The research and amelioration of pattern-matching algorithm in intrusion detection system. In: Proceedings of 2012 IEEE 14th international conference on high performance computing and communication & 2012 IEEE 9th international conference on embedded software and systems, pp 1712–1715
17. Xiong Z (2010) A composite boyer-moore algorithm for the string matching problem. In: Proceedings of 2010 international conference on parallel and distributed computing, applications and technologies, pp 492–496
18. Raita T (1992) Tuning the boyer-moore-horspool string searching algorithm. Softw Pract Exp 22(10):879–884. https://doi.org/10.1002/spe.4380221006
19. Xie L et al (2010) Improved pattern matching algorithm of BMHS. In: Book improved pattern matching algorithm of BMHS, Series improved pattern matching algorithm of BMHS. IEEE Computer Society, pp 616–619
20. Biba M et al (2010) A novel structure refining algorithm for statistical-logical models. In: Proceedings of 2010 international conference on complex, intelligent and software intensive systems, pp 116–123
21. Baeza-Yates RA (1989) String searching algorithms revisited. In: Proceedings of algorithms and data structures. Springer Berlin Heidelberg, pp 75–96
22. Xuan W et al (2020) Uncertain string matching based on bitmap indexing. In: Book uncertain string matching based on bitmap indexing, Series uncertain string matching based on bitmap indexing. Association for Computing Machinery, pp 384–389
23. Benson DA et al (2017) GenBank. Nucleic Acids Res 45(D1):D37-d42. https://doi.org/10.1093/nar/gkw1070
24. Navarro G, Raffinot M (1998) A bit-parallel approach to suffix automata: fast extended string matching. In: Proceedings of combinatorial pattern matching. Springer Berlin Heidelberg, pp 14–33
25. Prasad R et al (2010) Efficient bit-parallel multi-patterns string matching algorithms for limited expression. In: Book Efficient bit-parallel multi-patterns string matching algorithms for limited expression, Series efficient bit-parallel multi-patterns string matching algorithms for limited expression. Association for Computing Machinery, pp. Article 10
26. Vajjhala NR et al (2020) Novel user preference recommender system based on twitter profile analysis. In: Proceedings of soft computing techniques and applications. Springer Singapore, pp 85–93
27. Peltola, H., Tarhio J (2003) Alternative algorithms for bit-parallel string matching. In: Proceedings of string processing and information retrieval. Springer Berlin Heidelberg, pp 80–93
28. Salmela L, Tarhio J (2007) Algorithms for weighted matching. In: Book Algorithms for weighted matching, Series Algorithms for weighted matching. Springer, pp 276–286
29. Ďurian B et al (2010) Bit-parallel search algorithms for long patterns. In: Proceedings of experimental algorithms. Springer Berlin Heidelberg, pp 129–140
30. Amir A, Nor I (2007) Generalized function matching. J Discrete Algorithms 5(3):514–523. https://doi.org/10.1016/j.jda.2006.10.001
31. Hazay C et al (2007) Approximate parameterized matching. ACM Trans Algorithms 3(3):29–es. https://doi.org/10.1145/1273340.1273345

32. Das S, Kapoor K (2017) Weighted approximate parameterized string matching. AKCE Int J Graphs Comb 14(1):1–12. https://doi.org/10.1016/j.akcej.2016.11.010
33. Fredriksson K, Mozgovoy M (2006) Efficient parameterized string matching. Inf Process Lett 100(3):91–96. https://doi.org/10.1016/j.ipl.2006.06.009
34. Kumar K et al (2010) Software maintenance by multi-patterns parameterized string matching with q-gram. SIGSOFT Softw Eng Notes 35(3):1–5. https://doi.org/10.1145/1764810.1764822
35. Mendivelso J et al (2020) A brief history of parameterized matching problems. Discrete Appl Math 274:103–115. https://doi.org/10.1016/j.dam.2018.07.017
36. Cole R, Hariharan R (2004) Faster suffix tree construction with missing suffix links. SIAM J Comput 33(1):26–42. https://doi.org/10.1137/s0097539701424465
37. Kosaraju SR (1995) Faster algorithms for the construction of parameterized suffix trees. In: Book Faster algorithms for the construction of parameterized suffix trees, Series Faster algorithms for the construction of parameterized suffix trees. IEEE Computer Society, p 631
38. Lee T et al (2011) On-line construction of parameterized suffix trees for large alphabets. Inf Process Lett 111(5):201–207. https://doi.org/10.1016/j.ipl.2010.11.017
39. Gusfield D (1997) Algorithms on stings, trees, and sequences: computer science and computational biology. SIGACT News 28(4):41–60. https://doi.org/10.1145/270563.571472
40. Ben Nsira N et al (2015) A fast Boyer-Moore type pattern matching algorithm for highly similar sequences. Int J Data Min Bioinform 13(3):266–288. https://doi.org/10.1504/ijdmb.2015.072101
41. Cantone D et al (2020) The order-preserving pattern matching problem in practice. Discrete Appl Math 274:11–25. https://doi.org/10.1016/j.dam.2018.10.023
42. Breslauer D, Galil Z (2014) Real-time streaming string-matching. ACM Trans Algorithms 10(4):Article 22. https://doi.org/10.1145/2635814

Facial Emotion Recognition Using Hybrid Approach for DCT and DBACNN

D. Anjani Suputri Devi, Ch. Satyanarayana, and D. Sasi Rekha

Abstract Recognition of facial emotions is crucial part under the discipline of computer vision, artificial intelligence and data science. We suggest in this study a technique called hybrid approach for Discrete cosine transform (DCT) and deep based attentive convolutional neural networks (DBACNN). By aggregating both regional and comprehensive feature extraction, we propose to use Discrete cosine transform (DCT) and Deep based attentive convolutional neural networks (DBACNN). It has the ability to concentrate on major parts of the face and aggregating both regional and comprehensive features. Regional features designate neighbourhood or local features, whereas comprehensive features designate complete or holistic features. This method is very efficient to elucidate the facial emotion issue with recognition. The frontal face image database, commonly known as CK+, Japanese Female Facial Expression (JAFFE) and FER-2013 is used as an input to test the suggested technique. Information in this database is then categorised using convolutional neural networks, and a frequency domain method called as the discrete cosine transform is used to categorise the data. Information in this database is then categorised using two CNN hierarchical layers in it. Regional characteristics are extracted from picture markers at one level, whilst comprehensive characteristics are extracted from the entire image at the second level. Information in this database is then categorised using regional traits include eyes, noses and lips. In this model, regional features indicate expressional information, whereas comprehensive features depict the expression's high-level semantic information. We combine both regional and global characteristics. On various scales, these two sorts of characteristics express emotions. Our suggested technique is more efficient than current single type of feature methods, and it proposes a unique pooling technique called expressional transformation invariant pooling for dealing with nuisance variations like noises, rotations, and so on. The Japanese Female Facial Expression (JAFFE) data sets and FER-2013

D. A. S. Devi (✉) · D. S. Rekha
Sri Vasavi Engineering College, Tadepalligudem, Andhra pradesh, India

Ch. Satyanarayana
JNTUK, Kakinada, India

© The Author(s), under exclusive license to Springer Nature Singapore Pte Ltd. 2022   411
C. Satyanarayana et al. (eds.), *High Performance Computing and Networking*,
Lecture Notes in Electrical Engineering 853,
https://doi.org/10.1007/978-981-16-9885-9_34

data sets are used to recognise outcomes on the well-known extended Cohn-Kanade (CK+) data set.

Keywords DBACNN · Deep-based attentive convolutional neural network · DCT—discrete cosine transform · Regional feature extraction · Comprehensive feature extraction · Feature aggregation

1 Introduction

Humans rely heavily on facial expressions to communicate their feelings. Recent studies have focussed on how to enhance emotional analysis. Facial expression analysis is an important aspect of emotional analysis. The primary goal of facial expression analysis is to categorise and classify various expressions.

Surprise, happiness, sorrow, fear, anger and disgust are the seven major facial expressions. Aside from these fundamental emotions, a number of additional emotions have been studied. Contempt, jealousy, discomfort, tiredness and a variety of micro emotions are amongst them. There are three phases to recognise facial expressions. The three approaches are face and facial component detection, feature extraction, and expression classification. Various strategies are employed for each phase. First, a face is recognised in an input picture, then there is the detection of facial expressions, components in the face region. Second, the face components are used to extract a variety of temporal information. Depending on whether or not class labels are utilised, feature extraction methods can be supervised or unsupervised. Many characteristics may be retrieved and trained for a reasonable face expression detection system using deep learning and notably convolutional neural networks (CNNs). Machine learning approaches should concentrate on the most significant elements of the face (such as the lips and eyes) and be less sensitive to other areas of the face, such as the ears and hair. DBACNN have made incredible development in the area of computer vision in recent years. Each layer's convolutional kernels are used to extract certain desirable characteristics, allowing it to adapt to a variety of classification tasks without requiring much prior information.

2 Related Work

In emotional analysis, identifying expressions has long been a tough process. Regular techniques are divided into two classes: act unit-founded techniques and feature-founded techniques. These approaches, which rely on deep learning algorithms, provide good results in the recognition of expressions, making them a viable option to solving the FER problem. There are just a few image operators. In expression analysis, local description patterns (LDP) [1], local binary patterns (LBP) [2] and local phase quantization (LPQ) [3] are used to extract crucial information from pictures.

Deep learning algorithms have gained popularity in recent years and utilised to recognise facial expressions. Some deep-based networks have been shown to accumulate and generate higher recognition results in a particular type of feature. We provide a distinct CNN branch to extract regional characteristics in this research. In expression analysis, the relevance of local specific information is critical which is highlighted in this paper.

3 Proposed Method

We suggest a deep-based approach frame work for facial expression recognition which proceeds the attentive mechanism to concentrate the important part of the face [4].

First, we gathered a collection of face expression data sets that included all seven main emotions. After that we detect and extract potentially valuable features using DCT [5], for feature extraction and dimensionality reduction, and then, we utilise an DBACNN classifier for classification, as shown in Fig. 1.

Pre-Processing

In our suggested technique, a very efficient algorithm called the Voila–Jones algorithm is employed to properly and precisely extract the face region. Following the extraction process, crop and resize the image. Image resizing stands as a main technique for displaying images on different devices. For feature extraction, this data are extra administered using a frequency domain method identified as discrete cosine transform (DCT).

Feature Extraction

The DCT is used in the digital signal processing field to tackle a variety of difficulties. With its unique capabilities, the discrete cosine transform may be used to extract differentiating characteristics from a given image and also as a tool for dimensionality reduction without sacrificing a significant amount of useful data.

DCT

DCT converts the whole picture into a series of various frequency cosine coefficients. Low, intermediate and high-frequency coefficients are the three types of DCT frequency coefficients. Each category contains details and information about the

Fig. 1 Proposed technique

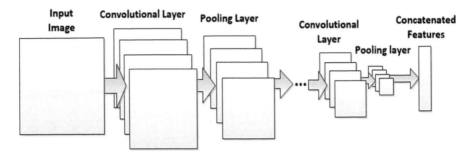

Fig. 2 Typical structure of CNN

entire image. The intensity of the picture, which is present in the low-frequency region of the DCT [5], is the most significant element necessary for facial identification. This model depends on a two-level CNN construction, as appeared in Figure 2. Here, we propose the extended transformation invariant pooling technique to change the normal construction of CNN, which frames the module CNN. In the proposed DBACNN model, a module CNN is a fundamental element for the extraction of features, and it aids removal of regional and comprehensive features from an information image.

3.1 Convolutional Neural Network

In current years, convolutional neural network was completely pragmatic in different jobs related to computer vision. CNN is a permutation of different convolutional layers and pooling layers. In our proposed work, CNN has a four-layer network architecture. Combination of convolutional layers and pooling layers is arranged in the form of stack and to form the strength of the CNN. The last layer is utilised for dispensation and acts as a high-level semantic representation of the input.

3.2 DBACNN for ETI Pooling

Varieties such as lighting or image revolution might distort the delegate limit of the separated features during the feature extraction phase. Data set expansion is a common way for dealing with this problem. In any event, there are certain drawbacks to this approach. Models built using data sets must learn to include feature representations independently for distinct data sets [6]. As a result, we are able to reduce the detrimental impact of picture variances whilst also overcoming the disadvantages of increasing the data set size. We proposed changing the CNN structure as a dynamic method for ETI pooling [7]. This approach was improved to accommodate several modifications at the same time.

Extended transformation invariant pooling [6] was introduced as a basic framework. To teach the organisation to delete expressional photos with invariant properties, we use tests from change sets, which contain a particular amount of expressional photos with the identical class name. Change sets are recognised as the organisations' contribution during the planning stage. A channel will be given to each picture in a change set, i.e. each expressional image will be assigned to a CNN module, and information image will pass via a CNN in each channel. Each channel yield is made up of vectorised characteristics that are represented by a linked component vector. The weight sharing amongst these equal channels is decided during the preparatory stage.

To designate the concatenated feature vector of the ith ($i = 1, 2, ..., M$) channel as

$$F^i = F^i_1, F^i_2, \ldots, F^i_t, ..F^i_N$$

where N is the dimension of the vector and $F^i_t (t = 1, 2, ..., M)$ is the tth element of the vector, the vector obtained after ETI pooling can be denoted as $F = (F_1, F_2, ..., F_t, ..., F_N)$. The non-linear operator performs an elements-by-elements fusion over all M channels, as follows: $F_t = \max(F^1_t, F^2_t, \ldots F^M_t)$. This activity just reacts the maximal components similarly situated amongst various element vectors, which brings down the likelihood of spreading an odd variety-related element to the accompanying features. In different words, extended transformation invariant pooling endeavours to develop the order execution by featuring the most discriminative feature components that are advantageous to most examples. Non-direct responsibilities boost competitiveness among various channels, forcing organizations to respond to distinctive qualities and inhibit data back propagation linked with vexing differences. Not at all comparable the maximum surveying system, extended transformation invariant pooling won't diminish the component of a representation. This makes it productively use all accessible and powerful data covered in various expressional pictures Fig. 3. The flowchart of our technique is shown.

3.3 Classification with DBACNNs

Single-branch CNNs are used in several modern deep models for facial expression analysis [8–10], which is focussed on the subject of extraction information from the entire image. A few studies have confirmed the effectiveness of nearby expressional characteristics in overcoming the FER problem. This revenues that for expressional analysis, both global and regional traits are important. Some current techniques [11–13] integrate characteristics from various representation spaces or

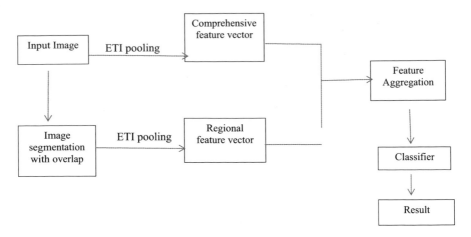

Fig. 3 Flowchart of the proposed method

total various attributes that achieve good presentation in various arranging undertakings. It is reasonable to assume that combined or cumulative characteristics include more successful characterisation data than a single type of feature.

Transformation sets are regarded the involvement of the CNN unit at the level of full feature extraction. The level's output is a comprehensive feature vector. It represents a collection of picture alterations. Original photos are consistently separated into picture patches on the other level. Individual CNN modules are updated to remove regional characteristics from each patch. All the means of regional include extraction are equivalent to those of the comprehensive feature extraction. The comprehensive feature vector is abbreviated as V_{C0}; the regional feature vector is abbreviated as V_{Rm}, and the listen concatenated feature vector is abbreviated as follows:

$$V_c = (V_{C0}; V_{R1}, V_{R2}, \ldots V_{RM})$$

The concatenated feature vector represents completely associated layer for feature fusion. Softmax is employed as a classifier in our technique, which can be described as follows.

$$f(z_j) = \frac{e^{zj}}{\sum_i e^{zi}}$$

Here, each element of expression represents distinctive expression class. Predicted class is the one with the highest element value. As a result, the loss function can be written as

$$L = \frac{1}{2}||y^p - y^g||^2 = \frac{1}{2}\sum_{c=1}^{C}(y_c^p - y_c^g)^2$$

where y^p is the predicted label; y^g is the ground truth table. C is the total class number of expressions.

3.4 For Expression Analysis, Learning Principle Marks is Essential

Expressions are, by definition, provincial variations in the look, with some facial muscles separating the progressions. This means that facial expression analysis may be linked to specific face areas. Some previous attempts at FER have relied on the research of adjacent areas. In this section, we define important marks as image fixes that have a significant impact.

Algorithm Input: set of principle feature set.

Output: anger, surprize, happiness, sadness, surprize emotions identified.
Begin

1. Using attentive CNN to identify the important face features and apply on DCT.
2. Applying extended transformation invariant pooling method to extract Comprehensive features and regional features.
3. To obtain combined feature vector of the ith (i = 1,2,…M) channel as $F^i = F_1^i, F_2^i, …F_t^i, ..F_N^i$ where N is the dimension of the vector, and F_t^i (t = 1,2,….M) is the tth element of the vector.
4. The vector that was created after extended transformation invariant pooling can be designated as F = (F$_1$, F$_2$,….,F$_t$, …, F$_N$).
5. The non-linear operator operates an operation that fuses items one by one across all M channels, expressed as

$$F_t = \max(, …,)$$

6. Applying softmax classifier and training loss converges.
7. Emotions are classified.
8. End

3.5 Experimental Evaluation Data Sets

Various trials are carried out in this section on three widely accessible facial expression data sets. Facial Expression Recognition (FER-2013) data sets, the Japanese Female Facial Expression (JAFFE) database. Experiments are being conducted in provision of the subsequent destinations:

1. Compare presentation of DBACNN on the FER job to several competing regs based on acknowledgement exactness.
2. Examine the protagonist of total features and extended transformation invariant pooling in addressing the FER problem.
3. Examine the influence of the principle feature erudition algorithm and its influence on acknowledgement exactness after removing certain inappropriate reinforcements.

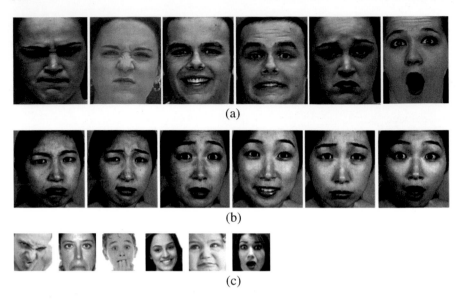

Fig. 4 Model of the six basic expressions. **a** CK + data set. **b** JAFFE data set. **c** FER-2013 data set. (left to right: anger, disgust, fear, happiness, sadness, surprise)

Fig. 5 A snapshot of data (left to right: anger, disgust, fear, happiness, sadness, surprise)

4. The CK+, JAFFE and FER-2013 data sets are used in the experiments. Six fundamental expressions are chosen as the goal of our classification job for each data set: anger, disgust, fear, happiness, sorrow and surprise. Figure 4 illustrates example basic expressions of CK+, JAFFE and FER-2013 data sets.

4 Result with Discussion

In this section, the enactment of the anticipated DBLCNN classifier for facial expression recognition is evaluated with the results of experiments conducted on MATLAB.

4.1 Databases

CK+ Data set

The CK+, facial expression database [14], is a publicly available data set for recognising action units and emotions. Both postured and non-postured expressions are included. A total of 593 sequences from 123 people make up the CK+. In most previous studies, the final frame of these sequences is chosen and used for image-based facial emotion detection.

JAFFE Data set

This data set comprises 213 photos of 10 Japanese female models posing with seven different face expressions. Six emotion descriptors were assigned to each image by 60 Japanese subjects [15].

FER-2013 Data set

This database was initially presented at the ICML 2013. Encounters in depiction knowledge [16], conference. This collection comprises 35,887 photos with a size of 48×48 pixels, the majority of which were captured in natural situations. There were 28,709 photographs in the training set, and 3589 photos in each of the validation and test sets. The Google image search was used to construct this database.

4.2 Performance Analysis Using CK + Data Set

Here, the concert of the proposed DBACNN classifier is analysed for the input images of the CK+ data set. The enactment of the proposed classifier is weighted against the existing methods, such as deep-based methods DTAN, MCSPL, Google Net, Bag of Words.

Discussion: Table 1 represents the confusion matrix of six facial expressions i.e. angry, disgust, fear, happy, sad and surprise. Table 4 represents the accuracy of the proposed method DBACNN is 94.67%, and it is 91.47% for DTAN, 91.12% for MCSPL, 89.45% for Google Net, 85.23% for Bag of words. In the above analysis, the proposed DBACNN method achieves better performance in terms of accuracy.

4.3 Performance Analysis Using JAFFE Data set

Here, the concert of the proposed DBACNN classifier is analysed for the input images of the JAFFE data set. The enactment of the proposed classifier is weighted against the existing methods, such as deep-based methods DTAN, MCSPL, Google Net, Bag of Words.

Discussion: Table 2 represents the confusion matrix of six facial expressions i.e. angry, disgust, fear, happy, sad and surprise. Table 5 represents the accuracy of the proposed method DBACNN is 94.87%, and it is 89.23% for DTAN, 87.56% for MCSPL, 85.58% for Google Net,86.89% for Bag of Words. In the above analysis, the proposed DBACNN method achieves better performance in terms of accuracy.

4.4 Performance Analysis Using FER-2013 Data set

Here, the concert of the proposed DBACNN classifier is analysed for the input images of the FER-2013 data set. The enactment of the proposed classifier is weighted against the existing methods, such as deep-based methods DTAN, MCSPL, Google Net, Bag of Words.

Discussion: Table 3 represents the confusion matrix of six facial expressions i.e. angry, disgust, fear, happy, sad and surprise. Table 6 represents the accuracy of the proposed method DBACNN is 89.78%, and it is 78.89% for DTAN, 77.67% for MCSPL, 77.89% for Google Net, 76.78% for Bag of Words. In the above analysis, the proposed DBACNN method achieves better performance in terms of accuracy.

4.5 Tables

See Tables 1, 2 and 3.

Classification accuracy of the DBACNN on the data set CK+, JAFFE and FER-2013

See Tables 4, 5 and 6.

Table 1 Confusion matrix on CK+

Expression	Angry	Disgust	Fear	Happy	Sad	Surprise
Angry	29	0	0	0	0	0
Disgust	0	34	1	0	0	0
Fear	0	0	30	0	0	1
Happy	0	1	0	30	1	1
Sad	0	0	0	0	31	0
Surprise	0	0	0	0	0	32

Table 2 Confusion matrix on JAFFE

Expression	Anger	Disgust	Fear	Happy	Sad	Surprise
Angry	30	0	0	0	0	0
Disgust	0	35	1	0	0	0
Fear	0	0	35	0	0	1
Happy	1	1	0	34	1	1
Sad	0	0	0	0	35	0
Surprise	0	0	0	1	0	35

Table 3 Confusion matrix on FER-2013

Expression	Angry	Disgust	Fear	Happy	Sad	Surprise
Angry	25	0	0	1	0	1
Disgust	0	30	1	0	0	0
Fear	0	0	31	0	0	1
Happy	1	1	0	29	1	1
Sad	1	0	0	0	24	0
Surprise	0	0	0	0	0	25

Table 4 Classification accuracy of the DBACNN on the dataset CK+

Method	Accuracy (%)
DBACNN	94.67
DTAN	91.47
MCSPL	91.12
Google Net	89.45
Bag of Words	85.23

Table 5 Classification accuracy of the DBACNN on the dataset JAFFE

Method	Accuracy (%)
DBACNN	94.87
DTAN	89.23
MCSPL	87.56
Google Net	85.58
Bag of Words	86.89

Table 6 Classification accuracy of the DBACNN on the dataset FER-2013

Method	Accuracy (%)
DBACNN	89.78
DTAN	78.89
MCSPL	77.67
Google Net	77.89
Bag of Words	76.78

Table 7 Confusion matrix on snapshot of data

Expression	Angry	Disgust	Fear	Happy	Sad	Surprise
Angry	34	0	0	1	0	1
Disgust	0	30	1	0	0	0
Fear	0	0	33	0	0	1
Happy	1	1	0	29	1	1
Sad	1	0	0	0	28	0
Surprise	0	0	0	0	0	28

Table 8 Accuracy of the proposed method DBACNN

No. of classes	Feature vector	Accuracy (%)
6	DBACNN	95.67
	DTAN	90.57
	MCSPL	90.13
	Google Net	88.55
	Bag of Words	80.33

4.6 Performance Analysis Using Snapshot Images

Here, the concert of the proposed DBACNN classifier is analysed for the input images of the snapshot images. The enactment of the proposed classifier is weighted against the existing methods, such as deep-based methods DTAN, MCSPL, Google Net, Bag of Words.

Discussion: Table 7 represents the confusion matrix of six facial expressions, i.e. angry, disgust, fear, happy, sad and surprise. Table 8 represents the accuracy of the proposed method DBACNN is 95.67%, and it is 90.57% for DTAN, 90.13% for MCSPL, 88.55% for Google Net, 80.33% for Bag of Words. In the above analysis, the proposed DBACNN method achieves better performance in terms of accuracy.

5 Conclusions

We proposed the DCT and DBACNN hybrid approach for face expression recognition in this research. This model contains two individual CNN levels. One of the level consists of comprehensive features extraction, whilst the other extracts regional features extraction. The fused features are created by concatenating both the comprehensive and regional characteristics, and classification is done using the fused features. The fused features are created by concatenating both the comprehensive and regional characteristics, and classification is done using the fused features. Broad tests openly applied on the data sets CK+, JAFFE and FER-2013. The proposed method attains a higher classification accuracy than other existing methods.

References

1. Datta Rakshit R, Nath SC, Kisku DR (2017) An improved local pattern descriptor for biometrics face encoding: a LC–LBP approach toward face identification. J Chin Inst Eng 40(1)
2. Alpaslan N, Hanbay K (2020) Multi-scale shape index-based local binary patterns for texture classification. IEEE Signal Process Lett 27. https://doi.org/10.1109/LSP.2020.2987474
3. Jiao J, Deng Z (2017) Deep combining of local phase quantization and histogram of oriented gradients for indoor positioning based on smartphone camera. https://doi.org/10.1177/155014 7716686978
4. Minaee S, Deep-emotion: facial expression recognition using attentional convolutional network. arXiv:1902.01019v1
5. Khan AS (2019) Facial expression recognition using discrete cosine transform & artificial neural network. IEEE. 978-1-7281-4001-8/19/$31.00©2019
6. Laptev D, Savinov N, Buhman JM, Pollefeys M (2016) Ti-pooling: transformation-invariant pooling for feature learning in convolutional neural networks. In: Proceedings of international conference computer vision pattern recognition, pp 289–297
7. Xie S, Hu H (2019) Facial expression recognition using hierarchical features with deep comprehensive multipatches aggregation convolutional neural networks. IEEE Trans Multimedia 21(1):211–220
8. Li J, Lam E (2015) Facial expression recognition using deep neural networks. In: Proceedings of IEEE international conference imaging system technology, pp 1–6
9. Mollahosseini, Chan D, Mahoor MH (2016) Going deeper in facial expression recognition using deep neural networks. In: Proceedings of IEEE Winter Conference applications computer vision, pp 1–10
10. Xu M, Cheng W, Zhao Q, Ma L, Xu F (2015) Facial expression recognition based on transfer learning from deep convolutional networks. In: Proceedings of 11th international conference on natural computation, pp 702–708
11. Islam B, Mahmud F, Hossain A (2018) High performance facial expression recognition system using facial region segmentation, fusion of HOG & LBP features and multiclass SVM. In: IEEE 10th international conference 2018
12. Liu Y, Zeng J, Shan S, Zheng Z (2018) Multi channel pose aware convolution neural networks for multi view facial expression recognition. In: 13th IEEE international conference
13. Jung H, Lee S, Yim J, Park S, Kim J (2015) Joint fine-tuning in deep neural networks for facial expression recognition. In: Proceedings of international conference on computer vision, pp 2982–2991
14. Lucey P et al (2010) The extended cohn-kanade dataset (ck+): A complete dataset for action unit and emotion-specified expression. In: IEEE computer society conference on computer vision and pattern recognition workshops (CVPRW). IEEE
15. Lyons M, Kamachi M, Gyoba J (2017) Japanese Femal Facial Expression (JAFFE) database. Version 2 Journal Contribution posted on 2017
16. Kaggle.com/msambare/fer2013, FER-2013 Learn facial expression from an image.Opendatabase,Usability 7.5,2020

SquashCord: Video Conferencing Application Using WebRTC

Adhiksha Thorat⊙ **and Avinash Bhute**⊙

Abstract WebRTC is a framework that helps to facilitate real-time communication between browsers. It provides services through application programming interface (API) and allows web applications and sites to exchange video and audio streams in real time. It is an open-source software developed by Google. The research presented in this paper delves into the development of a multi-peer video conferencing application that is developed using technologies like WebRTC, Node.js and Socket.io. WebRTC establishes a peer-to-peer network, and Socket.io (a library in Node.js) acts as a signalling mechanism for exchanging data necessary for establishing this network. The developed application works well on most web browsers and provides great user experience with rooms, live chat, games and many other features. The paper helps in understanding how these technologies can be used together to achieve a robust and secure application.

Keywords Node.js · WebRTC · Socket.io · Video conferencing

1 Introduction

During the pandemic, people started escalating towards virtual learning and virtual meetings which have been helping us to continue working. There are many tools in the market that facilitates video conferencing facilities with various other services. But recently a lot of these companies have been accused of possible breaches of user data. Hence, we wanted to make an application that would enhance the user's experience and provide maximum security. The application makes use of WebRTC which is a tool from Google, helps in serverless data transfer and establishes secure connections between user systems. The framework for this application is in Node.js. Also, building a video conferencing application is considered complicated because of the various components you need to master like P2P connection establishment,

---

A. Thorat · A. Bhute (✉)
MIT Academy of Engineering, Alandi(D), Pune 412105, India
e-mail: anbhute@mitaoe.ac.in

© The Author(s), under exclusive license to Springer Nature Singapore Pte Ltd. 2022   425
C. Satyanarayana et al. (eds.), *High Performance Computing and Networking*,
Lecture Notes in Electrical Engineering 853,
https://doi.org/10.1007/978-981-16-9885-9_35

streams exchange and room-wise management of users. Using a combination of WebRTC and Socket.io from Node.js helped us to overcome the difficulties. WebRTC multimedia applications have become popular these days because of the ease of adding the WebRTC APIs directly to our JavaScript code without having to use any other third-party plugins or proprietary software. This system can act as a great alternative to the server–client-based systems, where the servers can hoard user data.

Here, Socket.io acts as a signal data carrier which works with WebRTC to establish multi-peer connections. Socket.io also provides with rooms which are arbitrary channels that sockets can join and leave. It divides the user into subsets where the data and events can be broadcast. This paper provides a detailed view of our application and how the components work together.

Web real-time communication (WebRTC) is a state-of-the-art open technology that makes real-time communication capabilities in audio, video and data transmission possible in real-time communication through web browsers using JavaScript application programming interfaces (APIs) without plug-ins. This technology is open-source and has a lot of people intrigued by its functionalities and architecture. Hence, we have tried to research about this technology and build an application which is open source and would help people to understand this new technology better.

2   Related Work

There exist many video conferencing applications in the market these days. There are many unique features provided by different companies. Namely, we have Cisco WebEx, Microsoft Teams, Zoom, etc. All these applications do not make use of WebRTC instead use a proprietary protocol for the exchange of multimedia streams. But all the applications mentioned above have to be installed in your system for accessing the services.

We only have a few applications like Skype, Google Meet, UberConference, etc., that are making use of WebRTC. AppRTC sample is an application developed by Google which is truly an open-source WebRTC example. These applications do not need to be installed and can be directly accessed through Web browsers.

The journal article [1] implemented video conferencing application named Rendevous using WebRTC in their published research paper "Video conference System Based on WebRTC With Access to the PST". It uses Nodejs as a web and signalling server and allows the users with no Internet connectivity to exchange audio streams using dial and answer phone calls to/from the PSTN directly on the web browser.

The book [2] described the entire development cycle associated with WebRTC. Authors explained the step-by-step implementation of application development, and how the media streams could be associated with a PeerConnection object and what it represents. This book helps in understanding the WebRTC architecture and how to approach building an application using WebRTC.

The journal article [3] discussed the development of a video conferencing application using WebRTC and studied it in detail. The application is dynamic site designed under ASP.net using C# with JavaScript. The process of authorization is done by allowing the access to website pages depending on authorization level; password encrypted using encryption technique. This paper helps in understanding various features required for a making video conferencing application and analyses its compatibility with various browsers and devices.

The journal article [4] discussed the use of WebSockets with WebRTC as a signalling mechanism. This paper researched and analysed the core architecture and related technologies of WebRTC, including video input and output, multimedia transmission, the process of peer-to-peer connection establishment and signalling mechanism. It gave a brief idea of how the signalling mechanism and WebRTC can be used together to attain a successful videoconferencing application.

The journal article [5] suggested the development of a WebRTC video conferencing application using Node.js, Java and Kotlin. It guided about the steps of building your own signalling server. An extra feature is that the user can use various annotations or drawings to express themselves which can then be shared with other users in the network. The papers explain in detail the process of writing a signalling server simultaneously with WebRTC functions.

The journal article [6] proposed a system that allows users to communicate with high-speed data transmission over the communication channel using WebRTC technology, HTML5 and use Node.js server address. It gave a brief idea of the WebRTC API functions and has also implemented a Database in MySQL to store important user data. It has many features like Chat box, Post box, Friend Requests (Table 1).

3 SquashCord: Video Conferencing Application

This section discusses our proposed video conferencing application and its system architecture.

- Room-Wise Division of Users: The users must be able to create and join into rooms through a code or given link. They should be able to exchange messages and media exclusively to peers in the Room.
- Easy and Intuitive GUI: The user interface must be easy to use and flexible for different screen resolutions.
- Multiple Peers in one network: Connecting multiple peers by proper data transfer.
- Security of the users: The security of user's data is a major factor for developing this application. Using WebRTC provides the user's data high security.

Table 1 Summarising Literature survey

Reference no.	Approach	Pros	Cons
[1]	Uses WebRTC and PSTN for VOIP and IP PBX server as Signalling Channel	Poor network peers can join over Voice using PSTN	IP PBX server is very complicated
[2]	This is a book that illustrates the working and construction of WebRTC application. Any signalling mechanism is suggested	Properly explained examples with code samples	Not mentioned specific signalling mechanism
[3]	Uses WebRTC with ASP.net using C# as a programming language and JavaScript for WebRTC functions.	Great mobile application with WebRTC with high security	Does not have a signalling mechanism
[4]	Uses WebRTC in Node.js and WebSockets as a signalling mechanism	WebSockets are easy to implement with many features	Basic UI with limited features
[5]	Uses Node.js, Java and Kotlin to develop the videoconferencing application. Java for mobile app development	Low latency calls with many features	Only for android
[6]	Uses WebRTC with Nodejs. Uses Socket programming as a signalling mechanism.	Easy to implement and many features can be integrated	Not much information about Signalling mechanism

3.1   WebRTC Architecture

Here, we will be breaking down the WebRTC architecture into three parts for better understanding.

WebRTC establishes a peer-to-peer connection by transferring necessary stream information amongst the peers. To establish this multimedia connection, it is necessary to have audio technology, video technology and network transmission technology. Initially, the network connection is established between the peers and then, each peer captures the audio and video streams encodes it and transmits it over the network. When a peer receives this data, it decodes it and displays the streams accordingly. It provides a JavaScript API that can be directly integrated by the developers. The network between the peers is opened and established using **RTCPeerConnection**. The connection between local device and remote peers is setup using the STUN and TURN protocols. Media (MediaStreams) and/or Data Streams (RTCDataChannels) can be added to the connection once it is stable.

3.1.1   MediaStream

It is the stream of audio/video streams from our local device which are accessed using "GetUserMedia()" function.

3.1.2   RTCDataChannels

It is a bidirectional channel which the peers use to transfer data reliably. The basic steps that are followed in exchanging multimedia through WebRTC are as follows:

1. Peer A connects to the STUN server and receives a symmetric NAT in return. This helps the peer to get its public IP address.
2. Then the Peer A requests the TURN server for a Signal Channel to be established between Peer A and Peer B.
3. Peer A then sends an Offer SDP on the Signal Channel to Peer B.
4. Peer B processes the Offer SDP and sends an Answer SDP to Peer A.
5. Peer A receives the answer and then a channel is established between the two peers and Peer A will setRemoteDescription.
6. After the basic network is setup, peers exchange ICE candidates which contain information about the how to discover other peers on the network
7. After the ICEs are exchanged and the ICECandidates are added, a peer-to-peer connection is setup where they can now share multimedia streams like audio and video.
8. The peers then render the video stream to an HTML video element. WebRTC uses UDP protocol in the network layer for fast and reliable stream exchange.

3.1.3   SDP Offer and Answer

SDP stands for session description protocol which is used to describe the media communication sessions. It has various components like the system's IP address, information about the request, audio and video information, encryption type. SDP is of two types "offer" and "answer". The offer SDP is first sent over the channel and is responded back with an answer SDP.

3.1.4   ICE Exchange

ICE stands for interactive connectivity establishment, and it is mostly used to know how to connect to other peers. Once the connection is setup, the ICE candidates are generate and exchanges using NAT. ICEs are present in Candidate and Key pairs.

3.2 WebSocket Architecture (Signal Exchanging Data Carrier)

WebRTC does not provide much support when it comes to multiple peer network due to the fact that two peers exchange the ICEs without signalling the other peers in the network. Also, we cannot create features like rooms using only WebRTC. Hence, we need a signalling mechanism/channel to exchange data between peers. So, we have used Socket.io to help us establish a multi-peer network with WebRTC. Socket.io sets up webSockets that are bidirectional and have two ends, namely the client side and server side. The socket connection is established after handshake and on a particular port. The client side has WebRTC calls and functions that are local to every peer. The server side has all the Socket listeners and is connected to all the other sockets in the room. So, finally the browser and server are able to push data to each other. Whenever the user performs any actions on the web page like joining the room or leaving the room, the listeners on the client side will get triggered and will signal the server side about the change. The server will then broadcast this change to all the peers connected to the socket. Every peer/client will be listening to the socket, and after receiving the message about the change, the client side will call the related functions of WebRTC which makes the change happen.

Rooms are also features provided by Socket.io which help us to broadcast messages like ICEs and SDPs to the peers in the same room. When the user is connected and joins a room, Socket.io makes sure that user is connected to that room from the start.

3.3 Design of SquashCord: Video Conferencing Application

This is the basic architecture of how the system flow is (Fig. 1).

4 Our Approach for Implementation

The user will enter the room name and the user name. Every user is given a unique user ID(UUID). A new WebRTC peer is defined using setUpPeer() function. Then, the script will check if the user is the first one to enter the room, if so, it will create a new connection request to other peers and waits for other peers to connect. It creates a description and sends it to the server using socket.io. The server then broadcasts the message to all the peers in the room. If the user was not the first one to join the room, then the script will listen to all the messages broadcast by the server. If there is a description, the WebRTC peer will create an answer and send it to the server to broadcast. If the answer is received by other peers, then they will exchange ICEs. And finally, both the peers will exchange their video and audio streams using

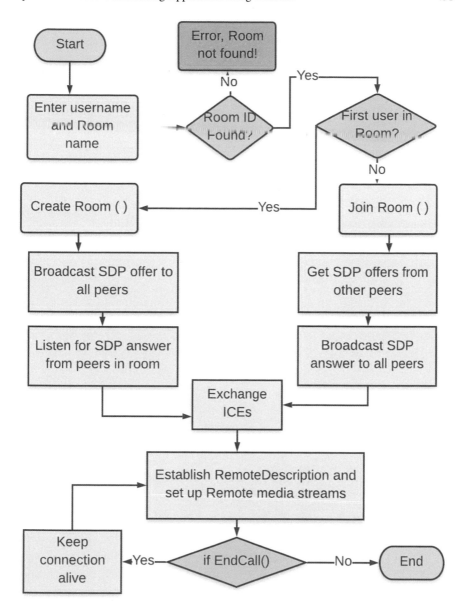

Fig. 1 Flow of diagram of the application

function gotRemoteStream(). Once the connection between them is established, they can exchange chat messages too using sockets.

4.1 Module-Wise Implementation

main.js: It sends and receives messages to the server. Has functions to establish and manage a WebRTC peer-to-peer connection. If user sends chat messages, the script will send them to server for broadcast. If any other user has sent a chat message, it receives the message from server and displays it to the screen.

server.js: It initialises the sockets and listens for messages from client side. It can also broadcast message to all peers who are only present in that room. It acts like a server and manages all users in a Room.

games.js: It has functions for initiating a game of HeadsUP between peers. One peer acts out the movie while other guess it. It uses Firebase FireStore to maintain previous room scores.

WebRTC Functions: It helps in setting up peers and handling them. Also, has functions to create offer and answer SDPs depending on what the status of connection is. The function gotMessageFromServer() handles most of the data like ICEs and SDPs that are received from other peers.

5 Security Measures

5.1 Protocol Layer Security

WebRTC uses strong encryption protocols for securing the data transmission between the peers. The various security features provided in this layer are:

Media Encryption: WebRTC mandates the encryption of all the voice, video and other data packets that are exchanged between the peers. It uses the Secure Real-Time Protocol (SRTP) to encrypt this data so that no one can attack the peer-to-peer connection and decode the information that is being exchanged. This is the feature that makes it more secure than the client–server-based applications.

Secure Encryption of Exchange Keys: The DTLS-SRTP protocol helps in exchange the session decryption keys to all the peers in the network, so that they can access the shared audio, video and other data. So, this ensures even more security from any sort of attacks.

Browser Security and Privacy Measures: WebRTC connections are usually established through web browsers, and browsers have their own security standards like IP protection and certificate validation. The OS also has many security measures preventing any attacks. WebRTC also asks for permission before accessing the user's audio or video channels using pop-up alerts.

User Authentication using Firebase: We are making use of Firebase Authentication for all users, so that user can access the protected data. Also, it helps in avoiding any malicious activities while starting the application.

5.2 Signalling Server Security

We are using Node.js—Socket.io library for exchanging data through sockets and are using STUN and TURN servers for NAT. Hypertext Transfer Protocol-Secure (HTTPS), this is the protocol used for transferring data between sockets and provides exceptional security services. Secure sockets layer (SSL) and transport layer security (TLS) are the protocols used for exchanging data in a HTTPS connection. We need an SSL certificate to establish the HTTPS connection, and we have generated one using "openssl" library. Hence, these encryption protocols make sure that the data being exchanged between the sockets is secure and can only be decrypted using the decryption keys.

The STUN and TURN servers do not pose much of a threat to the data security because they are never really used for data transmission but even these are secured using HTTPS protocol.

6 Result Analysis

The application successfully works on browsers like Firefox, Chrome and Edge. The pages are flexible and can be used on desktops as well as mobile phones. The landing page (index.html) makes the user to enter the username and choose the room he would like to join.

The next page (chat.html) has a URL with room name and username appended to it. So, the user can join by sharing the link as well.

We can monitor the performance of the WebRTC networks by using the website **"chrome://webrtc-internals"**. According to these stats, the following conclusions can be made:

1. The jitter is kept as low as possible, which means that the data is transmitted without much lag. It seems to increase with the increase in users per room.
2. The number of packets lost is zero, and hence, all the packets sent through the WebRTC media channels are received.
3. The fluctuation in the Internet connection can lead to a fluctuation in the frames received per second (fps). Frames received per second are stable.

Hence, the WebRTC media connections are pretty fast and reliable. Also, the signalling mechanism is effective in delivering the right data to the right peer. Hence, the combination of Sockets in Node.js and WebRTC work together seamlessly (Figs. 2, 3 and 4).

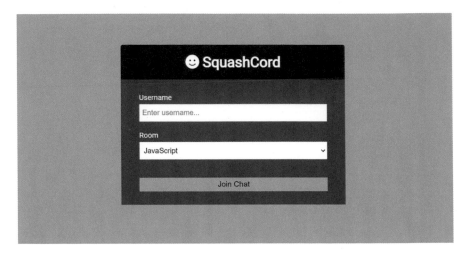

Fig. 2 Landing page of the application (index.html)

Fig. 3 Multiple users in the chatting room (chat.html)

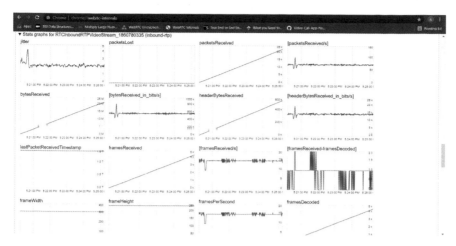

Fig. 4 Stats gathered from webrtc-internals site

7   Conclusion

In this paper, we first delved into understanding the architecture and implementation of WebRTC-based systems. Then, we have used Node.js framework with Socket.io library for transfer of SDPs, ICEs and other information amongst the peers. Also, sockets help us in managing and creating rooms and also facilitate transfer of chat messages. WebRTC provides high security data transmission between peers by a simple JavaScript API. The final system is compatible with multiple browsers and devices because of the interface being flexible. The application is open source as it proves as a practical and academic example of WebRTC and it is potential. The application currently allows four users in one room because of the increase in the jitter as the number of users increases. The application is much more secure than the traditional client–server applications because of all the security measures that are enforced by WebRTC.

References

1. Rosas AS, Martínez JLA (2016) Videoconference system based on WebRTC with access to the PSTN. Electron Notes Theoret Comput Sci 329:105–121
2. Loreto S, Romano SP (2014) Real-time communication with WebRTC: peer-to-peer in the browser. O'Reilly Media, Inc.
3. Mahmood S, Ercelebe E, Hadeed S (2018) Development of video conference platform based on Web RTC. Book
4. Cui J, Lin Z, Research and Implementation of WEBRTC Signaling via websocket-based for real-time multimedia communications. https://doi.org/10.2991/iccsae-15.2016.72
5. Pacaj K, Hyseni K, Sfishta D (2020) Peer to peer audio and video communication using WebRTC (No. 4304). EasyChair

6. Nayyef ZT, Amer SF, Hussain Z (2018) Peer to peer multimedia real-time communication system based on WebRTC technology. Int J Eng Technol 7(2.9):125–130
7. Jang-Jaccard J, Nepal S, Celler B, Yan B (2016) WebRTC-based video conferencing service for telehealth. Computing 98(1–2):169–193
8. Caiko J, Patlins A, Nurlan A, Protsenko V (2020) Video-conference Communication Platform Based on WebRTC Online meetings. In: 2020 IEEE 61th international scientific conference on power and electrical engineering of riga technical university (RTUCON). IEEE, pp 1–6
9. Alimudin A, Muhammad AF (2018) Online video conference system using WebRTC technology for distance learning support. In: 2018 International electronics symposium on knowledge creation and intelligent computing (IES-KCIC). IEEE, pp 384–387
10. Pandusadewa AR, Alimudin A (2019) Development of conversation application as english learning using WebRTC. In: 2019 International electronics symposium (IES). IEEE, pp 589–594
11. Suciu G, Stefanescu S, Beceanu C, Ceaparu M (2020) WebRTC role in real-time communication and video conferencing. In 2020 Global internet of things summit (GIoTS). IEEE, pp 1–6
12. Ha VKL, Chai R, Nguyen HT (2020) A telepresence wheelchair with 360-degree vision using WebRTC. Appl Sci 10(1):369
13. Bhute AN, Meshram BB (2014) Text based approach for indexing and retrieval of image and video: a review. Adv Vis Comput Int J (AVC) 1
14. Giri MB, Pippal RS (2017) Use of linear interpolation for automated drip irrigation system in agriculture using wireless sensor network. In: 2017 International conference on energy, communication, data analytics and soft computing (ICECDS). IEEE, pp 1599–1603
15. Ganjewar PD, Barani S, Wagh SJ, Sonavane SS (2018) Survey on data reduction techniques for energy conservation for prolonging life of wireless sensor network. Wirel Commun 10(2):17–25

A Hybrid Pipeline for the Segmentation of Eye Regions from Video Frames

Adish Rao, Aniruddha Mysore, Abhishek Guragol, Rajath Shetty, Siddhanth Ajri, Poulami Sarkar, and Gowri Srinivasa

Abstract An accurate tracking and, in turn, an accurate segmentation of key regions of the eye are a sine qua non to provide users with superior quality of immersive experiences in augmented reality (AR), virtual reality (VR), and mixed reality (MR) applications. In this paper, we present the detailed rationale and research behind the design of an image processing pipeline to perform pixel-wise segmentation of eye from the background and labeling key structures, viz. sclera, iris and pupil, of the eye. The images used in this study are from a dataset provided by Facebook as a part of the OpenEDS Challenge 2020 and are sampled frames from a video capture of the eye. The pipeline we present is a hybrid of traditional image preprocessing techniques (such as histogram equalization) with application-specific augmentation (such as emulating a glare pattern) and an ensemble of five powerful, deep learning-based segmentation networks derived from the U-Net and LinkNet, followed by post-processing that harnesses temporal information. With this pipeline, we obtain a final evaluation score of 0.9641, which is well above the baseline score of 0.840 (provided by Facebook as a part of the challenge) and comparable to the top scores reported in the public domain.

1 Introduction

The future of human–computer interaction is headed in the direction of augmented, virtual, and mixed reality technologies (AR, VR, MR). A key component of virtual and mixed reality is the head-mounted display, which allows users to interact with digital content and in the case of MR the real world as well. Eye movement-based

A. Rao · A. Mysore (✉) · A. Guragol · R. Shetty · S. Ajri · P. Sarkar
PES Center for Pattern Recognition, PES University Electronic City Campus, Bengaluru 560100, India

G. Srinivasa
Department of Computer Science and Engineering, PES Center for Pattern Recognition, PES University, Bengaluru, India
e-mail: gsrinivasa@pes.edu

C. Satyanarayana et al. (eds.), *High Performance Computing and Networking*,
Lecture Notes in Electrical Engineering 853,
https://doi.org/10.1007/978-981-16-9885-9_36

tracking has been identified as a possible solution to not only control and interact with head-mounted displays but also to enhance the quality of the virtual experience by increasing user immersion and engagement. This calls for accurate, efficient, and real-time computation of the human gaze [1].

Several eye-tracking methods can be found in the literature [2–6]. In almost all of these, the efficacy of tracking the eye is dependent on an accurate segmentation of key regions of the eye. Such a sensitivity to the accuracy of segmentation motivates a per pixel segmentation. Each pixel is thus classified as one of four different regions: the background, the sclera, the iris, and the pupil. There have been myriad research undertakings using segmentation in images, even in the specific field of segmenting the key regions of the eye. However, one of the more nascent applications in this domain is the use of segmentation to identify key features in video datasets from AR/VR headsets, which offers an additional temporal dimension.

In this work, we utilize the dataset published by Facebook as part of the OpenEDS Challenge 2020. This dataset contains sequential frames of footage captured from a head-mounted camera [7]. We explore numerous techniques to segment the afore-mentioned regions of the eye and present a complete pipeline to preprocess video frames, train, and validate the segmentation model, and fine-tune the predictions with image processing methods. Our model, a hybrid of traditional image process-ing techniques, deep learning-based segmentation networks, and post-processing that incorporates temporal data, achieves a high score for the mean intersection-over-union (mIoU) metric that significantly beats the baseline score achieved by the original OpenEDS paper and is on par with other state-of-the-art techniques for sparse semantic segmentation of features of the eye.

2 Related Work

Semantic segmentation of images and, in particular, semantic segmentation of the eye is a well-researched field. Previous work carried out in this domain explored various aspects of segmentation of the different regions of the eye, such as the segmentation of the iris region of the eye under visible and near-infrared light [2], and the segmentation of the sclera region of the eye [3]. Both these efforts, however, focus primarily only on segmenting out one out of the many different regions of the eye, rather than all regions simultaneously.

Research on the segmentation of multiple regions of the eye, including eyelashes as one of the segments, was not geared toward deployment on VR/MR headsets and thus do not delve into leveraging the temporal information present in the image data available or techniques to deal with the noise present due to light emitted from the headsets [4].

Other efforts in this direction, such as those undertaken as a part of the original OpenEDS challenge, address the task of segmentation of the different eye regions factoring in their use case in the VR/MR domain. The focus of these efforts is on fulfilling the segmentation challenge under the constraint of having a low complexity model for improved runs times [5, 6]. This constraint leads to faster prediction times but poorer accuracy of prediction. Furthermore, the original challenge made no mention of a temporal dimension. The need for a more accurate segmentation and a component in the pipeline that can harness the temporal dimension serves as the motivation behind the present work.

3 Dataset

The dataset provided by Facebook consists of video frames depicting the front view of the eye. The footage was gathered from a sample of 74 participants. The frames were extracted from 200 video sequences sampled at 5 Hz with about 150 frames/sequence, thereby resulting in 29, 476 extracted frames, for the segmentation task. Five percent of these images are labeled and constitute the base set. We further split the data, with a split ratio of 75 : 25, for model training and validation sets, respectively. The remaining unlabeled data was sampled by Facebook to generate a test set for evaluation purposes. The masks for the images were of dimensions 400 × 640 to represent the class each pixel in the image belongs to. The labels for the pixels are as follows: 0 for the background regions exterior to the eye, 1 for the sclera, 2 for the iris, and 3 for the pupil. These numbers are used to color code regions and are represented as masks. For representations of the image and mask refer Table 1

Some of the challenges in this data include extensive variations across the images. To begin with, not all images provide a view of the eyes being wide open that would make the task of semantic segmentation an easy one. Rather, many of the images depict the eye mid-blink or completely closed. Another major challenge is a saturation noise or glare on account of users wearing a pair of spectacles in addition to the headset, which creates patterns that pose a significant hurdle for segmentation. Further, some of the images are not sharp on account of motion blur. There are also

Table 1 A sample image from the dataset: (a) a video frame (image) showing structures of the eye and (b) the corresponding mask

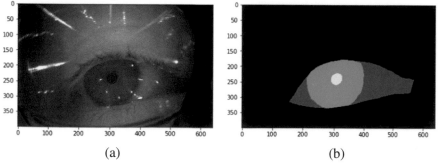

(a)   (b)

Table 2 Types of noise in images: (a) a normal image, (b) an image with glare, (c) mid-blink, and (d) an image with eyeliner/mascara

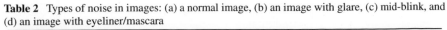

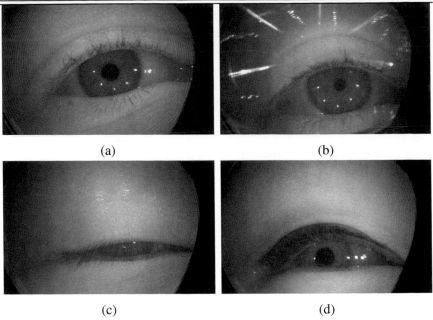

images where the user has a noticeable amount of makeup on, mainly eyeliner and mascara, which adversely impacts the segmentation task. A variation ascribed to the temporal aspect of the dataset is the transition between open and closed eye images, in the event of a blink, not being seemless. It should also be noted that the images are in grayscale and are not full color, i.e., red, blue, green (RGB) images, which makes an accurate prediction of boundaries a challenging task. These variations in the dataset can be seen in the images as depicted in Table 2.

4   Design of the Hybrid Pipeline for Segmentation

The design of the hybrid pipeline for segmentation of the regions of the eye evolved from exploring the most proven, off-the-shelf deep learning models to incorporating traditional image processing techniques to increase the accuracy and incorporating state-of-the-art deep learning-based segmentation networks with post-processing that harnesses temporal information. This evolution is explicated below with an explanation of the strength of the model and limitations, leading to the design of the final pipeline.

4.1 Dual-Model Approach and Image Augmentation

Our initial approach sought to leverage the convolutional neural network (CNN) model described in [8] used in the previous iteration of the competition. The authors demonstrated the efficacy of a dual-model approach to achieve greater accuracy while still utilizing an optimized model. We utilized the same approach, wherein the first model predicted the first three values of the segmentation masks that describe the relatively larger regions (the background, sclera, and iris), while the second model distinguished between the third and fourth values that describe more detailed structures (the iris and pupil). The results obtained were stitched together to obtain the final mask, delineating all four regions of interest. Images used for this experiment were scaled down from a dimension of 400 × 640 to an image size of 96 × 160. The value chosen was to ensure the dimensions were $M\%32 \times N\%32$ while still trying to retain the aspect ratio. This model, however, incorporated no preprocessing nor image augmentation techniques achieved an mIoU of only 0.84 on the validation set.

In an attempt to improve the performance, we integrated the ImageDataGenerator module from Keras to perform the inbuilt flip, rotate, shift, and zoom operations along with various custom augmentations such as adding noise in the form of random bright spots, image brightening, Gaussian blurring, and random white lines in a circular pattern to emulate the pattern caused due to the glare present in few images. With the addition of these augmentations, the model performance improved marginally to achieve an mIoU of 0.9 on the validation set. In a final attempt to improve performance, a technique known as attention gating [9] was embedded into the models which further increased the mIoU to 0.95 on the validation set. Although the model achieved good results on the validation set, the score achieved on the test set was only a marginal improvement over the benchmark score. This prompted a move from a dual-model structure to a single unified U-Net architecture as described in the next subsection.

4.2 Image Preprocessing and the Switch to U-Net

The dual-model approach in [8] was tailored for the constraints of the previous iteration of the OpenEDS challenge which imposed a size penalty on models. Given that this model parameter size restriction is not applicable for the dataset under consideration, we switched architectures to the U-Net architecture mentioned earlier [10].

The U-Net approach resulted in a significant increase in accuracy over the dual-model approach previously described. We further substituted the white-line augmentation used in the previous approach with a glare augmentation layer that was extracted from the original eye images to better represent the patterns present in the data. A key difficulty experienced by the model was the reflection present in images where the participants wore a pair of spectacles. This caused the sclera region to be misclassified. In order to amend this, we tried additional image preprocessing approaches.

We experimented with a variant of histogram equalization known as contrast limited adaptive histogram equalization, shortened to CLAHE, to reduce the sharp glare. CLAHE operates on tiles (subregions of the image) rather than the whole image. However, we found that the traditional histogram equalization from the OpenCV package resulted in better overall performance. Another noticeable aspect of the dataset was that most of the images were dark. To tackle this problem, we made use of image brightening methods which helped highlight the sclera of the eye more prominently, although it should be noted that the performance on the other regions of the eye had a negative impact. Finally, Gaussian blurring technique was applied in order to reduce the effect of noise present in almost all of the images.

Along with the vanilla U-Net architecture, we also tried a variation of U-Net that used the aforementioned attention gating mechanism. This technique, while providing a noticeable performance jump when compared to the vanilla U-Net, with scores considerably higher than the baseline score, still failed to match the performance of other state-of-the-art models. This prompted research into other models which yielded in the discovery of the segmentation models package that provided a variety of inbuilt models with multiple options that can be customized, such as altering the backbone architecture, varying the activation functions, etc. [11].

A key experimentation performed at this stage was leveraging the temporal information present in the data. The final prediction was a combination of the current prediction along with a weighted influence of the previous prediction. This was done as the images are sequential frames taken from a video, and thus, most of the regions locations from one image to another do not change drastically.

To achieve high performance, finding the optimal value of current to previous prediction ratio was imperative. To that extent, various weights ranging from 0.1 to 0.5 were experimented with and it was found that a weight of 0.2 to the previous image prediction gave the best accuracy.

$$X_n = X_n + (0.2 * X_{n-1}) \tag{1}$$

4.3 Segmentation Models, Experimentation with Loss Functions and Model Ensembling

Using the segmentation models package, we experimented with the U-Net architecture with a ResNet34 backbone. Dataset properties were also varied, with images being resized to 640 × 384 being the closet dimensions to the original data which is still M%32 × N%32. This is done to avoid a loss of information during the process of scaling. Other changes made were moving to single channel images, as opposed to the three channel images that were being used for training up until this point. The loss function was also changed to use more sophisticated losses, given the complexity of the problem, making a combination of dice loss and Jaccard loss as the final loss function of choice [12].

With the segmentation models package, it was now possible to use model ensembling given the variety of models offered. Our experimentation at this stage made use of an ensemble comprising U-Net and LinkNet architectures, both having ResNet34 backbone. Multiple U-Net and LinkNet models were trained on two sets of grayscale images, the original and an inverted counterpart (with pixel values being inverted), with one of the U-Net models in the ensemble being additionally equipped with CLAHE to preprocess the images.

Finally, we looked into freezing encoder weights by training the model for a few initial epochs and then training for a few more epochs where only decoder weights are tuned during training, but this specific technique did not yield any improvement in performance. All these experimentations led to the final model implementation which has been described in Sect. 5.

4.4 Experimentation with Nascent Techniques

There was no significant improvement in performance with the addition of other augmentation techniques and changes in model architecture which prompted us to further explore more nascent preprocessing and post-processing techniques such as conditional random fields (CRF) with superpixeling.

Superpixeling is the process of partitioning the image into multiple segments (superpixel) based on some common characteristics like pixel intensity. This helps in creating a clear delineation between the different regions present in an image which can potentially improve segmentation performance. Conditional random fields on the other hand are a discriminative statistical modeling method used when the class labels for the various inputs are not independent. CRF provides predictions for the data considering the input features along with the labels of all other inputs which are dependent on the current input. In CRF, the data is structured as a graph consisting of a set of nodes V and edges between the nodes E. An edge between a node i and a node j in the graph denotes the output label of data points i and j are dependent. CNNs sometimes fail to accurately predict the complex boundaries between classes at the pixel level resulting in slightly distorted image masks. Superpixel-enhanced pairwise conditional random fields are often used in segmentation to correct these minor inconsistencies and generate more accurate boundaries leading to a state of art accuracy. However, these techniques did not provide any boosts in performance and were thus dropped leading to the final implementation explained next.

5 Final Hybrid Pipeline and Results

A schematic diagram of the final hybrid pipeline is depicted in Fig. 1. The first step involves preprocessing using the best methods identified in the experimentation steps described above. The second step is to perform image augmentation, as shown in

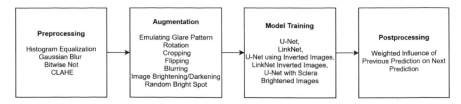

Fig. 1 A hybrid pipeline for the segmentation eye regions from video frames

Table 3, to increase the size of the training set. Then, the model ensemble is trained on the images. Finally, to account for the temporal dimension of the dataset, a post-processing step where the output from the previous prediction is weighted and fed back to influence the next iteration of training.

The ensemble comprises of five models which are a combination of U-Net and LinkNet architectures provided by the segmentation models package. The base model pair consists of a U-Net and LinkNet model duo trained on images preprocessed with the histogram equalization and Gaussian blurring techniques mentioned earlier. The secondary model pair is trained on images processed additionally using the inversion technique. This pair contributes to increasing inference accuracy over the iris region. The fifth component of the ensemble makes use of CLAHE and ConvertScaleAbs preprocessing methods that increase image brightness and the prominence of the sclera region. These images are trained using U-Net.

We define a custom loss function that uses the sum of Dice and Jaccard losses. All five models in the ensemble use this loss for the training process. The models are trained for 128 epochs using the Adam optimizer and fine-tuned for a further 16 epochs using SGD optimizer with following parameters—learning rate = 0.0001, decay = 10^{-6}, and momentum = 0.9.

The predictions from the individual models are averaged to compute the output mask. The masks are generated sequentially, one frame at a time. At each step, the mask prediction for the previous video frame is added to the current prediction as mentioned earlier in Eq. (1). This results in the final output mask for the frame. A visual depiction of the performance of the hybrid pipeline model is presented with representative images in Table 4.

The first column in Table 4 presents the original video frame, the second column presents the ground truth (annotated mask), and the third column presents the segmentation mask obtained using the hybrid pipeline. Visually, there is very little difference between the ground truth masks and those from the hybrid pipeline. To better understand the results, we present a quantitative comparison of the performance of various models in Table 5 to an accuracy of two decimal places. The hybrid pipeline model yields an mIoU of 0.9641, providing an accurate segmentation of even challenging images and making the most of the temporal information available. When used as a part of a larger pipeline such as gaze tracking, achieving as accurate a segmentation of the regions of the eye as possible would only ensure better efficacy for the larger system.

Table 3 Different transformations on the data for augmentation: (a) original image, (b) introducing a glare (starburst pattern), (c) rotating the image, (d) lateral inversion, (e) cropping (and resizing) the image, (f) reducing brightness, and (g) introducing random bright spots in the image

Data augmentation

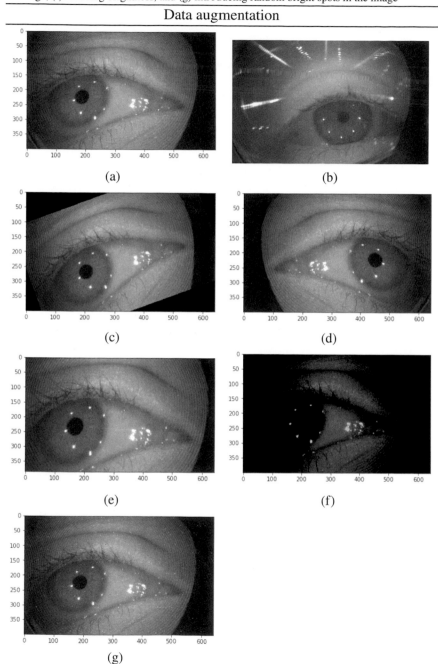

Table 4 A visual analysis of segmentation performance

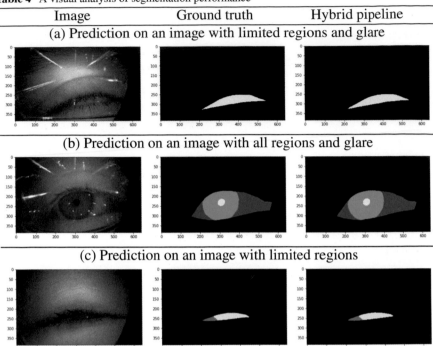

Image	Ground truth	Hybrid pipeline
(a) Prediction on an image with limited regions and glare
(b) Prediction on an image with all regions and glare
(c) Prediction on an image with limited regions

Table 5 A quantitative comparison of segmentation performance of various models

Segmentation model	mIoU
Dual-model CNN	0.84
Dual-model CNN + Data augmentation	0.90
Dual-model CNN + Attention gating	0.95
Hybrid segmentation model (see Fig. 1)	**0.96**

6 Conclusion

This paper details the rationale and evolution of models to develop a state-of-the-art pipeline to perform semantic segmentation of eye images obtained from video sequences recorded using VR/MR headsets. The final pipeline comprises a hybrid of traditional image preprocessing techniques with an ensemble of deep learning-based segmentation networks followed by a post-processing component that factors in temporal data, through using the mask generated on the previous image in the sequence to correct minor inconsistencies in the prediction. The use of standard architectures from the segmentation models package in the ensembled form contributes to the ease of training and execution. The final results achieved, quantified with an mIoU score of 0.9641 are seen to be very close to the ground truth. With the high mIoU score achieved, this pipeline is ideal for use in AR/VR/MR applications, to provide high quality, immersive, and interactive experiences or for any other applications, such as gaze tracking, that require a semantic segmentation of key regions of the eye.

References

1. Garbin SJ, Shen Y, Schuetz I, Cavin R, Hughes G, Talathi SS (2019) Openeds: open eye dataset
2. Sankowski W, Grabowski K, Napieralska M, Zubert M, Napieralski A (2010) Reliable algorithm for iris segmentation in eye image. Image Vis Comput 28(2):231 – 237. Segmentation of visible wavelength iris images captured at-a-distance and on-the-move. [Online]. Available: http://www.sciencedirect.com/science/article/pii/S0262885609001103
3. Das A, Pal U, Ferrer MA, Blumenstein M, Stepec D, Rot P, Emersic Z, Peer P, Struc V, Kumar SVA, Harish BS (2017) Sserbc 2017: Sclera segmentation and eye recognition benchmarking competition. In: 2017 IEEE international joint conference on biometrics (IJCB), pp 742–747
4. Rot P, Emersic Z, Struc V, Peer P (2018) Deep multi-class eye segmentation for ocular biometric. In: 2018 IEEE international work conference on bioinspired intelligence (IWOBI), pp 1–8
5. Boutros F, Damer N, Kirchbuchner F, Kuijper A (2019) Eye-mms: miniature multi-scale segmentation network of key eye-regions in embedded applications. In: Proceedings of the IEEE/CVF international conference on computer vision (ICCV) workshops
6. Perry J, Fernandez A (2019) Minenet: a dilated cnn for semantic segmentation of eye features. In: Proceedings of the IEEE/CVF international conference on computer vision (ICCV) Workshops
7. Palmero C, Sharma A, Behrendt K, Krishnakumar K, Komogortsev OV, Talathi SS (2020) Openeds2020: Open eyes dataset
8. Rao A, Mysore A, Ajri S, Guragol A, Sarkar P, Srinivasa G (2021) Automated segmentation of key structures of the eye using a light-weight two-step classifier. J Intell Fuzzy Syst, pp 1–7
9. Schlemper J, Oktay O, Schaap M, Heinrich M, Kainz B, Glocker B, Rueckert D (2018) Attention gated networks: learning to leverage salient regions in medical images
10. Ronneberger O, Fischer P, Brox T (2015) U-net: Convolutional networks for biomedical image segmentation. CoRR, vol. abs/1505.04597. [Online]. Available: http://arxiv.org/abs/1505.04597
11. Yakubovskiy P (2019) Segmentation models. https://github.com/qubvel/segmentation_models
12. Sudre CH, Li W, Vercauteren T, Ourselin S, Cardoso MJ (2017) Generalised dice overlap as a deep learning loss function for highly unbalanced segmentations. CoRR, vol. abs/1707.03237. [Online]. Available: http://arxiv.org/abs/1707.03237

EIDIMA: Edge-based Intrusion Detection of IoT Malware Attacks using Decision Tree-based Boosting Algorithms

D. Santhadevi and B. Janet

Abstract With the rise of smart gadgets and technology, anomalous traffic monitoring on the Internet has become a significant security challenge. Several assaults are causing havoc on the systems, lowering computing performance. Intrusion detection systems are one of the approaches that assist in determining the security of a system by raising an alert when an intrusion is detected. The EIDIMA framework is provided in this study as a distributed modular approach for detecting IoT malware network traffic during the monitoring phase instead of the attack phase. EIDIMA uses machine learning techniques, input vector databank, a decision-making module, and a subsample module for traffic categorization at edge devices. EIDIMA's classification performance is assessed using the F1-Score, accuracy, recall, and precision. This model is validated using the NSL-KDD and UNSW_IoT_Botnet benchmark datasets. The UNSW_IoT_Botnet dataset has an F1-score of 98.73% and an accuracy of 99.28%. On the NSL-KDD dataset, the F1-score and accuracy were both 99.50%.

Keywords IoT edge security · Machine learning · Gradient boosting ·
AdaBoosting · Histogram gradient boosting · Ensemble algorithms

1 Introduction

The Internet of things (IoT) [1] is a group of low-power intelligent gadgets that can communicate with cloud services via wired and wireless connections. Because IoT devices are more accessible to exploit than traditional PCs, criminals are increasingly targeting them with malware. This is due to various aspects [2], involving the accessibility of older devices that have not received defense updates, main concern placed on security during the development phase, and weak login credentials. Furthermore,

D. Santhadevi (✉) · B. Janet
National Institute of Technology, Tiruchirappalli, Tamil Nadu, India

B. Janet
e-mail: janet@nitt.edu

© The Author(s), under exclusive license to Springer Nature Singapore Pte Ltd. 2022   449
C. Satyanarayana et al. (eds.), *High Performance Computing and Networking*,
Lecture Notes in Electrical Engineering 853,
https://doi.org/10.1007/978-981-16-9885-9_37

with the rapid advancement of Internet technologies and the proliferation of IoT smart devices, the number of attacks has also increased [3]. Furthermore, many infected devices are projected to stay infected for an extended period. As a result, there is a strong incentive to identify these infected devices and take necessary action against them it does not do any more harm. However, as stated in [4], ensuring that all IoT devices are protected is pointless, and standard host-based finding and protecting techniques such as antivirus and firewalls are virtually impracticable to implement for IoT systems.

Hackers can send malicious traffic over ports like SMTP and HTTP that are frequently left open by systems. As a result, the need for advanced intrusion detection systems (IDS) grows. IDS is a key element of today's network security systems, monitoring network traffic, and looking for dangers. Signature-based detection and anomaly detection are the two types of IDS. An anomaly finding is based on establishing a regular activity summary of a system and detecting unknown attacks. Signature detection hunts only well-known patterns of attacks called harm signatures, whereas anomaly detection is established on an everyday activity summary of a system and detecting unknown attacks. In general, intrusion detection is seen to be a classification concern. In conventional classification tasks, the primary challenge is to reduce the risk of inaccuracy when making the classification decision. As a result, the most crucial consideration is how to select an accurate prediction strategy for developing reliable intrusion detection systems with good precision and minimal false positive rate. As a result, network-based instead of host-based secure mechanisms are required for the IoT environment.

In this study, a method for identifying IoT malware action in small and large-scale networks, such as business networks, was suggested. According to our suggested approach, machine learning (ML) techniques operating at the client entrance gateway; detect malicious movement based on scanning network traffic flow patterns. A databank retains network traffic patterns of malware and allows them to be retrieved or updated. After malicious gateway traffic is identified, a decision-making module determines the following line of action. It also comes with an optional packet subsampling module that may be used to link IoT devices to a single access gateway.

Further, this paper is divided into four portions. Section 2 summarizes the work being done in this area. The description of the dataset and the methodology utilized in this work are detailed in Sect. 3. Section 4 evaluates and discusses the findings. This research's findings and future direction are presented in Sect. 5.

2   Related Works

This section will investigate the research that has been done so far in the field of IoT intrusion detection. Reference [5] outlines an IoT device intrusion detection method based on an allow list (Heimdall). Reference [6] offers an intrusion detection system for IoT network infrastructures that identifies network assaults using two-layer dimensionality reduction and two-tier classification algorithms. The research community has recently become interested in IoT malicious bots and assault detection, resulting in a few articles addressing these issues. Anomaly detection using deep-autoencoders was utilized for identifying IoT botnet assaults in [7]. A few studies have concentrated on developing standard communication summaries for IoT devices that are unlikely to change significantly over time. DEFT [8] built standard device traffic fingerprints using machine learning techniques at software-defined network controllers and access gateways, while [9] provides a solution to automatically construct manufacturer usage descriptions for a wide range of consumer IoT devices. The authors in [10] presented a mechanism for classifying commonly utilized IoT gadgets into different device categories and creating regular traffic summaries, with any variation from some of those patterns being marked as abnormal activity.

Our research fills a few crucial holes in the narrative once it discriminates among IoT devices' legal and botnet traffic. The earliest research is on identifying botnets using their control and communication characteristics [5–7, 11] are meant for personal computer-based botnets, not for IoT botnets. Next, the goal is to detect network activity created by individual bots rather than botnets (networks of bots). Because IoT botnets often comprise tens of billions to millions of devices dispersed across broad geographic areas, so detecting up an entire IoT bot on the network is unfeasible. As a result, unlike [10, 11], this study does not involve the use of computationally intensive clustering techniques. Third, unlike [7, 10], the goal is to identify IoT malware activity during the monitoring phase, long before the actual assault. Finally, rather than fingerprinting IoT device traffic [8, 10] exploiting those fingerprints to identify anomalies and identifying malware-induced network traffic load created with compromised IoT gadgets. This is due to the limitation within the old technique, such as the risk of misclassifying contaminated devices as genuine devices, evaluation with simple malware. This can make it difficult to detect other types of malware. The final method has its own drawbacks since it is not immune to newly found malware when monitoring traffic features that have not been upgraded in the registry. This study advocate for a hybrid method that includes IoT gadget anomaly identification with scanning network traffic flow.

3 Materials and Method

3.1 Experimental Setup

The NSL-KDD and UNSW_IoT_Botnet datasets are utilized to develop the intrusion detection system. For categorization of assaults, a decision tree (DT)-based boosting technique is used. The NSL-KDD [12] is a benchmark dataset that contains 41 attributes. UNSW_IoT_Botnet [13] is created by building a realistic IoT network environment with primary components of network architecture, fabricated IoT facilities, and feature extraction techniques. The Argus tool was employed for extracting the necessary data features from the dataset. There are over 72 million records and 46 attributes in the generated dataset. The attribute assessment approach is used to reduce dimensionality, which aids in improving the intrusion detection system's performance in terms of time and space.

The models are trained and tested in the hardware environment of the Windows 10 operating system with an i7 processor along with GPU, 6 cores of CPU, 8 GB RAM. The scikit-learn machine learning library provides an experimental implementation of a machine learning algorithm that supports the boosting technique.

3.2 Proposed Method

EIDIMA is our suggested method for identifying scanning traffic created by IoT malicious nodes using a machine learning technique, as illustrated in Fig. 1. It is built with five separate modules:

The machine learning classifier module operates on the access gateway associated with IoT gadgets on the client's premises or in the company. It takes incoming traffic samples, derives selected features for those data, and classifies them using a machine learning model. The ML classifiers are discussed in further depth in the next section.

Machine learning model constructor trains the model for categorizing access gateway data packets using feature vectors and targeted labels. It has been taken from the database and given as input to the classification algorithm. The decision

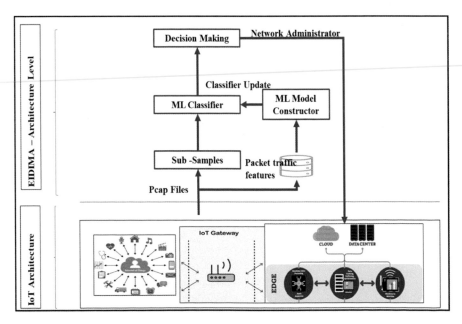

Fig. 1 EIDIMA framework for IoT environment

tree-based ensemble algorithms such as random forest, AdaBoost, gradient boosting, and histogram gradient boosting are used for classification. After that, the model is passed to the machine learning classifier. When a different malware variant is found, the machine learning model must be trained and evaluated to the current model's classification performance. The current ML model is used since there is no notable increase in concert; if not, the ML classifier module is updated with the trained-up ML model.

The databank contains a list of input feature vectors taken from network flow sections gathered from gateways linked to contaminated IoT devices and not afflicted devices. The databank is updated regularly to include newly found malware. The constructor retrieves the input features and matches target labels to train the ML classifier initially, and then, it will update the classifier whenever a new virus is detected. The group of researchers, business professionals, and consumers will employ honeypots, consumer access gateways, and other means to collect network traffic data to detect malicious activity. The network feature database is updated whenever a different pattern of traffic appears.

The decision-making module contains an inventory of policies set by network administrators that determine the plan of action to be performed once the ML classifier has categorized network flow from the edge gateway as mischievous. For instance, a network administrator can ban all bot activity and only let them back online once the device becomes normal from malicious activities.

The subsampling module collects packet data from IoT devices over time and across devices and feeds it into the machine learning classifier module. By giving only a portion of the coming packet data, this unit can significantly minimize the cost function of the ML classifier module.

3.3 Machine Learning Algorithms

The fundamental goal of machine learning is to create applications that learn from data and aid in improving decision-making processes or improve prediction accuracy over time. The machine learning algorithms help churn out a large amount of data that can be used to generate decisions and predictions based on a fresh batch of data. It consists of many statistical processing moves that have been trained to assist in the discovery of various patterns and characteristics. When this algorithm gives high accuracy, decision, and prediction, it is deemed to be superior. Five distinct machine learning algorithms are utilized: A decision tree and the others are ensemble boosting techniques based on decision trees. The main principle of constructing an ensemble model is to do it progressively by training each base model estimator one at a time using decision trees.

Random forest [14] is a method for learning in groups. The algorithm's core concept is that constructing a tiny decision tree with few attributes is a computationally inexpensive procedure. It can create multiple tiny, weak decision trees simultaneously, then average or using the majority vote to unite the trees into a single, powerful learner.

AdaBoost basically combines numerous week base learners, trained sequentially across numerous cycles of training data. Therefore, higher weights are applied to those misclassified learners throughout the training of week base learners.

A gradient boosting machine (GBM) [15] integrates predictions from several decision trees to provide final predictions. Every decision tree node uses a distinct collection of characteristics to choose the optimum split. Furthermore, each new tree takes into consideration the prior trees' flaws or faults. As a result, each consecutive decision tree is constructed on the prior trees' faults.

Histogram gradient boosting, the histograms formed during training that time the feature vector is continually bucketed into discrete bins. These bins are used to create feature histograms. Because it uses fewer resources and takes less time to learn, histogram-based estimators can be orders of magnitude faster than gradient boosting claim when the quantity of data is in the hundreds of millions.

Decision Tree Algorithm:

Step1: Tree begins with root node R and has complete dataset D.

Step2: Find the best features in the D applying Gini Index.

Step3: Divide the R into subtrees called subsets that have the best possible values of attributes.

Step4: Generate a decision tree node that has the best attribute.

Step5: Step 3 may be used to create new decision trees recursively. Carry on in this manner until it reaches the final node (leaf node), which cannot be categorized any further.

Random Forest Algorithm:

Step1: Select the random samples S from a dataset D.

Step2: It will construct the decision tree for each sample and predict the result.

Step3: Performed voting for selecting the predicted result from all samples.

Step4: Final prediction result will be selected based on the highest voted.

AdaBoost Algorithm:

Step1: Select training dataset D and initial weight of loss function $w_i = 1$.
Where $D = \{(X_i, y_i)\}_{i=1}^{N}$, $X_i \in R^k$, $y_i \in \{-1, 1\}$.

Step2: Set the number of weak learners $f_m(X) \in \{-1, 1\}$ and Loss function I.

$$I(f_m(X), y) = \begin{cases} 0, & \text{if } f_m(X) \neq y_i \\ 1, & \text{if } f_m(X) = y_i \end{cases}$$

Setp3: Fit the week classifier m.

　　　For I from 1 to N.

　　　For m = 1 to M do.

　　　　　Minimize the loss (objective function)

$$E_m = \frac{\sum_{i=1}^{N} w_i^{(m)} I(f_m(X) \neq y_i)}{\sum_i w_i^{(m)}}$$

$$\propto_m = \ln \frac{1 - E_m}{E_m}$$

　　　For all i do

$$w_i^{(m+1)} = w_i^{(m)} e^{\propto_m I(f_m(X) \neq y_i)}$$

　　End For
　　End For
　　End For

Step4: Repeat step 4 until the best prediction with lesser loss.

Gradient Boosting Algorithm:

Step1: Input training set $D = \{(x_i, y_i)\}_{i=1}^{N}$, a differentiable loss function $L(y, F(x))$. Model initialization with a constant value,

$$F_0(x) = \arg\min \sum_{i=1}^{n} L(y_i, \beta).$$

Step2: For m = 1 to M.

• Compute pseudo-residuals

$$r_{im} = \left[\frac{\partial L(y_i F(x_i))}{\partial F(x_i)} \right]_{F(x)=F_{m-1}(x)} \quad \text{for} \quad i = 1, \ldots, n.$$

- Fit the base learner $h_m(x)$ to pseudo- residuals and train the model.
- Compute multiplier β_m

$$\beta_m = \text{argmin} \sum_{i=1}^{n} L(y_i, F_{m-1}(x_i) + \beta h_m(x_i))$$

- Update the model

  o $F_m(x) = F_{m-1}(x) + \beta h_m(x)$

  Step 3: Final model $F_M(x)$.

4   Result Analysis

The proposed model is evaluated with the following performance metrics represented in the Eqs. (1) to (4).

$$\text{Accuracy} = \frac{TP + TN}{TP + TN + FP + FN} \tag{1}$$

$$\text{Precision} = \frac{TP}{TP + FP} \tag{2}$$

$$\text{Recall} = \frac{TP}{TP + FN}. \tag{3}$$

$$\text{F1 - Score} = 2* \frac{\text{Precision*Recall}}{(\text{Precision} + \text{Recall})} \tag{4}$$

Figures 2 and 3 represent the graphical representation of performance metrics of the proposed model, which is trained and tested with the UNSW_IoT_Botnet dataset and NSL-KDD dataset. Both accuracy and recall values were improved using the histogram gradient boosting classifier model, and it can be called the best classifier in this paper. This indicates that the model is capable of appropriately distinguishing between normal and attack situations. This is due to the network's subsampling and update of the ML classifier whenever unfamiliar patterns are discovered. Another factor for achieving higher accuracy is binning. This model utilizes 255 bins by default for each discrete input vector; however, this may be modified using the "max

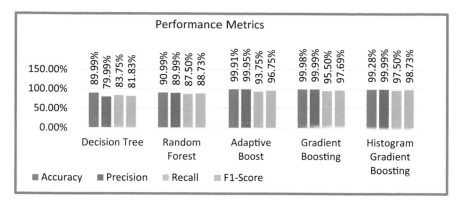

Fig. 2 Performance metrics of the proposed framework with ML model tested on UNSW_IoT_Botnet dataset

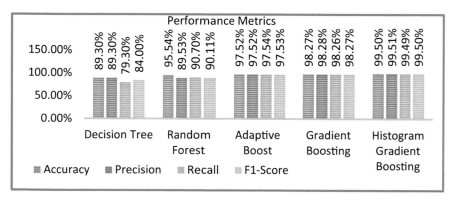

Fig. 3 Performance metrics of the proposed framework with ML model tested on NSL-KDD dataset

bins" option. The number of trees that can be planted is limited to 50 to achieve higher accuracy.

Figure 4 is the confusion matrix of the best classifier; it shows that false negative and true negative rates are meager in the UNSW_IoT_Botnet dataset, which means the classifier identifies the malware packets accurately. NSL_KDD dataset is a multiclass classifier; it has four malware classes and a normal. Malware is classified into classes 1 to 4 as DoS, probing, R2L, U2R, respectively, and class 0 represents normal. The best model classifies the malware classes 1 to 3 accurately and classes four as normal instead of malware due to the root access. Even though, this model raises lower false alarms than the other classifier.

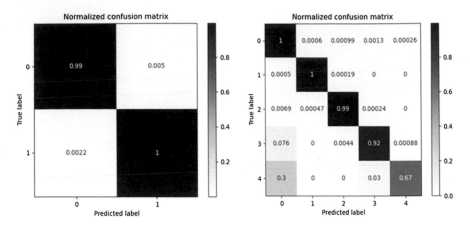

Fig. 4 Confusion matrix of best classifier (histogram gradient boosting)

5 Conclusion

In this paper, the preliminary results of the malware detection system using decision tree-based boosting algorithms have been presented. The proposed approach analyzes the malware activity captured by means of network traffic data at the edge of the IoT network gateway. The suggested framework increased accuracy, precision, recall, and F1-score, according to experimental data. The UNSW_IoT_Botnet dataset scored 99.28, 99.99, 97.50, and 98.73 for these four measures, while in the NSL-KDD dataset, it scored 99.50, 99.51, 99.49, and 99.50 for the same four criteria. This demonstrates that the new framework is prosperous and resilient in identifying destructive habits in IoT settings and the NSL-KDD traditional network traffic dataset. Future work will be dedicated to evaluating the scalability of the proposed methods and further improvements toward the knowledge transfer paradigm and real-time traffic analysis with deep learning concepts.

References

1. Al-Fuqaha A, Guizani M, Mohammadi M, Aledhari M, Ayyash M, Internet of things: a survey on enabling technologies, protocols, and applications. IEEE Commun Surv Tutorials 17(4):2347–2376
2. Yang Y, Wu L, Yin G, Li L, Zhao H (2017) A survey on security and privacy issues in internet-of-things. IEEE Internet Things J 4(5):1250–1258
3. Kumar S, Yadav A, Increasing performance of intrusion detection system using neural network. 2014 IEEE international conference on advanced communication control and technologies
4. Yu T, Sekar V, Seshan S, Agarwal Y, Xu C (2015) Handling a trillion (unfixable) flaws on a billion devices: rethinking network security for the internet-of-things. In: Proceedings of the 14th ACM workshop on hot topics in networks, ser. HotNets-XIV. New York, NY, USA: ACM, pp 5:1–5:7. https://doi.org/10.1145/2834050.2834095

5. Habibi J, Midi D, Mudgerikar A, Bertino E (2017) Heimdall: mitigating the internet of insecure things. IEEE Internet Things J 4(4):968–978
6. Pajouh HH, Javidan R, Khayami R, Ali D, Choo KKR (2016) A two-layer dimension reduction and two-tier classification model for anomaly-based intrusion detection in IoT backbone networks. IEEE Trans Emerg Top Comput PP(99):1–1
7. Meidan Y, Bohadana M, Mathov Y, Mirsky Y, Breitenbacher D, Shabtai A, Elovici Y (2018) N-baiot: network-based detection of IoT botnet attacks using deep autoencoders. CoRR abs/1805.03409. [Online]. Available: http://arxiv.org/abs/1805.03409
8. Thangavelu, Divakaran DM, Sairam R, Bhunia SS, Gurusamy M (2018) Deft: a distributed IoT fingerprinting technique. IEEE Int Things J 1–1
9. Hamza A, Ranathunga D, Gharakheili HH, Roughan M, Sivaraman V (2018) Clear as mud: generating, validating and applying iot behavioral profiles. In: Proceedings of the 2018 workshop on IoT security and privacy, ser. IoT S&P '18. New York, NY, USA: ACM, pp 8–14. [Online]. Available: https://doi.org/10.1145/3229565.3229566
10. Nguyen TD, Marchal S, Miettinen M, Dang MH, Asokan N, Sadeghi A (2018) Dïot: a crowdsourced self-learning approach for detecting compromised IoT devices. CoRR abs/1804.07474. [Online]. Available: http://arxiv.org/abs/1804.07474
11. Livadas C, Walsh R, Lapsley D, Strayer WT (Nov 2006) Using machine learning techniques to identify botnet traffic. In: Proceedings. 2006 31st IEEE conference on local computer networks. pp 967–974
12. Olusola AA, Oladele AS, Abosede DO (2010) Analysis of NSL KDD'99 intrusion detection dataset for selection of relevance features. Proceedings of the world congress on engineering and computer science, vol 1
13. Koroniotis N, Moustafa N, Sitnikova E, Turnbull B (2019) Towards the development of realistic botnet dataset in the internet of things for network forensic analytics: bot-IoT dataset. Futur Gener Comput Syst 100:779–796
14. Joshi S, Upadhyay H, Lagos L, Akkipeddi NS, Guerra V (2018) Machine learning approach for malware detection using random forest classifier on process list data structure. ACM-Comput Mach 98–102. https://doi.org/10.1145/3206098.3206113
15. Zhao D, et al (2013) Botnet detection based on traffic behavior analysis and flow intervals. Comput Secure 39(PARTA):2–16. https://doi.org/10.1016/j.cose.2013.04.007

Market Basket Analysis Recommender System using Apriori Algorithm

Samarth Vaishampayan, Gururaj Singh, Vinayakprasad Hebasur, and Rupali Kute

Abstract Market basket analysis is a data processing methodology for discovering relationships between different items. The primary goal of market basket analysis in retail is to provide information to the distributor about a customer's purchasing habits, which can aid the distributor in making the best choices. Market basket analysis can be performed using a variety of algorithms. This paper compares two popular market basket analysis techniques, to determine which approach is optimal for rule generation and visualization on a common dataset. The results can be used as a guide for cross-selling, creating promotions, and determining the best location for products in the store to boost sales.

Keywords Market basket analysis · Apriori algorithm · Association rule mining · Eclat algorithm · R programming

1 Introduction

Getting a shopping cart is usually the first thing to do when in the supermarket. Some things will be placed in the shopping cart. Most of these things may have been chosen based on a pre-planned shopping list, while others may have been chosen on the spur of the moment. It is assumed that the contents of the cart are registered when checking out of the supermarket because the supermarket wants to observe whether any patterns in selection occur from one consumer to the next [1]. A random pattern founds in supermarket sales data can be represented as a rule in the following

S. Vaishampayan · G. Singh (✉) · R. Kute
Department of Electronics and Communication Engineering, Dr. Vishwanath Karad MIT World Peace University, Kothrud, Pune 411038, India

R. Kute
e-mail: rupali.kute@mitwpu.edu.in

V. Hebasur
Distribution Business Unit, Cummins India Limited, Pune 411045, India
e-mail: vinayakprasad.hebasur@cummins.com

© The Author(s), under exclusive license to Springer Nature Singapore Pte Ltd. 2022
C. Satyanarayana et al. (eds.), *High Performance Computing and Networking*,
Lecture Notes in Electrical Engineering 853,
https://doi.org/10.1007/978-981-16-9885-9_38

manner: The rule {Lays Masala Magic, Cold drink} => {Five Star} If a client buys spicy Lays chips with a cold drink they are likely to buy Five Star as well.

The market basket analysis is one of the most prevalent and useful types of information analysis for selling and marketing. The goal of market basket analysis is to figure out which products customers will buy together. The term "market basket analysis" comes from the idea of customers putting all their purchases in a handcart or "market basket" when they shop at the grocery store. Knowing which products clients would buy in bulk can be extremely valuable to a distributor.

Implementing market basket analysis into inter-business marketing has various advantages. MBA examines the products that people frequently buy together. The data are then analyzed to determine whether goods can be cross-sold and as a result, should be promoted together [2].

Some of the advantages are given below:

Market Basket Analysis Aids in In-Store Logistics Optimization:

Prioritizing customers' purchase patterns help marketers optimize their in-store applications since market basket analysis is based on the collection of many data points, which includes getting data from multiple customer types. Optimized in-store applications let customers have better omnichannel experiences, which lead to more sales revenue and a higher return on marketing investment (ROMI) [3].

Marketing and Sales Promotion Optimization:

Market basket analysis in inter-business marketing aids in the enhancement of inter-business advertising campaigns by grouping products or offerings that have a greater possibility of purchase [4].

Aids in the assessment of customer behavior:

The identification and optimization of micro-environmental elements can be aided by a thorough examination of client behavior. Identifying and prioritizing major market participants aids marketers in cultivating long-term value exchanges between them and their customers [5].

Higher sales and improved return on investment:

Predictive sales analytics paves the way for higher sales efficiency and income. Market basket analysis in inter-business marketing enables retailers to tap into previously untapped revenue opportunities [6].

Gaining a larger sales figure:

Market basket analysis can be used to link purchases to demographic and socioeconomic information. Advertising of products aids in the enhancement of client behavior, resulting in increased sales revenue [4].

2 Literature Review

For several decades, data mining has become an integral component of marketing literature. Market basket analysis is one of the initial data mining techniques and the finest representation of mining association rules. Researchers have generated a set of algorithms for association rule mining (ARM) to assist users in accomplishing their tasks [7].

The Apriori algorithm was devised by Ramakrishnan Srikant and Rakesh Agrawal [8], and it is one of the classic techniques for identifying common patterns for Boolean association rules.

The authors expand on the idea of extracting quantitative rules from huge relational tables.

Julander [9] looked at the proportion of consumers who bought a certain product as well as the proportion of overall sales produced by that product.

Making such connections allows one to quickly determine which goods are the most popular and what percentage of sales they account for. Measuring which items are the most popular is critical since a significant number of customers are exposed to various product kinds daily. Because the departments with the most popular items create the most in-store traffic, it is critical to use this data to strategically place other specialized goods nearby. Because the departments with the most popular items create the most in-store traffic, it is critical to use this data to strategically place other specialized goods nearby. The method of developing association rules is another important area of research in the realm of exploratory analysis.

Berry and Linoff [10] focused on identifying buying trends by extracting connections or co-occurrences from transactional data from a retailer. Customers that buy bread frequently also buy milk, butter, or jam, which are all connected to bread. It makes sense to put these groups next to one other in a shopping mall so that shoppers can get to them easily.

3 Apriori Algorithm, Methodology, and Implementation

After experimentation on various parameters for both the algorithms "Apriori algorithm" and "Eclat algorithm", the Apriori algorithm was chosen for the implementation of market basket analysis on a standard dataset. The following flowchart was followed by the authors for implementation (see Fig. 1).

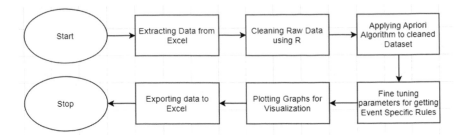

Fig. 1 Experimentation flowchart

3.1 Association Rule Mining

The process of extracting rules from a transaction object through an algorithm to analyze relationships between different items occurring in the dataset in an **{If} =>** **{Then}** format.

Marketing, basket data analysis (or market basket analysis) in retailing, clustering, and classification are some of the uses of association rule mining. By developing a set of rules known as association rules, the buying patterns of customers can be captured [11].

Example of Frequent Itemset:

{Product 3, Product 4}
Example of Association Rule Mining:
{Product 3} - > {Product 4}
The rules formed are assessed by 3 variables which are described as below:

Support:
Formula: (Frequency (A, B))/ (Total Transactions).
Support (Product 1 = > Product 3) = 3/5 = 0.6 (see Table 1).

Confidence:
Formula: (Frequency (A, B))/(Frequency(A)).
Confidence (Product 1 = > Product 3) = ¾ = 0.75 (see Table 1).

Lift:

Table 1 Standard transaction object

TID	Items
1	{Product 1, Product 2, Product 3, Product 4}
2	{Product 6, Product 3, Product 4, Product 7}
3	{Product 1, Product 2, Product 3, Product 7}
4	{Product 1, Product 2}
5	{Product 1, Product 3, Product 4, Product 5}

Formula: (Frequency (A, B))/(Frequency(A)* Frequency(B)).
Lift (Product 1 = > Product 3) = ¾*¼ = 3/16 = 0.1875 (see Table 1).

3.2 Apriori Algorithm

Apriori algorithms work in multiple iterations. The number of iterations depends on the support threshold set and the complexity of the transaction object.

The basic principle behind the algorithm is that the superset of any infrequent itemset is not tested. Apriori starts with comparing the individual items' support threshold and then goes on to increase the combination number over different iterations. Once the frequent itemset is generated, confidence is calculated for each itemset and the combination with the best confidence score is mined as a rule [6].

The Apriori algorithm is the most essential algorithm for creating association rules. This algorithm was created to work with transactional databases. It operates by generating association rules based on thresholds and finding items for a frequent item collection based on a minimal support [12].

4 Experimentation and Results

The experimentation involved two algorithms—"Apriori algorithm" and Eclat algorithm for market basket analysis. It was to compare these two based on various parameters and the algorithm which was best suited to the application was finally chosen.

The dataset on which the support was set, consisted of 29,265 rows and 2 columns being "invoice number" and "product ID". The total number of transactions was 17,767.

The correlation between the support and the number of rules for a fixed confidence threshold helps understand the dataset better. The correlation is always of the type "negative correlation" as support is lowered the number of rules increases. The reason behind this type of relationship also helps in understanding the working of these rule mining algorithms. As the support is lowered the sample space for algorithms to mine rules increases, hence results in the formation of more rules (see Fig. 2).

Fig. 2 Graph of minimum
support threshold versus
number of rules

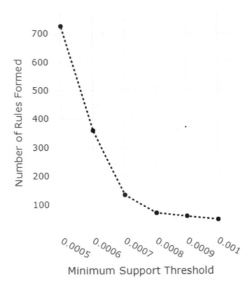

4.1 Visualization of Time Taken by Algorithms on Different Steps of Execution

(a)   Transaction Setting Time:

Transaction setting time is the time required for the algorithm to read the transaction object generated inside the algorithm system for its further analysis for rule generation.

The below graph shows the comparison between the transaction setting time in the 2 algorithms which are considered.

The X-axis contains the sample support threshold, and the Y-axis contains the transaction setting time in seconds (Fig. 3).

(b)   Pattern Finding Time:

Pattern finding time is the time required for the algorithm to read the transaction object and create relationships between objects in the dataset using predefined mechanisms, i.e., "transaction tree" in Apriori algorithm and "sparse bit matrix" in Eclat algorithm.

The above graph shows the comparison between the pattern finding time in the 2 algorithms under consideration.

The X-axis contains the sample support threshold, and the Y-axis contains the pattern finding time in seconds.

Rules writing time is the time required for the algorithm after analyzing the pattern received through either "transaction tree" or "sparse bit matrix" to output the rules in "if–then" format along with the support, confidence, lift, and count.

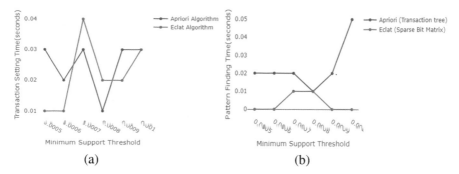

Fig. 3 **a** Graph of minimum support threshold versus transaction setting time (in seconds), **b** graph of minimum support threshold versus pattern finding time (in seconds)

Fig. 4 Graph of minimum support threshold versus rules writing time (in seconds)

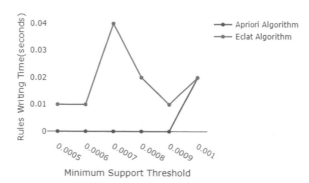

The below graph shows the comparison between the rules writing time in the 2 algorithms under consideration.

The X-axis contains the sample support threshold, and the Y-axis contains the pattern finding time in seconds (Figs. 4, 5, and 6).

After an assessment of various parameters, the Apriori algorithm was found to be better suited for this experiment.

4.2 Analysis after Experimentation

Analysis of Rule Formation using Apriori Algorithm:
See Fig. 7, which indicates the successful execution of the Apriori algorithm to the standard dataset.

Console output after applying Apriori algorithm in R language:
Apriori
Parameter specification:

	ID	Description			
			20	2350HZFH	HEINZ CHILLI SAUCE 300G
1	9320LWFW	1/3" STEALTH TWISTER FRIES 2.27KG	21	5461NVCR	BOTTEGA ZELACHI SHREDDED MOZZARELLA CHEESE 1KG
2	4250TSFR	ESPRIT DE TURSAN AOC WHITE	22	2561LBFM	CREMIERE DE FRANCE UHT WHOLE MILK 1L
3	1170FBCB	PETIT NORMAND U/S BUTTER FOIL 250G	23	2710WSFS	VIVO CLASSICO SHEET MARGARINE 1 KG
4	9230LWFW	1/4" SHOESTRING CUT - HIFRIES 2.04KG	24	2990JMFN	CREAM CHEESE 2KG
5	2320HZFH	HEINZ TOMATO KETCHUP 300G	25	2330HZFH	HEINZ TOMATO KETCHUP A10 3.3KG
6	2100UFFJ	UFC 100% PINEAPPLE JUICE 1L	26	2400HZFH	BELL ORTO PASTA SAUCE A10 2.98KG
7	2561LBFM	CREMIERE DE FRANCE UHT WHOLE MILK 1L	27	5410NVCR	BOTTEGA ZELACHI CHEDDAR CHEESE BLOCK 2KG
8	1690LBFN	FROMAGIO CHEESE GRATED 1KG	28	5490NVCR	BOTTEGA ZELACHI MARGARINE PALFFY U/S 5KG
9	1820BGFN	DAIRYMONT CREAM CHEESE 2KG	29	9110LWFW	LAMBWESTON GREEN PEAS 1KG
10	2710WSFS	VIVO CLASSICO SHEET MARGARINE 1 KG	30	2440HZFH	HEINZ YELLOW MUSTARD 255G
11	1560TAFC	TATUA WHIPPING CREAM 36% 1L	31	2480COFM	CONAPROLE UHT MILK FULL CREAM 1L
12	2440HZFH	HEINZ YELLOW MUSTARD 255G	32	7004ELFO	CRESPO SLICED BLACK OLIVES 2840ML
13	1520LBFN	FROMAGIO CHEESE BLOCK ~3.5KG	33	9290LWFW	SUPER SWEET CUT CORN 1KG
14	2480COFM	CONAPROLE UHT MILK FULL CREAM 1L	34	4300TSFR	ESPRIT DE TURSAN AOC RED
15	4290TSFR	ESPRIT DE TURSAN AOC ROSE	35	2610WSFS	MARGARINE PALFFY UNSALTED 15KG
16	5460NVCR	BOTTEGA ZELACHI SHREDDED MOZZARELLA CHEESE 1KG	36	9290LWFW	SUPER SWEET CUT CORN 1KG
17	9230LWFW	1/4" SHOESTRING CUT - HIFRIES 2.04KG	37	5461NVCR	BOTTEGA ZELACHI SHREDDED MOZZARELLA CHEESE 1KG
18	9260LWFW	1/2" REGULAR CUT 2.27KG			
19	3010HZFH	HEINZ CHILLI SAUCE 3.3KG			

Fig. 5 Description of product IDs

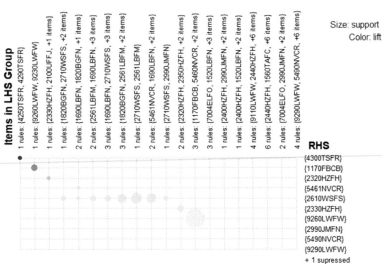

Fig. 6 Balloon plot

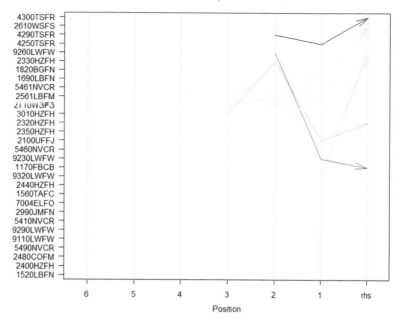

Fig. 7 Para-coord plot

confidence	minval	smax	arem	aval	originalSupport	maxtime	support	minlen	maxlen	target	ext
0.9	0.1	1	non	FALSE	TRUE	5	0.001	1	10	Rules	TRUE

Algorithmic control:

filter	tree	heap	memopt	load	sort	verbose
0.1	TRUE	TRUE	FALSE	TRUE	2	TRUE

Absolute minimum support count: 1/.

4.3   Visualization of Rules after Analysis

Below is the ItemID-Description matching table for reference during the visual analysis of the market basket through graphs.

Using Method Grouped

This method provides a grouped matrix-like visualization, its other name is balloon plot and provides efficient analysis with easy interpretation of the relationship between LHS and RHS using balloon-like figures. The size of the balloons represents the support of the relationship between the items and the color represents the lift.

Using method Para-Coord

This method of visualization focuses on uniquely representing rules. The thickness of the line determines the support of the rule formed, and the orientation of the line shows the relationship between the items present in the rules.

5   Conclusion

The greater choice of products available to customers, as well as the fierce competition among sales shops, has put new constraints on marketing decision-makers. There is a growing requirement to manage long-term relationships with clients. In data mining applications, association rules play a critical role in identifying interesting patterns in databases. Apriori is the most basic technique for extracting interesting threads from a customer's transaction dataset.

For market basket analysis of consumers' transaction data, pattern matching mining has been widely employed to reveal the hidden patterns that exist in transactional datasets.

This study examines the core of market basket analysis and focuses on the intensive comparison between the two prominent algorithms which are used to implement market basket analysis, Apriori, and Eclat. Following the experimentation, the study analyzes the implementation, visualization of market basket analysis with the superior algorithm (Apriori) after the experimentation, which fits the need for the given general transactional dataset.

Cross-selling, generating promotions, and identifying the optimal positioning for items in the shop to enhance sales may all be guided by this analysis.

Acknowledgements The authors would like to thank Cummins India Limited, Pune for sponsoring the project, and the teams involved for their invaluable support and guidance which led to this research work.

References

1. Loshin D (2013) Business intelligence, 2nd edn
2. Hemalatha M (2012) Market basket analysis—a data mining application in Indian retailing. Int J Bus Inf Syst 10:109–129. https://doi.org/10.1504/IJBIS.2012.046683
3. Chen J, Yang X, Chen L, Dong L, Fu Y (2010) An analysis of shopping basket in a supermarket. 2010 2nd IEEE international conference on information management and engineering. pp 486–489. https://doi.org/10.1109/ICIME.2010.5478116
4. Gupta N, Yadav ML (2014) An implementation and analysis of DSR using market basket analysis to improve the sales of business. 2014 5th international conference—confluence the next generation information technology summit (Confluence). pp 82–86. https://doi.org/10.1109/CONFLUENCE.2014.6949249
5. Maske A, Joglekar B (2018)Survey on frequent item-set mining approaches in market basket analysis. 2018 fourth international conference on computing communication control and automation (ICCUBEA). pp 1–5. https://doi.org/10.1109/ICCUBEA.2018.8697776
6. Maske A, Joglekar B (2018) Survey on frequent item-set mining approaches in market basket analysis. 2018 fourth international conference on computing communication control and automation (ICCUBEA). pp1–5. https://doi.org/10.1109/ICCUBEA.2018.869777
7. Setiawan A, Budhi GS, Setiabudi DH, Djunaidy R (2017) Data mining applications for sales information system using market basket analysis on stationery company. 2017 International conference on soft computing, intelligent system, and information technology (ICSIIT). pp 337–340. https://doi.org/10.1109/ICSIIT.2017.39
8. Agrawal R, Srikant R (Sept 1994) Fast algorithms for mining association rules. In: Processing of VLDB '94. Santiago, Chile, pp 487–499
9. Julander. Basket analysis: a new way of analyzing scanner data. Int J Retail Distrib Manage 20(7):10–18
10. Berry, Linoff (2004) Data mining techniques for marketing, sales and customer relationship management, (2nd edn). Hungry Minds Inc.
11. Nengsih W (2015) A comparative study on market basket analysis and Apriori association technique. 2015 3rd international conference on information and communication technology (ICoICT). pp 461–464. https://doi.org/10.1109/ICoICT.2015.7231468
12. Mittal M (2014) Efficient ordering policy for imperfect quality items using association rule mining. https://doi.org/10.4018/978-1-4666-5888-2.ch074

Meta-Analysis to Prognosis Myocardial Infarction Using 12 Lead ECG

N. Jothiaruna and A. Anny Leema

Abstract Cardiovascular disease is caused by heart or blood vessels. It creates immediate heart arrest or a blockage and leads to death. Nearly 70% of people are suffering from these diseases. One of the major diseases that affect the heart is myocardial infarction (MI). MI occurs when there is some damage to the heart muscle. There are various test measures for diagnosing myocardial infarction. A common way to diagnose heart diseases in the medical field is electrocardiogram (ECG). In diagnosing MI through ECG, the changes that occur in the ECG wave are ST-Elevation MI (STEMI), non-ST-elevation MI (NSTEMI), and left bundle branch block (LBBB). In this study, we discuss different classification methods for the diagnosis of MI. Before the classification of the diseases, preprocessing is a preliminary task to achieve accurate information. In comparison with KNN, SVM, and YOLOv3 algorithm, LSTM could give better classification results for the diagnosis of MI. In the future, our research can be carried out on automatic diagnosis of the diseases, by using current trends of deep learning models.

Keywords Myocardial infarction · STEMI · NSTEMI · LBBB · ECG · Cardiovascular · Preprocessing · Classification

1 Introduction

Myocardial infarction (MI) is a type of heart disease. Myocardial means muscle damage at the heart and infarction means tissue death [1]. It occurs when blood flow to the heart muscle is blocked at some point. Through arteries, blood and oxygen flow to the heart muscle is carried out [2]. While passing, some fatty or plaque formation occurs in a blood vessel, and blood flow to the heart muscle will stop or be blocked.

N. Jothiaruna (✉) · A. A. Leema
School of Information Technology and Engineering (SITE), Vellore Institute of Technology, Vellore, India

A. A. Leema
e-mail: annyleema.a@vit.ac.in

© The Author(s), under exclusive license to Springer Nature Singapore Pte Ltd. 2022   473
C. Satyanarayana et al. (eds.), *High Performance Computing and Networking*,
Lecture Notes in Electrical Engineering 853,
https://doi.org/10.1007/978-981-16-9885-9_39

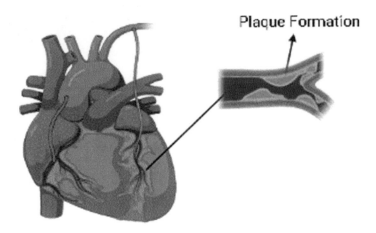

Fig. 1 Myocardial infarction [5]

If it stops blood flow will not occur, the supply of oxygen will also stop. If it happens tissue or muscle death will occur, then it leads to a heart attack (MI). Figure 1 shows the plaque formation [3] and clotting of blood circulation [4]. For diagnosing MI tests like electrocardiogram (ECG) which is 12 lead ECG, cholesterol level, and troponin I measures are used.

In this study, the discussion is mainly based on the existing work carried for classifying cardiovascular diseases using machine learning algorithms and also with different test measures undergone for diagnosing heart diseases. And in the future, we are planning to carry out work in the recent trend in deep learning methods and also with less time.

Different test measures are ECG [6], and blood test because for diagnosing a particular disease a test taken should be low cost, and at the same time, no side effects should be there. In ECG, there are no side effects, but in the case of an angiogram, it is more costly to take and has many side effects. An angiogram is a type of device which is inserted into the body for diagnosing heart disease [7]. Inserting a device in the human body causes many issues, likewise in an angiogram, a small device is inserted to diagnose MI, while inserting itself bleeding may occur or while doing an angiogram some patients will get a heart attack. Rather than using an angiogram, a blood test can be used to diagnose MI [8], and its name is called Troponin I test [9].

1.1 Electrocardiogram

Electrocardiogram gives a graphical representation of electrical activity in the heart [10]. In ECG, there are six waves P wave, Q wave, R wave, S wave, T wave, and U wave. Each wave describes the different electrical results. It gives a duration between

Fig. 2 Normal ECG wave

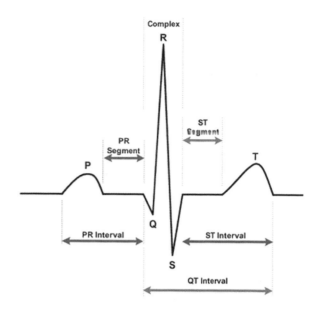

two waves; they are [11] *PR* interval, *QRS* interval, *QT* interval, and *RR* interval [12]. The length between the two segments is the *PR* segment, *ST*-segment as shown in Fig. 2. *PR* interval means that it will start at *P* and end at the start of the *Q* wave. Small square box represents 0.04 s and large square box represents 0.2 s (each large box have 5 small box so 0.04 * 5). An ECG signal will cover 10 large boxes which is equal to 2 s. *P* wave shows atrial depolarization. *Q* wave, *R* wave, and *S* wave show ventricular depolarization. *T* wave shows ventricular repolarization.

For checking the rhythm is normal or abnormal, the first check *RR* interval is the same or different. If the *RR* interval is the same, heart function is normal; otherwise, heart function is abnormal. To check *MI*, changes happened mainly in *ST*-segment [13]. The height of the *P* wave should be less than 2.5 mm in lead II and less than 1.5 mm in lead VI. Width is less the 0.12 s. This wave formation is produced from the 12 leads. Formation of 12 leads from 10 electrodes.

1.2 12 Lead ECG Position

In 12 lead ECGs, ten electrodes are placed on the human body, and each electrode is placed on a different location of the body. Each electrode records the electrical activity of the heart [14]. Twelve leads are divided into three types: (1) limb leads,(2) augmented limbs leads, and (3) chest or precordial limb leads. Limb leads [15] are bipolar, and they are classified into three types (I, II, III). Lead I describes the electrical difference between the positive left arm (*LA*) and negative right arm (*RA*) electrodes. Lead II indicates an electrical difference between the positive left leg (*LL*) and negative right arm (*RA*) electrode. Lead III indicates an electrical difference between positive left leg (*LL*) and negative left arm (*LA*) electrode [16] which is shown in Fig. 3.

Augmented limbs [17] are classified into three types (aVL, aVR, and aVF). Here, aV represents augmented voltage. Augmented limbs are unipolar. Wilson's center terminal (Vm) is the average perspective of the body that is the average of (*RA*, *LA*, and *LL*). Augmented leads are the same as limbs, but the only difference is augmented Goldberger's central terminal which is used. Augmented vector left (aVL) is a positive *RA* and negative combination of *LA* and *LL*. Augmented vector right (aVR) is a positive *RA* and a combination of negative *LA* and *LL*. Augmented vector foot (aVF) is a positive *LL* and a combination of negative *RA* and *LA*.

Chest leads or precordial leads [18] are classified into six types (V1, V2, V3, V4, V5, and V6) in Fig. 4. V1 is located between 4 and 5 ribs that are the fourth intercostal space but located at the right of the breastbone. V1 is located between

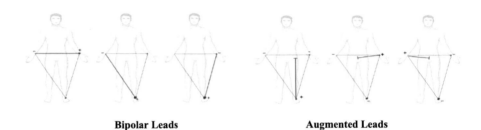

Bipolar Leads   **Augmented Leads**

Fig. 3 Bipolar leads **a** $I = LA - RA$ **b** $II = LL - RA$ **c** $III = LL - LA$ **d** $aVF = \frac{3}{2}(LL - Vw)$ **e** $aVL = \frac{3}{2}(LA - Vw)$ **f** $aVR = \frac{3}{2}(RA - Vw)$

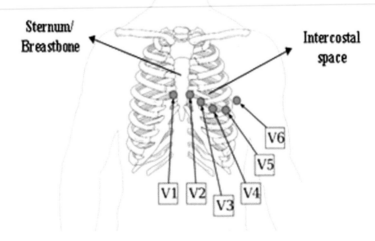

Fig. 4 Chest leads

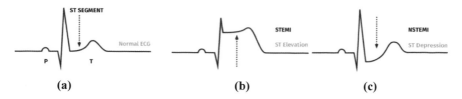

Fig. 5 **a** ST segment **b** STEMI **c** NSTEMI

4 and 5 ribs that are the fourth intercostal space but locates towards the left of the breastbone. V3 is located between V2 and V4 leads. V4 is located between 5 and 6 ribs that are fifth intercostal space but a line passing perpendicularly down to the surface of the body through the midpoint of the collarbone. V5 is located straight to V4 but through an auxiliary skin fold. V6 is located between V4 and V5 but through the top of the armpit.

2 Detection of MI Using 12 Lead ECG

2.1 ST-Segment

If blood and oxygen flow to the heart is normal, ECG wave is as shown in Fig. 5a. If the patients have MI, changes are shown mainly in ST-Segment [19]. STEMI and NSTEMI are the two types of changes. First, ST-elevation myocardial infarction (STEMI) occurs when blood flowing to the heart is blocked [20]. Figure 5b shows ST-elevation when blood flow to the heart is blocked means that the patient has MI. Another change is [21] non-ST-elevation myocardial infarction (NSTEMI) will happen when blood and oxygen flow to the heart is lower as shown in Fig. 5c but not fully blocked. STEMI is more dangerous when comparing with NSTEMI.

2.2 Lower Bundle Branch Block (LBBB)

Block happens when electrical impulses travel to make the heart beaten on both the left and right sides of the chamber. If a block occurs on the left side, it indicates MI [22]. LBBB changes shown in ECG Fig. 6 are changes happening mainly in QRS wave [23].

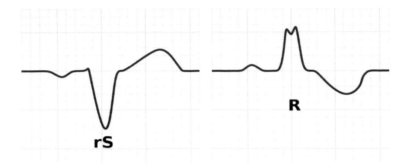

Fig. 6 LBBB changes in QRS wave [24]

3 Related Work

3.1 Data Acquisition

Data collection is the main challenge in health-based issues. Health-related research is a sensitive area. First, we need to consult experts (cardiologists) related to the topic that we have taken. Many researchers [25, 26] are collected data from the PTB diagnostic ECG database—PhysioNet Web site [27] and [28] acquired data from Zenodo annotated 12 lead ECG dataset [29]. Some researchers carried out their data collection in hospitals directly [30].

3.2 Preprocessing

Preprocessing is mainly used to remove the illumination or noises from an image or signal. If the data contains noise, while extracting the information from that data leads to misclassification. Likewise, in the ECG signal, one of the noises is called baseline wander. Baseline wander is a low-frequency signal, and it is difficult to extract the information. It is important to convert a low frequency to a high-frequency signal. Removal of baseline wanders from Fig. 7 in the ECG signal using an algorithm is proposed. Preprocessing is done by removal baseline wander in multi-lead ECG

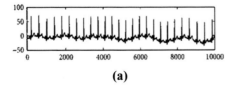
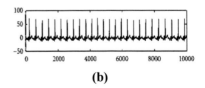

| (a) | (b) |

Fig. 7 **a** Original image **b** After removal of baseline wander [33]

signal. Multi-leads are represented in 3D (heartbeat, samples, and several leads) that is tensor structure, and the multiresolution pyramid is used to decompose the leads [31]. To eliminate false estimations induced by noise sources and to remove baseline drift, a simple and quick normalization procedure was adopted. The mean value and standard deviation of the sample values for each R-R interval of an ECG signal are calculated in this technique [32]. DB6 Mother Wavelet is used for the removal of baseline wander and noise in the ECG signal for segmentation purposes [33].

To extract the information in an RGB image, converting an ECG original image into a grayscale image is important. Then, the grayscale image is converted to a binary image for segmentation [34, 35]. Morphological techniques are applied in a binary image to make wave vision clear. Pan-Tompkins algorithm is used to extracts the feature in a segmented image [36]. There are several ways to convert an RGB image into a grayscale image, but lossless chrominance [37] conversion is important. A comparison of both conversions is performed for preserving chrominance information is calculated using CCFR (Color Content Fidelity Ratio), CCPR (Color Contrast Preservation Ratio), and E-Score [38]. Uneven illumination is the main issue for extracting the data accurately from an image, and here an adaptive filter algorithm is used to solve the illumination problem by segmenting the image into small blocks [39]. An automatic diagnose of STEMI in 12 lead ECG is proposed [40], this diagonalization is done by artificial neural network concept, and also deep learning concepts are used to analyze the ECG data [41].

3.3 Classification Algorithm

Gaussian mixture model (GMM)

GMM is an unsupervised learning algorithm. GMM is automatic detection of MI using 12 lead ECG signals which is proposed [42]. The labeling (leads) issue is the main challenge faced by many experts, but here labeling is not essential. After removal of baseline wanders in the ECG signal, a discrete cosine transform (DCT) is performed. Segmentation of the ST-elevation in each beat for classification of MI using multiple instance learning techniques is carried out [43]. Feature selection in all leads using hidden Markov model (HMM) technique is used to extract features. Gaussian mixture modal (GMM) and SVM technique are compared to classify (MI and Normal); GMM gives better classification result.

K-Nearest Neighbor

KNN is a supervised learning algorithm. The researcher mainly concentrated on a different database that the data which have been taken from three large-sized databases. Classification is done using a combination of Choi–Williams-based features and weighted KNN [44]. Comparison of the different classifiers with the IBA technique is shown in Fig. 8.

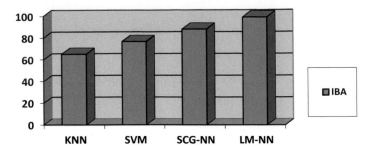

Fig. 8 Comparison of different classification algorithm [45]

Deep Neural Network

DNN is used when we have the bulk of data. It has neurons and works using the activation functions. Fourier Bessel series expansion-based empirical wavelet transform (FBSE-EWT) technique is used for decomposing the sub-bands in 12 lead ECG signals [44], a total of eight sub-bands are taken from 12 lead ECG signal, and deep neural network is used for classification of MI with entropy vector. It is a good classifier when the data is huge.

Support Vector machine

SVM performance is good when the data is structured and also unstructured. This algorithm is used when the data we have is lower and gives good accuracy. In the ECG signal continuously, boundary points and peak points are noted in each lead using the composite lead. Raw ECG signal and after removing noises using filters and by combining 12 lead signals, the composite signal is generated. Classification is done using the SVM algorithm, they compared SVM with using PCA, SVM without using PCA is proposed, and SVM without using PCA gives better accuracy results [26]. For smoothening the ECG image, Hanning filter multi-band is used. Normal ECG signals and abnormal ECG signals are used to extract data by comparing two signals using the technique normalized cross-correlation [46]. Recognition and localization of multi-lead ECG using multi-scale Eigen and multi-scale energy (MEES). Classification of healthy patients and MI patients is proposed [47]; a MEES technique is evaluated using radial basis function with SVM technique. Fig. 9 gives a comparison of a different algorithm using SVM. The researcher compared the result with matrix, vector, and tensor methods, and tensor gives a good performance using the SVM classification algorithm.

Multilayer Neural Network

It is a feed-forward neural network. Classification of acute myocardial infarction is proposed using the technique multilayer network [48]. In artificial intelligence, six-layered convolutional neural network is used to recognize MI [49], and 12 lead ECGs are used without reducing any leads because it will not make any issue. And they considered only ST-elevation. Convolutional neural network is used to diagnose

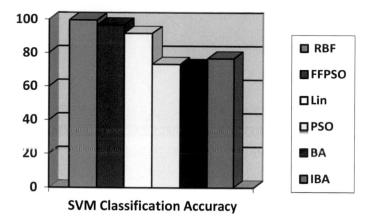

Fig. 9 Different classification accuracy level for MI detection

MI, and they have taken the test measure is STEMI and achieved a good accuracy level, if they consider the other test measure into an account for prediction it may give a higher accuracy level [50]. For diagnosing cardio diseases, neural network concepts are used, by comparing with five layers neural network [51] and six layers neural network with wavelet transform, five-layer NN gives 98.33%, and [52] six layer gives 97.5% accuracy level, but time complexity is high.

Large Margin Neural Network (LM-NN)

LM-NN is a distance metric algorithm. Extracting the heartbeat from the ECG signal using the BAT algorithm after removing the noise from an ECG image by using the smoothening technique called Sgolay FIR. Improved bat algorithm (IBA) is used for feature extraction, and it gives good feature extracting results when compared with bat algorithm (BA). LM-NN algorithm is used for classification purposes and gives good accuracy by comparing with KNN, SVM, and SCG NN. Levenberg–Marquardt neural network (LM-NN) is used because the consumption of time is very less [45]. By taking raw ECG, filtering and beat segmentation is performed; firefly algorithm with particle swarm optimization (FF-PSO) is used for the extraction of 20 samples per beat. Firefly amount of light gives the direction and attractiveness which gives the distance moved, both [45] and [53] use the LM-NN classifier algorithm, but here LM-NN with FF-PSO technique is used, and Fig. 10 gives high accuracy by comparing with a different algorithm using LM-NN [45].

Cross-validation

Cross-validation is used to avoid overfitting in data. Detection of normal ECG beats and abnormal ECG beats are proposed by using convolution neural network techniques. Here, 11 layer deep CNN is used and for classification purposes, tenfold cross-validation is used, advantage of [54] is automatically diagnosing MI with and without noise is performed. Both noisy and clear ECG signals are taken from the

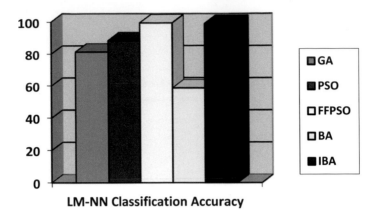

Fig. 10 Classification accuracy level for MI detection

database, then 18 features are extracted in the signal like fuzzy entropy, signal fractal dimension, and Renyi entropy. In that, t-test is carried out to decrease redundancy and to evaluate the significance of the features, and if the t-value exceeds the limit (that is > 2), it indicates that the feature is more important, but if the t-value is closest to zero, it indicates it is not unique. [25] To increase the robustness in this work, tenfold cross-validation technique is used. [55] For analyzing ECG signals, wavelet transform is used because the ECG signal is not static. Automatic detection of MI in 12 lead ECG signals using a deep convolutional neural network is proposed [56].

Long Short-Term Memory (LSTM)

LSTM is a recurrent NN. Each beat is segmented without except last and the first beat in ECG signal, and based on segmentation, the result feature extraction is done using three classes (DWT, DCT, and EMD) to classify normal, MI, coronary artery disease using KNN tenfold cross-validation [33] and classification using ensemble learning technique [57] is used for better classification of heart disease which is compared with bidirectional long short-term memory (BiLSTM). A combination of forwarding and backward LSTM is used for the classification of eight different diseases based on the heart for segmenting the information from each lead [58].

YOLO

A 12 lead ECG image is taken as input, and they carried out two steps to extract the data's from an image. First, in each lead text is detected. And then, using the detected text corresponding waves are detected with the help of bounding box technique. The bounding box technique is used to detect the object in the image using YOLOv3 [59]. To detect the exact object in the image and to detect weaker edges in the image, the non-maximum suppression technique gives better results [60]. A technique called multibox detector is used to detect the object in the image [61], and it is good in aspect ratio and predicting the location; Fig. 11 shows different bounding box techniques and their accuracy level.

Fig. 11 Comparison of different bounding techniques using VOC 2007 [66, 67]

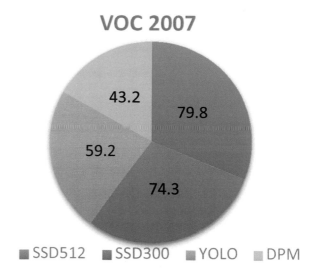

VOC 2007

43.2

79.8

59.2

74.3

■ SSD512   ■ SSD300   ■ YOLO   ■ DPM

ResNet.

After object detection, information is extracted from 12 leads. Based on the detection, classification is performed using classifier techniques. Residual network (ResNet), [62] which is used for classification to reduce the number of parameters and also reduce the computational time and DenseNet, adds zero for padding to reduce parameters [63, 64]. The whole ECG image is taken as input which makes the loss of data, but in the shallow neural network, input is given as 12 leads separately and there is no loss of data. A fusion of features like morphological, statistical, and temporal features is to classify the ECG [65].

DenseNet

A dense block is used for extracting a feature from an image, and also transition layer is used to decrease the parameter. Hereby comparing support vector machine (SVM), K-means and, DenseNet, DenseNet gives the higher classification accuracy rate shown in Fig. 12 [30]; lead extraction can be done if the image is of good quality. But if the ECG image has some issue like the lead name which is not clear or blurred text using the multi-branch network technique that cannot extract the information and if the lead names are clear, it is easy to extract the data.

4 Discussion and Future Work

In this paper, it found that for diagnosing myocardial infraction many tests has been taken and at a different time interval. First, we need to understand the reason for muscle damage which is happening, muscle damage is happening because blood

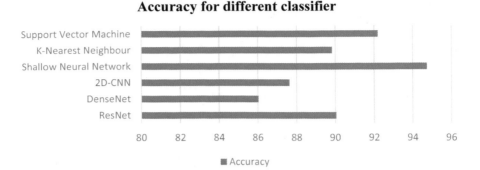

Fig. 12 Accuracy for different classifier

flow to the heart muscle is not regular, next why blood flow to the heart is abnormal. Abnormality is carried out because of plaque formation in arteries. The reason for plaque formation is cholesterol levels, and we know that HDL is good cholesterol and LDL is bad cholesterol. Both the cholesterol should a balanced manner, if the good cholesterol is low, the risk of plaque formation will increase and have a chance of MI.

Other than electrocardiogram, troponin I, and cholesterol level test, many other measures are there to diagnose MI that is angiogram. An angiogram is used to diagnose MI by inserting a device in a human body, but for taking this type of test, its cost is very high [68], and also it has many side effects like irregular heartbeat, while doing angiogram heart attack may occur for some patients and also while inserting the device inside the patient body bleeding may occur [69]. Aspirin medicine is a type of medicine that is used to reduce chest pain when chest pressure occurs, but it also has many side effects like breathing problems [70]. Troponin I test [9] is also used to diagnose MI by taking the blood samples in the skeleton muscle. When the heart muscle is damaged, it starts emitting the chemicals. Measuring the level of chemicals present in the blood gives the patient an MI or not and also the stages of MI [71]. This test gives 97% accuracy, and it detects MI at earlier as possible. A combination of ECG and troponin results gives an earlier diagnose of MI [72].

Future work can be done using diagnosing all types of heart diseases, and all stages of heart diseases should be carried out rather than diagnosing a single disease or particular wave, because many researchers concentrated on a single disease or particular, and after that intelligent decision-making system can be done to increase the scalability.

5 Conclusion

In this paper, we discussed different measures for diagnosing MI. Accurately diagnosing myocardial infarction is a challenging task nowadays, because a normal person can have a sudden heart attack which leads to death. Many studies have carried out the research work by considering ST-elevations that are STEMI and NSTEMI, but if the ST-elevation is normal and abnormality happens in the left bundle branch block, It gives a wrong prediction result. So further research could be taken by collecting all the possibilities for diagnosing MI. Cholesterol level is also the main factor for tissue death in the heart because heart abnormalities and heart issues are closely related to cholesterol. So by considering all the test measures, diagnosing ischemia has to be done to accurate prediction of MI that will save the life of a patient.

References

1. Graham DJ, Ouellet-Hellstrom R, MaCurdy TE, Ali F, Sholley C, Worrall C, Kelman JA (2010) Risk of acute myocardial infarction, stroke, heart failure, and death in elderly Medicare patients treated with rosiglitazone or pioglitazone. JAMA 304(4):411–418
2. Mechanic OJ, Grossman SA (2019) Acute myocardial infarction. In StatPearls [Internet]. StatPearls Publishing
3. Gulati R, Behfar A, Narula J, Kanwar A, Lerman A, Cooper L, Singh M (Jan 2020) Acute myocardial infarction in young individuals. Mayo Clinic Proc 95(1):136–156. Elsevier
4. Sedehi D, Cigarroa JE (2017) Precipitants of myocardial ischemia. Chronic coronary artery disease: a companion to Braunwald's heart disease, 69
5. https://www.shutterstock.com/image-vector/myocardial-infarction-3d-realostic-illustration-human-1079882426
6. Hedén B, Ohlin H, Rittner R, Edenbrandt L (1997) Acute myocardial infarction detected in the 12-lead ECG by artificial neural networks. Circulation 96(6):1798–1802
7. SCOT-Heart Investigators (2018) Coronary CT angiography and 5-year risk of myocardial infarction. New Engl J Med 379(10):924–933
8. Katus HA, Remppis A, Neumann FJ, Scheffold T, Diederich KW, Vinar G, Noe A, Matern G, Kuebler W (1991) Diagnostic efficiency of troponin T measurements in acute myocardial infarction. Circulation 83(3):902–912
9. Park KC, Gaze DC, Collinson PO, Marber MS (2017) Cardiac troponins: from myocardial infarction to chronic disease. Cardiovasc Res 113(14):1708–1718
10. Chen W (2018) Electrocardiogram. In: Seamless healthcare monitoring. Springer, Cham, pp 3–44
11. Kligfield P, Gettes LS, Bailey JJ, Childers R, Deal BJ, Hancock EW, Pahlm O, et al (2007) Recommendations for the standardization and interpretation of the electrocardiogram: part I: the electrocardiogram and its technology a scientific statement from the international society for computerized electrocardiology. J Am Coll Cardiol 49(10):1109–1127
12. Mason JW, Hancock EW, Gettes LS (2007) Recommendations for the standardization and interpretation of the electrocardiogram: part II the American college of cardiology foundation; and the heart rhythm society endorsed by the international society for computerized electrocardiology. J Am Coll Cardiol 49(10):1128–1135
13. Thygesen K, Alpert JS, White HD, Task force members: Chairpersons: Kristian Thygesen (Denmark); Alpert JS (USA)*, White HD (New Zealand)*, Biomarker group: Jaffe AS, Coordinator (USA), Apple FS (USA), Galvani M (Italy), Katus HA (Germany), Newby LK (USA),

Ravkilde J (Denmark), ECG Group: Bernard Chaitman, Co-ordinator (USA), Clemmensen PM (Denmark), Dellborg M (Sweden), Hod H (Israel), Porela P (Finland), ... Implementation Group: Wallentin LC Coordinator (Sweden), Francisco Fernández-Avilés (Spain), Fox KM (UK), Parkhomenko AN (Ukraine), Priori SG (Italy), Tendera M (Poland), Voipio-Pulkki L-M (Finland) (2007) Universal definition of myocardial infarction. circulation 116(22):2634–2653

14. Jowett NI, Turner AM, Cole A, Jones PA (2005) Modified electrode placement must be recorded when performing 12-lead electrocardiograms. Postgrad Med J 81(952):122–125
15. Mukherjee J, Das PK, Ghosh PR, Banerjee D, Sharma T, Basak D, Sanyal S (2015) Electrocardiogram pattern of some exotic breeds of trained dogs: a variation study. Vet World 8(11):1317
16. Npatchett, Contributes text and origin-nal graphics to English Wikipedia articles on medicine, biology, and chemistry (https://en.wikipedia.org/wiki/Electrocardiography)
17. Reilly RB, Lee TC (2010) Electrograms (ecg, eeg, emg, eog). Technol Health Care 18(6):443–458
18. Fotiadis D, Likas A, Michalis L, Papaloukas C (2006) Electrocardiogram (ECG): automated diagnosis. Wiley encyclopedia of biomedical engineering
19. White HD, Chew DP (2008) Acute myocardial infarction. The Lancet 372(9638):570–584
20. Barbagelata A, Bethea CF, Severance HW, Mentz RJ, Albert D, Barsness GW, ... Chisum B (2018) Smartphone ECG for evaluation of ST-segment elevation myocardial infarction (STEMI): design of the ST LEUIS international multicenter study. J Electrocardiol 51(2):260–264
21. Gholikhani-Darbroud R, Hajahmadipoorrafsanjani M, Mansouri F, Khaki-Khatibi F, Ghojazadeh M (2017) Decreased circulatory microRNA-4478 as a specifi c biomarker for diagnosing non-ST-segment elevation myocardial infarction (NSTEMI) and its association with soluble leptin receptor. Bratisl Med J 118(11):684–690
22. Jothieswaran A, Body R (2016) BET 2: diagnosing acute myocardial infarction in the presence of ventricular pacing: can Sgarbossa criteria help? Emerg Med J 33(9):672–673
23. Dodd KW, Elm KD, Smith SW (2016) Comparison of the QRS complex, ST-segment, and T-wave among patients with left bundle branch block with and without acute myocardial infarction. J Emerg Med 51(1):1–8
24. Left bundle branch block (29 Nov 2019) In Wikipedia Retrieved from https://en.wikipedia.org/w/index.php?title=Left_bundle_branch_block&oldid=928414830
25. Sharma M, San Tan R, Acharya UR (2018) A novel automated diagnostic system for classification of myocardial infarction ECG signals using an optimal biorthogonal filter bank. Comput Biol Med 102:341–356
26. Dohare AK, Kumar V, Kumar R (2018) Detection of myocardial infarction in 12 lead ECG using support vector machine. Appl Soft Comput 64:138–147
27. PhysioNet MITBIH (2017) Arrhythmia database. https://www.physionet.org/physiobank/database/mitdb
28. Ribeiro AH, Ribeiro MH, Paixão GM, Oliveira DM, Gomes PR, Canazart JA, Schön TB (2020) Automatic diagnosis of the 12-lead ECG using a deep neural network. Nat Commun 11(1):1–9
29. Ribeiro AH, Ribeiro MH, Gabriela M, Oliveira DM, Gomes PR (2020a) Annotated 12-lead ECG dataset. URL: https://zenodo.org/record/3765780. Xx1kLZ4zbIU/
30. Hao P, Gao X, Li Z, Zhang J, Wu F, Bai C (2020) Multi-branch fusion network for myocardial infarction screening from 12-lead ECG images. Comput Methods Programs Biomed 184:105286
31. Padhy S, Dandapat S (2017) Third-order tensor based analysis of multilead ECG for classification of myocardial infarction. Biomed Signal Process Control 31:71–78
32. Kayikcioglu İ, Akdeniz F, Köse C, Kayikcioglu T (2020) Time-frequency approach to ECG classification of myocardial infarction. Comput Electr Eng 84:106621
33. Luo Y, Hargraves RH, Belle A, Bai O, Qi X, Ward KR, ... Najarian K (2013) A hierarchical method for removal of baseline drift from biomedical signals: application in ECG analysis. Sci World J 2013

34. Sedaaghi MH, Khosravi M (July 2003) Morphological ECG signal preprocessing with more efficient baseline drift removal. In: Proceedings of the 7th. IASTED international conference, ASC. pp 205–209
35. Zhang ZN, Zhang H, Zhuang TG (Oct 1987) One-dimensional signal extraction of paper-written ECG image and its archiving. In: Visual communications and image processing II, vol 845. International Society for Optics and Photonics, pp 419–423
36. Hartati S, Wardoyo R, Setianto BY (2017) The feature extraction to determine the wave's peaks in the electrocardiogram graphic image. Int J Image, Graphics Signal Proc 9(6):1
37. Sowmya V, Govind D, Soman KP (2017) Significance of incorporating chrominance information for effective color-to-grayscale image conversion. SIViP 11(1):129–136
38. Jothiaruna N, Sundar KJA, Karthikeyan B (2019) A segmentation method for disease spot images incorporating chrominance in comprehensive color feature and region growing. Comput Electr Agric 165:104934
39. Wang S, Zhang S, Li Z, Huang L, Wei Z (2020) Automatic digital ECG signal extraction and normal QRS recognition from real scene ECG images. Comput Methods Programs Biomed 187:105254
40. Zhao Y, Xiong J, Hou Y, Zhu M, Lu Y, Xu Y, Liu Z (2020) Early detection of ST-segment elevated myocardial infarction by artificial intelligence with 12-lead electrocardiogram. Int J Cardiol
41. Hong S, Zhou Y, Shang J, Xiao C, Sun J (2020) Opportunities and challenges of deep learning methods for electrocardiogram data: a systematic review. Comput Biol Med 103801
42. Sun L, Lu Y, Yang K, Li S (2012) ECG analysis using multiple instance learning for myocardial infarction detection. IEEE Trans Biomed Eng 59(12):3348–3356
43. Chang PC, Lin JJ, Hsieh JC, Weng J (2012) Myocardial infarction classification with multi-lead ECG using hidden Markov models and Gaussian mixture models. Appl Soft Comput 12(10):3165–3175
44. Tripathy RK, Bhattacharyya A, Pachori RB (2019) A novel approach for detection of myocardial infarction from ECG signals of multiple electrodes. IEEE Sens J 19(12):4509–4517
45. Kora P, Kalva SR (2015) Improved Bat algorithm for the detection of myocardial infarction. Springerplus 4(1):666
46. Ramli AB, Ahmad PA (Jan 2003) Correlation analysis for abnormal ECG signal features extraction. In: 4th national conference of telecommunication technology, 2003. NCTT 2003 Proceedings. IEEE, pp 232–237
47. Sharma LN, Tripathy RK, Dandapat S (2015) Multiscale energy and eigenspace approach to detection and localization of myocardial infarction. IEEE Trans Biomed Eng 62(7):1827–1837
48. Dhawan A, Wenzel B, George S, Gussak I, Bojovic B, Panescu D (Aug 2012) Detection of acute myocardial infarction from serial ECG using multilayer support vector machine. In: 2012 annual international conference of the IEEE engineering in medicine and biology society. IEEE, pp 2704–2707
49. Makimoto H, Höckmann M, Lin T, Glöckner D, Gerguri S, Clasen L, Angendohr S (2020) Performance of a convolutional neural network derived from an ecG database in recognizing myocardial infarction. Sci Rep 10(1):1–9
50. Park Y, Yun ID, Kang SH (2019) Preprocessing method for performance enhancement in cnn-based stemi detection from 12-lead ecg. IEEE Access 7:99964–99977
51. Avanzato R, Beritelli F (2020) Automatic ECG diagnosis using convolutional neural network. Electronics 9(6):951
52. Li D, Zhang J, Zhang Q, Wei X (Oct 2017) Classification of ECG signals based on 1D convolution neural network. In: 2017 IEEE 19th international conference on e-health networking, applications and services (Healthcom). IEEE, pp 1–6
53. Kora P (2017) ECG based myocardial infarction detection using hybrid firefly algorithm. Comput Methods Programs Biomed 152:141–148
54. Acharya UR, Fujita H, Oh SL, Hagiwara Y, Tan JH, Adam M (2017) Application of deep convolutional neural network for automated detection of myocardial infarction using ECG signals. Inf Sci 415:190–198

55. Jayachandran ES (2010) Analysis of myocardial infarction using discrete wavelet transform. J Med Syst 34(6):985–992

56. Baloglu UB, Talo M, Yildirim O, San Tan R, Acharya UR (2019) Classification of myocardial infarction with multi-lead ECG signals and deep CNN. Pattern Recogn Lett 122:23–30

57. Baccouche A, Garcia-Zapirain B, Castillo Olea C, Elmaghraby A (2020) Ensemble deep learning models for heart disease classification: a case study from Mexico. Information 11(4):207

58. Mostayed A, Luo J, Shu X, Wee W (2018) Classification of 12-lead ECG signals with Bi-directional LSTM network. arXiv preprint arXiv:1811.02090

59. Novak B, Ilić V, Pavković B (May 2020) YOLOv3 algorithm with additional convolutional neural network trained for traffic sign recognition. In: 2020 zooming innovation in consumer technologies conference (ZINC). IEEE, pp 165–168

60. Magnusson LV, Olsson R (July 2016) Improving the canny edge detector using automatic programming: improving non-max suppression. In: Proceedings of the genetic and evolutionary computation conference 2016. pp 461–468

61. Liu W, Anguelov D, Erhan D, Szegedy C, Reed S, Fu CY, Berg AC (Oct 2016) Ssd: single shot multibox detector. In: European conference on computer vision. Springer, Cham, pp 21–37

62. He K, Zhang X, Ren S, Sun J (2016) Deep residual learning for image recognition. In: CVPR. pp 770–778

63. Jun TJ, Nguyen HM, Kang D, Kim D, Kim Y (2018) ECG arrhythmia classification using a 2-d convolutional neural network, arxiv.org/abs/1804.06812

64. Huang G, Liu Z, Maaten LVD, Weinberger KQ (2017) Densely connected convolutional networks. In: CVPR. pp 4700–4708

65. Golrizkhatami Z, Acan A (2018) ECG classification using three-level fusion of different feature descriptors. Expert Syst Appl 114:54–64

66. Redmon J, Divvala S, Girshick R, Farhadi A (2016) You only look once: unified, real-time object detection. In: Proceedings of the IEEE conference on computer vision and pattern recognition. pp 779–788

67. Erhan D, Szegedy C, Toshev A, Anguelov D (2014) Scalable object detection using deep neural networks. In: Proceedings of the IEEE conference on computer vision and pattern recognition. pp 2147–2154

68. Barrett BJ, Parfrey PS, Vavasour HM, O'Dea F, Kent G, Stone E (1992) A comparison of nonionic, low-osmolality radiocontrast agents with ionic, high-osmolality agents during cardiac catheterization. N Engl J Med 326(7):431–436

69. Tavakol M, Ashraf S, Brener SJ (2012) Risks and complications of coronary angiography: a comprehensive review. Global J Health Sci 4(1):65

70. Sorensen R, Hansen ML, Abildstrom SZ, Hvelplund A, Andersson C, Jørgensen C, Gislason GH (2009) Risk of bleeding in patients with acute myocardial infarction treated with different combinations of aspirin, clopidogrel, and vitamin K antagonists in Denmark: a retrospective analysis of nationwide registry data. The Lancet 374(9706):1967–1974

71. Twerenbold R, Boeddinghaus J, Nestelberger T, Wildi K, Gimenez MR, Badertscher P, Mueller C (2017) Clinical use of high-sensitivity cardiac troponin in patients with suspected myocardial infarction. J Am Coll Cardiol 70(8):996–1012

72. Sandoval Y, Smith SW, Love SA, Sexter A, Schulz K, Apple FS (2017) Single high-sensitivity cardiac troponin I to rule out acute myocardial infarction. Am J Med 130(9):1076–1083

Biometric Recognition from Face-Voice Using Rough-Neuro-Fuzzy Classifiers

B. V. Anil and M. S. Ravikumar

Abstract Reliable and prudent biometric person identification systems achieve authentication of the individual. In this work, eight distinct person identification algorithms are devised based on face recognition (FR), voice recognition (VR) and face-voice recognition (FVR) on video data. The lower face deformation caused by the movable jaw and the lip movement during speech is vectored into local voice-enabled face deformation profile (LVFDP). Feature fusion is employed between principal component analysis (PCA) features or linear discriminant analysis (LDA) with LVFDP and decision level fusion between FR methods, FR and VR methods. The eight algorithms are person identification using (i) VR by MFCC features and rough c-medoid clustering, (ii) VR by MFCC features and fuzzy c-medoid clustering, (iii) FR by PCA over LDA with fuzzy-multi-layer perceptron (fuzzy-MLP) classifier, (iv) FR by PCA over LDA and LVFDP with fuzzy-MLP classifier (v) FVR by PCA over LDA with f-MLP and MFCC with rough c-medoid (vi) FVR by PCA over LDA with f-MLP and MFCC with fuzzy c-medoid (vii) FVR by PCA over LDA and LVFDP with f-MLP and MFCC with rough c-medoid (viii) FVR by PCA over LDA and LVFDP with f-MLP and MFCC with fuzzy c-medoid. It is evident from the experimental results that fusion of LVFDP with facial features achieves increased recognition accuracy.

Keywords Face-voice recognition · Voice-enabled face deformation profile · Rough-neuro-fuzzy classifiers

1 Introduction

With the advent of digital electronic systems and compatible multimedia data representation techniques and networks that support integrated and synchronised audio and video, robust person identification is extremely important. It is indeed a certain fact that the physical characteristics and/or behavioural characteristics of a person

B. V. Anil (✉) · M. S. Ravikumar
K.V.G. College of Engineering, Sullia, Karnataka, India

© The Author(s), under exclusive license to Springer Nature Singapore Pte Ltd. 2022   489
C. Satyanarayana et al. (eds.), *High Performance Computing and Networking*,
Lecture Notes in Electrical Engineering 853,
https://doi.org/10.1007/978-981-16-9885-9_40

Table 1 Feature set, classifier model and fusion of eight algorithms; BM–biometrics

BM	Attribute vector	Classifier model	Fusion method
VR	MFCC	Rough c-medoid	Nil
VR	MFCC	Fuzzy c-medoid	Nil
FR	PCA over LDA	f-MLP	Decision
FR	PCA over LDA + LVFDP	f-MLP	Feature + Decision
FVR	PCA over LDA + MFCC	f-MLP & fuzzy c-medoid	Decision
FVR	PCA over LDA + MFCC	f-MLP & rough c-medoid	Decision
FVR	PCA over LDA + LVFDP + MFCC	f-MLP & fuzzy c-medoid	Feature + Decision
FVR	PCA over LDA + LVFDP + MFCC	f-MLP & rough c-medoid	Feature + Decision

form an extremely important entity to distinctly recognise individuals [1–4]. *Biometrics recognition* introduces the technology of person identification by machine after quantifying the physical and/or behavioural attributes with calculated precision and subsequently categorising them [2, 5]. Biometric recognition systems with excellent collaboration of learning-reasoning-granularization capability emerge from judicial hybridization of soft computing paradigms. Conventional systems authenticate individuals either by memory-oriented knowledge-based security and possession-oriented token-based security [3]. Real-world biometric systems must cope with multitude of obstacles such as *noise in sensed data, intra-class variations, distinctiveness, non-universality, spoof attacks* so forth. These obstacles faced by single mode biometrics are circumvented by *multimode biometrics,* and multimodal biometric systems increase recognition accuracy [3, 5]. Person identification by facial features and by voice features has the merits related to universality, collectability, acceptability and circumvention. Further, when the monomodal entities face biometric and voice biometrics considered individually, their performance is low [1, 2, 5, 6]. The proposed work is focussed on devising eight biometrics algorithms based on feature fusion and decision level fusion [7–9] listed in Table 1.

2   Related Works

The potential field of biometrics alleviates the necessity of possessions and remembrance and thereby allows authentication. This fact and its merits, demerits, spoof attack safety, fusion that leads to multimodal approach are detailed in [4, 5, 10]. Further, [5] highlights the fact that universality, permanence, collectability, acceptability, circumvention are relatively better for face and voice. This motivates the authors to investigate whether an approach with face-voice bi-modal biometrics contribute to increased performance. In [11], investigation is carried out on video to enhance the quality to achieve better facial recognition rate. The work enhances the frames by robust mean and covariance to achieve the recognition increase by 10%. Reference [12] depicts limitations of conventional histogram equalisation and the advantages of contrast-limited adaptive histogram equalisation. In [13, 14], non-linear colour space and spatiotemporal model for hierarchical segmentation is discussed which deals with the low-level joint processing of colour and motion for robust face analysis within a feature-based approach. Eigen face versus Fisher face comparison, merits, demerits, implementation details are found in [15]. Decision level fusion of subspace methods PCA and LDA is found in [16] with reported recognition accuracy. Reference [17] treats the FR problem as an intrinsically two-dimensional recognition problem rather than the three-dimensional geometric modelling. The intricacies of fusion, face-voice fusion and audio-visual biometrics are found in [6–9, 18]. Fuzzy-MLP as a classifier and its merits over conventional MLP and it is a choice for pattern recognition are found in [19–21]. Reference [22, 23] focusses on voice biometrics and soft computing for voice recognition. Algorithm for silence removal and end point detection is found in [24]. Rough stets, fuzzy sets and their emphasis in pattern recognition in an unsupervised manner are in [25–28]. Objective quantification of the measure of the recognition accuracy and recognition rate is found in [29]. Reference [30] deals with motion estimation in MPEG2 video encoding using a parallel block matching.

3 Person Identification by FR

Pose, expression, variation of faces in video frames becomes outliers and a serious impediment for the recognition accuracy [10, 11]. Avoiding the loss of potential information over brightness regions from mere histogram equalisation is the hallmark of CLAHE [12] shown in Fig. 1ii. Segmentation of the effective-region-of-face follows the pre-processing. Segmentation involves processing of the frames: (i) conversion from RGB space to YC_rC_b space (Fig. 1iii) (ii) skin colour filtering (Fig. 1iv) (iii) ARK face template grabber generation (Fig. 1v) and (iv) effective region-of-face extraction ((Fig. 1vi) of the frames in the video [2, 3, 13, 14]. The skin colour is investigated to set the threshold value, and the set threshold values are $C_{r\_skin} = [0.5, 0.6]$ and $C_{b\_skin} = [0.43, 0.59]$ for chrominance red and chrominance blue.

3.1 ARK Face Template Grabber and Effective Region-Of-Face Extraction

ARK template grabber can map the face pixels in the unsegmented domain onto a segmentation plane. Voila Jones' face detection algorithm on the segmented face-frame makes way to crop and remove the unwanted skin region shown in Fig. 1viii.

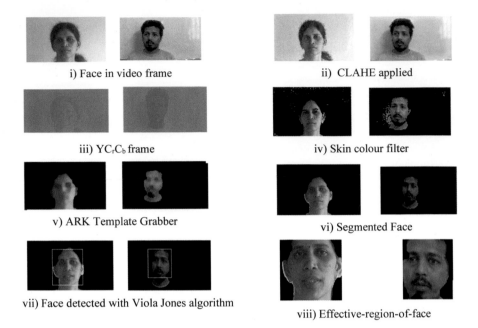

i) Face in video frame

ii) CLAHE applied

iii) YC$_r$C$_b$ frame

iv) Skin colour filter

v) ARK Template Grabber

vi) Segmented Face

vii) Face detected with Viola Jones algorithm

viii) Effective-region-of-face

Fig. 1 **i–viii** Face segmentation in video frames

3.2 Feature Extraction

The potentiality of appearance-based feature space fusion of LDA and PCA for face recognition or verification is discussed in [15–17]. PCA forms structural as well as statistical feature space also termed as Eigen space and is an appropriate choice in the recognition process of face biometrics. Incurring principal components allow the development of an excellent face template module with most needed feature vector dimensionality reduction [16, 17]. LDA forms a feature space also termed as Fisher space and is an attribute of choice in the recognition process of face biometrics.

3.3 Classifier Design–Fuzzy Logic to MLP

Artificial neural network aims at designing the *brain-behaviour* model based on chosen distributed architecture and iterative training process. Error back propagation technique is the supervised training algorithm that alter the free parameters of the feed forward MLP architecture to set the long-term memory. Fuzzy set theory is an extension of crisp set theory where in the degree of membership is gradual from perfect belongingness to absence of belongingness [19]. The membership function that defines the degree of membership is expressed as

$$Mf_A(x) : X \rightarrow [0, 1] \tag{1}$$

where X is the universe of discourse and $A \subset X$. Computational intelligence systems could be a synergetic integration of complementary technologies such as *feedforward-MLP* and *fuzzy logic* leading to *neuro-fuzzy* intelligent machines [19, 20]. The output of a neuron in any layer m, other than the input layer ($m = 0$), is given as

$$v_q^m = \frac{1}{1 + e^{-\lambda s_q^m}} \tag{2}$$

where

$$s_q^m = \sum_{p=0}^{n_{h-1}} v_p^{m-1} wt_{qp}^{m-1} \tag{3}$$

In Equation (2), v_p^{m-1} is the state of the pth node in the presiding ($m - 1$)th layer, and wt_{qp}^{m-1} is the free forms the network weight from the pth node in layer ($m - 1$) to the qth node in layer m [20, 21]. The implementation objective focusses on mapping the input attribute space to fuzzy domain which comprises of the set of membership values on overlapping partitions. These values have linguistic properties and are labelled as *exceptionally low, low, medium, high and extremely high* for an n-dimensional input space [23]. The weight adaptation and error estimation are computed using the expressions in Equations. (4), (5) and (6)

$$\Delta wt_{qr}^{m+1} = -\eta \sum_{q=1}^{n_{hid}} \frac{\partial Err}{\partial wt_{qr}} + \alpha \Delta wt_{qr}^m \tag{4}$$

$$\Delta wt_{pq}^{m+1} = -\eta \sum_{p=1}^{n_{inp}} \frac{\partial Err}{\partial wt_{pq}} + \alpha \Delta wt_{pq}^m \tag{5}$$

$$Err^P = \frac{1}{2} \left(\sum_{n=1}^{N_{pat}} Act_n^P - Des_n^P \right)^2 \tag{6}$$

where $n = 1, \ldots, N_{pat}$ number of output patterns, and $ip = 1, \ldots, P$ represents the number of input patterns. $\left(\sum_{n=1}^{N_{pat}} Act_n^P - Des_n^P \right)^2$ is the squared difference between actual response Act and the desired response Des. The pattern space comprising of n-dimensional vectors $F_{ip} = [f_{ip\,1}, f_{ip\,2}, \ldots, f_{ip\,n}]$ is modified and appended to form a $5n$–dimensional vector as

$$F_{ip} = \left[m_{f\,\text{exceptionally low}(f_{ip1})}(f_{ip1}), \ldots, m_{f\,\text{extremely high}(f_{ipn})}(f_{ip\,n}) \right] \tag{7}$$

where m_f represents the π membership functions, corresponding to the linguistic variables: *exceptionally low* (EL), *low* (L), *medium* (M), *high* (H) and *extremely high* (EH) along the feature axis. $U = [u_1^0, u_2^0, \ldots, u_{5n}^0]$ represents the activation of the 5n neurons in the input layer [19]. The π membership is computed based on the formulae:

$$\pi(F_j; cv, \Gamma) = \begin{cases} 2\left(1 - \frac{F_j - cv}{\Gamma}\right)^2, & \text{for} \frac{\Gamma}{2} \leq F_j - cv \leq \Gamma \\ 1 - 2\left(\frac{F_j - cv}{\Gamma}\right)^2, & \text{for } 0 \leq F_j - cv \leq \frac{\Gamma}{2} \\ 0, & \text{otherwise} \end{cases} \tag{8}$$

where the positive value Γ, and cv is the *radius* and *central* quantifiers of the π–function. The linguistic variables are expressed as [19]

$$\text{exceptionally low} = \left\{ \frac{0.95}{EL}, \frac{\pi\left(F_j\left(\frac{0.95}{EL}\right); cv_{jl}\Gamma_{jl}\right)}{L}, \frac{\pi\left(F_j\left(\frac{0.95}{EL}\right); cv_{jm}\Gamma_{jm}\right)}{M}, \right.$$
$$\left. \frac{\pi\left(F_j\left(\frac{0.95}{EL}\right); cv_{jh}\Gamma_{jh}\right)}{H}, \frac{\pi\left(F_j\left(\frac{0.95}{EL}\right); cv_{jeh}\Gamma_{jeh}\right)}{EH} \right\}$$

$$\text{low} = \left\{ \frac{\pi\left(F_j\left(\frac{0.95}{L}\right); cv_{jel}\Gamma_{jel}\right)}{EL}, \frac{0.95}{L}, \frac{\pi\left(F_j\left(\frac{0.95}{L}\right); cv_{jm}\Gamma_{jm}\right)}{M}, \right.$$
$$\left. \frac{\pi\left(F_j\left(\frac{0.95}{L}\right); cv_{jh}\Gamma_{jh}\right)}{H}, \frac{\pi\left(F_j\left(\frac{0.95}{L}\right); cv_{jeh}\Gamma_{jeh}\right)}{EH} \right\}$$

$$\text{medium} = \left\{ \frac{\pi\left(F_j\left(\frac{0.95}{M}\right); cv_{jel}\Gamma_{jel}\right)}{EL}, \frac{\pi\left(F_j\left(\frac{0.95}{M}\right); cv_{jl}\Gamma_{jl}\right)}{L}, \frac{0.95}{M}, \right.$$
$$\left. \frac{\pi\left(F_j\left(\frac{0.95}{M}\right); cv_{jh}\Gamma_{jh}\right)}{H}, \frac{\pi\left(F_j\left(\frac{0.95}{M}\right); cv_{jeh}\Gamma_{jeh}\right)}{EH} \right\}$$

$$\text{high} = \left\{ \frac{\pi\left(F_j\left(\frac{0.95}{H}\right); cv_{jel}\Gamma_{jel}\right)}{EL}, \frac{\pi\left(F_j\left(\frac{0.95}{H}\right); cv_{jl}\Gamma_{jl}\right)}{L}, \right.$$
$$\left. \frac{\pi\left(F_j\left(\frac{0.95}{H}\right); cv_{jm}\Gamma_{jm}\right)}{M}, \frac{0.95}{H}, \frac{\pi\left(F_j\left(\frac{0.95}{H}\right); cv_{jeh}\Gamma_{jeh}\right)}{EH} \right\} \tag{9}$$

$$\text{extremely high} = \left\{ \frac{\pi\left(F_j\left(\frac{0.95}{EH}\right); cv_{jel}\Gamma_{jel}\right)}{EL}, \frac{\pi\left(F_j\left(\frac{0.95}{EH}\right); cv_{jl}\Gamma_{jl}\right)}{L}, \right.$$
$$\left. \frac{\pi\left(F_j\left(\frac{0.95}{EH}\right); cv_{jm}\Gamma_{jm}\right)}{M}, \frac{\pi\left(F_j\left(\frac{0.95}{EH}\right); cv_{jh}\Gamma_{jh}\right)}{H}, \frac{0.95}{EH} \right\}$$

where $cv_{jel}, \Gamma_{jel}, cv_{jl}, \Gamma_{jl}, cv_{jm}, \Gamma_{jm}, cv_{jh}, \Gamma_{jh}, cv_{jeh}, \Gamma_{jeh}$ represent the centre value and radii of the five linguistic properties along the jth axis, and $F_j\left(\frac{0.95}{EL}\right), F_j\left(\frac{0.95}{L}\right), F_j\left(\frac{0.95}{M}\right), F_j\left(\frac{0.95}{H}\right), F_j\left(\frac{0.95}{EH}\right)$ denote the feature values F_j at which the five linguistic membership values attain 0.95.

The selection of centres of the overlapping π-sets is done by computing mean μ_j of the jth axis pattern vectors. Consider $[F_{jmin}, \mu_j)$ and $(\mu_j, F_{jmax}]$ as μ_{jL} and μ_{jH}, respectively. Furthermore, $[F_{jmin}, \mu_{jL})$ and $(\mu_{jH}, F_{jmax}]$ leads to μ_{jEL} and μ_{jEH}, respectively. F_{jmin} and F_{jmax} denote the upper and lower boundary of the dynamic range of the training set feature F_j. The centres and the radii of the five π-sets are therefore.

$cv_{jEL} = \mu_{jEL}, cv_{jL} = \mu_{jL}, cv_{jM} = \mu_j, cv_{jH} = \mu_{jH}, cv_{jEH} = \mu_{jEH}$ and $\Gamma_{jEL} = 2(\mu_{jL} - \mu_{jEL}), \Gamma_{jL} = 2(\mu_j - \mu_{jL}), \Gamma_{jH} = 2(\mu_{jEH} - \mu_j), \Gamma_{jEH} = 2(\mu_{jEH} - \mu_{jH})$, and finally

$$\Gamma_{jM} = \frac{\Gamma_{jEL}\left(F_{jmax} - \mu_{jL}\right) + \Gamma_{jL}\left(F_{jmax} - \mu_j\right) + \Gamma_{jH}\left(\mu_j - F_{jmin}\right) + \Gamma_{jEH}\left(\mu_j - F_{jmin}\right)}{F_{jmax} - F_{jmin}} \tag{10}$$

Let the number of categories be N_{pat}, which forces the response layer to have N_{pat} number of neurons. The distance vector of the training pattern $\mathbf{F}_i$ from nth class N_n is expressed as

$$dist_{in} = \sqrt{\sum_{j=1}^{m}\left(\frac{F_{ij} - \beta_{nj}}{\gamma_{nj}}\right)^2} \quad \text{for } 1 \leq n \leq N_{pat} \tag{11}$$

In (11), β_{nj} and γ_{nj} are the mean and standard deviation of jth component of the nth pattern vector. The ith pattern membership in class category n lying in the range [0,1] is computed by (12)

$$m_{fk}(F_i) = \frac{1}{1 + \left(\frac{z_{in}}{d_f}\right)^{e_f}} \tag{12}$$

where $d_f > 0$ and $e_f > 0$ are *denominational* and *exponential fuzzy generators*. Finally, the desired output of the jth neuron in the response layer is obtained as:

$$v_j = m_{f_j}(F_i) \tag{13}$$

4 Person Identification by VR

One of the stereo channels of the speech signal is segmented to three regions: *silence* (Φ), *unvoiced* (Ψ) *and voiced* (Ω). Algorithm to segment speech into Φ, Ψ and Ω

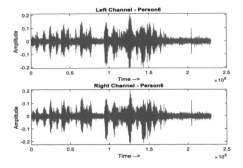
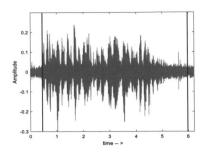

Fig. 2 i Left and right channels of the speech signal **ii** Beginning and end point detected and silence-removed speech

segments is carried out as mentioned in [24]. The resulting speech waveforms are shown in Fig. 2.

5   Classifier Design

5.1   Feature Extraction—MFCC

By placing frequency bands logarithmically on mel scale, the auditory system's response can be approximated. This leads to *mel frequency cepstral coefficients* (MFCC) [1, 6, 18, 22] features.

Fuzzy c-medoid clustering for classification

Fuzzification of the conventional hard c-medoid leads to fuzzy *c*-medoid [25–27]. This clustering technique minimises the objective function J_F expressed in (14)

$$J_F = \sum_{k=1}^{q} \sum_{n=1}^{c} (m_{fnk})^{f_z} \delta(y_k, \zeta_n) \tag{14}$$

where ζ_n represents the nth medoid. The fuzzy membership function of the object y_k to cluster ξ_n is given by

$$m_{fnk} = \sum_{l=1}^{c} \left(\frac{\delta(y_k, \zeta_n)}{\delta(y_k, \zeta_l)} \right)^{-1/f-1} \tag{15}$$

where nth medoid is represented by ζ_n. With $\sum_{n=1}^{c} m_{fnk} = 1, \forall k$ and $0 < \sum_{k=1}^{q} m_{fnk} < q, \forall n$ the new medoids are computed as $\zeta_n = y_j$

$$j = \arg \min \sum_{p=1}^{q} (m_{fnk})^{f_z} \delta(y_p, y_k); \ 1 \le k \le q \tag{16}$$

Rough c-Medoid clustering for classification

If lower and upper approximations of cluster ξ_n are denoted as $\underline{R}(\xi_n)$ and $\overline{R}(\xi_n)$, then $D(\xi_n) = \{\overline{R}(\xi_n), \backslash \underline{R}(\xi_n)\}$ is the boundary [27]. The rough medoid computation follows:

$$\xi_n = y_j \tag{17}$$

where j is given by (18)

$$j = \arg \min \begin{cases} \omega \times A + \tilde{\omega} \times B & \text{if } \underline{R}(\xi_n) \ne \emptyset, D(\xi_n) \ne \emptyset \\ A & \text{if } \underline{R}(\xi_n) \ne \emptyset, D(\xi_n) = \emptyset \\ B & \text{if } \underline{R}(\xi_n) = \emptyset, D(\xi_n) \ne \emptyset \end{cases} \tag{18}$$

where

$$A = \sum_{y_p \in \underline{R}(\xi_n)} \delta(y_p, y_k) \quad \text{and} \quad B = \sum_{y_p \in D(\xi_n)} \delta(y_p, y_k) \tag{19}$$

The lower approximation takes the weight ω, and the boundary weight is $\tilde{\omega} = (1 - \omega)$.

6   Local Voice-Enabled Face Deformation Profile–LVFDP

LVFDP is modelled in terms of instantaneous displacement vectors in the local parts of the lip-jaw face region. The lips and lower jaw movements are the key motion component that leads to the kinematics of deformation. The kinematics of deformation analysed results in six directional motion vectors. By the computation of the movement of the lips and jaw from the current frame to the succeeding frame, the deformation is estimated based on the motion vectors. In the BM technique, [30] employed a block of reference frame which is correlated with the blocks in its position and neighbouring positions in the next frame. This matching is with the minimisation of characteristic absolute error. For frames having non-overlapping blocks of $M \times N$ pixels, each block in frame t_n within a search window of size $S = (2W_1 + 1) \times (2W_2 + 1)$ in the preceding frame t_{n-1} is determined where W_1 and W_2 are the allowed displacement in horizontal and vertical directions, respectively. The criterion for BM vector computation is the sum of the absolute differences

Table 2 LVFDP vectors

S. No.	Vector direction	LVFDP
1	Lower lip lower arc	$\boldsymbol{LL}_{LA}$
2	Upper lip upper arc	$\boldsymbol{UL}_{UA}$
3	Lower lip flatten	$\boldsymbol{LL}_{FT}$
4	Upper lip flatten	$\boldsymbol{UL}_{FT}$
5	Lower jaw open	$\boldsymbol{LJ}_{OP}$
6	Lower jaw close	$\boldsymbol{LJ}_{CL}$

$$\text{SAD}(u_m, v_n) = \sum_{m=0}^{M-1} \sum_{n=0}^{N-1} |pb_n(x + m, y + n)$$
$$- pb_{n-1}(x + m + u_m, y + n + v_n) \tag{20}$$

where pb_n is the pixel intensity of block $\boldsymbol{b}_n$ in frame $\boldsymbol{t}_n$, and pb_{n-1} is the pixel intensity of block $\boldsymbol{b}_{n-1}$ in frame $\boldsymbol{t}_{n-1}$. The motion vector in (u_m, v_n) is defined as $(u, v) = \arg \min \text{SAD}(u_m, v_n)$. Lack of motion in each block is carried out by the mean value of the motion vector given by the expression:

$$\theta = \frac{1}{UV - 1} \sum_{m=0}^{U-1} \sum_{n=0}^{V-1} \sqrt{u_x^2(m, n) - u_y^2(m, n)} \tag{21}$$

$$\theta < \tau_{\text{no - motion}} \tag{22}$$

The six motion vectors corresponding to the displacement are listed in Table 2 and Fig. 3.

The six dominant motion vectors resulting after thresholding are depicted in Fig. 4.

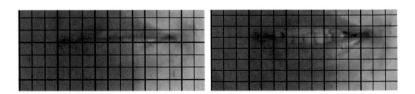

Fig. 3 Block formation

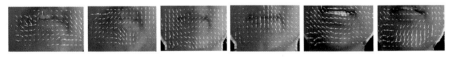

Fig. 4 LVFDP vectors reliable data on lips and jaw kinematics in speech production

Table 3 Recognition accuracy of the eight biometric algorithms with rough-neuro-fuzzy classifiers

BM	Attribute	Classifier	CAR	CRR	FRR	FAR
VR	MFCC	Rough c-medoid	73.24	71.12	18.76	19.88
VR	MFCC	Fuzzy c-medoid	86.24	84.36	15.71	15.28
FR	PCA + LDA	f-MLP	71.48	68.15	28.52	31.85
FR	PCA + LDA + LVFDP	f-MLP	94.88	94.53	6.83	5.22
FVR	PCA + LDA + MFCC	f-MLP & RCM	90.42	88.23	11.45	17.62
FVR	PCA + LDA + MFCC	f-MLP & FCM	92.63	91.51	7.89	8.51
FVR	PCA + LDA + LVFDP + MFCC	f-MLP & RCM	96.84	95.22	4.19	4.71
FVR	PCA + LDA + LVFDP + MFCC	f-MLP & FCM	98.47	98.73	2.09	2.26

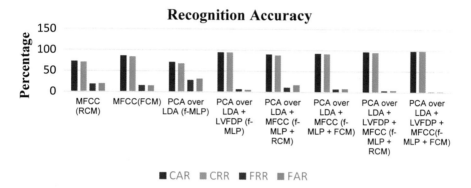

Fig. 5 Recognition accuracy of the eight-person identification algorithms

7 Experimental Results

"*I am presenting myself for person identification, my face and voice are my identity*"
is the text-dependent sentence pronounced by the individuals is captured as video.
Recognition accuracy is measured with *Correct Accept Rate (CAR), Correct Reject
Rate (CRR), False Accept Rate (FAR), False Reject Rate (FRR)* [29] (Table 3 and
Fig. 5).

8 Conclusion

It is evident from the experimental results that decision level fusion of facial features
PCA, LDA and LVFDP using fuzzy-MLP classifier and voice features MFCC
using fuzzy c-medoid algorithm has better overall accuracy. Hybridization of soft
computing paradigms of neuro-fuzzy computing as in fuzzy-MLP and granular

computing with reasoning as in rough fuzzy c-medoids may be investigated for better recognition accuracy over the methods.

References

1. Anil BV, Ravikumar MS (30, 31 Oct 2020) Voice based person identification using c-mean and c-medoid clustering techniques. Proceedings of IEEE discover 2020-international conference on distributed computing, VLSI, electrical circuits and robotics, SMVITM Udupi, India
2. Anil BV, Ravikumar MS (20–21 Sept 2018) Face segmentation in video frames using adaptive morphological face template. Proceedings of IEEE sponsored international conference on innovations in engineering, technology and science (ICIETS)
3. Anil BV, Ravikumar MS (6–7 May 2021) Face recognition in video frames using morphological face template grabber. Int Conf Advan Comput Commun Technol (ICACCT-2021)
4. Anil KJ, Ross A, Prabhakar S (Jan 2004) An introduction to biometric recognition. Invited Paper, IEEE Trans Circ Syst Video Technol 14(1):4–2
5. Anil KJ, Pankanti S, Prabhakar S, Hong L, Ross A, Wayman JL (Aug 2004) Biometrics: a grand challenge. Proceedings of international conference on pattern recognition. Cambridge, UK
6. Dupont S, Luettin J (Sept 2000) Audio visual speech modeling for continuous speech recognition. IEEE Trans Multimedia 2(3)
7. Ross A, Jain AK, Nandakumar K (2006) Levels of fusion in biometrics. In: Handbook of multibiometrics. International series on biometrics, vol 6. Springer, Boston, MA, pp 59–90. https://doi.org/10.1007/0-387-33123-9_3
8. Ross A, Jain AK, Qian J-Z (6–8 June 2001) Information fusion in biometrics. Proceedings of 3rd international conference on audio- and video based person authentication (AVBPAS). Sweden, pp 344–359
9. Mangai UG, Samanta S, Das S, Chowdhury PR (July–Aug 2010) A survey of decision fusion and feature fusion strategies for pattern classification. IETE Tech Rev 27(4):293–307
10. Jain AK, Ross A (2004) Multibiometric system. Commun ACM 47(1):34–40
11. Berrani SA, Garcia C, Enhancing face recognition from video sequences using robust statistics. 2015 IEEE, pp 324–329
12. Amburn EP, Austin JD, Cromartie R, Geselowitz A, Greer T, Haar Romeny B, Zimmerman JB, Zuiderveld K (Sept 1987) Adaptive histogram equalization and its variations. Comput Vis, Graph, Image Proc 39(3):355–368. Elsevier Inc
13. Liévin M, Luthon F (2004) Nonlinear color space and spatiotemporal MRF for hierarchical segmentation of face features in video. IEEE Trans Image Proc 13(1):63–71
14. Monwar MM, Paul PP, Islam MW, Rezaei S, A real-time face recognition approach from video sequence using skin color model and eigenface method. IEEE CCECE/CCGEI, Ottawa, May 6. pp 2181–2185
15. Belhumeur PN, Hespanha JP, Kriegman DJ (1997) Eigenfaces versus Fisher faces: Recognition using class specific linear projection. IEEE Trans Pattern Anal Mach Intell 19(7):711–720
16. Marcialia GL, Roli F (2006) Fusion of LDA and PCA for face recognition. Int J Image Graph, ©World Sci Publ Company 6(2):293–311; Department of Electrical and Electronic Engineering, University of Cagliari, Piazza D' Armi, I-09123 Cagliari, Italy
17. Turk M, Pentland A (March 1991) Eigenfaces for recognition. J Cogn Neurosci 3:71–86
18. Kumar K, Potamianos G, Navratil J, Marcheret E, Libal V, Audio visual speech synchrony detection by a family of bimodal linear prediction modals. https://www.researchgate.net/publication/290286223
19. Mitra S, Pal SK, Logical operation based fuzzy MLP for classification and rule generation. Contributed Article Neural Networks-1994, Elsevier Science Ltd, 7(2):353–373

20. Pal SK, Mitra S (1992) Multilayer perceptron, fuzzy sets, and classification. IEEE Trans Neural Netw 3(5):683–696
21. Bhattacharjee D, Basu DK, Nasipuri M, Kundu M (2010) Human face recognition using fuzzy multilayer perceptron. Soft Comput. https://doi.org/10.1007/s00500-009-0426-0
22. Markowitz JA (Sept 2000) Voice biometrics. Commun ACM 43(9):67–73
23. Jang J-SR, Chen J-J (1997) Neuro-fuzzy and soft computing for speaker recognition. Proceedings of 6th international fuzzy systems conference. pp 663–66
24. Saha G, Chakravarthy S, Senapathi S, A new silence removal and end point detection algorithm for speech and speaker recognition applications. pp 1–5. Available: https://www.researchgate.net/publications
25. Jain AK, Dubes RC, Algorithms for clustering data. Prentice Hall Inc, chapter 2. pp 7–50
26. Mitra S, Pal SK, Banerjee M, Rough fuzzy knowledge-based network—a soft computing approach. Rough fuzzy hybridization, Springer, pp 428–452
27. Maji P, Pal SK, Rough-fuzzy pattern recognition, applications in bioinformatics and medical imaging. IEEE computer society, Wiley, pp 161–180
28. Satish K (2013) Neural network a classroom approach, 1st edn. Tata Mc Graw Hill Publishing Company Limited, New Delhi, pp 42–65
29. Wang R, Bhanu B (2011) Prediction for fusion of biometrics systems, book chapter in "Multibiometrics for human identification". Cambridge University Press, pp 323–362
30. Grosu D, Galmeanu H, Motion estimation in MPEG2 video encoding using a parallel block matching algorithm, conference: processing of the 6th international symposium on automatic control and computer science (SACCS'98), vol II. At: Iasi, Romania

Early Breast Cancer Detection from Blood Plasma Using Hubness-Aware Adaptive Neural Network with Hybrid Feature Selection

S. Raja Sree and A. Kunthavai

Abstract Breast cancer is a complex and heterogeneous disease prevalent amongst women leading to mortality. Breast cancer diagnosis at the early stages of tumour development can increase the survival rate of women suffering from breast cancer. The most prevalent mammogram method for early screening of breast cancer results in a greater number of false positives for breast cancer detection in young women. Latest research in the field of genomics suggests that microRNAs (miRNAs) of circulating tumour cells, and gene expressions of circulating tumour cells in blood plasma are good candidate for the detection of breast cancer during early stages of cancer. Hence, it is proposed to develop a diagnostic machine learning model for early detection and effective treatment from the gene expression values of miRNA. Since gene expression data are complex and high dimensional, a hybrid feature selection is performed using molecular pathway information, and gene ontology information related to breast cancer and also most informative genes are selected using Laplacian score feature ranking. For the classification of samples into tumour and normal samples, a novel improved artificial neural network (ANN), namely hubness-aware adaptive neural network (HAANN) with adaptive learning rate is implemented. A novel strategy based on hubness score is adapted to adjust the learning rate of the neural network dynamically. Performance analysis of the proposed machine learning shows an improved performance compared to the traditional classification algorithms for intrinsic high-dimensional data.

Keywords MicroRNA · Circulating tumour cells · Gene expression · Hubness · Neural network · Adaptive learning rate

S. R. Sree (✉) · A. Kunthavai
Coimbatore Institute of Technology, Coimbatore, Tamilnadu, India
e-mail: rajasree.s@cit.edu.in

© The Author(s), under exclusive license to Springer Nature Singapore Pte Ltd. 2022
C. Satyanarayana et al. (eds.), *High Performance Computing and Networking*,
Lecture Notes in Electrical Engineering 853,
https://doi.org/10.1007/978-981-16-9885-9_41

503

1 Introduction

Breast cancer is a disease prevalent amongst women worldwide leading to death. Breast cancer can be treated successfully and cured by choosing the right treatment for the patient if it is diagnosed at the early stages of progression. If the diagnosis is performed at later stages of cancer development, the patient may not respond to the treatment as expected leading to further complications. At present, mammograms are used for breast cancer screening to detect cancer at early stages. However, mammograms are not accurate and may lead to false positive for young women aged less than forty due to dense breast tissues. Since cancer is one of the diseases caused due to mutations in the genes which controls the cell functionalities, current cancer research focuses on analysis of gene expression profiles associated with various cancer phenotypes.

During the early stages of cancer progression, tumour cells get mixed with the blood stream and keeps circulating as circulating tumour cells (CTCs). Latest microarray technologies are capable of separating the CTCs from the normal cells. MicroRNAs (miRNAs) from the CTCs are extracted and subjected to gene expression profiling in clinical laboratories. Extensive oncological studies have proved that the miRNAs are differentially expressed due to genomic alterations for breast cancer patients at all stages of cancer. Gene expression analysis of healthy individuals and breast cancer patients of various stages can be classified by machine learning methodologies for efficient prediction of breast cancer. Compared to mammograms and gene expression analysis of biopsy samples, analysis of gene expressions from blood is a non-invasive screening process requiring maximum of 10 ml of blood.

Analysing gene expressions are complex due to its high-dimensional nature and comparatively fewer samples. Data sets involved in the analysis contain gene expression samples of 100 to 200 patients, whereas the number of features for each patient would be more than 10,000. This leads to the problem of curse of dimensionality, and the classical machine learning algorithms may not perform well in these cases. To reduce the problem with high dimensions, an optimal feature selection is required to subset the most relevant features in the diagnosis process. From the selected features, efficient machine learning models addressing the challenges of high dimensional data are used to classify the gene expressions of CTCs as normal and healthy cells.

2 Related Works

Computational approaches are widely used in analysis and interpretations high-dimensional gene expressions to treat the patients with a detailed diagnosis. There are various works [1–5] proving the advantage of analysing CTCs for early detection of cancer using machine learning methodologies.

Zhang et al. [1] have proposed a method for biomarker selection to detect breast cancer in early stages using SVM with recursive feature elimination. Statistical significance test has been conducted after linear mixed modelling of the data to select the relevant features, and SVM-RFE method is used to classify the normal and healthy samples. The suggested model performed well for training data set, but the accuracy was around 55% for testing data set due to overfitting.

Zhang et al. [2] have improved the accuracy of their previous work for early detection of breast cancer in peripheral blood using multiple biomarker panels. Inclusion of multiple biomarker panels for feature selection has improved the accuracy of testing set from 58 to 78%. Classification model can be improvised to handle curse of dimensionality for more accurate results.

Chan et al. [3] conducted a study on the serum samples of healthy people and breast cancer patients to arrive at a signature for the early detection of breast cancer. Using paired T-test, relevant features are selected and grouped into healthy and tumour samples using unsupervised hierarchical clustering algorithm. Biologically informed feature selection based on pathway information regarding breast cancer can improve the predictive capability of the model.

Samarasinghe et al. [5] used an approach named bi-biological filter method for selecting the marker genes associated with breast cancer. A two-step process is followed for feature selection; first step selects the relevant genes based on the biological knowledge, and the second step uses a best first search with SVM wrapper. The output genes are passed to various classification algorithms such as artificial neural network and SVM. This work could be improved by testing the data with more samples and by handling the high dimensionality using better feature selection methods.

Huang et al. [6] have proposed a computational model for the early detection of colorectal cancer from peripheral blood. Dimension reduction of the gene expressions has been performed using principal component analysis and linear discriminant analysis and classified using logistic regression and support vector machine. Hyperparameters for the classification model have been chosen by random search, and the best learnt model has been chosen by k-fold cross-validation model.

There is a need for an efficient and accurate model for the early prediction of breast cancer from miRNAs in blood plasma. Existing approaches lead to an inference that the factors affecting the performance of the classical machine learning models developed for microarray expressions are as follows: (i) high dimensionality of the data (ii) intrinsic dimensionality (Large number of features and fewer samples). These challenges could be addressed using appropriate techniques for feature selection and choosing optimised values for hyper-parameters used in the machine learning model. A hybrid two-level feature selection is performed to filter the most informative genes from the high dimensional gene expression. First level of feature selection is performed using existing biological knowledge such as gene ontology and pathway information about the proteins and genes involved in breast cancer. Second-level feature selection is performed using unsupervised feature ranking method termed.

Laplacian Ranking: For classification, a novel improved multi-layer perceptron with back propagation model named hubness-aware neural network with adaptive learning rate for early breast cancer prediction is proposed and implemented.

3 Methodology

The objective of the proposed work is to predict early breast cancer in women from gene expression values of miRNA and plasma cells. The analysis of gene expressions from peripheral blood samples is performed using the proposed methodology illustrated as a schematic chart in Fig. 1. High-dimensional gene expressions are filtered using the first two steps. From the gene expression, relevant genes/miRNAs are selected based on the pathways related to breast cancer and gene ontology databases. From the genes relevant to breast cancer, the most informative genes required for the classification are filtered using Laplacian ranking method. Top-ranked genes are fed to hubness-aware adaptive neural network for early breast cancer prediction.

3.1 Ontology and Pathway Informed Gene Selection

Analysis of gene expression demands selection of gene sets that are relevant to the disease rather than using the entire gene expression. In this work, a gene subset is selected based on the existing knowledge regarding the association of genes to breast cancer development. Knowledge on the genes associated to breast cancer is curated from web-based ontology tools such as OMIM tool [16], gene ontology (GO) [13] and QuickGO [14].

Biological pathways are the set of actions involved in the cell cycle resulting in a product such as protein. If there are mutations in the genes involved in the pathways, then the resultant protein may become non-functional or over functional resulting in cancer. Hence, in addition to the genes associated with the disease, biological knowledge on pathways has been used to select the genes contributing to the production of proteins known to be associated with breast cancer. Kyoto Encyclopaedia of Genes and Genomes (KEGG) [12] and WikiPathways [15] databases have a collection of pathways involved in diseases for various organisms from the human pathway database. In this work, the pathways related to breast cancer have been queried from

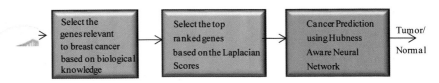

Fig. 1 Schematic diagram of early breast cancer prediction

WikiPathways database, and from the database, genes involved in the pathways are retrieved.

3.2 Feature Selection Based on Laplacian Score

Even after the selection of features based on the biological knowledge, the number of features in the data set is less compared to the number of samples. Hence, an unsupervised feature-ranking method based on Laplacian score is used to select the features with high locality preserving power. Locality preserving measure is calculated based on the probability that the data belonging to the same target class are close to each other. A good feature is the one that has a fair linear relationship with the neighbours of the data point. Laplacian score [8] is formulated based on the locality preserving property, and the most relevant features are ranked from the high-dimensional data for classification.

Laplacian score for each gene based on the similarity matrix is calculated using Eq. (1) from the k-neighbour values of the data points. Graph Laplacian matrix is constructed for each gene using Equation (2).

$$S = \begin{cases} S_{ij} = \frac{e^{-d(x_i, x_j)}}{t}, & j \text{ belongs to } k - \text{neighbors of } i \\ 0, & \text{otherwise} \end{cases} \tag{1}$$

$$\tilde{f}_r = f_r - \frac{f_r^T DI}{I^T DI} I \tag{2}$$

where

f_r set of all the sample values in the rth feature
D diag(S)
I Unit vector

Based on the similarity matrix and Laplacian score, Laplacian rank is calculated using Equation (3).

$$L_r = \frac{\tilde{f}_r^T L \tilde{f}_r}{\tilde{f}_r^T D \tilde{f}_r} \tag{3}$$

From the value of Laplacian rank L_r, top features are selected to perform classification.

3.3 *Early Cancer Prediction Using Hubness-Aware Adaptive Neural Network*

Multi-layer perceptron (MLP) is one of the best artificial neural networks applied in various fields such as image processing, pattern recognition, natural language processing and medical data mining. Architecture diagram of neural network is shown in Fig. 2. MLP is modelled with an input layer, output layer and two hidden layers. In the proposed work, the number of neurons in the input layer $I(x)$ is the number of selected genes for classification, and number of neurons in the output layer $O(x)$ is one, since the problem is a one class classification problem designed to predict if the given input sample is healthy or cancerous.

Number of neurons in the hidden layers is the same as in the input layer. The network between input layer and the first hidden layer is a fully connected network where all the input neurons are connected to all the neurons in the hidden layer. The connection between the first hidden layer and the second hidden layer is also the same as the number of input neurons and forms a fully connected network.

MLP learning takes place in two phases, namely feed forward phase and back propagation phase. In the feed forward phase, neurons are activated based on the input neurons and the connection weights as given in Equation (4). Activation value f_2 of the hidden layers h1, h2 in Fig. 2 and the output layer is calculated as given in Equation (4),

$$f_2(x_i) = f\left(\left(\sum_{i=1}^{n}(w_i x_i)\right) + b\right) \tag{4}$$

where

$f(x)$ $\max(0, x)$
b bias term

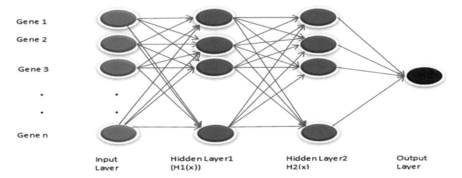

Fig. 2 Architecture diagram of neural network

In the proposed work, a linear activation function termed ReLU activation function f has been used between all the layers. For high dimensional data such as gene expressions, ReLU activation function gives better performance avoiding vanishing gradient problem.

In back propagation phase, weights are updated based on the absolute difference between the target value and actual output value from the output layer to the hidden layers in backward direction. The learning model is an iterative process starting with random weights $w0$. After completion of feed forward phase of iterations, the weights for the next iteration w_{i+1} are calculated using Equation (5).

$$w_{i+1} = w_i - \Delta w_i \tag{5}$$

where $\Delta w_i = \alpha |t - y| x_i$.

w_{i+1} updated weights for the next iteration.
w_i current weight of the connection
x_i current input value
α learning rate.

Learning rate is the hyper-parameter that controls the speed of learning in neural network. Usually, learning rate is set to a small constant value. In this paper, adaptive learning rate depending on the data points is used instead of constant learning rate to boost the performance of the learning model.

3.4 Adaptive Learning Rate for Neural Network

Learning rate has a major role in the back propagation of error from the output layer to the inner layers of the neural network. If the choice of the learning rate is too small, then the model takes a greater number of iterations for convergence. On the contrary, choice of large learning rate value results in inappropriate updates of error values. Hence, it is important to choose an optimum value for learning rate in the design of neural network model. Recent works [18] using neural network have used adaptive learning rate for efficient and faster convergence. In this paper, a hubness-aware adaptive learning rate is used based on the hubness score of the input data points.

High dimensional data such as gene expressions have a challenge named "Curse of Dimensionality" that makes all the data points look sparse, and the average distance between all the data points would be almost similar. In high-dimensional data, Tomasev et al. [9, 10] have observed the advantages of hubness property in various classification problems. Hubness is a measure quantified from the number of times a data point occurring as a neighbour to other data points in the data set. Same data occurring in the neighbour set of many other data points are termed as hubs.

Tomasev et al. [9, 10] have classified the hubness scores as good hubness score and bad hubness score. If a data point occurs in the k-neighbour set of other data point and the target label of the data points match, then the data points are added to the good hub score of the data point, whereas a mismatch would be added to bad hub score. Good hubness score of data point ($GH(x_i)$) is determined using Equation (6) from the count of k-neighbours with matching labels as that of x_i.

$$GH(x_i) = \left| x_j \in N_k(x_i), y_i = y_j \right| \tag{6}$$

where

$GH(x_i)$ Good hubness score of data point x_i.
$N_k(x_i)$ Set of neighbours of x_i.
y_i Target Label of x_i.

In this paper, a novel idea of using adaptive learning rate based on the good hubness score is used dynamically. Since good hubs are highly influential points, they are given more weightage in the back propagation phase, whereas data points with less good hub score are given low weightage. Thus, the learning rate would be higher for data points with high good hubness value and minimal for data points with less good hubness value.

Good hubness score values are normalised to values between 0 and 1 using probability distribution function given in Equation (7).

$$\alpha(x_i) = \frac{1}{\sqrt{2\pi}\sigma} \exp\left(\frac{-(GH(x_i) - \mu)^2}{2\sigma^2}\right) \tag{7}$$

where

μ Mean of good hubness score $GH(x)$.
σ Standard deviation of good hubness score $GH(x)$.

Thus, neural network model has been developed and fine-tuned by dynamically adjusting learning rate using hubness property observed in high-dimensional data.

4   Results and Discussion

Breast cancer can be detected by using machine learning methods from the gene expressions and microRNAs of plasma cells in the peripheral blood due to the presence of circulating tumour cells. Hubness-aware adaptive neural network model has been developed to predict the presence of circulating tumour cells in early stages of breast cancer from miRNA expressions of plasma and gene expression of plasma cells.

Gene expression and miRNA data sets from gene expression omnibus (GEO) [18] repository have been used to demonstrate the predictive performance of the proposed algorithm. The selected features and the labels are trained with hubness-aware neural

Table 1 Gene expression data sets used

GEO accession No.	No. of genes/miRNA	No. of genes/miRNA selected based on ontology	Accuracy achieved using proposed HAANN (First 50 genes)	Accuracy achieved using proposed HAANN (First 100 genes)	Accuracy achieved using proposed HAANN (First 150 genes)
GSE16443	11,217	767	0.9	0.88	0.778
GSE27562	54,675	1327	0.84	0.88	0.88
GSE73002	2540	152	0.99	0.99	0.99

network model using tenfold cross-validation. The best results obtained based on the accuracy values using tenfold validation by varying the number of genes are tabulated for gene expressions and miRNA. Accuracy of the proposed hubness-aware adaptive neural network is evaluated using the three different data sets in Table 1.

Table 2 shows the comparative performance of hubness-aware adaptive neural network is compared with the traditional classification algorithms such as k-nearest neighbour, random forest and neural network.

GSE16443 consists of 130 samples with 67 patients with breast cancer risk and 63 healthy samples. For GSE16443, hubness-aware neural network has achieved higher accuracy consistently compared to the traditional algorithms. By selecting the top 50 genes, hubness-aware neural network has achieved an accuracy of 90%. With 100 genes, accuracy of hubness-aware neural network is 88% resulting in a considerable improvement in performance compared to neural network's accuracy of 74%. With 150 genes, hubness-aware neural network gives a better performance of 77.8% compared to the other algorithms.

For the GEO series data set with accession number GSE27562, it is inferred that the hubness-aware neural network algorithm has consistent performance for various number of features. F1-score is 83% for the proposed neural network, and for the classical algorithms, the score ranges from 0.6 to 079. When executed with 100 genes, F1-score for hubness-aware adaptive neural network is 88%, same as that of KNN and random forest. With 150 genes, performance of random forest has drastically reduced to 50%, whereas KNN and random forest had an F1-score of 88%. Comparison of precision values has the maximum value of 100% in all three comparisons using various number of genes. Precision values of other algorithms vary between 50 and 100 for the classical algorithms. Recall score for hubness-aware adaptive neural network is around 80%, and the value is lesser compared to KNN and neural network. But, the recall value is higher for hubness-aware adaptive neural network than other algorithms when larger number of genes are used for classification.

Table 2 Performance evaluation of HAANN with classical algorithms

Data set	Number of genes	Algorithm	Accuracy	Precision	Recall	F1-score
GSE16443	50	KNN	0.778	1.0	1.0	0.8
		Random forest	0.75	1.0	0.75	0.75
		Neural network (NN)	0.75	1.0	0.75	0.85
		HAANN	**0.9**	**1.0**	**1.0**	**0.85**
	100	KNN	0.692	0.667	1.0	0.714
		Random forest	0.643	0.8	0.56	0.53
		Neural network (NN)	0.74	0.78	0.77	0.81
		HAANN	**0.88**	**0.82**	**0.85**	**1.0**
	150	KNN	0.7	0.667	0.82	0.727
		Random forest	0.68	0.8	0.4	0.5
		Neural network (NN)	0.69	0.7	1.0	0.75
		HAANN	**0.778**	**0.9**	**1.0**	**0.76**
GSE27562	50	KNN	0.812	1	1	0.6
		Random forest	0.667	0.5	0.05	0.5
		Neural network (NN)	0.812	1	1	0.784
		HAANN	**0.8375**	**1**	**0.82**	**0.832**
	100	KNN	0.84	0.9375	0.8	**0.882**
		Random forest	0.84	0.9375	0.8	**0.882**
		Neural network (NN)	0.67	0.82	0.81	0.67
		HAANN	**0.8853**	**1**	**0.82**	**0.882**
	150	KNN	0.621	0.95	0.8	0.882
		Random forest	0.714	0.831	0.4	0.55
		Neural network (NN)	0.8612	0.95	0.81	0.714
		HAANN	**0.8853**	**1**	**1**	**0.882**
GSE73002	50	KNN	0.9825	0.9591	0.95	0.95
		Random forest	0.9756	0.9466	0.95	0.9425
		Neural network (NN)	0.99	1	1	1
		HAANN	**0.9875**	**0.9925**	**1**	**0.99**
	100	KNN	0.9825	0.9591	0.95	0.95
		Random forest	0.9756	0.9466	0.9425	0.9425
		Neural network (NN)	0.99	1	1	1
		HAANN	**0.99**	**0.9925**	**1**	**1**

(continued)

(continued)

Data set	Number of genes	Algorithm	Accuracy	Precision	Recall	F1-score
	150	KNN	0.9825	0.9591	0.95	0.95
		Random forest	0.9756	0.9466	0.95	0.9425
		Neural network (NN)	0.99	1	1	1
		HAANN	**0.99**	1	1	1

GEO series with accession number GSE73002 contains the miRNA expression values of the circulating tumour cells in serum plasma from 4113 samples containing samples of breast cancer patients and non-breast cancerous samples with expression values of 2540 miRNAs. MiRNAs are mapped to the target genes using a tool named mirDB, and relevant miRNA was selected based on the existing biological knowledge from gene ontology and molecular pathway information. The miRNA data set gives high accuracy in the prediction of cancer from the selected genes when classified with classical algorithms and the proposed hubness-aware neural network. Neural network and hubness-aware adaptive neural network have accuracy score of around 99% for various number of genes, and the accuracy of KNN and random forest is around 98%. F1-score, precision and recall scores for neural network and hubness-aware adaptive neural network are around 100%. For KNN and random forest, the metrics values vary between 85 and 100.

From the comparative analysis of the various algorithms on the prediction of miRNA, it can be inferred that the algorithms predict accurately as the number of samples n are higher compared to the number of features, and the features selected for classification have high predicting capabilities.

5   Conclusion

Accurate inference by applying machine learning techniques on microarray data for effective cancer treatment is a challenge due to intrinsic nature of microarray data. In this paper, the number of features is reduced by applying two-level feature selection based on biological knowledge and using Laplacian score. Also, an efficient classification algorithm, named hubness-aware neural network (HAANN), capable of handling intrinsic high-dimensional data is implemented. Experiments have been conducted with three different data sets including gene expressions of plasma cells and miRNA expressions of plasma cells in blood. Experimental results show that the proposed algorithm outperforms the traditional algorithms such as k-nearest neighbour, random forest and artificial neural network in terms of various evaluation metrics for classification such as accuracy, precision, recall and F1-score. However, the performance of the algorithm fluctuates for intrinsically high dimensional gene expressions due to the randomness in the initial weight values applied to the neural network. Future works can be formulated to control the randomness in the initial weight values of neural network model. Comparison of the prediction performance of gene expressions and miRNA expressions shows that miRNA is better candidates for early-stage cancer prediction compared to gene expressions in plasma cells.

References

1. Zhang F, Kaufman HL, Deng Y, Drabier R (2013) Recursive SVM biomarker selection for early detection of breast cancer in peripheral blood. BMC Med Genomics 6(1):S4
2. Zhang F, Deng Y, Drabier R (2013) Multiple biomarker panels for early detection of breast cancer in peripheral blood. BioMed Res Int 2013
3. Chan M, Liaw CS, Ji SM, Tan HH, Wong CY, Thike AA, Tan PH, Ho GH, Lee AS-G (2013) Identification of circulating microRNA signatures for breast cancer detection. Clin Cancer Res 19(16):4477–4487
4. Chang Y-T, Huang C-S, Yao C-T, Su S-L, Terng H-J, Chou H-L, Chou Y-C et al (2014) Gene expression profile of peripheral blood in colorectal cancer. World J Gastroenterol: WJG 20(39):14463
5. Samarasinghe S, Kulasiri DD (2013) Gene expression based computer aided diagnostic system for breast cancer: a novel biological filter for biomarker detection
6. Huang S, Chong N, Lewis NE, Jia W, Xie G, Garmire LX (2016) Novel personalized pathway-based metabolomics models reveal key metabolic pathways for breast cancer diagnosis. Genome Med 8(1):34
7. Sfakianakis S, Bei ES, Zervakis M, Vassou D, Kafetzopoulos D (2013) On the identification of circulating tumor cells in breast cancer. IEEE J Biomed Health Inform 18(3):773–782
8. Liao B, Jiang Y, Liang W, Zhu W, Cai L, Cao Z (2014) Gene selection using locality sensitive laplacian score. IEEE/ACM Trans Comput Biol Bioinf (TCBB) 11(6):1146–1156
9. Tomašev N, Radovanović M, Mladenić D, Ivanović M (2011) Hubness-based fuzzy measures for high-dimensional k-nearest neighbor classification. In: International workshop on machine learning and data mining in pattern recognition. Springer, Berlin, Heidelberg, pp 16–30
10. Tomašev N, Buza K, Marussy K, Kis PB (2015) Hubness-aware classification, instance selection and feature construction: survey and extensions to time-series. In: Feature selection for data and pattern recognition. Springer, Berlin, Heidelberg, pp 231–262
11. Buza K (2016) Classification of gene expression data: a hubness-aware semi-supervised approach. Comput Methods Programs Biomed 127:105–113
12. Kanehisa M, Furumichi M, Tanabe M, Sato Y, Morishima K (2016) KEGG: new perspectives on genomes, pathways, diseases and drugs. Nucleic Acids Res 45(D1):D353–D361
13. Gene Ontology Consortium (2004) The gene ontology (GO) database and informatics resource. Nucleic Acids Res 32(suppl_1):D258–D261
14. Binns D, Dimmer E, Huntley R, Barrell D, O'donovan C, Apweiler R (2009) QuickGO: a web-based tool for gene ontology searching. Bioinformatics 25(22):3045–3046
15. Kelder T, Van Iersel MP, Hanspers K, Kutmon M, Conklin BR, Evelo CT, Pico AR (2011) WikiPathways: building research communities on biological pathways. Nucleic Acids Res 40(D1):D1301–D1307
16. Hamosh A, Scott AF, Amberger JS, Bocchini CA, McKusick VA (2005) Online mendelian inheritance in man (OMIM), a knowledgebase of human genes and genetic disorders. Nucleic Acids Res 33(suppl_1):D514–D517
17. Barrett T, Edgar R (2006) Gene expression omnibus: microarray data storage, submission, retrieval, and analysis. Methods Enzymol 411:352–369
18. Takase T, Oyama S, Kurihara M (2018) Effective neural network training with adaptive learning rate based on training loss. Neural Netw 101:68–78

Comparative Analysis of CNN Methodologies Used for Classification of Diabetic Retinopathy

P. Sudharshan Duth and Elton Grivith D. Souza

Abstract Diabetic retinopathy is currently one of the most common conditions that affects the eyes. It occurs when the blood vessels present on the light-sensitive tissue is damaged which results in blindness or vision loss. It is quite challenging to identify its symptoms in its early stages and can thus lead to delay in treatments. Hence, image processing was introduced to solve this classification problem. The problem domain mainly focussed its approach in classification speed and reliability. Thus, many classification methodologies were used to compute the symptoms according to varying levels of infection. In this work, we have acquired a fundus image data set categorised into five levels of infection and used it to compare different commonly used CNN methodologies to observe their behaviour in varying simulations.

Keywords Diabetic retinopathy (DR) · CNN · Image classification · Computer vision

1 Introduction

Diabetic retinopathy detection and classification are the process of using computations to identify the damaged blood vessels in the fundus images that exist on the light-sensitive tissue present at the back of the eye. This has been known as one of the most common cases leading to blindness. But, even though this increase, clinical diagnosis of this condition takes place manually where ophthalmologists examine the imaging results themselves. This makes the identification process arduous whilst consuming excessive time. Also, misdiagnosis due to false identification, lack of resources, etc. is quite common. Thus, automatic detection and classification of this condition are deemed necessary. The detected conditions can then be categorised into various levels depending on the amount of damage. This can then be used to

P. S. Duth (✉) · E. G. D. Souza
Department of Computer Science, Amrita School of Arts and Sciences, Amrita Vishwa
Vidyapeetham, Mysuru, India
e-mail: p_sudharshanduth@my.amrita.edu

detect and calculate the progress of the condition as well as monitor the effectiveness of the prescribed treatment.

In this paper, we have referred various CNN methodologies and compared them to observe the behaviour of different approaches in varying simulations. Different CNN algorithms have been used to classify image data into five stages of infection. This has been done using the retinal images provided by EyePACS which consists of more than 35,000 fundus images labelled between 0 and 4 to differentiate the different stages of infection. We will train multiple models based on this data set with different methodologies and data sizes and then compare the performance of these models with each other.

2 Literature Review

Zhang et al [1] developed a system called DeepDR that relies on transfer and ensemble learning to directly classify fundus images into infected and uninfected samples. The system developed is evaluated with nine different metrics. The system was built using high-quality retinal images trained with CNN and NN models. They have constructed an optimal model by exploring the connection between best component classifiers and the quantity of labels in the data frame. The model provides consistent results with high sensitivity which makes it easier for ophthalmologists to gain better insights. Gurcan et al [2] proposed a comprehensive study of a classification system based on the stages of processing, classification and feature extraction of images. Their work used InceptionV3 transfer learning approach with ml algorithms like SVM, logistic regression and random forest. Their model has shown competency in terms of accuracy without layer-wise tuning. Additionally, their study incorporates metrics of computational power, memory capacity, model complexity, etc. which provides researchers with a comparison of different methodologies. Krause et al [3] used quadratic-weighted kappa score and majority decision to assist grading of different stages of DR infection and AUC to analyse sensitivity and specificity. The authors concluded that adjudication reduced the errors in grading retinal images, and a small set of these adjudicated images resulted in significant improvement in algorithmic performance. Vo and Verma [4] proposed two CNN models, i.e. CKML Net and VGGNet with a hybrid colour space.

Their methodology incorporated transfer learning with two different data sets— EyePACS and Messidor. Their experiments conclude that results from CKML Net were better compared to GoogleNet, and that VNXK was better compared to the results from VGGNet on their data when using the LGI colour space. Their model showed improved results when implementing on the Messidor data set. Sayres et al [5] with the participation of 1612 patients studied the significance of deep learning diabetic retinopathy algorithms on physicians by using computer-assisted instructions (CAI). In their methodology, ophthalmologists read DR images according to ICDR disease severity scale in three conditions that include unassisted learning, grades only learning and grades with heat map. The sensitivity and specificity were adjusted according to adjudicated reference standard, and accuracy was measured with the five class level agreement and Cohens quadratically weighted k. Their analysis concluded that the classifiers were more accurate with the assistance from the model rather than without when using only the grades. And grades plus heat map showed improved accuracy for subjects infected with diabetic retinopathy. The authors concluded that DL algorithms can improve accuracy and confidence of the classifiers, whilst classifiers are assisted with the con of increased grading time. Kelly et al [6] published an article exploring the major challenges and limitations in the field of artificial intelligence in healthcare, and considerations needed to be able to take these technologies form research and put it into clinical practice. The authors state that the timely transition of safe artificial intelligence technologies into clinical practice that benefits everyone is difficult, and conclude that future work should focus on the concepts of algorithmic bias, reducing specificity and improving the generalisability and interpretability of ML algorithms and in doing so can lead to a technological transformation. Doshi et al [7] proposed a work which consisted of using various downscaling algorithms before feeding the retinal images into the network for classification. The authors used a multi-channel InceptionV3 model with the EyePACS and Indian Diabetic Retinopathy Image Data sets in experiments. Liu et al [8] proposed a new algorithm based on fractional integration for denoising and detecting noise based on fractional differential gradient. The author used neighbourhood information to detect anomalies based on contour, direction distribution of noise, etc. The implementation incorporated gradient-based architecture search to improve efficiency whilst maintaining quality. Zhou et al [9] proposed various conclusions derived from a publicly available medical image data set to provide additional parameters to the classifier. Their work draws a conclusion that intricate and critical data augmentation techniques, processing techniques and complex network architectures will not only fail to improve the network performance but can also hinder it, and that the architecture of the network is more important in segmentation rather than using other processing techniques. Bodapati et al [10] proposed a model that extracted features of DR images from multiple pre-trained transfer learning models, such as VGG16, Xception, ResNet, and NASNet. The authors then blended these features to get the final feature representations. These feature representations were then used to train the model. All experiments were executed on a Kaggle data set. The results achieved by the model are a kappa score of 94.82 for the identification of DR and a score of 71.1% for severity level prediction of the infection. Mateen et al [11] proposed a model regarding the classification of diabetic retinopathy that achieves a symmetrically optimised solution using Gaussian mixture model (GMM) for region segmentation, VGGNet to extract features, singular value decomposition (SVD) and principal component analysis for feature selection. A softmax layer was used to differentiate between the features in the retinal images. The research was conducted on a Kaggle data set of more than 35,000 images. Song [12] published a work relating to classification of DR using Messidor data set by formulating the grading system as multiple instances for the learning problem. This mechanism with the help of attention layers was developed to detect regions suspected of lesions. The model achieved an average of 76.4% accuracy over multiple experiments. Sagi and Rokach [13] published a survey on ensemble learning approaches. Their work compared traditional and novel ensemble learning techniques to provide an overview of the trends and challenges in this field. The paper provides a detailed explanation of the working of these methodologies as well as how and when to use these concepts. Xiu et al [14] have developed a deep learning DR classifier using DenseNet. They discuss about the challenges and impact of this infection and have developed a model from scratch and another model using transfer learning to compare the approaches and achieve better model accuracy. Sisodia et al [15] classified the DR images by examining the mean value and standard deviation that was extracted by identifying 14 different features using techniques such as histogram equalisation, image enhancement, green channel extraction, and resizing.

3 Proposed Methodology

3.1 Data Description

The data set comprising of retinal images was sourced from EyePACS available at Kaggle. The data set consists of more than 35,000 high-resolution images that were captured under different conditions. Each sample consists of the left and right eyes labelled according to the sample number (Example: 101_left.jpeg represents the left eye of subject 101). Each eye is given a label that categorises the images into five different levels—the highest signifying proliferative DR, and the lowest shows that there is no presence of DR symptoms.

These fundus images also vary with the imaging techniques that were used, exposure, angle of image, focus, contrast, etc. And like real-time images, this data set also has some amount of noise in both images and labels (Fig. 1).

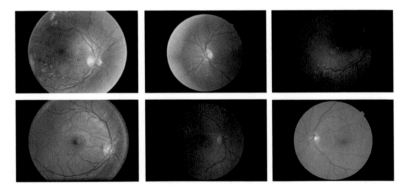

Fig. 1 Sample images from EyePACS data set

3.2   Transfer Learning

This is an approach to machine learning, wherein a model that was already trained is imported as a starting point for training another model. This enables the CNN to start with the imported weights instead of starting from scratch. The imported weights from the pre-trained model are generally trained on large amount of data These models generally consist of convolution, pooling and dense layers. The convolution and pooling layers help with object detection by relying on a small region of repetitive and consistent features, and the dense layers allow the model to train on all combinations of learning features. The pre-trained model is generally trained with a large data set of general images. This allows the model to be imported as a base to learn the spatial features which is useful for many computer vision tasks even if the new task belongs to an entirely different domain.

InceptionV3 is a commonly used pre-trained model that has achieved greater than 78.1% accuracy on the ImageNet data set. Large kennel sizes, MLPconv layers, batch normalisation, etc. have been used to reduce its parameters and complexity which has greatly contributed to its superior performance.

InceptionResNetV2 is a CNN trained on a large sample size of more than a million images on ImageNet. This model has a depth of 164 layers, and it can classify and categorise objects into 1000 different categories. It is a combination of inception with residual connections which can avoid degradation problems and can reduce training time.

VGG16 also known as OxfordNet has achieved 92.7% top-five accuracy on the ImageNet data set. The model consists of convolution layers, max pooling layers and fully connected layers that totals to 16 layers with five blocks, and each these blocks has its own max pooling layers.

ResNet50 is a widely used variant of the ResNet model which consists of 48 convolution lays with two pooling layers with 23 million parameters. The model can be used for image classification, object detection, object localisation, etc.

3.3   Machine Learning Algorithms

Extreme gradient boosting abbreviated as XGBoost is a boosting model that uses the architecture of the gradient descent algorithm. It minimises loss whilst adding new models. The boosting model works by creating new models that predict the prediction errors or residuals from the previous models and then uses them to produce the final prediction. A detailed explanation can be found in the work done by Chen and Guestrin [16].

Random forest is an ensemble learning method based on randomised decision trees. The classifications are given by the average result of individual classifiers. Random forests use a random feature during the process of induction, and each

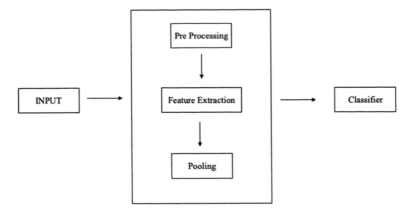

Fig. 2 Architecture of proposed system

decision tree is generated randomly. Further, explanation is available in the work done by Biau and Scornet [17].

Principal component analysis abbreviated as PCA is a dimensionality reduction algorithm that uses a sequence of matrix operations along with some linear algebra and statistics to project the original data with the same or fewer dimensions. Further, explanations can be seen in the work done by Wold et al [18].

3.4 Proposed Model

The pre-processed images are fed into the corresponding pre-trained model after which we extract its features in the initial layers. The model extracts abstract features from the initial layers and then extracts the more detailed features from the abstract features in the deeper layers.

The extracted features are the summarised with global average pooling (GAP) and then classified with various machine learning techniques. PCA was used on the summarised features to achieve lower dimensionality. Detailed explanations have been provided in the next section (Fig. 2).

4 Results

For XGBoost, parameters for max depth was considered between 3 and 5 with learning rate ranging between 0.001 and 0.006. The number of estimators ranged between 100 and 500.

For random forest, the estimators were searched between 100 and 500 with accuracy being optimal with the default number.

The models were trained on Python3.8 and scikit-learn 0.24.1. Table 1 gives the results of evaluation.

According to the results, XGBoost with InceptionV3 with 10% training data gave the best accuracy of 94.82% followed by InceptionResNetV2 with an accuracy of 92.89% on 10% training data with XGBoost. The lowest accuracy was 84.19% which was given by PCA | XGBoost on 90% training data with VGG16 as the pre-trained model.

The model was trained with four convolution layers and two dense layers. Pooling was done with two GAP layers for imported features and input features which were multiplied before passing onto the dense layers. The process was evaluated for 50 epochs with each batch having the size of 16. The input dimension was (512, 512, 3).

This work observed that the accuracy increased for smaller data sizes. This is probably due to ensemble methods reducing the risk of choosing weak individual classifiers. This in return improves model stability along.

5 Conclusion

The paper presents different CNN models that detects DR in fundus images. The models mainly focussed on pre-processing, feature extraction and classification whilst tweaking weights, learning rates, sample size and drop outs. Transfer learning is used to further improve results without training on the imported models layers. The experiments have yielded competitive results when compared to other models that had been trained on the same data set.

This paper is intended to serve as a reference for research relating to this domain, and the results are meant to be extensible to other applications using similar retinal images.

Table 1 Accuracy obtained by proposed method

Pre-trained model	Test_split	Method	Accuracy (%)	Loss
InceptionV3	0.1	XGBoost	94.82	0.849
		Random forest	90.17	0.885
		PCA + XGBoost	90.35	0.914
	0.5	XGBoost	91.71	0.829
		Random forest	89.68	0.855
		PCA + XGBoost	89.5	0.713
	0.9	XGBoost	91.42	0.810
		Random forest	88.00	0.892

(continued)

Table 1 (continued)

Pre-trained model	Test_split	Method	Accuracy (%)	Loss
		PCA + XGBoost	87.11	0.873
InceptionResNetV2	0.1	XGBoost	92.89	0.904
		Random forest	89.63	0.950
		PCA + XGBoost	87.24	0.881
	0.5	XGBoost	92.5	0.86
		Random forest	89.17	0.960
		PCA + XGBoost	86.00	0.818
	0.9	XGBoost	91.40	0.841
		Random forest	89.90	0.711
		PCA + XGBoost	86.5	0.963
VGG16	0.1	XGBoost	90.1	0.849
		Random forest	89.71	0.9
		PCA + XGBoost	88.32	0.853
	0.5	XGBoost	90.18	0.75
		Random forest	89.78	0.855
		PCA + XGBoost	87.74	0.818
	0.9	XGBoost	89.64	0.818
		Random forest	88.94	0.845
		PCA + XGBoost	84.19	0.712
ResNet50	0.1	XGBoost	91.86	0.875
		Random forest	88.53	0.996
		PCA + XGBoost	88.47	0.771
	0.5	XGBoost	91.3	0.950
		Random forest	88.9	0.923
		PCA + XGBoost	86.32	0.772
	0.9	XGBoost	89.5	0.940
		Random forest	88.71	0.941
		PCA + XGBoost	85.95	0.994

References

1. Zhang W, Zhong J, Yang S, Gao Z, Hu J, Chen Y, Yi Z (2019) Automated identification and grading system of diabetic retinopathy using deep neural networks. Knowl-Based Syst
2. Gurcan OF, Beyca OF, Dogan O (2021) A comprehensive study of machine learning methods on diabetic retinopathy classification. Int J Comput Intell Syst
3. Krause J, Gulshan V, Rahimy E, Karth P, Widner K, Corrado GS, Webster DR (2018) Grader variability and the importance of reference standards for evaluating machine learning models for diabetic retinopathy. Ophthalmology 125(8):1264–1272
4. H.H. Vo and A. Verma (2016) New deep neural nets for fine-grained diabetic retinopathy recognition on hybrid color space, IEEE. In: 2016 IEEE international symposium on multimedia

(ISM). San Jose, CA, USA, pp 209–215

5. Sayres R, Taly A, Rahimy E, Blumer K, Coz D, Hammel N, Webster DR (2019) Using a deep learning algorithm and integrated gradients explanation to assist grading for diabetic retinopathy. Ophthalmology 126(4):552–564

6. Kelly CJ, Karthikesalingam A, Suleyman M, Corrado G, King D (2019) Key challenges for delivering clinical impact with artificial intelligence. BMC Med 17(1):1–9

7. Doshi N, Oza U, Kumar P (2020) Diabetic retinopathy classification using downscaling algorithms and deep learning, IEEE. In: 2020 7th international conference on signal processing and integrated networks (SPIN). Noida, India, pp 950–955

8. Liu C, Chen LC, Schroff F, Adam H, Hua W, Yuille AL, Fei-Fei L (2019) Auto-deeplab: hierarchical neural architecture search for semantic image segmentation. In: Proceedings of the IEEE/CVF conference on computer vision and pattern recognition. pp 82–92

9. Zhou T, Ruan S, Canu S (2019) A review: deep learning for medical image segmentation using multi-modality fusion. Array 3:100004

10. Bodapati JD, Veeranjaneyulu N, Shareef SN, Hakak S, Bilal M, Maddikunta PKR, Jo O (2020) Blended multi-modal deep convnet features for diabetic retinopathy severity prediction. Electronics 9:914

11. Mateen M, Wen J, Song S, Huang Z (2019) Fundus image classification using VGG-19 architecture with PCAand SVD. Symmetry 11:1

12. Song R, Cao P, Yang J, Zhao D, Zaiane OR (2020) A domain adaptation multi-instance learning for diabetic retinopathy grading on retinal images. In: 2020 IEEE international conference on bioinformatics and biomedicine (BIBM). pp 743–750

13. Sagi O, Rokach L (2018) Ensemble learning: a survey. Wiley Interdisc Rev: Data Min Knowl Discovery 8(4):e1249

14. Xu X, Lin J, Tao Y, Wang X (2018) An improved densenet method based on transfer learning for fundus medical images. In: 2018 7th international conference on digital home (ICDH). pp 137–140

15. Sisodia DS, Nair S, Khobragade P (2017) Diabetic retinal fundus images: preprocessing and feature extraction for early detection of diabetic retinopathy. Biomed Pharmacol J 10(2):615–626

16. Chen T, Guestrin C (2016) Xgboost: a scalable tree boosting system. In: Proceedings of the 22nd ACM SIGKDD international conference on knowledge discovery and data mining. San Francisco, CA, USA, pp 785–794

17. Biau G, Scornet E (2016) A random forest guided tour. TEST 25(2):197–227

18. Wold S, Esbensen K, Geladi P (1987) Principal component analysis. Chemom Intell Lab Syst 2(1–3):37–52

19. Arun C, Prabhu A, Zeeshan M, Rani NS (2020) A study on various classifier techniques used in image processing. IEEE

20. Chandrajit M, Rani NS, Manohar N (2021) Robust segmentation and classification of moving objects from surveillance video. IOP conference series: materials science and engineering

21. Bipin Nair BJ (2018) A novel distributed algorithm with bitcoin for phylogeny analysis. Recent findings in intelligent computing techniques

22. Manohar N, Sharath Kumar YH, Rani R, Hemanth Kumar G (2019) Convolutional neural networks with SVM for classification of animal images, emerging research in electronics. Comput Sci Technol

23. Pushpa BR, Anand C, Mithun Nambiar P (2016) Ayurvedic plant species recognition using statistical parameters on leaf images. Int J Appl Eng Res

24. Samuel M (2020) Embedded imaging system based behavior analysis of dairy cow. J Electr 2(02)

25. Raj JS, Ananthi JV (2019) Vision intensification using augumented reality with metasurface application. J Inf Technol

Prediction of Diabetes and Recommendation of Insulin Dosage for Diabetic Patients

MD. Azmath Hussain, N. Sasi Kiran, A. Ravi Teja, Y. Nikhil,
G. Venkata Prasanth, and M. M. Meera Durga

Abstract Diabetes mellitus is a disorder that occurs when the human body produces insufficient levels of insulin and is not able to maintain normal levels of sugar in the blood. People with diabetes have high chance of getting other diseases related to eyes, heart, kidneys, nerve damage, and so on. Generally, in hospitals, diabetes diagnosis is done by various tests. Healthcare industries collect the data from the patients and they have large data of the patient's details. By applying this data to the machine learning classification algorithms, we can predict whether a person has diabetes. Here, we showed the accuracies of various machine learning algorithms in predicting the diabetes based on factors like BMI, age, Insulin, blood glucose levels, etc., and we have chosen the model which predicts more accurately than others. Further, we recommend the amount of insulin dosage to be given to the diabetic patients.

Keywords Diabetes mellitus · Machine learning classification algorithms ·
Glucose levels · Insulin

1 Introduction

Diabetes mellitus (DM) is one of the most common diseases that the people are suffering in the present world. It is caused when the human body either produces insufficient insulin or it becomes resistant to insulin. Most common are the type1 diabetes (T1DM) and type2 diabetes (T2DM). There are also other kinds which are rare. In type1 diabetes, the human body produces little insulin that is not sufficient for the glucose to be absorbed into the cells. In type2 diabetes, human body becomes

MD. Azmath Hussain (✉) · N. Sasi Kiran · A. Ravi Teja · Y. Nikhil · G. Venkata Prasanth ·
M. M. Meera Durga
Department of Computer Science and Engineering, V R Siddhartha Engineering College,
Vijayawada, India

M. M. Meera Durga
e-mail: mastan599@vrsiddhartha.ac.in

resistant to insulin. Nearly, 5% of all the people with diabetes are due to T1DM, and 95% of the people with diabetes are due to T2DM [1].

Over 10.5% of the population in United States are suffering from the diabetes [2]. In United States, diabetes was one of the major causes of death of the people in 2017 [3]. For the patients suffering from diabetes, diabetes management systems have been proposed to additionally assist them in self-monitoring the sickness. Predictive modeling of glucose metabolism is one of the primary goals of the diabetes management system. Because it could aid in the optimal patient response in critical conditions such as hypoglycemia. As a result, several recent studies have investigated enhanced data-driven methodologies for developing reliable predictive models of glucose metabolism [3]. Our main purpose is to check whether a person has diabetes or not and if a person is diabetic, then we assist diabetic patients by estimating the degree of insulin dosage intake required. Machine learning techniques (MLTs) may serve as a rescuer for early detection and prediction of diabetes. The estimated value is shown to the user, giving them an indication of how much insulin to take. Machine learning techniques (MLTs) can provide good results on the estimation of the insulin dosage. Linear regression and decision trees algorithms are used in the prediction of insulin dosage to be administered to the patients. This ensures that test data predictions are almost accurate.

2 Related Work

This part provides the previous work done in the diabetes prediction and insulin dosage recommendation to diabetic patients. While there has been a lot of work done in the prediction of diabetes, a little research has been done in recommending the insulin dosage to the diabetic patients. A report by the World Health Organization (WHO) says that the people with diabetes has increased from 108 million in 1980 to 422 million in 2014, and it will become one of the major causes of death by 2030 [4].

In [5], random forest algorithm was used for predicting the diabetes. The dataset they have used is from UCI learning repository. Observing the results, they have concluded that random forests can help in the early diabetes diagnosis with reasonable accuracy.

Menaria in [6] has predicted the diabetes using data mining techniques. They have chosen the Pima Indian dataset and R programming language to implement the algorithms. They used backpropagation, J48, and Naïve Bayes classifier algorithms. In backpropagation algorithm, they used simple neural network architecture. The prediction was more accurate for the backpropagation.

In [7], they used the random forest model for the risk prediction of type II diabetes. The dataset used was from the School of Medicine, University of Virginia. In [8], Decision stump classifier was used in decision support system to predict diabetes. The dataset was obtained from UCI.

In [9], An Amalgam KNN model was used to predict whether a person is having diabetes. Here, Pima Indians dataset was used. Amalgam KNN model gives predicts more accurate than the KNN model. In [10], they built an ANN model which is trained using backpropagation for the prediction of insulin dosage. ANN model consists of 3 layers such as Input layer, hidden layer, and an output layer. Sigmoid activation function was used in the hidden and output layers. The dataset used here is of patient's dataset containing information about patient's length, weight, blood sugar, and gender.

We have used the SVM, KNN, Naïve Bayes, logistic regression, random forest, and decision tree classifier algorithms for the prediction of diabetes. We have compared the accuracies of these models and have chosen the model with highest accuracy.

3 Methodology

The steps are followed as shown in Fig. 1.

3.1 Data Preprocessing

Dataset Collection

We considered the data with the information of 768 patients and are originally from the National Institute of Diabetes and Digestive and Kidney Diseases. The dataset has several dependent variables and one independent variable, outcome. Dependent variables include the number of pregnancies the patient has so far, their BMI, insulin level, blood pressure, skin thickness, and so on. After extracting the required features, we were down to work with 5 labels that have more impact on the prediction of diabetes, namely "glucose," "skin thickness," "BMI," "blood pressure," and "insulin."

In data preprocessing, duplicate rows are identified, if there are any, we should remove them from the data frame. If there are any null values in any column, they are replaced with the mean of that column.

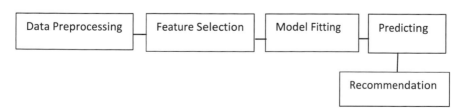

Fig. 1 Proposed system

Data Cleaning

Data cleaning is the primary step in the prediction of diabetes. During this step, we checked for the zero values and try to rectify them. In our dataset, there are four labels having zero values (glucose, blood pressure, skin thickness, insulin, BMI). We replace those zero values with the mean of those labels.

3.2   Feature Selection

A correlation matrix with a heatmap is used to identify the qualities that are most reliant on the target label. The features with correlation more than 0.2 are taken and incorporated into the model. The remaining functionalities are not included. As a result, the traits with the highest connection with the target label are chosen.

Data Visualization

The extracted features were plotted such that each graph represents the individual interaction or impact on the target label. Also, there is a visual representation of heatmap resembling the whole dataset into a correlation matrix as shown in Fig. 2. From the correlation heatmap, we can see that there is a high correlation between outcome and [pregnancies, glucose, BMI, age, insulin]. We can select these features to accept input from the user and predict the outcome. We visualized the dataset using the scatter plot as shown in the Fig. 3.

3.3   Model Fitting

Model fitting is how well the parameters are fitted to the model. Here, we tested the dataset on different models and the model with highest accuracy is SVM. The SVM model is developed, and the actual and estimated values are compared. This shows how the model is fitted.

SVM

We used different models to predict whether a person is having diabetes or not. Of all them SVM has highest test accuracy of 83.11%. So we chose SVM model for the prediction of diabetes. Support vector machines (SVMs) are one of the supervised machine learning algorithms that can be used for both classification and regression purposes. Here, we used SVM for classification purpose for predicting whether a person has diabetes or not. The advantage of using SVM is, it is efficient when the dataset has large number of attributes and when the number of attributes is greater than the size of the dataset. Fig. 4 shows the accuracies of various models.

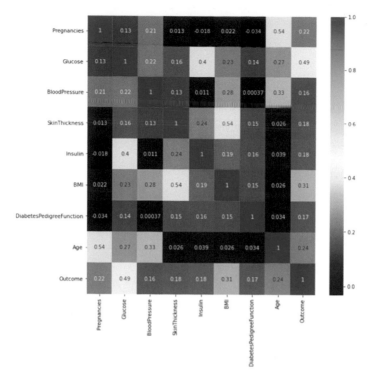

Fig. 2 Correlation matrix

3.4 Predicting

After the model is trained, then the target value is predicted based on the features. The model is 83% accurate. So, we can predict whether a person has diabetes or not.

3.5 Recommendation of Insulin

If a person is found to have diabetes, then we recommend the dosage of insulin to be given based on the calories taken, gender, and blood glucose levels.

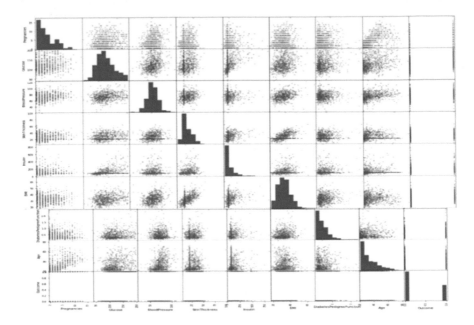

Fig. 3 Scatter plot of the labels in the dataset

Classification Algorithm	Test Accuracy
Logistic Regression	77.2%
KNN	74.6%
Naïve Bayes	74%
Decision Tree	79.2%
SVM	83.11%
Random Forest	81.1%

Fig. 4 Accuracies of various classification algorithms

4 Results

Prediction of Diabetes

The trained model is provided with the test data and accuracy is calculated. The SVM model gave 83.11% accuracy. Figure 5 shows the prediction of diabetes.

Recommendation of Insulin

The person if found to be diabetic, we recommend the insulin dosage to be taken based on the person's blood glucose levels, calories taken, and gender. Recommendation of insulin is shown in Fig. 6.

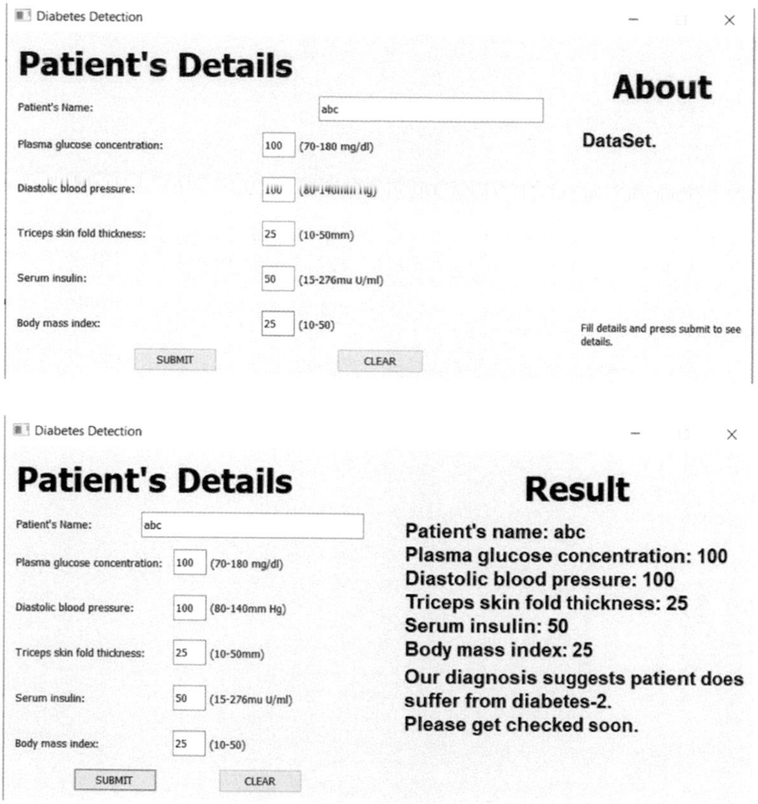

Fig. 5 Prediction of diabetes

5 Conclusion and Future Work

So, we have chosen SVM model for the diabetes prediction which has higher accuracy and recommend the insulin dosage to be taken by a person. For the prediction of diabetes, we used SVM model which gives better accuracy compared to the other classification algorithms. A better model can be developed using neural networks for the prediction of diabetes. Future research can be done in this area by using artificial neural networks.

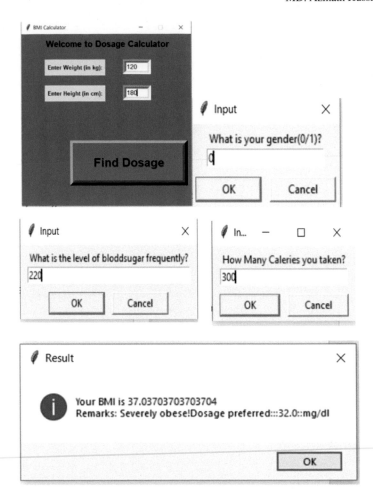

Fig. 6 Recommendation of insulin

References

1. Parker RS, Doyle FJ, Peppas NA (2001) The intravenous route to blood glucose control. IEEE Eng Med Biol Soc Mag 20:65–73
2. Centers for Disease Control and Prevention. National Diabetes Statistics Report, 2020. Atlanta, GA: Centers for Disease Control and Prevention, U.S. Dept of Health and Human Services; 2020.
3. Centers for disease control and prevention. National center for health statistics. Underlying cause of death 1999–2017 on CDC WONDER online database, 2018. Accessed at http://wonder.cdc.gov/ucd-icd10.html on 10 Oct 2019
4. Global report on diabetes by world health organization (2016) ISBN 978-92-4-156525-7
5. VijiyaKumar K, Lavanya B, Nirmala I, Caroline SS (2019) Random forest algorithm for the prediction of diabetes. 2019 IEEE international conference on system, computation, automation and networking (ICSCAN). pp 1–5. https://doi.org/10.1109/ICSCAN.2019.8878802

6. Woldemichael FG, Menaria S (2018) Prediction of diabetes using data mining techniques. 2018 2nd international conference on trends in electronics and informatics (ICOEI). pp 414–418. https://doi.org/10.1109/ICOEI.2018.8553959

7. Xu W, Zhang J, Zhang Q, Wei X (2017) Risk prediction of type II diabetes based on random forest model. 2017 third international conference on advances in electrical, electronics, information, communication and bio-informatics (AEEICB). pp 382–386. https://doi.org/10.1109/AEEICB.2017.7972337

8. Vijayan VV, Anjali C (2015) Prediction and diagnosis of diabetes mellitus—a machine learning approach. IEEE Recent Adv Intell Comput Syst (RAICS) 2015:122–127. https://doi.org/10.1109/RAICS.2015.7488400

9. NirmalaDevi M, alias Balamurugan SA, Swathi UV (2013) An amalgam KNN to predict diabetes mellitus. 2013 IEEE international conference ON emerging trends in computing, communication and nanotechnology (ICECCN). pp 691–695. https://doi.org/10.1109/ICECCN.2013.6528591

10. Zahran B (2016) A neural network model for predicting insulin dosage for diabetic patients. Int J Comput Sci Inf Sec (IJCSIS) 14

A Cloud Based Breast Cancer Risk Prediction (BCRP) System

Madhavi B. Desai and **Vipul H. Mistry**

Abstract Breast cancer is one of the main causes of cancer across the world for women. Early diagnostics of cancer considerably increases the chances of correct treatment and survival. However, this diagnosis process is tedious and often leads to a disagreement between pathologists. Machine learning algorithms and computer aided tools have significant potential for improvement in diagnosis process. It is a need of time to implement an Artificial Intelligence based breast cancer risk prediction system. In this paper our aim to develop a cloud based model that is capable of detecting the breast cancer at an early stages. In the pre-processing stage, missing values are replaced by mean and one hot encoding method is used for converting categorical attributes of dataset into numeric. This paper also analyzes the performance of various classification models i.e., Logistic Regression, Decision Tree, Naïve Bayes, Gradient Boosting, Random Forest, KNN, Linear Discriminant Analysis and Multilayer Perceptron. The implementation of a machine learning model is done in python using jupyter notebook. This model is deployed in cloud using IBM cloud services. This application will be useful to doctors for making decision whether a patient is benign or malignant.

Keywords Breast cancer · Prediction · Machine learning · KNN · Logistic regression · Gradient boosting

1 Introduction

A recent statistics from World Health Organization [1] show that breast cancer impacts 2.1 million women each year. It causes highest number of cancer related deaths among women. It is estimated that 15% of women died because of breast

M. B. Desai (✉)
R. N. G. Patel Institute of Technology, Gujarat Technological University, Ahmedabad, Gujarat, India

V. H. Mistry
Picus Tech Software Pvt. Ltd., Surat, Gujarat, India

© The Author(s), under exclusive license to Springer Nature Singapore Pte Ltd. 2022
C. Satyanarayana et al. (eds.), *High Performance Computing and Networking*,
Lecture Notes in Electrical Engineering 853,
https://doi.org/10.1007/978-981-16-9885-9_44

535

cancer among all cancer deaths. Breast cancer begins with the abnormal increase of breast cells. These cells divide more rapidly and continue to accumulate than the healthy cells. It results into lumps or mass. The majority of women died were diagnosed in late stages and this is the major cause of death in breast cancer. Breast cancer varies with different age groups. There are two early detection strategies for breast cancer: (i) screening (ii) early diagnosis. Screening includes testing of women to identify cancer before any of the symptoms. The early diagnosis means timely access to cancer treatment.

The goal is to increase the proportion of breast cancer identification at an early stage and that can be done by computer aided diagnosis. If one has to propose the solution with computer aided diagnosis than machine learning is the first option. In recent years, machine learning techniques have been used for detection of diseases like cancer, diabetes, heart disease [2–4]. The purpose of this paper is to develop a model for risk prediction of breast cancer. There is no evidence that single machine learning model can work on various diseases. The performance of the models gets varied with different disease. In the medical domain, we can predict risk of disease on the basis of patient symptoms.

In this paper, we have taken standard dataset from UCI machine learning repository. For handling the missing value and for the conversion of attributes into numerical attribute, we have applied pre-processing techniques. For choosing best model we have done experimentation on various machine learning classification methods. We have also created web application for our model. Hence, doctors, physician and medical representative can use it easily.

The rest part of the paper is organized as follows. Section 2 describes the related work for the breast cancer prediction. Supervised Machine learning algorithms used in this paper are described in Section 3. Section 4 describes the proposed methodology. Section 5 discusses experiment results and Section 6 summarizes the paper.

2 Related Work

Machine Learning works on the principal of "learning from examples". We have to train a model by providing symptoms of patients for breast cancer. Model must have generalization capability i.e., one pass the symptoms of unknown patient than also model must work accurately. In medical domain accuracy of positive and negative class both must be accurate. This is because if patient is identified as benign, she will get relaxed and at later stages this will become the reason for death. On the other side, benign person if identified as malignant then cancer treatments may lead to severe health issues.

In recent years, researchers have worked on risk prediction of breast cancer using machine learning approaches. In 2014, Shen et al. [4] proposed an intelligent model for breast cancer prediction using data mining technique. Author proposed to use feature selection method INTERACT for selecting sensitive features. Afterward, selected features were passed to upport Vector Machine classification method and achieved 92% classification accuracy. In 2014, Vikas et al. [5] investigated different data mining techniques using WEKA tool. Through experiments results authors proposed Sequential Minimal Optimization which gives 96% accuracy. Huang et al. [6] proposed to use SVM and SVM ensemble based breast cancer prediction model in the year 2017. This paper evaluated the performance of SVM and SVM ensembles for breast cancer prediction. For the small size dataset, it was concluded that linear SVM with bagging method and SVM ensemble with RBF kernel gave better performance whereas for large dataset SVM ensemble model with RBF kernel and boosting can perform better than other models. Kanimozhi et al. [7] proposed fuzzy temporal based breast cancer prediction system in 2019. The proposed model and fuzzy rules were validated through domain expert of disease. In 2019, Dhanya et al. [8] made a comparative study of feature selection methods and classification methods for breast cancer prediction system. Experimental results proved that random forest classification model performed better with feature selection model than other classification models. It was also concluded that f-test performed better for small dataset and sequential forward selection for large datasets. In 2020, Mohammed et al. [9] analyzed the performance of different machine learning models on breast cancer. Performance of Decision tree, Naïve Bayes and sequential optimization were validated on two different standard datasets.

From the literature, it is analyzed that there is need of a computer based system that can help in early diagnosis of malignant cancer tissues. This paper presents a cloud based online Breast Cancer Risk Prediction (BCRP) system. The model is implemented in python and deployed on cloud using IBM cloud services.

3 Classification Models

The machine learning methods used in this paper are briefly described in this section.

3.1 Decision Tree Classifier

Decision tree has structure like flowchart, where each non-leaf node represents test on attribute and branch of node represents test on particular attribute. Leaf nodes of decision tree are the class labels, and top node is represented as root node. For selection of root not and internal node various attribute selection measures can be applied like information gain, gain ratio and gain index.

Once the decision tree is created using training attributes, unknown tuple is passed to the trained model. It is traced from root node to leaf node and will reach to class prediction. Decision tree can be converted to decision rules. This classifier does not require any domain knowledge. Hence it is popular machine learning model.

3.2 Gradient Boosting Classifier

The three basic elements of gradient boosting algorithms are:

- Optimized loss function
- Decision trees as the weak learner
- A gradient descent procedure to add trees and minimizing loss function.

As compared to basic gradient boosting algorithm, gradient boosting algorithm is a greedy algorithm. The basic enhancements over basic gradient algorithm include:

- Tree constraints like tree depth, number of trees, number of observations for split and number of nodes
- Weighted updates
- Random sampling of training dataset and
- Penalized gradient boosting.

3.3 KNN Classifier

In nearest neighbor classification, each data instance is represented in n-dimensional space. When new data instance will pass to model, k nearest neighbor model will find the k nearest trained data instances which are nearest to new data instance. These nearest data instances are known as k nearest neighbors of new tuple and new tuple will be assigned to the nearest neighbor's class label.

3.4 Multilayer Perceptron Classifier

Multilayer Perceptron (MLP) is a class of feed-forward neural network that consists of three node layers i.e., input, hidden and output layer. MLP uses back propagation for the training. The multiple layers and activation function differentiate MLP from a liner perceptron. MLP learns based on amount of output error compared to actual values and changes the weights after each instance of data is processed.

3.5 Gaussian Naïve Bayes Classifier

Gaussian Naïve Bayes classifier is an extension of Naïve Bayes classifier that works on real-valued attributes with an assumption of Gaussian distribution. This classifier is easy to implement as one has to estimate the mean and standard deviation from the training data. However it is to be noted that when using Gaussian Naïve Bayes classifier one has to remove the outliers i.e., values that are more than 3 to 4 standard deviations from the mean value.

3.6 Logistic Regression Classifier

A logistic regression makes use of logistic function called sigmoid function. Sigmoid function accepts any real-valued number and maps the value between 0 and 1. Logistic regression classifier is used for two class classification problem. It recognizes the association between different attributes of the dataset. If the value is less than or equal to 0.5 than it return 0 otherwise it returns 1. This classifier is better choice for binary classification. The coefficients of the logistic regression are estimated using maximum-likelihood estimation. This classifier model focuses on getting best weights and regression coefficient.

3.7 Random Forest Classifier

The fundamental principle of random forest classification is that it trains several decision tree models with the bagging. This model divides whole datasets into different subsets. It creates and trains decision tree of each individual subsets parallel. For the final decision, it aggregates the decision of each decision tree classification model. This method reduces the variance of each classifier and having high generalization capability. It also solves the problem of over fitting and under fitting.

3.8 Linear Discriminant Analysis

Linear Discriminant Analysis (LDA) is used for prediction in multiclass classification problems. In LDA, it is assumed that all inputs have same variance. LDA model represents statistical properties i.e., mean and variance of each input data, calculated for each class. LDA attempts to represent the data as a linear combination of variables. LDA has continuous independent data and dependent categorical class labels.

4 Methodology

The goal of this paper is to develop an online system that can predict whether a patient is malignant or benign. This section of the paper explains the development steps of the Breast Cancer Risk Prediction (BCRP) system. Before making online deployment, various popular machine learning models are evaluated on Wisconsin (Diagnosis) cancer dataset. The model with best prediction performance is used further for the online deployment and user interface creation using IBM.

4.1 Training and Testing Dataset

The machine learning models are trained using Wisconsin cancer dataset [11]. The dataset contains information of total 569 instances. Each instance has total 30 breast cancer diagnosis features, patient id and label information as malignant or benign. Classification model is built to evaluate whether the patient is having breast cancer tissue classification as malignant or benign. The dataset contains 357 benign and 212 malignant instances out of total 569 samples. Table 1 describes all the 30 attributes of the dataset and their statistical values.

Each instance of dataset contains 10 basic features. Mean, standard error and worst or largest mean of the three largest mean values are used to make total of 30 features which are used to train the machine learning based classification models.

4.2 Classification Model

This segment of the paper refers to the design of classification model using dataset. Figure 1 illustrates the basic block diagram of the cloud based Breast Cancer Risk Prediction (BCRP) system.

The model is built in python using jupyter notebook. As illustrated in Fig. 1, the dataset is first imported from the cloud storage. This data is pre-processed before it is used to train the machine learning algorithms. The pre-processing steps are as follows:

- Identification of empty cells and filling the data with mean values of the features
- One hot encoding for labels
- Feature scaling.

Once the data is pre-processed, it is divided in two parts: training set and testing set. We have used 80% of the instances as training set and remaining 20% as testing set. The training instances are used to train the machine learning algorithms where features and labels are given to the model. Once the model is trained, the testing instances are used to evaluate the model performance. The trained model is evaluated based on various statistical parameters like confusion matrix, accuracy of detection, recall, AUC, precision and F_measure.

The classification models were built for different classifiers which include Logistic Regression. Linear Discriminant Analysis, KNN, Gaussian Naïve Bayes, Decision Tree, Gradient Boosting classifier, Random Forest and Multilayer Perceptron classifier. The performances of various prediction models are compared, and best model

Table 1 Dataset attributes statistics and description

Attribute	Numeric values (Min, Max)	Description
Radius_mean	6.98, 28.1	Mean of distances center point to points on perimeter
Texture_mean	9.71, 39.3	Standard deviation of gray-scale pixel values
Perimeter_mean	43.8, 189	Mean size of tumor
Smoothness_mean	0.05, 0.16	Mean of local variations in radius
Compactness_mean	0.02, 0.35	Mean of compactness
Concavity_mean	0, 0.43	Mean value of severity of concave proportions of contour
Concave points_mean	0, 0.2	Mean of total number of concave proportions in contour
Symmetry_mean	0.11, 0.3	
Factal_dimension_mean	0.05, 0.1	Mean value of coastline approximation-1
Radius_se	0.11, 2.87	Standard error for the mean of the distances from center to points on the perimeter
Texture_se	0.36, 4.88	Standard error of standard deviation of gray-scale pixel values
Perimeter_se	0.76, 22	Standard error of size of tumor
Area_se	6.8, 5.42	
Smoothness_se	0, 0.03	Standard error for local variation in radius length
Compactness_se	0, 0.14	Standard error for compactness
Concavity_se	0, 0.4	Standard error for concavity proportions
Concave_points_se	0, 0.05	Standard error of no of concave points in contour
Symmetry_se	0.01, 0.08	Standard error of symmetry
Fractal_dimension_se	0, 0.03	Standard error for coastline approximation-1
Radius_worst	7.93, 36	Worst case mean of distances from center to points on perimeter
Texture_worst	12, 49.5	Worst case mean of standard deviation of gray-scale pixel values
Perimeter_worst	50.4, 251	Worst case mean of perimeter
Area_worst	85, 4250	Worst case area mean
Smoothness_worst	0.07, 0.22	Worst case value of local variation in radius lengths
Compactness_worst	0.03, 1.06	Worst or largest mean of compactness

(continued)

Table 1 (continued)

Attribute	Numeric values (Min, Max)	Description
Concavity_worst	0.1, 25	Worst case mean of severity of concave proportions of countour
Concave points_worst	0, 0.29	Worst or largest mean for number of concave proportions of countour
Symmetry_worst	0.16, 0.66	Largest mean value of symmetry
Fractal_dimenstion worst	0.06, 0.21	Worst or largest mean of coastline approximation-1

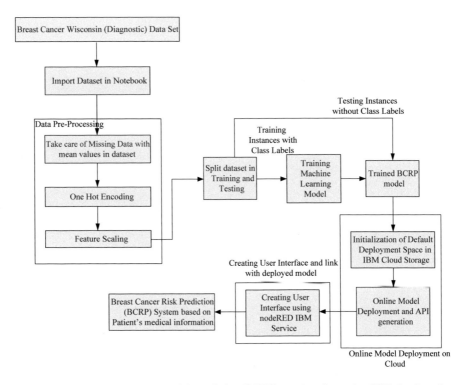

Fig. 1 A cloud based breast cancer risk prediction (BCRP) user interface using IBM cloud services and machine learning algorithms

is used for online deployment using IBM cloud services. The next section describes the process of model deployment and user interface creation using trained model.

4.3 Online Deployment of BCRP Model

This section illustrates the deployment of trained model on cloud and interfacing of this model with user interface. The trained model is used for online deployment and user interface.

The online user interface is developed using following IDM cloud services [10].

1. IBM Watson Studio
2. IBM Machine learning service
3. NodeRED application
4. Cloud Object Storage.

The architecture of the system is shown in Fig. 2.

As shown in Fig. 2, the IBM cloud storage is used to store the database. Following steps are followed to develop the UI.

1. Database is imported from cloud storage to jupyter notebook using IBM Watson Studio.
2. Watson machine learning service is used to build a classification model.
3. Creation of default deployment space with IBM Client service.
4. Deployment of trained model in cloud space.
5. Designing of user interface using nodeRED flow application of IBM cloud.
6. Interfacing nodeRED flow with API of deployed model.

NodeRED is a browser based editor to create flow for the user interface. IBM nodeRED application contains various nodes for different IBM services and user interface creation. Figure 3 illustrates the design of BCRP system UI nodeRED flow. As shown in Fig. 3, user input is passed to the http client with UI credentials. These inputs are parsed to function node which gets the values of the user input and passes

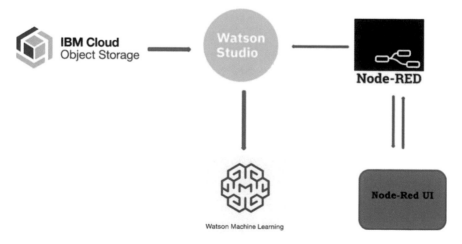

Fig. 2 Breast cancer risk prediction system using IBM services

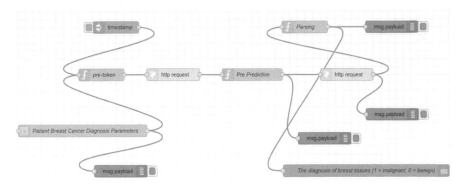

Fig. 3 NodeRED Flow to make user interface for diagnosis of breast cancer tissues (Malignant or Benign)

it to http node using API keys of the deployed trained model. The prediction output of the model is parsed using output function node.

5 Results and Discussion

The performance of the model is evaluated using Wisconsin cancer dataset [11]. As explained in Fig. 1, various machine learning algorithms are quantitatively compared using different design metrics. The model with highest quantitative performance is used for the UI creation. Finally the UI is evaluated with various user instances. The commonly used design metrics are described below.

5.1 Confusion Matrix

The confusion matrix contains information about total number of cross-classifications for actual and predicted classes. Table 2 shows the confusion matrix for the BCRP system.

Table 2 Confusion matrix structure

Confusion matrix			
Total number of samples		Predicted class	
		Benign	Malignant
True Class	Benign	True negative (TN)	False positive (FP)
	Malignant	False Negative (FN)	True Positive (TP)

The meanings of various terms of the confusion matrix are as follows:

- TP: Malignant is classified as Malignant
- TN: Benign is classified as Benign
- FP: Malignant is classified as Benign
- FN: Benign is classified as Malignant.

5.2 Quantitative Measures

One of the most commonly used parameter for the evaluation of machine learning algorithm is accuracy. Accuracy is used to demonstrate how many instances of the total test instances are correctly classified i.e., Malignant is classified as Malignant and Benign is classified as Benign.

$$\text{Accuracy} = \frac{TP + TN}{TP + FP + TN + FN} \tag{1}$$

$$\text{Precision} = \frac{TP}{TP + FP} \tag{2}$$

$$\text{Recall} = \frac{TP}{TP + FN} \tag{3}$$

$$\text{F\_Measure} = \frac{2 * \text{Precision} * \text{Recall}}{\text{Precision} + \text{Recall}} \tag{4}$$

Precision indicates correct number of classifications out of total malignant instances from the testing dataset. Recall represents number of malignant classifications out of total number of malignant instances. F_measure is the weighted harmonic mean of recall and precision.

5.3 Receiver Operating Characteristic

Receiver Operating Characteristic (ROC) is one more widely used parameter for the evaluation of the machine learning models. ROC is obtained by plotting True Positive Rate (TPR) versus False Positive Rate (FPR) values while varying the threshold for the positive classification over its probability range. Figure 4 shows the ROC obtained for different machine learning models under evaluation. TPR and FPR are defined as follows:

$$\text{TP Rate} = \frac{TP}{TP + FN} \tag{5}$$

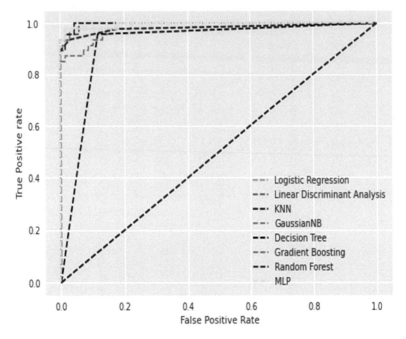

Fig. 4 Receiver operating characteristic for various machine learning models under consideration

$$\text{FP Rate} = \frac{FP}{FP + TN} \tag{6}$$

5.4 AUC

AUC is defined as area under the curve. The curve is plotted between precision vs recall while varying threshold of positive classification is varied across the predicted probability range of 1 down to 0. It is observed that when threshold is set high, FP will occur and high precision is obtained. As we decrease threshold, recall increases and precision decreases. There is always a trade-off between precision and recall. Area under this curve (AUC) is an important statistical measure for the binary classification.

5.5 Comparative Evaluation

Table 3 demonstrates the quantitative comparison between popular machine learning algorithms. As demonstrated by the results, gradient boosting algorithm and multi-layer perceptron algorithms gives comparatively better results compared to other classifiers like logistic regression, linear discriminant analysis, KNN, Gaussian Naive Bayes, decision tree and random forest. It has been observed that linear discriminant analysis and KNN provide 100% precision, but fail to achieve the similar performance over other quantitative measures. AUC is an important measure when there is imbalance in positive and negative test samples. This is the reason that has enabled us to select gradient boosting algorithm for online deployment and UI.

In order to create an online user interface gradient boosting classifier model is used. The API of this model is used to link the nodeRED flow and generate the UI. Figure 5 shows the final UI where 30 medical features are passed as an input for the benign class and correct classification of benign is obtained.

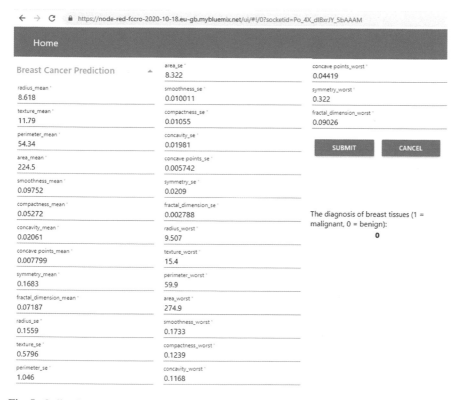

Fig. 5 Online breast cancer risk predictions UI

Table 3 Comparative evaluation of various machine learning algorithms on Wisconsin breast cancer dataset

Performance parameter	Logistic regression	Linear discriminant analysis	KNN	Gaussian Naïve Bayes	Decision tree	Gradient boosting	Random forest	Multilayer perceptron (MLP)
Accuracy	96.5	96.5	95.6	90.4	91.2	97.4	95.6	97.4
Precision	95.7	100	100	87.5	84.9	95.8	93.8	95.8
Recall	95.7	91.5	89.4	89.4	95.7	97.9	95.7	97.9
F_measure	95.7	95.6	94.4	88.4	90.0	96.8	94.7	96.8
Area under curve (AUC)	99.33	99.71	98.23	98.41	91.90	99.75	99.74	99.56

6 Results and Discussion

Computer based diagnosis tools can immensely help in improving the cancer diagnosis accuracy and reduce the chances of death. With this motivation, this paper presented a cloud based online system for prediction of breast cancer tissues using gradient boosting machine learning approach. Section 5 illustrates the performance of various machine learning models on Wisconsin cancer dataset. After analyzing the quantitative results gradient boosting algorithm based machine learning classification model is deployed using IBM Cloud services. Gradient boosting algorithm provides the accuracy of 97.4%, recall of 97.9% and F_measure of 96.8% along with AUC of 99.74%. The model is capable of correctly predicting the malignant and benign classes from the patient's health features. The UI made for an early prediction of breast cancer will help the doctors and pathologists to efficiently diagnosis cancer at an earlier stage and it will help them in timely and correct treatments which may lead to increased chances of patient's survival.

References

1. World Health Organization link: https://www.who.int/cancer/prevention/diagnosis-screening/breast-cancer/en/
2. Almustafa KM (2020) Prediction of heart disease and classifiers' sensitivity analysis. BMC Bioinform 21:278
3. Vizhi K, Dash A (2020) Diabetes prediction using machine learning. Int J Adv Sci Technol 29(06):2842–2852
4. Shen R, Yang Y, Shao F (2014) Intelligent breast cancer prediction model using data mining techniques. 2014 sixth international conference on intelligent human-machine systems and cybernetics. Hangzhou, pp 384–387
5. Chaurasia V, Pal S (Jan 2014) A novel approach for breast cancer detection using data mining techniques (June 29, 2017). Int J Innovative Res Comput Commun Eng (An ISO 3297:2007 Certified Organization) 2(1)
6. Huang M-W, Chen C-W, Lin W-C, Ke S-W, Tsai C-F (2017) SVM and SVM ensembles in breast cancer prediction. PLoS ONE 12(1):e0161501
7. Kanimozhi U, Ganapathy S, Manjula D et al (2019) An intelligent risk prediction system for breast cancer using fuzzy temporal rules. Natl Acad Sci Lett 42:227–232
8. Dhanya R, Paul IR, Sindhu Akula S, Sivakumar M, Nair JJ (2019) A comparative study for breast cancer prediction using machine learning and feature selection. 2019 international conference on intelligent computing and control systems (ICCS). Madurai, India, pp 1049–1055
9. Mohammed SA, Darrab S, Noaman SA, Saake G (2020) Analysis of breast cancer detection using different machine learning techniques. In: Tan Y, Shi Y, Tuba M (eds) Data mining and big data. DMBD 2020. Communications in computer and information science, vol 1234. Springer, Singapore
10. IBM Cloud Services link: https://www.cloud.ibm.com
11. Dataset link: UCI Machine Learning Repository: https://archive.ics.uci.edu/ml/datasets/Breast+Cancer+Wisconsin+%28Diagnostic%29 last accessed on 19 Oct 2020

Automatic Road Network Reconstruction from GPS Trajectory Data using Curve Reconstruction Algorithms

Philumon Joseph, Binsu C. Kovoor, and Job Thomas

Abstract Reconstructing the road networks using GPS trajectory data is important in vehicle traffic management. In this paper, a novel approach using representative point extraction and curve reconstruction algorithms that convert GPS trajectories to the routable road network is proposed. In this approach, GPS trajectories are simplified by a representative point extraction algorithm. With the resulting reduced point set from input GPS trajectories, a curve reconstruction algorithm to create a graph of nodes and edges that represent the road network structure is developed. The usefulness of the proposed model is demonstrated using the GPS trajectories collected from public roads and GPS traces from the public map database OpenStreetMap. The results show that this approach can build the road network from single and multiple GPS vehicle trajectories. The performance of the representative point extraction algorithm is evaluated in terms of trajectory reduction rate and it was found to be 93%. This indicates that the proposed model reconstructs the traffic scenario quite accurately.

Keywords Road network generation · Curve reconstruction · Delaunay triangulation

1 Introduction

Nowadays, almost all public vehicles are equipped with global positioning system (GPS), which generates an enormous amount of trajectory data every day. These vehicle trajectory data contain a lot of information about the shape of the road network, sequence of location, and time information. Recently, many researchers use these vehicle trajectory data to map the traffic in road networks. Lane-level routable digital map reconstruction[1], urban road network extraction[2], and generate maps from trajectories [3] are the very recent works in this area. Road network structure has a key role in developing smart cities, route planning, vehicle navigation systems,

P. Joseph (✉) · B. C. Kovoor · J. Thomas
School of Engineering, Cochin University of Science and Technology, Kochi, Kerala 682022, India

© The Author(s), under exclusive license to Springer Nature Singapore Pte Ltd. 2022   551
C. Satyanarayana et al. (eds.), *High Performance Computing and Networking*,
Lecture Notes in Electrical Engineering 853,
https://doi.org/10.1007/978-981-16-9885-9_45

logistics, emergency rescue, and location-based services. The road network reconstruction problem can be linked with the curve reconstruction problem [4]. The input GPS trajectory data are represented as a set of polygonal curves and each curve represents a trajectory. Curve reconstruction is an active research problem in computational geometry. For reconstructing a curve from a set of sample points, Voronoi diagram and its dual Delaunay triangulation-based algorithms are being used [5, 6].

Delaunay triangulation (DT) is one of the most powerful data structures in the field of computational geometry. Recently, the road network reconstruction, road boundary extraction, and road centerline extraction problems have received great attention in which the computational geometry plays an important role. The models such as Mores theory and topological simplification are applied to road network reconstruction and map integration [7]. Delaunay triangulation is used to extract road boundary information [8–11].

Road network information collection and update technologies can be large-scale divided into three kinds (i) volunteered geographic information (VGI)-based [12] data collection. This is a tool to create, assemble, and disseminate geographic information provided voluntarily by individuals. These methods are costly and intensive. Wikimapia [13] and OpenStreetMap [14] are some of the examples of VGIs. (ii) Satellite/aerial image processing [15–17]. This method extracts road network information from high-resolution satellite images or aerial photographs. After getting the image, it needs some manual adjustments in areas like treetops, buildings that are hard to map. Due to the high purchase cost of images, low real-time performance and limited image processing technology, this method is inefficient. (iii) Specialized vehicle-based data collection [18, 19]. Skilled data gathers drive specialized vehicles with mapping devices and collect road information. This requires an experienced person and a specialized vehicle, so a large investment is needed to collect the road network information.

During recent years, with the development of GPS and sensor technologies, many researchers utilize GPS trajectory data to create and amend the road network information. GPS trajectory data consist of spatiotemporal information and have turned out to be a new data source for generating road network structure information. Vehicle trajectory data are obtained from the GPS device installed on the vehicle and it generally contains latitude, longitude, time, speed, and direction attributes. GPX is a GPS exchange format that is designed as a common GPS data format for various software applications [20]. GPX format is open and can be used without the need to pay license fees. GPX is an XML schema and it is supported by hundreds of software applications and Websites. GPS visualizer [21] is an online utility that quickly visualizes GPX files and other geographic data.

The road network information about a particular region is very much important for traffic services improving, updating of existing road network structure, creating new traffic plans, vehicle navigation, and location-based services. The road network information is changing rapidly due to the new road construction, road maintenance, road accidents, etc. The generation and updation of road networks from the maps obtained by field survey and high-resolution remote sensing images are an expensive and time-consuming process. It is very important to generate a road network quickly and inexpensively. The information from GPS trajectories of vehicle data is very useful as it gives rich information about the road structure. The GPS trajectories of vehicle data are unique because the road status is changing along with the road structure. The GPS vehicle trajectory data reveal the shape of the road network, and this data are very useful for generating road networks.

2 Related Works

The current strategies for creating a road network using vehicle trajectory data may be more or less labeled into the following 3 groups. They are point clustering, incremental track insertion, and intersection linking. A brief review of these methods is given below.

2.1 Point Clustering

This method takes the GPS sample points as input and form cluster centers using different clustering algorithms. Then, cluster centers are connected to form a complete road network map. Li and Kulik [22] developed a spatial-linear cluster (SLC) technique to infer road segments from the GPS trace. This algorithm can locate missing roads and verify that the present road network is correct. Edelkamp and Schrodl [23] used a clustering technique based on k-means algorithm. This method first creates cluster centers from sample points of the trajectories, and the cluster centers are updated based on new points. After processing, the centers of the clusters become the node of the map. Zang et al. [24] newly developed graph-based clustering algorithm to cluster the unmatched sampling points into different linear clusters. They propose an automatic method for detecting and updating newly added roads from low-quality GPS trajectory data.

2.2 Incremental Track Insertion

In this category, the road network is constructed by incrementally inserting the vertices of trajectory into an empty graph. Ni et al. [25] proposed a road network generation based on incremental learning of vehicle trajectories. This algorithm continuously receives vehicle trajectories and it was pre-processed to ensure its correctness. The road network is then incrementally generated or modified based on the location and timing information learned from input trajectory online. Ahmed and Wenk [26] provide a easy and workable incremental modal based on a partial matching of the trajectories to the graph. Through fundamental graph structure learning and tree linking approach, Huang et al. [27] present an auto-generate road map from massive low-quality GPS trajectory data. This approach is unaffected by noise, low sampling rate, and perhaps an uneven density distribution.

2.3 Intersection Linking

This method first determines the intersection vertices of the road network and then linked the intersection by interpolation. Fathi and Krumm [28] use a local shape descriptor that perfectly discriminates between intersection and non-intersections. They next looked for roads that connected the intersection and utilized the iterative closest point (ICP) technique to optimize the location of the intersection. Karagiorgou et al. [29] proposed an algorithm that first identifies intersection using turns in vehicle trajectories and then creates a link between intersections to build a meaningful road network graph.

Another approach that converts the GPS trajectory data into images and image processing techniques are used to extract the geometry of the roads from an image [30]. The longitude and latitude of the vehicle's trace information are transformed into the image and morphological operations are used to generate digital road maps. Yuan and Cheriyadat proposed [31] a method to infer road networks from GPS trace data and accurately segment road regions in high-resolution aerial images.

Recently, several algorithms have been proposed to road network generation and updation based on Delaunay triangulation. Ni et al. [25] used DT formed by the representative points of vehicle trajectory for interpolating the connecting segments. In [24], the DT is firstly generated for all unmatched GPS points and generates subgraphs in the road map generation process. Tang et al. [32] suggested an incremental road map construction and employing constrained Delaunay triangulation for higher accuracy during the GPS trace merging process. To generate road boundary descriptors, Yang et al. [33] construct the DT and Voronoi diagram within interpolated tracking lines.

To extract the road geometry information, the GPS trajectory data should be processed. This pre-processing step is called GPS trajectory dilution [34] or representative point extraction [25] or trajectory compression [35]. Before the road map generation algorithms are applied, it should ensure that the trajectory points are distributed on the road surface and dilute the trajectory by removing the redundant points. A graph-based approach proposed by Diansheng et al. [36] used a circular window for smoothing GPS points and to extract representative points. Delaunay triangulation is constructed for efficiently search neighbors of a given point. Wang et al. [37] adopt kernel density function to eliminate the outliers that have a low spatial density in the GPS trajectory. Ni et al. [25] proposed an algorithm for representative point extraction and updating algorithm. The algorithm looks for the nearest representative point that is no more than r meters away. The K-d tree is used to implement the nearest neighbor search in this method. Yuan and Cheriyadat [31] use initial filtering by eliminating non-trace segments based on the spatial density of the tracepoints by applying a Gaussian kernel with σ set to 3 m.

3 Methodology

For generating road networks from vehicle trajectory data, an approach is proposed that consists of two algorithms. The representative point extraction algorithm identifies the representative points from GPS trajectory data, and the reconstruction algorithm generates a road network from representative points, Figure 1 gives an overview of the proposed approach for road network generation.

3.1 *Representative Points Extraction Algorithm*

By extracting representative points from GPS trajectory points, it will suit for representing the road network, because of (1), it will effectively eliminate the noise points that are generated due to the error of the GPS device, (2) it reduces the data redundancy, (3) it eliminates the stationary points that are generated when the vehicle is stopped for a long time period, (4) it almost uniformly distributed from spatially unevenly distributed GPS trajectories, so the shape of the road is preserved, (5) it identify the true structure of the road from the collection of low-frequency GPS trajectories. Figure 2 illustrate the stationary, high density, low-density points, and noise point in the trajectories.

Algorithm 1 for representative point extraction takes two inputs, one is the GPS trajectories in GPX format and another is external parameter ω. GPX file contains

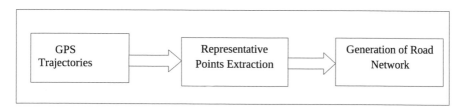

Fig. 1 Overview of the proposed method

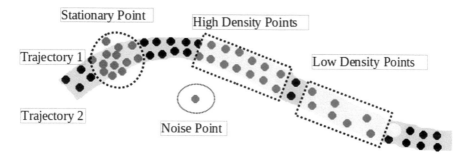

Fig. 2 An illustration of stationary, high density, low-density points, and noise point in the trajectories

the latitude and longitude values. This GPX file mapped onto the map and save it as an image using GPS visualizer. In step 2, it create a point set R that corresponding GPS points from the image. Then, DT is constructed with all points in R and check for a valid flower structure [38] present or not (steps 4 to 12). Take each vertex x in DT with a set of incident edges L. Find the shortest edge, say xz , and the longest edge, say x y. The ratio of x y to x z is lower than 2, then there exists a valid flower structure consisting of a set of triangles associated with x. Then, remove all the points inside the disk with center x and radius ω.

Algorithm 1: Representative Point Extraction
Input: GPX file and parameter ω
Output: Representative Points

Steps:
    1   Map the GPX file onto map and save it as an image
    2   Create a point set R, sampled from the image corresponding to GPS points
    3   Generate Delaunay Triangulation (DT) with all points in R
    4   for each vertex x in DT do
    5   for each incident edge xy of x
    6   Determine the x y length and hold it in the array len[].
    7   end
    8   *short*= shortest(len*[]*)
    9   *long*= longest(len*[]*)
    10   if(*long*<2*short)
    11   delete all the points within the disc that have middle x and radius ω.
    12   end
    13 end

A total of 241 points of 20 GPS traces are mapped onto the map and saved to an image that is shown in Fig. 3a. This trajectory set contains high-density points, low-density points, and stationary points. The representative point extraction algorithms are applied to point set S that is sampled from the image corresponding to GPS

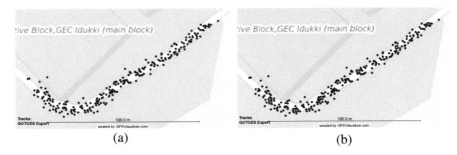

                (a)   (b)

Fig. 3 Representation points extraction. **a** GPS points shows in map. **b** Representative GPS points shown in red color

points. In Fig. 3b, it shows the only 6 representative points (red color) extracted from the sampled GPS point set with the user given parameter ω is set to 80.

3.2 Reconstruction of Road Networks

After representative points are extracted from GPS trajectories, the curve reconstruction algorithm is applied to the reduced point set. In this stage, peeling the longest algorithm [38] is used to generate the road network. Peeling the longest means that the longest edge is removed from each triangle in Delaunay triangulation of the reduced point set. Figure 4a shows the single GPS trace is plotted on the map.

For generating the road network, the algorithm first constructs the Delaunay triangulation of the input point set that is sampled from the map image. Then, the longest edge of each triangle is deleted from the Delaunay triangulation. In the resultant graph, for each point p with more than two as degree, at most two shortest incident edges are retained. Self-intersection happens only on the vertices that has degree one. For handling self-intersection, find all the points q with the disk of radius $\|pq\| < \vartheta \times l$, where l is the smallest edge length in the neighborhood of p and ϑ is a user given parameter. The edges from all q to p are identified and added it to the curve C. The resultant curve that represents the road network is shown in Fig. 4b.

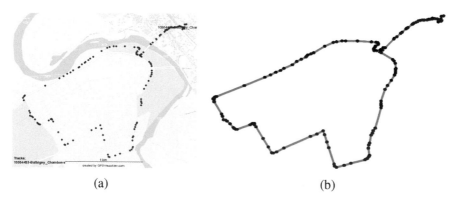

(a)   (b)

Fig. 4 **a** Map image of a single GPS trace, **b** Generated road network corresponding to the GPS trace

4 Experiments and Result

Experimental platform: Representative point extraction algorithm and generation of road networks are implemented in C++ using computational geometry algorithms library [39]. The outputs are viewed using OpenGL framework. For the experimentation study, first, GPS trajectories data sets that are collected from smartphone application. Second experiment based on the GPS traces collected from OpenStreetMap (OSM). OSM is regarded as one of the most successful and well-known voluntary geographic information (VGI) projects, providing open access to a vast amount of geographic data [40]. Before applying the algorithm to GPS trajectories, first, GPS trajectories are mapped using GPS visualizer and save it to an image. Then GPS points are sampled to create a point set. For that, WebPlotDigitizer tool [41] is used for sampling. This tool is a standard tool that is used for sampling purposes [5, 6, 38].

4.1 Experiment on GPS Trajectories Collected from Public Roads

In this experiment, trajectory data are collected from Geo Tracker app [42] installed in a smartphone and deployed in the vehicle. The vehicle roams around various roads and collect GPS Trajectory data. The GPS trajectory data are in the GPX file format. This GPX file consists of latitude and longitude values, elevation values, and time at various points.

Three sets of GPS trajectories are used for experimentation. The first set consists of 6 GPS trajectories and the total number of GPS points is 254. After applying the representative points extraction algorithm, the representative points became reduced to 18 points. The external parameter ω is set to 20 in all cases to the extraction of representative points. The trajectory reduction rate (*TRRn*) is calculated by the equation

$$TRRn = 1 - \left(\frac{TNGPn}{NRPn} \right) \tag{1}$$

Where TNGPn is the total number of points in GPS trajectory set n and NRPn is the number of representative points after the extraction of representative points. The variable n represents the particular GPS trajectory set, say 1, 2, and 3. Each column of Table 1 shows the number of GPS trajectories that constitute a particular set, the total number of GPS points, number of representative points after the representative points extraction algorithm, and the trajectory reduction rate of each GPS trajectory sets. On an average, the trajectory reduction rate is 93%.

Table 1 GPS trajectory sets with the trajectory reduction rate

	Number of GPS trajectories	Total number of GPS points	Number of representative points	TRRn (%)
GPS trajectory set 1	6	254	18	92.91
GPS trajectory set 2	5	742	44	91.07
GPS trajectory set 3	9	566	45	92.05

Figure 5 shows the results of experiment 1. Figures (a), (d), and (g) are the three GPS trajectory sets that are mapped onto the map image. Figures (b), (e), and (h) are the result of representative points, and Figures (c), (f), and (i) are the generated road network.

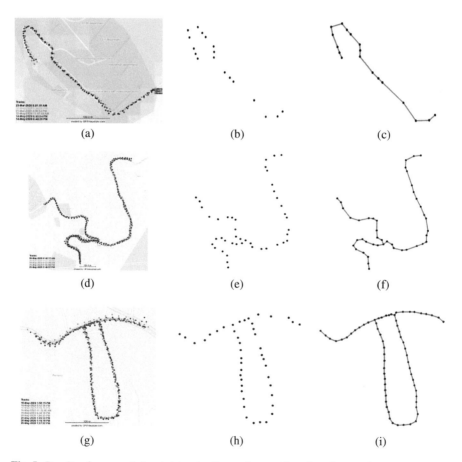

(a) (b) (c)

(d) (e) (f)

(g) (h) (i)

Fig. 5 Results of representative point extraction and generation of road network

Experiments are also carried out on single GPS trajectories collected using a smartphone application. Here, the reconstruction algorithm is directly applied for generating a road network from a single GPS trajectory. Figure 6 shows the results

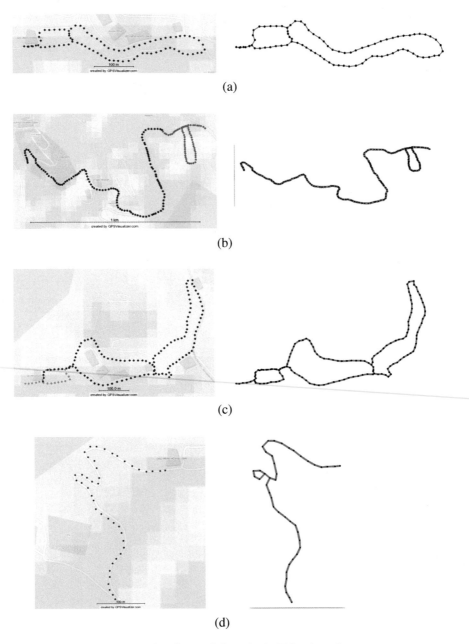

(a)

(b)

(c)

(d)

Fig. 6 Results of generation of road network from single GPS trajectories

of road network generation from a single GPS trajectory. In this study, 50 single GPS trajectories are used. Road network generated from a single GPS trajectory merged two single GPS trajectories and merged three single GPS trajectories are shown in Fig. 6a–c. As observed in Fig. 6d, this approach is not correctly generated the road network when the GPS trajectory contains a sharp curve like structure.

4.2 Experiment on Public Map Database

The experiment utilizes the public GPS traces from OpenStreetMap, an open-source map database. In this study, 50 single public GPS traces are taken from OpenStreetMap. All GPS traces in OpenStreetMap are GPX format and it converted to a map image using GPS visualizer. The points set from the map image is used as input to the reconstruction algorithm to generate the road network.

The reconstruction algorithm is tested with the 50 single traces taken from OSM are correctly generate the road network. Some of the results are shown in Fig. 7a–d.

5 Conclusion

This paper presents an approach for generating road network from GPS vehicle trajectories. GPS vehicle trajectory data of road contain several GPS points. The representative point extraction algorithm has a major role in extracting representative points. The proposed algorithm correctly extracts representative points from high density, low density, noise, and stationary points in the set of GPS vehicle trajectory. The reconstruction algorithm perfectly generates the road network from the representative points as well as from the single GPS traces. Experiments are carried out on the GPS vehicle trajectories collected from the public road and also on the public map database. The experimental results show that this approach is well suited for generating road network from GPS vehicle trajectory data. The trajectory reduction rate shows that this approach is generating a very less number of resultant point sets and it reduces the storage requirement. The vector form of the output will be used for trajectory classification and matching application. The method described in this paper has certain discrepancies when dealing with a sharp curve like trajectory.

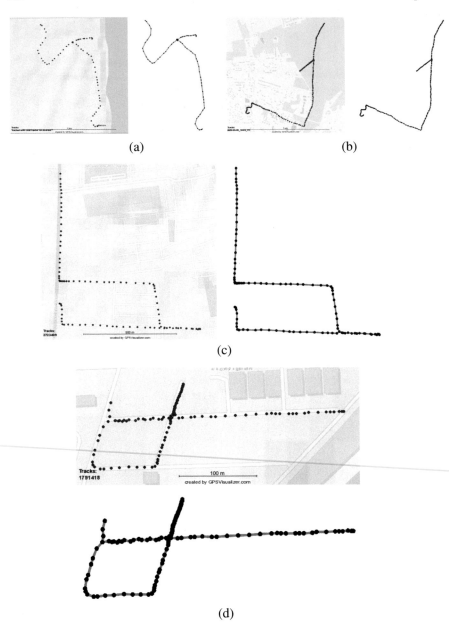

(a)

(b)

(c)

(d)

Fig. 7 Results of generation of road network from OSM single GPS traces

References

1. Mohammad AA, Chris MJT (August 2021) Lane-level routable digital map reconstruction for motorway networks using low-precision GPS data transportation research part C: emerging technologies. Elsevier, p 129
2. Song G, Mingxiao L, Jinmeng R, Gengchen M, Timothy P, Joseph M, Yingjie H (2021) Automatic urban road network extraction from massive GPS trajectories of taxis. In: Werner M, Chiang YY (eds) Handbook of big geospatial data. Springer, Cham
3. Zhongliang F, Liang F, Yangjie S, Zongshun T (March 2020) Density adaptive approach for generating road network from GPS trajectories. IEEE Access, pp 1–1
4. Chen D, Guibas L, Hershberger J, Sun J (17–19 Jan 2010) Road network reconstruction for organizing paths. In: Proceedings of the twenty-first annual ACM-SIAM symposium on discrete algorithms, SODA 2010. Austin, Texas, USA
5. Methirumangalath S, Parakkat AD, Muthuganapathy R (2015) A unified approach towards reconstruction of a planar point set. Elsevier Comput Graph 51:90–97
6. Parakkat AD, Muthuganapathy R (2016) Crawl through neighbors: a simple curve reconstruction algorithm. Computer graphics forum
7. Wang S, Wang Y, Li Y (3–6 Nov 2015) Efficient map reconstruction and augmentation via topological methods. In: Proceedings of the 23rd SIGSPATIAL international conference on advances in geographic information systems. Seattle, Washington, DC, USA, pp 1–25
8. Yang W, Ai T, Lu W (2018) A method for extracting road boundary information from crowdsourcing vehicle GPS trajectories. Sens (Basel) 18(4):1261
9. Tang L, Ren C, Liu Z, Li Q (2017) A road map refinement method using delaunay triangulation for big trace data. ISPRS Int J Geo-Inf 6(2):45
10. Xupeng M, Qiange W, Tiancheng Z (2016) Road network generation from low frequency GPS trajectory data. Chinese control and decision conference (CCDC). Yinchuan, pp 6254–6258
11. Yang W, Ai T (2017) The extraction of road boundary from crowdsourcing trajectory using constrained delaunay triangulation. Acta Geod Cartograph Sin 46(2):237–245
12. Goodchild MF (2007) Citizens as sensors: the world of volunteered geography. Geo J 69:211–221
13. https://wikimapia.org
14. https://www.openstreetmap.org
15. Hu J, Razdan A, Femiani JC, Cui M, Wonka P (2007) Road network extraction and intersection detection from aerial images by tracking road footprints. IEEE Trans Geosci Remote Sens 45:4144–4157
16. Dal Poz AP, Zanin RB, do Vale GM (2006) Automated extraction of road network from medium-and high-resolution images. Pattern Recogn Image Anal 16:239–248
17. Sghaier MO, Lepage R (2016) Road extraction from very high resolution remote sensing optical images based on texture analysis and beamlet transform. IEEE J Sel Top Appl Earth Obs Remote Sens 9:1946–1958
18. Lili C, John K (2009) From GPS traces to a routable road map. 17th ACM SIGSPATIAL international conference on advances in geographic information systems (ACM SIGSPATIAL GIS 2009), November 4–6, Seattle, WA
19. El-Sheimy N, Schwarz KP (1998) Navigating urban areas by VISAT—a mobile map ping system integrating GPS/INS/digital cameras for GIS applications. Navigation 45:275–285
20. https://en.wikipedia.org/wiki/GPS_Exchange_Format
21. https://www.gpsvisualizer.com/
22. Li H, Kulik L, Ramamohanarao K (24–28 Oct 2016) Automatic generation and validation of road maps from GPS trajectory data sets. In Proceedings of the 25th ACM international conference on information and knowledge management. Indianapolis, IN, USA, pp 1523–1532
23. Edelkamp S, Schrödl S (2003) Route planning and map inference with global positioning traces. In: Klein R, Six H-W, Wegner L (eds) Computer science in perspective. Springer, Berlin/Heidelberg, Germany, pp 128–151

24. Zhang Y, Liu J, Qian X, Qiu A, Zhang F (2017) An automatic road network construction method using massive GPS trajectory data. ISPRS Int J Geo-Inf 6:400
25. Ni Z, Xie L, Xie T, Shi B, Zheng Y (2018) Incremental road network generation based on vehicle trajectories. ISPRS Int J Geo-Inf 7:382
26. Ahmed M, Wenk C (2012) Constructing street networks from GPS trajectories. In: Epstein L, Ferragina P (eds) Algorithms—ESA 2012. ESA 2012. Lecture notes in computer science, vol 7501. Springer, Berlin, Heidelberg
27. Huang J, Deng M, Tang J, Hu S, Liu H, Wariyo S, He J (2018) Automatic generation of road maps from low quality GPS trajectory data via structure learning. IEEE Access 6:71965–71975
28. Fathi A, Krumm J (2010) Detecting road intersections from GPS traces. In: Fabrikant SI, Reichenbacher T, van Kreveld M, Schlieder C (eds) Geographic information science, proceedings of the 6th international conference on geographic information science, Zurich, Switzerland, 14–17 September 2010. Springer, Berlin/Heidelberg, Germany, pp 56–69
29. Karagiorgou S, Pfoser D (Nov 2012) On vehicle tracking data-based road network generation. Proceedings of the 20th international conference on advances in geographic information systems. pp 89–98
30. Chen C, Cheng Y (21–22 Dec 2008) Roads digital map generation with multi-track GPS data. In: Proceedings of the IEEE international workshop on education technology and training, 2008 and 2008 international workshop on geoscience and remote sensing ETT and GRS 2008, vol 1. Shanghai, China, pp 508–511
31. Yuan J, Cheriyadat AM (2016) Image feature based GPS trace filtering for road network generation and road segmentation. Mach Vis Appl 27:1–12
32. Tang L, Ren C, Liu Z, Li Q (2017) A road map refinement method using delaunay triangulation for big trace data. ISPRS Int J Geo Inf 6:45
33. Yang W, Ai T, Lu W (2018) A method for extracting road boundary information from crowdsourcing vehicle GPS trajectories. Sensors 18:1261
34. Gotsman R, Kanza Y (2013) Compact representation of GPS trajectories over vectorial road networks. In: Nascimento MA, et al (eds) Advances in spatial and temporal databases. SSTD 2013. Lecture notes in computer science, vol 8098. Springer, Berlin, Heidelberg
35. Vishen R, Silaghi MC, Denzinger J, GPS data interpolation: Bezier versus Biarcs for tracing vehicle trajectory. In: Gervasi O, et al (eds) Computational science and its applications—ICCSA 2015. ICCSA 2015. Lecture notes in computer science, vol 9156. Springer, Cham
36. Diansheng G, Shufan L, Hai J (2010) A graph-based approach to vehicle trajectory analysis. J Location Based Ser 4(3–4):183–199
37. Wang J, Rui X, Song X, Tan X (2014) A novel approach for generating routable road maps from vehicle GPS trajectories. Int J Geogr Inf Sci 29:69–91
38. Parakkat AD, Methirumangalath S, Muthuganapathy R (2018) Peeling the longest: a simple generalized curve reconstruction algorithm. Comput Graph 74
39. https://www.cgal.org/
40. Haklay M, Weber P (2008) Openstreetmap: user-generated street maps. IEEE Pervasive Comput 7:12–18
41. https://apps.automeris.io/wpd/
42. https://play.google.com/store/apps/details?id=com.ilyabogdanovich.geotracker

Power Aware Energy Efficient Virtual Machine Migration (PAEEVMM) in Cloud Computing

Tajinder Kaur and Anil Kumar

Abstract In Cloud computing, Energy Efficiency is a latest research area. These days the dependency of industry on cloud is increasing day by day that leads to requirement of large number of datacenters as well as size of virtual machines. It needs migration of virtual machine along with energy saver. This paper has proposed a method for migrating the virtual machine based on virtual machine temperature's threshold value named as Power Aware Energy Efficient Virtual Machine Migration (PAEEVMM) Method. This method migrates the high loaded virtual machine to the less loaded virtual machine based on temperature. The simulation is performed on CloudSim Plus and results are compared with other traditional first fit algorithm. The experiment shows that the proposed algorithm works better in terms of power usage and CPU utilization.

Keywords Cloud Computing · Energy efficient · CPU utilization · Power usage · Virtualization

1 Introduction

Cloud Computing offers the resources such as computational power, infrastructure, memory and many more [1]. This paradigm is based on the virtualization concept. According to this, multiple virtual machines work on a single physical machine which shares the hardware configurations with other VMs such as memory, Network Interface card and USB Ports. This further minimizes the resource underutilization and idle-time of CPU [2]. With this, the hardware requirement will be minimized that will help to less power usage. During this time, to maintain the energy efficiency has become the valuable research topic in cloud computing [3]. It has been

T. Kaur (✉) · A. Kumar
Guru Nanak Dev University, Amritsar, India

A. Kumar
e-mail: anil.dcse@gndu.ac.in

© The Author(s), under exclusive license to Springer Nature Singapore Pte Ltd. 2022
C. Satyanarayana et al. (eds.), *High Performance Computing and Networking*,
Lecture Notes in Electrical Engineering 853,
https://doi.org/10.1007/978-981-16-9885-9_46

concluded that the virtualized environment requires less energy as compared to traditional systems because the traditional systems do not utilize the nodes in appropriate manner. This would prevent the system from underutilization and over utilization [4]. Underutilization is defined as the node of the system is not working and it is idle whereas over utilization means system is working beyond its capability [5]. So with all these conditions, when virtual machine migrates from one place to other best host place dynamically known as Live Migration [6]. Along with this, to find the over utilized host is a major challenging task because this task also helps to make it power efficient.

To manage the workload and perform the migration is a NP–hard Problem. For these type of problem heuristics techniques are used. There are various kinds of heuristic techniques such as local heuristics and meta-heuristics, to find the optimal solution for such problems, meta-heuristics techniques are more suitable. The proposed algorithm is also considered as meta-heuristic one because it has given optimal solution.

The rest of the paper is organized as follows: The first section introduces the term cloud computing and live migration. The next section reviews the papers, in which authors focused on migration of workload in cloud computing. The third section describes the algorithm used in this paper along with its flowchart. The fourth section contains the experimental setup and the results obtained from the simulation. The last section concludes the paper.

2 Literature Survey

In the area of virtual migration in cloud computing [7], lot of research work is being done. Many authors have proposed different methods to make the data centers power efficient. Mainly the dynamic virtual machine migration means to migrate the working VM from one of the running nodes to the other running node. This section discusses the various research works done by other authors:

In [8] the author has considered the problem of power and energy that are usually faced on cloud data centers. The proposed technique works on the basis of resources such as local and global range. In local range, power management of operating system's cover and in global range, all the information and data of local range are to be managed. While the worldwide supervisor gets the data from the local range virtual machines with respect to the current resource scenario and afterward applies its approaches to choose if the virtual machine requirement is there.

In [9], the author focused on reducing the power that is consumed by various web applications. According to their proposed method, the nodes which are idle are considered to be power off. The workload of each node is measured periodically to check which idle node needs to be power on. This procedure helps to reduce the power usage. The main limitation shown in this paper is, if the master node is turn off then it can create major problem in whole of the system.

In [10], the author has not focused on cloud data centers, they have focused on host centers of Internet. The challenging task of this paper is need and allocation of resources. They have proposed a method that creates a bid of number of resources those are available. The system makes a list of servers those are in work mode. With this, power saving mode is achieved.

In [11], the author has focused on management of power and used the LLC algorithm known as Limited Lookahead Control. They have used this method into heterogeneous environment. As the requests come from user end, it estimates the situation and filters are applied for the reallocation of virtual machines. But the limitation of this paper is that the execution time is very large.

In [12], the author worked on resource management. Here, in this paper, the author has taken a time stamp range in the form of hours and seconds. They considered different time scale ranging from hours to seconds. This paper has performed various actions such as reallocation of virtual machines, place the load and requests on the servers, allocates resources to the virtual machines, and applied an approach of setting up the fixed utilization threshold value, which was not that efficient.

In [13] the author has optimized the consumption of energy and SLA. For this, they have used traditional machine learning techniques to optimize energy consumption and SLA. Their proposed approach was designed for the High-Performance Computing (HPC) where concept of deadline constraint occurs making it unsuitable for the mixed workload.

In [14] the author has reviewed the migration of the multiple virtual machines from multiple source hosts towards multiple destination hosts by taking into consideration the network connection.

In [15] proposed an algorithm that aimed to decrease the consumption of energy along with the maintenance of high-level SLA. A novel adaptive heuristic for dynamic consolidation of VMs was the approach used to analyze the historical usage of resources of the VM.

A novel approach called EnaCloud that allows live placement of applications dynamically while considering energy optimization in a cloud infrastructure was proposed in [16]. In EnaCloud, a Virtual Machine was used to provide the application that supports the live migration and applications scheduling to prune the number of active machines, in order to conserve maximum amount of energy. Particularly, the application placement is considered as the bin packing problem. Moreover a power aware heuristic algorithm was offered to obtain the appropriate result. In addition, the over-provisioning scheme was proposed to manage the changing the resource demands of applications.

Two power aware migration strategies were proposed in [17]. The overall energy consumption was minimized by restricting the number of migrations. The clock speed was altered at the time of migration by using dynamic voltage and frequency scaling (DVFS) approach to further decrease energy consumption. *The following* Table 1 *illustrates the two power aware migration strategies.*

Table 1 Power Aware Migration Strategies

Author and Year	Strategy	Approach	Characteristics
Wang et al.[18] 2008	Process level migration	Proactive	The deteriorating machine is detected to trigger live migration 70% failures can be avoided by implementing this proactive approach Number of checkpoints is considerably reduced resulting in efficient utilization of available storage space
Jin et al. [19] 2009	Live virtual machine migration with adaptive, memory compression	Proactive	Adaptive compression of migrated data In every round, the transferring of the data at the source node is compressed by this algorithm and decompressed on achieving the target Migration time was reduced

3 Algorithm Used

The main aim of this work is to propose the power aware energy efficient algorithm for placing the virtual machines in data center. This proposed work helps to minimize the consumed energy. That has been compared with first fit algorithm and resulted best. The proposed approach takes the input of host and its parameters such as bandwidth, ram and processing elements. More than 100 cloudlets are initialized and this approach monitors the temperature, CPU Utilization and power consumption of different hosts.

The average power consumption is calculated using Eq. (1)

$$\text{Power} = \frac{P1 + P2 + P3 + \ldots\ldots + Pn}{n} \tag{1}$$

P1 and P2 are factors corresponding the power consumed when there is no workload (idle mode) and addition power required during execution of various jobs. 70% of overall power is consumed by a system in idle mode. CPU utilization increases dynamically as the workload increases.

Energy consumption can be calculated by Eq. (2)

$$\text{Energy}_i = \frac{\text{CPU}_{\text{Utilization}_i}(P1 + P2)}{\text{Power}_i} \tag{2}$$

4 Methodology

Energy efficiency is the primal challenges these days. Different architectures, frameworks, algorithms and policies have been proposed to make the cloud computing environment energy efficient. However, there is limited research which considers this parameter. This proposed work focuses on power efficient algorithm which monitors system's thermal behavior to reduce the overall temperature so that failures which may occur due to rising temperature can be avoided by using migration strategy. Moreover, the energy required to operate the data center cooling systems can be saved. The power aware reallocation approach is used such that virtual machine on deteriorating physical machine can be reallocated to optimal physical machine, which further saves energy. Moreover, the restricted presence of assets e.g., memory and energy executing cloudlets or tasks becomes a critical issues while conserving energy in base system.

Input: Host list: all the active hosts, VM list: all VMs currently available in the pool, Threshold value: 60.

1. Initialize temperature to each VM.
2. Evaluate average power consumption of each VM using equation.

$$\text{Power} = \frac{P1 + P2 + P3 + \ldots\ldots + Pn}{n} \tag{1}$$

3. Evaluate energy consumption of each VM using equation.

$$\text{Energy}_i = \frac{\text{CPU}_{\text{Utilization}_i}(P1 + P2)}{\text{Power}_i} \tag{2}$$

4. Sort VMs on the basis of energy consumption.
5. Given Name to minimum one VM_{Min}
6. Assign Load to host.
7. Check if the VM requires to place on basis of temperature
   If (Temperature > Threshold).
   Migrate VM to optimal destination selected from list of VMs.
   Else (Energy > Threshold).
8. Use Eq. (1) and (2) to check for power and energy consumption.

Output: Power consumption and CPU utilization.

5 Experimental Setup and Results

The experiment was conducted using CloudSim Plus simulator. The simulated cloud infrastructure comprised of one data center in which the hosts were created dynamically in accordance with number of jobs which are taken as input from user. Each host had the capacity of ten virtual machines. The proposed approach is implemented and results are expressed in terms of energy consumption and CPU Utilization.

Cloudlets indicating tasks are varied in each simulation run. Difference in energy consumption has been noted as shown in Fig. 1.

Total execution time indicates the delay or time consumed in order to execute entire simulation. As the cloudlet increases, the total time taken for the completion of task also increases.

Here, in this paper, the proposed algorithm is compared with the traditional first fit algorithm. Figure 1 shows the results for energy consumed in cloud systems with different number of tasks. Figure 2 shows the results of utilization of processor in percentage while performing the migration.

Result comparison proves the worth of the study as prime objective of conserving energy is accomplished efficiently through power aware energy efficient migration mechanism proposed through this literature.

In this simulation, Fig. 3 shows the results of usage of host in different interval of time during the migration.

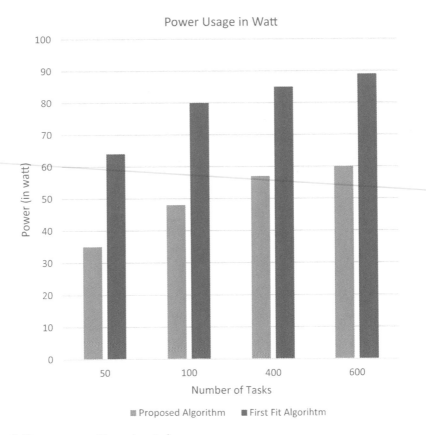

Fig. 1 Power consumed by various tasks

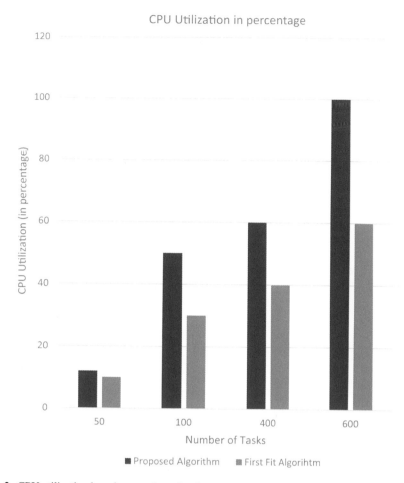

Fig. 2 CPU utilization based on number of tasks

6 Conclusion and Future Scope

In current cloud computing technology, energy efficiency is main research area. The virtualization concept in cloud computing extends from single system servers to multiple virtual machines such as data centers and they consume more and more energy. So, energy management is essential for this technology. In this paper, we have proposed a PAEEVMM algorithm that gives the optimized way to use the energy. The proposed algorithm results are compared with the first fit algorithm. In future it can be enhanced with the use of load balancing along with same migration algorithm.

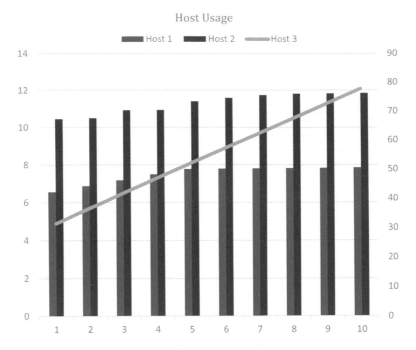

Fig. 3 Host usage in different interval of time

References

1. Buyya R, Yeo CS, Venugopal S, Broberg J, Brandic I (2009) Cloud computing and emerging IT platforms: vision, hype, and reality for delivering computing as the 5th utility. Futur Gener Comput Syst 25(6):599–616
2. Chiueh SNTC, Brook S (2005) A survey on virtualization technologies. Rpe Report 142
3. Behl A (Dec 2011) Emerging security challenges in cloud computing: an insight to cloud security challenges and their mitigation. In: 2011 world congress on information and communication technologies. IEEE, pp 217–222
4. Lee YC, Zomaya AY (2012) Energy efficient utilization of resources in cloud computing systems. J Supercomput 60(2):268–280
5. Feller E, Rilling L, Morin C (May 2012) Snooze: a scalable and autonomic virtual machine management framework for private clouds. In: 2012 12th IEEE/ACM international symposium on cluster, cloud and grid computing (ccgrid 2012). IEEE, pp 482–489
6. Clark C, Fraser K, Hand S, Hansen JG, Jul E, Limpach C, Pratt I, Warfield A (2005) Live migration of virtual machines. In: Proceedings of the 2nd conference on symposium on networked systems design and implementation. pp 273–286
7. Kaur T, Chana I (2015) Energy efficiency techniques in cloud computing: a survey and taxonomy. ACM Comput Surv (CSUR) 48(2):1–46
8. Nathuji R, Schwan K (2007) Virtualpower: coordinated power management in virtualized enterprise systems. ACM SIGOPS Oper Syst Rev 41(6):265–278
9. Pinheiro E, Bianchini R, Carrera EV, Heath T (2001) Load balancing and unbalancing for power and performance in cluster-based systems
10. Chase JS, Anderson DC, Thakar PN, Vahdat AM, Doyle RP (2001) Managing energy and server resources in hosting centers. ACM SIGOPS Oper Syst Rev 35(5):103–116

11. Kusic D, Kephart JO, Hanson JE, Kandasamy N, Jiang G (2009) Power and performance management of virtualized computing environments via lookahead control. Clust Comput 12(1):1–15

12. Zhu X, Young D, Watson BJ, Wang Z, Rolia J, Singhal S, McKee B, Hyser C, Gmach D, Gardner R, Christian T (2008) Integrated capacity and workload management for the next generation data center. In: ICAC08: proceedings of the 5th international conference on autonomic computing

13. Berral JL, Goiri Í, Nou R, Julià F, Guitart J, Gavaldà R, Torres J (April 2010) Towards energy-aware scheduling in data centers using machine learning. In: Proceedings of the 1st international conference on energy-efficient computing and networking, (ACM, 2010). pp 215–224

14. Deshpande U, Keahey K (2017) Traffic-sensitive live migration of virtual machines. Futur Gener Comput Syst 72:118–128

15. Beloglazov A, Buyya R (2012) Optimal online deterministic algorithms and adaptive heuristics for energy and performance efficient dynamic consolidation of virtual machines in cloud data centers. Concurr Comput: Pract Exp 24(13):1397–1420

16. Li B, Li J, Huai J, Wo T, Li Q, Zhong L (Sept 2009) Enacloud: an energy-saving application live placement approach for cloud computing environments. In: 2009 IEEE international conference on cloud computing. IEEE. pp 17–24

17. Arroba P, Moya JM, Ayala JL, Buyya R (2017) Dynamic voltage and frequency scaling-aware dynamic consolidation of virtual machines for energy efficient cloud data centers. Concurrency Comput: Pract Experience 29(10):e4067

18. Wang C, Mueller F, Engelmann C, Scott SL (Nov 2008) Proactive process-level live migration in HPC environments. In: SC'08: proceedings of the 2008 ACM/IEEE conference on supercomputing. IEEE, pp 1–12

19. Jin H, Deng L, Wu S, Shi X, Pan X (August 2009) Live virtual machine migration with adaptive, memory compression. In: 2009 IEEE international conference on cluster computing and workshops. IEEE, pp 1–10

Automotive RADAR Human Classification Algorithm Through Simulation Analysis: Basics and Practical Challenges

Anto Jeyaprabu James and Kayalvizhi Jayavel

Abstract In the automotive domain, Advanced Driver-Assistance System (ADAS) sensors are game changers which bring science fiction movies into real life with the help of Automotive Radar and imaging sensors. This paper will summarize the types of radar, algorithms, and its features from the Advanced Signal Processing (ADSP) concepts. Especially in the urban roads, vehicle drivers need to make a quick decision on pedestrian classification behind other objects. Also, the pedestrians' unique actions need to be predicted while crossing the road. There are multiple reasons where radars are unable to make a right decision, but behind the obstacles/objects scenario the Emergency Brake Assist (EBA) feature is more sophisticated to make a perfect decision better than humans (drivers). This paper will assist the researchers to visualize the open points behind the pedestrian nature and possible ways to improve the EBA feature. Also, this paper will help researchers to find the suitable algorithms and hardware from the automotive market. Hope this paper will also bridge the gap between academic researchers and industrial trends.

Keywords Machine learning (ML) · Advanced driver-assistance system (ADAS) · Emergency brake assist (EBA)

1 Introduction

Automotive Radars are developed to ensure a comfortable environment, road safety with certain limitations and freedom. The term RADAR is a well-known acronym for **Ra**dio **D**etection **a**nd **R**anging. In general, two types of Radars' use cases are

A. J. James (✉)
Department of Computer Science and Engineering, School of Computing, SRM Institute of Science and Technology, Chennai, Tamil Nadu, India
e-mail: aj7273@srmist.edu.in

K. Jayavel
Department of Information Technology, School of Computing, SRM Institute of Science and Technology, Chennai, Tamil Nadu, India
e-mail: kayalvij@srmist.edu.in

© The Author(s), under exclusive license to Springer Nature Singapore Pte Ltd. 2022
C. Satyanarayana et al. (eds.), *High Performance Computing and Networking*,
Lecture Notes in Electrical Engineering 853,
https://doi.org/10.1007/978-981-16-9885-9_47

available for the defense usage as well as commercial usage based on scope. Globally the most common one is electromechanical scanning radar and other one is electronic scanning radar. In terms of features and application wise, both types of radars have a greater number of differences.

Electromechanical scanning radar has moveable parts with heavy payload with 360 or ±180-degree FOV (Field of View) operation with long-range detection, and it is operated on the low frequency which can travel up to few kilometers in the open space. Also, there is no better object classification because of the ambiguities and environment losses. These radars are gigantic in size and mostly used for the defense, aerospace, and satellite communication.

Other side electronic scanning radar/beam steering radar works within a few hundred meters. It is operated on high frequency with limited range (less than 400 m) and short FOV (±50 degree) operation with high accuracy of object detection in the real time, as well as being very compact in the size and used for the automotive application. In this paper, human classification is mainly described through the automotive radar and its features. The rest of the paper is divided as follows: automotive radar types & specific application, problem statement, global techniques & constraint, signal processing based proposed solution, results, and conclusion.

1.1 Automotive Radar Types Overview and Specific Applications

Primarily radar is used to detect objects (vulnerable road users and obstacles) [1] near the vehicle and to find their object range as well as velocity and angle of arrival from the radar mounting position. There are two major types of safety systems followed in automotive world.

i. Active safety
ii. Passive safety.

Sensors, cameras, and all radar products would come under active safety components. In terms of frequency range, two types of radar categories are available in the market (Table 1).

ISM refers to Industrial, Scientific, and medical bands or unlicensed bands.

The calculated distance R from the reflecting object

$$R_r = (C_o|\Delta t|)/2$$

Table 1 Frequency versus wavelength and range	Frequency	24 GHz (ISM band)	77 GHz (77 to 81 GHz)
	Wavelength	12.49135 mm	3.89341 mm
	Detection range	Less than 100 m	Less than 300 m

R_r Range/distance from the Reflecting Object.
C_o Speed of the light (3e8 m/s).
Δt Delay time in sec.

While in a vehicle-to-vehicle collision scenario, the driver should be aware of the relation between activation speed and the deceleration/required detection distance described in the EUNCAP documents.
The detection range to apply brake could be calculated through this formula:

$$D_{min} = V_T * t_d - \left(\frac{d^2(t_B - t_d)^2 - (d(t_B - t_d)) - (V_{mas} - V_T))^2}{2d} \right)$$

D_{min} Minimum distance decided by OEM in meter

$$V_{mas} = d * (t_B - t_d) + V_T - \sqrt{d^2 * (t_B - t_d)^2 - 2 * a * (V_T * t_B - D_{min})}$$

V_T Speed of the target vehicle (Ex: 16.6667 m/s = 130kph).
d deceleration of the target vehicle.
t_B Time to stop the Ego vehicle before reaching the target.
t_d Remaining time gap of the ego vehicle to meet deceleration of the target vehicle.
V_{mas} to avoid collision at minimum activation speed m/s.
D_{min} minimum distance decided by OEM in m.

With reference to the maximum detection range, it is also categorized like short-range and long-range radar [2]. The short-range radar (SRR) would help the driver by warning depending on the feature and function description except the brake request. The warning could be a sound alert or light indication, but the long-range radar (LRR) would try to help the driver by warning and apply a "brake" request to the ECU (meanwhile applying brake) too. These kinds of automotive radars are manufactured from tier1 companies like Continental, Bosch, Veoneer, Denso, etc.

At present, the automotive radar works with a series of FMCW [3] signals and a well-studied research field. Inside the radar box, the PCB (Printed circuit Board) will be divided into two levels. Front side of the radar (Looking for the signal from reflected objects) is called RF (Radio Frequency) or HF (High Frequency) PCB and Rear side located PCB of the Radar are connected with power supply and all signal communication, which is called LF (Low Frequency) PCB. All the DSP (Digital signal processing) algorithms work in the LF PCB.

The software package would be released with all kinds of OEM (Original Equipment Manufacturer) interested features. Also, it would be readily available to make a synchronized decision with other sensors through local CAN (Controller Area Network). ADAS's domains well-known features are:

i.   Emergency Brake Assist (EBA) (Fig. 1) or Advanced Emergency Brake (AEB)

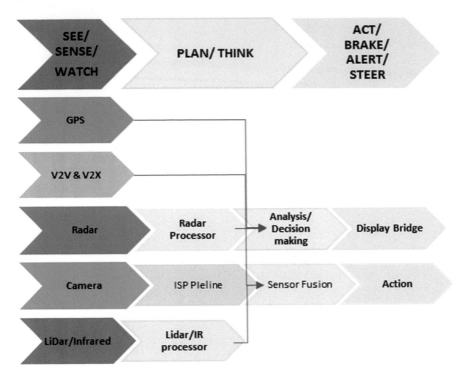

Fig. 1 EBA function overview

ii.   Cruise control
iii.   Road sign recognition
iv.   Speed limit assist
v.   Lane-change warning and lane-change assist
vi.   Parking assist
vii.   Traffic Jam assist.

All these special characteristics would provide safety features in the combination of radar with camera. In this paper, our focus would be on the EBA. EBA will keep an eye on the road in all the environmental conditions [4]. At the time of emergency or unpredictable fast-moving driving scenarios EBA would warn the driver. Then the driver will control the car, in case, if the driver reacts slowly or has no reaction, EBA will start applying brakes automatically and try to avoid the collision/collision with low speed. The car will stop and reach the zero speed smoothly. In this scenario, there are a lot of parameters to consider such as road conditions, driving speed, tire pressure, eco vehicle or target vehicles speed, driver's reaction, etc.

When the trigger is initiated by radar, the engine ECU/ADAS ECU would separate this complete EBA operation into multiple parallel on module wise work. So, the Radar's final confirmation could save many human beings at the right time on the road. This EBA operation is subdivided into 3 major categories such as,

i.   EBA-Pedestrian,
ii. EBA-Bicyclist
iii. EBA-Car/Truck.

2 Problem Statement

The EBA-Pedestrian feature is again classified into two types like adult pedestrian classification and child pedestrian classification [5]. Detection of the pedestrian is highly complicated with real time other objects like streetlight poles, road sign boards, traffic light signal poles, advertising poles, and pedestrian crossing sign poles.

The countryside (non-highway) roads are less informative while compared to wider organized highways [6]. In this case, the existing two types of pedestrian classification [7] are not effective. It would go more challenging behind the parked car/truck, junction point at the street. The existing algorithms [5] are more efficient and suitable for the moving pedestrian scenario (8kph). Our focus should be trying to address the slow-moving (less than 5 kph) pedestrians [8] and elders (Senior Citizen) classification. Also, the similar classification for the standing pedestrian stands behind the high reflecting objects.

3 Discussion of Global Techniques and Constraints

3.1 Field of View (FOV)

FOV is like the front most visible area for the radar. FOV has certain constraints. The biggest area volume, which could be achieved for the Field of View (FOV) [9] of a phased array antenna, will be 120° maximum (60° left and 60° right) in terms of PCB printed antenna.

FOV considered for two types of scanning [10]

– Azimuth scan
– Elevation scan.

Radar could gain the maximum value of field intensity pattern equal to the main lobe. In simple words, our human natural eyes will be able to visual ±110 degrees in their front side. Radar is also able to scan the field in the same way, which is called FOV (Fig. 2).

While calculating FOV, the OEM will consider Auto SAR coordinate system instead of Cartesian coordinate system.

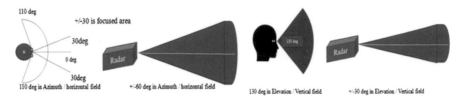

Fig. 2 Radar's FOV (Azimuth and Elevation) comparison with human vision

3.2 Radar Signals

All measured raw signals are given to RSP (Radar Signals Processing) and RDP (Radar Data Processing). The preprocessed echo signals would also help to calculate antenna parameters. These antenna parameters will be used to plot the radar's bird eye view.

The analog raw signal would carry magnitude (in-phase), direction (quadrature) values, and noise included as an echo signal in time domain/analog signals. In general, these time domain signals would be converted into frequency domain/digital signals. The RDP is the part of signal processing [11], which concerns only the information about a target after suppressing the noise or generic object like road, and guardrail. In parallel there is a process of measuring the XYZ coordinates of any reflecting object.

RSP focuses on the two major detections; they are Stable or Non-moving object and Unstable or moving object. Based on the feature algorithm's requirement, both types of objects will be considered for tracking on the vehicles own speed while crossing or passing the scenario.

3.3 Antenna Types and Pattern

In the automotive industry, micro strip antennas and array antennas are the most popular antennas. Antenna could be used as a transmitting antenna or receiving antenna which supports electrical power into electromagnetic waves and vice versa. Their antennas are mostly printed on the PCB like loop, patch inverted F and meander line.

MIMO [2] has multiple transmitters and multiple receivers to cover the wider front of the car. The maximum power radiation at the zero degree is called the main lobe (Fig. 3). All the other lobes are called side lobe, and the exact opposite power radiation to the main lobe is called back lobe.

Currently, automotive domain applications micro strip patch antennas, waveguide antennas are most reliable and cost effective as well as less power dissipation. On the other side, on a single PCB both the transmitter and receiver antennas are fabricated to reduce the radar size. To cover a wider area multiple transmitter and receiver,

Fig. 3 Antenna gain

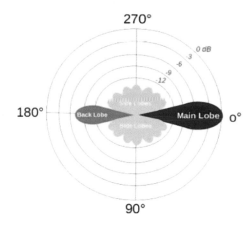

these are connected like a tree structure. The entire antenna structure is powered through a qualified single chip transceiver [12] like NXP, Texas Instruments (TI), and Qualcomm.

$$G = D * \eta$$

G   Antenna Gain.
D   Directivity of the antenna.
η Efficiency.

Before fabrication into PCB, antenna designer would try to visualize and analyze the far field, directivity pattern of the antenna. The below comparison represents the preprocessing of 24 GHz SRR antenna through a coupling solution in sensor's EM simulation (Fig. 4).

3.4 Mounting Position

With respect to OEM features, the Radars are mounted at either four corners of the car or at the car's front middle or rear middle [13] (behind logo). Most of the EBA features Radars are mounted behind the logo of the front middle car or behind the number plate. From the outside these radars would not be visually available since this radar is mounted behind the pumper. Radar could not give the maximum efficiency due to this complex mounting location. In some cars, this kind of power/efficiency loss would be up to 40%.

To improve the radar efficiency and accuracy of the object detection, better algorithms are required, because physically the Radar mounting positions cannot be modified and this solution differs with respect to different colors and shape of the car. Certain limited freedom is available from OEM (Table 2).

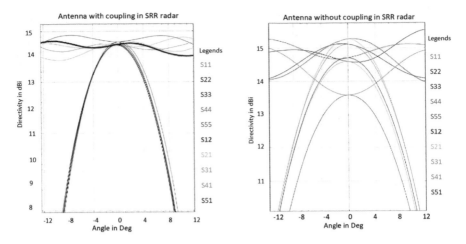

Fig. 4 L.H antenna with coupling, R.H antenna without coupling in SRR radar

Table 2 Combination of coordinates in Azimuth versus Elevation	Tolerance on each direction	Azimuth	Elevation
	Yaw (Z)	±3°	± 3°
	Roll (X)	±5°	± 3°
	Pitch (Y)	±3°	± 5°

3.5   Object of Interest (OOI)

In the EBA application pedestrians [9], cyclists, cars, trucks are the most interested objects from the real city roads and parking scenarios. The algorithms are always looking for the separation between moving objects versus non-moving objects. Some OEMS are looking for four to six cars in the EBA object list [14] in the highway and traffic scenarios. In the city, roads are highly mixed with all these kinds of objects which make the EBA algorithm more complicated to make quick autonomous decisions.

3.6   Object Detection

Object detections are done with the help of Object of Interest (OOI) tracker and Radar Cross Section (RCS). RCS value will be calculated based on the below formula.

$$\text{Radar Cross - Section} \left(\Sigma^0 \right) = |RCS_i / A_i|$$

Here,

Table 3 Relative permittivity of selected materials

Material	Relative dielectric number (εr)	Applicability
Polypropylene	2.33	Best
ABS	2.7	Ok
Polyamide	2.73	Ok
Polycarbonate	2.8	Ok
PP/EPDM	3.5	TBD

- RCS_i–The radar cross-section of a particular object
- A_i–The area of the ground associated with that object.

RCS values play a vital role in the EBA algorithm to differentiate the adult pedestrians versus child pedestrians [1, 15] and bicyclists versus moped riders. The detected objects will be listed in an array with its XYZ coordinates. Each detected object would be grouped with on time so those detected objects will vary continuously while the car is moving or crossing toward the targets [16] (vehicle/pedestrians/bicyclists).

Considering the above dynamic situation, the algorithms are expected to provide the effective result. In parallel all the environmental effects (heavy rainfall/snowfall/water/mud and dirt on the bumper) would be considered along with noises. The material thickness of the bumper plays a very crucial role here.

The radar needs the overall optimized thickness of the car bumper material. Through that value it will look for high permeability achievement.

$$T_o = \frac{n * C_o}{2 * f * \sqrt{\varepsilon_r}}$$

T_o optimized thickness of the car bumper material.
C_o Speed of the light (3e8 m/s).
ε_r Relative permeability.
f Operating frequency of the Radar.

The intention to find the below value is to make the bumper work like a transparent layer (Table 3).

3.7 Object Classification

Object classification is to separate the desired and interested objects from the group of detected similar as well as dissimilar groups of other objects. It is the main input for the algorithm to track the objects from the static object by that scenario. For example, while developing the algorithm, the number of similar objects groups will be considered as a main input for the tracker (JPDAF-Joint Probabilistic Data-Association Filter) [17]. To classify each object RCS [13], the object speed (Doppler) [7] will be the main input. Differentiating the slow-moving pedestrian among the normal standing pedestrian will be challenging work.

In this case, 70% of the detection is based on the pedestrian gesture and the remaining is based on their hand and the leg movements. There is a wider possibility to misclassify the pedestrian when there are no hands and leg movements, for example, when hands are inserted in their pockets [8]. The main goal of this work is to provide an optimal solution for this kind of issue in real time along with other classified objects.

4 Systems Engineering and Advanced Signal Processing Based Existing Solution

The random variables, statics and probability, machine learning, and deep learning theories are utilized. Earlier, the suitable equations from the above-mentioned theories were converted into software functions with the help of embedded C programming language. At present, the Systems Engineering (SE) team's consistent effort would reduce the complexity into multiple chapters. Also, they can get detailed diagnoses results and traceability matrix for each software and hardware module individually.

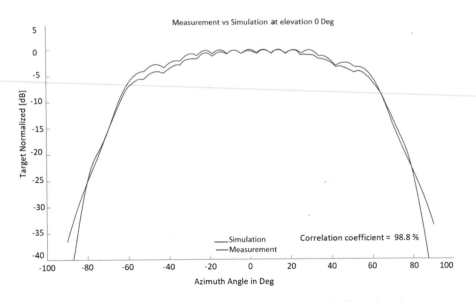

Fig. 5 The target normalized (TargertNormS) azimuth angle results (Fig. 5) are plotted as a comparison between Simulation vs Measured at the Elevation 0 degrees. Here the DBF maximum values are considered from all antennas. The correlation factor is 98.8% within ±60 deg FOV

Table 4 Algorithms based accuracy, snapshot, antenna array, grid required

Antenna Array	Algorithm	Imaging technique	Required Grid
I/ II	DBF (low)	1 shot	No
I	MUSIC (High)	10 + shots	No
I/ II	OMP (High)	1	No
I/ II	IAA (High)	1	No
I	ESPIRIT (High)	10 + shots	Yes

Instead of chip-based IDE (Integrated Development Environment) and software development tools, MATLAB code generation toolbox could be used alternatively. MATLAB can reduce the software documentation work and it is easy to update throughout the entire software functions in case of multiple versions and revisions. It heals the embedded hardware platform related issues at PC/Laptop level debugging itself. Then the source code will be ready for the multiple analyses like HIL (Hardware-In-Loop) SIL (Software-In-Loop) and PIL (Processor-In-Loop). AUTOSAR based software environment components could easily get synchronized through MATLAB software [18] to other vendor products like Lidar, camera, and ADAS ECU. This will reduce the script development effort across the sensors, and it will help in great number for the fusion strategies [19] through synchronized clock in common.

Currently, two types of antenna fabrication techniques are used on PCB level.

I. ULA–uniform linear array,
II. SLA–sparse linear array (Table 4).

There are different estimation DoA (Direction Of Arrival) algorithms in automotive radar industry [2]. They are:

- DBF–digital beam forming algorithm (Fig. 6)
- IAA–iterative adaptive approach
- MUSIC–Multiple Signal Classification Algorithm
- ESPRIT–Estimation of Signal Parameters via Rotational Invariance Techniques
- OMP–Orthogonal matching pursuit algorithm (Table 5).

MUSIC and ESPIRIT have been considered as a super resolution algorithm in machine learning.

The frequency bandwidth and number of elements in the antenna have been used as a system parameter in ML estimator when compared to the Rayleigh limit set. STAP (space and time adaptive processing) and CFAR (Constant false alarm rate) processing could be actively used to reduce the effect of clutter. The reflected data from unwanted/not-interested objects are called clutter. Ex: side walls, garbage on the road.

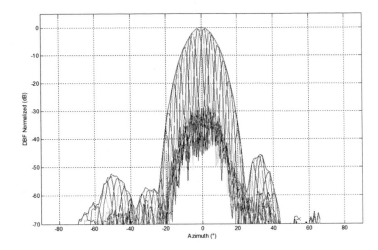

Fig. 6 DBF (digital beam forming) algorithm's fairfield power data from the radar measurement

Table 5 Algorithms based rank, robustness, difficulty, signal processing

Algorithm	Clutter rank estimation	Robustness	Difficulty	Signal processing effort
DBF	No	Strong	Low	Medium
MUSIC	Yes	Medium	High	Low
ESPIRIT	Yes	Medium	Medium	Low
OMP	No	Medium	High	Medium
IAA	No	Strong	High	Medium

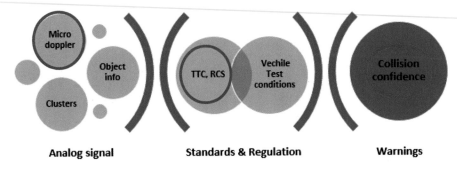

Fig. 7 Warning sequence for EBA-pedestrian classification algorithm

Table 6 LRR angle deviation comparison results

Angle error (deg)	−80	−20	0	+20	+80
Measurement versus 3D EM simulation (deg)	< 3.5°	< 1.5°	< 1°	< 1.5°	< 3.5°

5 Results

As per the proposed below Fig. 7 algorithm strategy, The EBA feature would be able to provide good agreement on the classification but to fix the collision confidence the sensors angle deviation error should be less or equal to zero.

In the closed environment lab condition, SRR sensor sample Measurement and EM Simulation results are compared using Matlab software. The below Table 6 provides Angle deviation comparison in azimuth axis. This angle deviation comparison would help the feature developers to understand the pedestrian classification algorithm's final accuracy at the high level.

This comparison study results would be available the quote base of the project with the Sample OEMS Radome and bumper (with and without multi-layer of different color paints). The results create high confidence of the project beginning success agreement between OEM and Tier 1suppliers and bumper manufactures too.

6 Open Topics for the Future Researchers

In the ADAS RADAR field, testing data collection with individuals or groups of real pedestrians crossing scenarios is not allowed, since the high-speed cars involved.

(a) Not allowed to do any research activities with the risk of human life, so dummy pedestrians used which is not 100% equal to human reactions.

(b) In simple words, a large dataset is found to be missing [20] with fusion strategies.

(c) It is not easy to store the raw data and reproduce the scenarios back with multiple sensor combinations. Ex: GPS co-ordination, Day-light condition, Environments effects [14]

(d) The Real-time challenges are required to update back as a continuous learning/reinforcement learning via IOT (Internet of Things) and OTA (over-the-air) software update in the existing hardware.

(e) To solve the above issues, we need to do a few 100 simulations [18] at each mounting location for each scenario Ex: Road crossing with moving VRU (Vulnerable Road Users), Junction assist, EBA functions.

(f) On the other hand, it takes time in weeks to complete the EM simulation [21] for each car, and the high cost is also incurred for the analysis. But Simulations are a powerful and highly optimized way to reduce months duration of fielding testing and data transfer between locations [6].

(g) For example, to make this one blue line pattern scanning measurement in between the range ± 90 deg azimuth direction, testing engineers need to spend at least 3 min. The same process must be repeated for 180 times. So, the one complete measurement takes almost 9 + hours. There are multiple ways to conduct similar measurements [22], but each one has its own advantages and disadvantages.

(h) In the Micro-Doppler radar development, estimation algorithms and target tracking algorithms are essentials, and the challenging module for the small RCS values is like child detection.

7 Conclusions and Future Works

In this automotive field, ADAS plays a vital role for autonomous driving and pedestrian safety. It is almost equally powerful to one supercomputer. ADAS decision making processors are supposed to function similarly like the human brain at the rate of microsecond time. In this article/paper, we summarized a few types of radar and its working principles, features relevant to ADAS industry, OEMs problems with existing radar modules and signal processing techniques [17] as well.

In the last three decades, automotive radar has been improved a lot by solving the unknown parameters through the software up scaling. Here we have proposed the medium range of cost-effective hardware and parallel processing well-structured software at each level of processing. The raw data preprocessing needs to do with high accuracy and less noise. To maintain the good compensation in the RF transmission and receiving side, Antenna materials and spacing are very important. The advanced signal processing techniques will help us to balance the software and hardware load in the real-time environment.

There few problems are easily addressed by better mechanical design as well as experts through better radome design and materials selection. The Tier 1 automotive suppliers are looking for the better freedom to place their radars in the car as well as the best price and are looking for hands-on knowledge sharing while designing the new model cars and NCAP assessment. On the other hand, the OEMs are not required to lose their customers by ugly appearance, design, and low-cost materials which make no sense, and an uncorrectable high risk in passenger's safety and market downscaling.

In future, autonomous cars will assist the human's world like a contacts list option in every mobile phone. For that, we need better RF regulations and safety standards like NCAP assessment [23]. Last but not the least, there are few topics which are not covered in this paper such as RF interference mitigation, Field testing, product life cycle, development, and Research cost analysis.

References

1. Rasouli A, Tsotsos JK (2020) Autonomous vehicles that interact with pedestrians: a survey of theory and practice. IEEE Trans Intell Transp Syst 21(3):900–918. https://doi.org/10.1109/TITS.2019.2901817
2. Sun S, Petropulu AP, Poor HV (2020) MIMO radar for advanced driver-assistance systems and autonomous driving. advantages and challenges. IEEE Signal Process Mag 37(4):98–117. https://doi.org/10.1109/MSP.2020.2978507
3. Hyun E, Jin Y (2020) Doppler-spectrum feature-based human–vehicle classification scheme using machine learning for an FMCW radar sensor. Sensors (Switzerland) 20(7)
4. Cheng H, Zheng N, Zhang X, Qin J, Van De Wetering H (2007) Interactive road situation analysis for driver assistance and safety warning systems: framework and algorithms. IEEE Trans Intell Transp Syst 8(1):157–166. https://doi.org/10.1109/TITS.2006.890073
5. Senigagliesi L, Ciattaglia G, De Santis A, Gambi E (2020) People walking classification using automotive radar. Electron 9(4). https://doi.org/10.3390/electronics9040588
6. Chipengo U (2018) Full physics simulation study of guardrail radar-returns for 77 GHz automotive radar systems. IEEE Access 6:70053–70060. https://doi.org/10.1109/ACCESS.2018.2881101
7. Aßmann A, Izzo A, Clemente C (2016) Efficient micro-doppler based pedestrian activity classification for ADAS systems using Krawtchouk moments. Int Conf Math Signal Process 11(December):1–6
8. Hervas BR (2015) Novel classification of slow movement objects in urban traffic environments using wideband pulse doppler radar
9. Gandhi T, Trivedi MM (2007) Pedestrian protection systems: issues, survey, and challenges. IEEE Trans Intell Transp Syst 8(3):413–430. https://doi.org/10.1109/TITS.2007.903444
10. Häcker P, Yang B (2010) Single snapshot DOA estimation. Adv Radio Sci 8:251–256. https://doi.org/10.5194/ars-8-251-2010
11. Patole SM, Torlak M, Wang D, Ali M (2017) Automotive radars: a review of signal processing techniques. IEEE Signal Process Mag 34(2):22–35. https://doi.org/10.1109/MSP.2016.2628914
12. Kumar C, Killedar YBA. mmWave radar—ADAS applications
13. Deep Y et al (2020) Radar cross-sections of pedestrians at automotive radar frequencies using ray tracing and point scatterer modelling. IET Radar, Sonar Navig 14(6):833–844. https://doi.org/10.1049/iet-rsn.2019.0471
14. Hsu YW, Lai YH, Zhong KQ, Yin TK, Perng JW (2019) Developing an on-road object detection system using monovision and radar fusion. Energies 13(1). https://doi.org/10.3390/en13010116
15. Zhao Z et al (2020) Point cloud features-based kernel SVM for human-vehicle classification in millimeter wave radar. IEEE Access 8:26012–26021. https://doi.org/10.1109/ACCESS.2020.2970533
16. Kim Y, Alnujaim I, You S, Jeong BJ (2020) Human detection based on time-varying signature on range-doppler diagram using deep neural networks. IEEE Geosci Remote Sens Lett 1–5. https://doi.org/10.1109/lgrs.2020.2980320
17. Hakobyan G, Yang B (2019) High-performance automotive radar: a review of signal processing algorithms and modulation schemes. IEEE Signal Process Mag 36(5):32–44. https://doi.org/10.1109/MSP.2019.2911722
18. Topak AE, Hasch J, Zwick T (2011) A system simulation of a 77 GHz phased array radar sensor. Int Radar Symp IRS 2011—Proc (June):175–180
19. Darms M, Foelster F, Schmidt J, Froehlich D, Eckert A (2010) Data fusion strategies in advanced driver assistance systems. SAE Tech Pap 176–182. https://doi.org/10.4271/2010-01-2337
20. Ouaknine A, Newson A, Rebut J, Tupin F, Perez P (2020) CARRADA dataset: camera and automotive radar with range-angle-doppler annotations. arXiv
21. Wien A, Simon W, Kress R (2019) 77 GHz automotive radar simulation. ISAP 2018–2018 Int Symp Antennas Propag (Isap):517–518

22. Hartmann J, Habersack J, Gmbh A (2002) Antenna measurement in compact ranges. Meas Tech (April):1–13
23. Euro NCAP (2015) 2020 roadmap: European new car assessment programme. (March):1–19

A Study on Defensive Issues and Challenges in Internet of Things

K. Venkateswara Rao⑩, D. Sri Latha, K. Sushma⑩, and Kolla Vivek⑩

Abstract The Internet of Things (IoT) has become a focal point of study in the near years. IoT applications include many fields including wearable devices, intelligent houses, intelligent towns, factory automation, and many more. There are several forms of problems and difficulties with IoT's strong intelligence. For IoT systems, software, and networks, protection is one of the key concerns. This study outlines the advancement of IoT's studies to address this crucial feature of the IoT and finds that a range of safety problems and concerns ought to be addressed and defined momentarily. Internet of Things (IoT) essentially implies that all things—more accurate devices—are joined together and talk to each other through a contact platform beyond user interaction or involvement. Protection is critical since IoT has no human–machine interaction. Protection and secrecy are now one of IoT's main issues. This study outlines the IoT design and the ultimate execution of what IoT is with several explanations and faces IoT protection issues and mitigation measures.

Keywords IoT · IoT security issues and loopholes · IoT security problems and mitigation measures

1 Introduction

The IoT inserts advanced sensors and circuits into any conceivable real-world entity surrounding us. Each sensor transmits useful information. This knowledge helps one to grasp how devices operate and that data is then processed to be valuable to us.

K. V. Rao (✉)
Vignan's Lara Institute of Technology & Science, Vadlamudi 522213, India

D. S. Latha
Vasireddy Venkatadri Institute of Technology, Namburu 522508, India

K. Sushma
Vignan's Institute of Information Technology, Duvvada 530049, India

K. Vivek
QIS Institute of Technology, Ongole 523001, India

© The Author(s), under exclusive license to Springer Nature Singapore Pte Ltd. 2022   591
C. Satyanarayana et al. (eds.), *High Performance Computing and Networking*,
Lecture Notes in Electrical Engineering 853,
https://doi.org/10.1007/978-981-16-9885-9_48

The challenge is why these instruments interlink and how we profit from the data they create. The sensors use a global ground and link safely with the IoT system in addition to communicating with one another. The information from the sensors is gathered and then integrated with insights to delete relevant and helpful data for software packages that respond to distinctive demands of the business or customers through the prevalent IoT system [1–3]. Only envision that after 10–25 years, your life is associated with your residence, your body is associated with your vehicles, etc. And both of these will communicate with the other systems surrounding them to predict this functional ability and fulfill our interests best.

2 IoT Structured Framework

The structured framework of IoT is represented in Fig. 1. Four subsystems can be seen in this structured framework [1, 2], and each subsystem is discussed separately here.

Fig. 1 IoT structured framework

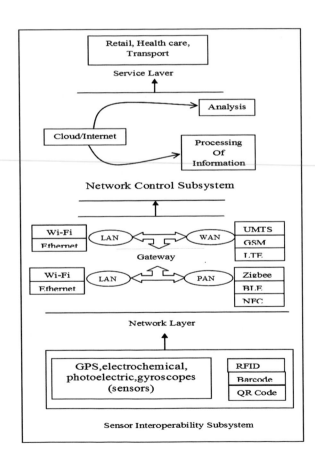

Fig. 2 Sensor connectivity layer

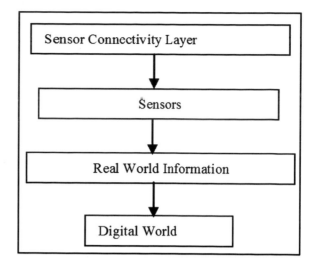

2.1 Sensor Subsystem for Interoperability

The sensor communication subsystem comprises a vast number of intelligent systems embedded with smart objects that collect and transfer data from the physical environment to the electronic environment. We may then assume that sensor systems interfere with the physical environment and the rest of the electronic environment. Data is then forwarded to the subsequent modules to analyze and evaluate the results. We have sensors that can record a range of metrics, such as activity tracking, humidity, pollution levels, health information, and much more. In such smart devices, higher capacity sensors are integrated. These sensors are known as automotive sensors, robotics, and body sensors. The sensor communication subsystem is shown in Fig. 2.

2.2 Network Layer

IoT's development is shown in Fig. 3. The electronic receptor generalizes loads of trillions of details. We also require a good data transfer method. This is why we have got interfaces. Interfaces are also used to minimize data from one end to the other. Certain interfaces also transmit online data to network nodes. Interface communication is two-way. This subsystem combines multiple networking styles under one IoT framework. Interface development can be done in two methods for IoT [3, 4]: (a) Simple gateway: It just transports or transmits the data produced by sensors and actuators. (b) Embedded control gateway: This interface supports a wide range of basic access points, but includes adaptive sorting and smart management of multiple nodes. The interface will define different types of data. This lowers nodes' costs and complexities. It offers interaction and connectivity.

Fig. 3 Simple interface

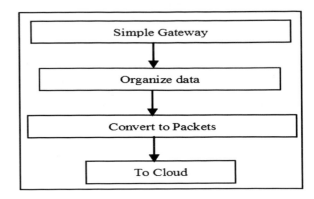

2.3 Network Control Subsystem

This subsystem deals with data analysis, threat control, administration of devices, and network management [5]. The functionalities of this subsystem are shown in Fig. 4.

In reality, this subsystem manages data in two classifications: (a) Continuous: IoT devices' sensor data need processing in this situation. This implies that we can use these processed data for analysis, operation, and control sensors. All the processed data is completed. (b) Discrete: The information is handled, managed, or transmitted without processing immediately to the recipient. Immediate transmission and response of sensor data from certain IoT units are needed [6]. For instance, information linked to the patient from the sensor. If a patient's heart sends erratic measurements, then information needs to be transmitted immediately which is shown in Fig. 5.

2.4 Service Layer

Service subsystem is the final module in the standardized IoT system [7]. This level will move the stored information from the existing level. This subsystem delivers services to customers and end-users. In pretty nearly every segment, IoT can be applied. Requests are subdivided into two major groups.

Partition-Based Applications. In different fields, such as transit, hospitals, commerce, electricity, and armed units, IoT will contribute. IoT sensors can aid in tracking the impacts of climate change in multiple urban environments. These tools may be used to look at different surrounding ecosystems properties, such as aquatic environment, lithosphere, sunshine, and plants. To achieve this mission, different sensors are used. Automobiles can be connected to IoT systems, so that all automobiles can interact on the highway with others [8]. The owner may have full vehicle info. Medical equipment allowed by IoT will be used to protect patient safety. It will

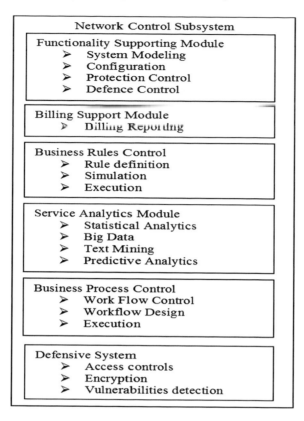

Fig. 4 Network control subsystem

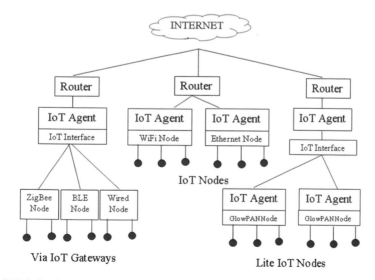

Fig. 5 IoT design interface

Table 1 Implementation areas of the service layer

Horizontal marketing system	IoT applications
IoT-based home surveillance system	World Wide Web (WWW) connection, entertainment
IoT-based smart cities	Urban administration, control of resources, control of transportation, control of crises
IoT-based farming	Moisture detecting, detecting field, violation, warning for water requirements, detecting smoke
Intelligent transportation system	Smart devices, road traffic monitoring, GPS service, technologies of smart vehicles, road traffic condition
IoT for smart energy systems	Refinery control, an indicator of fluid levels

also help doctors' evaluations. In the shopping industry, a smarter shop may be an instance of IoT. The smart store contains technologies such as linked consumers, sales forecasting, equipment control to prevent loss, energy usage, and other problems [9].

IoT Applications Using Horizontal Marketing System. In this section, IoT relates to flood control, inventory regulation, business logistics administration, recording, and surveillance of citizens which is given in Table 1.

3 Security Concerns

Web services are not the major concern here; IoT machines can be used anywhere in your workplace, in your vehicle, in your residence, and simply by logging your information and monitoring stuff. Safety cannot, however, be undermined here [10–12]. Client-side systems such as Google Chrome create a "Sandboxing" functionality that will improve the safety of the client. Every Web site we launch is an individual operation in the Internet browser. Each window or tab that is launched in the browser is a different operation. When one of the tabs has trouble or it fails, the remaining tabs will not be affected. Sandboxing thus introduces a defensive shield across each of these systems [13]. If you inadvertently open a dangerous Web address or compromised domain, the sandbox feature functions, so that malware does not affect your computer. The malware is within the sandbox, avoiding any harm to other tabs in the browser. Therefore, the malware has gone once the tab is closed. Sandboxing thereby manages to deter our network's risk and attack. Many virus protection applications such as Avast may also be used for sandboxing. These strategies should be used to safeguard our network. Figure 6 illustrates the cloud service's internal framework and its functions [14].

Table 2 shows cyber threats and their development. The intelligent systems are attached to frequency-hopping spread spectrum-based radio technology or Wi-Fi microcontrollers [15]. These embedded systems operate either on Linux or real-time operating system which has a great deal of image processing, and computational abilities and attackers can take over them to launch DDOS assaults [16]. So safety

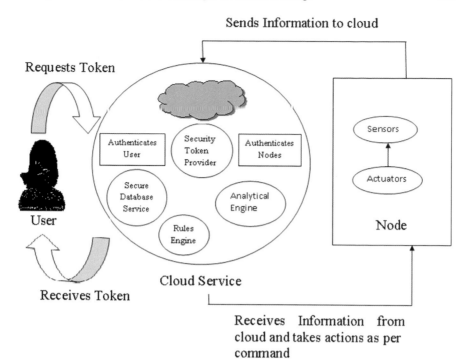

Fig. 6 Cloud service architecture

Table 2 IT threats and its progression

Period	Threats
1985–1997	Crackers, phone *Phreaking*
1997–2005	Mail bomb spywares, malwares, viruses and worms, creepers, polymorphic viruses, fake account generator
2005–2008	Spear phishing, government espionage, corporate espionage, denial-of-service attacks
2008–2011	Vulnerabilities using malicious SQL code, cyber warfare, destructive attacks
2011–2015	Indiscriminate attacks, stealing credit card info, e-mail addresses, login credentials and financial info, medical-related data
2015-till date	Zero-day attacks, e-mail phishing, man-in-the-middle attacks, cryptojacking, machine learning poisoning, angular *Template Injection,* ransomware, telegram hijack, etc.

on the Internet of Things is undoubtedly a significant problem. Companies that are developing IoT systems should be concerned about these devices in terms of safety and security [17].

4 Solutions

Previously underestimated, IoT protection has now grown into an extremely troubling problem [18, 19].

4.1 Machine Learning for IoT Security

For protecting IoT systems, machine learning (ML) and deep learning (DL) techniques are becoming more common [20]. These methods necessitate the creation and processing of massive quantities of security data to train and develop supervised and unsupervised learning frameworks that are reliable and adaptable to a variety of security frameworks and implementation configurations. A variety of ML and artificial intelligence (AI) methods are being used by the IoT security world currently. Different sorts of IoT infrastructures, such as wireless sensor networks (WSN) and smart grids, as well as different kinds of threats, such as malicious software identification and infiltration identification, have recently been introduced. Various learning methods, such as DL and reinforcement learning, have also been used. ML and DL methods for detecting, evaluating, and in certain instances forecasting security threats are not novel ideas; generic strategies have been documented in the research for two years. Moreover, as computing and storage innovations advance, new frontiers in the implementation and application of ML and AI strategies for IoT security open up. Data mining methods are also consistently compatible with IoT architectures, including applicable reference models, for security analysis and verification. ML methods aid in improving deduction accuracy and protecting IoT devices that are susceptible to DoS attacks. Q-learning and Dyna-Q are examples of ML methods that can be used to secure IoT devices from eavesdropping. The task of ML is to use and train models to identify intrusions in IoT devices or any inappropriate behavior occurring in an IoT system to avoid data leakage or other problems. As a result, ML offers a promising forum for overcoming the challenges of securing IoT devices.

4.2 Software Defined Networking (SDN)-Based IoT Frameworks

Studies suggest a network-level security framework to protect IoT devices in [21]. The protected system makes use of a secure channel that is capable of recognizing various types of networked devices. Furthermore, the device employs mitigation mechanisms to remove possible threats. For classifying a system as vulnerable or invulnerable, ML methods are used. Device type recognition, as well as data from vulnerability databases, are fed into an ML system that can predict insecure network nodes. Such solutions are feasible for intelligent ecosystems that can make decisions at the hardware level due to the network's global visibility. Since SDN is a developing framework that is not being fully exploited, several proofs of concepts are being introduced to supplement the need for SDN-based IoT deployment.

4.3 IoT Security Using Fog Computing

The solutions that fog computing offers or may provide to combat certain potential risks are addressed further down.

1. **Man-in-the-middle attack**: Between the end-user and the cloud or IoT device, fog serves as a layer of security. All vulnerabilities or infiltrations on IoT systems must pass through the fog layer in the center, which can detect and minimize suspicious activity until it reaches the device [22].
2. **Data transit attack**: When contrasted to IoT systems, data collection and management on stable fog nodes are significantly good. When information is held on fog nodes rather than end-user computers, it is better covered. Fog nodes also aid in the accessibility of user information.
3. **Eavesdropping**: Instead of route discovery across the overall infrastructure, fog nodes facilitate interaction only between the end-user and the fog node. Since the network traffic is limited, the risks of an intruder attempting to eavesdrop are greatly diminished [23].
4. **Issues with IoT device constraints**: Most IoT devices have limited resources, which adversaries take full advantage of. They attempt to smash the IoT devices and use them as weak points to gain access to the system. IoT devices can be supported by fog nodes, which can protect them from such attacks. The much more complex security operations needed for safety can be performed by a neighboring fog node.

4.4 IoT Security Using Blockchain

For IoT data, blockchain is a powerful, protected, decentralized, and open data framework. The use of blockchain in IoT systems has several benefits. Table 3 summarizes several basic IoT security issues and their potential blockchain solutions [24]. The following sections go into the main advantages of using blockchain in IoT

Table 3 Blockchain solutions to IoT threats

IoT challenges	Blockchain solution
Privacy	Permissioned blockchain
Traffic and cost	Decentralized blockchain
Heavy load	Records updated on network nodes
Defective architecture	Verifying the data cryptographically

systems. (1) Blockchain can be used to archive IoT data. (2) Blockchain's decentralized behavior allows for safe information storage. (3) The hash key is used to encipher data, which is then checked by miners. (4) Data loss, security breaches, and impersonation attacks are avoided. (5) The use of blockchain technology to avoid unauthorized access. (6) The use of centralized cloud servers is no longer necessary.

5 Conclusion

IoT is going to transform the future, but if engineers do not concentrate on IoT protection, confidence in consumers that IoT systems safety will not evolve. Measures can also be put in place to ensure that IoT systems are resistant to cyber threats. Importance should be granted to individuals' data protection, and information should be protected.

References

1. Almolhis N, Alashjaee AM, Duraibi S, Alqahtani F, Moussa AN (2020) The security issues in IoT-cloud: a review. In: 2020 16th IEEE international colloquium on signal processing & its applications (CSPA). IEEE, pp 191–196
2. Swamy SN, Kota SR (2020) An empirical study on system level aspects of internet of things (IoT). IEEE Access 8:188082–188134
3. Sokolov SS, Alimov OM, Nekrashevich PS, Moiseev AI, Degtyarev AV (2020) Security issues and IoT integration in Russian industry. In: 2020 IEEE conference of Russian young researchers in electrical and electronic engineering (EIConRus). IEEE, pp 517–520
4. Hasan T, Adnan A, Giannetsos T, Malik J (2020) Orchestrating SDN control plane towards enhanced IoT security. In: 2020 6th IEEE conference on network softwarization (NetSoft). IEEE, pp 457–464
5. Duangphasuk S, Duangphasuk P, Thammarat C (2020) Review of internet of things (IoT): security issue and solution. In: 2020 17th international conference on electrical engineering/electronics, computer, telecommunications and information technology (ECTI-CON). IEEE, pp 559–562
6. Mohanta BK, Jena D, Ramasubbareddy S, Daneshmand M, Gandomi AH (2020) Addressing security and privacy issues of IoT using blockchain technology. IEEE Internet Things J
7. Das S, Mohanta BK, Jena D (2020) IoT commercial drone and its privacy and security issues. In: 2020 international conference on computer science, engineering and applications (ICCSEA). IEEE, pp 1–4
8. Alwarafy A, Al-Thelaya KA, Abdallah M, Schneider J, Hamdi M (2020) A survey on security and privacy issues in edge computing-assisted internet of things. IEEE Internet Things J
9. Singh S, Singh K, Saxena A (2020) Security domain, threats, privacy issues in the internet of things (IoT): a survey. In: 2020 fourth international conference on I-SMAC (IoT in social, mobile, analytics, and cloud) (I-SMAC). IEEE, pp 287–294
10. Portal G, de Matos E, Hessel F (2020) An edge decentralized security architecture for industrial IoT applications. In: 2020 IEEE 6th world forum on internet of things (WF-IoT). IEEE, pp 1–6
11. Niraja KS, Rao SS (2020) Security challenges and counter measures in the internet of things. In: 2020 international conference on computer communication and informatics (ICCCI). IEEE, pp 1–3

12. Li Y, Li Y, Liu J (2020) Discussion on privacy issues and information security in the internet of things. In: 2020 Chinese control and decision conference (CCDC). IEEE, pp 4968–4972
13. Anwar RW, Zainal A, Abdullah T, Iqbal S (2020) Security threats and challenges to IoT and its applications: a review. In: 2020 fifth international conference on fog and mobile edge computing (FMEC). IEEE, pp 301–305
14. Anwer M, Ashfaque A (2020) Security of IoT using blockchain: a review. In: 2020 international conference on information science and communication technology (ICISCT). IEEE, pp 1–3
15. de Oliveira Conceição CM, da Luz Reis RA (2020) Security issues in the design of chips for IoT. In: 2020 IEEE 6th world forum on internet of things (WF-IoT). IEEE, pp 1–5
16. Khursheeed F, Sami-Ud-Din M, Sumra IA, Safder M (2020) A review of security mechanism in the internet of things (IoT). In: 2020 3rd international conference on advancements in computational sciences (ICACS). IEEE, pp 1–9
17. Sharma P, Kherajani M, Jain D, Patel D (2020) A study of routing protocols, security issues, and attacks in network layer of internet of things framework. In: 2nd international conference on data, engineering, and applications (IDEA). IEEE, pp 1–6
18. Abuladel A, Bamasag O (2020) Data and location privacy issues in IoT applications. In: 2020 3rd international conference on computer applications & information security (ICCAIS). IEEE, pp 1–6
19. Zaldivar D, Lo'ai AT, Muheidat F (2020) Investigating the security threats on networked medical devices. In: 2020 10th annual computing and communication workshop and conference (CCWC). IEEE, pp 0488–0493
20. Roukounaki A, Efremidis S, Soldatos J, Neises J, Walloschke T, Kefalakis N (2019) Scalable and configurable end-to-end collection and analysis of IoT security data: towards end-to-end security in IoT systems. Global IoT Summit (GIoTS) 2019:1–6. https://doi.org/10.1109/GIOTS.2019.8766407
21. Iqbal W, Abbas H, Daneshmand M, Rauf B, Bangash YA (2020) An in-depth analysis of IoT security requirements, challenges, and their countermeasures via software-defined security. IEEE Internet Things J 7(10):10250–10276. https://doi.org/10.1109/JIOT.2020.2997651
22. Venkateswara Rao K (2020) Disease prediction and diagnosis implementing fuzzy neural classifier based on IoT and cloud. Int J Adv Sci Technol (IJAST) 29(5): 737–745. ISSN : 2005-4238, May 2020
23. Venkateswara Rao K (2019) A novel approach towards smart agriculture using IoT. Int J Res 8(4):273–278. ISSN: 2236-6124. Apr 2019
24. Venkateswara Rao K, Gopi A (2017) Internet of things and big data towards a smart city. IJIEET 3(2):01–06. ISSN: 2455-3182, Mar-Apr 2017

A Deep Convolutional Neural Network for COVID-19 Chest CT-Scan Image Classification

L. Kanya Kumari and B. Naga Jagadesh

Abstract A novel corona virus (COVID-19) is a new dangerous disease which affects the global economic growth and challenge to the doctors and scientists. This disease is escalating gradually which impacts world's financial system at risk. Due to increase in COVID-19, the role of artificial intelligence, machine learning, and deep learning is crucial in this situation. Deep learning is a dominant tool to control this pandemic outbreak by predicting the disease in advance. Deep learning techniques deal with several types of data sources that put together to form the user-friendly platforms for physicians and researchers. The proposed methodology is based on convolutional neural network which classifies the COVID-19 chest CT-scan images into infected or not infected. We have done the experiment on publicly available dataset in GitHub which consists of 360 positive and 397 negative chest CT-images which are collected from 216 patients. In our proposed CNN model, we used Adam optimizer with learning rate 0.001 and obtained the classification accuracy 88.4%. The experimental results show that our methodology can handle current pandemic situation in a better manner.

Keywords CT-images · Artificial intelligence · Machine learning · Deep learning · Convolutional neural networks

1 Introduction

A corona virus disease (COVID-19) is generated from a severe acute respiratory syndrome corona virus 2 (SARS-COV-1) which is becoming a pandemic worldwide [1, 2]. It was first seen in China, which spreads quickly around the world within a month [3]. It is a deadly disease where many people lose their lives. Whole world

L. K. Kumari (✉)
Department of Information Technology, Andhra Loyola Institute of Engineering and Technology, Vijayawada, Andhra Pradesh, India

B. N. Jagadesh
Department of Computer Science and Engineering, Srinivasa Institute of Engineering and Technology, Amalapuram, Andhra Pradesh, India

© The Author(s), under exclusive license to Springer Nature Singapore Pte Ltd. 2022   603
C. Satyanarayana et al. (eds.), *High Performance Computing and Networking*,
Lecture Notes in Electrical Engineering 853,
https://doi.org/10.1007/978-981-16-9885-9_49

is suffering with this disease [4]. Previously, several viruses like flu, SARS, MERS, etc., came into the picture, but they affected few days or few months [5–7]. But this novel corona virus is affecting people since more than one year. Typical symptoms of this virus are dry cough, head ache, fever, and dyspnea [8], but in some cases, it is like asymptomatic too. This initially affects throat of the body which in turn suffers with breathing. Infected people of this virus [9] should be in isolation. This easily transfers from one person to other person when people are moving closely [10]. Globally as of March 29, 2021, there are 126,890,643 confirmed COVID-19 cases including 27,78,619 deaths, and in this, 29,921,591 are from America [11, 12].

Medical imaging [13] is a technique to evaluate and forecast this virus in a human body. The imaging modalities used are computer tomography (CT-scan) and chest X-ray [14]. Many more diagnosis techniques were applied to predict this virus like X-ray images, plasma therapy [15, 16], etc. The recent studies described that the CT-scan examination for COVID-19 virus is fast, accurate, and gives good sensitivity [16]. China addressed that CT-scan modality is besides being helping in diagnosing COVID-19 but also in monitoring the development of the disease and also in finding the therapeutic efficacy [17]. It is preferable to use CT-scan screening because of its versatility and three-dimensional pulmonary view [18, 19].

Artificial intelligence (AI) is the much more software technology in medical imaging [20–22]. Some systems are using pre-trained models with transfer learning [23, 24], and some systems are customizing the networks [25–27]. ML and data science are also using for corona disease prediction and detection [28–30].

DL techniques are artificial neural networks that work similar to the human neurons. Convolutional neural network (CNN) is the DL technique that is proven as effective and successful technique in the medical image classification [31]. DL methods are helping in the areas like drug discovery [32], biomedicine [33], medical image analysis [34], etc. DL steps are collecting the data, preprocessing, feature extraction, classification, and calculating the performance [35]. In data collection stage, the patients' data is collected from the various hospitals or publicly available datasets which are in Kaggle and Gitthub. This data is converted into appropriate format called data preparation. Preprocessing is also involved in this step which includes noise removal, augmentation, resizing, etc. The main important phase in DL is feature extraction and classification and then assessed by performance metrics based on confusion matrix. The main objectives of the proposed methodology are given below.

1. To develop and analyze the DL based approach to detect COVID-19 disease from CT-scan images.
2. To design a model used to classify the COVID-19 images into infected or non-infected patients based on CT-scan images using CNN, so that the spreading of the disease can be controlled and also can increase the life span the patient through early diagnosis.

This paper is systematized as follows: Sect. 2 discusses the related work, Sect. 3 represents the dataset used, Sect. 4 describes the proposed methodology, and Sect. 5

focuses on experimental results and performance analysis and finally described conclusion and future scope.

2 Related Work

New technologies like AI, ML, and DL are used for early detection of disease, development of drugs, prediction of future likely cases, contact tracing, etc., [36, 37]. Several studies have been carried out in classifying the CT-scan images using deep learning algorithms. DL techniques are more efficient that can help in medical science. This mainly is helpful in detecting the heart problems, diagnosing cancer, medical image analysis, and many other applications. So, it can be used to classify COVID-19 images as positive and negative. CTnet-10 was designed with 82.1% accuracy and also used multiple pre-trained models and found that VGG-19 is best in classifying CT-images and obtained the accuracy of 94.52% [38].

Recurrent neural networks was used to handle the nonlinearity and data dependencies [39]. DL approaches used in this were VGG 16, ResNet50, inceptionV3, DenseNet124, and DenseNet 201. Decision of all these models was combined and achieved better efficiency in detecting the disease. A comparative study was done by the authors to forecast the COVID-19 disease.

The authors [31] proposed a recommender system to diagnose the COVID-19 disease. The authors used a DL-based approach to detect the COVID-19 infected people and achieved 97.48% accuracy. The authors developed a CNN model to analyze the pneumonia based on chest X-ray images.

Further, the authors have developed an AI tool used on X-ray and CT-scan images and applied DL techniques and transfer learning algorithms to detect the COVID-19 disease. They have used a pre-trained model called AlexNet and customized CNN model and achieved accuracy 98% and 94.1%, respectively [40]. They have developed two different classifiers like binary and multiclass. They used DarkNet methodology for classification in used chest X-ray to detect COVID-19 virus. They designed an architecture that follows projection-expansion-projection-extension for classification into positive case or negative case. They obtained the accuracy of 92.4% for the proposed model [41].

From the literature mentioned in Table 1, it is observed that chest X-ray and CT-images are very much useful for diagnosing the COVID disease, and deep learning is playing an important role in classifying these images.

Table 1 Literature survey

Reference number	Dataset	Methodology	Performance measure
[3]	Two publicly available datasets	Projection-expansion -projection-extension	Accuracy = 92.4%
[14]	Chest X-ray	Inception 3 Xception ResNeXt	Accuracy Xception = 97.9%
[16]	Chest CT-images	Deep CNN	AUROC = 0.883 F1-score = 0.867
[16]	CT-images	VGG-19	Accuracy = 94.52%
[31]	Chest X-ray	Xception ResNet 50 MobileNet Inception V3	Accuracy Xception = 98.1% ResNet 50 = 82.5% MobileNet = 98.6% Inception V3 = 97.4%
[42]	CT-images	SLSTM ARIMA LSTM	AUC = 0.9

3 Methodology

3.1 Dataset

As this is a new disease, limited data sources are available and also limited expertise in labeling the data [4]. The dataset used is available in GitHub in which 360 images are positive cases and 397 images are negative chest CT-images which are collected from 216 patients. These images are of different sizes to height and width. Sample images are represented in Figs. 1 and 2. All the images in this dataset are portable network graphics (.png) format and resized to $128 \times 128 \times 3$.

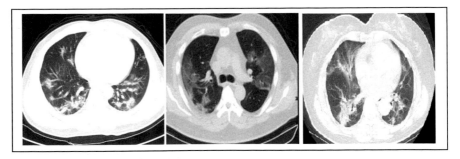

Fig. 1 Sample COVID-19 images

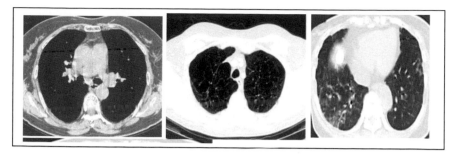

Fig. 2 Sample non-COVID-19 images

3.2 Proposed Methodology

The proposed model is a four-step process which is represented in Fig 3. Initially, the chest CT-images are acquired and then augmentation is applied. These images are given as input to the convolutional neural network. This network extracts the features and classifies the images as COVID-infected patient or COVID non-infected patient.

Our proposed CNN architecture consists of four convolutional blocks to categorize the chest CT-images into infected/1 or uninfected/0 which is represented in Fig. 4.

Fig. 3 Proposed
methodology

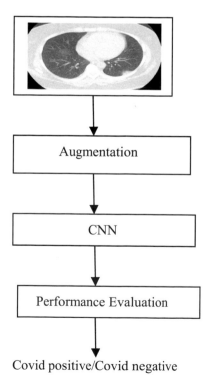

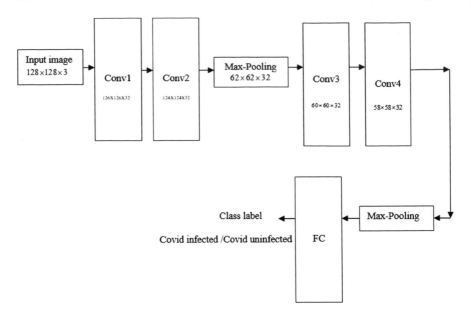

Fig. 4 A proposed deep CNN architecture

The images are resized to $128 \times 128 \times 3$ and given as input to the network. Convolution layer is the important building block of neural network. Pooling layers reduce the number of computations. Rectified linear unit (ReLU) activation function is used to help in understanding the complex patterns. Initially, the input image is given as input to the convolutional blocks of size $126 \times 126 \times 32$, $124 \times 124 \times 32$, respectively. This is passed to a max-pooling layer of size $62 \times 62 \times 32$ followed by other two convolutional blocks of size $60 \times 60 \times 32$, $58 \times 58 \times 32$, respectively. Then, it is passed to the pooling layer of size $29 \times 29 \times 32$. The result is given to fully connected (FC) layer to predict the class label which is represented in Fig. 4.

4　Experimental Results

The experiment is done in Kaggle freely accessible graphical processing unit (GPU) environment. This model is developed using Python Keras library with Tensor Flow as backend. This model is evaluated with 10 and 15 epochs, on the 70% training dataset and 30% for testing. The experiments are done by using different optimizers like stochastic gradient descent (SGD), Adam, and RMSprop with learning rate 0.001. The performance metric used to evaluate the methodology is accuracy. The accuracy for SGD optimizer obtained is 72.3, 71.1% for 10 and 15 epochs, respectively. For Adam optimizer, the accuracy is 88.4, 81.6% with 10 and 15 epochs. Similarly,

Table 2 Accuracy of proposed methodology

Optimizer	Learning rate	Epoch	Accuracy (%)
SGD	0.001	10	72.3
		15	71.1
Adam	0.001	10	88.4
		15	81.6
RMSprop	0.001	10	71.2
		15	71.8

Table 3 Accuracy of proposed methodology with learning rate 0.001

Optimizer	Epoch	Accuracy (%)
SGD	10	72.3
Adam	10	88.4
RMSprop	15	71.8

for RMSprop optimizer, the accuracy is 71.2% and 65.8% for 10 and 15 epochs, respectively. Table 2 represents the accuracy of the model.

By observing Table 2, we conclude that SGD optimizer is good for 10 epochs, Adam optimizer is good for 10 epochs, and RMSprop is good for 15 epochs. This is represented in Table 3. The graphical representation is shown in Fig. 5.

We conclude that a deep CNN model with Adam optimizer, learning rate as 0.001, and the epochs are 10 is achieved good accuracy which classifies the chest CT-images into infected or non-infected.

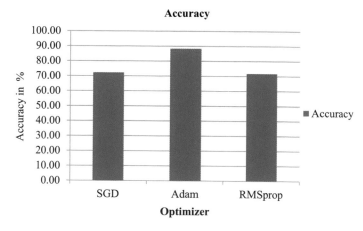

Fig. 5 Accuracy of the model

5 Conclusion

AI, ML, and DL are the important technologies which can be applied to solve the problems in medical field. Our goal is to study the role of deep learning in controlling the spreading of COVID-19. A CNN is an effective and efficient DL algorithm which helps the radiologists and physicians in diagnosing the disease. In our paper, a new deep CNN architecture is designed to classify COVID-19 images into infected or not infected images. Our CNN model extracts better features and classifies the images which yield better accuracy than compared to other models. This architecture is tested on chest CT-images which has given better accuracy as 88.4% with Adam optimizer, learning rate 0.001, and number of epochs are 10. From the results, it can be observed that a deep CNN model has a huge impact on the spreading of COVID-19 by providing the fast screening.

References

1. Wu F, Zhao S, Yu B, Chen YM, Wang W, Song ZG (2020) A new coronavirus associated with human respiratory disease in China. Nature 579(7798):265–269
2. Cucinotta D, Vanelli M (2020) WHO declares COVID-19 a pandemic. Acta Biomed 91(1):157–160
3. Ye Z, Zhang Y, Wang Y et al (2020) Chest CT manifestations of new coronavirus disease 2019 (COVID-19): a pictorial review. Eur Radiol 30:4381–4389
4. Gozes O, Frid-Adar M, Greenspan H, Browning PD, Zhang H, Ji W, Bernheim A, Siegel E, Rapid AI development cycle for the coronavirus (COVID-19) pandemic: initial results for automated detection & patient monitoring using deep learning CT image analysis. arXiv.org
5. Wong KT, Antonio GE, Hui DS, Lee N, Yuen EH, Wu A, Leung CB, Rainer TH, Cameron P, Chung SS, Sung JJ (2003) severe acute respiratory syndrome: radiographic appearances and pattern of progression in 138 patients. Radiology 228(2):401–406
6. Xie X, Li X, Wan S, Gong Y (2006) Mining x-ray images of SARS patients. In: Data mining. Springer, Berlin, pp 282–294
7. Huang C, Wang Y, Li X, Ren L, Zhao J, Hu Y, Zhang L, Fan G, Xu J, Gu X, Cheng Z (2020) Clinical features of patients infected with 2019 novel coronavirus in Wuhan, China. Lancet 395(10223):497–506
8. Vetter P, Vu DL, L'Huillier AG, Schibler M, Kaiser L, Jacquerioz F (2020) Clinical features of COVID-19. BMJ 4
9. Roosa K, Lee Y, Luo R, Kirpich A, Rothenberg R, Hyman JM, Yan P, Chowell G (2020) Real-time forecasts of the COVID-19 epidemic in China from February 5th to February 24th, 2020. Infect Dis Modell 5:256–263
10. Yan L, Zhang HT, Xiao Y, Wang M, Sun C, Liang J, Li S, Zhang M, Guo Y, Xiao Y, Tang X (2020) Prediction of criticality in patients with severe Covid-19 infection using three clinical features: a achine learning-based prognostic model with clinical data in Wuhan. medRxiv
11. https://Covid19.who.int/. Last accessed on 10 Apr 2021
12. https://www.worldometers.info/coronavirus/worldwide-graphs/ 01/04/2021
13. Xu B, Meng X A deep learning algorithm using CT images to screen for corona virus disease (COVID-19)
14. Jain R, Gupta M, Taneja S et al (2021) Deep learning based detection and analysis of COVID-19 on chest X-ray images. Appl Intell 51:1690–1700

15. Positano V, Mishra AK, Das SK, Roy P, Bandyopadhyay S (2020) Identifying COVID19 from Chest CT images: a deep convolutional neural networks based approach. J Healthcare Eng
16. Shah V, Keniya R, Shridharani A et al (2021) Diagnosis of COVID-19 using CT scan images and deep learning techniques. Emerg Radiol
17. Fang Y, Zhang H, Xie J et al (2020) Sensitivity of chest CT for COVID-19: comparison to RT-PCR. Radiology
18. National Health Commission of the People's Republic of China (2020) The diagnostic and treatment protocol of COVID-19. China. Last accessed 30 Mar 2021
19. Kim H, Hong H, Yoon SH (2020) Diagnostic performance of CT and reverse transcriptase polymerase chain reaction for coronavirus disease 2019: a meta-analysis, Radiology 296(3):E145–E155
20. Ye Z, Zhang Y, Wang Y, Huang Z, Song B (2020) Chest CT manifestations of new coronavirus disease 2019 (COVID-19): a pictorial review. Eur Radiol 30(80):4381–4389
21. Shi F et al (2021) Review of artificial intelligence techniques in imaging data acquisition, segmentation, and diagnosis for COVID-19. IEEE Rev Biomed Eng 14:4–15
22. McCall B (2020) COVID-19 and artificial intelligence: protecting health-care workers and curbing the spread. Lancet Digit Health 2(4):e166–e167
23. Vaishya R, Javaid M, Khan IH, Haleem A (2020) Artificial intelligence (AI) applications for COVID-19 pandemic, Diabetes metabolic syndrome. Clin Res Rev 14(4):337–339
24. Panwar H, Gupta PK, Siddiqui MK, Morales-Menendez R, Singh V (2020) Application of deep learning for fast detection of COVID-19 in X-rays using nCOVnet, Chaos. Solitons Fractals 138
25. K. El Asnaoui and Y. Chawki.: Using X-ray images and deep learning for automated detection of coronavirus disease. J. Biomol. Struct. Dyn 7, 1–12 (2020).
26. Oh Y, Park S, Ye JC (2020) Deep learning COVID-19 features on CXR using limited training data sets. IEEE Trans Med Imag 39(8):2688–2700
27. Fan DP, Zhou T, Ji GP, Zhou Y, Chen G, Fu H, Shen J, Shao L 92020) Inf-net: automatic COVID-19 lung infection segmentation from CT images. IEEE Trans Med Imag 39(8):2626–2637
28. Pereira PM, Bertolini D, Teixeira LO, Silla CN, Costa YMG (2020) COVID-19 identification in chest X-ray images on flat and hierarchical classification scenarios. Co Comput Methods Programs Biomed 194
29. Albahri AS, Hamid RA, Alwan JK, Al-qays ZT, Zaidan AA, Zaidan BB, Albahri AOS, Alamoodi AH, Khlaf JM, Almahdi EM, Thabet E, Hadi SM, Mohammed KI, Alsalem MA, Al-Obaidi JR, Madhloom HT (2020) Role of biological data mining and machine learning techniques in detecting and diagnosing the novel coronavirus (COVID-19): a systematic review. J Med Syst 44(7)
30. Muhammad LJ, Islam MM, Usman SS, Ayon SI (2020) Predictive data mining models for novel coronavirus (COVID-19) infected patients' recovery. Social Netw Comput Sci 1(4)
31. Latif S, Usman M, Manzoor S, Iqbal W, Qadir J (2020) Leveraging data science to combat COVID-19: a comprehensive review. IEEE Trans Artif Intell 1(1):85–103
32. Sethi R, Mehrotra M, Sethi D (2020) Deep learning based diagnosis recommendation for COVID-19 using chest X-rays images. In: 2020 second international conference on inventive research in computing applications (ICIRCA), Coimbatore, India, pp 1–4
33. Chen H, Engkvist O, Wang Y, Olivecrona M, Blaschke T (2018) The rise of deep learning in drug discovery. Drug Discovery Today 23(6):1241–1250
34. Wainberg M, Merico D, Delong A, Frey BJ (2018) Deep learning in biomedicine. Nat Biotechnol 36(9):829–838
35. Shen D, Wu G, Suk H (2017) Deep learning in medical image analysis. Annu Rev Biomed Eng 19:221–248
36. Nath MK, Kanhe A, Mishra M (2020) A novel deep learning approach for classification of COVID-19 images. In: 2020 IEEE 5th international conference on computing communication and automation (ICCCA), Greater Noida, India, pp 752–757

37. Raju V, Mohd J, Haleem KI, Abid H (2020) Artificial intelligence (AI) applications for COVID-19 pandemic. Diab Metab Syndr 14(4):337–339
38. Naud'e W (2020) Artificial intelligence against COVID-19: an early review, IZA Institute of Labor Economics, IZA DP No. 13110
39. Zhu X, Fu B, Yang Y, Ma Y, Hao J, Chen S, Liu S, Li T, Liu S, Guo W, Liao Z (2018) Attention-based recurrent neural network for influenza epidemic prediction. BMC Bioinf 20
40. Devaraj J, Elavarasan RM, Pugazhendhi R, Shafiullah GM, Ganesan S, Jeysree AK, Khan IA, Hossain E (2021) Forecasting of COVID-19 cases using deep learning models: is it reliable and practically significant? Results Phys 21
41. Maghdid HS, Asaad AT, Ghafoor KZ, Sadiq AS, Khan MK (2020) Diagnosing COVID-19 pneumonia from X-ray and CT images using deep learning and transfer learning algorithms. arXiv preprint arXiv:2004.00038
42. Hewamalage H, Bergmeir C, Bandara K (2020) Recurrent neural networks for time series forecasting: current status and future directions. Int J Forecast 37(1):388–427

Clinical Text Classification of Medical Transcriptions Based on Different Diseases

Yadukrishna Sreekumar and P. K. Nizar Banu

Abstract Clinical text classification is the process of extracting the information from clinical narratives. Clinical narratives are the voice files, notes taken during a lecture, or other spoken material given by physicians. Because of the rapid rise in data in the healthcare sector, text mining and information extraction (IE) have acquired a few applications in the previous few years. This research attempts to use machine learning algorithms to diagnose diseases from the given medical transcriptions. Proposed clinical text classification models could decrease human efforts of labeled training data creation and feature engineering and for designing for applying machine learning models to clinical text classification by leveraging weak supervision. The main aim of this paper is to compare the multiclass logistic regression model and support vector classifier model which is implemented for performing clinical text classification on medical transcriptions.

Keywords Clinical text mining · Transcriptions · Natural language processing · TF-IDF vectorization · scispaCy · Multiclass logistic regression · Support vector classifier

1 Introduction

In the medical world, a lot of digital text documents from several specialties are generated like patient health records or documentation of clinical studies. Clinical text contains valuable information about symptoms, diagnoses, treatments, drug use, and adverse (drug) events for the patient that can be utilized to improve healthcare for other patients. The physician also writes her or his reasoning for the conclusion of the diagnosis of the patient in the patient record [1].

Since there is enormous data being generated in the healthcare sector, it becomes a great deal for people to get the required information. There comes the relevance of text mining and classification in biomedical and clinical data. We have to make use of

Y. Sreekumar · P. K. Nizar Banu (✉)
Department of Computer Science, CHRIST (Deemed to be University), Bangalore, India
e-mail: nizar.banu@christuniversity.in

© The Author(s), under exclusive license to Springer Nature Singapore Pte Ltd. 2022 613
C. Satyanarayana et al. (eds.), *High Performance Computing and Networking*,
Lecture Notes in Electrical Engineering 853,
https://doi.org/10.1007/978-981-16-9885-9_50

several text mining algorithms for fetching the information from heap data [2]. The main aim of this paper is to compare two major algorithms that classify and summarize the potential factors, signs, or symptoms from unstructured textual descriptions of patients. For extracting the potential information from the transcriptions, we will be using various natural language processing techniques. Once after extracting the potential information, we will be trying to diagnose the diseases based on the symptoms extracted using various machine learning models. Here, we will be having a comparison of the multiclass logistic regression model and support vector classifier model which are used to classify the transcriptions. There is an enormous volume of biomedical data as well as clinical data generated, so that there is increasingly more demand for accurate biomedical text mining tools for extracting information from the literature [3].

Healthcare systems and specifically health record systems contain both structured and unstructured information as text [1]. More specifically, it is estimated that over 40% of the data in healthcare record systems contains text, so-called clinical text, sometimes also called electronic patient record text. Clinical text or biomedical text literature can be seen as a large unstructured data repository, which makes text mining come into play. In the next session, we will be having a background study to know what exactly happening in medical text classification before we move on to proposed methodology [4]. Sect. 3 presents the methodology and details about the dataset. Section 4 discusses on the results obtained. Section 5 concludes the paper.

2 Background Study

In dictionary-based approach, they have taken the data from Pub Med and Medline, using part-of-speech (POS) tagging, phrase block's formulation, and designed VWIA algorithm to identify entities for matching biomedical concepts. With the data collected from PubMed and Medline, they have created a literature database from that literature they used to take one of each literature [5]. Here, they have used a model called conditional random fields (CRF) model. This combines the best of both HMM and MEMM [6]. Dynamic biomedical information is extracted, namely association between biomedical entities which is often extracted based on entity co-occurrence analysis with statistics theory [7]. For that purpose, they were using an algorithm called mining multiclass entity association (MMEA) [8].

Another set of researchers have collected information Medline and ScienceDirect [9], and used NLP methods are based on prior knowledge on how language is structured and on specific knowledge on how biological information is mentioned in the literature [10]. The analysis results show that pre-training BERT on biomedical corpora helps it to understand complex biomedical texts [11] (Table 1).

Table 1 Literature review table

Authors	Name of the paper	Technology/algorithm	Accuracy (%)
Lee	BioBERT: a pre-trained biomedical language representation model for biomedical text mining	BERT	95
Pereira	Text mining applied to electronic medical records	Variable-step window identification algorithm (VWIA)	75
Gong	Application of biomedical text mining	Conditional random fields (CRF) model	74.50
T. Fadi	MCAR: multiclass classification based on association rule	Mining multiclass entity association	
M. Simmons	Text mining for precision medicine: bringing structure to EHRs and biomedical literature to understand genes and health	General idea about medical documents	
G. Tancev	Mining and classifying medical documents	General idea about biomedical text mining	

3   Methodology

In this paper, we have implemented a model to correctly classify the medical diagnosis based on the given medical transcriptions. Our basic aim is to correctly classify the medical specialties based on the transcription text. Flowchart of the process what we have followed in our methodology is given in Fig. 1.

3.1   Dataset

This dataset contains sample medical transcriptions for various medical specialties. Medical data is extremely hard to find due to HIPAA privacy regulations [12]. This dataset offers a solution by providing medical transcription samples. This dataset contains sample medical transcriptions for various medical specialties. This data was scraped from mtsamples.com. MTSamples.com is designed to give us access

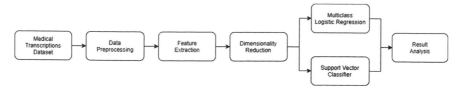

Fig. 1 Block diagram of the proposed model framework

Unnamed: 0		description	medical_specialty	sample_name	transcription	keywords
0	0	A 23-year-old white female presents with comp...	Allergy / Immunology	Allergic Rhinitis	SUBJECTIVE:, This 23-year-old white female pr...	allergy / immunology, allergic rhinitis, aller...
1	1	Consult for laparoscopic gastric bypass	Bariatrics	Laparoscopic Gastric Bypass Consult - 2	PAST MEDICAL HISTORY:, He has difficulty climb...	bariatrics, laparoscopic gastric bypass, weigh...
2	2	Consult for laparoscopic gastric bypass	Bariatrics	Laparoscopic Gastric Bypass Consult - 1	HISTORY OF PRESENT ILLNESS: , I have seen ABC ...	bariatrics, laparoscopic gastric bypass, heart...
3	3	2-D M-Mode. Doppler	Cardiovascular / Pulmonary	2-D Echocardiogram - 1	2-D M-MODE: , 1. Left atrial enlargement wit...	cardiovascular / pulmonary, 2-d m-mode, dopple...
4	4	2-D Echocardiogram	Cardiovascular / Pulmonary	2-D Echocardiogram - 2	1. The left ventricular cavity size and wall ...	cardiovascular / pulmonary, 2-d, doppler, echo...

Fig. 2 Sample data description of medical transcription dataset

to a big collection of transcribed medical reports. These samples can be used by learning, as well as working medical transcriptionists for their daily transcription needs [13].

This dataset contains six columns—'description,' 'medical_specialty,' 'sample_name,' 'transcription,' and 'keywords' as shown in Fig. 2.

In total, there are 140,214 sentences in the transcription's column and around 35,822 unique words in the transcriptions column which is the vocabulary. And also, there are around 40 categories of medical specialties in the dataset. The categories are like allergy/immunology, autopsy, cardiovascular/pulmonary, gastroenterology, endocrinology, etc. As part of pre-processing, we have filtered out the categories which have more than 50 samples, so the number of categories got reduced from 40 to 21. If we see the number of transcriptions based on the medical specialties also, we can see that surgery has 1088 transcription records, and there are also few categories which has a smaller number of records, for example, emergency room reports, pain management, psychiatry/psychology, etc. We have also plotted the classes of filtered data categories, so we have around 21 categories of medical specialties. Figure 3 portrays the various medical specialty categories and number of records in every category.

If we look at the plot, we can clearly state that it is a data imbalance problem. There are a huge number of records belonging to the class surgery, which is almost thrice when compared with some of the other classes in the dataset. Since we are trying to classify the medical specialities based on medical transcriptions, we need only the 'transcription' and 'medical_specialty' columns in the dataset.

3.2 Data Pre-processing

As part of data pre-processing, the transcription columns which are empty or null are removed. After removing the empty cells in the transcription columns, there are a total of 4597 transcriptions in the whole dataset. In order to make the data perfect, we had removed the punctuations, digits, and white spaces in the transcriptions. Also, we had converted the data into lowercase for more convenience. Then, we have performed lemmatization on the text. Lemmatization [14] is a text normalization technique, which reduces the inflected word properly assuring that the root word

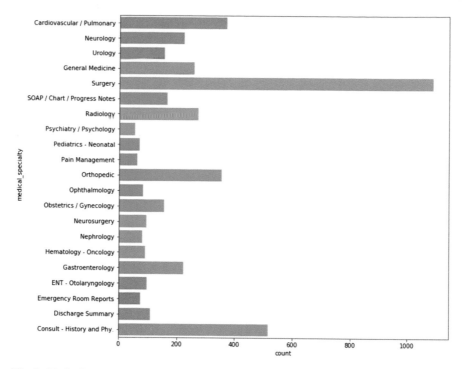

Fig. 3 Medical speciality category details in dataset

belongs to the language. It will be replacing the words with similar meaning, so that it will reduce the number of words present in the transcription column. It reduces the variability in the words, so that the words with similar meaning will be mapped together.

3.3 Feature Extraction

In order to extract the features from the dataset, we have used TF-IDF vectorizer. In information retrieval, TF-IDF or TFIDF, short for term frequency–inverse document frequency, is a numerical statistic that is intended to reflect how important a word is to a document in a collection or corpus. It is often used as a weighting factor in general [15]. We have used term frequency—inverse document frequency as a feature extraction method over here. Also, we set that word or bigram appears in more than 75% of the document, then we do not consider it as a feature, and also, we were looking for maximum features, so that we have set the maximum feature count as 1000. Then, we fit the TF-IDF vectorizer on our transcription column. We have to visualize the TF-IDF features using t-sne plot. So, if you look at the feature extraction process, we have extracted close to 1000 features, so from 1000 features, we are trying to visualize that in a two-dimensional space. If we look at the t-sne plot, we can see that most of the classes are quite close to each other and the majority class surgery overlaps the other classes here. So, the data points are quite close to each other.

3.4 Dimensionality Reduction

We have performed PCA for reducing the dimensionality in the features for further processing. PCA [16] is commonly used for dimensionality reduction by projecting each data point onto only the first few principal components to obtain lower-dimensional data while preserving as much of the data's variation as possible. We have performed PCA in TF-IDF matrix, so after doing PCA the number of features reduced from 1000 to 614. While doing PCA, we retained the components which has variance more than 0.95, which captures more than 95% of the dataset.

3.5 Classification Using Support Vector Classifier and Multiclass Logistic Regression

Then, we have used the train–test split in scikit learn to split the data into test (25%) and train (75%) data. Also, we have used stratified methods here because some of the classes are minority classes. We have applied support vector classifier to learn on training data, to learn a classifier, and to predict on the test data. Once after completing the training, predict the results on the dataset. SVC is a nonparametric clustering algorithm that does not make any assumption on the number or shape of the clusters in the data. In our experience, it works best for low-dimensional data, so if the data is high-dimensional, a pre-processing step, e.g., using principal component analysis, is usually required. Several enhancements of the original algorithm were proposed that provide specialized algorithms for computing the clusters by only computing a subset of the edges in the adjacency matrix [17]. We got an accuracy of 39% which is comparatively less. So, we need to add a few more methods to increase the accuracy. Transcriptions for surgery could belong to any of the categories like, for example, heart surgery, so if it is heart surgery, it could belong to cardiology, but it is still present in surgery. Similarly, if it is something related to bone, then it could belong to orthopedic. So, we can say that surgery class is a superset of all other classes. Also, we have classes like discharge summary, office notes, emergency room report, etc., which will be a super set of all other classes. So, we have removed these classes from the dataset. Also, we have done some mapping on neurosurgery and nephrology since both of those come under neurology and urology, respectively. After performing all the mapping and removal, now we will be having around 12

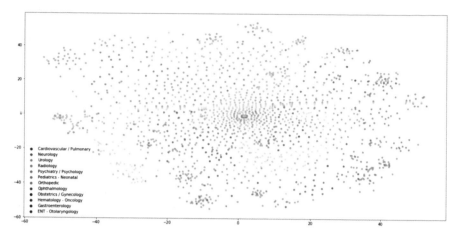

Fig. 4 T-sne plot for data points after applying scispaCy package

categories of medical specialities. Now all the medical specialities are separate and unique. Now the total transcriptions in the dataset are 2324.

The next step is to apply scispaCy models to detect medical entities in our text. ScispaCy is a Python package containing spaCy models for processing biomedical, scientific, or clinical text. So, we will be using spaCy to implement scispaCy model which will be detecting the medical terms. So again, we will be processing all the 12 categories of data with this scispaCy package to detect the medical entities. Once the medical entities are detected, we will be again doing the lemmatization and cleaning the text which we had done earlier. Again, we will be applying TF-IDF vectorizer and extracting the maximum features from the data. Figure 4 shows the T-sne plot for various categories after applying scispaCy package.

Now if we see the t-sne plot of updated dataset, there are few more clusters created, but still we can see a lot of overlapping in the dataset. One way to deal with addressing imbalanced datasets is to oversample the minority class. The least complex methodology includes copying models in the minority class, albeit these models do not add any new data to the model. By considering all the things, new models can be integrated from the current models. This is a sort of information increase for the minority class and is referred to as the synthetic minority oversampling technique, or SMOTE for short [18].

Table 2 Confusion matrix details for different algorithms

Models	Precision	Recall	$f1$-score	Accuracy (%)
Support vector classifier	0.35	0.39	0.32	38.80
Multiclass logistic regression	0.63	0.64	0.63	64
MLR with SMOTE	0.65	0.67	0.65	67

4 Results and Discussion

4.1 Support Vector Classifier

The goal of the SVM algorithm is to create the best line or decision boundary that can segregate n-dimensional space into classes, so that we can easily put the new data point in the correct category in the future. This best decision boundary is called a hyperplane. SVM chooses the extreme points/vectors that help in creating the hyperplane. These extreme cases are called as support vectors, and hence, algorithm is termed as support vector machine [19].

We have applied a support vector classifier to learn on training data, to learn a classifier, and to predict the test data. The results are analyzed using the confusion matrix, and classification results are depicted in Table 2. If we analyze the confusion matrix, the classification is done properly, but here most of the dataset is classified in the surgery class. Then, if we observe the classification reports here, the overall accuracy is 39% which is very low. And if we see the classification results in the bigger classes like surgery, the results are quite better, but if we see the minority classes like neurosurgery and hematology—oncology, etc., the results are very poor.

4.2 Multiclass Logistic Regression

Logistic regression, by default, is limited to two-class classification problems. Some extensions like one versus rest can allow logistic regression to be used for multiclass classification problems, although they require that the classification problem first be transformed into multiple binary classification problems [20]. Since the accuracy is very less, we have to apply some domain knowledge to improve the results. After adding the data to the scispaCy model, we have applied another machine learning algorithm called logistic regression to classify the medical transcriptions. Since there are multiple output classes, we should use multiclass logistic regression for the classification purpose. After doing all the pre-processing task, the multiclass logistic regression is applied on the training data, and then, it is classified and the results are presented in Table 2.

But now if we see the confusion matrix after the prediction, we can see that certain classes are getting classified very well over here. But again, certain classes are not getting classified properly. But the overall accuracy improved from 39 to 64%.

4.3 Multiclass Logistic Regression with SMOTE

Since some classes are in minority, we can use synthetic minority oversampling technique (SMOTE) to generate more sample form minority class to solve the data imbalance problem. In machine learning and data science, we often come across a term called imbalanced data distribution, which generally happens when observations in one of the class are much higher or lower than the other classes. As machine learning algorithms tend to increase accuracy by reducing the error, they do not consider the class distribution. Synthetic minority oversampling technique (SMOTE) is one of the most commonly used oversampling methods to solve the imbalance problem. It aims to balance class distribution by randomly increasing minority class examples by replicating them.

SMOTE helps to generate new samples from the existing minority classes of data. It generates the virtual training records by linear interpolation for the minority class. These synthetic training records are generated by randomly selecting one or more of the k-nearest neighbors for each example in the minority class. After the oversampling process, the data is reconstructed, and several classification models can be applied for the processed data [21].

Initially, we have used support vector classifier for classifying the transcriptions based on the diseases. After using SVC, we got an accuracy of 39% which was slightly on the lower side of accuracy. So, we have used multiclass logistic regression along with scispaCy package for attaining for accuracy. This time we got an accuracy of 64%. Basically, we will not be able to attain more accuracy as there is a problem of data imbalance with the dataset. Synthetic minority oversampling technique in Python is one of the solutions for data imbalancing problem. Even after using SMOTE, we got an accuracy of 67% which was on the higher side compared to another two algorithms.

5 Conclusion

We have used support vector classifier on the medical transcription dataset, and we have tried to classify the medical specialties (diagnosis) based on the available medical transcriptions. As presented in the results section, though we use any of the advanced techniques, expecting increased accuracy is a very challenging task as it is a class imbalance dataset. On the other hand, we understood that the data itself is noisy, and if we could use some customized feature extraction technique, we can expect better results. Future work will be focusing on using more suitable machine learning techniques to generate more samples from minority classes to address the class imbalance problem and also using an ensemble approach for better classification.

References

1. Dalianis H (2018) Clinical text mining: secondary use of electronic patient records. Springer, Stockholm
2. Tancev G (2019) Mining and classifying medical documents, 25 Oct 2019. [Online]. Available: https://towardsdatascience.com/mining-and-classifying-medical-text-documents-1876462f73bc. Accessed on 02 Apr 2021
3. Lee J1 LW (2020) BioBERT: a pre-trained biomedical language representation model for biomedical text mining. Bioinformatics 36(4):1234–1240
4. Singhal A, Simmons M, Lu Z (2016) Text mining for precision medicine: bringing structure to EHRs and biomedical literature to understand genes and health. Adv Exp Med Biol 939:139–166
5. Rijo R, Martinho R, Pereira L, Silva C (2015) Text mining applied to electronic medical records. Int J E-Health Med Commun 6(3):1–18
6. Blog G (2018) Complete tutorial on text classification using conditional random fields model (in Python). Analytics Vidhya, 13 Aug 2018. [Online]. Available: https://www.analyticsvidhya.com/blog/2018/08/nlp-guide-conditional-random-fields-text-classification/. Accessed on 05 Apr 2021
7. Gong L (2018) Application of biomedical text mining. IntechOpen I:427–428
8. Thabtah F, Cowling P, Peng Y (2005) MCAR: multi-class classification based on association rule. ResearchGate
9. ScienceDirect, 05 Apr 2005. [Online]. Available: https://www.sciencedirect.com/. Accessed on 05 Apr 2021
10. Fleuren WW, Alkema W (2015) Application of text mining in the biomedical domain. Sci Direct 74(1):97–106
11. Lee J, Yoon W, Kim S, Kim D, Kim S, So CH, Kang J (2019) BioBERT: a pre-trained biomedical language representation model for biomedical text mining,.Cornell University, pp 10–11
12. Boyle T (2020) Medical transcriptions—Kaggle," Kaggle, Apr 2018. [Online]. Available: https://www.kaggle.com/tboyle10/medicaltranscriptions. Accessed on 25 Oct 2020
13. MTSAMPLES.COM (2021) "mtsamples, 1 Apr 2021. [Online]. Available: https://www.mtsamples.com/index.asp. Accessed on 05 Apr 2021
14. Srinidhi S (2020) Lemmatization in natural language processing (NLP) and machine learning, towards data science, 26 Feb 2020. [Online]. Available: https://towardsdatascience.com/lemmatization-in-natural-language-processing-nlp-and-machine-learning-a4416f69a7b6. Accessed on 05 Apr 2021
15. Wikipedia (2021) Wikipedia—the free encyclopedia, 08 Mar 2021. [Online]. Available: https://en.wikipedia.org/wiki/Tf%E2%80%93idf. Accessed on 05 Apr 2021
16. Jolliffe IT, Cadima J (2016) Principal component analysis: a review and recent developments. Royal Soc Publishing 374(2065)
17. Ben-Hur A (2008) Scholarpedia. 2008. [Online]. Available: http://www.scholarpedia.org/article/Support_vector_clustering. Accessed on 05 Apr 2021
18. Brownlee J (2020) Machinelearningmastery—SMOTE for imbalanced classification with Python, 17 Jan 2020. [Online]. Available: https://machinelearningmastery.com/smote-oversampling-for-imbalanced-classification/. Accessed on 03 Apr 2021
19. Javatpoint, [Online]. Available: https://www.javatpoint.com/machine-learning-support-vector-machine-algorithm

20. Brownlee J (2021) Machinelearningmastery—multinomial logistic regression with Python, 1 Jan 2021. [Online]. Available: https://machinelearningmastery.com/multinomial-logistic-regression-with-python/. Accessed on 02 Apr 2021
21. "GeeksforGeeks—ML|handling imbalanced data with SMOTE and near miss algorithm in Python, 30 June 2019. [Online]. Available: https://www.geeksforgeeks.org/ml-handling-imbalanced-data-with-smote-and-near-miss-algorithm-in-python/. Accessed on 20 June 2021

A Hybrid Acoustic Model for Effective Speech Emotion Classification by the Deep Fusion of Spectral and Prosodic Features Using CNN and DNN

Maganti Syamala [ID]**, N. J. Nalini** [ID]**, and Lakshmana Phaneendra Maguluri** [ID]

Abstract To explore and enhance the need of speech emotion classification (SEC) for improving customer quality of service, this paper classified the speech into different emotions by analyzing speech features using neural network fusion-based feature extraction mechanism. This paper proposed a deep learning framework by fusing deep features extracted from spectrograms and prosodic features. Implemented a 2D convolutional neural network (CNN) to extract features from Mel-scale spectrogram. The drawbacks in the traditional methods are dealt by the fusion of CNN with deep neural network (DNN) for deep feature extraction. The experimental results are derived from RAVDESS emotional speech database and demonstrate the significant emotion accuracy improvement by combining para-lingual spectrogram and prosodic features using CNN and DNN. Compare the proposed model in terms of classification accuracy using various machine learning and deep learning techniques. Comparison was made with the traditional models where features are extracted from chroma gram, spectrogram, Mel-frequency cepstral coefficient (MFCC), and tonal centroid feature extraction techniques. The results obtained from the proposed model are outperformed when measured in terms of accuracy, precision, recall, and *F*-score. The classification accuracy of deep fusion feature extraction is 83%, and there is a comparable difference with the traditional state-of-the-art models.

Keywords Classification · Emotions · Extraction · Feature · Para-lingual · Quality · Recommender · Speech · Machine learning · Validation

M. Syamala (✉) · L. P. Maguluri
Koneru Lakshmaiah Education Foundation, Vaddeswaram, Guntur, Andhra Pradesh 522502, India

M. Syamala · N. J. Nalini · L. P. Maguluri
Annamalai University, Annamalai Nagar, Chidambaram, Tamil Nadu 608002, India

© The Author(s), under exclusive license to Springer Nature Singapore Pte Ltd. 2022
C. Satyanarayana et al. (cds.), *High Performance Computing and Networking*,
Lecture Notes in Electrical Engineering 853,
https://doi.org/10.1007/978-981-16-9885-9_51

625

1 Introduction

The actual content qualifying the context can be extracted by using different feature extraction and machine learning techniques. For example, in text analytics for improving the quality of customer service in the form recommendation, sentiment analysis is one of the fields of research where the expression expressed is analyzed using various machine learning and NLP techniques [1]. This process in speech is actually carried out by mapping the audio signal with the best matching word sequences from a trained dataset. This process requires building an acoustic model for extracting audio feature vectors and a language model for defining the pre-defined word sequences. Taking all the speech utterances into consideration may lead to dimensionality problem [2]. A set of pre-defined statistical values are interpreted with the input model to map and match the emotion. This process of capturing is treated to be a dependent statistical model. Most of the statistical measures used are pre-defined like calculated mean, threshold set for maximum, and minimum values for extracting the features [3].

Most of the research in present days is been carried out using deep learning techniques. Many neural network architectures are been invented, and most of the studies depicted [4] that the essential speech signal features are being captured depending on several factors in neural network architecture like layers in a network, memory-based network models, auto-encoder network models, etc. While modeling the context, the machine learning and deep learning techniques that are used should be dependent on the outliers [5]. Figure 1 describes the flow of feature extraction and emotion classification in SEC using the mechanism of traditional machine learning and deep learning algorithms.

The significance and contributions of the work are:

- A hybrid acoustic model is proposed by combining spectral and prosodic features for efficient emotion classification.
- The deep feature fusion mechanism using 2D CNN and DNN for emotion classification is validated using various machine learning algorithms and combination of existing deep learning techniques.

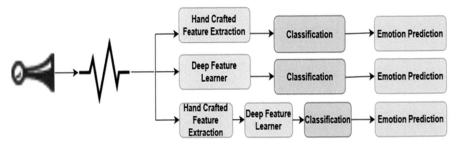

Fig. 1 Flow of feature extraction and emotion classification in SEC using the mechanism of traditional and deep learning

- The experimental results evolved is compared against the traditional model where features are extracted by considering only spectral features.

The second part of the paper Sect. 2 describes the literature carried out on SEC, and Sect. 3 presents the proposed methodology. Experimental results performed are presented in Sect. 4, and in Sect. 5, conclusion was made.

2 Related Work

The research in this paper is carried out to depict four discrete unique emotions like angry, sad, happy, and neutral. There is an abundant research taking place in the field of speech signal processing for speech emotion recognition. Various feature extraction techniques and machine learning, deep learning techniques are evolved. Most of the researchers cope up with new ideas for extracting and training the features to derive more classification accuracy, and some of the research carried in this area is presented below.

The research gap that is identified from the existing works is:

- Traditional handcrafted features were used for emotion classification [6].
- An CNN and LSTM, RNN models [7] are used for feature extraction, but the work is limited in considering only spectral features mostly MFCC.
- Also, it was proved that the complex structure of LSTM, BLSTM, and RNN make the training process difficult [8].
- SVM, ELM algorithms are mostly used for emotion classification from the extracted features using neural networks [9].
- The existing works limit to consider only spectral features resulting in classification inaccuracy. Drawing and training the handcrafted features results in low-level features, and the evolution of learning techniques made the prediction process more efficient and effective [10]. This made my work to derive toward the deep feature fusion using deep learning techniques combing spectral and prosodic features.
- There are existing studies where prosodic features are trained for feature extraction, but it is limited in using machine learning algorithms like SVM and RF.
- The fusion done by considering both spectral and prosodic features derived a hybrid acoustic model for effective SEC.

In the proposed work, the spectral features from a spectrogram and prosodic features are feed into 2D CNN and DNN for SEC. For validation, compare the proposed model with the machine learning algorithms and combination deep learning techniques to determine the truly predicted instances in terms of accuracy, precision, recall, and F-score. The performance derived by deep fusion of spectral and prosodic features for SEC has dealt the problem of classification inaccuracy and is analyzed using confusion matrix.

3   Proposed Methodology

In the proposed work, a combination of spectral and prosodic features is learned through neural networks. 2D CNN and DNN are used as feature learning techniques from spectrograms and prosodic features. The proposed framework is presented in the following sub-sections, and the architecture describing this process is illustrated in Fig. 2.

3.1   Pre-processing

It is a pre-computing stage applied prior to actual process of SEC for pre-processing the unnecessary signals by considering some set of descriptors. It mainly concerns on the estimation of signal energy envelop, short time Fourier transform (STFT), and sinusoidal harmonic modeling. At each time frame, the peaks of the STFT for the windowed signal segment ($W[n]$) are estimated as given in Eq. (1). The peaks of this frame close to multiples of the fundamental frequency are then chosen to estimate the sinusoidal harmonic frequency and amplitude.

$$S^1[n] = W[n] * S[n] \tag{1}$$

$$S^1[n] = S[n] - \alpha * S[n-1] \tag{2}$$

Equation (2) represents the mechanism of filtering the lower-order frequencies from the input signal $S[n]$ to derive the boosted higher frequency signal $S^1[n]$.

The parameter α has assigned a positive value (<1) which is meant for controlling the degree of filtering in pre-emphasis.

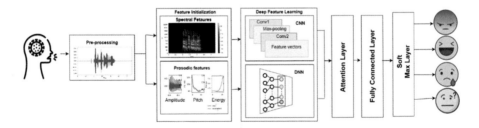

Fig. 2   Proposed methodology architecture

3.2 Feature Extraction

A combined fusion mechanism is employed for extracting the features. Compared to the traditional state-of-the-art methods, the proposed neural network-based fusion mechanism captures the emotion relevant higher-level features more efficiently for SEC.

Mel-spectrogram

Mel-spectrogram uses short time Fourier transform (STFT) to analyze the frequency content of signals varying with time. Discrete Fourier transform (DFT) is used to understand how the energy in the signal gets changed over time and frequency. It is a straight forward extension where it applies DFT by taking segments of the signal window through sliding the window to next segment. The sliding process fixes the window size rather than fixing the data record for deriving loss less information.

$$\text{Fourier Transform } X[n,\lambda] = \sum_{m=-\alpha}^{\alpha} x[n+m] \cdot w[m] \cdot e^{-j\lambda m} \tag{3}$$

n Location in time
λ Continuous frequency.

sample λ at $X_k = \frac{2\pi}{N}k$

$$X[n,\lambda] = \sum_{m=0}^{L-1} x[n+m] \cdot w[m] \cdot e^{-j\frac{2\pi}{N}km} \tag{4}$$

Computation of DFT and FFT in order to transform each window from time domain to frequency domain is given in Eqs. (3) and (4).

Prosodic features

Prosodic features are also known to be acoustic features mainly used for capturing three types of speech features like pitch derived from frequency of a speech signal, stress denoting the energy in the speech signal, and time duration representing the length of the signal. Prosodic features are suprasegmental features and inherent the above speech features. In the proposed work, the prosodic features are trained into DNN for extracting high-level features. Prosodic features can be extracted from continuous speech for effective emotion classification. Computing prosody of speech signal includes 103 different features of pitch, energy, and duration. The prosody features including pitch, energy, and duration are computed for each voiced and unvoiced segment by means of average, mean, skewness, and Kurtosis.

3.3   Learning Techniques: A Fusion Mechanism

Convolutional Neural Network (CNN)

Convolutional neural network (CNN) is a feed-forward neural network mostly used to make use of spatial information efficiently in image data. The spatial information in image if passed to CNN derives effective higher-level features from low-level raw pixel information. In the proposed work, Mel-spectrogram generated from the input speech signal is given as input to 2D CNN. 2D CNN architecture is designed to have three layers, namely convolutional layer, pooling layer, and fully connected (FC) layer.

Convolutional layer makes the use of in-built convolutional filters to produce feature maps by extracting local patterns from the input Mel-spectrogram. The output of the feature map is mathematically represented in Eq. (5).

$$(h_k)_{i,j} = (W_k * q)_{ij} + b_k \tag{5}$$

i, j 2D input elements
h_k Feature map output of kth element
q Input features
W_k kth filter
b_k bias
$*$ 2D spatial convolution.

Deep Neural Network (DNN)

Deep neural network (DNN) is a feed-forward neural network with fully connected layers and hidden layers. When working with huge complex data, this DNN makes the process simple to derive heuristic features. In the proposed model, the prosodic features extracted are feed into DNN and DNN acts as a learning model to derive high-level features. Adam is used as an optimizer to optimize cross entropy loss. DNN uses the following mathematical equations in the forwarded process is represented in Eqs. (6) and (7).

$$h^{(l)} = y^{(l-1)}w^{(l)} + b^{(l)} \tag{6}$$

$$y^{(l)} = \emptyset\left(h^{(l)}\right) \tag{7}$$

$h^{(l}$ Output of lth hidden layer
$y^{(l-1)}$ Input to lth hidden layer
$w^{(l)}$ Weight matrix for layer l and bias b.

3.4 Emotion Classification

There are various classifiers in machine learning that can be used for SEC. Here, in this model, the features extracted from deep fusion of 2D CNN + DNN are validated using different machine learning classification algorithms. The classification or prediction of emotion in deep fusion mechanism is carried out by SoftMax classifier. It derives the probability value for each class and the gives the percentage of emotion detected in the input speech as output. The SoftMax layer maps the output to N number of emotion classes. SoftMax function is mathematically represented in Eqs. (8) and (9).

$$S_i = \sum_j A_j W_j \tag{8}$$

$$\text{SoftMax } (S)_i = F_i = \frac{e^{S_i}}{\sum_{j=1}^{n} e^{S_i}} \tag{9}$$

S_i SoftMax input
F_i Fully connected hidden layer having one label (class) per node
W_{ji} Weight connected between S_i and F_i.

Finally, the target emotion label of the predicted class is given by Eq. (10)

$$\hat{t} = \arg\max_i F_i \tag{10}$$

It is proved that the emotion classification results obtained from deep fusion of combined features are more effective than traditional models when measured in terms of accuracy. The results obtained for SEC is presented in detail in the experimental analysis section.

4 Experimental Analysis

To enhance the performance of the SEC, the research work was carried out on two emotional datasets, namely Ryerson audio-visual database of emotional speech and song dataset (RAVDESS). RAVDESS dataset contains the emotional utterances of 24 actors, holding 12 male and 12 female actors' speech in North American accent. On total, 1440 utterances with eight different emotions are made available in RAVDESS dataset. Among the available emotions, the proposed model was trained against four emotions, namely angry, sad, happy, and neutral.

The proposed work was implemented in Python 3.6.9 using Jupyter notebook as integrated development environment (IDE). TFlearn, a deep learning library, is used for implementing neural networks like CNN, DNN, LSTM, etc. The performance measure metrics used in the model are evaluated using the library sklearn.

In the proposed work, the model is evaluated by taking 80% of data as training data and 20% of the data as testing data. The performance of deep fusion mechanism is evaluated when Mel-spectrograms features and prosodic features are trained into CNN and DNN. The results obtained are compared with the traditional feature extraction techniques when trained using different machine learning and deep learning algorithms. The experimental results are evaluated using the spectrograms trained by individual and combinational neural networks for enhancing the performance. And also, the features extracted from traditional techniques are validated using machine learning techniques. The experimental results obtained made a comparison in terms of correctly classified instances, accuracy, precision, and recall.

4.1 Emotion Classification Using Deep Learning

In the proposed work, the speech files recorded in WAV format are considered as input. The speech features that are extracted independently by using traditional feature extraction methods and by various neural network architectures are compared to analyze the efficiency in SEC. The low-level features extracted need to be distinguished among themselves for deriving better classification accuracy. For this reason, experiments are carried out to train the speech features independently and as well as combined into different neural network architectures like CNN, DNN, and LSTM. To achieve the above-discussed criteria, experimental results are carried out and are detailed in the following section.

Emotion Classification Using CNN

CNN captures the spectrogram as input to derive the high-level speech features from low-level descriptors. Initially, the spectrogram generated is a frame-level feature and was obtained by framing the window of size 2048 and 512 hop length. A well-known Python library, Librosa, is used to map the speech signal into spectrogram. STFT is used to transform each window from time domain to frequency domain. The experimental results obtained when spectrograms are trained into CNN model for SEC are analyzed using confusion matrix and is depicted in Fig. 3.

Emotion	Angry	Sad	Neutral	Happy
Angry	0.80	0.02	0.01	0.17
Sad	0.02	0.88	0.03	0.07
Neutral	0.03	0.08	0.89	0.00
Happy	0.08	0.04	0.03	0.85

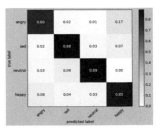

Fig. 3 True positive-false negative analysis and confusion matrix plot for CNN

Emotion Classification Using DNN

As similar to CNN, DNN is also a feed-forward neural network, and a three hidden layer architecture is designed for SEC. As part of evaluation, performance of spectral features was analyzed using neural networks as learning models. In this section, DNN is used as a learning model for training the low-level features of spectrogram in order to derive the high-level features and extreme learning machine algorithm (ELM) for extracting utterance level features. The experimental results obtained when spectrograms are trained into DNN model for SEC are analyzed using confusion matrix and is depicted in Fig. 4.

Emotion Classification Using CNN + LSTM

An end-to-end learning model by a combination of CNN and LSTM is evaluated for SEC. In this model, CNN acts as an encoding layer to capture the high-levels features from spectrogram, and LSTM acts as a decoding layer to derive global utterances by including temporal dependencies. LSTM is bidirectional that captures the temporal dependencies in both the directions and known to be BLSTM. The experimental results obtained when spectrograms are trained into CNN + LSTM model for SEC are analyzed using confusion matrix and is depicted in Fig. 5.

Emotion	Angry	Sad	Neutral	Happy
Angry	0.85	0.08	0.02	0.05
Sad	6.41	70.51	3.85	6.41
Neutral	2.56	8.97	84.63	0.00
Happy	15.38	7.69	2.58	71.79

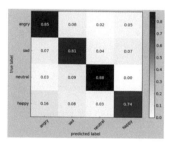

Fig. 4 True positive-false negative analysis and confusion matrix for DNN

Emotion	Angry	Sad	Neutral	Happy
Angry	0.90	0.05	0.05	0.00
Sad	0.05	0.85	0.02	0.08
Neutral	0.06	0.10	0.79	0.05
Happy	0.08	0.05	0.03	0.84

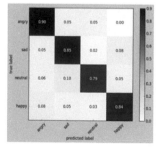

Fig. 5 True positive-false negative analysis and confusion matrix for CNN + LSTM

4.2 Emotion Classification Using Machine Learning

Unlike deep learning, emotions can also be classified using machine learning (ML) techniques. There exist various studies in SEC where deep learning neural architectures are used as learning models for feature extraction and machine learning algorithms for classification. There exist various traditional spectral feature extraction techniques like chroma gram, spectrogram, Mel-frequency cepstral coefficient (MFCC), and tonal centroid. In this study, the results obtained from these techniques are validated using machine learning techniques like support vector machine (SVM), decision tree (DT), random forest (RF), K-nearest neighbor (KNN), and logistic regression (LR). The experimental results obtained when features extracted from traditional feature extraction methods for SEC using machine learning algorithms are analyzed using confusion matrix and is depicted in Fig. 6.

The features extracted by traditional feature extraction methods are classified using various machine learning algorithms, and the performance is analyzed using accuracy, precision, recall, and F-score measures in Table 1 and Fig. 7.

4.3 Deep Fusion of CNN + DNN

In the traditional state-of-the-art methods, most of the research that is been carried out in SEC at feature extraction level is limited to extract either spectral features

Emotion	Angry	Sad	Neutral	Happy
Angry	0.60	0.01	0.11	0.28
Sad	0.02	0.52	0.21	0.25
Neutral	0.04	0.10	0.52	0.34
Happy	0.07	0.08	0.14	0.72

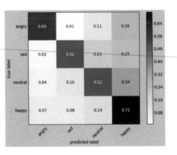

Fig. 6 True positive-false negative analysis and confusion matrix for ML

Table 1 Performance analysis of machine learning algorithms

Classifier	Accuracy (%)	Precision (%)	Recall (%)	F-score (%)
DT	74	74	73	73
LR	68	68	68	67
RF	67	68	67	66
SVM	64	64	63	63
KNN	55	57	58	56

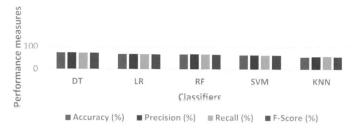

Fig. 7 Performance analysis of machine learning algorithms

or prosodic features. As per our study, spectral features contain lower frame-level features and if include individually may result in classification inaccuracy. Prosodic features qualify an individual speaking style which has a great impact on detecting the emotion efficiently. The combination of these two features by a deep fusion mechanism using CNN and DNN have yielded better results.

The spectral features from spectrograms are given as input to CNN model and the prosodic features that are stated in the proposed methodology section are trained into DNN. For high-level feature extraction, DNN model with three hidden layers, each containing 3000 nodes is used. Both CNN and DNN act as feature learning models for extracting the global utterances of speech features for effective SEC. The input feature vectors are added into attention layer to align the features obtained from both these networks, and the corresponding output is feed into fully connected layer having four neurons. A SoftMax activation function is used in full connected layer for emotion label classification. The experimental results obtained when spectrograms and prosodic features are trained into CNN and DNN for SEC are analyzed using confusion matrix and is depicted in Fig. 8.

The experimental results obtained from the proposed model are compared with the existing work carried out in the area of SEC, and the results are analyzed using the performance measure accuracy and the same is depicted in Table 2.

Emotion	Angry	Sad	Neutral	Happy
Angry	0.90	0.03	0.02	0.05
Sad	0.03	0.88	0.02	0.07
Neutral	0.02	0.06	0.92	0.00
Happy	0.10	0.05	0.02	0.83

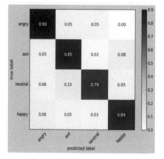

Fig. 8 True positive-false negative analysis and confusion matrix for CNN + DNN

Table 2 Model performance analysis of existing work

Authors	Features	Model/architecture	Classes	Accuracy (%)
Zeng et al. [11]	Spectrograms	Convolutional layers	08	64.48
Jalal et al. [12]	Log-spectrogram	BLSTM + CNN	08	61.08
Bhavan et al. [13]	Spectral features	Bagged ensemble of SVM	08	75.69
Mustaqeem et al. [14]	Spectrograms	DSCNN	08	79.05
Shegokar et al. [15]	Continuous wavelet transforms, prosodic coefficients	SVM	08	60.01
Proposed model	Spectral + Prosodic features	CNN + DNN	04	83.33

A comparison was made, the performance of the proposed model is analyzed by training the spectrograms using various models of neural networks, and the results are analyzed in Table 3 and Fig. 9.

Table 3 Comparison of performance with respect to the proposed model

Architecture	Feature	Train Acc. (%)	Validation Acc. (%)	Test Acc. (%)
CNN	Mel-spec.	100.00	68.64	65.90
DNN	Mel-spec.	99.28	67.30	68.70
CNN + LSTM	Mel-spec.	97.88	67.86	69.23
ML	Combined spectral features	97.57	65.23	64.32
CNN + DNN	Spec. and prosodic	100	89.12	83.33

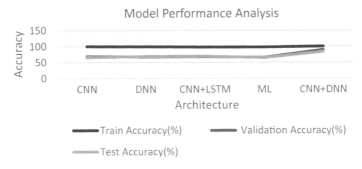

Fig. 9 Comparison of performance with respect to the proposed model

5 Conclusion

The proposed work in this paper depicts the importance of spectral and prosodic features for SEC. A deep fusion framework is designed using CNN and DNN to extract the high-level features for effective SEC. The evaluations were analyzed using various performance measures like accuracy, precision, recall, F-score, and correctly classified instances. The results are compared with the traditional deep learning and machine learning models. In comparison, the deep learning models are used as learning and training models to classify the high-level features obtained from spectral features, while the machine learning algorithms are used only to train the spectral features extracted from traditional feature extraction methods for predicting the emotion class. From the analysis, we came to know that the deep learning models used for learning and training the features are more effective in deriving the better results. So, this made our work to drive toward deep learning for SEC and also to overcome the problem of classification inaccuracy found in baseline models because of capturing the low-level features.

The proposed model is an end-to-end learning model which is capable of capturing the global utterances of the speech features for effective SEC. The proposed model overcomes the problem of classification inaccuracy which was reported as the most common problem in the traditional state-of-the-art models. In terms of correctly classified instances, the proposed deep fusion framework was superior to all the traditional baseline models. The combination of spectral, prosodic features, and deep fusion of CNN and DNN for deriving high-level features for SEC is the two basic highlights of the proposed model.

References

1. Noekhah S, Salim N, Zakaria N (2017) Evaluation of data mining features, features taxonomies and their applications. Kurdistan J Appl Res 3:131–141
2. Zhang J, Yin Z, Chen P, Nichele S (2020) Emotion recognition using multi-modal data and machine learning techniques: a tutorial and review. Inform Fusion 59:103–126
3. Chen L, Mao X, Xue Y, Cheng LL (2012) Speech emotion recognition: features and classification models. Digit Signal Process 22:1154–1160
4. Khalil RA, Jones E, Babar MI (2019) Speech emotion recognition using deep learning techniques: a review. IEEE Access 7:117327–117345
5. Khalil RA, Jones E, Babar MI, Jan T, Zafar MH, Alhussain T (2019) Speech emotion recognition using deep learning techniques: a review. IEEE Access (7):117327–117345
6. Griol D, Molina JM, Callejas Z (2017) Combining speech-based and linguistic classifiers to recognize emotion in user spoken utterances. Neurocomputing 30:1–9
7. Cho J, Pappagari R, Kulkarni P, Villalba J, Carmiel Y, Dehak N (2018) Deep neural networks for emotion recognition combining audio and transcripts. Int Speech Commun Assoc 10:247–251
8. Hossain MS, Muhammad G (2018) Emotion recognition using deep learning approach from audio-visual emotional big data. Inf Fusion, 1–24
9. Heracleous P, Mohammad Y, Yoneyama A (2019) Deep convolutional neural networks for feature extraction in speech emotion recognition. LNCS-Springer Nature (11567):117–132

10. Lu Z, Cao L, Zhang Y, Chiu CC, Fan J (2019) Speech sentiment analysis via pre-trained features from end-to-end ASR models. arXiv:1911.09762v1, pp 1–5
11. Zeng Y, Mao H, Peng D, Yi Z (2019) Spectrogram based multi-task audio classification. Multimed Tools Appl 78:3705–3722
12. Jalal MA, Loweimi E, Moore RK, Hain T (2019) Learning temporal clusters using capsule routing for speech emotion recognition. In: Proceedings on interspeech, pp 1701–1705
13. Bhavan A, Chauhan P, Shah RR (2019) Bagged support vector machines for emotion recognition from speech. Knowl Based Syst 184:1–7
14. Mustaqeem, Kwon SA (2020) CNN-assisted enhanced audio signal processing for speech emotion recognition. Sensors (183):1–15
15. Shegokar P, Sircar P (2016) Continuous wavelet transform based speech emotion recognition. In: 10th international conference on signal processing and communication systems. IEEE, Australia, pp 1–8

Application of Relay Nodes in WBAN-Based Smart Healthcare for Energy Conservation Explained with Case Studies

Koushik Karmakar, Sohail Saif, Suparna Biswas, and Sarmistha Neogy

Abstract Wireless sensor network has vast applications in different fields. One of the major applications is of WSN is in healthcare sector. Tiny sensor nodes are used to collect physiological data from the patients. Collected data are then sent to the doctor's server maintained in a remote cloud through analysis. This is one of the most popular smart healthcare techniques used worldwide. In this method, heterogeneous nodes are used for data collection from the patient's body. Heterogeneous nodes include sensor nodes and relay nodes as well. Relay nodes do not collect data directly from the patient's body but used to carry forward them that come to them from the previous nodes. It is energy saving and also increases the longevity of the wireless body area network (WBAN) system. It also helps in data routing and thus maintaining postural mobility and seamless data connectivity. In this paper, we have described a case study on how the use of relay nodes in designing a WBAN helps us making the system more energy efficient. We have calculated total energy used in both the cases and proved that use of relay node is beneficial as it is energy saving and ensures thus longevity of the network.

Keywords Sensor node · WBAN · Healthcare · Relay nodes · Energy efficiency

1 Introduction

Significant research works are carried out in different fields like sensor nodes, smart devices, healthcare monitoring system, Internet of things (IoT), and many other similar things. Among them, one of the important areas of research is healthcare using sensor nodes. This is because with the increase in human life there is an

K. Karmakar (✉)
Narula Institute of Technology, Kolkata, India

S. Saif · S. Biswas
Maulana Abul Kalam Azad University of Technology, West Bengal, Kolkata, India

S. Neogy
Jadavpur University, Kolkata, India

© The Author(s), under exclusive license to Springer Nature Singapore Pte Ltd. 2022
C. Satyanarayana et al. (eds.), *High Performance Computing and Networking*,
Lecture Notes in Electrical Engineering 853,
https://doi.org/10.1007/978-981-16-9885-9_52

increase of chronic diseases too. As a side effect of it related expenditure due to healthcare is also growing. But, its quality is declining with time. This is really a great problem for us. Sensor-based health monitoring system is, therefore, very important [1, 2]. It shows a new method for health monitoring. As per this method, small sensor nodes are sometimes attached to the patient's body or implanted. They collect different human physiological parameters and send them to a remote server. It is generally stored at doctor's chamber. All the data are stored and analyzed there. This is called wireless body area network (WBAN) [1–3]. This is written in IEEE standard 802.15.6. However, the design of the system is should be perfect and also energy efficient. Sensor nodes used in health data monitoring should be very much energy efficient as replacement of the battery is very difficult. Relay nodes help achieve this goal in a very successful way. Not only in making the system as energy efficient one, but also it helps achieve other goals like maintaining user mobility and handling data routing seamlessly. In the current paper, we have shown how relay nodes help achieve this goal in an efficient way.

Organization of this paper is briefly described here: In Sect. 2, a brief state of the art literature survey was done. In Sect. 3, application of relay nodes in WBAN design is explained. Energy consumption is explained in Sect. 4. Experimental results are explained in Sect. 5. Section 6 concludes our paper.

2 Literature Survey

There are three layers in WBAN, respectively, called as tier-I, tier-II, and tier-III. Sensor nodes used for remote health monitoring can be wearable or implanted on human body. A diagram for a standard WBAN communication architecture is described in Fig. 1 [1–3]. In first layer, sensor nodes collect and transmit physiological parameters to a sink node. In the subsequent layer, these data are then transmitted

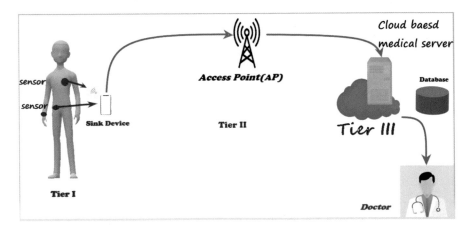

Fig. 1 WBAN data communication architecture

to the external access point (AP). At last, it is send to a server stored at cloud for details analysis.

Research works were done for last few years on WBAN, sensor nodes, IoT, and other smart devices. A brief introduction is given here. A routing method [4] was invented called ERRS which was designed based on forwarder node selection and rotation method. Simulation was done in MATLAB. In this paper [5], the protocol was designed which takes different factors into consideration like latency, temperature, and energy. Based on the sensor path, optimum routing path is selected. In this paper [6], a critical data routing code is used for data transmission known as critical data routing (CDR). In some paper [7], a block chain-based routing protocol (ATEAR) was advocated. It was simulated in OMNET++ for result analysis. In this paper [8], a data priority-based method was suggested. Sensor data classification is done based on weighted energy and QoS (WEQ)-based algorithm. It was also simulated in OMNET++. In this paper [9], a link-quality and thermal awareness-based routing protocol were developed called LATOR. It improves packet delivery rate (PDR) WBAN. In this paper [10], an energy efficient routing technique was suggested. In this work [11], a thermal aware routing algorithm is proposed. This is based on data priority considers only those data having higher priority. A MAC-based protocol is used for data classification which that classifies data into three different factors. In this paper [12], a routing protocol (MHRP) was developed that takes care of various types of user mobility. It was proved to be better in different respects. Another protocol M-SIMPLE [13] was developed which suggests a better approach regarding factors like the throughput, residual energy consumption, and path loss. A brief study report of the above routing methods is shown below (Table 1).

3   Application of Relay Nodes in WBAN Design

Sensor nodes in WBAN are used for collecting and sending information to the sink node which in turn send them to the access point (AP). A lot of energy is wasted in this process. Sending data to a long distance always requires high energy. In this case, use of relay nodes is beneficial. It is a special types of nodes which do not sense anything but retransmit the data which have been previously sensed and transmitted by the previous sensor nodes. It is used for different purposes like providing seamless connectivity, mobility management, fault tolerance, and proving seamless connectivity. In Fig. 2, we have shown an example of WBAN formation without using any relay node. In Fig. 3, the same WBAN formation is shown using relay nodes. In this Fig. 3, sensor nodes read information and then transmit them to the relay node. Relay node will transmit them to the sink node. From sink node information goes to the access point (AP). Different sensor nodes placement is shown in Fig. 4.

Table 1 Comparison of different routing techniques in WBAN

Authors, year	Technology used and application	Simulation environment	Results
Ullah et al. [4], 2021	A new routing method has been proposed	Simulation carried out using MATLAB	Throughput is better, energy saver, and provides lesser path loss
Banuselvasaraswathy and Rathinasabapathy[5], 2020	Sensor node temperature is measured and from there optical path is selected	Simulation carried out using MATLAB	Better network life time, delay, power, and energy efficiency
Sagar et al. [6], 2020	Critical data routing method (CDR) was invented which can transmit data between inner body and on body nodes	Simulation was done in MATLAB	Average packet delivery ratio is good
Shahbazi and Byun [7], 2020	It is based on the block chain-based routing protocol known as ATEAR	Simulation was done in OMNET++	Provides better output with respect to energy, latency, and node temperature
Ibrahim et al. [8], 2020	A method called weighted energy and QoS (WEQ) has been developed that selects optimal path and then sends normal as well as high normal data	Simulation was carried out in OMNET++	Better performance with respect to different parameters
Caballero et al. [9], 2020	A new protocol was designed which considers sensor node temperature and also the overheating problem	Simulation carried out in OMNET++	Provides better packet delivery rate
Ahmed et al. [10], 2019	During routing, weighted average of three factors is considered	Simulation was done in MATLAB	Provides better output
Kathe and Deshpande[11], 2019	A MAC-based algorithm was developed which considers different factors for computing	Simulation carried out in discrete event-based environment	Provides better output

(continued)

Table 1 (continued)

Authors, year	Technology used and application	Simulation environment	Results
Khanna et al. [12], 2018	One routing method (ERRS) was developed that works on forwarder node selection and rotation method	Simulation done in MATLAB	Longer stability period and network lifetime are achieved
Karmakar et al. [13]. 2017	To take care of postural mobility, one protocol (MHRP) was developed	Results calculated analytical	Provides better output in terms of delay, mobility handling, fault tolerance

Fig. 2 WBAN formation without relay node

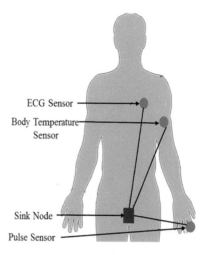

Fig. 3 WBAN formation with relay node

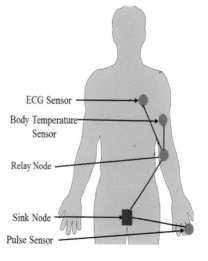

Fig. 4 Sensor node position
in WBAN

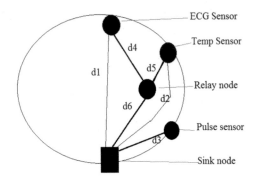

4 Energy Consumption

Energy consumption by the system can be calculated by the following rules. In this work, energy consumption refers to the communication energy consumption only as this is the main energy consumption type for a wireless sensor node. Other types of energy consumptions are minimal [14]. As per the basic radio model for WBAN, the following equations are applicable:

$$E_{TX}(t, d) = E_{TX\text{elec}} * t + E_{\text{amp}}(n) \times t * (d)^n \tag{1}$$

$$E_{RX}(t) = E_{RX\text{elec}} * t \tag{2}$$

In the above two equations, E_{TX} indicates transmission energy and E_{RX} indicates receiver energy. $E_{TX\text{elec}}$ and $E_{RX\text{elec}}$ indicate the energy level of internal system of the transmitter as well as receiver, respectively. E_{amp} indicates the energy level of the transmitter system and t indicates number of the transmitted bits. In this equation, n indicates path loss coefficient which is 3.38 in case of line-of-sight propagation (LOS). The value of n is 5.9 where the object is at non-line-of-sight (NLOS).

In Table 2, a Nordic nRF2401 transceiver along with its hardware values are mentioned [14]. We use these values in energy calculation.

Table 2 Nordic nRF2401 transceiver values [14–16]

Parameters	nRF2401
$E_{TX\text{elec}}$	16.7 nJ/nit
$E_{RX\text{elec}}$	36.1 nJ/bit
$E_{\text{amp}}(3.38)$	1.97e-9 J/bit
$E_{\text{amp}}(5.9)$	7.99e-6 J/bit

5   Experimental Results

5.1   Case 1: Energy Consumption Using Without Using Relay Nodes in WBAN

In the first case, we consider WBAN cluster formation without using any relay node (Fig. 2). Here, sensor nodes send their information directly to sink. Three sensor nodes will send collected information to the distance $d1$, $d2$, and $d3$. In this case, total energy consumption will be the sum of their individual energy.

We have taken the measurement from an adult man with a height of around 1.8 m. Respective distances for $d1$, $d2$, and $d3$ are measured as follows:

$$d1 = 0.45\,\text{m}; \quad d2 = 0.45\,\text{m}; \quad d3 = 0.2\,\text{m}.$$

5.2   Case 2: Energy Consumption Using Relay Nodes in WBAN

In the second case, we consider WBAN cluster is formed using relay node (Fig. 3). Here, sensor nodes send their information to the relay nodes only which will send it to sink node. Three sensor nodes will transmit the information to the distance $d3$, $d4$, and $d3$. Total energy consumption will be the sum of their individual energy consumption. We have collected this data from an adult man with a height of around 1.8 m. Respective distances for $d1$, $d2$, and $d3$ are measured as follows:

$$d4 = 0.3\,\text{m}; \quad d5 = 0.25\,\text{m}; \quad d3 = 0.2\,\text{m}.$$

In our WBAN system, sink node is always at LOS position from the sensor nodes. So, in this case, path loss coefficient (n) will be 3.38. Also we consider that the transmitter of the sender nodes sends 8 bit data. So, the value of t will be 8 and we put these values in the two Eqs. (1) and (2) and calculate the consumed energy by all the sensor nodes. Values obtained in this way are described in Table 3.

Table 3 Consumed energy by the sensor nodes in WBAN

Parameters	Total consumed energy by all sensor nodes (nJ)	Average consumed energy by all sensor node (nJ)
Without relay node	20.72 nJ	6.9 nJ
With relay node	5.74 nJ	1.91 nJ

6 Conclusion

In the current work, the proposed WBAN system has been designed for cardiac monitoring of the patients. We have taken three types of sensor nodes for that like ECG sensor node, temperature sensor node, and pulse sensor node. Initially, we designed this system without any relay node but later we have included a relay node in the design itself. In both the cases, consumed energy by all the sensor nodes has been calculated. It is found that the consumed energy by all the sensor nodes in presence of relay node is much lower than that of the same without the relay node. Use of relay node also helps in smooth routing in the WBAN, mobility management, and seamless connectivity. Use of relay node in WBAN design is, therefore, recommended and widely used.

References

1. Chen M, Gonzalez S, Vasilakhos A, Cao H, Leung VCM (2011) Body area networks: a survey. Mobile Netw Appl 16(2):171–193. https://doi.org/10.1007/s11036-010-0260-8 (in Springer)
2. Ullah S, Hignis H, Braem B, Latre B, Blondia C et al (2012) A comprehensive survey of wireless body area networks. J Med Syst 36(3):1065–1094
3. Latre B, Braem B, Moerman I, Blondia C, Demeester P (2011) A survey of wireless body area network. J Wirel Netw 17(1):1–18. https://doi.org/10.1007/s11276-010-0252-4 (Springer)
4. Ullah F, Khan MZ, Faisal M, Rehman HU, Abbas S, Mubarek FS (2021) An energy efficient and reliable routing scheme to enhance the stability period in Wireless Body Area Networks. Comput Commun 165:20–32 (Elsevier)
5. Banuselvasaswathy B, Rathinasabapathy V (2020) Self-heat controlling energy efficient OPOT routing protocol for WBAN. Wirel Netw (Springer)
6. Sagar AK, Singh S, Kumar A (2020) Energy-aware health monitoring using critical data routing (CDR). Wirel Personal Commun (Springer)
7. Shahbazi Z, Byun YC (2020) Towards a secure thermal energy aware routing protocol in wireless body area network based on block chain technology. MDPI Sensor
8. Ibrahim A, Bayat O, Ucan ON, Salisu S (2020) Weighted energy and QoS based multi-hop transmission routing algorithm for WBAN. In: 6th International engineering conference "Sustainable Technology and Development", IEC, Erbil, Iraq
9. Caballero E, Ferreira VC, Lima RA, Albuqerque C, Muchaluat-Saade DC (2020) LATOR; link-quality aware and thermal aware on-demand routing protocol for WBAN. In: Proceedings of the IWSSIP
10. Ahmed G, Mahmood D, Islam S (2019) Thermal and energy aware routing in wireless body are networks. Int J Distrib Sens Netw 15(6)
11. Kathe KS, Deshpande UA (2019) A thermal aware routing algorithm for a wireless body area network. Wirel Personal Commun (Springer)
12. Khanna A, Chaudhary V, Gupta SH (2018) Design and analysis of energy efficient wireless body area network (WBAN) for health monitoring. Springer-Verlag
13. Karmakar K, Biswas S, Neogy S (2017) MHRP: a novel mobility handling routing protocol in Wireless BodyArea Network. In: Proceedings of the 2017 international conference on wireless communications, signalprocessing and networking (WISPNET), Chennai, India, 22–24 March 2017, pp 1939–1945
14. Huynh TT, Dinh-Duc AV, Tran CH (2016) Delay-constrained energy-efficient cluster-based multihop routing in wireless sensor networks. J Commun Netw 18(4)

15. Reusen E, Joseph W, Latre B, Brahem B, Vermeeren G, Tanghe E, Mrtens L, Moerman I, Blondia C (2009) Characteristics of on body communication channel and energy efficient topology design for wireless body area networks. IEEE Trans Inf Technol Biomed 13(6):933–945

16. Chepkwony RC, Gwendo JO, Kemei PK (2015) Energy efficient model for deploying wireless body area networks using multiple network topology. Int J Wirel Mobile Netw (IJWMN) 7(5)

Design and Implementation of Intelligent Treadmill with Fitness Tracker Using Raspberry Pi and IOT

Padmaja Sardal, Kshitija Shinde, Umesh Sangade, and Ashwini Shinde

Abstract Treadmill users mostly prefer automated treadmills having better construction and various speed levels over a manual treadmill. But using a treadmill with clickable buttons or screen sometimes becomes a dangerous task for newbies and people in their old ages. They find it difficult to reach the controller board and change the commands as per their need, having achieved a considerable fast speed, which results in injuries due to slip off from the mill. To avoid these situations, the proposed system changes the touch-operated controller to voice-operated one, to reduce the accident rates and provide a great user experience. Deep neural network handles sound input, Mel-spectrogram is used to achieve higher efficiency results which is the base of the audio processing technique in python that uses automatic speech recognition (ASR). The proposed system focuses on easing the treadmill speed control using ASR and also has features like checking the weight of a person standing on the mill, calculating his BMI, and time of run which is then stored on cloud platform ThingSpeak, for analysis of workout and a built-in music player which solely operates on speech recognition principle using Google APIs.

Keywords Google API · IOT · ThingSpeak · Speech recognition · Raspberry Pi

1 Introduction

People think of having a treadmill whenever a cardio workout is necessary, but the treadmill can be attributed to various foot, knee, and hip pain. These treadmills also provide inclination features that help to harden the workout routine which often causes accidents. In 2017 emergency rooms recorded 24,000 injuries regarding the treadmill, according to the United States Consumer Product Safety 3 Commission. There were 30 reported deaths Related to treadmills for the more than 10 year Time span from 2005–2015. Nowadays Gym equipment is getting more technologically advanced and has more software inclusion for powering them. To keep pace with it,

P. Sardal (✉) · K. Shinde · U. Sangade · A. Shinde
Pimpri Chinchwad College of Engineering, Pune, India

© The Author(s), under exclusive license to Springer Nature Singapore Pte Ltd. 2022   649
C. Satyanarayana et al. (eds.), *High Performance Computing and Networking*,
Lecture Notes in Electrical Engineering 853,
https://doi.org/10.1007/978-981-16-9885-9_53

we will be automating our traditional treadmill using a voice recognition mechanism. In the proposed system, all the basic operations like start, stop [1], changing the speed of the treadmill from low to high also checking the weight of the person, the sound system will be operated using voice commands i.e., controlling the speed of the motor with voice commands [2], building a voice-operated music player, building a fitness assistant based on previously filled information or earlier captured data. This will help to achieve ease in operation of the treadmill also to those who are not familiar with the machine or those who have been using it for a long time. The voice commands will be fed into the system with the help of which even any guest could use the machine without having prior knowledge. So a voice command control treadmill will help to reduce accidents and for a better Customer-friendly experience.

The paper is organized into five sections. Section 2 describes the background with the literature survey. Section 3 explains the detailed working of the proposed intelligent treadmill. Section 4 demonstrates different voice command-wise experimental results. At the end, Sect. 5 gives a conclusion with future scope.

2 Background

Reference [1] is related to the development of a speech recognition system for a voice-controlled car. The robotic device's voice commands are sent through Bluetooth. They are then received by the car's motor driver. It is an important part of the car's operation and delivers commands to the car through a wireless system and the BitVoicer Server is used as a database that enables speech processing and synthesis. It was designed to work seamlessly with low-power devices.

In Ref. [2], voice input is sent by the mobile phone to the Bluetooth module of Arduino UNO. It is converted into a radio signal with a frequency of 2.4 GHz and transmitted through the Arduino UNO. The device is programmed to output a width modulated signal. The same width modulated signal is then converted into a pulse driving signal. DC motor and voice recognition application is interfaced in this paper to achieve fast and reliable voice control.

In Ref. [3], author stored the voice commands of specific person. With utilization of voice recognition, accurate transcription is achieved. A Speaker-dependent system uses a training concept. The voice command is sent through the microphone to the voice recognition module and converts into pulses and which are given to the microcontroller and compared with store value.

In Ref. [4], the author has explained various feature extraction techniques used for the development of the Automatic Speech Recognition (ASR) System. The comparative study of Linear Predictive Coefficients (LPC), Mel Frequency Cepstral Coefficient (MFCC), and other techniques. It was observed that technique has some limitation, sometimes reliability and performance of the system is affected. Also, it observed that the LPC has a recognition rate of 91.4% for the English language. It is the most useful technique for encoding good quality of speech, and the reason for

MFCC being most commonly used for extracting features is that it is nearest to the actual human auditory speech perception.

In Ref. [5] author used speech recognition methodology to control vehicle wiper, indicator, etc. using voice commands. MFCC, power spectral density, F0, energy features are used for speech recognition. Simulation is done through proteus software and it uses a Raspberry Pi 3b controller. System performance is verified with the use of six different voice commands. Better accuracy can be achieved with introduction of machine learning in controlling the voice commands.

In Ref. [6], MFCC features are extracted through voice commands and classification is done by Hidden Markov Model (HMM) classifier. This system is made speaker-independent so that every member of the house can access it. Voice recognition is done using Google API. Controller ATmega328P is used to switch on and off the fan using the voice recognition principle. The proposed system has achieved accuracy far better than offline features.

Smartphone plays a vital role in today's world and can be used to control various electronic systems. Various domestic appliances can be controlled by speed control of DC motors. Along with these in [7] author used mobile phone with GSM, Wi-Fi, and ZIGBEE. It deals with wireless communication. System can be independently used by a touchscreen or voice commands.

In Ref. [8], speed control is achieved through pulse width modulation (PWM). This system uses 8051 microcontrollers through the serial port. In addition, system objective is to introduce a computer software that can help minimize the constraints related with use of single motor. Instead the controls can be controlled from a series of individual devices.

Goal of system in Ref. [9] is to help disabled person to operate magnetic door remotely using an android smartphone.

Nowadays physical health matters a lot to survive while working on laptops or working in domains that keep you seated for a long time at one place. To maintain good physical health, one should keep a proper diet and work out. For a workout, most of the time people prefer gyms or having one of the gym instruments like a treadmill at home. Gym instruments have come a long way in the case of automation, still, we get to hear about accidents in the gym. Consumers can report and research safety hazards with a wide variety of products on SaferProducts.gov, an online database. According to this, more than 80 treadmills owned by different companies have been recalled for the past 10 years. Whenever a person on a treadmill is in motion, he could not regulate this workout on the mill by operating the switch on the controller. When speed gets uncomfortable to users accidents do happen, which may lead to bone fractures. As treadmills are not like running on the road, it is necessary to handle them simply and efficiently i.e., using voice instructions [3]. To do this, in ASR (Automatic speech recognition) first audio signal is digitized i.e., it is recorded to store in .mp3/.wav compressed format, which is then decompressed to an array where amplitudes of the signal are stored in memory [4], after which Mel-spectrogram is created which will serve as input to the deep learning model. Pre-processing of the signal is done by spectrogram augmentation and then MFCC (Mel Frequency Cepstral Coefficient) [5] helps by extracting small but highly relevant features which capture high-quality

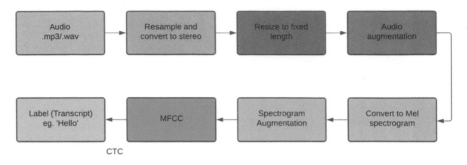

Fig. 1 Speech to text converter

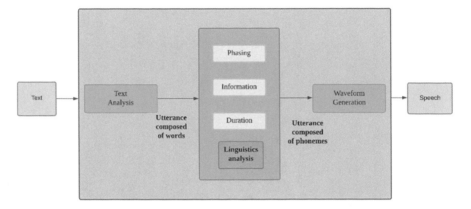

Fig. 2 Text to speech converter

sound [6]. At last, the CTC (Connectionist Temporal Classification) algorithm is used to create the correct sequence of uttered words. As shown in Fig. 1. Also, to get a response from the system according to scripts written for specified tasks, TTS (Text to speech) is carried out, as shown in Fig. 2, which includes analysis of provided text, phrasing, and intonation according to the language selected and punctuation marks, duration of response which makes phonemes when converted to waveforms and fed to transducers give human-understandable speech output.

3 Proposed System

To control the treadmill using voice commands for powering it ON and OFF, also changing its speed using voice recognition [7] principle and PWM technique [8], to reduce the accident cases on treadmills, also providing supplementary features like weight measurement of a person on the treadmill, calculating BMI (Body Mass

Index), time of run after the session, building voice-operated music player using a raspberry pi controller with python and storing it on ThingSpeak cloud platform.

Figure 3 presents the block diagram of an intelligent treadmill. The voice commands are given through the microphone. The microphone will convert the sound signal into an electrical signal which is given to the raspberry pi. Even android phones act as microphones [9]. A load cell is a transducer that converts a force such as tension, compression, pressure, or torque into an electrical signal that can be measured and standardized. The Memory card or SD card is part of the Raspberry Pi which is mainly used for storage for information like voice commands, music, a previous database of a person. Raspberry Pi 3B is used as a microprocessor and is programmed using python 3.8 to carry out all functions proposed. It is easy to interface with the keyboard and monitor and other peripherals used in the proposed system such as mic & speaker. It also has onboard WLAN which helps connect to the internet to carry out speech recognition also, for data storage and analysis tasks as proposed for BMI calculation further. It adds future scope to enhance the functionalities of this system. The L298D motor driver IC is used to control two sets of DC motors simultaneously. Using the PWM technique, speed is varied and thus the DC motor will acquire the best speed accordingly and does function as programmed. The Speaker is connected to the raspberry pi to get the audio output. LCD Display is connected to the raspberry pi to display information regarding the status of the system, function it is executing, and to show outputs such as the weight and BMI of that person, also to show his previously recorded workout session data from the cloud.

'Activate' voice command will activate and the system (wake up keyword), after powering it ON. There will be 3 options of voice commands are available after activation, such as

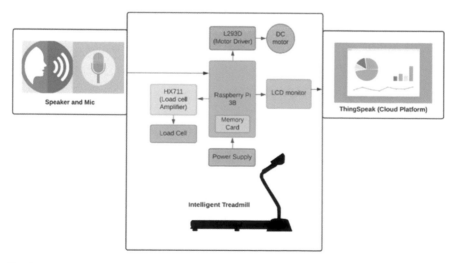

Fig. 3 Block diagram of proposed system

- 'Check my weight'
- 'Start treadmill'
- 'Play music'.

For the voice command 'Check my weight', the system will check the person's weight and it will be displayed on LCD. Also, the weight will be stored in memory.

For voice command 'Start treadmill', system will start mill at base speed.

For voice command 'Start music', music will be played. Music player with stored songs will be started as per the user's choice while running.

For every different speed, a number will be given to call the speed achieved without jerks. If the user uses the voice command 'Lock the speed', the user won't be able to change the speed further, unless he stops the system. If a person suddenly stops the system, the speed will be reduced by the next lower speed till it matches the base speed and finally, it is stopped. BMI will be calculated based on his weight and height also speed of run at the end of the session, further which he can deactivate using the keyword 'Deactivate'. The detail working of intelligent treadmill is explained in the flowchart in the Fig. 4.

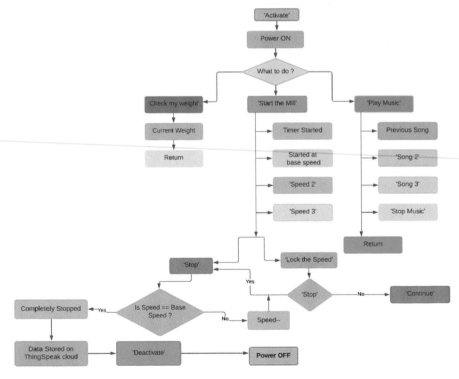

Fig. 4 Flowchart of intelligent treadmill

4 Experimental Results

The experimental results of the proposed system have been explained in three subparts as per the three different voice commands inputs.

4.1 Checking User Weight and Calculating BMI

In the proposed system, load cell with HX711 module is used to measure the weight of an object placed on it, which will then be converted in kg and shown at the output window, rounded to 2 decimal places. After this system will ask whether to calculate body mass index (BMI) or not. A user says 'yes' system will ask the user to input for his height in centimeters (cm), which then is converted to meters (m), BMI will be calculated given as output according to the formula (Fig. 5). The system also stores the BMI calculated by equation such as

$$\text{Body Mass Index (BMI)} = \frac{\text{Weight (Kg)}}{\text{Height (m}^2\text{)}}$$

Body mass index (BMI) is used as a basic parameter for fitness of individual person. Table 1 shows the standard values for BMI according to person's height.

The proposed system will give an estimate of the fitness of the person who is using the intelligent trademill based on the his or her daily usage. The intelligent trademill uasge data such as time of run, person's weight and height will be stored on ThingSpeak cloud. Based on this data, fitness tracker feature of proposed system will be

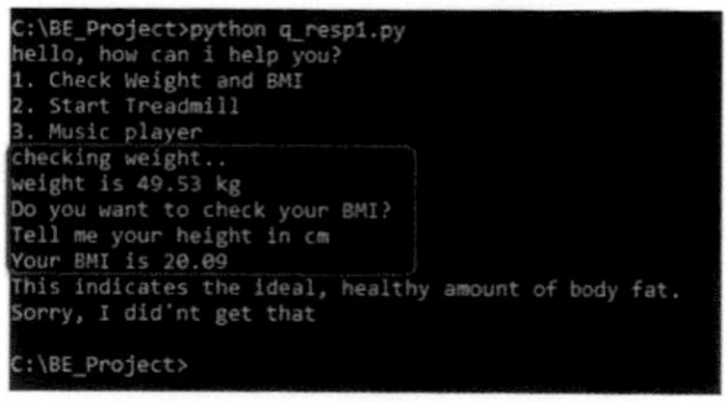

Fig. 5 Output of voice command 'Check my weight'

```
C:\BE_Project>python q_resp1.py
hello, how can i help you?
1. Check Weight and BMI
2. Start Treadmill
3. Music player
checking weight..
weight is 49.53 kg
Do you want to check your BMI?
Tell me your height in cm
Your BMI is 20.09
This indicates the ideal, healthy amount of body fat.
Sorry, I did'nt get that

C:\BE_Project>
```

Table 1 Standard values for Body Mass Index (BMI)

Sr. No	Nutritional Status	BMI Category
1	Underweight	<18.5
2	Normal	18.5–22.9
3	Overweight	23–24.9
4	Pre-Obese	25–29.9
5	Obese	≥30

 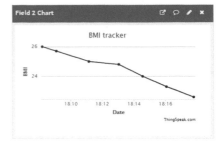

Fig. 6 Graph of time of run on tradmill and BMI fitness tracker w.r.t day

able to estimate the user's fitness level such as underweight/overweight/in a healthy range based on Table 1.

This data of BMI will be sent on Internet of Things (IOT) ThingSpeak cloud platform along with the time of run after the treadmill session has ended. Figure 6 shows the Graph of Time of run on treadmill and BMI FitnessTracker with respect to day of a user. For example, here in Fig. 6, a person gets an estimate of how his BMI has come in a healthy range. With increase in time of run, BMI gets reduced. Hence one can figure out how much time of the run is sufficient for his body to maintain a healthy BMI.

4.2 Operation of Treadmill

After activation of system using voice command 'activate' and on next voice command 'Start the mill', the treadmill acquires speed 1 (base speed) set as minimum speed for a smooth start and the timer will start (Fig. 7). It gradually increases in 5 s (corresponds to 5 km/hr). After switching to speed 2 by voice command, 'Speed 2' system gains intended speed in 8 s (corresponds to 10 km/hr) of duration and speed continues till the user asks for a different speed. If user changes to speed 3 by voice command 'Speed 3', it achieves it in 10 s (corresponds to 24 km/hr). This is shown in Fig. 8. During the stop function, the treadmill gradually decreases the speed from speed 3 to speed 1 in 10 s, 5 s, 3 s respectively which is as shown in Fig. 9. In between users can switch any speed from speed 3 to speed 1 and the motor changes

Fig. 7 Output of voice command 'Start the Mill' and changing the speed

```
C:\BE_Project>python q_resp1.py
hello, how can i help you?
1. Check Weight and BMI
2. Start Treadmill
3. Music player
starting the mill at base speed and the timer

Turning speed to level two
Current Speed:two
Turning speed to level three
Current Speed:three
```

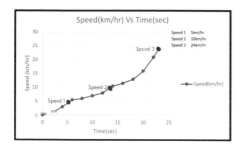

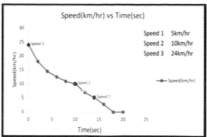

Fig. 8 Gradual speed change at starting and at stopping treadmill

Fig. 9 Output of voice
command 'Music Player'

```
C:\BE_Project>python q_resp1.py
hello, how can i help you?
1. Check Weight and BMI
2. Start Treadmill
3. Music player
which song do you want to listen?

Music playing
You finished the song
which song do you want to listen?
Turning off music player, back to previous menu
```

the speed gradually to avoid the jerk. At the end of the session, the timer will stop, and collected information about the time of the run is stored in system memory.

4.3 Music Player

When voice command 'play music' is given by user, the system will ask the user to tell user's choice about a song to listen to. Corresponding input will be given by the user. This input voice command will be then be converted to a string with the .mp3 extension and matched with stored songs. The song with the same name will be played by the system. Voice command 'finish command' is used to stop the song. At that instance system will ask again for a choice of song to play. Voice command 'Finish music' will take user back to the previous menu.

5 Conclusion

The proposed system makes use of an ASR to convert speech signal to text using python with GoogleAPI libraries and feeds it to the Raspberry Pi. The system checks user weight, BMI when it is asked for and gives an estimate of whether it is in a healthy range or not. Treadmill changes its speed according to changes given and collects the time of the run, which is then stored on cloud platform ThingSpeak along with BMI. The proposed system has added songs to the memory card so that required songs can be searched and played from memory, but it could also be extended by using online audio streaming services like Spotify to search for a variety of songs and play it. Also, to track fitness, data stored on the cloud (time of run and BMI) could be analyzed to get an estimate of the required workout for the user to maintain his BMI in a healthy range. In future, android mobile phones application can be used for inputting voice instructions with more advanced graphical user interface. Also, the system's scope could be enhanced by adding a speaker recognition algorithm to provide access to its authenticated users as well as more fitness features such as body temperature, heart rate can be integrated for better performance. The system limitation is, it has to rely on input height provided by user, as it cannot measure it on its own. Also system has limitations in emergency situations like power failure.

References

1. Maddileti T, Jammigumpula M, Jagadish Kumar H, Sai Sashank KV (2019) Voice controlled car using arduino and bluetooth module. Int J Eng Adv Technol (IJEAT) 9:1062–1065
2. Mathurri Sail T, Keerthi Kumar S (2016) Speed control of Dc motor using voice commands. In: International conference on computation of power, energy information and communication (ICCPEIC), pp 800–803
3. Prabhu S, Sahul Hameed A, Sureshkumar V, Arun S (2014) Voice-enabled speed control of AC Motor. Int J Res Eng Technol 3:564–567
4. Kurzekar PK, Deshmukh RR, Waghmare VB, Shrishrimal PP (2014) A comparative study of feature extraction techniques for speech recognition system. Int J Innov Res Sci Eng Technol 3:18006–18016
5. Pagar SD, Pote SJ, Anmulwar AS, Shinde AS (2020) Voice controlled vehicle dashboard. Int J Recent Technol Eng (IJRTE) 9:1022–1027
6. Chougle SR, Kulkarni NR, Kamble SM, Desai GR (2018) Smart home system using voice recognition. Int Res J Eng Technol (IRJET) 5:1592–1595
7. Gokul B, Karthi K, Thiyagaseelan A, Santhosh Kumar V (2016) Android based closed loop speed control of dc motor using voice recognition via bluetooth. Int J Adv Res Electr Electron Instrum Eng 5:1379–1385
8. Meha SA, Haziri B, Gashi LN (2011) Controlling DC motor speed using PWM from C# Windows application. In: 15th international research and expert conference, "Trends in the development of machinery and associated technology" TMT 2011, Prague, Czech Republic, pp. 481–484
9. Ismail NH, Tukiran Z, Shamsuddin NN (2014) Android-based home door locked application via Bluetooth for disabled people. In: IEEE international conference on control systems, pp 227–231

CXR-15: Deep Learning-Based Approach Towards Pneumonia Detection from Chest X-Rays

Sneha Rao, Vishwa Mohan Singh, Sumedha Sirsikar, and Vibhor Saran

Abstract Pneumonia detection and recognition have been one of the major challenges, and the machine learning community has been trying to tackle. Pneumonia is identified in X-ray images by the virtue of haziness in the lung region created due to the air sacs filled with fluid or pus. As pneumonia affects around 7% of the world's population and kills over 700,000 children annually, the research in this field has become more prominent. In severe cases of COVID-19, people also get pneumonia. Earlier attempts using CNN, ChexNet, ensembles of transfer learning models have been carried out to solve this problem. However, work in this field has not been keeping up with the advancements in neural network happened in past few years. In this work, a 15-layer CNN architecture called CXR-15 is proposed. The performance of the architecture was tested on a dataset with 5856 images and compared with various existing architectures. CXR-15 outperformed most of the existing architectures used for pneumonia detection like ChexNet, Xception, InceptionResNetV2, VGG16, EfficientNet-B5, CNN as feature extractors and MobileNetV2 by achieving an accuracy of 95.2%

Keywords Pneumonia · Deep learning · Transfer learning · Chest X-rays · Convolutional neural networks (CNNs)

1 Introduction

Machine learning and artificial intelligence have been play a crucial role in the medical domain. One of the major applications of ML is the diagnosis of pathological reports and identification of diseases. One such disease which is very prominent is pneumonia. This disease causes inflammation in the air sacs in the lungs and the

S. Rao (✉) · V. M. Singh · S. Sirsikar
School of Computer Engineering and Technology, Dr. Vishwanath Karad MIT World Peace University, Pune, India

V. Saran
Turtle Shell Technologies Pvt. Ltd, Bangalore, India

severity can range from mild to life threatening. This can be really harmful for children and people older than 65 along with those who have a medical history of heart diseases [1]. According to statics, in the United States alone, there are almost a million adults every year that seek care in hospitals due to pneumonia and around 50,000 succumb to the same [2]. Diagnosis of pneumonia has become more prominent in the current pandemic since it is a symptom of some severe cases of COVID-19.

Various tests like X-rays, CT scans, MRI scans and ultrasound are used to diagnose pneumonia [3]. But the problem with these tests is that we need trained radiologists to study them, these facilities are not available in rural areas where healthcare is yet not developed and sometimes even radiologists take a lot of time in studying the different scans. Hence, there is a need of system which can automate this task by taking an image as input and detecting whether the person is normal or suffering from pneumonia. Recent work has been carried out for pneumonia detection in which authors have used convolutional neural network (CNN) as feature extractors, created ensembles of transfer learning models like InceptionV3 [4] and VGG16 [5] and created custom architectures like ChexNet. Our goal in this work is to improve the efficiency of pneumonia detection whilst reducing the weight of the architecture.

In this paper, we are proposing a 15-layer convolution neural network inspired from VGG16 architecture which takes an X-ray image as input and classifies it as normal or pneumonia.

2   Literature Survey

One of the first methods to detect pneumonia out of X-ray images was proposed in Ref. [6]. This method uses the eigen analysis of the image in order to make the classification. Work in this field has advanced since then with the increasing use of methods like neural networks and CNNs.

In Ref. [7], the authors have used DenseNet-169 as feature extractor followed by support vector machine (SVM) classifier for classifying the image as normal or pneumonia. The authors were able to achieve a AUC score of 0.8002 on ChestX-ray14 dataset.

ChexNet [8] is 121-layer convolutional neural network (CNN) which is trained on ChestX-ray14 dataset consisting of 14 labels and it achieved 0.7680 AUROC score for pneumonia detection.

The authors of Ref. [9] have trained 5 different convolutional neural networks, namely AlexNet, VGGNet, ResNet, GoogleNet and LeNet, on Radiological Society of North America (RSNA) dataset consisting of 26,684 images.

Authors of Ref. [10] have trained four convolutional neural networks for pneumonia detection having different number of convolutional layers on chest X-ray images (Pneumonia) dataset. The first, second, third and fourth blocks consist of one, two, three and four convolutional layers, respectively. They have also employed dropout regularization for reducing overfitting.

More of these works have been discussed in detail in [11].

We are proposing CXR-15 architecture for pneumonia detection in this paper. CXR-15 is a 8 block structure and consists of Depthwise separable convolutional layer, batch normalization layer and exponential linear unit layer in each of the blocks. All the layers are explained below.

Depthwise Separable Convolutional Layer [12]: This layer consists of a Depthwise convolution followed by pointwise convolution. This allows the network to deal with both the spatial and the depth dimension of the input data.

Batch Normalization [13]: This involves normalizing the output of every layer by scaling and recentring in order to regularize the network better and increase the convergence rate faster.

Exponential Linear Unit [14]: We have used exponential linear unit activation function in this paper as it overcomes the vanishing gradient problem and is useful in increasing nonlinearity of layers.

3 Methodology

3.1 Dataset Description

We have used pneumonia dataset consisting of 5856 images divided as 4883 images in training set, 624 images in test set and 349 images in validation set. It consists of normal and pneumonia chest X-ray images. The width and height of images are set to 150.

For training set, we have performed data augmentation, rescaled the images by dividing it by 255, vertically flipped the images using ImageDataGenerator. For test set, we just rescale the images by dividing it by 255.

The following Fig. 1 shows some of the images generated by ImageDataGenerator.

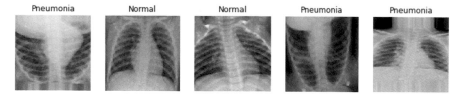

Fig. 1 Pneumonia dataset images

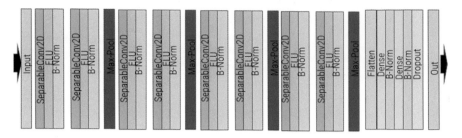

Fig. 2 CXR-15 architecture

3.2 Network Architecture

CXR-15 is a 15-layer convolutional neural network inspired from VGG16 architecture. In this architecture, we have added batch normalization and exponential linear unit (ELU) layers on top of Depthwise separable convolutional layers followed by max pooling layers. As we are dealing with two classes, we have used sigmoid activation function in the output layer. Apart from this, we have used dropout regularization [15] for preventing overfitting on the training set by randomly discarding neurons.

We have compiled the architecture with stochastic gradient descent optimizer and binary cross entropy loss as we are dealing with binary classification problem.

The architecture consists of 8 Depthwise separable convolution layers, 10 batch normalization, 8 exponential linear unit (ELU) layers, 4 max pooling layers, 1 flatten layer, 2 fully connected layers and 1 output layer.

We have trained the network for 25 epochs and set the batch size as 19.

The following Fig. 2 shows the architecture of CXR-15.

In CXR-15, we have used kernel size of 3×3 and a stride of 1 for each of the Depthwise separable convolution layers. For the max pooling layer, we have used a kernel size of 2×2. One block consists of 2 Depthwise separable convolutional layers and one max pooling layer. We start with 32 filters for the first block and double the number of filters for every subsequent block. Following these blocks, we have aggregated the results using two dense layers consisting of 128 and 64 neurons, respectively.

4 Results

4.1 Evaluation Metrics

The first and most essential metric is accuracy. It is the ratio of total number of predictions which were correct divided by total number of samples.

It is given by

$$Accuracy = \frac{\text{Total no. of correct predictions}}{\text{Total no. of samples}}$$

The next metric is the ROC-AUC score [16]. Receiver operating characteristic curve is the plot of the true positive rates to the false positive rates. AUC stands for 'area under the curve' which is plotted using the ROC score.

The third metric we have used is log loss [17], whose value depends upon the severity of error, the model has in the prediction. This means, the larger the deviation forms the actual value, the larger the value of the error.

For $y_j \in S_i$ and $\lambda = p(y_i)$, log loss is given by

$$loss = \frac{-1}{|N|} \sum_{i=1}^{|N|} \log(\lambda_j)y_j + \log(1 - \lambda_j)(1 - y_j)$$

The final metric, which is the $F1$ score, which combines the precision and the recall score to get a common metric.

$$F1 = \frac{1}{|L|} \sum_{j=1}^{|L|} \frac{2 \times p_j \times r_j}{p_j + r_j}$$

where L is the number of labels.

4.2 Performance Comparison

The following Table 1 compares the result of CXR-15 with existing architectures like MobileNetV2 [18], Xception [12], ChexNet, InceptionResNetV2 [19], VGG16, EfficientNet-B5 [20], ResNet-50 [21] and NASNetMobile [22].

From the above table, it is evident that CXR-15 outperformed all the architectures tested in terms of accuracy, $F1$-score and log loss. The only metric where it is outperformed by another is ROC-AUC score.

The following Fig. 3 shows some the graphical representation of aforementioned results.

Table 1 Comparison table of different models tested

	Accuracy	ROC-AUC	F1-score	Log loss
CXR-15	*95.2*	94.74	*96.13*	*1.66*
MobileNetV2	94.07	93.78	95.27	2.048
Xception	92.47	91.79	93.92	2.602
ChexNet	95.03	94.31	95.95	1.716
InceptionResNetV2	95.03	95.14	96.08	1.716
VGG16	94.87	95.93	96.04	1.771
EfficientNet-B5	89.9	88.9	91.59	3.487
ResNet-50	95.05	*96.02*	96.08	1.665
NASNetMobile	86.7	85.6	89.06	4.594

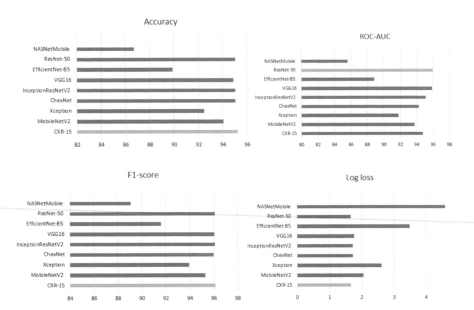

Fig. 3 Graph showing the performance of different architectures

5 Conclusion

A new deep learning architecture CXR-15 was proposed in the paper to accurately classify images into pneumonia and normal classes. We achieved an accuracy of 95.2%, $F1$-score of 96.13% and log loss of 1.66. The results achieved were better or comparable to existing transfer learning methods. It is also working better than other custom architectures such as ChexNet. Hence, we can establish that a lighter architecture performs better in case of the dataset considered.

The above results show that if we provide a bigger dataset, the architecture will be able to learn well and we might achieve better accuracy. Apart from this, CXR-15 can also be deployed in the real-time scenarios to assist the lab technicians. By deploying in real-world scenario, more data can be generated and can act as a feedback to the proposed algorithm.

References

1. Pneumonia, https://www.mayoclinic.org/diseases-conditions/pneumonia/symptoms-causes/syc-20354204. Last accessed 17 June 2021
2. American Thoracic Society Top 20 Pneumonia facts—2019, https://www.thoracic.org/patients/patient-resources/resources/top-pneumonia-facts.pdf. Last accessed 17 June 2021
3. Pneumonia, https://www.radiologyinfo.org/en/info/pneumonia. Last accessed 17 June 2021
4. Szegedy C, Vanhoucke V, Ioffe S, Shlens J, Wojna ZB (2016) Rethinking the inception architecture for computer vision. https://doi.org/10.1109/CVPR.2016.308
5. Simonyan K, Zisserman A (2014) Very deep convolutional networks for large-scale image recognition. arXiv 1409.1556
6. Bones PJ, Anthony PHB (2004) Eigen analysis for classifying chest x-ray images. Image reconstruction from incomplete data III, vol 5562. International society for optics and photonics
7. Varshni D, Thakral K, Agarwal L, Nijhawan R, Mittal A (2019) Pneumonia detection using CNN based feature extraction, pp 1–7. https://doi.org/10.1109/ICECCT.2019.8869364
8. Rajpurkar P, Irvin J, Zhu K, Yang B, Mehta H, Duan T, Ding D, Bagul A, Langlotz C, Shpanskaya K, Lungren M, Ng A (2017) CheXNet: radiologist-level pneumonia detection on chest X-Rays with deep learning
9. Militante SV, Sibbaluca BG (2020) Pneumonia detection using convolutional neural networks. Int J Sci Technol Res 9(04):1332–1337
10. Kaushik V, Nayyar A, Kataria G, Jain R (2020) Pneumonia detection using convolutional neural networks (CNNs), pp 471–483. https://doi.org/10.1007/978-981-15-3369-3_36
11. Karki S, Rao S, Walvekar R, Ladda S, Sirsikar S (2021) X-ray, ECG and digital pathology analysis using deep learning. ICICITES-2021
12. Chollet F (2017) Xception: deep learning with depthwise separable convolutions, pp 1800–1807. https://doi.org/10.1109/CVPR.2017.195
13. Batch normalization, https://en.wikipedia.org/wiki/Batch_normalization. Last accessed 17 June 2021
14. Clevert D-A, Unterthiner T, Hochreiter S (2015) Fast and accurate deep network learning by exponential linear units (elus). arXiv preprint arXiv:1511.07289
15. Srivastava N, Hinton G, Krizhevsky A, Sutskever I, Salakhutdinov R (2014) Dropout: a simple way to prevent neural networks from overfitting. J Mach Learn Res 15(1):1929–1958
16. AUC-ROC Curve in Machine Learning Clearly Explained, https://www.analyticsvidhya.com/blog/2020/06/auc-roc-curve-machine-learning/. Last accessed 17 June 2021
17. Binary Cross Entropy aka Log Loss- The cost function used in Logistic Regression, https://www.analyticsvidhya.com/blog/2020/11/binary-cross-entropy-aka-log-loss-the-cost-function-used-in-logistic-regression/. Last accessed 17 June 2021
18. Sandler M, Howard A, Zhu M, Zhmoginov A, Chen L-C (2018) MobileNetV2: inverted residuals and linear bottlenecks, pp 4510–4520. https://doi.org/10.1109/CVPR.2018.00474
19. Szegedy C, Ioffe S, Vanhoucke V, Alemi A (2016) Inception-v4, Inception-ResNet and the impact of residual connections on learning. In: AAAI Conference on Artificial Intelligence

20. Tan M, Le Q (2019) EfficientNet: rethinking model scaling for convolutional neural networks
21. He K, Zhang X, Ren S, Sun J (2015) Deep residual learning for image recognition, vol 7
22. Zoph B, Vasudevan V, Shlens J, Le Q (2018) Learning transferable architectures for scalable image recognition, pp 8697–8710. https://doi.org/10.1109/CVPR.2018.00907